THE TRAGEDY OF THE CHINESE REVOLUTION

THE TRAGEDY OF THE CHINESE REVOLUTION

Harold R. Isaacs

THE TRAGEDY OF THE CHINESE REVOLUTION
Harold R. Isaacs

First Published in India 2015

ISBN 978-93-5002-296-2

Published in agreement with Haymarket Books, Chicago, Illinois, USA for publication and sale only in the Indian Subcontinent (India, Pakistan, Bangladesh, Nepal, Maldives, Bhutan and Sri Lanka)

Published by
AAKAR BOOKS
28 E Pocket IV, Mayur Vihar Phase I, Delhi 110 091
Phone : 011 2279 5505 Telefax : 011 2279 5641
aakarbooks@gmail.com; www.aakarbooks.com

Printed at
Sapra Brothers, Delhi 110 092

CONTENTS

Foreword

"Facts are stubborn things," John Adams wrote in 1770, "and whatever may be our wishes, our inclinations, or the dictates of our passion, they cannot alter the state of facts and evidence."

I don't know if my father, Harold Isaacs, knew that quotation. But the principle it expresses was central to his character and his work. The stubborn facts documented in *The Tragedy of the Chinese Revolution*, his first book, have not been persuasively challenged, to my knowledge, in the nearly three-quarters of a century since it was originally published. It is also probably safe to say that much more than most histories, this book didn't just document facts, but rescued them from extinction. Without it, much of the truth about the fateful events in China in the 1920s would have been lost, covered over by layers and layers of totalitarian lies like an ancient, forgotten city lying under desert sand.

It is a measure of Isaacs's respect for facts that changes in his political judgments and beliefs did not necessitate revisions in his account of what happened (something that could not be said of many others caught up in the ideological passions of the middle third of the twentieth century). The original edition of *The Tragedy* that is reprinted here, first published in Great Britain in 1938, is most often labeled as Trotskyist. It remains true that Isaacs drew the same conclusion as Trotsky about Chinese events—that China's revolutionaries and the millions of Chinese they led were betrayed by Soviet policies—but that is a question of historical fact, not ideology. His position on Trotsky's underlying beliefs is a different matter. At the time he researched and wrote *The Tragedy*, Isaacs approached his subject "as a revolutionist," as Trotsky approvingly noted in his foreword to the original edition. But those views fairly quickly changed. As Isaacs explained in a preface to a revised edition published thirteen years after the first one—and I know would want to explain again to readers of the present book—he no longer agreed with the fundamental Leninist principles that Trotsky held until his death in 1940: in particular, the principle that a proletarian dictatorship led by a single revolutionary party must exercise sole power in a revolutionary state.

Whether Trotsky might have modified those views if he had lived longer is impossible to know, but for my father, the course of events in the world and in Stalin's Soviet Union in particular showed that the issue was not just that Stalin had "deformed" the workers' state, as the Trotskyist formula had it, but that the workers' state itself, as the Bolsheviks conceived and constructed it, was antidemocratic and inhumane. The Soviet experience "taught us that the contradiction between authoritarianism and democratic socialism is complete," he wrote. "The one-party monopoly of political life, developing into a bureaucratic oligarchy, an outcome that clearly rose out of some of the basic premises of Bolshevism, cannot serve socialist ends. No broader democracy can come from a political system based on force and lacking in institutional safeguards against the corruptions of power and violence."

When he wrote those words in 1951 he still referred to himself as a democratic socialist, although, he added, "one feels compelled to add that political labeling nowadays has become virtually a form of abuse, driving one to try to make a political philosophy out of the defense of simple human decency." In later years, he rejected all labels and was suspicious of all isms—most of all, perhaps, revolutionism (to borrow Trotsky's word), which preached a better world but made the twentieth century an era of unprecedented butchery and drowned its believers' hopes in vast seas of blood.

◆ ◆ ◆

When *The Tragedy of the Chinese Revolution* was published in 1938, my father was twenty-eight years old. He had spent the first half of the decade in China, where he arrived, as he put it, as "a twenty-year-old tyro journalist in search of experience and definition." Early travels far into the hinterland awakened him to the terrible poverty, injustice and oppression that weighed on the lives of the great majority of Chinese. That awakening led to contacts with members and supporters of the Chinese Communist Party, then being hunted down in a brutal suppression campaign waged by Chiang Kai-shek's Guomindang (Nationalist) government.* Under orders from Moscow delivered through the Communist movement's international arm, the Comintern, the Chinese Communists had allied with the Nationalists in the 1925–27 struggle to overthrow warlords and unify China under a single government. In 1927, as soon as he felt strong enough to rule without them, Chiang turned on his former Communist allies, imprisoning and executing them by the tens of thousands in a bloodbath that lasted well into the following decade.

Isaacs absorbed that history as a sympathizer with the revolution and its aims, and with the victims of Chiang's repression. But to the extent that he began to

---

* In the text the name appears as Kuomintang, the customary spelling under the now outdated Wade-Giles system of transliteration.

understand the Comintern's role and its deep complicity in the revolution's defeat by the Nationalists, he was also stepping onto heretical ground, learning things the Chinese Communist leadership and its Comintern mentors and their masters in Moscow did not want anyone to remember, ever. (For its part, the Guomindang also had every interest in suppressing the facts and its own bloodstained record, and did what it could toward that end.) Toward the end of his years in China, and after a final break with his associates in the organized Communist underground, Isaacs—now joined by my mother, Viola Robinson, who had come to China in 1932 to marry him—undertook a more systematic effort to uncover the events of the recent past. With the help of a few sympathetic collaborators, he accumulated, translated, and transcribed hundreds of contemporary documents, most of them from personal collections whose owners had kept them hidden in the intervening years. That record was the raw material for *The Tragedy,* which appeared three years after he and my mother left China in 1935.

Seventy years later, it is still an important work: "the book," as Isaacs once wrote, that he liked to think "made it impossible for the Stalin version of the history of events in China in the 1920s to stand up under serious scrutiny." That sentence is from his last book, *Re-Encounters in China*, published just a year before his death. In that book he recounted his return to China in 1980, his first visit after being banned from the country for thirty-five years—first by the Nationalists, who expelled him in 1945 when he was assigned there as a war correspondent for *Newsweek* magazine, and then by the Communists for another three decades after what they chose to call the "liberation" of the country from Nationalist rule. That last book also tells, more fully and revealingly than he had ever told it elsewhere, the story of his experiences in the 1930s that led to the writing of *The Tragedy.* For that reason, I believe readers of the present volume would get added value from reading *Re-Encounters* as well; I hope some will do so.

The story of what made that last visit possible, after all those years on the Communists' enemies list, is too long and convoluted to be retold here. What is pertinent to this essay is that the invitation came from the Chinese Writers Association, making it possible for Isaacs to make contact with a sprinkling of writers and others he had known a half-century before, and others he had not known but who had shared the experience of that time. They had shared something else, too: longer and crueler repression under the revolutionaries they had supported than was ever inflicted by the Guomindang regime they struggled against. Under Mao Zedong, whose era had ended just four years before Isaacs's return, Chinese intellectuals had endured more than two decades of purges and persecution, first in the anti-Rightist campaign of the late 1950s and then in the mass insanity of Mao's Great Proletarian Cultural Revolution, which ravaged the country for the last ten years of his life.

By 1980, Mao was dead, his virulent widow and the other top leaders of the Cultural Revolution were disgraced and in prison, and Deng Xiaoping was beginning to set China on an entirely new course. But the air was far from free enough for the men and women Isaacs met in those re-encounters to go very far beyond the approved Communist Party formulas in discussing their experiences. For the most part my father was left to guess what they really felt and what meaning they had really found in their lives and their country's life under the regime they had sacrificed to create. And eventually he heard the answer in his own voice, not theirs, when he burst out to one of them: "This has not been your experience alone. Our whole generation everywhere went through it in different ways, dreaming the great socialist dream, then having it crushed, by Stalin and his murderous regime in Russia and now again here in China. We were left to find some better way to human betterment, something better than prisons and labor camps and killings and oppression worse than before, and we haven't been very successful."

If a man or a book can be judged by the enemies they make, my father was entitled to take some pride in being the author of *The Tragedy* and in his later work on China, including his reporting during World War II. The latter earned him expulsion by the Chiang Kai-shek regime; the former earned enough enmity from the Communists for them to keep him on their blacklist long after they began welcoming right-wing anti-Communists such as Richard Nixon to Beijing. To be the enemy of Chiang's Nationalists and Mao's Communists at the same time was no small honor, considering the deeds and nature of those two regimes. If facts are stubborn, as John Adams wrote, it is also true that some facts become known only if truth-tellers are stubborn, too. This book, now available to a new generation of readers, is a reminder that my father spent his life as one of those stubborn truth-tellers. I salute his memory.

Arnold R. Isaacs
September 2009

Introduction by Leon Trotsky

First of all, the mere fact that the author of this book belongs to the school of historical materialism would be entirely insufficient in our eyes to win approval for his work. In present day conditions the Marxist label would predispose us to mistrust rather than to acceptance. In close connection with the degeneration of the Soviet State, Marxism has in the past fifteen years passed through an unprecedented period of decline and debasement. From an instrument of analysis and criticism, it has been turned into an instrument of cheap apologetics. Instead of analyzing facts, it occupies itself with selecting sophisms in the interests of exalted clients.

In the Chinese Revolution of 1925–27 the Communist International played a very great role, depicted in this book quite comprehensively. We would, however, seek in vain in the library of the Communist International for a single book which attempts in any way to give a rounded picture of the Chinese Revolution. Instead, we find scores of "conjunctural" works which docilely reflect each zigzag in the politics of the Communist International, or, more correctly, of Soviet diplomacy in China, and subordinating to each zigzag facts as well as general treatment. In contrast to this literature, which cannot arouse anything but mental revulsion, Isaacs' book represents a scientific work from beginning to end. It is based on a conscientious study of a vast number of original sources and supplementary material. Isaacs spent more than three years on this work. It should be added that he had previously passed about five years in China as a journalist and observer of Chinese life.

The author of this book approaches the revolution as a revolutionist, and he sees no reason for concealing it. In the eyes of a philistine a revolutionary point of view is virtually equivalent to an absence of scientific objectivity. We think just the opposite: only a revolutionist—provided, of course, that he is equipped with the scientific method—is capable of laying bare the objective dynamics of the revolution. Apprehending thought in general is not contemplative, but active. The element of will is indispensable for penetrating the secrets of nature and society. Just as a surgeon, on whose scalpel a human life depends, distinguishes with extreme care between the various tissues of an organism, so a revolutionist, if he has a serious attitude toward his task, is obliged with strict conscientiousness to analyze the structure of society, its functions and reflexes.

To understand the present war between Japan and China one must take the Second Chinese Revolution as a point of departure. In both cases we meet not only identical social forces, but frequently the same personalities. Suffice it to say that the person of Chiang Kai-shek occupies the central place in this book. As these lines are being written it is still difficult to forecast when and in what manner the Sino-Japanese war will end. But the outcome of the present conflict in the Far East will in any case have a provisional character. The world war which is approaching with irresistible force will review the Chinese problem together with all other problems of colonial domination. For it is in this that the real task of the second world war will consist: to divide the planet anew in accord with the new relationship of imperialist forces. The principal arena of struggle will, of course, not be that Lilliputian bathtub, the Mediterranean, nor even the Atlantic Ocean, but the basin of the Pacific. The most important object of struggle will be China, embracing about one-fourth of the human race. The fate of the Soviet Union—the other big stake in the coming war—will also to a certain degree be decided in the Far East. Preparing for this clash of titans, Tokyo is attempting today to assure itself of the broadest possible drill-ground on the continent of Asia. Great Britain and the United States are likewise losing no time. It can, however, be predicted with certainty—and this is in essence acknowledged by the present makers of destiny—that the world war will not produce the final decision: it will be followed by a new series of revolutions which will review not only the decisions of the war but all those property conditions which give rise to war.

History Is No Pacifist

This prospect, it must be confessed, is very far from being an idyll, but Clio, the muse of history, was never a member of a Ladies' Peace Society. The older generation which passed through the war of 1914–18 did not discharge a single one of its tasks. It leaves to the new generation as heritage the burden of wars and revolutions. These most important and tragic events in human history have often marched side by side. They will definitely form the background of the coming decades. It remains only to hope that the new generation, which cannot arbitrarily cut loose from the conditions it has inherited, has learned at least to understand better the laws of its epoch. For acquainting itself with the Chinese Revolution of 1925–27 it will not find today a better guide than this book.

Despite the unquestionable greatness of the Anglo-Saxon genius, it is impossible not to see that the laws of revolutions are least understood precisely in the Anglo-Saxon countries. The explanation for this lies, on the one hand, in the fact that the very appearance of revolution in these countries relates to a long-distant past, and evokes in official "sociologists" a condescending smile, as would childish pranks. On the other hand, pragmatism, so characteristic of Anglo-Saxon thinking, is least of all useful for understanding revolutionary crises.

The English Revolution of the seventeenth century, like the French Revolution of the eighteenth, had the task of "rationalizing" the structure of society, i.e., cleansing it of feudal stalactites and stalagmites, and subjecting it to the laws of free competition, which in that epoch seemed to be the laws of "common sense." In doing this, the Puritan revolution draped itself in biblical dress, thereby revealing a purely infantile incapacity to understand its own significance. The French Revolution, which had considerable influence on progressive thought in the United States, was guided by formulas of pure rationalism. Common sense, which is still afraid of itself and resorts to the mask of biblical prophets, or secularized common sense, which looks upon society as the product of a rational "contract," remain to this day the fundamental forms of Anglo-Saxon thinking in the domains of philosophy and sociology.

Yet the real society of history has not been constructed, following Rousseau, upon a rational "contract," nor, as according to Bentham, upon the principle of the "greatest good," but has unfolded "irrationally," on the basis of contradictions and antagonisms. For revolution to become inevitable class contradictions have to be strained to the breaking point. It is precisely this historically inescapable necessity for conflict, which depends neither on good nor ill will but on the objective interrelationship of classes, that makes revolution, together with war, the most dramatic expression of the "irrational" foundation of the historic process.

"Irrational" does not, however, mean arbitrary. On the contrary, in the molecular preparation of revolution, in its explosion, in its ascent and decline, there is lodged a profound inner lawfulness which can be apprehended and, in the main, foreseen. Revolutions, as has been said more than once, have a logic of their own. But this is not the logic of Aristotle, and even less the pragmatic demi-logic of "common sense." It is the higher function of thought: the logic of development and its contradictions, i.e., the dialectic.

The obstinacy of Anglo-Saxon pragmatism and its hostility to dialectical thinking thus have their material causes. Just as a poet cannot attain to the dialectic through books without his own personal experiences, so a well-to-do society, unused to convulsions and habituated to uninterrupted "progress," is incapable of understanding the dialectic of its own development. However, it is only too obvious that this privilege of the Anglo-Saxon world has receded into the past. History is preparing to give Great Britain as well as the United States serious lessons in the dialectic.

Character of Chinese Revolution

The author of this book tries to deduce the character of the Chinese Revolution not from *a priori* definitions and not from historical analogies, but from the living structure of Chinese society and from the dynamics of its inner forces. In this lies the chief methodological value of the book. The reader will carry away not only a better-knit picture of the march of events but—what is more important—will learn to understand their social mainsprings. Only on this basis is it possible correctly to appraise political programs and the slogans of struggling parties—which, even if neither independent nor in the final analysis the decisive factors in the process, are nevertheless its most manifest signs.

In its immediate aims the uncompleted Chinese Revolution is "bourgeois." This term, however, which is used as a mere echo of the bourgeois revolutions of the past, actually helps us very little. Lest the historical analogy turn into a trap for the mind, it is necessary to check it in the light of a concrete sociological analysis. What are the classes which are struggling in China? What are the interrelationships of these classes? How, and in what direction, are these relations being transformed? What are the objective tasks of the Chinese Revolution, i.e., those tasks dictated by the course of development? On the shoulders of which classes rests the solution of these tasks? With what methods can they be solved? Isaacs' book gives the answers to precisely these questions.

Colonial and semi-colonial—and therefore backward—countries, which embrace by far the greater part of mankind, differ extraordinarily from one another in their degree of backwardness, representing a historical ladder reaching from nomadry, and even cannibalism, up to the most modern industrial culture. The combination of extremes in one degree or another characterizes all of the backward countries. However, the hierarchy of backwardness, if one may employ such an expression, is determined by the specific weight of the elements of barbarism and culture in the life of each colonial country. Equatorial Africa lags far behind Algeria, Paraguay behind Mexico, Abyssinia behind India or China. With their common economic dependence upon the imperialist metropolises, their political dependence bears in some instances the character of open colonial slavery (India, Equatorial Africa), while in others it is concealed by the fiction of state independence (China, Latin America).

In agrarian relations backwardness finds its most organic and cruel expression. Not one of these countries has carried its democratic revolution through to any real extent. Half-way agrarian reforms are absorbed by semi-serf relations, and these are inescapably reproduced in the soil of poverty and oppression. Agrarian barbarism always goes hand in hand with the absence of roads, with the isolation of provinces, with "medieval" particularism, and absence of national consciousness. The purging of social relations of the remnants of ancient and the encrustations of modern feudalism is the most important task in all these countries.

The achievement of the agrarian revolution is unthinkable, however, with the preservation of dependence upon foreign imperialism, which with one hand implants capitalist relations while supporting and re-creating with the other all the forms of slavery and serfdom. The struggle for the democratization of social relations and the creation of a national state thus uninterruptedly passes into an open uprising against foreign domination.

Historical backwardness does not imply a simple reproduction of the development of advanced countries, England or France, with a delay of one, two, or three centuries. It engenders an entirely new "combined" social formation in which the latest conquests of capitalist technique and structure root themselves into relations of feudal or pre-feudal barbarism, transforming and subjecting them and creating a peculiar relation of classes.

Bourgeoisie Hostile to People

Not a single one of the tasks of the "bourgeois" revolution can be solved in these backward countries under the leadership of the "national" bourgeoisie, because the latter emerges at once with foreign support as a class alien or hostile to the people. Every stage in its development binds it only the more closely to the foreign finance capital of which it is essentially the agency. The petty bourgeoisie of the colonies, that of handicrafts and trade, is the first to fall victim in the unequal struggle with foreign capital, declining into economic insignificance, becoming declassed and pauperized. It cannot even conceive of playing an independent political role. The peasantry, the largest numerically and the most atomized, backward, and oppressed class, is capable of local uprisings and partisan warfare, but requires the leadership of a more advanced and centralized class in order for this struggle to be elevated to an all-national level. The task of such leadership falls in the nature of things upon the colonial proletariat, which, from its very first steps, stands opposed not only to the foreign but also to its own national bourgeoisie.

Out of the conglomeration of provinces and tribes, bound together by geographical proximity and the bureaucratic apparatus, capitalist development has transformed China into the semblance of an economic entity. The revolutionary movement of the masses translated this growing unity for the first time into the language of national consciousness. In the strikes, agrarian uprisings, and military expeditions of 1925–1927 a new China was born. While the generals, tied to their own and the foreign bourgeoisie, could only tear the country to pieces, the Chinese workers became the standard-bearers of an irresistible urge to national unity. This movement provides an incontestable analogy with the struggle of the French Third Estate against particularism, or with the later struggle of the Germans and Italians for national unification. But in contrast to the first-born countries of capitalism, where the problem of achieving national unity fell to the petty bourgeoisie, in part under the leadership of the bourgeoisie and even of the landlords (Prussia!), in China it was the proletariat that emerged as the primary motive force and potential leader of this movement. But precisely thereby, the proletariat confronted the bourgeoisie with the danger that the leadership of the unified fatherland would not remain in the latter's hands. Patriotism has been throughout all history inseparably bound up with power and property. In the face of danger the ruling classes have never stopped short of dismembering their own country so long as they were able in this way to preserve power over one part of it. It is not at all surprising, therefore, if the Chinese bourgeoisie, represented by Chiang Kai-shek, turned its weapons in 1927 against the proletariat, the standard-bearer of national unity. The exposition and explanation of this turn, which occupies the central place in Isaacs' book, provides the key to the understanding of the fundamental problems of the Chinese Revolution as well as of the present Sino-Japanese war.

The so-called "national" bourgeoisie tolerates all forms of national degradation so long as it can hope to maintain its own privileged existence. But at the moment when foreign capital sets out to assume undivided domination of the entire wealth of the country, the colonial bourgeoisie is forced to remind itself of its "national" obligations. Under pressure of the masses it may even find itself plunged into a war. But this will be a war waged against one of the imperialist powers, the one least amenable to negotiations, with the hope of passing into the service of some other, more magnanimous power. Chiang Kai-shek struggles against the Japanese violators only within the limits indicated to him by his British or American patrons. Only that class which has nothing to lose but its chains can conduct to the very end the war against imperialism for national emancipation.

Grandiose Historical Test

The above developed views regarding the special character of the "bourgeois" revolutions in historically belated countries are by no means the product of theoretical analysis alone. Before the second Chinese Revolution (1925–1927) they had already been submitted to a grandiose historical test. The experience of the three Russian revolutions (1905, February and October 1917) bears no less significance for the twentieth century than the French Revolution bore for the nineteenth. To understand the destinies of modern China the reader must have before his eyes the struggle of conceptions in the Russian revolutionary movement, because these conceptions exerted, and still exert, a direct and, moreover, powerful influence upon the politics of the Chinese proletariat and an indirect influence upon the politics of the Chinese bourgeoisie.

It was precisely because of its historical backwardness that czarist Russia turned out to be the only European country where Marxism as a doctrine and the Social Democracy as a party attained powerful development before the bourgeois revolution. It was in Russia, quite naturally, that the problem of the correlation between the struggle for democracy and the struggle for socialism, or between the bourgeois revolution and the socialist, was submitted to theoretical analysis. The first to pose this problem in the early eighties of the last century was the founder of the Russian Social Democracy, Plekhanov. In the struggle against so-called Populism (Narodnikism), a variety of socialist Utopianism, Plekhanov established that Russia had no reason whatever to expect a privileged path of development, that like the "profane" nations, it would have to pass through the stage of capitalism and that along this path it would acquire the regime of bourgeois democracy indispensable for the further struggle of the proletariat for socialism. Plekhanov not only separated the bourgeois revolution as a task distinct from the socialist revolution—which he postponed to the indefinite future—but he depicted entirely different combinations of forces. The bourgeois revolution was to be achieved by the proletariat in alliance with the liberal bourgeoisie, and thus clear the path for capitalist progress; after a number of decades and on a higher level of capitalist development, the proletariat would carry out the socialist revolution in direct struggle against the bourgeoisie.

Lenin—not immediately, to be sure—reviewed this doctrine. At the beginning of the present century, with much greater force and consistency than Plekhanov, he posed the agrarian problem as the central problem of the bourgeois revolution in Russia. With this he came to the conclusion that the liberal bourgeoisie was hostile to the expropriation of the landlords' estates, and precisely for this reason would seek a compromise with the monarchy on the basis of a constitution on the Prussian pattern. To Plekhanov's idea of an alliance between the proletariat and the liberal bourgeoisie, Lenin opposed the idea of an alliance between the proletariat and the peasantry. The aim of the revolutionary collaboration of these two classes he proclaimed to be the establishment of the "bourgeois-democratic dictatorship of the proletariat and the peasantry" as the only means of cleansing the czarist empire of its feudal-police refuse, of creating a free farmers' system, and of clearing the road for the development of capitalism along American lines. Lenin's formula represented a gigantic step forward in that, in contrast to Plekhanov's, it correctly indicated the central task of the revolution, namely, the democratic overturn of agrarian relations, and equally correctly sketched out the only realistic combination of class forces capable of solving this task. But up to 1917 the thought of Lenin himself remained bound to the traditional concept of the "bourgeois" revolution. Like Plekhanov, Lenin proceeded from the premise that only after the "completion of the bourgeois democratic revolution" would the tasks of the socialist revolution come on the order of the day. Lenin, however, contrary to the legend later manufactured by the epigones, considered that after the completion of the democratic overturn, the peasantry, as peasantry, could not remain the ally of the proletariat. Lenin based his socialist hopes on the agricultural laborers and the semi-proletarianized peasants who sell their labor power.

An Internal Contradiction

The weak point in Lenin's conception was the internally contradictory idea of the "bourgeois-democratic dictatorship of the proletariat and the peasantry." A political bloc of two classes whose interests only partially coincide excludes a dictatorship. Lenin himself emphasized the fundamental limitation of the "dictatorship of the proletariat and the peasantry" when he openly called it bourgeois. By this he meant to say that for the sake of maintaining the alliance with the peasantry the proletariat would, in the coming revolution, have to forego the direct posing of the socialist tasks. But this would signify, to be precise, that the proletariat would have to give up the dictatorship. In that event, in whose hands would the revolutionary power be concentrated? In the hands of the peasantry? But it is least capable of such a role.

Lenin left these questions unanswered up to his famous *Theses of April 4, 1917*. Only here did he break for the first time with the traditional understanding of the "bourgeois" revolution and with the formula of the "bourgeois-democratic dictatorship of the proletariat and the peasantry." He declared the struggle for the dictatorship of the proletariat to be the sole means of carrying out the agrarian revolution to the end and of securing the freedom of the oppressed nationalities. The regime of the proletarian dictatorship, by its very nature, however, could not limit itself to the framework of bourgeois property. The rule of the proletariat automatically placed on the agenda the socialist revolution, which in this case was not separated from the democratic revolution by any historical period, but was uninterruptedly connected with it, or, to put it more accurately, was an organic outgrowth of it. At what tempo the socialist transformation of society would occur and what limits it would attain in the nearest future would depend not only upon internal but upon external conditions as well. The Russian revolution was only a link in the international revolution. Such was, in broad outline, the essence of the conception of the permanent (uninterrupted) revolution. It was precisely this conception that guaranteed the victory of the proletariat in October.

But such is the bitter irony of history: the experience of the Russian Revolution not only did not help the Chinese proletariat but, on the contrary, it became in its reactionary, distorted form, one of the chief obstacles in its path. The Comintern of the epigones began by canonizing for all countries of the Orient the formula of the "democratic dictatorship of the proletariat and peasantry" which Lenin, influenced by historical experience, had acknowledged to be without value. As always in history, a formula that had outlived itself served to cover a political content which was the direct opposite of that which the formula had served in its day. The mass plebeian, revolutionary alliance of the workers and peasants, sealed through the freely elected Soviets as the direct organs of action, the Comintern replaced by a bureaucratic bloc of party centers. The right to represent the peasantry in this bloc was unexpectedly given to the Kuomintang, i.e., a thoroughly bourgeois party vitally interested in the preservation of capitalist property, not only in the means of production but in land. The alliance of the proletariat and the peasantry was broadened into a "bloc of four classes": workers, peasants, urban petty bourgeoisie, and the so-called "national" bourgeoisie. In other words, the Comintern picked up a formula discarded by Lenin only in order to open the road to the politics of Plekhanov and, moreover, in a masked and therefore more harmful form.

To justify the political subordination of the proletariat to the bourgeoisie, the theoreticians of the Comintern (Stalin, Bukharin) adduced the fact of imperialist oppression which supposedly impelled "all the progressive forces in the country" to an alliance. But this was precisely in its day the argument of the Russian Mensheviks, with the difference that in their case the place of imperialism was occupied by czarism. In reality, the subjection of the Chinese Communist Party to the Kuomintang signified its break with the mass movement and a direct betrayal of its historical interests. In this way the catastrophe of the second Chinese revolution was prepared under the direct leadership of Moscow.

Significance of Russian Marxism

To many political philistines who in politics are inclined to substitute "common sense" guesses for scientific analysis, the controversy among the Russian Marxists over the nature of the revolution and the dynamics of its class forces seemed to be sheer scholasticism. Historical experience revealed, however, the profoundly vital significance of the "doctrinaire formulas" of Russian Marxism. Those who have not understood this up to today can learn a great deal from Isaacs' book. The politics of the Communist International in China showed convincingly what the Russian Revolution would have been converted into if the Mensheviks and the Social Revolutionaries had not been thrust aside in time by the Bolsheviks. In China the conception of the permanent revolution was confirmed once more, this time not in the form of a victory, but of a catastrophe.

It would, of course, be impermissible to identify Russia and China. With all their important common traits, the differences are all too obvious. But it is not hard to convince oneself that these differences do not weaken but, on the contrary, strengthen the fundamental conclusions of Bolshevism. In one sense czarist Russia was also a colonial country, and this found its expression in the predominant role of foreign capital. But the Russian bourgeoisie enjoyed the benefits of an immeasurably greater independence from foreign imperialism than the Chinese bourgeoisie. Russia itself was an imperialist country. With all its meagerness, Russian liberalism had far more serious traditions and more of a basis of support than the Chinese. To the left of the liberals stood powerful petty bourgeois parties, revolutionary or semi-revolutionary in relation to czarism. The party of the Social Revolutionaries managed to find considerable support among the peasantry, chiefly from its upper layers. The Social Democratic (Menshevik) Party led behind it broad circles of the urban petty bourgeoisie and labor aristocracy. It was precisely these three parties—the Liberals, the Social Revolutionaries, and the Mensheviks—who for a long time prepared, and in 1917 definitely formed, a coalition which was not yet then called the People's Front but which had all of its traits. In contrast to this the Bolsheviks, from the eve of the revolution in 1905, took up an irreconcilable position in relation to the liberal bourgeoisie. Only this policy, which achieved its highest expression in the "defeatism" of 1914–1917, enabled the Bolshevik Party to conquer power.

The differences between China and Russia—the incomparably greater dependence of the Chinese bourgeoisie on foreign capital, the absence of independent revolutionary traditions among the petty bourgeoisie, the mass gravitation of the workers and peasants to the banner of the Comintern—demanded a still more irreconcilable policy—if such were possible, than that pursued in Russia. Yet the Chinese section of the Comintern, at Moscow's command, renounced Marxism, accepted the reactionary scholastic "principles of Sun Yat-sen," and entered the ranks of the Kuomintang, submitting to its discipline. In other words, it went much further along the road of submission to the bourgeoisie than the Russian Mensheviks or Social Revolutionaries ever did. The same fatal policy is now being repeated in the conditions of the war with Japan.

New Methods of Bureaucracy

How could the bureaucracy emerging from the Bolshevik Revolution apply in China, as throughout the world, methods fundamentally opposed to those of Bolshevism? It would be far too superficial to answer this question with a reference to the incapacity or ignorance of this or that individual. The gist of the matter lies in this: together with the new conditions of existence the bureaucracy acquired new methods of thinking. The Bolshevik Party led the masses. The bureaucracy began to order them about. The Bolsheviks won the possibility of leadership by correctly expressing the interests of the masses. The bureaucracy was compelled to resort to command in order to secure its own interests against those of the masses. The method of command was naturally extended to the Communist International as well. The Moscow leaders began quite seriously to imagine that they could compel the Chinese bourgeoisie to move to the left of its interests and the Chinese workers and peasants to the right of theirs, along the diagonals drawn in the Kremlin. Yet it is the very essence of revolution that the exploited as well as the exploiters invest their interests with the most extreme expression. If hostile classes could move along diagonals, there would be no need for a civil war. Armed by the authority of the October Revolution and the Communist International, not to mention inexhaustible financial resources, the bureaucracy transformed the young Chinese Communist Party from a motive force into a brake at the most important moment of the revolution. In contrast to Germany and Austria, where the bureaucracy could shift part of the responsibility for defeat to the Social Democracy, there was no Social Democracy in China. The Comintern had the monopoly in ruining the Chinese Revolution.

The present domination of the Kuomintang over a considerable section of Chinese territory would have been impossible without the powerful national revolutionary movement of the masses in 1925–1927. The massacre of this movement on the one hand concentrated power in the hands of Chiang Kai-shek, and on the other doomed Chiang Kai-shek to half-measures in the struggle against imperialism. The understanding of the course of the Chinese Revolution has in this way the most direct significance for an understanding of the course of the Sino-Japanese War. This historical work acquires thereby the most *actuel* political significance.

War and revolution will be interlaced in the nearest future history of China. Japan's aim, to enslave forever, or at least for a long time to come, a gigantic country by dominating its strategic centers, is characterized not only by greediness but by wooden-headedness. Japan has arrived much too late. Torn by internal contradictions, the empire of the Mikado cannot reproduce the history of Britain's ascent. On the other hand, China has advanced far beyond the India of the seventeenth and eighteenth centuries. Old colonial countries are nowadays waging with ever greater success a struggle for their national independence. In these historic conditions, even if the present war in the Far East were to end with Japan's victory, and even if the victor himself could escape an internal catastrophe during the next few years—and neither the former nor the latter is in the least assured—Japan's domination over China would be measured by a very brief period, perhaps only the few years required to give a new impulse to the economic life of China and to mobilize its laboring masses once more.

The big Japanese trusts and concerns are already following in the wake of the army to divide the still unsecured booty. The Tokyo government is seeking to regulate the appetites of the financial cliques that would tear North China to pieces. If Japan were to succeed in maintaining its conquered positions for an interval of some ten years, this would mean, above all, the intensive industrialization of North China in the military interests of Japanese imperialism. New railways, mines, power stations, mining and metallurgical enterprises, and cotton plantations would rapidly spring up. The polarization of the Chinese nation would receive a feverish impulse. New hundreds of thousands and millions of Chinese proletarians would be mobilized in the briefest possible space of time. On the other hand, the Chinese bourgeoisie would fall into an ever greater dependence on Japanese capital. Even less than in the past would it be capable of standing at the head of a national war, no less a national revolution. Face to face with the foreign violator would stand the numerically larger, socially strengthened, politically matured Chinese proletariat, called to lead the Chinese village. Hatred of the foreign enslaver is a mighty revolutionary cement. The new national revolution will, one must think, be placed on the agenda still in the lifetime of the present generation. To solve the tasks imposed upon it, the vanguard of the Chinese proletariat must thoroughly assimilate the lessons of the Chinese Revolution. Isaacs' book can serve it in this sense as an irreplaceable aid. It remains to be hoped that the book will be translated into Chinese as well as other foreign languages.

1

Seeds of Revolt

On the fringes of big Chinese cities the shadows of lofty factory chimneys fall across fields still tilled with wooden ploughs. On the wharves of seaports modern liners unload goods carried away on the backs of men or shipped inland on primitive barges. In the streets great trucks and jangling trams roar past carts drawn by men harnessed like animals to their loads. Sleek automobiles toot angrily at man-drawn rickshaws and barrows which thread their way through the lanes of traffic. Streets, lined with shops where men and women still fashion their wares with bare hands and simple tools, lead to huge mills run by humming dynamos. Airplanes and railways cut across vast regions linked otherwise only by footpaths and canals a thousand years old. Modern steamers ply the coasts and rivers, churning past junks of ancient design. Throughout the towns and villages, and on the tired land of the vast river valleys that stretch from the sea to the heart of Asia, these contradictions and contrasts multiply. They embody the struggle of nearly half a billion people for existence and survival.

The pattern of Chinese life is jagged, torn, and irregular. Modern forms of production, transport, and finance are superimposed upon, and only partially woven into, the worn and threadbare pattern of the past. That ancient fabric was already giving way a century ago when the West invaded China with its commodities, its guns, its greed, and its ideas. The result of that impact was catastrophic and revolutionary. Chinese economy was forcibly transformed. Classes of society, for so long stable, entered upon a period of violent change. Forms of government, habits, and the entire social equilibrium were upset. The process of change was intricate. It posed the immense historical task of creating a new framework in which China's productive forces could thrive. It created conflicts which soon accumulated, gathered momentum, and flowed swiftly toward a solution on the battlefields of the class struggle.

The backwardness of Chinese economy was determined primarily by the stagnation of productive forces over a lengthy historical period. Introduction of the iron plough led, some two thousand years ago, to an increase of agricultural productivity. Partially as a result of this impetus, land was at that time converted into private property. Land held in fief or cleared by imperial grant became alienable, that is to say, it could be bought and sold. Labor thus released and capital thus acquired were in part absorbed by the state in the construction of great public works, dams, canals, palaces, walls and fortifications. But capitalist modes of production did not develop. Feudal forms of exploitation were perpetuated in the village. Chinese society remained organized in small agricultural units. Home or local handicraft industries supplied the major supplementary needs of the community. The state took direct part in trade and manufacture. It exercised monopolies, for example, in salt and in iron. Both the system of production and the internal market were rigidly controlled by the state apparatus and all-embracing guilds of merchants and artisans. Urban centers of production and commerce grew up but seem to have been restricted to luxury products and regional specialities, fine silks, lacquer, chinaware, carvings, ironwork. Only further research into the nature and extent of the internal market, the operations of commercial capital, and the relative isolation of the small communities, will illuminate what Marx called the "Asiatic mode of production," with its remarkable capacity for self-renewal.[1]

The whole structure rested solidly on the mass of peasants who paid rent to the landlords, interest to the merchants and moneylenders, and taxes, in labor, in kind, and in money, to the state. The latter was represented by local officials joined in a loose hierarchy stretching up through the provincial viceroys to the emperor. These officials joined with the landlords and merchants in the process of the exploitation of the peasantry. To meet the ever-increasing tax demands, the landlords multiplied their exactions from the men who actually worked the soil. Small landholders mortgaged themselves to the moneylenders and were gradually reduced to the status of tenants or agricultural laborers. As each succeeding dynasty passed its peak and went into decline, its financial demands increased and the corruption of its officials deepened. When the burden of accumulated rent, debts, and taxes became intolerable and the prevailing hardships further weighted by repeated natural disasters, local revolts against rent and tax collectors broadened into great peasant wars.

Military cliques, headed by landholding nobles, took the field at the head of scattered peasant detachments and provincial soldiery, overthrew the dynasty, and fought for primacy among themselves. Attempts at drastic social and agrarian reforms usually featured the period of civil war and confusion which often lasted decades and at one time several centuries. The most famous of these were the attempted reforms of Wang Mang after the fall of the Han dynasty at the beginning of the first century of the Christian era, and those advocated by Wang An-shih after the collapse of the T'ang dynasty and the rise of the Sung at the end of the tenth century. Some of their proposals went as far as a primitive sort of nationalization of land, i.e., the abolition of private property rights in the land and its reversion to its original owner, the state. Others provided for the establishment of an embryonic state capitalism. None of these reforms, however, matured. The peasant wars which provoked them invariably exhausted themselves. One of the warring cliques would finally assert its supremacy and erect a new dynasty. While the new emperor and his immediate descendants consolidated their rule and gradually suppressed all rival claimants to the throne, the original social forms in the village were reproduced and the same gradual process of expropriation resumed.

The Manchus came to power in the mid-seventeenth century by taking advantage of one of these peasant rebellions. Once established as alien rulers, they had a natural interest in preserving China from any other external contact while they completed the subjugation of the country. During this period Europe was locked in the bitter wars which accompanied the birth of Western capitalism. European contacts with Cathay were occasional and episodic. The early Manchu emperors were left free to enjoy the period of their ascendancy. With the passing of another two centuries, however, a remarkable growth of population brought renewed and sharpened pressure on the land. The Manchu dynasty had already entered upon its decline. Its rule was already disintegrating and it had been compelled to make heavy levies on the population to meet repeated revolts in different parts of its domain. Chinese society was on the brink of a new era of political breakdown and chaos when the first waves of expanding Western capitalism broke against China's shores. The advent of the new barbarians who came from across the seas deepened, transformed, and immensely complicated the inner divisions in the classes of Chinese society. Their coming meant that the old solutions, arrived at in the old manner, would no longer suffice.

Driving forward irresistibly toward the expansion of trade and the accumulation of capital resources, the Western nations smashed the barriers that had until now divided the Celestial Empire from the rest of the world. Out of this impact profound economic, political, and social changes had at last to come. Capitalist economy was drawing the whole world into its orbit. China's isolation was at an end. For capital was a new type of conqueror, hitherto unknown in Chinese history. Invading hordes which had swept down across the northern frontiers had in the past been assimilated with little difficulty into the more highly organized framework of the older Chinese civilization. These new barbarians possessed technical equipment and a material level which nothing in China could match. Mere traditions could not cope with cannon, any more than the hand could cope with the machine or the palanquin with the railway. Against the driving force and weapons of the Western barbarians, China could pit only the sheer weight of its age, its size, and numbers. These could determine the length and agony of this uneven conflict, not its outcome.

The Chinese economic and social structure, already in crisis, reacted swiftly at top and at bottom to the corrosive influence of the foreign invasion. Economically, China was laid prostrate. With the help of opium, the foreign traders established a balance permanently in their favor. Silver, heavily imported during the first period of the foreign trade, started draining away by 1826. Ten years later opium replaced silver as the medium of payment for Chinese tea and silk.[2] Through the breach made by the drug and widened by British and French cannon in the Opium Wars of 1842 and 1858, manufactured commodities made their way. British cotton goods stopped the export of Chinese woven cloth (nankeens) which practically disappeared from the export list by 1833. The curve of Chinese exports dropped sharply with the corresponding spectacular rise of opium imports during the first quarter of the nineteenth century. Cotton imports advanced steadily, and by 1870 cotton goods accounted for 31 percent of China's imports and a few years later replaced opium at the top of the list. The rapid strides in industrial organization and technique in the West, the opening of the Suez Canal, and the development of steam navigation, stimulated the China trade, which doubled between 1885 and 1894. The flow of commodities was soon followed by capital investments and loans. Foreign shipping companies, cotton mills, railways, and telegraph lines occupied by the end of the century all the commanding positions in Chinese economic life.

This economic conquest was facilitated by the establishment of foreign political control. The Manchu regime was reduced to impotence. Its early attempts to check the silver drain by restricting the opium trade were battered down in a series of wars in which it suffered humiliating defeats and for which it had to pay heavy penalties. Humbled by the Westerners, the Manchu regime lost immeasurably in prestige and authority over the Chinese. Treaties exacted by the foreigners at the cannon's mouth[3] provided for the free propagation of Christianity, the spearhead of Western penetration, and legalized the trade in opium.[4] But their most important provisions opened coastal and river ports to trade, limited the Chinese tariff to a nominal 5 percent, granted territorial footholds and concessions whence later came the different foreign "spheres of influence," and set up the system of extraterritoriality which exempted the foreigners from the jurisdiction of Chinese law and the payment of Chinese taxes. China became in all but name a subject land, saved from outright division and colonization only by the acute rivalries among the imperialist freebooters.

The spread of opium, the drain of silver, and the influx of machine-made commodities heightened to an acute degree the crisis in the countryside which derived from the rapid growth of the population and the shortage of cultivable land.[5] The widespread use of opium caused a flow of wealth from the countryside to the towns and led to an alarming contraction of the internal market.[6] The silver shortage caused by the drain resulted in a 20 to 30 percent depreciation of the copper currency in common use and a sharp rise in the cost of living. Debased coinage came into use.[7] Foreign cotton goods and other commodities drove Chinese handicrafts to the wall, especially in the southern provinces. The weavers who had produced the 3,359,000 pieces of cloth exported in 1819 lost their means of livelihood when the export dropped to 30,600 pieces in 1833 and almost to zero in the three subsequent decades.[8] Finally, as if man and his works were not sufficiently malignant, nature joined in the physical destruction of the old order of things. Scarcely a year passed in the middle decades of the nineteenth century without its quota of floods and famines, droughts and plagues, in the great river valleys and beyond.

The accumulative result of all these agencies of dissolution was mass pauperization and the creation of a large floating population. Sporadic revolts and outbreaks among the racial minorities of the Miao tribes in the southwest and the Muslims in the northwest heralded the beginning of a new peasant war which, in the traditional course of events, would have confirmed the exhaustion of Heaven's mandate to the ruling dynasty and led to the rise of a new reigning house. But while an essentially peasant revolt was brewing in the provinces, the Chinese ruling class was finding resources for renewing itself by participating, directly and indirectly, in the profits of the foreign trade.

Merchants and officials in the seaports had early begun to accumulate great fortunes through their dealings with the foreigners. Prior to 1830 when foreign ships still arrived at Canton laden with silver dollars to pay for the tea and silk carried back to Europe and the United States,[9] little of this wealth had found its way back to the ultimate producers. Most of it remained in the hands of the port merchants and mandarins.[10] Members of the co-hongs, special merchant monopolies officially established to deal with the foreigners, and local officials, who had a free hand in levying special taxes and "contributions," acquired great wealth, especially in the contraband opium trade. Membership in the co-hong was often worth as much as 200,000 taels. One Canton merchant boasted a fortune of $26,000,000 over and above the huge sums he had paid to the local officials in return for their benevolent support.[11]

From these merchants and officials a new class took shape, the class of compradores, brokers for foreign capital on the Chinese market. This was one of the first direct effects of the imperialist invasion upon the fabric of Chinese society. The commanding economic positions which imperialism secured for itself effectively blocked the main channel of indigenous, independent capitalist development. These Chinese merchants and officials stemmed, to begin with, from the landed gentry. The new wealth accumulated through the foreign trade went not into capitalist enterprise but into land, a process which visibly hastened the growth of large landed estates and the expropriation of petty landholders.[12] Landlords sent their sons into the cities to join in the lucrative business of compradoring. Rare was the compradore who was not an absentee landlord. Their profits went back not only into the land but into usurious loans to the peasants who had to borrow to bridge the gap between their decreasing incomes and the rising cost of living and taxes. Unable to compete with the superior force and material technique of the foreigners, the old landlord-merchant bourgeoisie was converted into a class of brokers, moneylenders, and speculators, with interests divided between town and country.

In this process the whole state structure took part. The Manchus had been defeated by the British in the Opium Wars "with an ease that shook their own confidence in the prowess and destiny of their race and completely dispelled its prestige of military power in the eyes of the subject Chinese."[13]

Broken by military defeats, the Manchu bureaucracy was soon undermined by bribery and the attractive profits from the smuggling of opium.[14] Edicts from Peking often remained inoperative. Peking was far away and the clink of foreign silver near and enticing. Chinese officialdom, theoretically virtuous, already had an ancient tradition of corruption. The dependence of officials on tax revenues for their own sustenance had from time immemorial placed a premium upon official honesty. The riches of the foreign trade crowned this tradition with a new source of illegitimate income. With the decline of the dynasty, the falling off of revenue to the center, and growing financial stringency, all pretense at virtue was thrown to the winds and official position became an object of open barter. The plums of power were acquired not by the learned but by those who had the price. Naturally it was the already wealthy merchant or compradore who could buy his son or his brother a mandarin's button. As the practice became common, the merchants, landlords, and officials became even more distinctly the branches of the same class tree. This class, fundamentally concerned with the preservation of all the inequalities on the land from which it profited, became one of the chief instruments of foreign penetration and control. Imperialism, on its part, having battered the imperial government into submission and adapted the upper strata of Chinese society to its uses, became the protector of the Chinese rulers against the wrath of a ravaged people. This was to become the basic formula of imperialist control in semi-colonial China. The whole Chinese economic, social, and political structure had been thrown into solution by imperialism, but new elements had barely begun to form when imperialism found itself compelled to join with everything conservative, oppressive, and backward in the nation to resist and smash agencies of revolutionary change.

This relationship crystallized during the Taiping Rebellion which threatened to overthrow the Manchu Dynasty in the middle of the nineteenth century. Repeated revolts, engendered by intolerable economic conditions, culminated in 1850 in a mighty anti-dynastic peasant rebellion which swept northward from Kwangsi and established its power for a period of eleven years in the Yangtze Valley. Beginning as a tiny religious sect of neo-Christian "God-worshippers" who came into conflict with local authority in the south, the Taiping movement developed swiftly into a social upheaval of the first magnitude. All the discontented and rebellious of the land flocked to its standard. Ancient anti-Manchu secret societies, never entirely extinguished, came once more to life. Chinese intellectuals and members of the lesser gentry, dispossessed from their land, weary of Manchu exactions, and angered by Manchu racial discrimination, joined its leading ranks. In the flush of anti-Manchu sentiment, the queue, badge of subjection, was abolished and the old Ming costumes restored. But above all and primarily, the great masses of pauperized peasants, migrating artisans, and seekers of land, long in revolt against local officials, landlords, and tax collectors, gave the movement its flesh and blood and stamped it with the traditional features of the peasant uprisings which in the past had led to dynastic changes.

Military successes were rapid and spectacular. Manchu authority was swept from the provinces of the south and the Yangtze Valley. Taiping armies reached almost to the gates of Peking. Hung Tsui-chuen, the fanatically religious leader of the movement, assumed the title Tien Wang, or Heavenly King, and established his capital at Nanking. At its height the movement was characterized by the independent seizure of land by the peasants in many places. This fundamental agrarian radical tendency was not supported at the top, although its pressure produced unenforced decrees for the destruction of land titles and plans for a collective sharing of landed property.[15] Beside the agrarian reforms carried out by the peasants at the base, it is also a significant fact that wherever the Taiping regime was relatively stabilized not unsuccessful efforts were made to suppress the opium trade, check the silver drain, stimulate the internal market, standardize taxation, and increase agricultural productivity. It is a fact of utmost interest, for example, that during the Taiping period the export of silk from the Kiangsu districts to the coast reached new high levels. The Taipings, if some accounts are to be believed, made repeated efforts to conciliate the foreigners on a basis of free exchange and suppression of the ruinous opium trade. Thus the Taiping Rebellion, primarily a peasant war of the primitive or traditional variety, also revealed tendencies, neither too directly nor clearly, but unmistakably, toward a "normal" bourgeois development.

The Taiping movement came into collision with all the forces of privilege on the land and in the cities. The rebellion destroyed the authority and position of the old official class. The agrarian measures of the peasants brought them into direct conflict with the landholding class as a whole and with the compradores and merchants who were so heavily involved in landed property through loans and mortgages. The "destructiveness of the Taipings," states a typical "standard" history, "antagonized the influential classes."[16] The "influential" Chinese classes were ranged solidly on the side of the Manchus.

For the imperialists the Taipings represented in their earlier stages a possibly more satisfactory alternative to the Manchus as the rulers of China. The Christian character of the movement aroused a certain sympathy among the missionaries. The Taipings, moreover, gave some promise of stimulating trade and restoring the tranquillity which the Manchus were unable to preserve. Nevertheless, despite all these factors, the foreigners soon threw their full weight to the side of the Manchus. The opium trade, it must be remembered, was still the most lucrative division of the Chinese market for the foreigners. It corresponded to the need for continued primitive accumulation and laying up of balances which only at a later date would make the marketing of more legitimate commodities more profitable. The fact that the Taipings opposed the trade in the drug placed them in opposition to the immediate interests of the foreigners.[17]

The civil war provided the imperialists with an excellent opportunity for strengthening their grip and extending their economic and political positions. In 1854 foreign guns prevented the anti-Manchu Triads from capturing Shanghai and took advantage of the complete collapse of local authority to assume control of the customs administration[18] and extend the domain of the foreign settlement. In 1858 French and British guns hammered away at the weakened Manchu forces in the north and forced the signature of new treaties fully satisfactory to foreign interests. The opium trade was legalized and the entire country was thrown open to foreign penetration. With the signing of these treaties, the foreigners had a definite stake in the preservation of the existing regime. The subjugation of the government was completed by the campaign of 1860 with its brutal sacking of the Summer Palace. Now a fully pliable instrument, the dynasty became an asset definitely worth protecting. The Taipings were transformed in the eyes of the foreigners "from possibly friendly successors to the Manchus into mere rebels who interfered with the carrying out of the new agreement."[19]

The Taiping version of Christianity, no less reasonable, certainly, than other variations on the themes of Jesus, was promptly perceived to be the rankest blasphemy. The Christian General Gordon took the field with the fervor of a crusader and stopped at nothing, treachery included, to deal with the Taipings as Jehovah's chosen people dealt with the Amalekites and all the worshippers of Baal. British and French forces, throwing aside all formal pretence at "neutrality," intervened actively in the struggle with decisive results. The battle for the preservation of the Manchu Dynasty was fought and won by two Chinese statesmen, Tseng Kuo-fan, representative of the landed interests, and Li Hung-chang, spokesman and leader of the new compradore class. They organized and led the defense of the Dragon Throne and they in turn succeeded only because foreign military and naval forces swamped the ill-armed Taipings before whom the Manchu troops were helpless.

The final defeat and dispersal of the Taipings in 1865 took place when the movement was already itself internally exhausted. The ravages of the civil war, which cost heavily in lives and laid waste large sections of the land, dissipated the resources of the peasant war. The leaders of the Taiping movement were unable to give a consistent lead to the agrarian movement which degenerated, inevitably, into partisan warfare and banditry. The leadership split into warring cliques of hopeless adventurers. The great Taiping Rebellion failed and the status quo was preserved because there was no class in Chinese society capable of leading the country out of its impasse. The weight of imperialism, stifling the free growth of China's own productive forces, at the same time made forever impossible a repetition of the old cycle of peasant war, dissolution, and dynastic change.

Here emerged the central contradiction around which the class struggle in China would henceforth revolve. The very coming of foreign imperialism, the end of Chinese isolation, and the appearance of the machine-made commodity on the Chinese market inexorably decreed the revolutionary transformation of Chinese society. Once entrenched, imperialism threw its weight into the balance for the perpetuation of all that was archaic and retrograde in that society. Revolutionary change for China now required the destruction of the old system of landholding and the release of pressure on the land. Imperialism joined in propping up the sway of the landlords, merchants, and officials who kept the mass of peasants in bondage and who provided the channels for the flow of foreign commercial capital into the remotest hinterland. Solution of China's economic, social, and political problems urgently demanded the unity of the country to ensure the best possible exploitation of its resources. The rivalries of the imperialist powers perpetuated internal conflicts which undermined the central authority by their unceasing exactions. Economic progress was contingent upon national independence. The maintenance of imperialist privilege demanded continued subjection.

The Taiping Rebellion was the last attempt to respond to a need for change in the "traditional" Chinese manner. It failed because the path to that solution was cut off by the entirely new conditions created by the imperialist invasion. Exhausted by twenty years of revolt and defeat, the Chinese masses had to await renewal in a new generation under entirely new circumstances before they could again intervene. At the base of Chinese society in the ensuing period all the contradictions responsible for chronic mass poverty profoundly deepened. The concentration of land continued. The flow of commodities and commercial capital into the villages broadened and gripped the lives of all toilers. Meanwhile, at the top of the social structure and in the developing urban centers, fundamental revisions were taking place, giving new form and new content to the struggle for China's future.

From the struggle against the Taipings and other sporadic revolts which lasted until 1880, the Manchu Dynasty emerged a spent force. Having barely sustained the shocks of internal rebellion, famines, and repeated natural disasters, it had again to face blows from without. In the face of a new imperialist offensive on the fringes of the Empire, it was helpless. France occupied Cambodia and Annam in the late sixties and "legalized" its acquisitions by a brief war in 1884–85. The next year Britain added Burma to its Indian Empire. Across Asia on the northern frontier, czarist Russia laid the course of a new railway and established in North Manchuria its "sphere of influence." In these same years Japan, responding more unifiedly and more quickly to the imperialist impact, had razed most of its feudal structure and with the Meiji Restoration embarked upon its remarkable course of adaptation to Western modes of production and organization. It was already reaching across the narrow strip of sea, seeking a continental foothold. In 1894 the new island power inflicted a humiliating defeat upon its aged and hitherto venerated neighbor. The amputation of Korea and the establishment of Japanese influence in South Manchuria was the signal for a new scramble among the powers for territories and concessions. Buffeted and helpless, the Imperial Court signed treaty after treaty. The dismemberment of China and the absorption of its several parts into the colonial empires of the Western nations seemed imminent.

Renewed imperialist pressure, however, brought to life new movements of reform and revolution quite different in character and class origin from the great mass revolts of the mid-nineteenth century. These new agencies of change developed in the upper strata of Chinese society. Foreign pressure had hammered the Chinese ruling class into a shape fitting imperialist requirements and foreign privilege closed most doors to native capitalist development. Nevertheless, the accumulation of wealth by this class could not fail in the nature of things to stimulate efforts to compete with the foreigners on their own ground. Imperialism had destroyed the old economic base. It could hinder but not entirely prevent the erection of a new one. Li Hung-chang, compradore-in-chief, himself initiated the first independent Chinese capitalist enterprises. The first rice-cleaning mill was built in Shanghai in 1863. The Kiangnan shipyard was established in 1865. Seven years later the China Merchants Steam Navigation Company was organized to compete with the foreign monopoly in coastal and river shipping. The next year the first modern silk filature was built, and in 1876 the first railway, a twelve-mile span from Shanghai to Woosung, came to confound the spirits of the ancestors of frightened peasants. A modern coal mine began operations at Kaiping in 1878, and in 1890 the first cotton spinning and weaving mill was built at Shanghai and the first ironworks at Wuchang. Match factories and flour mills had followed by 1896. The industrialization of China had begun.[20]

China's trade position, especially in cotton and cotton goods, visibly improved during this same period. An unfavorable balance in raw cotton was transformed into an export excess in 1888. The export of native woven cotton cloth, which had dropped almost to zero after 1833, recovered ground after 1868, rising from 238 piculs* that year to 30,100 piculs in 1900, the sharpest rise occurring after 1883,

---

* 1 picul equals 133 $^{1}/_{3}$ pounds.

although the import of manufactured cotton goods enjoyed at the same time an uninterrupted growth.[21] With the initial development of industry and the relative improvement in trade, transport, communications, and banking facilities were developed, although at a slower pace. A modern postal system came into existence in 1878. A telegraph line was laid between Shanghai and Tientsin in 1881. The Commercial Bank of China was organized in 1896 with all-Chinese capital. Other lines, other banks, soon followed in increasing numbers.

From the outset, Chinese capital fought a losing battle against foreign competition. The Treaty of Shimonoseki which concluded the Sino-Japanese War in 1895 established the right of foreigners to build industrial plants in China, and enterprises quickly sprang up to enjoy the benefits of cheap and plentiful Chinese labor. The superior technical equipment and knowledge of the foreigners, the economic and political privileges enjoyed by them, placed their Chinese rivals at an immediate disadvantage. In addition to being subject to technical limitations and tax burdens from which the foreigners were free, the Chinese were dependent upon the foreign market for credit facilities, machinery, and the great variety of manufactured commodities which China could not yet produce. The budding Chinese industrialists tried to overcome these disadvantages through the more intensive exploitation of labor. But it was not long before the desire to create more favorable conditions for the operations of Chinese capital forced its way into the political arena in the form of agitation for changes in a regime that no longer corresponded to the needs of newly growing economic interests.

In the period following the defeat of the Taiping Rebellion, Li Hung-chang sponsored a series of meager attempts to modernize the regime. Initiating new industrial enterprises on the one hand, Li also introduced the beginnings of a modern army and navy, urged changes in the schools, and sent student groups abroad to acquire for China the secrets of Western economic and political power. His efforts were cut short, however, by the Japanese War. The defeat, the loss of territory, and the new drive of the powers which followed brought new political tendencies to the surface. Quicker, more drastic changes were sought.

Two distinct currents dominated Chinese political life after 1895. The first hoped to reform the dynasty and adapt it to the new requirements. It dreamed of an emperor who would play the role of Peter the Great, and of a government that would resemble England's constitutional monarchy. The second advocated the overthrow of the Manchu Dynasty and the establishment of a Chinese republic along American or French lines. Entering upon the final period of its decline, the Manchu rulers gave way gradually before the reformers. By submitting to changes entirely incompatible with its own essential structure, the dynasty hastened its eventual abdication in favor of the revolutionists.

The reformers began by revising Confucius. They daringly represented him, not as the classic defender of the status quo, but as a progressive liberal. Into the old channels of Chinese social, political, and economic conceptions, they tried to pour the ideas of Adam Smith, John Stuart Mill, Herbert Spencer, and Thomas Huxley, whose works began to appear in Chinese translations. They profoundly believed that the nation could be transformed by imperial rescript and thought their cause won when in 1898 they gained the ear of the young emperor Kwang Hsu and launched the famous "Hundred Days" of reform. A series of sweeping decrees were issued to replace the archaic government of the Manchus with a modern state instrument. They called for the establishment of schools, election machinery, the elimination of tax abuses and official corruption. They ordered state aid to industry and agriculture and the democratization of the regime. Unhappily for the zeal of the reformers, the stream of new ideas that flowed out of the austere gates of the Forbidden City swirled only into the moat and there stagnated. To the old mandarins and magistrates it seemed that the emperor had gone mad, for his orders seemed designed to strip them of all the perquisites of office and to destroy all the institutions canonized by centuries of usage. Edict after edict begged that the imperial will be obeyed, but it seemed doubtful whether that will any longer enjoyed the sanction of Heaven. These doubts were swiftly confirmed at the Imperial Court itself where resistance to the reforms crystallized around the Empress Dowager. In September, 1898, she imprisoned her nephew and with a few strokes of her brush effaced all the reforms he had sponsored. Some of his advisers she executed. Others, including Kang Yu-wei and Liang Chi-chao, barely escaped into exile with their lives. These intellectuals had attempted during the "Hundred Days" to adapt the Manchu regime to Western ideas by working from the top down. The Chinese bourgeoisie was too immature, its economic base still too narrow and its interests still too divided, to impose its influence more aggressively upon the march of events. So the bourgeois intellectuals who sought reforms placed their reliance in an enlightened monarch. Unfortunately the "imperial will" proved impotent as an instrument of social change. The emperor only personified his own state apparatus. When he commanded it to destroy itself, it is not strange that it stolidly resisted. Against the inertia of the mandarinate, the reformers were helpless.[22]

The conservative Manchu bureaucracy could check the thin trickle of reforms supported only by a few individuals, but it could not resist the powerful and varied factors that were encompassing its doom. It was staggered by blow after blow from the imperialists. The closing years of the century were marked by the exaction of territorial, trade, and railway concessions by one power after another.[23] Within the country the destruction of the old handicraft economy, the high cost of living, new floods and droughts, led to the rise of a new primitive mass revolt, this time in the northern provinces where ancient secret societies revived and flourished and turned the wrath of an outraged people against all the foreign barbarians, Manchu and Western alike. Recoiling from the reform movement, the Manchu bureaucracy, headed by the Empress Dowager, fell back on the dangerous expedient of turning this mass revolt against itself into a whip with which to lash the hated foreigners. Open official support was given to the I Ho Chuan (Fists for the Protection of Public Peace), the insurgent society known to the foreigners as "Boxers." The rebels changed their slogan from "Down with the Manchus! Protect the Chinese!" to "Down with the Foreigners! Long Live the Imperial Dynasty!"[24]

Only disaster could follow. The fierce, primitive local uprisings were crushed by foreign arms and shattering penalties were imposed upon China by the victors, including an indemnity of U.S. $350,000,000 and sweeping military advantages under the Boxer Protocol of 1901. In the ensuing years China became the helpless spectator and victim of the rivalries and conflicts among the powers. The fate of railways, of concessions, and of whole Chinese provinces was decided in European chancelleries. Control of Manchuria and Korea was determined by a war fought across Chinese territory by Russia and Japan and settled by a treaty which freely bartered Chinese possessions without consulting the Chinese government. The Manchu Court no longer spoke for any effective section of the Chinese population, nor could it offer any resistance to the gradual destruction of its sovereignty.

From hopes in reform the Chinese intelligentsia turned to propaganda for revolution. The realization that the dynasty had outlived itself took firm root. Students and intellectuals turned their backs on Kang Yu-wei and began to listen more closely to the voice of another exile, Sun Yat-sen.

Sun had been among those who in 1895 had addressed reform memorials to the emperor. His political development, however, was the product of currents different from those which influenced the more prominent reformers of that day. Born in a village near Canton the year after the final suppression of the Taiping Rebellion, Sun in his early manhood came into contact with underground radicals steeped in the Taiping tradition of armed revolt. Sent as a youth to Honolulu, he became a Christian and along with the holy writ absorbed American notions of democracy. At the very beginning of his political career, Sun took the road of conspiratorial organization of the overthrow of the monarchy. His first attempt in 1895 failed and Sun went into foreign exile, seeking and winning support among overseas Chinese for his revolutionary program.

Sun's connections with overseas Chinese were of decisive importance for the course of the first Chinese Revolution. Chinese capitalism at home suffered from all the disabilities of foreign competition and the organic link between urban Chinese capital and semi-feudal exploitation on the land. Hindering independent capitalist development, these factors also prevented the emergence of any strong, clear-cut bourgeois nationalist revolutionary movement. Chinese overseas, however, in the Indies, the South Seas, in Europe, and the United States, laborers and merchants, came into direct contact with modern democracy. The strong protection afforded foreign nationals in China contrasted sharply with the defenselessness of overseas

Chinese in the face of racial discrimination and abuse. Among them a strong Nationalist sentiment took form long before it developed in China itself. Powerful racial, family, and traditional ties bound these emigrants to their native land and from them came the first financial and moral support for the revolutionary movement. It is interesting that only a few of the more wealthy overseas Chinese joined in the struggle for a strong and independent Chinese republic. Most of the money Sun raised came in small sums from contract workers and small merchants who proved ready before anyone else to support Sun's program.

This program, focused on the idea of overthrowing the monarchy by military conspiracy, attracted large sections of the disillusioned reformers and most of the new generation of students, especially those who flocked to Japan after 1895 and in much greater numbers after 1900. In China, the movement forged links with the secret societies. The new elements from the intelligentsia of town and country gave these organizations a Nationalist and Democratic coloration they had never before possessed. Students who went abroad and returned bulging with new ideas and radical fervor found recruits everywhere. Discontent with the existing order of things grew. Democratic and Nationalist ideas made headway. Russia's 1905 revolution made an impression on the Chinese intellectuals and had a very specific influence in driving the Court toward concessions.[25] Chinese merchants and capitalists began to assert themselves more boldly. Nothing showed this more clearly than the boycotts against the United States in 1905 and against Japan in 1908.

These movements took on a broad, popular character. They were supported by the merchant guilds and the newly grown popular press. The use of the economic weapon in China against the abusive attitude of Americans toward Chinese in the United States revealed the rise of a new spirit of confidence and solidarity among the merchants and petty capitalists. The campaign tightened the bonds between the Chinese in the United States and those at home. It helped break down sectional barriers. The boycott was strongest in Canton, most of the Chinese in America being Cantonese, but it was accompanied by demonstrations and boycott activities in Singapore, Shanghai, and Tientsin. Perhaps most significant was the conduct of the boycott in open defiance of imperial authority which had, in response to American diplomatic pressure, issued an edict against the boycott. The anti-Japanese boycott in 1908 was even more specifically anti-government in character. It arose from the cringing submission of the Chinese authorities to Japan in connection with a shipping incident. Merchants burned Japanese merchandise and workers at the docks refused to unload from Japanese vessels, perhaps the first direct participation of Chinese workers in the anti-imperialist struggle of the present century.[26]

One of the demands that arose in connection with the anti-American boycott had been for the cancellation of the concession granted to an American firm for the construction of the Canton-Hankow Railway. It was around the issue of railway concessions that opposition to the Imperial Court now developed among the wealthy provincial merchants and gentry. Plans for the construction of railways linking Canton, Hankow, Changsha, and Chengtu had already been drawn up and companies had been established with Chinese capital to carry the plans through. The Peking government, now a compradore instrument which found the game of granting concessions to foreign interests extremely profitable, used foreign money to buy up Chinese holdings already invested in various railway schemes in order to turn over the projects to the foreigners. Resistance to this flared among the incipient railway magnates, especially in Hunan, Hupeh, and Szechwan. The underground revolutionary societies[27] made broad agitational use of the issue which helped to identify the Manchu regime with the hated foreign exploiter and rival. This drew new strata of the upper classes into the struggle against the monarchy. It was an outbreak over precisely this issue, in Szechwan, which finally provoked open rebellion.

The threat of utter collapse was present during the whole last decade of the dynasty's existence. It was put off only by surrender to the pressure for reforms. The empress dowager and her advisers were compelled to realize that the growing critical unrest after the Boxer episode had to be met by compromise. It was a question, it seemed, of giving in or going down. In 1906 the Manchu Court, absolute ruler of the Celestial Empire for nearly three hundred years, grudgingly recognized the "principle" of constitutional government. After this initial dilution, the birthright of the emperors was gradually watered down. The dynasty was already doomed when its last vigorous representative disappeared from the scene. The empress dowager died at the end of 1908. With her to the grave went the imprisoned emperor Kwang Hsu. Her oldest advisers soon followed. On the Dragon Throne sat the three-year-old emperor Hsuan Tung.* A foolish and incompetent man reigned as regent. The Court degenerated into a swamp of petty nepotism and clique rivalries. Paper reforms, more numerous but more niggardly and unreal, were admitted. In 1910 provincial viceregal assemblies, closely resembling the zemstvos under the czar in Russia, came into existence as a result of rigorously limited "popular" elections.[28] These had only the right to debate, and to debate only certain topics prescribed by the throne. But even these carefully hand-picked "long-gowned" assemblies came into conflict with the Court. They urged that a broader, more responsible government would alone preserve the monarchy. Delegates of the provincial assemblies joined in a national body in Peking and over Court resistance tried desperately to hasten parliamentary reform. Formal changes were introduced but the hand of the old regime, still heavy upon the new bodies, reduced them to hopeless fictions. The assembly, composed of imperial appointees and eminently safe friends of the viceroys, tried to drag the monarchy behind it to

* Otherwise known as Henry Pu Yi, destined to become Emperor Kang Teh of Japan's puppet state, Manchukuo.

the illusory salvation summed up in the magic word "parliament." While they wrangled, revolution overtook them and the Court they hoped to save.

A local outbreak against the imperial officials in Szechwan in September 1911 was followed in October by the revolt of the garrison at Wuchang. When imperial troops stationed at Lanchow refused to march against the rebels, the days of Manchu rule were at long last numbered. While the revolt spread, the Court abjectly offered to surrender all claims to authority in return for the semblance of rule. But it was too late. The empire crumbled and fell. With it went the "national assembly" whose banner it had tried feebly to wave in the face of an unalterable destiny.

Internal corrosion had already reduced the dynasty to a cipher. Only a tiny push was needed to erase it. The revolution of 1911 generated only enough energy to produce this tiny push, no more. From it emerged no class capable of directing the transformation of the country, capable of solving the agrarian crisis and of regaining the national independence which alone could protect China from the continued incursions and pressure of the imperialist powers. The identity of the Chinese bourgeoisie with the semi-feudal interests on the land predetermined its inability to lead the impoverished peasantry out of its difficulties. Nor were the revolutionists of 1911 driven even to make the attempt. The masses of the peasantry played no role in the overthrow of the dynasty. Their passivity made it possible for the old provincial military and civilian apparatus to preserve the status quo minus only the dynastic label and the queues imposed upon the people as a badge of subjection by the Manchu conquerors.

With the disappearance of nominal central authority, power passed into the hands of provincial or regional satraps committed to the preservation of the whole existing exploitative system. Through them the foreign stranglehold on the country's economic and political life was tightened. The regional powers that came into existence corresponded in the main to the respective "spheres of influence" of the great powers. Militarists in Yunnan and southern Kwangsi drew sustenance and support from France. The river valleys economically controlled by Hong Kong and Shanghai passed more definitely under British influence. The north became largely Japan's special domain. The civil wars that soon broke out among these rival governments came to reflect, primarily, the conflicts among the principal imperialist powers jockeying for key economic positions. It is this fact which distinguishes the post-1911 period from similar periods of division, civil wars, and confusion following the collapse of earlier dynasties.

The bourgeois intellectuals who had participated in the revolution proved helpless as these new divisions unfolded and took form. Their strategy in the fight against the dynasty had never been able to acquire the form of an authentic popular movement because of the economic immaturity and political impotence of the class they represented. The preservation of its interests on the land meant the preservation of all that was backward in rural China, the feudal family system, illiteracy, superstition, of everything on which the old system rested. Its interests in the city were subordinated, and therefore subjected, to foreign capital. The struggle of the bourgeois intellectuals therefore took the form of military conspiracies which always failed. The downfall of the monarchy had occurred almost independently of their efforts. Afterwards they became mere appendages of the militarists who seized power. The parliaments and constitutions they elaborated were not organs of actual political control, but window-dressing tolerated or utilized at will by the militarists they depended upon for protection. Thus Sun Yat-sen, who had returned to China in triumph and had been elected first president of the Chinese Republic, was quickly compelled to give way to Yuan Shih-kai, a general of the old regime who took command in Peking.

Those intellectuals who did not become secretaries or jobholders under illiterate generals fell away from the movement into passivity and apathy. Sun Yat-sen and the remains of his party, the Kuomintang, fell prey to parliamentary cretinism, inscribing the slogan "Protect the Constitution" on the party banner. But the only protection they sought was in the camp of one set of generals pitted against another. At this game they lost with consistent regularity. Only the generals won.

The overturn of the monarchy, itself a progressive act of immense historical importance, seemed to have brought the country from bad to worse. The civil wars and the reign of the generals deepened the misery in the countryside. Exactions increased. Land was laid waste. Agricultural production declined. China was compelled to begin importing rice and wheat. Famines and unchecked disasters took heavy tolls in human life. Millions of peasants, driven off the land, swelled the hordes of the militarist armies or took to banditry. Harsh taxation and militarist requisitions hastened the destruction of Chinese rural economy and condemned the overwhelming majority of the population to chronic starvation. Domestic industry could not, and seemingly never would, absorb the large labor surplus. But it was precisely in this sphere that swift and sudden changes began to occur as a direct result of the Great War.

The war absorbed the undivided attention and the full industrial output of all the nations involved. Native Chinese producers unexpectedly found themselves with a great market open before them in their own country under conditions temporarily relieved of the constant pressure of foreign capital. Thanks to the war demands, China's unfavorable trade balance dropped abruptly to record depths, amounting to only Tls. 16,000,000 in 1919, with exports rising sharply. Taking 1913 as 100, imports were 91.6 in 1914 and 105.9 in 1919. Exports rose from 83.8 in 1914 to 140.1 in 1919. In effect imports remained nearly stationary for the war years, giving the export trade a chance to leap forward.[29]

Far more spectacular was the spurt of industrial growth made possible by the breathing space of the war. Imports of industrial machinery rose from Tls. 4,380,749 in 1915 to Tls. 56,578,535 in 1921. Cotton mills increased from forty-two in 1916 to 120 in 1923, spindles from 1,145,000 to 3,550,000. Silk filatures rose from fifty-six in 1915 to ninety-three in 1927. Four cigarette factories in 1915 grew to 182 by 1927.[30] If we take the year 1913 as 100, we have the following indices for 1923: coal production, 183.5; iron ore production, 180.6; silk exports, 152.3; bean oil exports, 432.5; cotton spindles, 403.9. At the same time there were smaller but appreciable increases in transport and shipping.

This growth was accompanied by extensive alterations in the Chinese business structure. Corporate forms were adopted. Banking facilities were expanded. As machines replaced handicraft production in swiftly increasing measure, the old master-journeyman-apprentice relationship gave way in decisive economic sectors to the stockholder-manager-worker relationship.

This rise of productive forces brought aspiring Chinese capital automatically into collision with entrenched foreign interests and the existing structure of foreign economic and political privilege. It also brought the new class of workers into conflict with their employers, foreign and Chinese alike. From these new springs flowed fresh Nationalist currents which swept China into the upheavals of the next decade.

2 Problems of the Chinese Revolution

Social change came belatedly to China. That is why it is today a land of such deeply chiseled contrasts. It is forced by the pull of a whole world system to make the leap from wooden plough to tractor, from palanquin to airplane. Imperialism forced the Celestial Empire to find its place in a terrestrial world that had already advanced far beyond it, economically, culturally, and politically. For China there was no gradual grade to ascend nor the opportunity to pass through the historical stages of development the rest of the world had already left behind. To come abreast it had to take a mighty leap forward. The West had taken centuries to make the changes China had to make in a few decades. This wrench could not occur without the most profound convulsions. Hence the turmoil, the speed, the scope, the depth, the explosive character of events in China during the last thirty years.

To lift itself to the material and cultural plane the new times so imperiously demanded, China had not only to break sharply with its own past. It had to transform its present. Old fetters and new both had to be sundered. Imperialist penetration introduced the most modern of techniques in production, transport, communications, and finance, the instruments of modern capitalism. Yet by adapting to its own uses the merchants, the landlords, the officials, and the militarists, imperialism helped to perpetuate the pre-capitalist forms of Chinese social organization. Foreign-built factories, foreign-built railroads, were used to extract super-profits out of the backwardness that still prevailed in China as a whole. By commanding all the strategic positions in Chinese economy and drawing off its tribute for the benefit of investors abroad, imperialism stifled the "normal" or independent development of China's resources in the interest of a raised standard of living for the Chinese people. If the Chinese people were to be lifted from privation to the beginnings of plenty, productive forces had to be freed of all that fettered them. Land had to be restored to those who tilled it and the imperialist grip on Chinese economic life had to be broken. These were the inseparable elements of the problems of the Chinese revolution. Their solution, to be sure, could not be envisaged within China's national framework alone. In modern conditions of world economy, the problems of one nation could no longer be divorced from the problems of the world as a whole. In China, in the most immediate sense, the nature of its historic tasks brought their solution into direct collision with the imperialist powers. This dictated at once the international character of Chinese social and political conflicts. Reorganization of Chinese society could be only a factor in the economic and social reorganization of the whole world. At the same time China had now become part of this world, a gigantic element in the activity, the calculations, and the conflicts of opposing forces on a world scale. The development and ultimate solution of China's internal crisis could not fail to exert an important, and perhaps a decisive, influence far beyond its own borders.

No radical revision in Chinese economic life could even be contemplated if in the first instance the revolution did not restore to the peasant the land and the product of his toil. Only in this way would the old land-holding system be destroyed. Without this indispensable first step, the eventual transformation of rural economy and the growth of agricultural productivity in new forms and by new methods were unthinkable. More than three-quarters of China's population, or more than 300,000,000 people, depend upon the land for their livelihood. The problem of these millions is the problem of China. Their poverty is China's poverty. In the release of the gigantic productive energies of this great mass of people alone lies the hope for China's future. Today they are pauperized by a social system that takes from them the produce they wring from the land as well as the land itself and gives them nothing in return.

Chinese rural economy is characterized by the following main features: (1) The increasingly swift concentration of land ownership in the hands of a constantly narrowing section of the population; (2) the passage of title in much of the land to absentee landlords, government officials, banks, and urban capitalists, who control the commercial capital penetrating to the remotest villages through the local merchants and usurers, who in turn are controlled and dominated by foreign finance capital and the regime of the world market; (3) the dislocation and decline of agricultural production as a result of the uneconomic use of increasingly parcellized land, the preservation of the most backward farming methods, the harsh impositions of landlord, usurer, and the state, exposure to the ravages of famine, flood, and drought, and civil wars fought by armies swollen by dispossessed peasants.

Only recently, surveys, for the first time competently and scientifically conducted, finally destroyed the illusion, once so common, that China was a land of relatively comfortable small land-holders. From sectional studies made under his direction, Professor Chen Han-seng has estimated that no less than 65 percent of the peasant population is either entirely landless or land-hungry, that is, possessing land in parcels too small and too burdened by the backward methods of production and the harshness of the regime to provide a living, even on the barest subsistence level.[1] Differences in land owned and used and in the labor applied or exploited on the land revealed the profound cleavages within the peasant population into the categories of rich, middle, and poor.*

Conditions of land tenure mirror class relations in agriculture. One official estimate made in 1927 held that 55 percent of the Chinese peasantry was entirely landless and 20 percent holders of inadequate land. It was calculated that 81 percent of the cultivable land was concentrated in the hands of 13 percent of the rural population.[2] These figures have been in the main substantiated by later investigators. In the north, where individual land-holders predominated, study of a sample district showed that although only 5 percent of the farming population consisted of landless tenants, 70 percent of the total held less than 30 percent of the cultivated land in average plots of 10.9 mow, or less than two acres. In another district it was found that 65.2 percent of the population held 25.9 percent of the land in parcels of less than seven mow, or a fraction above one acre. Landlords and rich peasants, together comprising 11.7 percent of the farming population, held 43 percent of the land and middle peasant families held the rest.

In the far more densely populated Yangtze River Valley and in the south, where imperialist influence had first been felt and where the commercialization of agriculture was consequently more advanced, the disproportions were found to be much greater. In one district of Chekiang province investigators found that 3 percent of the population owned 80 percent of the land. In Wusih, another district of Central China, 68.9 percent of the farming families owned only 14.2 percent of the land in individual average holdings of 1.4 mow, or less than a quarter of an acre. Landlords and rich peasants, 11.3 percent of the families, owned 65 percent of the land.[3]

A separate survey made in the southern province of Kwangtung[4] revealed that owners of land in different sections of the province comprised 12 to 32 percent of

---

* Professor Chen defined these categories as follows: "When a peasant family is barely capable of self-support from the land, and in its agricultural labour not directly exploited by, nor exploiting, others, we may say that such a family belongs to the class of middle peasants. The status of the middle peasants helps us to determine that of the other two classes of peasantry. When a peasant family hires one or more agricultural labourers by the day or by the season during busy times, to an extent exceeding in its total consumption of labour power that required by the average middle peasant family for self-support, or when the land which it cultivates surpasses in area the average of the land used by the middle peasant, we shall then classify this family as that of a rich peasant. Where we see families cultivating twice as much land as the middle peasants in their village, we safely classify them as those of rich peasants without further considering the labour relations. The poor peasants are comparatively easy to recognize. All peasant families whose number of cultivated mow (one mow is one-sixth of an English acre) falls below that of the middle peasants and whose members, besides living on the fruits of their own cultivation have to rely upon a wage income or some income of an auxiliary nature, belong to the poor peasants in general. Those poor peasants who do not cultivate any land, either their own or leased, but hire themselves out, or who cultivate a mere patch of land but have to support themselves chiefly by selling their labour power in agriculture, are called hired agricultural labourers, but still belong to the peasantry."

— Agrarian Problems in Southernmost China, Shanghai, 1936, p. 8.

the population and tenants and agricultural laborers 68 to 88 percent. Of the poor peasants representing 64.3 percent of the population in one area, investigators found that 60.4 percent were landless. An average of all the districts studied showed that more than half the farming population owned no land. Of all the land tilled by the poor peasants, only 17.2 percent was owned and 82.8 percent leased. The average area owned by a poor peasant family was found to be .87 mow and the average area cultivated, including leased land, 5.7 mow. The number of mow necessary to provide the barest subsistence for a peasant family was found, in different districts, to vary between six and ten and double that many for tenant farmers.

This extreme concentration of ownership in the land came about partially through the gradual alienation of the once considerable state, temple, or community lands and the conversion of the large collective holdings of the rural clans into the virtual private property of small groups of powerful clan leaders. The steady decline in agricultural production and increasing weight of the burden placed on the peasant's shoulders soon lost him what land he had left. Not all his skill on his tiny plot of ground could meet the scientific advances made elsewhere in agriculture or provide him with means to deal with the decreasing productivity of his land. China's chief commercial crops, tea and silk, surrendered their positions in the world market because better products were more efficiently produced by more modern competitors.[5]

The backwardness of the country as a whole, the lack of communications adequate to meet the demands of the modern market, the primitiveness of the peasant's methods, combined to ruin the agricultural producer as soon as the penetration of commercial capital into the deepest hinterland and with it the influx of cheap manufactured commodities brought an end to his old self-sufficiency. He had to produce for sale in order to exist, yet the smallness of his land and the primitive character of his farming proved an impassable bar to doing this successfully. He not only could not produce enough to provide his needed surplus, but had to go into debt, for fertilizer, for food to tide him over until the harvest, for seed, for the rent and use of implements. For these he mortgaged his land, at rates never lower than 30 percent and more often 60, 70, 80 percent and even higher. The crushing burden of taxes and the rapacious extortions of the militarists who came to rule over him drove him more deeply into debt and placed him and his land at the mercy of the usurer and the tax collector.[6] He was fleeced at will by the merchant because he could not ship his tiny crop to more distant markets and hope for a return. Crops were freely cornered and prices manipulated. Invariably new debts and not a surplus became the result of the season's toil. They followed him into the next year and unto the next generation. Losing his land, he became a tenant. To the landlord he had to surrender 40 to 70 percent of his crop and a substantial additional percentage in special dues, gifts, and obligations borne through the centuries from the dim feudal past, including the duty of free labor on special occasions fixed by ancient tradition. Famines, floods, and droughts, against which he was defenseless, cost him his crop, his land, if he had any, his family, and most often his life. Even in the best years, however, he lived on the slimmest borderline of starvation. He was little better than a bonded slave to the landlord, the tax collector, the merchant, and the usurer.

This process, in its manifold aspects, plunged the great mass of the peasantry into chronic, unrelieved pauperism. Millions driven off the land begged, starved, took to banditry, or swelled the armies of the warlords. From the south they streamed abroad, to the Americas, to Malaya, and to the Indies. From the north they emigrated to the undeveloped lands of Manchuria. Millions clogged the cities and towns on the rivers and on the seaboard, an inexhaustible source of cheap manpower that the new industries could not absorb. Their labor was still cheaper than that of animals, and throughout the length and breadth of China men did the work of beasts of burden. More and more land was left untilled. China, one of the greatest of agricultural countries, was compelled to begin importing foodstuffs in steadily increasing measure.[7] The internal and external markets entered upon a disastrous decline. The whole economic structure rotted at its core.

These conditions meant that the release of the land for more productive use (and this meant the release of the peasant from his burdens) had become the indispensable first step in any effort to revive and revitalize Chinese economy. This could be realized, however, only if the economy of the country as a whole were at the same time freed to develop and coordinate the nation's resources in accordance with its needs. This it would never be so long as existing imperialist economic and political privileges remained intact. Foreign capital occupied dominant positions in all the basic economic sectors, sucking the country leech-like of its resources. It owned nearly half the cotton industry, China's largest. It owned a third of the railways outright and held a paralyzing mortgage on the rest. It owned and operated more than half the shipping in Chinese waters and carried in its own bottoms nearly 80 percent of China's foreign and coastal trade. Favored by their technical superiority and their political and economic privileges, the imperialists subjected China to a steady drain. The country's adverse trade balance accumulated between 1912 and 1924 to the staggering total of $1,500,000,000,* which was more than doubled in the subsequent decade. Between 1902 and 1914 foreign investments doubled and doubled again in the ensuing fifteen years, reaching an estimated total of $3,300,000,000. More than four-fifths of it was directly invested in transport and industrial enterprises and the rest in loans which converted Chinese governments into docile tools of the imperialists and gave the latter a strangling grip on the nation's internal and external revenues.[8]

To regain control of its own productive forces, China had to recapture this lost ground. It had to unify itself by cutting across the sectional rivalries perpetuated by

---

* Calculated in U.S. dollars at par

the imperialist-supported warlords in the foreign "spheres of influence." Only in this way could internal peace be restored, the incubus of militarism removed, the internal market expanded and developed. Only in this way could Chinese industry become the basis for a raised standard of living for the whole people. To solve the impasse on the land, China had to free itself from imperialism. To free itself from imperialism it had to galvanize the great masses of the peasantry by offering them hope of release from their intolerable burdens. An anti-imperialist movement that inscribed the slogans of agrarian revolt on its banners alongside those of national liberation would alone find the strength to bring imperialism to heel.

How and by whom could this be done? The answer resolves itself automatically into an estimate of class forces and relationships, for each section of the population stood in distinct and different relation to the land and to imperialism. Each would necessarily take the road of political struggle with different objectives in view. The peasantry, comprising the great majority of the petty bourgeoisie, as history has abundantly proved, cannot function independently in the political arena. It is deeply cleft into layers with sharply conflicting economic interests. It is the most scattered and the most backward section of the population. It is localized and limited, economically and psychologically. For these reasons the village has always followed the town. The peasantry has always been subject to the urban class able to centralize, weld, control, and command. Without the centripetal force of the city, around which rural economy must inevitably revolve, the peasant is helpless, especially the poorest peasant, the most exploited and the nearest to the soil. His own attempts to better his own lot, without the aid or in defiance of the dominant city class, have invariably taken the form of isolated acts of violence without permanent issue.

This was true of Russia and is especially true of China, a vast land of impoverished millions, darkened by illiteracy and superstition, so divided sectionally that customs, habits, and the spoken language differ sharply from province to province, from town to town and even from village to village. China's great peasant wars had invariably ended in a restratification within the peasantry, for the revolting peasants were always taken in tow by a section of the ruling class that sought not a new society but a new dynasty. When the fighting was done, a new emperor sat on the Dragon Throne and the landlords rose anew. Only an urban ally capable of transforming all social relations, of destroying the old state in its entirety and erecting a new one on its ruins, could release the peasantry from this vicious historical circle, free it from its own exploiting minority in the countryside, and help it bridge the cultural gap separating town and country.

In Europe the bourgeois revolutions of two and three centuries ago had played this historic role. The rising capitalists had to extend the rights of bourgeois property to the land and free labor from serfdom for the wage slavery of the newly rising industrial system. The most radical sections of the petty bourgeoisie came forward to help the peasantry break the bonds with which feudalism kept it chained to the soil and laid the foundations of strong national bourgeois states. In China of the twentieth century a different social pattern forced different solutions. The bourgeoisie could not liberate the peasantry because, as a result of the peculiar conditions and the belatedness of its growth, it was the bourgeoisie that directly exploited the peasantry. It has already been shown how the bourgeoisie rose, not as a distinctly urban grouping, but out of the old ruling classes and how it remained bound by a thousand ties to the pre-capitalist or semi-feudal system of exploitation on the land in which it directly participated. The peasant was subject to the depredations of landlord, usurer, merchant, banker, war lord, tax-collector, and local officials. The interests of these exploiters fused and became the interlaced interests of the ruling class as a whole. Not uncommonly, the collector of rent, of interest, of feudal dues, and of taxes was one and the same person. "Quite unlike the landlords in France *sous l'ancien régime*, the landlords in China are often quadrilateral beings," wrote Professor Chen Han-seng.

> They are rent collectors, merchants, usurers, and administrative officers. Many landlord-usurers are becoming landlord-merchants; many landlord-merchants are turning themselves into landlord-merchant-politicians. At the same time many merchants and politicians become also landlords. Landlords often possess breweries, oil mills, and grain magazines. On the other hand, the owners of warehouses and groceries are mortgagees of land, and eventually its lords. It is a well-known fact that pawnshops and business stores of the landlords are in one way or another affiliated with banks of military and civil authorities.... While some big landlords practise usury as their chief professions, nearly all of them have something to do with it. Again, many landlords are military and civil officers.[9]

This is the real physiognomy of the Chinese ruling class and of the system of exploitation that grinds the peasant. The fundamental relations that govern it are bourgeois in character. Feudalism, in its classic form, disappeared from China many centuries ago when land, the basic means of production, became alienable. The penetration of commercial capital into the village established there essentially bourgeois forms of exploitation within an economic structure that retained many of its pre-capitalist features. The bourgeois of today, the landlord-merchant-banker-politician-tax collector, derives his income from usury, market speculation, land mortgages, state taxes, and ground rent. Himself a product of the backwardness of Chinese economy, he also benefits, to no small degree, from the pre-capitalist forms of exploitation embedded in the social structure. He extracts toll by methods strongly feudal in character and in origin, militarist requisitions, dues to the landlord in free labor and gifts, rent in kind, forced labor, military service, miscellaneous local taxation, and *likin*, or district customs taxes.

Under the molding pressure of imperialism, the most important sections of the Chinese bourgeoisie had become brokers, once, twice, or thrice removed, for the operations of foreign or foreign-controlled capital, just as the warlords and their governments had been converted, in their respective spheres, into pawns on the chessboard of inter-imperialist rivalries. While aspiring Chinese industrialists and bankers, envisaging an independent capitalist development of their own, would naturally want to loosen the imperialist grip, they were confronted with the fact that the gulf that separated them from the exploited masses in the country was far more profound and unbridgeable than the antagonism between them and the foreign rivals upon whom they still depended for so much. From the imperialists the bourgeoisie could and would try to exact concessions, to demand and secure a larger share of the spoils, but it could not hope to satisfy the masses without undermining itself. Land could not be restored to the peasantry without upsetting all existing property relations and destroying the economic base of the bourgeoisie in town and country alike. This fundamental fact predetermined the unity of the Chinese and foreign exploiters against the exploited. It also meant that the solution of China's revolutionary tasks passed into the hands of the newest and youngest class, the urban proletariat, organizing and drawing behind it the millions of toilers and artisans in the towns and on the fields. Its interests alone were consistent with the radical revision of the whole of Chinese economic life.

The idea that the proletariat, a tiny minority in a teeming country, could assume the responsibilities of political leadership had ceased to be a theory and became a condition, in Russia in 1917. There the proletariat of a backward country had taken over the tasks a bankrupt bourgeoisie proved unable to shoulder. The October revolution had shown how the combination of a proletarian insurrection—the culmination of the new class antagonisms—and a peasant war—the carry-over of the old—offered the only way out for a backward country in the modern world of imperialism. Like Russia, China had to solve tasks that belonged historically to the past epoch of bourgeois revolutions. Russia had demonstrated that this could be done in the twentieth century only by radically transforming all class relations and the whole social structure. This was achieved by telescoping the bourgeois and proletarian revolutions.

The experience of the October revolution was decisive for the whole backward East, and especially for China. The bourgeois revolutions of the past had taken place in the early dawn of capitalism before the emergence of the proletariat as a distinct class. Yet even those revolutions were brought to their historical fruition only by the determined intervention of the plebeian masses. The artisans and city poor of Holland fought for a century to throw off the dead hand of Spanish feudalism and clear the path for the economic expansion of the Dutch bourgeoisie. It was the artisan and peasant in the ranks of Cromwell's armies who laid the foundations of the British bourgeois commonwealth. In France, the land of the classic bourgeois revolution, the peasant insurrection drove the frightened burghers of the Third Estate back into the arms of the nobility. The city plebeian, the embryo proletarian, the pauper, the sans-culotte, rose from the gutters of Paris again and again to drive the revolution forward. It was the Jacobin republic of 1793, not the

National Assembly of 1789, that finally smashed the chains of feudalism and freed the peasant, although it had to hand him over to the new slavery of the bourgeois order of which he became an integral part.

Between these events and the Russian revolution a whole historic epoch intervened, profoundly transforming all society and consequently the methods and instruments of social change. Capitalism established the division of labor on a world scale. Sweeping technological advances and the automatic expansion of capital wealth soon collided with the national barriers originally erected to facilitate reorganization of the internal country market and the productive system that fed it. Rival national groups fought for markets, for fresh sources of raw material, for cheap labor and higher profits. Out of these conflicts colonial empires grew. All the backward sections of the world became subjected to the more advanced countries and were drawn irresistibly into the orbit of world capitalist economy. Asia and Africa became the theaters of stupendous economic, political, and military conflicts. Out of the ruthless competition that lay at the heart of this swiftly unfolding process emerged the tendency toward concentration of capital wealth, the rise of monopolies on the basis of mass production in large-scale industries, the division of the world into a decreasing number of increasingly mighty economic and political groups, incessantly at war with one another, by economic or military means. Industrial control was transformed into financial control that crossed seas and the highest mountains and even battered down the walls of old China. When backward Russia and the newly awakened East ripened for revolution, the world had already advanced far into the epoch of imperialism.

To the backward countries this transformed world came ready-made. The tardy had to make gigantic leaps forward, combining in single historical stages the progressive steps the rest of the world had already left behind. The high degree of interdependence between the advanced and the backward nations linked their political fate, destroying the possibility of any gradual, isolated national development for the latter. Economically they had to leap from the most primitive of pre-capitalist forms of production to the latest techniques of industry, transport, and market organization. No less a leap had to be taken on the political plane, folding into brief compass the long and relatively gradual development of modern democratic political institutions. This was not all, for the point to which society had already developed on a world scale forced the backward countries not merely to come abreast but to surge beyond. Capitalism was already a fetter on productive forces. Its national barriers blocked the further development that was possible now only on an international scale. For this, the capitalist world could offer only the solution of a catastrophic war. If in the advanced countries capitalism and its democratic political institutions already failed to correspond to the basic needs of expanding economy, for the backward countries the hope for peaceful capitalist development in a democratic political framework had entirely disappeared. To move forward at all, they had to step over a whole historical epoch and move directly toward Socialist development through the establishment of the transitional proletarian dictatorship. This is precisely what happened in Russia in 1917. Only the young proletariat proved capable of grappling with the problems inherited from the past and those posed by the present.

The October revolution was victorious because the course of historical development made the growth of productive forces dependent upon the elevation of the proletariat to power. In Russia the workers were able to rise to this historic occasion because they were led by a party that had developed to an extraordinary degree the consciousness of the class mechanics of history. This it drew from the revolutionary experiences of Europe in the mid-nineteenth century and from the more recent Russian past. It was generalized and made intelligible by those first great Communists, Marx and Engels, and after them, the Russian Marxists, Lenin and Trotsky, four men who have stamped their imprint on a whole historic epoch as few men have ever done.

It was not enough that the dialectics of history had taken the lever of social progress out of the hands of the bourgeoisie and placed it in the hands of the proletariat, in the advanced and backward nations alike. Rising against their class enemy in the economic domain, the workers had to acquire through their own experience a consciousness of their political and historical role and had to forge the necessary weapon, the political party which could lead them to independent action on the political arena.

The history of the class struggle is in one very direct sense the history of the liberation of oppressed classes from servility and dependence upon their oppressors. When the burghers no longer cringed before the barons, the struggle for the creation of the bourgeois state came on to the order of the day. The democratic movements in Europe in 1848 were abortive because the petty bourgeois democrats, frightened by the workers and the plebeian masses, betrayed the peasants to the feudal reaction and permitted Cavaignac and his German and Austrian counterparts to crush the nascent working-class movement. With a rising proletariat at its back, the bourgeoisie could no longer solve the agrarian crisis or establish a stable democratic power. It submitted itself instead to the Bismarcks and the Louis Napoleons, seeking partial and niggardly solutions of the impasse by other than revolutionary means.

Out of these events proletarian revolutionary thought crystallized. Marx and Engels, who had charted the course of history by illuminating its past and were already actively engaged as proletarian revolutionists, perceived that the workers had to achieve complete organizational and political independence as a distinct social grouping to whom the future belonged. "The proletarian party," they wrote to the German Communists in 1850, must henceforth "appear in the arena as united and as independent as possible if it is not to be exploited and taken in tow by the bourgeoisie as was the case in 1848." It had to avoid becoming an "appendage of the official bourgeois democracy" and work for "the establishment of an independent...organization of the workers...and make every municipality a centre and a nucleus of workers' societies in which the position and interests of the proletariat should be discussed independently of bourgeois influences." Against any common enemy, a "momentary connection" with the petty bourgeois democrats was possible, but only on the basis of vigilant distrust of these allies and the uncompromising presentation of the workers' own demands "in contradistinction to the demands put forward by the bourgeois democrats." Marx and Engels still saw the bourgeois democracy as the urban ally of the peasantry and therefore envisaged the establishment, in Germany, of a bourgeois democratic regime. It was the task of the workers' party, however, to see that the revolution did not stop there.

"It is in our interest and it is our task," they wrote, "to make the revolution permanent, until all propertied classes are more or less dispossessed, the governmental power acquired by the proletariat and the association of proletarians achieved, not only in one country, but in all the important countries of the world.... With us it cannot be a mere matter of a change in the form of private property, but of destroying it as an institution; not in hushing up class antagonisms but in abolishing all classes, not in the improvement of present-day society, but in the foundation of a new society."[10]

A few years later Marx put his finger on the essential factor in the permanence of the revolution: "The whole thing in Germany will depend," he wrote to Engels in 1856, "on the possibility of covering the rear of the proletarian revolution by a second edition of the Peasants' War. Then the affair will be splendid."[11] It did not turn out that way in Germany, but for what happened in Russia fifty years later it was an almost mathematically perfect forecast.

The lessons of 1848 and of the Paris Commune of 1871, which gave the world its first rough outline of the dictatorship of the proletariat, were the headwaters of the Russian Marxist current known as Bolshevism. While in the more advanced countries the "Marxists" watered down the international and revolutionary content of Marxism to fit it to their National Socialist, evolutionary conceptions, backward Russia embraced the hardiest of all revolutionary doctrines, just as it had taken over the boldest of capitalist techniques. Bolshevism, fashioned by the genius of Lenin, was rooted firmly in the conception of the unconditional independence of the working class, in its organization and in its policies. It based its whole notion of Russia's future on the international character of the revolution, on the collaboration of the workers of the more advanced countries. The other current in the Russian labor movement, known to history as Menshevism, based itself on the practice of class collaboration, on the idea that Russia's was a bourgeois revolution and that the workers had therefore to subordinate themselves to the bourgeoisie. In sharpest contrast to this, Lenin held that the bourgeois revolution would be achieved and carried through to the end only if the peasant were drawn behind the worker, not behind the bourgeois. The nature of the state that would emerge from this worker-peasant bloc Lenin left an open question, expressing it in the abstract formula of "the democratic dictatorship of the proletariat and the peasantry." Following Lenin, Trotsky made a bold theoretical thrust forward and declared that the collaboration of worker and peasant in the bourgeois revolution would and could be realized only through the dictatorship of the proletariat, drawing behind it the peasant millions. This was Trotsky's famous theory of the permanent revolution. Its fundamental premise was that the bourgeois revolution in Russia would have to grow over into a socialist, proletarian revolution, whose final victory, in turn, would be realized only on a world scale. Events, far sooner than most men dreamed, synthesized the thought and action of these two titans.[12]

The 1905 revolution revealed the readiness of the liberal bourgeoisie to content itself with crumbs from the autocracy's table and in the years of reaction that followed the idea of proletarian independence became Lenin's incessant theme. Bolsheviks, he wrote, "need not fear to inflict blows upon the enemy hand in hand with the revolutionary bourgeois democracy under the absolute provision: not to amalgamate organizations, to march separately and strike unitedly, not to conceal the conflict of interests, to watch its allies as much as its enemy."[13] When in 1917 the Mensheviks tried to canalize the revolution into bourgeois channels, Lenin wrote: "All the bourgeois politicians in all the bourgeois revolutions have fed the people with promises and stupefied the workers. Our revolution is a bourgeois revolution, therefore the workers must support the bourgeoisie; that is what the worthless politicians from the camp of the Liquidators* say. Our revolution is a bourgeois revolution, say we Marxists; therefore the workers must open the eyes of the people to the deception of the bourgeois politicians, must teach it to put no trust in words, to rely on its own forces, its own organizations, its own unity, its own arms."[14]

This was the cornerstone of Bolshevism. The Russian autocracy was a brake on the productive forces of a country where, as in China, capitalist and feudal forms of exploitation were entwined and held the great mass of peasants in their grip. This meant for the Bolsheviks not the unity of all classes against the czar, but, on the contrary, the unfolding of the mutual struggle among these classes and the emergence of the proletariat as the real leader of the peasantry. The October revolution provided the "algebraic formula" of Lenin of the democratic dictatorship of the proletariat and peasantry with its arithmetical content, or to use Lenin's own words, "life brought it out of the realm of formula into the realm of reality, clothed it with flesh and blood, concretized it and thus changed it."[15] It proved to be the dictatorship of the proletariat which alone could crown the peasant war with victory. Looking to the workers in the rest of the world to join them, the Bolsheviks and the Russian workers translated daring theory into dazzling reality. When the war tore the last props out from

* The Liquidators were those Mensheviks who after the defeat of the 1905 revolution wanted to adapt the labor movement to czarist legality.

under czarism, they transformed a vast backward nation into the first proletarian state in history.

The revolutionary stimulus that radiated from workers' Russia across a war-weary world found responding impulses throughout the colonial empires of the great powers. The war had strained the imperialist world until it had broken at its weakest link and the October revolution caused the whole structure to totter. War had led to convulsions in Europe. It also stimulated colonial and national revolts in the East, near and far. Across Turkey, Syria, Egypt, Arabia, Afghanistan, India, Indonesia, Indo-China to China and Korea, subject peoples tried to break the chains the war had weakened. For all of them the experience of backward Russia was of decisive importance, for the underlying theoretical-strategic lessons it concretized, and for the new objective factor it introduced into world politics, the challenge of the first workers' state, opposing its proletarian internationalism to the oppressive weight of imperialism. The men who led the proletariat to power in Russia staked everything on the further advance of the world revolution and defined their internationalism as "the subordination of the interests of the proletarian struggle in one nation to the interests of that struggle on an international scale and the capability and the readiness on the part of one nation which has gained a victory over the bourgeoisie, of making the greatest national sacrifices for the overthrow of international capitalism."[16]

They based this not on sentimental considerations, but on the fact that the socialist transformation of the world could be realized only through "the creation of a unified world economy based on one general plan and regulated by the proletariat of all the nations of the world," carrying forward and perfecting the world economic system already established by capitalism. This created "the urgent necessity of transforming the dictatorship of the proletariat and changing it from a national basis (i.e. existing in one country and incapable of exercising an influence over world politics) into an international dictatorship (i.e. a dictatorship of the proletariat of at least several advanced countries capable of exercising a determined influence upon world politics)."[17] This transformation depended upon the confluence of two main streams, the struggle of the proletariat for power in the advanced countries and the struggle for national liberation in the vast subjected countries comprising between half and three-quarters of the world's area and of the world's population. At its founding under the leadership of Lenin and Trotsky, the Communist International based its entire world revolutionary strategy upon the collaboration of the workers of the West and the oppressed peoples of the East. Guided and helped by the former, the latter would be able to emerge from their varying stages of backwardness to direct participation in the socialized reorganization and administration of the world's productive forces, skipping over the stage of capitalism. This bold conception was the firmly-rooted basis of the internationalism with which the name of Lenin is indissolubly associated.

The striving toward national liberation in the colonies and in those other subjected nations more indirectly subjected to the powers (semi-colonies) took on forms determined by their relative economic development and consequent class structure. The revolutionary party of the worker had not merely to support national movements, progressive as a whole, but had to understand what classes in the subject countries were capable of conducting the struggle against imperialism most resolutely by solving the internal problems of the nation and in so doing moving the country in the direction of a noncapitalist development. In his discussion of these problems at the Second World Congress of the Communist International in 1920, Lenin heavily stressed the distinction between bourgeois-democratic and national-revolutionary movements in the colonial and semi-colonial countries. The former tended towards striking a bargain with imperialism on terms satisfactory to the upper trust of the native ruling classes. The latter sought to unite the masses of the population in a struggle against imperialism on the basis of the solution of their most pressing internal social and economic problems. It was in this stream that the proletarian revolutionists had to find their way, marshalling the masses against their native exploiters as the only means of carrying the national liberation movement to fruition.[18]

"It is of special importance to support the peasant movements in backward countries," wrote Lenin in his colonial theses for the Second Congress,[19]

> against the landowners and all feudal survivals. Above all we must strive as far as possible to give the peasant movement a revolutionary character, to organize the peasants and all the exploited into Soviets....
>
> It is the duty of the Communist International to support the revolutionary movement in the colonies and in the backward countries for the exclusive purpose of uniting the various units of the future proletarian parties—such as are Communist not only in name—in all backward countries and educate them to the consciousness of their specific task, i.e. to the tasks of the struggle against the bourgeois-democratic tendencies within their respective nationalities. The Communist International must establish temporary relations and even unions with the revolutionary movements in the colonies and backward countries, without, however, amalgamating with them, but preserving the independent character of the proletarian movement, even though it be still in its embryonic state.

To guard against being "taken in tow" by national bourgeois movements seeking to exploit the authority and prestige of the October revolution, Lenin injected a specific warning "to wage determined war against the attempt of quasi-Communist revolutionists to cloak the liberation movement in the backward countries with a Communist garb."

In a supplementary document adopted by the same congress these ideas were concretized as follows:

> There are to be found in the dependent countries two distinct movements which every day grow farther apart from each other. One is the bourgeois democratic

Nationalist movement, with a program of political independence under the bourgeois order, and the other is the mass action of the poor and ignorant peasants and workers for their liberation from all sorts of exploitation. The former endeavour to control the latter, and often succeed to a certain extent, but the Communist International and the parties affected must struggle against such control and help to develop class consciousness in the working masses of the colonies. For the overthrow of foreign capitalists, which is the first step toward revolution in the colonies, the co-operation of the bourgeois Nationalist revolutionary elements is useful. But the foremost and necessary task is the formation of Communist parties which will organize the peasants and workers and lead them to the revolution and to the establishment of Soviet republics. Thus the masses in the backward countries may reach Communism, not through capitalist development, but led by the class-conscious proletariat of the advanced capitalist countries.

The real strength of the liberation movements in the colonies is no longer confined to the narrow circle of bourgeois democratic Nationalists. In most of the colonies there already exist organized revolutionary parties which strive to be in close connection with the working masses. (The relation of the Communist International with the revolutionary movement in the colonies should be realized through the mediums of these parties or groups, because they are the vanguard of the working class in their respective countries.) They are not very large today, but they reflect the aspirations of the masses and the latter will follow them to the revolution. The Communist Parties of the different imperialist countries must work in conjunction with these proletarian parties of the colonies and, through them, give all moral and material support to the revolutionary movement in general....

The revolution in the colonies is not going to be a Communist revolution in its first stages. But if from the outset the leadership is in the hands of a Communist vanguard, the revolutionary masses will not be led astray, but will go ahead through the successive periods of development of revolutionary experience.... In the first stages the revolution in the colonies must be carried on with a program which will include many petty bourgeois reform clauses, such as division of land, etc. But from this it does not follow at all that the leadership of the revolution will have to be surrendered to the bourgeois democrats. On the contrary, the proletarian parties must carry on vigorous and systematic propaganda for the soviet idea and organize the peasants' and workers' soviets as soon as possible. These soviets will work in co-operation with the Soviet Republics in the advanced capitalistic countries for the ultimate overthrow of the capitalist order throughout the world.[20]

In these words, the Communist International summarized and applied to the problems of the East the fruits of a half-century of revolutionary thought and experience, and above all and most concretely, the experiences of the Russian revolutions and what they revealed about the internal dynamics of the bourgeois revolutions in backward countries under twentieth-century conditions.

For China the lessons of the Russian revolutions bore a peculiar cogency. The fate of the two countries was joined, in the first place, by a contiguous frontier crossing Asia for a distance of nearly six thousand miles. Both composed of different races and nationalities with specific cultures and characteristics, the two countries and the two groups of peoples did not clash at a barrier, but tended gradually to merge across the Turkestan and Mongolian frontiers. In both the agrarian population overwhelmingly predominated, with the proletariat a small but decisive minority. Like the Russia of the czars, China on the morrow of the Great War was a backward nation which combined the beginnings of capitalism with the holdovers of a feudal past, an anomaly that spelled ruin and impoverishment for the great mass of the peasantry. Whereas in Russia the autocracy fettered the productive forces of the country and perpetuated the barbarism of the past, in China imperialism in a far more drastic manner paralyzed the country's economic growth. The backwardness in economy and social organization condemned the masses of both countries to conditions of helotry supported by the blackest superstitions, ignorance, and the burden of traditions centuries old. In the circumstances created by the war, the youthful Russian proletariat proved that it alone could release the latent creative energies of the nation, open the path to industrialization of its resources, and thence, with the aid of workers in other lands, to the establishment of a socialist economy on a worldwide basis.

Backward as Russia was, China was more backward still because it came much later into the mainstream of world history and because imperialism was a far more potent obstacle in its path than the rotting autocracy of the Romanoffs. The 1905 revolution in Russia, which clearly demarcated the dividing lines of the classes and occurred at a time when backward Russia had become an imperialist nation in its own right, was one of the world-historical factors that led to the explosion in China in 1911, toppling the last Ching emperor from his throne. While in Russia the 1905 events had already introduced into the most advanced sections of the Russian working class a consciousness of its historic role, in China the revision of the economic structure and the emergence of new class divisions had not yet, in 1911, developed to the point where they could find expression in terms of political power. The bourgeoisie, stifled by imperialism, was too weak to replace the Manchus by a unified and modern state of its own. The proletariat was scarcely yet born. Power fell, therefore, to the militarists, whose warring satrapies thinly masked the interplay of imperialist antagonisms. The 1911 revolution had nevertheless ushered in a transitional epoch which could no longer lead, as in the past, to the rise of a new dynasty, but had to lead to a complete transformation of the economic and class structure of the country and of the state superimposed upon it. The spectacular growth of productive forces during the years of the war brought a modern Chinese proletariat into being. The momentary weakening of the imperialist pressure had given certain layers of the Chinese bourgeoisie a dazzling glimpse of unfettered growth and undreamed-of profit. Its hope for capitalist expansion collided, however, with the impassable barrier of the competition and the mutual rivalries of the imperialists, the enormous tribute extracted by foreign capital for its investment in production goods, supplementary raw materials, and manufactured goods. Moreover, it could not revitalize its internal market without solving the agrarian problem and the agrarian problem could not be solved without upsetting the whole existing structure of property relations.

The Russian revolution offered a new and radical point of departure. World revolution, on which the Russian Bolsheviks so firmly counted as the only possible condition for the preservation of their own victory, assumed the rational reorganization of world economy and the rational distribution of the world's goods in accordance with the needs of those who people it. This meant abolition of the anarchy of the world market under capitalism. Taking its place in the new order, China would be assured the planned and systematic aid of the more advanced countries, working harmoniously in the interests of a general elevation of the economic and cultural level of all peoples. This was the only sense in which China would truly achieve its national liberation. The path to this lay through the mobilization of the great masses of the country for struggle against exploitation, native and foreign alike. The bourgeoisie, vassal to imperialism, could not lead such a struggle. The youthful proletariat, new and raw at its machines, was confronted at once with the task of guiding the greater mass of their people into the future. No other class could do so.

The political role of the proletariat in Chinese society was determined more by its specific gravity than by its bulk in relation to the rest of the population. It was no more a question of the "maturity" of the country for socialism, any more than it had been for Russia. It was a question of the "maturity" of the world as a whole for socialist reorganization. It was not so much a question of the actual numbers of the proletariat in relation to the whole population as it was the economic and political position held by the workers in the mutual relations of the different classes. Yet it is interesting to note that the factory population of Russia in 1905 was one and a half million, and the workers in city and village together were estimated at ten million.[21] The industrial spurt in China during and just after the war created a class of factory workers estimated at about one and a half million. Industrial workers, inclusive of the factory population, were put, in 1927, at about two and three-quarter million, and the handicraft workers at more than eleven million.[22] Even when properly weighted for distribution and density of population and taken in conjunction with the disparate totals, these figures nevertheless reveal a striking similarity. There was a similarity, too, in the militancy and combative qualities of the Russian and Chinese workers. The latter had only come into being as a class during the war, and the first unions, in the modern sense, appeared only in 1918. Yet a year later China's working class was already intervening in the political life of the country, striking in support of Nationalist students against the Japanese rape of Shantung and the treachery at Versailles. Six years later one million workers participated in strikes, many of them on the basis of directly political demands. Two years after that the Chinese unions counted nearly three million members and the Shanghai workers carried out a victorious insurrection that placed power in their grasp. The intensity of this unprecedented growth was in part a source of weakness, yet it was also expressive of the profound reservoirs of strength of the Chinese working class, for all its youth. Here mere comparison must end and give way to the criterion of historical continuity. One of the deepest sources of this strength was the fact that the Russian working class had already triumphed and already ruled over the first workers' state in the world.

If the Chinese workers were comparatively weak because they were so young as a class, they were far stronger than the Russian workers had been before them precisely because this workers' state now existed as a gigantic objective factor in the class struggle viewed on a world scale. The influence of the October revolution was expressed in China not only in the intangible impulses it radiated or in the significant historical lessons it taught. It existed tangibly. Behind the Chinese workers rising fresh to the struggle stood the whole might of the Russian proletariat, the Russian proletarian state, and the most advanced sections of the workers of all the advanced countries united in the ranks of the Communist International. This was the world factor which more than any other single circumstance entitled the youthful Chinese proletariat to make its audacious claim to leadership of a nation of four hundred millions. Yet it was precisely at this point that a historical contradiction intruded itself and began to transform this decisively favorable circumstance into its opposite, the Chinese revolution's greatest asset into its heaviest liability.

When the new and fresh forces of the Chinese revolution began to gather momentum, the revolutionary wave in Europe was already declining. The Soviet state in Russia was driven, internally and externally, to seek respite. The economic structure it had inherited from czarism was ravaged by the war and had been strained to the utmost of its meager limits by the needs of "war Communism." The proletarian dictatorship was compelled to retreat to the New Economic Policy to win a breathing space for an exhausted people. Circumstances forced this strategic withdrawal primarily because the expected aid from the workers of advanced Europe had not materialized. The Social Democrats of the Second International at the head of the European labor movement had degenerated from internationalists in words to nationalists in deeds as soon as the outbreak of war put their professions to the test. They had handed over the workers for defense of the bourgeois fatherlands of Europe. In the convulsions that followed the war's end, they proved to be the firmest pillars of the bourgeois order. They dammed the proletarian tide and handed political power back, intact, to the bourgeoisie. Absence of a firmly consistent revolutionary leadership prevented the victory of the new revolutions upon which Lenin and the Bolsheviks calculated. Instead of the ready aid of European workers' states, Soviet Russia fated the menacing bayonets of the imperialist intervention. It drove back its enemies, but was compelled in the end to find means of establishing a temporary truce with the rim of hostile capitalist states that surrounded it.

Lenin said and repeated a thousand times that the workers' state in backward Russia could not stand without the aid of the workers in at least several advanced countries. When he was compelled to lead the retreat to the New Economic Policy, he recognized the dangerous rise of hostile class influences that bore down upon the proletarian dictatorship from within and without as the revolutionary wave in Europe and the tension of the Russian masses began to recede. Through the Communist International and with the positive intervention of the Soviet state, the Bolsheviks hoped that a new conjuncture of events on the world scene would quickly enable them to shift the relationship of forces back in favor of the proletariat. The first four Congresses of the Communist International provided the ideological armament for the parties abroad upon whom this new conjuncture depended to no small extent. Yet it took more than the genius of a Lenin or a Trotsky to make history to order. Amid conditions of isolation and recession of the masses from the political arena, especially after the last great battles of the civil war were fought, bureaucratic reaction, refracting the pressure of hostile classes at home and abroad, grasped the machinery of the new state. It began to entrench itself long before the young revolutionary organizations of Europe could lead the workers once more to the threshold of political power.

This bureaucratic stratum which began to solidify on the outer crust of the newly formed Soviet state took Russia's national isolation as its starting point. It began the shift in Soviet policy from the premise of world revolution to the narrowly conceived conservative national interests of the bureaucracy, identifying itself with the workers' power. Lenin fought this tendency in his last years, but it was stronger than he. Too soon his struggle ended and power fell to representatives of the new bureaucratic caste, personified in Joseph Stalin. The Bolshevik opposition to the usurpers centered around Trotsky and the best elements of the proletarian core of the Bolshevik Party. They swam against the current, but they could not dam or divert it. The new leadership still espoused in words the extension of the proletarian revolution, but began to replace it in practice by consolidation of the privileges of the bureaucracy. The defeats of the revolution in Europe, above all the defeat in Germany in 1923, engendered moods of disillusionment and punctured the confidence in the capacity of the Western proletariat to win power. Out of these roots and these moods sprang the theory of "Socialism in one country" brought forward by Stalin for the first time in 1924. He superimposed it upon the uncompromising internationalism of Lenin and established it as the main axis of latter-day revised "Bolshevism."

This Nationalist degeneration, proceeding under the corrosive influence of Soviet isolation, led inevitably to a departure from the proletarian basis of Soviet policy at home and abroad. Internally the regime entered upon a flirtation with the petty bourgeoisie, the rich peasants (kulaks) and the Nepmen. Externally it pursued a policy which more and more tended to subordinate the interests of the proletarian movements abroad to the diplomatic requirements of the new Soviet bureaucracy. It became no longer a question of "making the greatest national sacrifices for the overthrow of international capitalism," but of making the greatest international sacrifices for the preservation of Russia's national "socialism." This evolution took more than a decade and a whole series of dizzy zigzags to reach full flower in the Communist parties of the Western countries. Its effect was sooner felt in the countries of the East where the desire to find strong bourgeois nationalist allies, and the loss of confidence in the power of the working class, led to the application of policies that stemmed not from Bolshevism and the October revolution, but directly from Menshevism, with its insistence upon the leading role of the bourgeoisie in the bourgeois revolution and its readiness to subordinate the interests of the workers to those of the bourgeoisie. The pedantic and mechanical concept of rigidly chronological "stages" in the bourgeois revolution replaced the living experience of October which had shown how these stages were fused or telescoped.

It was not at all accidental that Stalin and with him many of the top ranks of the "Old Bolsheviks" slid so easily down this path. Prior to Lenin's arrival in Russia in April 1917, all of them, without exception, had assumed the inviolability of the bourgeois power that had emerged from the first phase of the revolution. Stalin had been the author of the famous formula of support to the bourgeois Provisional Government in March 1917, against which Lenin fought to the point of threatening to break with the party leadership. "In so far as the Provisional Government fortifies the steps of the revolution," declared Stalin at the party conference in March that year, "to that extent we must support it, but in so far as it is counter-revolutionary, support to the Provisional Government is impermissible."[23] To this Lenin a few days later sharply counterposed in his historic April thesis: "No support to the Provisional Government. Exposure of the utter falsity of all its promises.... Unmasking, instead of admitting, the illusion-breeding demand that this Government, a Government of capitalists, cease being imperialistic. . ."[24] To a Bolshevik Party conference he declared: "Even our own Bolsheviks show confidence in the government. This is the death of Socialism. You, comrades, have faith in the government. In that case our ways part. I would rather be in the minority."[25] When he demanded that the party steer a course towards workers' power and declared that the old idea of a "democratic dictatorship" was fit only for "the archive of 'Bolshevik' pre-revolutionary antiques,"[26] the horrified "old Bolsheviks," Stalin stunned among them, accused him of "jumping over the bourgeois democratic stage of the revolution." Lenin's course prevailed, and the October revolution rolled over the heads of the defenders of the "bourgeois-democratic stage." When the wave receded and left power in their hands, it found them still clinging to their "pre-revolutionary antiques." The experience of October had passed, barely leaving a trace upon them. The "antiques," not the living reality that replaced them, were refurbished and stamped with the labels of Bolshevism and the October revolution to bolster the authority of the new ruling caste. By the time the revolution began to stir in China and the Soviet bureaucracy turned its attention to the east, the dynamic Bolshevism of Lenin and Trotsky had given way to the empiricism of Stalin clothed in the scholastic formulas of Bukharin. Not the interests of the proletariat in China, but the desire to find a strong national bourgeois ally became the fundamental motivation of their policies. The Mensheviks Martinov and Rafes emerged as the "interpreters" of Bolshevism for the Orient. Their axis was not the proletariat but the bourgeoisie.

The Chinese workers had already embarked spontaneously on the revolutionary path. The impulses they radiated from the cities were already beginning to stir great layers of the peasants into action. The Chinese bourgeoisie, its hopes for expansion fluttering, was already reaching out to control this nascent movement and was already attempting to cloak itself, as Lenin foresaw it would, with the authority of Communism and the October revolution. On the other hand, with the heroism, the courage, the capacity for sacrifice and endurance that is his distinguishing mark, the humble Chinese coolie was pitting himself against a society that tried to keep him a dumb and docile animal. To fill in the gap of his political immaturity, he needed the aid of the workers' state. Above all, he needed a revolutionary party, armed from the ideological arsenals of the October revolution, backed by the strength of the Communist International, and impregnated with a consciousness of its historic role. With these forces, the Chinese revolution had an incomparable opportunity to inflict a smashing blow on imperialism and break down the isolation of the Soviet state by galvanizing the whole subjected East and destroying the basis of imperialist power.

In a few short, swift years a stupendous mass movement rose from the streets of Chinese cities and the tired land of Chinese fields and threatened to destroy or transform all that was old, corrupt, and rotting in Chinese society. But those who put themselves at the head of these denim-clad ranks did not teach them to break forever with the deadening tradition of submission, but yoked them, even as they rose to struggle, to the political chariot of their exploiters. The whole weight and authority of the October revolution and the Communist International were thrown not behind the proletariat as an independent force, but behind the national bourgeoisie. As a result of this the masses were halted at the height of their forward surge, their organizations were shattered, their leaders decapitated. The shaken foundations of the system of exploitation they challenged settled back and still stood. This was the tragedy of the Chinese revolution.

The New Awakening

When China's economic transformation began during the World War it quickly opened all the sluices of change. Along a thousand channels new ideas, new thoughts, new aspirations found their way into the country and crashed against the dead weight of the past like mighty waves against a grounded hulk. Among the intellectuals the mood of despair and discouragement engendered by the failure of the 1911 revolution gave way to the beginnings of a rich cultural renaissance which rapidly drew a whole new generation into its orbit. New leaders, new forces came to the fore. From out of the thinned ranks of the revolutionary intellectuals of 1911 emerged the figure of Chen Tu-hsiu, scion of an Anhwei mandarin family, who began posing the tasks of revolt more boldly, more clearly, more courageously than anyone who had preceded him. To his side rallied the men who with him were going to make over the life of a whole generation and who in later years would enter and lead opposing armies on the battlefields of social conflict.

The task of the new generation, proclaimed Chen Tu-hsiu, was "to fight Confucianism, the old tradition of virtue and rituals, the old ethics and the old politics...the old learning and the old literature." In their place he would put democracy and modern science.

"We must break down the old prejudices, the old way of believing in things as they are, before we can begin to hope for social progress," wrote Chen in 1915 in his famous magazine, *New Youth*.

> We must discard our old ways. We must merge the ideas of the great thinkers of history, old and new, with our own experience, build up new ideas in politics, morality, and economic life. We must build the spirit of the new age to fit it to new environmental conditions and a new society. Our ideal society is honest, progressive, positive, free, equalitarian, creative, beautiful, good, peaceful, co-operative, toilsome, but happy for the many. We look for the world that is false, conservative, negative, restricted, inequitable, hide-bound, ugly, evil, war-torn, cruel, indolent, miserable for the many and felicitous for the few, to crumble until it disappears from sight.

"I hope those of you who are young will be self-conscious and that you will struggle." Chen also wrote,

> By self-consciousness I mean that you are to be conscious of the power and responsibility of your youth and that you are to respect it. Why do I think you should struggle? Because it is necessary for you to use all the intelligence you have to get rid of those who are decaying, who have lost their youth. Regard them as enemies and beasts; do not be influenced by them, do not associate with them.
>
> Oh, young men of China! Will you be able to understand me? Five out of every ten whom I see are young in age, but old in spirit; nine out of every ten are young in health, but they are also old in spirit.... When this happens to a body, the body is dying. When it happens to a society, the society is perishing. Such a sickness cannot be cured by sighing in words; it can only be cured by those who are young, and in addition to being young, are courageous.... We must have youth if we are to survive, we must have youth if we are to get rid of corruption. Here lies the only hope for our society.

This memorable call heralded the new awakening. When it was published, wrote one student, "it came to us like a clap of thunder which awakened us in the midst of a restless dream.... Orders for more copies were sent post-haste to Peking. I do not know how many times this first issue was reprinted, but I am sure that more than two hundred thousand copies were sold."[1] From it flowed the forward-looking iconoclasm and the slashing courage with which the youth set out to erect a new life and a new world for itself. It was the intellectual fountainhead of the great movements which were soon to electrify the nation and bring millions from their knees to their feet. From it sprang the new nationalism, quickened by the unease and unsettlement stirring oppressed peoples everywhere as a result of the Great War.

This mood collided at once with Japanese imperialism, which had seized the opportunity of the war years to impose upon China the infamous Twenty-One Demands of 1915 and to occupy the province of Shantung. The shining phrases of Woodrow Wilson, his promises of self-determination and social justice for all peoples had bred the hope that in the general readjustment China too would come into her own. When at Versailles these illusions were cynically spiked by the imperialist horse-traders,[2] the new youth rose in fury against the treachery of the corrupt Japanophile Peking government. On May 4, 1919, there were huge student demonstrations in Peking. The homes of traitorous ministers were attacked and wrecked. The movement spread across the country. In it a new note sounded. Workers in factories struck in support of the student demands.

The growth of industry had brought a modern proletarian class on to the scene. At the end of 1916 there were already nearly one million industrial workers and their number nearly doubled by 1922. To the Western front in Europe went an army of nearly 200,000 Chinese laborers, who learned there to read and write a little and, what was more important still, came into contact with European workers and the higher European standard of living. They returned with new ideas of how men struggle for better lives. They had seen the great nations locked in conflict and they came back determined to free their own. Many on their way back from Europe refused to land at Japanese ports during the furor over Shantung. When strikes began to deepen the roar of the May 4 movement, the returned laborer was already regarded as "the stormy petrel of the Chinese labor world."[3] Within the great new body of Chinese industrial labor this army of toilers fresh from the war formed a solid, conscious nucleus that helped the infant class face the adult tasks with which it was confronted, almost at birth. The young industrial proletariat, taking the lead of some ten million transport workers, coolies, shop employees, artisans, and apprentices,[4] began to group itself into its own organizations. While the old family firms and partnerships were giving way to corporations, the guilds were breaking up and giving way to labor unions and chambers of commerce. The Chinese workers, new to their machines, were thrust at once into political struggle. Their strikes in Shanghai and other cities in 1919 forced the release of the arrested student demonstrators in Peking and the resignation of the offending government officials.

The tide of May 4 engulfed the entire country. It ushered in the epoch of the second Chinese revolution. The rumble of the falling ramparts of the old traditionalism echoed throughout the land, awakening unrest in the hearts of its youth. They were drawn from town and village into the turmoil of the generation emerging to take command of China's future. They boldly broke the shackles of authority and marched forward to batter down what remained of the walls of old China. The inertia of the old ways of doing and thinking remained, looming large and formidable in the coming agony of revolution and readjustment, but the gates were down, never again to be raised. The eyes of the new youth turned from Versailles to Russia where the October revolution offered them an example and an inspiration infinitely more compelling in its reality. With it came to China belated tributaries of all the main currents of European social thought, democracy, anarchism, syndicalism, and Marxism, opening up new horizons and stimulating a veritable revolution in thought, morals, and literature which rapidly deepened the channels of political change and social conflict. All classes of society entered the political arena. Old political organizations took on fresh life. New organizations came into being.

When these fresh political currents began to flow in 1919, the Kuomintang, party of the 1911 revolutionists, had been reduced to sterile impotence. Its "right" elements, conservative bourgeois intellectuals, had become the helpless dependants of the warlords. Sun Yat-sen, leader of the more radical wing of the bourgeois intelligentsia, was pursuing his schemes for revolution by military means through utilizing the lesser against the greater militarists. He had evolved a political philosophy, summed up in his Three People's Principles, whose distinguishing feature was not their crystal clarity nor the concrete and bold manner in which they approached the social problems of the Chinese revolution. His principle of Nationalism suggested nothing of a struggle against China's imperialist masters. Indeed, as first president of the republic, Sun displayed an attitude of cringing servility before the powers, promising them that their perquisites and privileges, extracted by main force from the overthrown dynasty, would remain intact, and that the payments due them on their loans would be taken over by the republic.[5] After the Great War, Sun saw hope for China only in some form of benevolent cooperation among the powers. To this end he submitted to the various foreign governments a naive plan for "sincere" collaboration among the imperialists in the development of China's economic resources. He actually envisaged an idyll in which the foreign freebooters would forego their greed and join in a "socialistic scheme" from which all would benefit. "It is my hope," wrote Sun, "that as a result of this, the present spheres of influence can be abolished, international and commercial war done away with, internecine capitalistic competition can be got rid of, and last but not least, the class struggle between capital and labor can be avoided."[6]

Sun's "nationalism" also included the prospect of transforming the oppressed Chinese state into an oppressor of minority nationalities within the Empire. He envisaged the "assimilation" of the Manchus, Mongols, Mohammedans, and Tibetans, in a great China ruled by the Han. The self-determination of nations, like the struggle against imperialism, entered his thinking somewhat later.

His second principle, Democracy, provided mainly for a period of "political tutelage" during which the enlightened leaders would gradually guide the dark and miserable masses toward the light of self-government. There was nothing in common between Sun Yat-sen's concept of democracy and the idea of the direct conquest of political rights and liberties by the people.

The third principle, of the People's Livelihood, embodied Sun's political thinking on the vital subject of the future form of Chinese economic organization and the all-pervading question of the land and the peasantry. Sun advocated "restriction of capital" and "equalization of rights in the land," two formulas subjected to broad and various changes and interpretations by Sun himself and by his disciples in the ensuing years. By "restriction of capital," through means never clearly designated, Sun hoped to preserve China from the blights of capitalism. By "equalization of rights in the land," Sun Yat-sen meant a plan to adjust the inequalities that throttled rural China so that "those who have had property in the past will not suffer by it."[7] His plan was to have land values fixed by agreement with the landlords and for all future increment in these values to revert to the State. By the power of purchase the state would proceed to establish more favorable conditions for the landless or land-hungry sections of the peasant population. But for years Sun Yat-sen never ventured to propagate even this theory too openly for fear of alienating his military allies and many of his own followers. Sun rejected on all counts the idea of a class struggle and the participation of the masses in political life. He hoped to evolve means of transforming Chinese society peacefully and without convulsions after securing power for himself and his followers by purely military means. This was the aim of his endless series of invariably fruitless military adventures and alliances.[8]

Nevertheless the rise of the new political tendencies and the mass movement after 1919 energized Sun Yat-sen's declining party and the Kuomintang's activity revived. Sun began appearing before student gatherings and, when General Chen Chiung-ming permitted him to establish a government in Canton, he established contact with the newly organized trade unions there and in Hong Kong.

By this time embryonic proletarian political organizations had come into existence. Marxist journals began to appear in the schools and universities, opening up new perspectives of thought and action to the petty bourgeois intellectuals and before long to the working class itself. Groups that formed in 1918 and 1919 expanded into socialist societies and from these it was but a step, in 1920, to the foundation of the Chinese Communist Party. Its founders were the leading figures of the May 4 movement, chief among them Chen Tu-hsiu, then a professor at Peking National University. To the first national conference of the Communist Party in Shanghai in July 1921, came delegates drawn from widely differing backgrounds. Few were proletarian. Many were petty bourgeois nationalists, stirred by the new awakening. Untrained, untested, they mingled in a temporary solution which was quickly precipitated by events. Sooner than most of them expected, the class struggle leveled at every man its deadly white light. Its impact hurled them in many different directions. Not a few, drawn by sentiment or by quickly stifled anarchist leanings, dropped away at once and found their way into the bourgeois camp.* Some among the founders lapsed into passivity and disappeared from the political scene. Others, like Li Ta-chao, were destined to lose their lives in the coming struggle. Of the remaining leaders, men like Chen Tu-hsiu, Mao Tse-tung, and Chang Kuo-tao, were to trace devious threads through the fabric of latter-day Chinese history, beginning with their initial dedication to the cause of Communism on that hot summer day in 1921 when all these skeins were still unraveled. The Communist Party, born in the glow of the Russian October, set itself at that conference the task of building organizational weapons for the Chinese working class. This work had already begun in Changhsintien, near Peking, where railway workers had formed a union and where night schools had been established by Communist students. A labor secretariat was set up in Shanghai. The headway was slow, the beginnings

* Among the founders was Tai Chi-tao, who left the Communist Party within a few months of its formation under the pressure of a stinging rebuke from Sun Yat-sen. He later became the chief bourgeois ideologist of the Kuomintang. Others who soon broke away included Chen Kung-po, Shao Li-tze, and Chow Fu-hai, all later luminaries in the Kuomintang regime that massacred thousands of Communists and workers and peasants.

were small, the problems vast and difficult, for history had imposed adult problems on a class still in its infancy.

First of the Communist Party's problems was the question of its relationship, as a proletarian party, to the bourgeois nationalist Kuomintang. The form and method of Communist participation in the nationalist movement was decisive for the whole future course of events. Such participation was dictated by the indisputably progressive character of the national revolutionary movement. As we have already seen Lenin had pointed out at the Second Congress of the Communist International how, in the imperialist epoch, the national liberation movements in the colonial and semi-colonial countries could be led to merge with the mainstream of the international proletarian revolutionary movement. Cooperation with nationalist movements was desirable and necessary, with the all-important proviso that the independence of the proletarian organizations be preserved, "even in their embryonic form."

A project for a two-party alliance between the Chinese Communists and the Kuomintang was put forward at the second national conference of the Communist Party in 1922. When this plan was laid before Sun Yat-sen by Dalin, a Russian delegate of the Young Communist International, Sun rejected it. He told Dalin he might permit Communists to join the Kuomintang, but would countenance no two-party alliance. Shortly afterward, Maring, the first delegate of the Comintern in China who had already been in contact with Sun in the south, met with the Communist Central Committee at West Lake, Hangchow, and proposed that the Communists join the Kuomintang and utilize its broad loose organizational structure as a means for developing their propaganda and contacts among the masses.

Maring based his proposal on three factors.* The first was his own experience in Java. There prior to the war the left-wing social democrats participated in the Saraket Islam, a mixed economic, social, and religious movement directed against the exploitation of the Javanese by their European colonizers. Its left wing had accepted the aid of the Indian Social Democratic Association, which Maring had helped organize. Within the Saraket Islam it began to develop the idea of trade union organization and during the war years was responsible for the growth of a considerable left-wing movement. Maring based himself secondly on the strategic and tactical conclusions of the Second Congress of the Comintern which he felt were especially applicable because—and this is the third factor—of the connections already established between the Kuomintang and the growing labor movement in the south where the unions under Sun Yat-sen's influence were already participating in the nationalist movement and offered the most fruitful field for the expansion of Communist activity.

* This information is based on notes of a conversation with Maring at Amsterdam in 1935.

According to Maring, the majority of the Chinese Central Committee accepted these views. Those who opposed his proposal did so on the grounds that they questioned the weight of the Kuomintang as a political force and doubted its capacity for developing into a mass movement. Chen Tu-hsiu, listed by Maring among those who agreed with the plan to enter the Kuomintang, has written an account of the Hangchow conference of 1922 which differs on this point.[9] He says that all the members of the Communist Central Committee opposed Maring's view. He assigns a fundamental political character to this opposition, claiming that they believed entry into the Kuomintang "would confuse class organizations and curb our independent policy." But there is no evidence that in those early years the Chinese Communist leaders opposed collaboration with the bourgeoisie. On the contrary, this idea dominated them completely. "Co-operation with the revolutionary bourgeoisie," wrote Chen Tu-hsiu in 1922, "is the necessary road for the Chinese proletariat."[10] Opposition to entering the Kuomintang, whether it came from all or some of the Communist leaders, would seem to have been based more on the belief that the Kuomintang was defunct. This, in effect, says Maring, was the view expressed by Chang Kuo-tao, strongest of the opponents of the entry at the Hangchow parley. In the end, however, the proposal was adopted, although doubt remained as to whether the leaders of the Kuomintang would welcome it.*

The Communists entered the Kuomintang as individuals in hopes of winning to Communist influence the workers in the south who had already affiliated with the Kuomintang.[11] Sun Yat-sen, however, remained cold to their proposals for reorganizing the party on the basis of a program capable of attracting popular support. Only when Sun was forced once more to flee for his life, following a revolt by General Chen Chiung-ming in Canton in June, 1922, did he grow more receptive to the arguments of Maring, supported by Liao Chung-kai, the most radical of Sun's immediate entourage. Sun was still unattracted by the potentialities of the mass movement as a political weapon, but he had begun to be attracted by the prospects of direct and concrete aid from Russia.

Several factors combined to help turn Sun Yat-sen's attention to the possibilities of an alliance with the Soviet Union. His naive plan for the international

---

* According to Chen Tu-hsiu, the entry was voted when Maring invoked the discipline of the Comintern. Maring denies this, pointing out that there was ample opportunity for appeal against him to the higher organs of the Communist International, but that no such appeals were made. "Moreover, I possessed no specific instructions from the Comintern," he added, "I had no document in my hand." Further light on this point undoubtedly exists in the unpublished and unavailable archives of the Comintern. According to P. Mif, of the Far Eastern Bureau of the Comintern, the first formal instructions "to co-ordinate the activities of the Kuomintang and the young Communist Party of China," were contained in a special communication of the Executive Committee of the Comintern dated January 12, 1923. By that time the Communists had already entered the Kuomintang, although the formal decision to do so was not taken until the Third Conference of the Chinese Communist Party in June 1923. Cf. P. Mif, Heroic China, New York, 1937, pp. 21–22.

development of China had met with rebuffs or polite indifference in all the imperialist chancelleries. The wolves would not lie down together with the lamb.[12] They were intent only upon fighting to determine who should devour it. To settle this question was the purpose of the Washington Conference of 1921–22. The parley had again revived Chinese hopes of imperialist benevolence, but these were quickly dissipated. The Washington Conference, to borrow Wang Ching-wei's summary, "freed China from the Japanese policy of independent violent encroachment" only to leave it victim "to the co-operative slow encroachment" by all the powers.[13] It was called to serve not the interests of Chinese national liberation but the interests of American imperialism. Realization of this fact helped dispel persisting illusions in the benevolent friendship of the powers. It also forced upon the consciousness of the Chinese Nationalist leaders the fact that the new Soviet power, so successfully and spectacularly defeating the united interventionist forces of the World War victors, could prove a mighty lever in the attempt to extract concessions from the imperialists in China.

As early as July 25, 1919, the Soviet government had proclaimed its readiness to renounce all the imperialist privileges held by czarist Russia in China. It renewed this offer in a further declaration on October 27, 1920, and unofficial Soviet representatives began making efforts in Peking to negotiate a new treaty on this basis. The angry hostility of the powers, who were seeking by every possible means, political and military, to isolate and destroy the Bolshevik regime, blocked these efforts, although the Russian offer to treat with China on a basis of complete equality made a profound impression in China and greatly heightened the prestige of the newly established Soviet power in the eyes of a growing group of Chinese intellectuals.

The initial efforts of Soviet representatives to establish contacts in China were a striking although still isolated example of the tendency to give the apparent immediate state interests of the Soviet Union precedence over revolutionary objectives. The Peking government was in the hands of the notorious pro-Japanese Anfu clique when the first unofficial Soviet agents, sent by the Chita government and the Irkutsk Bureau of the Comintern, arrived in China. The puny Nationalist movement led by Sun Yat-sen did not impress them as a point of support for Soviet interests. They were more attracted by the military strength of the warlord Wu Pei-fu who sought the overthrow of the Anfu regime. When Wu took power in Peking in 1920 and set up a puppet cabinet of his own, a Soviet Far Eastern "expert" of *Izvestia,* Soviet government organ, wrote that "Wu Pei-fu has hung out his flag over the events which are taking place in China and it is clear that under this flag the new Chinese cabinet must take an orientation in favor of Soviet Russia."[14] But Wu proved to be an instrument of British imperialism, no friend at all to Bolshevik Russia. The Union Jack had merely replaced the Rising Sun at the back door of the Peking government. That was why the 1921 negotiations proved fruitless.

When Maring came to China in the spring of 1921 and established connection with Sun Yat-sen, whom he visited in Kwangsi, he decided that the mainstream of the Chinese Nationalist movement was with Sun's Kuomintang. This belief ripened into conviction when in January 1922, during the seamen's strike in Hong Kong, he visited Canton and there discovered that substantial connections already existed between the Kuomintang and the most active section of the young Chinese labor movement. Reversing the tendency of the Irkutsk Bureau, until then the Comintern's only link with the Far East, Maring proposed to the Chinese Communists at Hangchow the entry into the Kuomintang. When Sun Yat-sen, expelled from Canton, arrived in Shanghai in August 1922, Maring met him again and urged him to substitute a campaign of mass propaganda for any attempt to recapture Canton by purely military means. The Washington Conference had helped to change the minds of the Kuomintang leaders, and Maring found his views more warmly welcomed, for Sun Yat-sen had definitely begun to think in terms of Soviet assistance. This was the report Maring took back with him to Moscow the next month. On the basis of his findings, the Comintern abandoned the "Irkutsk line" and turned its attention to Sun Yat-sen. Maring's views in favor of collaboration with the South China movement were published in the Communist press.[15] The Soviet government, on its part, sent Adolph Joffe, one of its first rank diplomats, to establish formal contact with Sun Yat-sen.

Joffe met Sun in Shanghai where on January 26, 1923, they issued a joint statement in which Joffe agreed that "conditions do not exist here for the successful establishment of Communism or Socialism," that "the chief and immediate aim of China is the achievement of national union and national independence." Joffe assured Sun that in seeking these aims, the Nationalist movement "could depend on the aid of Russia."[16] This diplomatic formula inaugurated the entente with Sun, upon whom it finally dawned that the Russians were offering him and his party the prestige of the October revolution, backed up with arms, money, and advisers.

Almost at once, however, the same formula was interpreted to mean that the Chinese Communists had to subordinate themselves completely to the job of helping to make the Kuomintang a worthy ally. When Michael Borodin took his post as adviser to Sun Yat-sen in the fall of the same year, he came not as a representative of the Communist International to work with the Chinese Communist Party, but as adviser to the Kuomintang delegated by the political bureau of the Communist Party of the Soviet Union. This distinction was far from purely formal. Borodin's job was to reorganize and pump new life into the Kuomintang. All efforts—primarily those of the Chinese Communists—had to be concentrated now to that end.

The independent political perspectives of the Communist Party disappeared from the calculations of the moment. "In so far as the independent working-class movement in the country is weak," decided the Executive Committee of the Comintern on January 12, 1923, "in so far as the central task confronting China is to carry out the national revolution against the imperialists and their feudal agents within the country, and in so far as the working class is directly interested in the solution of this national revolutionary problem but is not yet sufficiently differentiated as an absolutely independent force, the E.C.C.I. considers that it is necessary to co-ordinate the activities of the Kuomintang and of the young Communist Party of China."[17] Proletarian independence was projected into the uncertain future, but the Chinese Communist Party was nevertheless "not to merge" with the Kuomintang nor to "furl its own banner." In practice, if the Communists had to give up the idea of functioning as the representatives of an "absolutely independent force" in favor of the "central task" of coordinating their activities with those of the Kuomintang, the result was necessarily a loss of their independence. The third conference of the Communist Party in June 1923, silenced internal opposition to the Kuomintang entry and the slogan was raised: "All work to the Kuomintang!" The conference manifesto declared that "the Kuomintang should be the central force of the national revolution and should stand in the leading position."[18]

The course thus laid before the Communists led directly and unavoidably to the idea that the national struggle against imperialism preceded or temporarily postponed the struggle between the classes. The very idea that classes with opposing interests could unite in a single party was based on the assumption that imperialism temporarily welded the interests of the various classes instead of deepening the antagonism between them. It assumed that the bourgeoisie could and would play not only a revolutionary role, but the leading role in the national revolutionary movement. This was a radical shift from the broad line of strategy laid down by Lenin at the Second World Congress of the Comintern for it immediately canalized the Nationalist movement onto bourgeois-democratic lines and put an end to the political and organizational independence of the Communist Party. The latter from the outset, in 1923, recognized the "leading position" of the Kuomintang. The Comintern did likewise and rationalized this blurring of class lines by developing the theory that the Kuomintang was not the party of the bourgeoisie, but the party in which all classes united in common cause against the foreign interloper. This conception, first established in practice, soon made its way into the official documents of the Comintern and guided the whole future course of its strategy.

Borodin set out to convince Sun Yat-sen that what the Kuomintang needed was a disciplined party organization with a powerful mass movement behind it. When in November Chen Chiung-ming again threatened Canton where Sun had managed to re-establish himself, Borodin gave a concrete example of how a few promises could arouse the workers and peasants to the defense of the regime. The ease with which Chen's threat was averted clinched Borodin's argument.[19] With Sun's support, Borodin drafted[20] a program based upon cooperation between the Kuomintang and the Soviet Union and the Communist Party, the idea of a militant anti-imperialist struggle, and a platform of liberal reforms for the workers and peasants. Borodin took over Sun's "equalization of rights in the land" and "restriction of capital," concretizing them only to the extent of a plank for a 25 percent reduction in land rent and the promise of a labor code.[21] The new program was adopted and the Kuomintang thoroughly reorganized at its first national congress in January 1924. The day the congress opened Lenin died, a historical coincidence that did not lack its own irony, for the Soviet Union and the Communist International he had helped create were abandoning in China the idea of irreconcilable proletarian independence that was Lenin's richest legacy.*

The Kuomintang was organizationally transformed into a rough copy of the Russian Bolshevik Party and Bolshevik methods of agitation and propaganda were introduced. To correct the dependence on feudally minded militarists which had hitherto been one of the Kuomintang's chief weaknesses, the Russians founded in May 1924 the Whampoa Military Academy to lay the basis for a corps of officers for a new Nationalist army. This academy was supplied and run with Russian funds.[22] Before long shiploads of Soviet arms were coming into Canton harbor to feed the armies which rallied to the new banner as soon as the Kuomintang began to display the strength with which the activities of the Comintern and the Communist Party endowed it.

In accordance with the demands of their work within the Kuomintang, which now began to develop swiftly, the Communists limited themselves to the slogans and demands of the bourgeois national revolution, and these were naturally limited by the interests of the Chinese bourgeoisie. The cadres of the Communist Party, recruited first mainly from among students and later in increasing measure from the ranks of the skilled workers, were educated in a purely bourgeois-national revolutionary, not proletarian revolutionary, sense. Their activities and their propaganda were restricted to achieving the purely anti-militarist and anti-imperialist aims acceptable to the bourgeoisie. This fact converted the Communist Party into a left-wing appendage of the Kuomintang.

Communists were distinguished from "pure" Kuomintang members not by the profound ideological gulf that lay between Marxism and the vague populism of

---

* The late Arthur Ransome gave an astute summary of the Comintern's contribution to the Chinese revolution when he wrote in February 1927 that Russia taught the Kuomintang "how to turn Dr. Sun's pious programme of a raised standard of living for the workers into a stout weapon of offence and defence. Borodin may be said to have taught Dr. Sun to rely on classes rather than on individuals after having taught him to rely on a party instead of on himself. Borodin could show how the Revolution of 1905 was brought about by the work-men...for the benefit of the Russian bourgeoisie. He could show how agrarian revolution in France...crushed the feudal lords for the benefit of the French bourgeoisie.... These are dangerous weapons, but no other could have brought about the result achieved. In bringing these weapons into active operation the obvious agents to use were the Chinese Communists, and on them will fall the heaviest blows if and when the Chinese revolution finds it necessary to blunt them."

— *The Chinese Puzzle*, London, 1927.

Sun Yat-sen, nor by any difference in program, for the whole movement was carried forward under the banner of Sun Yat-sen's Three People's Principles and nothing more.*

They were distinguished from the upper ranks of the Kuomintang by the fact that they alone brought to the party and the movement the heroism, self sacrifice, and Communist enterprise which sprang from their devotion to the workers' and peasants' cause they believed they were serving. The Communists, advancing at no time any political perspective of their own nor appearing at any time before the masses under their own name and banner, tirelessly poured the steel of organization and mass power into the Kuomintang mold. In the initial stages, however, the ultimate significance of this fact was partially concealed by the spectacular growth of the mass movement. For neither the tactics of the Communists nor the requirements of the Kuomintang brought the mass movement into being. Conditions for its rise were embedded like ore in rock in the existing structure of Chinese social organization.

In foreign-owned and Chinese factories in Canton, Shanghai, Hankow, Tientsin, and other cities, factory workers lived and toiled in conditions comparable only to the helotry of workers in England in the early stages of the industrial revolution. Men, women, and children toiled, as they still do, for twelve, fourteen, and sixteen hours for wages as low as eight cents a day without the most elementary guarantees for their safety or the slightest provisions for human hygiene. A vicious apprentice system provided small producers and shopkeepers with an inexhaustible supply of child labor working daily up to eighteen and twenty hours in return for a bowl of rice and a board to sleep on. From such conditions of labor, employers, especially the foreigners with their superior technique, could extract the maximum surplus value and more, for the life of a laborer was cheap and no one knows the mortality rate in China.[23] Against these conditions the Chinese workers, their ranks swelling with the growth of industry, soon took up cudgels.

The organized labor movement began to take form immediately after the Great War. Strikes had begun to occur even before the May 4 movement in 1919. In 1920 the Mechanics Union in Canton staged the first large-scale strike, and in 1922 the Hong Kong seamen electrified the entire country by winning a smashing strike victory over the British imperialists, securing recognition of their union and

---

* In 1924 Sun attempted to reconcile his doctrines with the ideas of Communism, identifying the latter with his own principle of the "people's livelihood." The resultant muddle confused many of his own disciples and does not make for easy reading. He remained true, however, to the fundamental bourgeois principle of the inviolability of private property. For an ably documented study of the evolution of Sun's ideas, see Shu-chin Tsui, "The Influence of the Canton-Moscow Entente upon Sun Yat-sen's Political Philosophy," *The Chinese Social and Political Science Review*, Peiping, April, July, October 1934.

sizable wage increases.[24] These strikes laid the groundwork for a rapid flow of workers into unions. In May 1922, the first national labor conference met in Canton under the triumphant leadership of the seamen. The conference united the delegates of 230,000 organized workers. Under the pressure of this new and powerful force, Sun Yat-sen's Kwangtung government revised the penal code to legalize union organization and the path was cleared for further growth.[25]

In Central and North China the fight for higher wages and for the right to organize and bargain collectively was also beginning. Chief of these struggles was that waged by the workers of the Peking-Hankow Railway culminating in the massacre of February 7, 1923, at Chengchow, Honan. Wu Pei-fu, the reigning militarist in North China, ordered his soldiers to break up an organization conference. Sixty workers were murdered. This repression only temporarily checked the efforts of the railway workers to secure a national organization. Almost a year later to the day the National Conference of Railway Workers took place and a national committee was formed to carry on the fight for "improvement of our conditions, respect for our fate, education for us and our children, the right to form individual unions, to forge solidarity among all railway workers."[26]

In Shanghai by the beginning of 1923, there were already 40,000 workers organized into twenty-four unions. The battle front rapidly widened. In 1918, there were twenty-five recorded strikes involving less than 10,000 workers. In 1922, there were ninety-one strikes involving some 150,000 workers in all parts of the country.[27] The movement grew with astonishing rapidity and militancy. On May Day, 1924, 100,000 workers marched through the streets of Shanghai and twice that number in Canton. Contemporary reports describe how in Wuchang, Hanyang, and Hankow, despite rigid martial law, red flags appeared over working-class quarters. The traditional May Day slogan, the eight-hour day, thrilled workers who had just begun to dream of working fourteen instead of sixteen, twelve instead of fourteen, ten instead of twelve hours a day.

"Eight hours of work, eight hours of education and recreation, eight hours of rest—how reasonable this program is!" ran the leaflets of the day. "For forty years the working class has poured out its blood for its realization. The time is past when proletarians are but cannon fodder for the bosses. They will not cede but to Revolution? Then they shall have it!"[28]

"Remember today, fellow workers, that you are men, just as the bosses are. Demand then that you be treated as men. Organize! Numbers give strength! Comrades will extend to you their hand!" They marched through the streets singing new songs: "Work shall be a pleasure, our offering to Fraternity. We shall be called to it by the bells of Liberty. Join hands and sing—Long Live the Workers!"[29]

It is clear that by the time the Kuomintang was reorganized in 1924, the proletarians of China were already rising to their feet and organizing themselves in a movement strikingly characterized by its militancy and courage. It was inoculated too with a healthy spirit of skepticism and suspicion of bourgeois "allies," too soon to be stifled by the demands of the Kuomintang-Communist alliance. On May Day, 1924, Sun Yat-sen told the Canton workers: "The difference between the Chinese workers and foreign workers lies in the fact that the latter are oppressed only by their own capitalists and not by those of other countries.... The Chinese workers are as yet not oppressed by Chinese capitalists.... They are oppressed by foreign capitalists."[30] Similar statements were made by a Kuomintang speaker at the first conference of transport workers of the Pacific held at Canton the next month. Of this conference G. Voitinsky, Comintern delegate in China, who was destined to play a large role in yoking the labor movement to bourgeois leadership, wrote:

> The delegates of the Chinese railway workers, who had traveled thousands of miles, illegally, to attend the conference, with vivid memories of the bloody events of the Peking-Hankow strikes and the shooting of workers in May of this year, and also the Javanese comrades, constituted the Left wing of the conference. They gave a cold and dubious reception to the declaration of the responsible representative of the Kuomintang who called upon the workers to form a united front with the peasants and intellectuals, but not under the hegemony of the proletariat. The Javanese comrades, who had also experienced a big and serious railway strike in May last year and who detached a considerable Left wing from the Pan-Moslem organization, Saraket Islam, joined in the appeal for a united anti-militarist front, but under the leadership of the real revolutionary organizations in which there is sufficient Communist influence.[31]

Voitinsky and his friends soon taught the Chinese workers how to receive responsible representatives of the Kuomintang properly.

The peasants, too, had begun to hammer out organizational weapons of their own. The modern Chinese peasant movement was cradled in Haifeng, in the East River districts of Kwantung, by Peng Pai, one of the most striking and heroic figures of the Chinese Revolution. Son of a wealthy Haifeng landlord, Peng Pai became a school teacher in his native village. He was one of the first Communists and he soon tried to make his way among the peasants with his ideas. Dismissed from his school for staging a May Day demonstration of his pupils in 1921, Peng went out into the countryside to arouse the peasants to the need for organization. The story of his early rebuffs, his first successes, and the initial struggles of the Haifeng Peasant Union, he has himself left behind in a precious sheaf of personal notes and reminiscences.[32] First received by the peasants with mistrust and hostility—was he not the son of a landlord?—Peng Pai finally fired the imaginations of a few peasant lads. By combining conjuring tricks and a gramophone with speeches on how to win freedom from the oppression of the landlords, Peng and his little group of young comrades finally won the confidence of the peasants. After that the first Peasant Association was formed, grew swiftly, and almost at once had its first baptism of fire under the attack of Chen Chiung-ming's soldiers.

Thus begun, the organization spread rapidly to the neighboring districts, and the framework of a Provincial Peasant Association was set up before the middle of 1923. "It is not true," ran one of the manifestos of the new body, "that the landowners' land was acquired by purchase. The fathers and the grandfathers of the present landowners took it by force from the peasants. Even supposing that it was bought, it was paid for only once while the landlords have received rent for it annually for hundreds and thousands of years.... The landowners receive the greater part of the harvest without doing any work. How much money and sweat have we and our peasant forefathers expended on this land!"[33] These were simple phrases. They described a situation which the peasants had been taught was immutable and endowed with the sanctions of Heaven. When the peasant unionists suggested it could be changed by their own efforts—and proceeded to prove that it could be—it was as though the world had changed its face. Heaven seemed to have smiles for the peasants as well as for the landlords. These ideas seeped quickly through the countryside like rain into the earth. Rapidly they bore fruit. Peasant struggles against the landlords and against all the forces of the magistrates, the police, and the soldiers, multiplied throughout the East River districts and ignited similar conflicts in the west and north of the province. Demands for reduction of land rent passed almost immediately over to demands for its complete abolition. Even in 1923, in Kaoyao district, "some of the unionist farmers had the courage to refuse to pay rentals to the landowners, and the latter had to resort to the army and police to make collections."[34] Sharp skirmishes were fought in every case. The peasant movement was launched. By the time the Kuomintang was reorganized in 1924, it was well under way.

To workers and peasants alike the Kuomintang program, carried into the factories and out into the country by the Communists, seemed to offer a clear opportunity to better the conditions of their life through fighting organizations. Naturally, they made the Kuomintang's enemies their own, and there were many to be fought and overcome before the Kuomintang could claim to be the governing power, not only of Kwangtung province, but of the city of Canton itself. In the summer of 1924 Kuomintang rule in Canton was challenged by the Merchants' Volunteers, armed and financed by the British and by the wealthy compradores of Hong Kong and Canton. It was organized by Chen Lim-pak, chief compradore for the Hong Kong and Shanghai Banking Corporation, chief British financial institution in the Far East. On August 10, Sun Yat-sen seized a boatload of arms consigned to Chen and prepared, after considerable vacillation and delay, to suppress the armed corps that threatened his rule.

On August 26, the British Consul-General delivered a virtual ultimatum which threatened British naval intervention in the event of an attack on the Merchants' Volunteers. Sun protested to Britain's Labour prime minister, Ramsay Macdonald, whose silence proved that the reforms promised by the Labour Party did not include any modification of British imperialist policy. Sun wired, too, to the League of Nations, but that institution of world peace did not quite see where it was concerned and it, too, remained silent. Finally, in October, a force composed of Whampoa cadets, workers' battalions, and peasant guards descended on the Merchants' Volunteers, and after a brief but sharp battle defeated and disarmed them. The British river gunboats did not carry out their threats.[35]

Four months later, in February 1925, Canton was threatened by Chen Chiung-ming, Sun Yat-sen's former militarist ally who still enjoyed military control over a large part of the province. The Kuomintang forces carried the fight into his own East River strongholds. Chen Chiung-ming was rendered helpless by the activities of the peasants in Haifeng, Lufeng, Huiyang, and Wuhua, who demoralized his defenses by attacking his rear, cutting his lines of communications, and seizing his supplies. Peasants of Tungwan, Siapen, and neighboring districts fought side by side with the Kuomintang troops and also functioned as guides, spies, and transport corps. Against this offensive which seemed to rise against him from all sides in his own territory, Chen was impotent. He was forced to fall back and give up his plan for an attack on Canton.[36]

On May Day, 1925, Canton witnessed an impressive demonstration of the phenomenal growth of the workers' and peasants' movement when the Second National Labor Conference and the First Provincial Assembly of the peasant associations simultaneously convened. The labor conference brought together 230 delegates of 570,000 organized workers in all the principal cities of China.[37] The peasant associations were still confined to twenty-two *hsien* (counties) in Kwangtung, but there were nevertheless 117 delegates representing 180,000 peasant unionists.[38] Jointly the worker and peasant delegates, accompanied by thousands of Canton workers and peasants who poured into the city from the surrounding countryside, paraded through the flag-decked streets of the city in the first gigantic demonstration of worker-peasant solidarity ever staged in Chinese history. Hard of hand and brown of face, they marched to the assembly halls of various Canton schools and colleges which were thrown open to them for their ten-day sessions. Students and political workers addressed their meetings. They heard for the first time of the new mechanical implements whose use promised a lightening of their toil. They wandered through classrooms and libraries. They got their first dazzling glimpse of the world from which centuries of labor and sweat had relentlessly cut them off.

A few weeks later, the streets of Canton again rang with rifle and machine-gun fire. Canton was still then under the military control of the Yunnanese generals, Yang Hsi-min and Liu Chen-han, who hoped, like many others, to derive advantage for themselves from cooperation with the Kuomintang. But the gulf between them and the mass movement was too great for them to straddle. Once again the Whampoa cadets and armed workers fought side by side. The result was a foregone conclusion. The Yunnanese troops were demoralized and scattered and the generals expelled from the city. Peasants in the West River districts completed the job by cutting off the retreating remnants and effectively removing them from the scene after a brief, sharp engagement at Kiangtun.[39] Meanwhile a new thunderous voice was roaring out of Shanghai. The high tide of the mass movement was only just coming in.

Shanghai workers had launched their drive against the slave-labor conditions which prevailed, particularly in the cotton mills. A series of hammer-like strikes during the early months of 1925 were conducted for wage increases and against the brutality of foremen, especially in the Japanese mills. The shooting down of striking workers in Tsingtao and the murder of a Chinese worker by a Japanese foreman in Shanghai brought mass resentment boiling to the surface. It vibrated along the line of march in Shanghai's streets when students and workers joined in a demonstration of protest. Several were arrested and the demonstrators marched to the police station to demand the release of their comrades. A panic-stricken British officer shouted orders to fire. Students fell writhing to the ground. Twelve of them died. It was the afternoon of May 30.

The effect was swift, tumultuous, electric. Shanghai, the great imperialist stronghold with its foreign banks and mills, was paralyzed by a general strike which even drew Chinese servants from the homes of foreigners. Like a giant awakened, the seemingly inert mass of Chinese toilers rose with a rumble that struck fear into the hearts of employers, Chinese and foreign alike, and passed beyond the seas to shake the doors of imperialist chancelleries. Arrogant foreigners, for decades accustomed to regarding Chinese toilers as just so many dirty but docile and necessary pack animals, blanched when this unrecognizable mass rose and shook its mighty fist in their faces. The tie-up was so complete that "it was difficult for foreigners to do anything except serve as part of the local defence units."[40]

The rising was country-wide. Incomplete statistics collected by a labor investigator recorded 135 strikes arising directly out of the May 30 shootings, involving nearly 400,000 workers from Canton and Hong Kong in the south to Peking in the north.[41] The May 30 massacre in Shanghai was soon followed by shootings in Hankow and Canton. At Hankow on June 11, a landing party of British sailors opened fire on a demonstration of workers, killing eight and wounding twelve.[42] In Canton, Chinese seamen employed on British lines walked out on June 18, and three days later were joined by practically all the Chinese workers employed by foreign firms in Hong Kong and Shameen, the Canton foreign concession area. On June 23, a demonstration of students, workers, and military cadets paraded through the streets of Canton. When they passed the Shakee Road Bridge, British and French machine-gunners on the concession side of the creek opened fire on the marchers. Fifty-two students and workers were killed and 117 wounded.*

* The foreigners claimed in justification that they were fired upon first. They had a difficult time

A boycott of British goods and a general strike were immediately declared. Hong Kong, fortress of British imperialism in China, was laid prostrate. Not a wheel turned. Not a bale of cargo moved. Not a ship left anchorage. More than 100,000 Hong Kong workers took the unprecedented action of evacuating the city and moved en masse to Canton. The strike, which brought all foreign commercial and industrial activity to an abrupt stop, drew 250,000 workers out of all the principal trades and industries of Hong Kong and Shameen.[43]

In Canton the workers cleaned out gambling and opium dens and converted them into strikers' dormitories and restaurants. An army of 2,000 pickets was recruited from among the strikers and an impassable barrier was thrown around Hong Kong and Shameen. The movement was superbly organized. Every fifty strikers named a representative to a Strikers' Delegates' Conference which in turn nominated thirteen men to function as an executive committee. Under the auspices of this working-class body, the first embryo soviet in China, a hospital and seventeen schools for men and women workers and for their children were established and maintained. Special committees handled funds and contributions, the auctioning of confiscated goods, and the keeping of records. A strikers' court was set up which tried offenders against the boycott or other disturbers of public order.[44]

Police and judicial functions devolved upon the striker-pickets, who performed these duties with characteristic proletarian dispatch and vigilance. The picket barrier was tight as a drum. "The boycott against British goods in Canton," wrote a foreign observer,

> is controlled by a strike committee which operates through pickets whose work it is to prevent breaches.... Wherever in Kwangtung there is a highway for the transfer of goods, the pickets are present, ready to examine cargo, to open packages, to search individuals.... Foreigners as well as Chinese are subjected to search.... The strikers' rule is that no goods, not even foodstuffs, are to be taken to and from the Shameen.... If there is an infraction of the boycott, the guilty person is brought before the strikers' tribunal for punishment.... The boycott is complete.... (It) must be regarded as a war on Hong Kong and Great Britain and the pickets as the soldiers in that war. There is no other possible interpretation of the completeness and ruthlessness with which it is carried out.[45]

The task of covering all lines of communication along the Kwangtung coast and at all ports was carried out with the cooperation of the peasant associations. Peasant pickets patrolled the coast at Swatow, Haifeng, Pingshang, and other points, to make the blockade complete.[46]

---

trying to prove it. The section of the demonstration passing the bridge when shooting began was composed entirely of students and workers who were marching unarmed. And the fact remains that only two foreigners were killed in the affair whereas fifty-two Chinese were killed by the murderous machinegun fire which swept across the bridge.

Shameen, with its isolated little colony of bitter, fuming, vindictive foreigners, was cut off from all contact with the rest of Canton. Pickets rigidly guarded all entrances to the concessions. Only occasional ships coming up from Hong Kong, mainly warships or British vessels manned by volunteer foreign crews, kept it supplied with the bare necessities of life. British communities in other cities suffered the same fate. "More food must come from Hong Kong—no fresh milk here. The Club is empty, servants gone," plaintively reported a Swatow Briton to the *North China Daily News*.[47]

The strikers enjoyed the spectacle of the haughty foreigners doing their own cooking and washing. Under strike conditions the removal of refuse was apparently not all that it might have been, for the strikers changed the Chinese name of Hong Kong from Shiang Kong (fragrant harbor) to Tzo Kong (stinking harbor), and as the strike and boycott strangled the rich British colony, they began to call it Sze Kong (dead harbor).[48]

"An attack has been made upon us, as representing the existing standards of civilization, by the agents of disorder and anarchy!" cried the governor of Hong Kong.[49] "Disorder and anarchy" were costing the standard-bearers of civilization some £250,000 or two million dollars in Chinese currency daily.[50] "The number of British steamers which entered into the harbour of Canton...from August to December 1924, varied between 240 and 160 each month," reported an official of the British Chamber of Commerce. "During the corresponding period of 1925 the number varied between 27 and 2."[51] Demands for armed intervention in defense of "civilization" were shouted loudly from Hong Kong's forsaken house-tops. "Responsible British and Chinese residents of Hong Kong are convinced that intervention by the British Government and local action is imperative...." Otherwise "it is hopeless to expect the Canton anti-Reds to succeed without British assistance." Prompt military action, it was urged, could "easily place alternative and friendly Chinese authorities in power at Canton."[52]

But Whitehall saw more wisely than the over-heated and hysterical gentlemen in Hong Kong and other ports that "alternative and friendly Chinese" could be better won without the direct use of British armed forces. There was probably not a militarist or a bandit leader in Kwangtung province who did not in this period see the color of British money and who did not in return raid the picket lines or organize military opposition to the Canton regime.

However, the strike and boycott continued unbroken. On the strength of the mass movement the Kuomintang was able to consolidate its power and at the end of June organize a national government. In September, Kuomintang troops, supported by the peasant associations on both sides of the fighting line, finally cleared Chen Chiung-ming from the East River districts, despite the heavy financial and material aid given him by Hong Kong.[53] During the remaining months of 1925,

Southern Kwangtung was cleared of the last hostile militarist elements. The Kuomintang was supreme in Kwangtung.

Thus in less than two years a mighty mass movement had lifted the Kuomintang from the depths of political sterility and impotence to a position of power and prestige which enabled it to challenge all the forces which stood in the way of its supremacy. Having unified Kwangtung, it was able to look northward toward the vast array of enemies in Central and North China who watched its growing strength with unconcealed trepidation. All this the Kuomintang had achieved thanks only to the mass movement of the workers and peasants, and the mass movement was able to develop its power and cohesion only through the enterprise and initiative of the Chinese Communists. A mighty weapon had now been forged. How it was to be wielded and who would wield it were the questions that now pushed themselves forward on to the order of the day. The mass movement had stirred all layers of Chinese society into action. Quickly the classes grouped into new alignments. The iron realities of class struggle forced their way into the open arena.

4

Canton: To Whom the Power?

Sun Yat-sen used to be fond of saying that there were neither rich nor poor in China—only the poor and less poor. Had he lived a little longer (he died in March 1925), he would have seen what happens when the desire of the "poor" to become "less poor" clashes with the ambition of the "less poor" to become richer. He would have seen how, with a logic as relentless as time itself, the so-called "anti-imperialist united front" constituted in the Kuomintang resolved itself into irreconcilably divided camps, the masses of the incredibly poor against the handfuls of comfortably "less poor." He would have seen a massive demonstration of a social fact which he had died without recognizing—the class struggle. For as the mass movement rose steadily to higher levels, as it grew in extent and intensity, all the class issues it evoked were driven to the forefront. The worker could not be expected long to continue making a formal distinction between the Chinese employer and the foreign. Nor could the peasant be expected to remain satisfied with meager promises or to refrain from taking action in his own interest. Against the workers who soon overstepped their limits, all the forces of property, the employers of labor, and the owners of land, rapidly took up the counteroffensive.

Naturally the Chinese bourgeoisie preferred compromise with the foreigners on a booty-sharing basis to the alternative which the growing mass movement seemed to suggest. This was true of the interests of the ruling class as a whole. This did not mean it would react uniformly. The whole social process was too greatly accelerated, the normal social balances too profoundly shaken by the intervention of the masses. Political crystallization of the classes was taking place simultaneously with the development of the struggle. The Chinese bourgeoisie was itself undergoing changes, and within this class this was nowhere even and uniform. In the end the fundamental community of interest of the various divisions of the Chinese ruling class would whip them into a common front against the menace of the exploited, for the basic aim of the national revolution from their point of view was the establishment of a new, stronger bourgeois power, more stable and more amenable to control than the regime of the warlords, and more capable of commanding better terms from the imperialists who held the real reins of power. Yet, on the basis of differing immediate interests and gradations from conservative to radical within the bourgeois fold, the counter-offensive against the mass movement in 1925 deployed along varying and sometimes conflicting routes.

The compradores, the brokers for foreign capital, represented a powerful section of the bourgeoisie, whole interests, intertwined with those of the imperialists, collided most directly with the nationalist aims of their rivals, who dreamed of competing with the imperialists in industry and trade. This section of the population fought the new nationalism from the outset, utilizing the old militarists and acting as the channel along which the imperialists backed the militarist defense of the status quo. In some cases, as in Canton in 1924, they organized their own fighting detachments and directly challenged the government of Sun Yat-sen. In general, however, the caste of old militarists, based upon the landlords in the countryside and the compradores in the towns, were the main instruments of this resistance.

The political representatives of this section of the bourgeoisie were the oldest, most corruptly conservative, and therefore the most nearsighted, right-wing elements of the old Kuomintang, who had long since become clerks and appendages to the warlords. They rejected from the outset the new tri-cornered policy of Sun Yat-sen, alliance with the Soviet Union, cooperation with the Communists, and mobilization of the masses. When the first congress of the party adopted this course in 1924, they repudiated it and immediately organized an opposition for the avowed purpose of saving the Kuomintang from the perdition which they believed threatened it. They felt that the path to effective compromise with the foreign powers was being irretrievably blocked.

"Since the admission of the Communists into the Kuomintang," ran one of their manifestos, "their propaganda about overthrowing the imperialists of Great Britain, France, the United States, and Japan is aimed at the destruction of the international good will of the Kuomintang.... Their intention is to obliterate the Kuomintang."[1] Various organizations for "saving the party" sprang up. Their members attached themselves to the entourages of the reactionary militarists in North China and Manchuria. They scurried between Peking, Tientsin, Shanghai, and Hong Kong, organizing, propagandizing, intriguing, and conspiring. After Sun Yat-sen died, they soon raised the slogan of saving the purity of Sun Yat-senism from the "Bolshevism" of the epigones, and one of their principal groupings took the name "Sun Yat-senist Society." In November 1925, they gathered for a conference in the Western Hills, just outside of Peking, and from that meeting took the name by which they were subsequently known—the Western Hills Conference group. They considered themselves the guardians of the policy of compromise with the imperialist powers. In practice they served the purpose of keeping clear the path to such compromise against the day when it would become more propitious.

The foreigners, on their part, were rocked to their heels by the impact of the mass movement. Signs of their willingness to cooperate with the Chinese bourgeoisie on a compromise basis were not long in coming forth. In the beginning they seemed to believe that the freebooting methods of the Opium Wars and the Boxer days would suffice. But the more intelligent among them soon realized, with no small sense of shock, that the times had changed. The British threat to use force in support of the Merchants' Volunteers in Canton did not prevent the smashing of that reactionary force a few months later. The rattle of imperialist gunfire the next year at Shanghai, Tsingtao, Hankow, and Canton, far from cowing the Chinese, only laid bare the culture in which the germs of revolt seemed to thrive. Foreign bullets sown in Chinese soil brought springing to life thousands and tens of thousands of new revolutionary recruits. Without forsaking their strong-arm policy, the powers sought supplementary outlets by lending active support to every available anti-nationalist force. We have already seen how during the East River Wars in 1925, Hong Kong openly fed Chen Chiung-ming with munitions and cash. Unfortunately for them, General Chen paid no dividends. When the pro-nationalist Kuominchun ("People's Army") of Feng Yu-hsiang in the north launched an offensive against the Manchurian warlord Chang Tso-lin late in 1925, Japanese arms and money bolstered up the defenses. When the revolt of Kuo Sung-lin, one of Chang's subordinates, made his position almost untenable, Japanese military forces were thrown into the breach[2] and the anti-Chang offensive smashed, putting an end for some time to the further growth of nationalist tendencies in North China.

Appeals for solidarity between foreign and Chinese exploiters began to be heard. "We know by long years of friendly association with you that you do not sympathize with the rioters and strikers," said the arch-imperialist *North China Daily News* to Shanghai's men of property at the height of the Shanghai general strike. It called upon them to show that they had "no fellowship with the unfruitful workers of anarchy and ruin.... How long this threat to your peace, your welfare, and your safety is to last depends largely on you."[3] The foreigners hastened to show that they were prepared to discuss compromises of a concrete character designed to bolster their puppet Peking government against the nationalist threat. Arrangements made at the Washington Conference in 1922 to take up the questions of Chinese tariff rights and extraterritoriality, long unimplemented, were hastily revived. In October 1925, a special tariff conference opened at Peking which ended by promising tariff autonomy to China by January 1, 1929. At the end of the year an international commission on extraterritoriality was formed to assist in bringing about legislative and judicial reforms which, in the terms of the Washington resolution, "would warrant the several powers in relinquishing, either progressively or otherwise, their respective rights of extraterritoriality." Early in 1926, Britain sent out a special commission to decide upon the allotment of the British share of the

Boxer Indemnity Funds. Thus from these several strings the powers dangled hopes and promises before the Chinese bourgeoisie.

They found a growing response. The rising strike wave had not confined itself to foreign enterprises alone. Even Chinese "liberals" of the type who were willing to admit that the labor movement had "created a nation-wide social consciousness which is essential toward the building of a new and vigorous republic" watched uneasily the movement's "foolish excesses, like the rapid increase of strikes in China's industries."[4] That the labor movement was useful was gingerly acknowledged. Had it not already wrung from the foreigners the promise of conciliatory compromise? But the feeling, nevertheless, grew that "it is one thing to utilize the workers...but quite another to let them bite off more than they can chew." It was a good thing to enjoy "the benefits of strong organized labor"—"but too much of a good thing is often harmful."[5]

It was cause for rejoicing when the workers struck heavy blows at the strongholds of the foreign capitalists. It was quite another thing when the workers, Sun Yat-sen to the contrary notwithstanding, failed to make the desirable distinction between foreign and Chinese employers. This deplorable lack of discrimination soon made the Chinese factory-owner realize that he was in much the same boat as his foreign rival. Every advance in the working-class movement brought this into sharper relief. Moreover, the ties that bound the weakling Chinese industrialists to the boot-straps of the foreigners were only too painfully apparent. In Shanghai, the principal industrial center of the country, Chinese factories were even dependent upon a foreign power plant for their electricity. When the general strike followed the events of May 30, 1925, the foreigners retaliated by cutting off the power and stopping all wheels in Chinese-owned factories. This brought the gentlemen of the Chinese Chamber of Commerce quickly to their knees. They flocked to the council chambers of the foreigners with drastic modifications of the sweeping economic and political demands originally put forward by the striking workers. Readily they laid the basis for an entente between themselves and the foreigners. Their own profits depended upon such a compromise. They choked off the flow of funds that poured in for the strikers' support. Gradually the back of the strike was broken. At the end of the summer the Fengtien military, who had assumed control of Shanghai, in cooperation with the foreign settlement authorities and with the full sanction and support of the Chinese Chamber of Commerce, closed down the Shanghai General Labor Union, raided and sealed some hundred and twenty workers' clubs and other organizations. The strike wave in Shanghai was temporarily stifled and remained so during the winter months of 1925–26.

During this period the flirtation between foreign and Chinese men of property became more audacious. There was no difficulty about the preliminaries. Both sides organized their own anti-Communist leagues, published violent anti-Communist propaganda, and pounded their chests on public platforms. "I appeal to you to save for China the priceless heritage of its ancient civilization!" cried a British Mr. Jones.[6] The devotion of these gentry to the heritage of China's past was genuinely moving.

Board chairmen counted up their fading earnings and to their shareholders said: "It is to be hoped that the authorities will in future take drastic steps to curb the activities of professional agitators."[7] What they meant by "drastic steps" was demonstrated on the afternoon of March 18, 1926, in Peking when the troops of Tuan Chi-jui, head of the government, opened fire on a student demonstration, killing scores of boys and girls who were protesting Tuan's readiness to submit to a foreign ultimatum concerning the demilitarization of Tientsin harbor.[8] The massacre was the Peking backdrop for an unusual scene in Shanghai.

At the Majestic Hotel there that night, the members of the foreign Municipal Council sat down to dine with the pillars of Shanghai Chinese bourgeois society. The event was called "another milestone in the history of Shanghai." It was "the first time in the history of this municipality when any such gathering has taken place."[9] It was indeed an unaccustomed role for these arrogant foreigners, used to sending Chinese of all classes around to the back doors of their clubs. For the Chinese present—bankers, brokers, merchants, and officials—the smooth flattery of the barbarians was gloss to their vanity. "We, your hosts," said the American chairman, speaking for his British and Japanese colleagues, "count ourselves fortunate in having been able to secure the attendance of so distinguished a company of Chinese gentlemen.... We have with us a representative gathering of the men who mold and guide that vast and wonderful force known as public opinion."[10]

The speaker, Stirling Fessenden, came directly to the point. The authorities saw trouble ahead and it was necessary "to devise counter-measures." Force might have to be used, but this method had its drawbacks. Its use might "quickly lead to an international situation of extreme gravity. This has happened before." Attempts at arbitration "would probably end in failure." The workers of Shanghai, it seems, were the gullible victims of "third parties" who lured them from the security of their factories. Why not, then, take advantage of the "extreme credulousness of the Chinese working classes...why not take advantage of it—for their good and for ours? Why not set up a different kind of leadership from that to which they had been accustomed—a leadership they would be inclined to follow at least as readily as any other?...It needs, I suggest, men like some whom we have with us here tonight."

"We are all fully aware of the exceedingly tense situation," rose Yu Ya-ching, banker and compradore, to reply. "It is no exaggeration to say that spontaneous combustion is apt to take place at the slightest provocation, which may quickly lead to a worse conflagration than that of last year. For our respective and common interests we must by all means prevent it." Time was short and drifting dangerous. "It is most important for us, through the combination of local initiative and concerted action on a national and international scale, to provide the earliest and most satisfactory settlement of our outstanding problems." Peace was desirable, said Yu bluntly, "but speaking frankly, we do not care to have it 'at any price.'" The foreigners had to give some recognition to the principles of "racial equality" and "sovereign rights." More specifically for the moment, they had to give the Chinese bourgeoisie a hand in the administration of Shanghai.

Three weeks later the annual meeting of foreign ratepayers approved the participation, for the first time, of three Chinese members on the Shanghai Municipal Council. It was a bargain.

The "Majestic" dinner was a strikingly clear symbol of the basic attitude of the Chinese bourgeoisie toward the imperialists. They frankly fixed a price—and a modest one, too—and when it was met they openly proceeded together to organize resistance against the workers' movement. They consciously marshalled their joint forces and became increasingly conscious, alert, and deliberate in all their moves. Their influence was by no means confined to Shanghai and the north, but reached down into the heart of the nationalist movement in Canton itself.

Your simple-minded men of money, Chinese and foreign alike, were prone to see nothing but red whenever they looked in the direction of Canton. Others, more acute, were beginning to become aware that the reality was quite otherwise. The foreigners had to learn a great deal in those harried months and the sharpest of them learned quickly. They had to understand that the solution lay not in the use of force on their own part, but in the class differentiations within the movement that seemed to threaten their interests. "The serious mistake made by foreigners," wrote one of them, "was to emphasize Communism as the cause of all the troubles in 1925.... As long as anti-Communism was in any way identified with pro-foreignism, there was little hope of the better elements among the Chinese really opposing the Communists."[11] The Chinese politicians and others with whom they were rapidly cementing new contacts had to teach their more obtuse associates that Canton, far from being of a single hue, in reality reflected all the colors in the class spectrum. The spectrum had to be broken down with the utmost care if the red was to be crowded from the screen.

For at Canton, closest to the mass movement, class antagonisms smouldered and grew. The old guard "Rights" of the Kuomintang had broken away because they believed that cooperation with the Communists would prevent compromise with the powers. But at Canton, the so-called "Lefts," those who dared to use dangerous weapons, saw to the contrary that the mass movement would give them a mighty lever in bargaining with the imperialists. In the Communists they found the ready instruments of this policy. The result had been the organization of mass forces on a grand scale and the consolidation and strengthening of the Kuomintang regime in Kwangtung. But the rise of this movement brought sharply onto the order of the day the question of leadership. It had to be made certain that this mass movement would remain under the control of the bourgeoisie. Thanks to the acquiescent policy of the Communists this was bloodlessly accomplished. To follow this process as it actually occurred, we need only plunge into the maze of intrigues and the clash of individual wills which composed the political life of Canton, find and trace a single thread, the career of Chiang Kai-shek.

Chiang Kai-shek is another of those historical personalities who emerge from a class to lead it because their personal ambitions, background, and history fit them to serve the given needs of their class at a given historical moment. What Engels called an "endless array of contingencies," which we term chance because their inter-connections are so often untraceable, brings them forward when these needs arise. Reaching out for the values they deem desirable, be they on the one hand the satisfaction of participating in the building of a better world or, on the other hand, the lust for power, wealth, or "face," they fulfill the demands which their times make upon them. They are all part of the general design woven out of the clash of classes in society, but they help, too, to determine the quality and color of the new patterns that constantly take form. What seems to be in the lives of such men an accumulation of fortuitous chances corresponds in the end to inescapable historical necessities. Such a man, in his own time and place, was Chiang Kai-shek, whose ambition, fathered by ruthless cunning and an utter lack of scruple, brought him now to the center of the Chinese political scene.

Scion of a well-to-do Chekiang merchant family, Chiang Kai-shek was at the military school in Tokyo when the first revolution broke out in 1911. He hurried back to Shanghai where he joined the staff of General Chen Chi-mei. Under Chen's patronage Chiang met Sun Yat-sen. He also came into contact with Yu Yaching, the compradore, and Chang Ching-chiang, who was adding to the fortune his father had left him by engaging in banking and dealing in curios and beancurd. Chiang became associated with Hwang Ching-yung, one of Shanghai's notorious underworld chieftains, and is generally believed to have become a member at this time of the most powerful secret society and gang in Shanghai, the Green Circle. From these gangs, from the scum and riff-raff of the treaty ports, he recruited his soldiers. Gangsters, bankers, military men, murderers, crooks, smugglers, and brothel-keepers drew the original lines of the portrait the world was to come to know as Chiang Kai-shek. Far from being effaced as time passed, they deepened. In the years to come Chiang was destined to lean upon and be leaned upon by these early mentors. The fleshpots of Shanghai apparently suited his taste and for a time we find him operating as a petty broker on the Shanghai Stock Exchange. Either through cupidity or ignorance—the records are not clear on this point—he was soon penniless and on the streets. Chang Ching-chiang and his other sponsors helped him out of a situation which seems to have been exceedingly precarious. They made good some shady losses, lined his pockets, and shipped him off to Canton to link his fortunes with those of Sun Yat-sen. Few investments have ever paid greater dividends.

After Sun Yat-sen established contact with the Soviet government, he sent Chiang, who had meanwhile become a member of his staff, to Moscow to study Red Army methods and the Soviet system. Chiang left China in July 1923, and remained in Russia for six months. Few in Moscow probably noticed the youthful, thin-lipped Chinese officer whose cold, beady black eyes probably noticed a great deal. Coming from a country overrun with hordes of mercenary soldiery, Chiang must have regarded the morale and methods of the Red Army with awe. He saw an army of the people rising out of revolution and civil war and observed the integral connection between the army and the masses. He saw millions who had just thrown off the sodden garments of oppression and ignorance. If this gigantic spectacle stirred in him any response, any desire to help his own people rise out of the muck of centuries, nothing in his later career gives evidence of it. For him the things he observed were just so much capital that could be turned to his own account. He saw, perhaps, how the strength of an idea could call forth limitless sacrifices and loyalty. Above all, he saw the power of the masses as a political and military weapon. So Chiang returned to China with knowledge that gave him an enormous advantage over his fellow militarists. For as long as it suited him, he could now shout: "Long Live the World Revolution!" This was the cry he had heard galvanize millions. It was a cry with which he hoped to build his own power. All his deeply embedded class instincts warned him that it was a dangerous game to play; but Chiang Kai-shek, if he was anything, was a gambler. He laid his stakes on the table and boldly plunged.

On his return to Canton at the end of the year, Chiang became the dark-haired darling of Borodin and the Russian military advisers. When in May 1924 the Whampoa Military Academy was established with Russian funds and under Russian auspices, Chiang, the only military man of rank who had been to the Soviet Union and seen Soviet military methods at first hand, was the logical choice for director. Whampoa bred a new type of military man for China, but it also became the breeding ground of Chiang's power. To it flocked some of the best youth of the land. From it came some of the sturdiest fighters of the revolution. But the growth of the mass movement, the rising power of the labor unions and the peasant associations, soon drove the dividing line of class through the ranks of Whampoa's cadets. In the early period, in the suppression of the Merchants' Volunteers in Canton, in the expeditions to the East River, in the war against the Yunnanese generals, in the southern campaign, the Whampoa cadets distinguished themselves in the van of the fighting. Chiang was their military leader and each of these campaigns successively heightened his prestige, power, and influence, especially after the Whampoa cadets began to graduate and take their places as officers in the various military units. As the mass movement grew, however, particularly as the peasants began to use the weapons of organization to challenge the rights and privileges of the landlords, many of these young men, themselves the sons of landlord families, began to align themselves against the masses and against the Communists. Within the ranks of the Whampoa cadets this class differentiation quickly took the organized forms which it had already assumed on the broader political stage. The Sun Yat-senist Society, already actively functioning in Central and North China, secured a firm foothold among the Whampoa cadets. The Communist cadets and their more radical Kuomintang allies organized themselves into their own League of Military Youth. During the military campaigns in 1925 these two groups openly clashed on several occasions. Chiang Kai-shek endeavoured to maintain the balance between them, just as on the broader political scene he was already beginning to play a like role in relation to the Kuomintang and the Communist Party. When the armies got back to Canton after the second successful expedition to the East River in October 1925, Chiang gathered his young officers at a banquet. "He pounded on the table and scolded them"[12] and demanded that the warring organizations make peace. For the time being, at any rate, he demanded the semblance of unity.

In this question of "unity" Chiang Kai-shek met Borodin on common ground. The consonance of their attitudes clearly reflected the manner in which the Communist policy was dovetailing with the requirements of the bourgeoisie. Chiang's power, like that of his class, was by no means as yet firmly entrenched. He still needed the Communists, the mass movement, the Russians, their advice, their guidance, and their material support, to consolidate his position. Chiang himself was still on uncertain ground. Politically he was still subordinate to the civilian leaders of the Kuomintang, chief among them Hu Han-min and Sun Yat-sen's favorite, Wang Ching-wei. In the military domain, he still had many rivals in the group of generals who had also hitched their fortunes to the Kuomintang star. Chiang Kai-shek counted on the momentum of the mass movement to sweep him forward to a vantage point from which he could command. This, too, was precisely the aim and the need of the Chinese bourgeoisie.

Borodin, as well as his mentors in Moscow and the leaders of the Chinese Communist Party, proceeded from the premise that the cooperation of the bourgeoisie was vital to the success of the revolution. To them the independent, and by that time mighty, organized strength of the workers and peasants never suggested the necessity for orienting on the direct interests of these classes, even and especially when they clashed with those of the bourgeoisie. Instead the notion solidified and became official Comintern doctrine that the Kuomintang was not the party of the liberal bourgeoisie with whom the Communists were in a temporary bloc, but that "the Kuomintang...represents a revolutionary bloc of the workers, peasants, intellectuals, and urban democracy (read: bourgeoisie) on the basis of a community of class interests of these strata in the struggle against the imperialists and the whole militarist-feudal order for the independence of the country and for a single revolutionary-democratic government."[13]

The basic orientation was on the "community of class interests," not their clash. It fathered the illusion that the bourgeoisie on the one hand and the great masses of workers and peasants it exploited on the other were opposed to the imperialists on common ground. That was why Borodin thought he saw in Chiang Kai-shek the most reliable kind of "ally" in the Kuomintang leadership. The other militarists in Canton still formed part of the past, with its warlords and its militarist anarchy. It was obvious, even to Borodin, that their paramount interest was self-interest. Chiang Kai-shek seemed a more legitimate representative of that section of the bourgeoisie which the Comintern believed would really conduct a struggle against the imperialists. Moreover, Chiang wrapped himself in radical phrases and presented himself to Borodin and to the masses as the red hope of the revolutionary army. Borodin therefore employed every possible political stratagem to drive Chiang to the top of the heap. Chiang did not object if Borodin, in doing this, believed he was serving the interests of the masses. To the contrary, it has been recorded that he "often quoted a saying of Dr. Sun to him that in taking Borodin's advice he would be taking his (Dr. Sun's) advice. Borodin reciprocated by exhorting that 'no matter whether Communist or Kuomintang, all must obey General Chiang.'"[14] When Borodin "advised" the enhancement of Chiang's power, the latter had no difficulty hearing the ghostly voice of the late great Leader issuing from the lips of his Russian counsellor.

In August 1925, a right-wing Kuomintang conspiracy in Canton culminated in the assassination of Liao Chung-kai, political director of the Whampoa Military Academy, who stood at the extreme left wing of the Kuomintang. Hu Han-min, the senior leader of the Kuomintang, and General Hsu Chung-shih, commander of the Cantonese Army, were deeply involved.[15] This open manifestation of the menace of the right wing in Canton was handled by Borodin entirely behind the scenes in "maneuvers" designed to eliminate the undesirables. By skillful dickering, of which he was evidently very proud,[16] Borodin succeeded in forcing Hu to go abroad. General Hsu and a number of others linked to the plot likewise left Canton. The workers of Canton suddenly discovered that their new leaders were Wang Ching-wei, who became head of the party, the government, and the military council, and Chiang Kai-shek, who succeeded to the command of the Canton Army. For this it had been only necessary for Chiang to click heels, salute, and cry: "Long Live the World Revolution!"

Yet while Borodin and after him the Communist leaders were engrossed in dealing out new combinations with dubious allies at the top, the mass movement had already assumed great proportions. The Canton–Hong Kong strike, country-wide economic and political strikes involving nearly one million workers, the phenomenal growth of the peasant associations, the beginnings of the war against the landlords in the countryside, all marked the sharply rising curve of the masses on the march. Workers' and peasants' struggles had led to the creation of independent organizational forms through which the masses reached out instinctively for their own class aims.

The Canton–Hong Kong strikers, organized in their own strike committee and united with the rest of Canton's workers in the Workers' Delegates' Conference, were seeking to defend their own class interests. The police power of Canton was virtually in their hands. The peasants were already, in the language of an official report, "openly warring against the landlords in six or seven *hsien*."[17] The army offered a clear field to the Communists, especially after the 1925 campaigns in the East River districts and elsewhere in Kwangtung which were won primarily because of the direct participation of the workers and peasants. Only by grace of these victories did the Canton government exist at all. Its power rested squarely on the achievements of the Canton–Hong Kong strikers and the Kwangtung peasantry. Even Chiang Kai-shek publicly recognized this fact. The organized masses and the decisive sections of the soldiery had become the driving power of the whole movement. Despite all this, the bloc at the top prevented them from extracting from the government erected over their heads a single effective measure in their own interest. A few minor tax burdens were lifted. A few of the more glaring official abuses were eliminated. The sacred precincts of private property remained unviolated.

The Communists were never taught the necessity for giving this mighty mass movement a political orientation of its own, a perspective and a banner which would enable it to intervene in its own way, in its own interest, in the field of the class struggle. Instead it was dulled by a leadership which, far from inoculating the masses with the indispensable suspicion and mistrust of their Kuomintang allies, taught them to rely completely on the bourgeois nationalists at the head of the movement.

To the Kuomintang and its leadership, all the power and all the glory. This was the dictum of the Comintern and above all of the leaders of the Communist Party of the Soviet Union. Joseph Stalin and the other members of the presidium of the fourteenth party conference of the C.P.S.U. in January 1926, sent the following telegram to the presidium of the Second Congress of the Kuomintang: "To our Party has fallen the proud and historical role of leading the first victorious proletarian revolution of the world.... We are convinced that the Kuomintang will succeed *in playing the same role in the East, and thereby destroy the foundation of the rule of the imperialists in Asia*...if the Kuomintang strengthens the alliance of the working class and the peasantry in the present struggle and allows itself to be guided by the interests of these fundamental forces of the revolution..."[18] (Emphasis in original.)

Stalin had already produced his original notion that the Kuomintang was not the "united front" with the bourgeoisie, but the political expression of the alliance of the workers and peasants. In China, he told a group of students on May 18, 1925, the Nationalist bloc could "assume the form of a single party of workers and peasants, like the Kuomintang."[19]

Discussion of the prospects of "proletarian hegemony" in the revolution began to appear in some Comintern accounts of the events in China; but the central organ of the Comintern informed its sections that "a Kuomin (people's) Government, closely resembling the Soviet system, was formed in Canton on July 1, 1925," and proudly quoted the speeches of Chiang Kai-shek and Wang Ching-wei at the Kuomintang Congress. Said Chiang: "Our alliance with the Soviet Union, with the world revolution, is actually an alliance with all the revolutionary parties which are fighting in common against the world imperialists to carry through the world revolution." Said Wang Ching-wei: "If we wish to fight against the imperialists we must not turn against the Communists. (Loud applause.) If we are against the Communists we cannot at the same time describe ourselves as antagonists of imperialism. (Loud applause.)" The report concluded: "The work and struggles of the Kuomintang prove that Sun Yat-sen's disciples have remained true to his fundamental idea."[20]

The Sixth Plenum of the Executive Committee of the Communist International, which met in February 1926, applauded the Kuomintang's condemnation of its right wing and declared that this condemnation "strengthens the revolutionary trend of the Canton Government and ensures the Kuomintang the revolutionary support of the proletariat."[21] Yet at this plenum the delegates, under the tutelage of the Soviet leaders, reserved their most enthusiastic applause for the appearance of Hu Han-min, one of the outstanding leaders of the Kuomintang Right! Exiled from Canton because he was implicated in the murder of Liao Chung-kai, Hu went to Moscow, where he was promptly elected to the ruling body of the Krestintern, the Peasants' International, as a "representative of the Chinese farmers!"[22] To the opening session of the Sixth Plenum he was invited to bring the fraternal greetings of the Kuomintang to the general staff of the world proletarian revolution.

Andreyev Hall, the former throne room of the czars, "presented an unforgettable picture," says the official record, "when the Generalissimo of the Canton Army* stepped up to the tribune in military uniform. For several minutes the speaker was unable to commence speaking on account of the continually renewed applause. The solidarity between the revolutionary proletariat of the West and the oppressed peoples of the East was expressed here with striking clearness."[23]

There was applause, too, for the representative of the Chinese Communist Party, but after all, he only represented the oppressed proletariat of the East. "An even greater pitch of enthusiasm was reached when Comrade (!) Hu Han-min...ascended the platform. These demonstrations of enthusiasm lasted several minutes and punctuated nearly every sentence of the speaker."[24] Hu's speech is

---

* In Moscow, Hu made full use of the honorary title of "Generalissimo," which he inherited from Sun Yat-sen.

worth citing, for let us not forget that Hu was not merely one of that large group of Kuomintang leaders who only later on would suddenly emerge as butchers of the masses. He stood on that Comintern platform already an exile from Canton for his part in the murder of a left-wing leader!

"On behalf of the Chinese people," said Hu,

> of the Chinese workers and peasants, of the oppressed Chinese masses, I express gratitude for being able to attend personally this international session. There is only one world revolution and the Chinese revolution is part of this world revolution. The slogan of our great leader, Sun Yat-sen, is identical with the slogan of Marxism and Leninism. No one has faith any longer in the Second International. The influence of the Third International has considerably increased in China of late. The movement embraces intellectuals as well as large sections of workers and peasants, the entire proletariat.
>
> The Kuomintang slogan is: For the masses, i.e., seizure of political power together with the workers and peasants! All these slogans coincide with the policy of the Third International.... I feel I am one of the fighters for the world revolution and I greet the session of the Communist International. Long live the solidarity of the proletariat of the world! Long live the victory of the world revolution! Long live the Third International! Long live all the Communist Parties of the world! Long live the comrades present here![25]

The Comintern's influence embraced the "entire Chinese proletariat." The Chinese bourgeoisie had every reason to be grateful for the chance to cover itself with the prestige of Comintern support. (Even the Canton Chamber of Commerce signed its manifestoes with the slogan: "Long Live the World Revolution!") Hu Han-min could afford to be prodigal in dispensing his wishes for long life. It would enable him, one short year later, to help Chiang Kai-shek brutally shorten the lives of the best of China's young Communists. In return for Hu's good wishes (and that is all the Comintern ever got out of its Chinese bourgeois allies), the Sixth Plenum of the Comintern proclaimed that "the Canton Government is the vanguard in the liberation struggle of the Chinese people (and) serves as a model for the future revolutionary-democratic order of the whole country," and urged upon the Chinese revolutionists unity within "a single national revolutionary front of the widest strata of the population (workers, peasants, bourgeoisie) under the leadership of the revolutionary democratic organizations."[26]

For this reason in Canton Borodin was far from pleased by the spectacular advance of the Communists in the mass movement.

> The prominent position which the Communist members occupied in the new revolutionary system...not unnaturally caused anxiety among the leaders of the Kuomintang and the Communist Party. Borodin, too, was greatly concerned about it and often during 1925 he discussed the question with Wang (Ching-wei), Liao (Chung-kai), Hu (Han-min), and Chiang (Kai-shek). "Ever since the Reorganization in 1924 the Kuomintang was divided into two parties, those supporting and those opposing the Reorganization. This division, however, is not serious, for the

> Leftists are bound to be victorious. What would be serious, however, is that there might be a division in the Left itself," he said, foreseeing a split between the Kuomintang and the Communist Party. "The only way to surmount future difficulties is, therefore, for the leaders of the Left to present a united opinion."[27]

The only way, said Borodin, lay in unity among the leaders of the so-called left. This meant the "unity" of the Communist Party with the Kuomintang. It meant subjecting the masses to the political leadership of the bourgeoisie. In a work which attempts to justify the official Comintern policy in China, it is argued that radical reforms could not be introduced at Canton nor the agrarian revolution carried out because the Kuomintang, "in view of its mixed class composition," could not "undertake the confiscation of private property."[28] The "mixed class composition" of the Kuomintang required the protection of bourgeois interests. Inside the Kuomintang the Communists were bound to observe the inviolability of private property. In other words the Kuomintang was not the party in which all classes cooperated (to say nothing of a "workers' and peasants' party!"), but was the party in which the bourgeoisie compelled the other classes to drag at its tail.

Why was it not possible to organize an independent working-class offensive? Because the Canton proletariat was "weak." Borodin thought that "we could have seized power in Canton, but we could not have held it. We would have gone down in a sea of blood."[29]

Wherein lay the "weakness of the Canton proletariat"? The Canton government had been raised to power on the wave of the mass movement and stood or fell on the question of continued organized mass support. In this respect the workers of Canton and the peasants of Kwangtung occupied a decisively strategic position. Their "weakness" lay in the absence of an independent political perspective for these powerful mass organizations. If it was not at the outset, perhaps, a direct question of workers' power, it was certainly a question of smashing the counter-offensive of the bourgeoisie which was being openly mobilized on all sides. This could have been done only by arming the workers and peasants with a class policy of their own, by leading them to the creation of soviets capable of holding the club of mass power over the heads of the Chinese Kerenskys who sat in the nominal seats of power. Was the Canton proletariat too "weak" to do this? The Canton–Hong Kong strike committee and the Delegates' Conference united to the Canton Workers' Delegates' Council already provided the framework of the dual power. These organizations, which had assumed police powers and such state functions as the establishment of schools, courts, and hospitals, and which had even taken on the job of building a road from Canton to Whampoa, were instinctively reaching out for the exercise of full political power. They were already functioning as soviets function. United with delegates of the army and the provincial peasant associations, they represented the real sources of whatever power there was in Kwangtung.

But the question of a working-class offensive along these lines was never raised or even considered by the Communist leadership. Why? Because the possibility that such an offensive might involve the violation of bourgeois property meant that the "united front" with the bourgeoisie would be disrupted.

"But let us admit," wrote Trotsky, "that the Cantonese workers were still too weak to establish their own power. What, generally, is the weak spot of the masses? Their inclination to follow the exploiters. In this case the first duty of revolutionists is to help the workers liberate themselves from servile confidence. Nevertheless, the work done by the bureaucracy of the Comintern was diametrically opposed to this. It inculcated in the- masses the notion of the necessity to submit to the bourgeoisie and it declared that the enemies of the bourgeoisie were their enemies."[30]

Borodin says that the workers would have been "drowned in a sea of blood" had a more aggressive policy been pursued. Success, to be sure, is never guaranteed in advance. It would be impossible and futile to assert now that any other policy would certainly have triumphed. Yet it is clear that the policy of submission in Canton in 1925 disoriented the workers and only postponed the blood-letting until the bourgeoisie was better prepared to strike and the masses completely disarmed by the policies of their own leaders. An aggressive, independent, proletarian policy might conceivably have led to defeat. That would have depended on many factors. But such a defeat would have been suffered in the open, against known and recognized enemies like the defeat of the Russian revolution of 1905. The result would have been a hardening of the cadres and a new stage in the education of the Chinese workers, leading more clearly, more surely, toward a Chinese 1917. To reject an independent course, however, for fear of disrupting the "united front" guaranteed defeat under conditions infinitely more costly and demoralizing for the worker stabbed in the back by those they had been taught to trust.

The workers, wrote Marx and Engels seventy-five years earlier, "must not permit themselves to be corrupted by the phrases of the Democrats, as for example, that the Democratic Party will be split because of the independent action of the workers, and that it will make possible the victory of the reaction. When such phrases are used, the final result is that the proletariat will always be swindled."[31]

Those phrases were used and the Canton proletariat was swindled.

5 Canton: The Coup of March 20, 1926

Chiang Kai-shek guarded the interests of his class like the three-headed Cerberus who stood at the gates of Hades. One head faced right and looked like Tai Chi-tao, who had become the leading ideologist of the conservative wing of the Kuomintang in Canton. Tai was the link between the openly functioning right wing in Shanghai and the north and the covert right wing in Canton. The scope of his activities and influence in the Kuomintang capital amply refuted the crude classification into right and left on the sole basis of approval or disapproval of the 1924 reorganization, which proved to be a comforting over-simplification cherished by Borodin and his fellow functionaries like an iced drink on a blistering Canton afternoon. Yet ice melts under the sun, just as political fictions dissolve in the glare of the class struggle. What appeared to be a profound cleavage between two violently differing political tendencies proved in fact to be only a division of labor between two sections of a fundamentally homogeneous group. The Rights in the north were the bridge across which the Canton "Lefts" would march to compromise with the powers. In Canton, as early as July, 1925, when the national government was formed, Tai Chi-tao had already begun clearing the approaches.

With the tacit protection of Chiang Kai-shek, he began issuing anti-Communist and anti-Marxist pamphlets. He proclaimed the inalienable right of the "conscious" sections of the population to guide and govern the "unconscious." Communism, he declared, had nothing in common with the precepts of Sun Yat-sen and he urged the preservation of the Leader's doctrines from the menace of Communist adulteration. Tai boldly organized on behalf of the Sun Yat-senist Society, which sought carefully to distinguish itself from the Western Hills group in the north. The Sun Yat-senists "declared that they differed from the Western Hills people on three points. (1) The Western Hills group were against the reorganization of 1924, while they supported it. (2) The former consisted only of corrupt and reactionary bureaucrats and anarchists, while they were active revolutionaries. (3) The object...(of the Western Hills group)...was the overthrow of Wang and Chiang while they accepted them as their leaders. But while belonging to the Left, they were as actively and energetically opposed to the Communists as were the Western Hills people. They also desired to break with the Communist Party."[1]

The second head of Cerberus faced left. It looked more like Chiang Kai-shek, but it dripped phrases of fealty to the revolution.

> I too am willing to lie beside the graves of those who have already fallen martyrs to the National Revolution, the Three People's Principles, and Communism. The revolution cannot do without Dr. Sun's Three People's Principles. Neither can the international revolution neglect Communism. We cannot deny that the Chinese Revolution is part of the World Revolution. The realization of the Three People's Principles means the realization of Communism. Knowing that we cannot separate the Chinese Revolution from the World Revolution, why should there be any quarrel amongst us about the Three People's Principles and Communism?[2]

Cerberus's third head held the center and looked forward, the jealous guardian of sprouting ambition. To his left Chiang heard his own voice establishing an identity between Communism and Sun Yat-senism. To the right he heard Tai Chi-tao's voice proclaiming the ineradicable contradiction between them. From the left he drew sustenance, prestige before the masses, Russian arms, money, and counsel; but it was from the right that he drew the material to fashion the cogs in his own machine. In making appointments to keyposts, his selections were rigidly confined to non-Communists. In building up this strictly "pure" Kuomintang political structure, Chiang had the full cooperation of the pallid, handsome weakling, Wang Ching-wei, chief of the petty bourgeois radicals, fated forever to be putty in the hands of his stronger big bourgeois allies.

In the Kuomintang party organization several prominent Communists functioned as members of the Central Executive Committee, but none were permitted to hold places in the party secretariat. The Military Council employed a number of Russian technical advisers and the Political Department of the army was in most places dominated by individual Communists, but from the General Staff and the Financial Bureau of the army, Communists were rigidly excluded. In the national government itself there were no Communists, only Borodin in an advisory capacity, but in the mass organizations and in the lower layers of the government and party machinery Communists and their sympathizers bore the brunt of the daily tasks. From them the left wing of the Kuomintang drew the strength which enabled it to reign supreme over the second National Congress of the Kuomintang which met in January 1926.

At this congress the clash of class interests and of personalities was concealed, although thinly, under the shadow of the mass movement. The number of organized workers throughout the country had reached 800,000. Peasant associations in Kwangtung had expanded to a membership of more than 600,000. Hong Kong was paralyzed by the strike, and in Canton the pickets patrolled the streets and wharves of the city. With the lessons of the unification of Kwangtung fresh in their minds, the representatives of the bourgeoisie understood that they were going to need this mass weapon in the battles to come. They passed with acclaim resolutions which reiterated the half-hearted promises and glowing phrases of the Kuomintang's "worker peasant policy." They frowned on Cerberus No. 1 by mildly reprimanding Tai Chi-tao for his anti-Communist propaganda. They smiled on Cerberus No. 2 by electing him, for the first time, to the Central Executive Committee of the Kuomintang. He was present to accept and dutifully to hail "the alliance with the Soviet Union, with the World Revolution."[3] But Cerberus No. 3 left the congress severely alone, for here the supreme figure was Wang Ching-wei, head of the party and government, chairman of the Military Council, holder of all the Kuomintang posts to which Chiang aspired.

For Chiang Kai-shek had early come to regard himself as chief among the disciples of Sun Yat-sen. The assassination of Liao Chung-kai and the removal of Hu Han-min left only Wang to rival his claims. Chiang was still merely head of the Whampoa Academy and commander of the First Army, while Wang, as head of the party and government, not only exercised the leading civil power, but as chairman of the Military Council represented civilian control over the military machine. Under these conditions other military commanders who had linked themselves to Canton's fortunes enjoyed an intolerable equality of treatment in the distribution of political and material advantages, especially in arms. In February when the Soviet military delegation banqueted the Kuomintang leaders, a Russian officer made a toast in which he placed Wang's name before Chiang's. A fellow-guest says he saw Chiang go white and tight-lipped. Chiang "did not utter a word for the rest of the evening."[4] Chiang was fiercely jealous of Wang's manifold prerogatives and the bourgeoisie, for its part, knew how to play on the keyboard of Chiang's vanity. The old guard of the right-wing Kuomintang had early realized that through Chiang Kai-shek they would succeed in regaining mastery over the party. At the Western Hills Conference, which Tai Chi-tao helped organize, they had adopted the slogan: "Ally with Chiang to overthrow Wang," an idea which Chiang at the time publicly repudiated but secretly nursed. When the rump congress of the right wing met in Shanghai in January 1926, and insistently repeated its overtures, Chiang proved more receptive. Although the "Left" had seemingly triumphed and from Moscow the Comintern had greeted "the transformation of the Kuomintang into a resolute fighting force, into a real party of the Chinese revolution,"[5] the influence of the right wing was plainly discernible in Canton.

"The Right or anti-Red wing of the Kuomintang, with headquarters at Peking and Shanghai...has no small backing on the part of the less radical Kuomintangites in the southern capital. This has been felt by General Chiang and other comrades," wrote a perspicacious Chinese correspondent from Canton.[6] This influence was no longer indirectly communicated. Chang Ching-chiang, the young general's benefactor, had personally come down to look after his investment. He had joined Chiang Kai-shek's entourage and had become his chief political aide and counsellor.

What the bourgeoisie now needed and what Chang Ching-chiang advised his protégé to secure was the guarantee of its hegemony over the growing mass movement. It was necessary to ensure that the mass movement would not exceed the limits of bourgeois interests. For this, concretely, it was necessary to whip the Communists into line, to regularize and define their position as auxiliaries to the bourgeois Kuomintang. It was time, in short, to cut the political wages of the Communists in order to increase the political profits of the bourgeoisie, and to place at the latter's disposal the immense capital reserves of the mass movement. It was a question of stabilizing the leadership at the top. For this a sharp blow, damaging but not fatal, had to be dealt the Communists and their petty bourgeois radical allies. If Canton's coterie of politicians and generals was rift and rent by criss-crossing intrigues, it was only because many strove to strike this blow first. Thanks to Borodin, Chiang was in the favored position and it was he who decided to act.

The influence of the imperialists acted on the right wing and, through Chang Ching-chiang and the Sun Yat-senist Society, it reacted on Chiang Kai-shek. Their desires fused with his ambition, his cunning, his envy of political and military rivals, his unmistakable lust for power. To level the Communists was to win bourgeois hegemony over the masses. To subdue his rivals was to secure for himself the leading place in the exercise of that hegemony. All the vari-colored threads in this pattern were drawn swiftly into a knot. It fell to Chiang Kai-shek to sever it and to create in so doing a new pattern. His evolution into what Marx called "a man who did not decide at night and act during the day, but decided during the day and acted at night," was thorough and sure.

Several hours before dawn on the morning of March 20, 1926, Chiang's troops moved. The pretext was the allegedly threatening attitude of the gunboat *Chungshan* which had anchored off Whampoa during the night. The night's incidents brought together the lines of many complicated intrigues far too devious to be traced here, for the clashing wills of many dubious would-be Kuomintang heroes were involved.* These were brushed aside, however, as Chiang proceeded systematically with his plan. All Kuomintang delegates to the military units under his command, some fifty men, most of them Communists, were arrested. The headquarters of the Canton–Hong Kong strike committee were disarmed. All Soviet advisers in the city were placed under house arrest. Teng Yen-ta, a Communist sympathizer who had succeeded Liao Chung-kai as political director of Whampoa Military Academy, was detained. Chiang had caught all his victims quite literally napping.

* Li Chih-lung, the Communist head of the Naval Bureau who all unwittingly became the chief nominal object of the night's operations, has recorded a good part of the story in a pamphlet, *The Resignation of Chairman Wang Ching-wei*, not published until a year later at Wuhan.'

Li Chih-lung, the Communist head of the Naval Bureau, was one of those dragged from their beds and carted off to the military prison. Grey morning saw Chiang Kai-shek master of Canton. It also found the other Kuomintang leaders in a state of utmost confusion. All "were utterly unprepared and did not even dream the coup was coming," records a Communist historian.[7] Everyone crumpled in fright.

Members of the Kuomintang Central Committee hurriedly gathered. "Since Chiang Kai-shek has always struggled for the revolution, it is hoped that he will realize his mistake in this event," they ventured in a resolution, but "in view of the present situation," they decided, "the comrades of the Left should temporarily retreat."[8] For Wang Ching-wei this meant a literal removal from the scene. He fell conveniently ill. His biographer relates that he "considered that the best way to solve the situation was for him to retreat and to allow Chiang to take charge of affairs for the time being."[9] After an ignominious scene at the Mint, during which he handed over the seals of his authority to Chiang, he withdrew, first to a village outside of Canton and a few days later to European exile. Before leaving he wrote Chiang imploring him to keep to the "revolutionary" path. "If he would only do so, Wang did not mind sacrificing himself."[10]

The Kuomintang "Lefts" weakly capitulated because Chiang's sudden descent upon them brought no corresponding pressure from the real left, from the organized masses who were confused and completely uninformed as to what was taking place at the top.[11] One foreign observer who arrived at Canton a few days later was delighted to discover that the Communists were in hiding and that the Russian advisers were packing to leave.[12] It was not Chiang's intention as yet, however, to strike directly at the mass movement. He sought only to bring that movement under the assured control of the bourgeoisie and to concentrate that control in his own hands. Having successfully put the leaders of the "Left" to flight, he came forward with explanations to the workers. The events of March 20 and, in particular, the raid on the strike headquarters were due to a "misunderstanding," he told them, and promised to reprimand the officers responsible. The Communists themselves were so completely confused that they did not know whether to believe him or not.[13]

Meanwhile right-wing politicians, until now on the outside looking in, poured into Canton from their Hong Kong and Shanghai refuges. A plenary session of the Kuomintang Central Executive Committee was called for May 15 and, as the date for that meeting approached, a deliberately manufactured pogrom atmosphere enveloped the city. Walls were covered with posters warning against mysterious "provocations" and rumors of an impending Communist coup against the government were set in circulation. A run was staged on the Central Bank. On the eve of the conference martial law was suddenly clamped down on the city. No one outside of Chiang's immediate entourage had the faintest notion of what to expect.[14]

At the opening session Chiang introduced and hammered through a special resolution "for the readjustment of Party affairs." It was framed to limit and define within the closest possible bounds the organizational activity of the Communist members of the Kuomintang. Communists were required "not to entertain any doubt on or criticize Dr. Sun or his principles." The Communist Party was required to hand over to the Standing Committee of the Kuomintang Executive a list of its membership inside the Kuomintang. Communist members of municipal, provincial, and central party committees were limited to one-third of the committee membership. Communists were banned from serving as heads of any party or government department. Kuomintang members, on the other hand, were enjoined "not to engage in any other political organization or activity." That is, Communists could join the Kuomintang, but members of the Kuomintang could not join the Communist Party without forfeiting their Kuomintang cards. All instructions henceforth issued by the Communist Central Committee to its own members were to be submitted first to a special joint committee of the two parties for approval.[15]

Thoroughly lacing the Communists into this political straitjacket, Chiang simultaneously proceeded to centralize all power in his own hands. The coup of March 20 had destroyed the authority of the civilian Military Council and the removal of Wang Ching-wei had left Chiang in undisputed control of all party and government affairs. The May 15 plenary session regularized these changes. Chiang was formally put at the head of the party and he promptly deputized Chang Ching-chiang to act for him as chairman of the Central Executive Committee. Plans for launching a northern military expedition were also approved and Chiang Kai-shek was appointed commander-in-chief of all the expeditionary armies. Subsequently a set of special decrees conferred emergency powers upon Chiang for the duration of the campaign. All government and party offices were subordinated to the headquarters of the commander-in-chief. The Military Council, originally conceived as a civilian check on militarist ambitions, passed entirely into Chiang's hands. He became arbiter of the government's finances. He controlled the political department, the arsenals, the general staff, the military and naval schools. The Canton government was transformed into a military dictatorship. Chiang's victory was complete.

This seizure of power by Chiang Kai-shek in Canton bloodlessly established bourgeois hegemony over the national liberation movement. It established in China precisely that bourgeois control over the mass movement against which Lenin had warned the Communist parties in the backward countries to struggle with all their might. Those men in the Kremlin who had assumed responsibility for the Chinese revolutionary movement had embalmed the living Lenin with the dead. They mumbled fragments from his writings on state occasions and at congresses and meetings, like the Kuomintang politicians who murmured platitudes from Sun Yat-sen at their weekly memorial meetings in honor of the dead leader. Yet Lenin was not merely bringing tablets down from Sinai when he wrote that Communists had to support national revolutionary movements for the "exclusive purpose" of uniting the elements of Communist parties and educating them "to the tasks of the struggle against the bourgeois democratic tendencies within their respective nationalities," nor when he urged the preservation of the independent character of the proletarian movement, "even though it be still in its embryonic form."[16] The whole experience of Bolshevism was summed up in the reminder that the Communist International and its parties in the backward countries would have to struggle against attempts to establish bourgeois control of mass movements seeking "liberation from all sorts of exploitation"; that "it did not follow at all" from the backward character of colonial and semi-colonial economy "that the leadership of the revolution will have to be surrendered to the bourgeois democrats."[17]

Events in China were again testing and again confirming this analysis. But the Kremlin's axis was no longer a proletarian policy. In China it believed that bourgeois leadership of the Nationalist movement would more quickly produce badly needed allies. The moral and material support of the Soviet state and the Communist International was not extended through the Communist Party to the mass movement but through the bourgeois Kuomintang, rationalized into an all-class party to which the Communists and the masses had necessarily to be subordinated. This had led directly to the coup d'état of March 20. If, unlike Lenin, the leaders of the Comintern could not foresee the event, they were at least now confronted with the accomplished fact. It was late, but not too late. The empiricists in the Kremlin could still take up the struggle against bourgeois control—or else completely "surrender the leadership of the revolution to the bourgeois democrats"—and in this case to bourgeois who were not democrats but the creators of a military dictatorship.

The Comintern leaders, Stalin and Bukharin, adopted the latter course and tried to hide it by concealing from the ranks of the International that the Canton coup had taken place.

They suppressed all news of its occurrence. The facts were kept not only from the Russian workers and the other sections of the Comintern, but from its Executive Committee and even from the other members of the Executive Committee's presidium. For this there is the testimony of members of both those bodies.[18] When news of the coup appeared in the imperialist press in China and abroad—with specific facts often garbled, but containing the essentially true assertion that power in Canton had passed into the hands of Chiang Kai-shek—the centrally geared machinery of the Comintern press started turning out vehement denials.

"Reuter's Telegraphic Agency…recently issued the statement that in Canton, Chiang Kai-shek, the supreme commander of the revolutionary troops (whom Reuter had hitherto described as a red), had carried out a coup d'etat. But this *lying report* (emphasis in original) had soon to be denied…. The Kuomintang is not a tiny group with a few members, but is a mass party in the true sense of the word and the revolutionary Canton troops and the revolutionary Canton Government are founded on this basis. It is, of course, impossible there to carry out a coup d'état overnight," wrote the central organ of the Comintern on April 8, 1926.[19]

Far from being converted into an instrument of bourgeois policy, the Canton government was more than ever "aiming at the world revolution" and extending its power into the neighboring provinces as a "Soviet government."

"The perspectives for the People's Government in Canton were never so favourable as they are now," the same Comintern report continued. "The province of Kwangsi will shortly form a Soviet Government...*the power of the generals, as a result of the national revolutionary movement, is beginning to disappear.* (Emphasis in original.) The Kuomin Government is now proceeding to organize all district and town administrations within the province of Kwantung according to the Soviet system."[20]

"The reactionary British Press at Hong Kong and in London have spread sensational stories of disruption within the Nationalist Government in an effort to further their imperialist propaganda," said a Moscow dispatch to the New York *Daily Worker*, on April 21, 1926.

> These reports have no real basis. They are nothing but provocative manoeuvres of British imperialism. There has been no insurrection in Canton. The basis of the reports seems to be certain differences (!) between a general of the Canton Army, Chiang Kai-shek, and the Canton Government. These differences were not concerned with matters of principle and had no connection with an armed struggle for power. The differences have since been abolished and Canton remained the stronghold of the movement for the emancipation of the Chinese people. The attempt of British imperialism to utilize the unimportant differences in Canton in its own interests has failed.... The Moscow Press regards this provocative manoeuvre of the British reactionary Press as an exposure of the real plans of British imperialism with regard to Canton. *Izvestia* writes: "The wish was the father of the thought and the British imperialists presented their real intentions as a fait accompli."[21]

Should these denials be laid, by some chance, to mere ignorance, the same could not be said of the report of the Comintern's own representative in China: "The British imperialists...were vainly attempting to provoke an insurrection in Canton and at the same time trumpeting forth to the whole world that the Canton Government had already fallen, that the Right wing of the Kuomintang had seized power and formed a Government which had agreed to a compromise with the British and was arresting partisans of the Left Kuomintang as well as the Communists. All this proved to be an invention of the imperialists," wrote Voitinsky. "The Canton Government, which was 'overthrown'~ by the imperialist Press, is now actually stronger than ever."[22]

At the end of 1926 this ostrich policy was carried over into the deliberations of the highest body of the Comintern, which adopted a resolution on the Chinese question which, as will be shown, made no mention whatever of the March events in Canton or their sequel. By this silence the Comintern tops hoped to conceal the significance of the March coup and to facilitate the acquiescence of the Chinese Communists, directed thereto by the Comintern's representatives in China.

Borodin, who had been on a trip to the north, returned to Canton after the coup, but before the Kuomintang plenary session of May 15. One sharp foreign observer, who was already at that time in connection with some of Chiang Kai-shek's closest advisers (and who later entered the service of Chiang's government), arrived in Canton a few days later. According to his account:

> The Russians seemed to believe the game was up. Most of the Chinese Communists were in hiding.... The anti-Communists were jubilant.... Borodin had it out with Chiang. Chiang wanted to know how far Russia would support him in a military expedition against the north. Borodin had heretofore opposed the Northern Expedition. Chiang's attitude toward the continuance of the Russian alliance depended upon Borodin's attitude toward the Northern Expedition. They came to an agreement. The Russians would support the Northern Expedition. The Russian alliance was continued. The Communists were reinstated.[23]

Subsequently, according to other accounts, "Chiang's relations with Borodin became more cordial than ever,"[24] and all the decisions of the May 15 Kuomintang session "were fully endorsed by M. Borodin."[25] It is further recorded that all the emergency powers delegated to Chiang after his appointment as commander-in-chief were so delegated "at the advice of Borodin."[26] It is in any case a fact that Borodin and, after him, the leaders of the Chinese Communist Party, submitted without question to the military dictatorship established as a result of the March 20 coup. Borodin even saw to it that the Russian military advisers who had incurred Chiang's displeasure because they wanted to distribute their advice and material aid equally among all the armies instead of exclusively through Chiang were dismissed and replaced by more amenable colleagues. Having secured all this with far less difficulty than he himself must have imagined possible, Chiang turned without compunction on some of the right-wing conspirators who had helped him execute his coup and expelled them from Canton. He needed more than ever now to garb his leadership in a cloak of leftism. His associates of the right wing returned to Shanghai. He could and would call upon them when he needed them again.

Historians who draw political inspiration as well as their information from the Moscow bureaucracy have usually dismissed the March 20 coup in a few paragraphs, entirely concealing or distorting its significance. Moscow cynically ignored the significance of the coup when it took place and naturally would like to have history written without notice being given to that fact. Louis Fischer, for example, describes the sequel to March 20 as follows: "But Chiang, whose distinguishing characteristic was not courage, apparently had been frightened by his own action and sent...a humble letter begging Borodin to return south without delay." When Borodin got back, Chiang "overflowed with apologies.... What, he asked of

Borodin, must he do? 'Prepare for the Northern Expedition,' Borodin replied." Then it was "because Borodin wished to repair some of the damage (!) done by the coup of March 20" that "Chiang engineered a second coup...this time against the Right."

"But why did not Borodin, the Left Kuomintang, and the Chinese Communist Party eliminate Chiang Kai-shek?" he continues. "Because they were too weak," he replies, after Borodin.

> They had wide mass sympathy, but in Canton they wielded insufficient forces to overcome Chiang and the bourgeoisie which supported him.... Both sides knew that the struggle between them was inevitable. But rather than engage now in blood-letting from which only the Cantonese militarists could gain, they tacitly agreed to postpone the issue until they reached the Yangtze. The resolution to commence the Northern Expedition was adopted by the Kuomintang Central Committee on May 15. At that meeting the expressed sentiments of each faction amounted to this: "Gentlemen, we know we must fight one another. But we need a wider area. Let us delay the day of reckoning and meanwhile go forward to a common goal."[27]

Fischer conveniently neglects to mention the other resolutions adopted on May 15 which hog-tied the Communist Party. The bloodletting was indeed postponed until they reached the Yangtze, but the March coup, the May decisions, and the Communist capitulation to them had guaranteed in advance that the blood shed would be that of the workers. The "common goal" was the victory of the bourgeoisie over the mass movement. Borodin is represented here as desiring to give future battle to Chiang Kai-shek—and preparing for it by handing over to him well in advance all the weapons. If Chiang Kai-shek possessed any quality at all, it was the ability to strike and strike hard in the interests of his class, the bourgeoisie. Not the same could be said of Stalin-Bukharin-Borodin & Co. with regard to the interests of the workers. Acting under their orders, the Chinese Communists were compelled to capitulate, and even to grovel, before the new master of the Nationalist movement.*

Chiang Kai-shek had carried out the March coup and put through the May decisions on the pretext that the Communists were plotting a coup d'état of their own. There were, to be sure, rival conspiracies in Canton directed against Chiang Kai-shek, but none, unfortunately, was even contemplated by the Chinese Communist

---

* Another particularly crude example of historical distortion with regard to the March 20 coup will be found in the writings of the ex-czarist general, V. A. Yakhontoff, who found his way without difficulty into Stalin's camp a few years ago. According to Yakhontoff, "in less than two months (after the coup) the 'Rights' and the 'Centrists' were forced to compromise and agree to many concessions to the 'Lefts' in order to gain the support of the masses.... In May, therefore, the factions were reconciled and Chiang Kai-shek became leader of the Kuomintang and commander-in-chief of the Revolutionary armies" (V. A. Yakhontoff, *Russia and the Soviet Union in the Far East,* New York, 1932, p. 151.) Chiang "conceded" and "compromised" by making himself master of Canton!

Party. Nothing was farther from its mind than the organization of a working-class insurrection in March 1926. Chiang and his right-wing helpers manufactured the rumors of Communist "plots" out of the material which the logic of the situation itself presented to them. It was they—and not the Communists—who saw that the working class, with its growing organizations, its armed picket forces, its militancy, and its might, was capable at that time of seizing and holding the hegemony of the revolutionary movement. It was they, therefore, and not the Communists, who realized that the time had come to act. When they acted forthwith, no one was more shocked, more pained, more aggrieved than the Chinese Communist leaders that they should be charged with planning a working-class offensive.

"First of all," wrote Chen Tu-hsiu, general secretary of the Chinese Communist Party,

> unless the Communist Party is a party of madmen, certainly it does not want to establish a workers' and peasants' government in Canton. Secondly, Chiang Kai-shek is one of the pillars of the national revolutionary movement. Unless the Communist Party were the tool of the imperialists, it would surely not adopt such a policy of disrupting the unity of the Chinese revolutionary forces!...The policy of the Communist Party, contrary to the declarations of the Rights, is not only that the revolutionary forces in Kwangtung should not be split, but that the revolutionary forces of the whole country shall be united. Otherwise one cannot fight the enemy.[28]

In an open letter addressed to Chiang Kai-shek on June 4, Chen Tu-hsiu protested further: "At this time to conspire for the overthrow of Chiang Kai-shek in Canton—what a help to the reactionary forces this would be! If the Chinese Communist Party is such a counter-revolutionary party, it should be got rid of.... If among the comrades of the Communist Party there are any who harbor ideas of such a counter-revolutionary conspiracy, you should shoot them without the least ceremony. But I know, I am convinced, that in our party nobody has any such idea in mind."[29]

As evidence that such ideas did exist in the minds of Communists, Chiang Kai-shek, in a speech at Canton shortly after March 20, recalled the remark of a certain Communist, who had said: "In our organization there is a Tuan Chi-jui,* and in order to overthrow the northern Tuan Chi-jui we must first overthrow the Tuan Chi-jui in our midst." The Communist who had made the offending speech hastened into print with an open letter to Chiang explaining that he had meant "Tuan Chi-jui ideology," that is, old feudal ideas, and that since he spoke Anhwei dialect and not Cantonese, there had been a mistake made by the interpreter.

> I never slandered you in my words, and it is everywhere open and clear that what I said was to love and protect you for the sake of the National revolution.... I

* Tuan Chi-jui was head of the notoriously corrupt government at Peking.

> remember that after March 20 I met you .. . and earnestly expressed to you my attitude of everlasting confidence in you. If you truly regarded me as a comrade, you should have taught me; or if you saw anything wrong in me, you should have severely blamed me or chastised me and made me correct my error. But you only mildly and indifferently replied, 'Never mind, never mind, nothing, nothing. . .' So now why do you charge me with slander and ulterior motives?[30]

The man who wrote this letter, Kao Yu-han, was not an obscure individual but a leading comrade of the Communist Party, who also held office on the Supervisory Committee of the Kuomintang.

While the March 20 coup was met with aggrieved denials and reproaches, the resolutions of the May 15 plenary session were unquestioningly accepted, the Communists seeking every devious means of rationalizing and justifying them. "When the imperialists saw it (the resolution on the readjustment of party affairs) they may have suspected that your party had fallen into their trap and had voluntarily broken the revolutionary front in order to turn to the right," said an official letter from the Central Committee of the Communist Party to the Kuomintang,

> but it *may be* that your party did this because the form of co-operation between our party and yours has for several years aroused suspicion and jealousy in certain quarters.... Therefore you tried to make several changes in the form of co-operation in order to do away with unnecessary suspicion and jealousy, and later to purify the ranks, deal blows against the reactionaries, consolidate the revolutionary front and proceed to fight against the imperialist and militarist rule and oppression with all your might. If this is the case, then there is no fundamental conflict in the policy of co-operation with our party. The principal thing is to consolidate the revolutionary forces against imperialism, no matter what the form of consolidation and co-operation is. If such is the case, the spirit of alliance between our two parties will not be dampened.... Your resolution...is a question for your own party, and no matter what you decide in connection therewith, (we) have not the right to accept or reject.[31]

On May 26, the Canton correspondent of the Communist *Guide Weekly*[32] wrote that in view of the fact that the May 15 plenary session had adopted a "declaration for the consolidation of all revolutionary elements against the reaction, no fundamental change in the policy of co-operation had taken place," and that "a mere resolution on party affairs is not sufficient to indicate a rightward development of the Kuomintang Central Executive Committee. The Communists clearly recognize that the present situation of the revolution demands a strong and consistent revolutionary front. Their attitude toward the new resolution of the Kuomintang Central Executive Committee is guided by this criterion. The Communist fraction in the Kuomintang plenary session did not dispute in the least...the internal organization of the Kuomintang."*

This cringing policy did not go unchallenged in the ranks of the Communist Party. In Shanghai a group of comrades raised the demand for the immediate withdrawal of the party from the Kuomintang, declaring that it was impossible for the Communists to work effectively under the conditions laid down by the May 15 Kuomintang plenary session. Both the Central Committee in Shanghai and the Kwangtung party organization vigorously opposed this instinctively correct proletarian demand. The Kwangtung committee (later represented as more "radical" than the Shanghai Central Committee) considered that "to withdraw from the Kuomintang would mean to abandon the toiling masses, to abandon the banner of the revolutionary Kuomintang to the bourgeoisie. This would be an irretrievable loss. At this time a policy of temporary retreat must be pursued in order to remain in the Kuomintang."[33]

Nevertheless, even the leadership of the party which carried out, under Comintern orders, the policy of capitulation after March 20 began to feel the need for a revision of the party's course. The voices that called for resumption of independence made themselves heard to such an extent that even Chen Tu-hsiu wrote to the Comintern proposing substitution of a two-party bloc outside the Kuomintang instead of work within the Kuomintang.[34] A decision to this effect was actually adopted by the Communist Central Committee at its plenary session in June 1926. It was immediately and drastically condemned by the Comintern, in which the Russian Opposition led by Trotsky had already begun likewise to pose the problems of the Chinese revolution in a way that sought to orient the Chinese Communists away from the stifling stranglehold of the Kuomintang. The same official article which nearly one year later revealed for the first time that the March 20 coup had placed the Chinese Nationalist movement under the control of the right wing of the Kuomintang also disclosed, likewise for the first time, that the Communists in China had demanded their freedom, and that this demand had been ordered "revised." Even the Chinese Communist proposal to organize left-wing fractions within the Kuomintang—a shocking revelation that the so-called left did not even have a fractional organization of its own—was likewise condemned in favor of a policy of "directing the entire Kuomintang to the left and in guaranteeing it a stable left policy."[35]

In China Borodin firmly clamped down on the tendencies within the Chinese Communist Party toward the pursuit of an independent political policy. "The present period is one in which the Communists should do coolie service for the Kuomintang!" he declared.[36] Proposals to withdraw from the Kuomintang were squelched because they meant "abandoning the banner of the revolutionary Kuomintang to the bourgeoisie." The bourgeoisie had not waited, however, for the Communists. After March 20, the Kuomintang banner was firmly in their hands, and the masses were never apprised of that fact but were left to learn it suddenly

---

* The author of this report, Tsao Sze-yuan, was destined to suffer the consequences of not having disputed "in the least" the bourgeois offensive. A year later he died a martyr's death at the hands of Chiang Kai-shek's executioner.

and catastrophically. Instead of carrying the fight to the bourgeoisie on the battlefield of the class struggle at the head of the great labor and peasant organizations—in whose leadership Communists predominated and upon whose strength the Canton regime still rested—the Chinese Communists were compelled to offer only servile apologies. The coup of March 20, 1926, presents the remarkable spectacle of a mighty mass movement under Communist leadership painlessly deflected from the course of its own independent development, brought under the leadership and control of its class enemy, and kept in ignorance of this fact by its own leaders, who protested that they never dreamed of leading the masses except under the direction of the bourgeoisie.

Thanks only to this, the representatives of the bourgeoisie could still appear before the masses as "revolutionary leaders" between whom and the Communists there was little discernible difference. In May 1926, Chiang Kai-shek came before the Third National Labor Conference, where 500 delegates represented 400 unions and 1,240,000 organized workers, of whom 800,000 had participated in more than two hundred political and economic strikes since the previous May.[37] With mock modesty Chiang referred to himself as *shun ti*—"your younger brother." With cool cynicism he paid tribute to the decisive role played by the workers and peasants in the East River and southern campaigns during 1925. "In this period," he said, "the worker-peasant masses...hastened the unification of Kwangtung, swept away all the counter-revolutionaries, and consolidated the basis of the National government. From this one can see that the workers and peasants are already able to fight imperialism with their own forces, without reliance upon the forces of the army!"[38]

Chiang Kai-shek dared to tell the Chinese workers what the Communists dared not—that they were in a position to depend upon their own forces to fight and win their own battles. He could end his speech with "Long Live the World Revolution!" and step down from the rostrum amid cheers in which Communist voices mingled with all the others. He could now go ahead with preparations for the Northern Expedition, secure in the knowledge that the mass movement was still available for his use. The preliminary battle for control had been fought without a single bourgeois casualty. Indeed, it was not a battle but a successfully performed maneuver. Thanks to the Communist policy of retreat and acquiescence, it had taken place away from the arena of mass struggles. The organized workers and peasants, who at the call of the Communists would have hurled their weight into the scales where they belonged—*against* the bourgeoisie—were now called upon to march into the battles of the Northern Expedition under conditions which guaranteed to the bourgeoisie the fruits of their victories. The armies of the expedition marched northward in July, and were soon sweeping from victory to victory on the crest of a new revolutionary wave that surged torrent-like across Kiangsi, Hunan, and Hupeh, drawing fresh millions into the struggle and before long engulfing Wuhan and Shanghai.

Meanwhile in Canton the consequences of the March 20 coup made themselves felt. From covert maneuvers the bourgeoisie passed over to overt repression. The "temporary retreat" of the Communists in Canton became a permanent rout. On July 29, Chiang Kai-shek's headquarters proclaimed martial law. Public organizations, assemblies, the press, workers' and peasants' volunteer corps, strikes, all came within the orbit of military authority. Three days later an order was issued "forbidding all labor disturbances for the duration of the Northern expedition." While the authorities nominally held themselves aloof, the gangsters of Canton were mobilized into a "Central Labour Union." The offensive against the revolutionary workers was carried into the streets.

Startled sharply out of the specious calm in which their leaders had lulled them, the workers grabbed up arms, clubs, bamboo sticks, knives, an occasional revolver and rifle, and defended themselves. In six days' street fighting more than fifty workers were killed. On August 9, the authorities stepped in with regulations for the compulsory arbitration of all labor disputes under government auspices. Workers were forbidden to bear arms of any description, to assemble, or to parade. "Any attempt during the period of the war against the North to make trouble at home will be considered an act of counterrevolution and treason against the Kuomintang," read a police order. Military patrols took possession of the streets. Members of the "Central Labour Union" were called in to break a printing strike which had paralyzed the city's press. The Workers' Delegates' Conference, a revolutionary organization representing 170,000 Canton workers and shop employees, threatened a general strike. But their threat was months too late. It never materialized. The few small gains which the workers of Canton had wrested from their employers after years of struggle, were wiped out. The vicious contract system, which had made the workers the helpless slaves of the bosses, and which had been partially abolished in Canton, was restored. Public abuses, like licensed gambling and opium dens, which had been obliterated by the government under the influence of the mass movement, resumed a flourishing existence with the rates of official "squeeze" boosted far above those of the pre-Nationalist days.[39]

In the Kwangtung countryside the March 20 coup was the signal for the launching of a vicious offensive of the landlords against the revolting peasants. A report of the Kwangtung Provincial Peasant Association, made in February 1927, listed scores of attacks, murders of peasant leaders, smashing of peasant associations, which began in Kwangtung in June 1926, and never ended until the revolutionary peasant movement was blotted out of the province. Even in the language of this report, the Communist leaders of the peasant movement continued to cloak the real authors of this counteroffensive. The March 20 affair "really had no influence upon the policy of our Kuomintang," it read,

> but avaricious officials, corrupt gentry, and rowdies took advantage of it to spread rumors such as "the peasant associations are to be dissolved," and "the Kuomintang

> is discontinuing the worker and peasant policy...The resolution passed on May 15 by the Central Executive Committee plenary session was merely to deal adequately with the problems of the Kuomintang's internal affairs, but it was taken by the unprincipled landlords, the corrupt gentry, and the avaricious officials to indicate that the Government was about to dissolve the peasant associations and that the Kuomintang had abandoned the worker and peasant policy.[40]

The landlords and their minions correctly took their cue from Chiang Kai-shek's coup. The peasants never understood that the attacks upon them were thoroughly "lawful," that the March 20 coup had, indeed, put the peasant revolt beyond the pale of Kuomintang "legality" upon which the peasant leaders so helplessly depended. The same transformation brought to a fruitless close the strike of the Canton–Hong Kong workers.

Negotiations for a settlement of the great strike were resumed shortly after the March coup. They had been suspended in January when the British categorically rejected the demands of the Hong Kong strikers and the Canton government still insisted that it could negotiate only as an intermediary between the Hong Kong authorities and the strikers. In June 1925, at the outset of the strike, the newly established National government had demanded the retrocession of the Shameen concessions and the withdrawal of all foreign naval vessels from Kwangtung waters. The workers of Hong Kong had demanded freedom of speech and press, the right to vote in the selection of Chinese representatives in the government of the Crown Colony, improvement in working conditions, prohibition of child labor, the enforcement of an eight-hour day, and withdrawal of the general house rent increases scheduled to go into effect on July 1 that year.

The British had refused all negotiations and sat on their Hong Kong rock fulminating while the strike and boycott continued. "Only the unlawful activities of the Canton Strike Committee, instigated by Bolshevik intrigue, prevent the resumption of normal relations between Canton and Hong Kong on the old, familiar footing," declared the governor of Hong Kong on February 4, 1926. "We expect and require the Canton government to put an end to these illegalities. I also wish it to be clearly understood that the Hong Kong government will never agree in principle to strike pay or to compensation for non-reinstatement of laborers."[41] What His Excellency expected and required came to pass a few short weeks after his utterance. The transformation wrought in Canton by the March coup of Chiang Kai-shek made possible a resumption of relations on the "old familiar footing."

Unofficial contact between Hong Kong and Canton was resumed on April 9 when a Mr. Kemp, attorney-general of the Hong Kong government, conferred with C. C. Wu, the Canton foreign minister, in what was officially described as a "hearty talk."[42] A few days after the adjournment of the May plenary session of the Central Executive Committee, the Canton government officially approached

Hong Kong for a reopening of negotiations. The British readily agreed. The delegates met in July. The original demands of the Canton–Hong Kong workers were mutually deprecated. "These demands," said Eugene Chen, who had now taken over the Foreign Office, "were conceived and formulated in the unusual circumstances immediately following the shooting of June 23, and they included terms which my Government, actuated by a sincere desire to arrive at a satisfactory settlement, is prepared to review in order that nothing incompatible with the real dignity and interest of Great Britain as a trading power in China shall continue to obstruct the path of settlement."[43] It was no longer a question of strike pay for the workers. It became instead a question of a $10,000,000 loan from the British to the Canton Government, conditional upon "the complete cessation of the boycott and of all other anti-British manifestations throughout the territory controlled by the Canton Government."[44] The Chinese delegates no longer even pretended to represent the interests of the strikers. When the Strike Committee demanded a voice in the parleys, Chiang Kai-shek issued an order "instructing the Canton chief of police to prevent any interference by labor unions with the Canton–Hong Kong Conference now in progress."[45]

During the negotiations squads of soldiers and police patrolled the main streets of the city and a close check was kept on labor union leaders

> to prevent any movement among the workers which will create an opinion that the Kuomintang is unable to command the Canton situation and that any arrangement with the Kuomintang relative to the strike settlement...will be futile. The Canton Strike Committee is still clamouring that it should be heard, if not admitted to the negotiations now in progress in which the workers are chiefly concerned; and it is understood that should there be no objection from either side, in certain matters a sub-committee or the whole conference may hear representations from the workers. In Canton Chinese opinion has been that the whole matter has been straightened out among the Kuomintang leaders and General Chiang Kai-shek before the meeting of the...delegations of July 15, and they cannot see how any agitation among the workers will change the policy already formulated. Any attention to the Strike Committee will be more a matter of courtesy than anything else.[46]

"Courtesy" for the workers and $10,000,000 for Chiang Kai-shek! Not a bad bargain. But the negotiations ended inconclusively since the bargaining position of the Canton government collapsed as soon as it was apparent that it no longer spoke for the workers and, in fact, was as anxious to end the strike as the British themselves. Thereupon, Britain dispensed with parleys and instead, on September 3, a British naval landing party cleared the wharves of the Canton West Bund of worker-pickets. In protest against this act, Eugene Chen asked for the "retirement of the British gunboats now moored along the jetties to their usual anchorage off the Shameen."[47] A far cry, this, from the demand for the removal of all British vessels from Kwangtung waters! But the back of the strike and boycott was broken. On October 10, 1926, the Canton government unconditionally called off both strike and boycott. The Kuomintang and the strike committee explained that this step was required "by the change in the national situation brought about by the extension of Nationalist power and influence to the Yangtze." The abrupt termination of a historic fifteen months' struggle without a single concession to the demands of the workers who conducted it was termed "not a defeat but a great victory."[48]

"Imperialism either had to capitulate to China," explained Borodin, "...or China acknowledge defeat. Since, however, defeat could not be countenanced, it became necessary to terminate the battle in this corner in order to start out with greater vigor to fight imperialism throughout China—on the wider base."[49] Defeat could not be "countenanced." It had to be rationalized into a victory. It was necessary to conceal the fact that the strategic moment and decisive positions had long since been surrendered to the enemy without a struggle. The Hong Kong strike and boycott had opened wide the door to an independent working-class perspective and had incomparably demonstrated the ability of the workers to function in their own interests. Under the mentorship of the Comintern and Borodin, the Chinese Communists had let the opportunity slip by without ever realizing it. The workers of Canton and Hong Kong had to pay dearly for this "victory."

Following the voluntary liquidation of the strike and boycott, the governor of Hong Kong happily declared that "we may reasonably hope that a determined effort will now be made by the Cantonese authorities to re-establish law and order." Hong Kong desired to see in Kwangtung and Kwangsi "a strong, stable, and enlightened government; of such a government we should gladly be close friends and staunch supporters."[50] With the departure of the national government to the Yangtze in December, the task of re-establishing "law and order" in Kwangtung passed to the Kwangsi militarist, Li Chi-sen, who took over full control. Strict police measures were enforced against the workers. A set of stringent regulations was issued providing for compulsory arbitration of all disputes between workers and employers, forbidding workers to possess or carry arms, to make arrests, to picket shops or factories.[51]

In reply to these measures, the pickets and other workers' volunteer groups were "instructed by the Workers' Delegates' Conference, acting under the auspices of the Communist Party, to remain indoors for the present, pending readjustment of their standing."[52] Anxious only to propitiate Li Chi-sen, the Communists abruptly put an end to their agitation for a popular re-election of delegates to the various provincial Kuomintang organizations.[53] They offered no protests when Li Chi-sen put through a sweeping reorganization during which he filled all important posts with his own appointees. No effort was made to organize any resistance to this reactionary offensive. Canton was tight in the militarist grip. The capitulation of the Communists was complete.[54]

This was Canton when a delegation of the Communist International composed of Earl Browder, Tom Mann, and Jacques Doriot, arrived on February 17,

1927. They inspected the outer shell of the mass movement that still remained and were feted by the dictator, Li Chi-sen, who told them that "never, never, would the Nationalist government proceed against the interests of the working class."[55] They sent their greetings to Chiang Kai-shek, who wired back his welcome.[56] Their first reports to the international press glowed with pride in "revolutionary Canton," and were unmarred by the slightest suggestion of discord.[57] At the graves of the Hong Kong pickets killed in action during the great strike they laid wreaths with an inscription that read: "The martyred Hong Kong pickets symbolize the great contribution of the Chinese working class to the Chinese revolution and the world revolution."[58]

Six months later, after events had long since taken their course, the delegation wrote the following of its visit to Canton:

> The Northern Expedition was in full swing and the Canton merchants cleverly utilized the slogan of the united revolutionary front in order to free themselves from all obligations to the working class.... Some of the leaders of the Canton proletariat were far from clear in their policy in the face of this clever and demagogic tactic of the bourgeoisie.... (They) neglected...the fundamental class interests of the proletariat for fear of breaking the united front with the bourgeoisie.... The only class, it seems, which took the slogan of the "united front" of all anti-imperialist and anti-militarist forces seriously was the proletariat and its revolutionary leaders.... This was undoubtedly a mistake which later cost the Chinese working class much sacrifice and good blood.[59]

6 From Canton to the Yangtze

The Kuomintang marched its forces northward to replace the power of the older militarists with its own. It marched not to fight imperialism, but to compromise with it. Deluded into the belief that a Kuomintang victory would bring a thorough change in their conditions of life and livelihood—of this the Communists made no attempt to disabuse them—the masses rose in a tidal wave which swept the expeditionary armies to the banks of the Yangtze.

Success was swift and spectacular. Armed forces merely supplemented the huge propaganda machine which swept forward, unleashing the forces which levelled all opposition like a line of tanks clearing the way for infantry. Before this onslaught the mercenary forces of Wu Pei-fu and his allies were helpless and demoralized. They either fell back in confusion or with their commanders sought the safety of an alliance with the Nationalists. A foreign eyewitness relates how "an indigenous intelligence service...was ready waiting to assist the incoming army, reliable guides were available to serve whenever wanted; in some cases days before the army arrived, towns and cities were taken possession of by little groups (!) of enthusiasts...in the name of the national government."[1] In the actual fighting peasant detachments were found wherever the clash was fiercest. Railway and telegraph workers paralyzed the enemy's communications. Peasant intelligence made all the enemy staff secrets almost instantly available to the advancing Nationalists.

Tang Sheng-chih, a Hunan militarist who was among the first to leap upon the Nationalist bandwagon, occupied Changsha on July 12. A few weeks later the expeditionary forces faced the northern defenses at Yochow on the Yangtze. Their way had been cleared by the independent action of the peasants at Pingkiang and of the workers of the Canton-Hankow and Chuchow-Pinghsiang railways. Peasant guides led the Nationalists to a ford unknown to the northerners which enabled them to cross one of the adjacent tributaries of the Yangtze and fall upon

Yochow's defenders from the rear. "The enemy thought the army had come from Heaven," gleefully reported a Canton newspaper.[2] Twelve hours later on the morning of August 22, Nationalist troops entered Yochow. Nationalist forces converged on the three great cities located at the confluence of the Han and Yangtze rivers, Hanyang, Hankow, and Wuchang. The arsenal workers in Hanyang struck. The northern garrison retreated from the city in confusion, the Nationalists taking possession of Hanyang on September 6 and of Hankow two days later. Wuchang's defenders held out inside that city's mighty walls for nearly a month before the charges of the famous "Ironsides" army battered the gates in. By mid-October the flag of the Kuomintang was firmly established over the heart of the Yangtze Valley.

Meanwhile in the east the advance of Chiang Kai-shek through Kiangsi had been less spectacular and less successful. Chiang had restricted the activities of the propaganda machine and had already along the line of march adopted repressive measures against the mass movement. This enabled Sun Chuang-fang, military overlord of the five eastern provinces, to put up a hardier resistance. Chiang's progress was so slow that in October he loosened slightly the restrictions on propaganda and matters then moved more swiftly. Nanchang was finally taken, and on November 5 Chiang's forces reached Kiukiang on the banks of the Yangtze.

The victories of the Northern Expedition coincided with a vast extension of the mass movement. In Hunan labor unions spread from five to forty *hsien* and their membership rose from 60,000 to 150,000 by the end of November. In Wuhan within two months of the Nationalist occupation more than 300,000 workers and shop employees were mobilized in more than 200 unions united under the banner of the Hupeh General Labor Union. To the workers the Nationalist victory was the signal for militant efforts to revise the miserable living standard to which they were subjected by Chinese and foreign employer alike. Wuhan was rocked by a terrific series of strikes.[3]

Even more spectacular was the growth of the peasant movement. By the end of November there were in Hunan fifty-four organized *hsien* with a total registered membership in the peasant associations of 1,071,137. By January 1927, this number had passed 2,000,000.[4] The peasants first demanded rent reduction, abolition of the miscellaneous tax burden, and arms to fight the village gentry. Village authority fell largely to the peasant associations and in Hunan the step from refusal to pay all rent to the outright seizure of land was quickly taken.

It was in these circumstances that the national government moved in December from Canton to the Yangtze. The flush of victory and the glow of the mass movement enabled the vacillating petty bourgeois politicians of the "Left" to shed temporarily the inferiority complex which Chiang Kai-shek's show of power in Canton had thrust upon them. They strutted back and forth on the platform of power erected by the masses and gushed a torrent of radical phrases. Before the realities of the class struggle, however, they shrank. Soon the traditional cry of the petty bourgeois radical rose like a wail in the meeting chambers of government committees—"The masses are going too far!"

In the face of the strike wave the Hankow capitalists stiffened into resistance. On December 3, the General Chamber of Commerce threatened a general strike of capital unless measures were immediately taken to limit the workers' struggles. Borodin, the Communist leaders, and their Kuomintang associates hastened to comply. Three days later a board of arbitration was set up to "recognize reasonable (?) increases of wages, advise different trades to follow traditions (!) in fixing working hours, to improve materially the social treatment of the workers, and to leave the power of employing and dismissing labourers entirely in the hands of the employers."[5] The personnel of the board was made up of representatives of the Kuomintang, the General Labor Union, and the Chamber of Commerce. Its decisions were to be "binding on both employer and employees." An attempt was made to introduce labor legislation which fixed a minimum wage of thirteen dollars a month—a ruling which never took effect, miserable as it was—and at the same time forbade workers to interfere in matters "of management and employment; but in cases of obvious disadvantage to the workers they may present protests."[6] This meant the establishment of a system of compulsory arbitration, against which Communists had always taken a principled position precisely because such a system is designed to sap the initiative of the working class, vitiate the fighting strength of its organizations, and in general to deflect them from methods of militant class struggle.

Borodin and the Wuhan Kuomintang radicals similarly tried to evade taking responsibility for the peasant movement. The task of formulating a concrete program of peasant demands was avoided. Even the 25 percent rent reduction provided for in the 1924 program of the Kuomintang was never applied. Instead peasant "excesses" were deplored and the fear prevailed that the peasants, by going "too far," might prejudice the united front of the classes. The period of the Northern Expedition offered an incomparable opportunity to liberate the masses from bourgeois influence and from the bourgeois leadership established by Chiang Kai-shek in Canton. The Communist leadership did not seize this opportunity, however. Instead it clung to the flabby bourgeois radicals of the Kuomintang "Left." A striking picture of the Communist leadership and the policies of the Comintern delegate was given by three more critical-minded Comintern functionaries in Shanghai in a letter to Moscow dated March 17, 1927:

Up to October 1926, the question of the peasantry...was never raised in a more or less serious form either by the representative of the E.C.C.I. (Executive Committee of the Communist International) or by the C.C. (Central Committee) of the Chinese Communist Party, except for the decisions of the June plenum of the C.C., which completely hushed up the peasants' struggle and appealed for a bloc with the "good gentry."...In October a programme of peasants' demands was worked out, but the representative of the E.C.C.I. as well as the Party leaders considered it only as a programme for the Party congress. For a period of three to four months the programme did not pass beyond the walls of the C.C., and only in January was it sent out to the local organizations. But up till now, nothing has been essentially changed in the tactics of the Party on the peasant question. The old line of curbing the struggle in the village and applying the brakes to the peasants' movement as a whole still prevails.... The fear of the peasants' movement has existed and still remains in the Party. The realization of peasant possession of land (that is, the occupation of the land by the peasants) is called by the C.C. "a dangerous infantile disease of Leftism." It continues to speak of the "united front with the good gentry and the small and middle landlords against the bad gentry and the blackguards." (Report from Hunan of December 30.) The expression "good gentry" is found to this day in all Party documents, in articles by leading comrades. This replacement of social categories by moral categories is essentially a suspension of the revolutionary movement in the village.

At the December plenum of the C.C. a resolution on the peasant question was adopted with the participation of the representative of the E.C.C.I. Not a word is to be found in this resolution on an agrarian programme and on the struggle of the peasantry. The resolution does not answer a single one of the most burning questions of the day; the question of the peasants' power is answered negatively. It says, the slogan of a peasants' power must not be raised so as not to frighten away the petty bourgeoisie. From the neglect of the peasants' revolution springs the suspension by the leading Party organs of the arming of the peasantry....

The tactic of the Party in the workers' movement is no different from its tactic in the peasants' movement. Above all, there is an absolute under-estimation and lack of attention to it. The C.C. has no trade union department. More than a million organized workers have no guiding centre. The trade unions are separated from the masses and remain to a large degree organizations at the top. The political and organizational work is replaced everywhere by compulsion, but the main thing is that reformist tendencies are growing inside as well as outside the revolutionary trade union movement...there occur refusals to support and defend the economic demands of the workers. Out of fear of the elementary growth of the labour movement, the Party in Canton consented to compulsory arbitration, then it did the same thing in Hankow (the idea of compulsory arbitration itself comes from Borodin). Especially great is the fear of the Party leaders of the movement of the non-industrial workers....

The report of the C.C. at the December plenum says:

It is unusually difficult for us to decide our tactics in relation to the middle and petty bourgeoisie, since the strikes of non-industrial and office workers are only conflicts within the petty bourgeoisie themselves. Both sides (i.e. the employers and the workers) being necessary for the national united front, we can support neither of the two sides, neither can we be neutral.... The employees in concerns producing vital necessities (rice, salt, coal, fuel, etc.) must never resort to strikes if there is the slightest possibility of attaining concessions in a peaceful manner.'

Thus the Party abandons the defence and support of the non-industrial workers, i.e., the majority of the Chinese working-class, and covers it up with the necessity of the united front with the petty bourgeoisie. Incidentally, it is quite clear that it is not so much a question of the petty bourgeoisie, especially of the artisans, as of the commercial middle bourgeoisie.... The Party leadership also fears the arming of the workers....

A characterization of the Party attitude towards the army was given by comrade Chow En-lai in his report. He said to the Party members: "Go into this national revolutionary army, strengthen it, raise its fighting ability, but do not carry on any independent work there." Up to recently there were no nuclei in the army. Our comrades who were political advisers occupied themselves exclusively with military and political work for the Kuomintang....

With the aid of all sorts of combinations, oppositions, etc., our comrades hoped to maintain a balance of forces in the army, but it never occurred to them to capture it.... With particular ardour does the representative of the E.C.C.I. deny the possibility of political work in the army. The December plenum of the C.C. adopted a decision to build nuclei in the army (only of commanders, to be sure, with the prohibition against taking in soldiers), and in January of this year, when the other Russian comrades (not for the first time), raised the question of work in the army, comrade V.* already expressed himself sharply against the organization of nuclei. First he told comrade M.** that Moscow had decided not to form nuclei and then he showed the impossibility of organizing them; first, because the military commanders, especially Chiang Kai-shek, would see in it the machinations of the Communists, which would strain relations; second, because the Cantonese army was not susceptible to influence from below. When it was proposed to draw workers and Communists into the army on a mass scale...as well as peasants and members of the Peasant leagues, he laid it aside with pretexts, declaring that nobody would take them into the army anyway, nothing would ever come of it, there is no recruiting going on now, etc. And since he did not dare to appear as an opponent in principle in the question of arming the workers, he discovered a thousand difficulties, and showed that the arming of the workers is absolutely unthinkable, that we cannot get weapons anywhere, etc.

Besides, there are dozens of company commanders and a few regiment commanders who are Communists and have a colossal influence, there is a Communist regiment, and through all these channels an enormous work could be conducted. But out of fear of revolutionizing the army which pervades some Party leaders, isolated comrades working in the army became detached from the Party, were transformed into "individual" Communist commanders.... Despite the fact that the representative of the E.C.C.I. after a long resistance admitted to us that the work of the Party in the army must be reorganized, he subsequently did nothing to carry through this reorganization. We do not even know if he spoke of it to the C.C.[7]

---

* Voitinsky

** Mandalyan

In all this the functionary critics were careful not to say that Borodin and Voitinsky were only carrying out in China the policies dictated by Stalin and Bukharin in Moscow. The fatal policies of the Chinese Communist leadership, sponsored by Borodin and Voitinsky, flowed irrevocably from the course pursued by the Comintern. In March 1926, on the very eve of Chiang Kai-shek's coup, the Sixth Plenum of the Executive Committee of the Comintern had sanctified the bloc of the workers and peasants with the bourgeoisie and ensured to the latter the support of the proletariat. After the March 20 coup it deliberately concealed the shift of power in Canton to the hands of the extreme right wing of the Kuomintang under the aegis of Chiang Kai-shek. Shortly afterward the Political Bureau of the Communist Party of the Soviet Union, against one adverse vote—Trotsky's—approved the admission of Chiang Kai-shek's Kuomintang, as a "sympathizing party," into the Communist International.*

"In preparing himself for the role of an executioner," wrote Trotsky, Chiang Kai-shek "wanted to have the cover of world Communism—and he got it."[8]

In October 1926, the Stalin-Bukharin leadership in Moscow wired the Chinese Communists to keep the peasant movement in check in order not to drive away the generals leading the victorious march northward. When confronted with the fact,[9] Stalin later admitted that such a telegram had been sent and, more remarkably still, confessed that it had been "a mistake," hastily adding that it had been "cancelled" a few weeks later.[10] The "cancellation" consisted of the directives of the Seventh Plenum of the Executive Committee of the Communist International, which were more careful to stress, in general terms, the importance of the agrarian revolution to the Chinese anti-imperialist struggle. At the same time, by the system of double bookkeeping that had now become the rule in the Comintern, the specific and concrete program laid down for the Chinese Communists required them, more than ever, to check the tumultuous uprising of the peasant millions.

This cleavage between profession and practice flowed from the opportunism of the Comintern, which professed, abstractly, the principle of the political independence of the proletariat while it practiced, concretely, a policy of capitulation to the bourgeoisie. In their word-laden, over-cunning resolutions, Stalin, Bukharin & Co. united these antithetical elements and presented them as a synthetic whole. When their practices led to disaster, they could always cite their professions and shift the blame to the practices of others.

The theses on the Chinese question,[11] adopted by the Seventh Plenum of the Comintern Executive in November 1926, observed that "the progressive aban-

---

* The participation of Shao Li-tze, of Chiang's personal entourage, as fraternal delegate of the Kuomintang in the Seventh Plenum of the E.C.C.I. in November 1926, confirms the membership status of the Kuomintang in the International.

donment of the revolution by the big bourgeoisie is historically inevitable." This phrase was later worn thin when quotations were needed to prove that the Comintern "foresaw" and "predicted" everything. Its original context, however, included the following passages: "This does not signify that the bourgeoisie is totally eliminated, as a class, from the struggle for national independence, since side by side with the small and middle bourgeoisie, even a certain section of the big bourgeoisie can for a certain time still march with the revolution.... The proletariat must, of course, broadly utilize those strata of the bourgeoisie which at present are actively co-operating in the revolutionary struggle against imperialism and militarism."

The theses warned that the "bourgeoisie" was trying to "smash the revolution," but the worker closely following the actual events in China would look in vain in the pages of this document for a translation of this dire "warning" into the names, dates, parties, and places directly involved in the Chinese events. "Smashing the revolution" implied an activity of an extremely concrete nature. Who was smashing it? Where, when, and how? Of this the theses speak no word. What of Chiang Kai-shek, the March 20 coup, the repression of the workers in Canton and the massacres of the peasants in the province of Kwangtung and in the wake of Chiang Kai-shek's northward advancing armies? Of all this no word, not a single solitary word. The theses contained a single reference, unexplained and unelaborated, to the fact that "the labour and peasant movement, even in Kwangtung province, have had to surmount many difficulties." In his report, Tang Ping-shan, delegate of the Chinese Communist Party, referred mysteriously to "the March affair this year in Canton" as "an attempt on the part of the bourgeoisie to take the leadership of the revolution away from the proletariat," but he never mentioned it again, nor did anyone else, if the official record is to be believed.[12]

Stalin himself assured the members of the Chinese commission on November 30 that the "big national bourgeoisie is extremely weak...the role of leader of the Chinese peasantry must inevitably fall into the hands of the Chinese proletariat which is better organized and more active than the Chinese bourgeoisie."[13] The sections of the Comintern and their delegates were left secure in their belief that while the "bourgeoisie" might be trying to "smash" the revolution, Chiang Kai-shek was leading it from victory to victory. When Chiang's personal representative, Shao Li-tze, appeared on the rostrum as the fraternal delegate of the Kuomintang, they gave him a stormy ovation and rose to sing the "International" in his honor. When "in the name of the Kuomintang," Shao—referred to in the record as "comrade" Shao—declared that "we expect the support of the Comintern and all its affiliated parties.... Long live the Comintern! Long live the world revolution!" the enthusiasm was indescribable.[14]

Stalin was perfectly aware that the advance of Chiang Kai-shek's armies had meant in Canton and in scores of towns and villages the bloody suppression of strikes, the destruction of trade unions, and repression of the peasant movement,[15] yet of Chiang Kai-shek's Northern Expedition he said: "The advance of the Canton troops meant a blow aimed at imperialism, a blow aimed at its agents in China. It meant the freedom of assembly, freedom to strike, freedom of the Press, freedom of coalition for all the revolutionary elements in China in general and for the workers in particular.... In China it is not the unarmed people against the troops of their own government, but the armed people in the form of its revolutionary army. In China armed revolution is fighting against armed counterrevolution. This is one of the peculiarities and one of the advantages of the Chinese revolution.

"What is important," continued Stalin, "is not the bourgeois democratic character of the Canton government, which forms the nucleus of the future all-Chinese revolutionary power. The most important thing is that this power is an anti-militarist power, and can be nothing else, that every advance of this power is a blow aimed at world imperialism and is therefore a stroke in favor of the world revolutionary movement."[16]

The "bourgeoisie" would indeed "inevitably abandon" the revolution, but its chief agent, Chiang Kai-shek, was the heroic leader of the "armed revolution," and its chief agency, the Canton government, was the shining spearhead of struggle against the militarists and against imperialism, which, "despite its bourgeois-democratic character, essentially and objectively contains the embryo of a revolutionary-democratic-petty-bourgeois dictatorship of the revolutionary bloc of the proletariat, the peasantry, and the urban petty bourgeoisie."[17] How more to disorient and confuse the communists of all countries, and above all the communists in China?

On the agrarian revolution the theses of the Seventh Plenum spoke bold words: "The agrarian question...is the central point of the present situation.... Not to deal boldly with the agrarian question, not to support in their entirety the political and economic aims of the peasant masses would be a real danger for the revolution. It would be false not to place the program of the peasant movement first in the programme of national liberation for fear of alienating the uncertain and perfidious co-operation of a part of the capitalist class."[18]

This was, presumably, the "cancellation" of the October telegram that ordered a restraining hand on the peasants precisely to assure the continued "uncertain and perfidious" cooperation of the bourgeoisie. But examine this new boldness a few lines farther, where the theses declare: "While recognizing that the Communist Party of China must proclaim the nationalization of land as the fundamental demand of the agrarian programme of the proletariat, it must nevertheless for the present differentiate its agrarian tactic according to the economic and political peculiarities of the different sections of Chinese territory."

Light is shed on this cryptic qualification in the concrete agrarian program laid down for the Chinese communists to follow. Exceeding in no respect the liberal-reform program of the Kuomintang, the Comintern asked for rent reductions, tax adjustments, credit aids, governmental support of the peasant organizations, arms, and "confiscation of church and convent land and of land belonging to the reactionary militarists." Stalin suggested the same kind of "tactical differentiation" when he spoke of the programmatic demands of the proletariat and raised the slogan of nationalization of industry. "This raises above all," he immediately added, "the question of nationalization of those undertakings whose owners have distinguished themselves by special hostility and special aggressiveness towards the Chinese people."[19]

This reproduced the categories of "good" and "bad" gentry already in common usage in China. It extended them to the idea of "reactionary" (as against "progressive"?) militarists, and "especially hostile" (as against "friendly"?) exploiters of industrial labor. This mechanism served here simply to "cancel" completely the specious radicalism of the theses and to conceal, however thinly, the Comintern's capitulation to the bourgeoisie. The Communists were ordered to support "in their entirety" the demands of the peasants—and the peasants were already demanding the land. At the same time the Communists were required to limit themselves to agitating for the confiscation only of the land of the "reactionary militarists." Was it not a fact that every local satrap joined the Kuomintang as soon as it reached his bailiwick? He thus became part of the "armed revolution" and his land became theoretically inviolate, along with the land of all his satellites, his relatives, his supporters—i.e. all the local owners of land for whom he ruled. Peasants in Kwangtung, Hunan, and Kiangsi were already discovering this as they reached out to take the land for their own. Protection of the "officers' land," sanctified here by the Comintern, served as a noose for the agrarian revolution. Supported by the Communists, it became the main prop in the defense of the landlords as a whole.

This was the kind of "agrarian revolution" that even Chiang Kai-shek gladly supported. Said "comrade" Shao Li-tze to the plenum: "Comrade (comrade!) Chiang Kai-shek declared in his speech before the members of the Kuomintang that the Chinese revolution would be unthinkable if it were unable to solve correctly the agrarian, i.e. the peasant, question.... We are convinced that the Kuomintang, under the leadership of the Communist Party and the Comintern, will fulfill its historic role!"[20]

There was a grim truth in Chiang Kai-shek's conviction that under the "leadership of the Comintern" the Kuomintang would "fulfill its historic role." So long as this leadership kept the Chinese Communists, and with them the masses, lashed to the chariot of the bourgeoisie and its government, there could be no doubt of it. On this point the theses were emphatic. The whole program was to be achieved through and by the Kuomintang government. "The task of the Communist Party," said the theses, "is to see that the Canton government carries out these measures as a transition toward a further development of the agrarian revolution." Casually the theses admitted that "since its creation, this government has really been in the hands of the right wing of the Kuomintang," and then added: "Recent events indicate that the Communists must enter the national government to support the left wing in its struggle (?) against the feeble (?) and wavering (?) policy of the right." The "recent events"—again unspecified—had really shown that the "left" was the feeble and wavering prisoner of the aggressive and powerful right. To order the Communists into this government and cut them off from a powerful independent offensive of their own only ensured that they in turn would remain obedient prisoners of the "left."

All power and unquestioning obedience to the Kuomintang regime! "What is essentially new and original," Bukharin told a Leningrad party meeting, "is that now the Chinese revolution already possesses a center organized into a state power. This fact has enormous significance. The Chinese revolution has already passed the stage of evolution in which the popular masses struggle against the ruling regime. The present stage of the Chinese revolution is characterized by the fact that the forces of the revolution are already organized into a state power with a regular, disciplined army...the advance of the armies, their brilliant victories...are a special form of the revolutionary process."[21]

The popular masses had no longer need of struggle against "the ruling regime." The ruling regime still represented the interests of the exploiters in town and country, and its generals were already clamping the lid on the mass movement, but this was "a special form of the revolutionary process." Tang Ping-shan unconsciously summed up the dilemma:

"We must safeguard the interests of the peasantry, but on the other hand we must maintain and solidify the united front of the national revolutionary movement. In so contradictory a situation it is not easy (!) to maintain a correct tactical line...In this question we stand completely on the standpoint of Comrade Bukharin: the development of the Chinese peasant movement, while at the same time maintaining the united front of all strata of the population in the national revolutionary movement against imperialism."[22]

This was the attempt to reconcile the irreconcilable. To "develop" the peasant movement and still preserve the bloc with the bourgeoisie was impossible if this "development" was carried to its logical conclusion, the expropriation of the landlords. The Chinese Communists were asked to ride two horses pulling in opposite directions, and those in the Russian Opposition and in China who raised their voices to say that this could not be done were condemned out of hand. Stalin and other speakers at the plenum sharply rapped the demand of the Chinese Communists for withdrawal from the Kuomintang. "It would be the greatest mistake," said Stalin.[23] When P. Mif, later chief of the Stalinist experts on maintaining the "national united front," chanced to reread the theses of Lenin and came forward with a proposal for the creation of soviets in the Chinese countryside, Stalin called him brusquely to order, and he quickly subsided.

The Seventh Plenum resolution spoke about the "path of non-capitalist development" and the "agrarian revolution," but it laid down a policy that based itself, not on the interests of the workers and peasants, but on the sacrifice of those interests for the sake of a get-rich-quick bloc with the Chinese bourgeoisie. Preservation of this bloc at all costs was the task assigned to the representatives of the Comintern in China, to Borodin in Hankow and Voitinsky in Shanghai, whose counsel helped petrify the Chinese Communist leadership in the mold of class collaboration. They did not teach the Chinese Communists to go out into the factories and the fields with faith in the power of the millions who entered the struggle against their exploiters during the closing months of 1926.

The spectacular growth of the peasant movement coincided with a strike wave of unparalleled depth and intensity in all the major industrial centers throughout the year 1926. Incomplete records show a total of 535 strikes in 1926 as compared with 318 in 1925. Well over one million workers were directly involved. Most of the strikes were fought on the battleground of economic demands, for wage increases, and improvement in working conditions. More than half of them were fully or partially successful. Counting only those strikes for which full data were available, one investigator calculated that 49.70 percent were wholly successful, 28.01 percent were partially successful, while only 22.29 percent failed.[24] These statistics tell their own story. The workers of China were raising their heads as never before. By the end of the year the strike wave was already reaching beyond the plane of economic demands to that of open political struggle. With a single, spectacular stroke the Hankow workers took the course of the anti-imperialist struggle into their own hands.

On the afternoon of January 3, 1927, a great demonstration took place at the boundaries of the Hankow British Concession. The British, with memories of May 30, 1925, still fresh in their minds, voluntarily withdrew their naval landing party the next day. Frightened even more than the British by the demonstrations in the streets, the leaders of the Nationalist government agreed to take over responsibility for policing the British area after the marines and volunteer guards were withdrawn. In mid-afternoon on January 4, the workers again gathered at the Concession boundary. "Finding that the Concession was merely being policed by their own men, and that it had not actually been taken away from the British, the cry went up to 'Take it now!'...Squads of coolies then started a round of the Concession removing the barricades. Sandbags which had been stacked up at the entrances to all the Concession roads were torn open, the sand scattered in the street and the sacks taken away. Barbed-wire barricades were removed bodily, as were all other obstructions.... The foreigners' day was done on the streets of the British Concession."[25] Along the wires to Shanghai and to the world outside raced reports of "mobs," of looting and pillage. As a matter of fact, as eyewitnesses were compelled to admit, the victors "were riotously excited and jubilant in the Concession thoroughfares for a day or two, and there were some instances of insolence and threats toward foreigners; but no personal violence was done and no houses entered."[26]

At Kiukiang two days later the British Concession was similarly recovered when the British hurriedly evacuated from the city under the threat of mass action. Similar stories of vandalism were circulated. Six weeks afterwards the well-known British journalist Arthur Ransome visited Kiukiang and inspected some of the "violated" premises which had been especially sealed for investigators. "The looting seemed to me to have been very inefficient," he wrote, "floors covered with torn-up papers which must have been left by foreigners while preparing to leave; corners of sofas and mattresses ripped up.... Very little furniture was broken and no windows, not even a very ugly ostentatious hanging lamp, which I should have liked to smash myself.... It is curious to observe that at 6 p.m. of that day (January 7) a party of fifteen, two men and the rest women, who had come down...from Kuling, came through the Chinese streets into the Concession and down to the ships without molestation."[27]

The seizure of the British Concession in Hankow was a spontaneous act of the Hankow workers. "Nobody foresaw the events of January 3," wrote the three Comintern functionaries in their letter from Shanghai. "The occupation of the Concession by the Hankow workers took place spontaneously, without any leadership, either from the government, from the Kuomintang, or from our party. They were all confronted by an accomplished fact, by a spontaneous act of the masses, and all of them had to reckon with it."[28]

For the imperialists, and for the British in particular, the Hankow events served to hasten the policy of retreat before the mass movement that had already begun to manifest itself during the course of 1926. This policy had a dual character. It consisted first in making concessions sufficiently attractive to the Chinese bourgeoisie to establish a new basis for united action against the mass movement. This was accompanied, however, by a display and a use of force designed to remind the bourgeoisie that imperialist privileges could not and would not be surrendered without a struggle. The policy combined cajolery with menace. On August 31, 1926, the powers signed an agreement for the rendition of the Shanghai Mixed Court to become effective on January 1, 1927. A few days after the accord was reached, British gunboats ruthlessly shelled the Yangtze town of Wanhsien, inflicting heavy casualties on the civilian population in retaliation for a minor shipping scuffle. It was a reminder that "gunboat policy" still held good.

Early in December, when the Nationalist government moved to Hankow, the British minister, Sir Miles Lampson, was sent there on an official mission to explore possible channels of compromise. The Japanese and United States governments likewise sent special diplomatic representatives to treat with the Wuhan regime. On December 18, 1926, to the horror and angry consternation of the British community in China, the British government circulated a memorandum to the other signatories of the Washington treaties of 1922 proposing progressive relinquishment of foreign treaty privileges. On January 27, 1927, it followed this up with similar proposals addressed impartially to the Peking and Wuhan governments. The same week the U.S. secretary of state announced his government's readiness to participate in a compromise arrangement. In line with this policy, the British government accepted the fait accompli at Hankow and opened negotiations which ended with the signature of the Chen-O'Malley notes of February 19 and March 2, which returned the Hankow and Kiukiang Concessions to Chinese jurisdiction, a surrender that seemed like the end of the world to the British residents of other treaty ports.[29] For them, however, there was the satisfaction of freshly arriving troops and warships. Caressing with one hand, the imperialists were prepared to strike with the other. The threat of armed intervention was held over the head of the Chinese bourgeoisie, hut the imperialists still counted on their Chinese minions to smash the mass movement in their joint behalf, and their major strategy was directed to this end.

When the petty bourgeois politicians of Hankow recovered from their fright at the audacity of the workers, the spectacle of a retreating and conciliatory Britain gave them new heart. They readily stepped in to negotiate and emerged dazzled with the Chen-O'Malley accord. It was greeted as a "diplomatic victory" for Eugene Chen, but it was the humble Hankow coolie and his comrades who had brought the mighty Britain to heel.

The Communist leaders, on their part, were dazed. "How did the Central Committee of the Communist Party react to the events in Hankow? At first it did not want to react at all.... The C.C. was of the opinion that the foreigners and the petty bourgeoisie need not have been irritated."[30] Again: "The seizure of the British concession by the Wuhan workers...was not only carried out without the knowledge of the Party leadership, but afterward the Central Committee regarded it as having been incorrect."[31]

Nevertheless the psychological effect of the January 3 events was to stiffen the attitude of the left leaders at Wuhan, if only temporarily, toward Chiang Kai-shek. Chiang had established himself at Nanchang, capital of Kiangsi, where the politicians of the right wing gathered about him and go-betweens like Huang Fu and C. T. Wang scurried to and fro seeking an entente with the Japanese and even with

Chang Tso-lin through the latter's emissary, Yang Yu-ting. Chiang's eyes were fixed on Shanghai, the principal economic and political base of compradorism, the stronghold of foreign and Chinese finance capital. Pending conquest of that vital center with its ready funds and its direct access to the big bourgeoisie, Chiang Kai-shek maneuvered to keep control of the party in his own hands. He demanded that the seat of the government be established at Nanchang. He wanted the Central Executive Committee of the Kuomintang to meet there under his auspices. He even made a swift trip to Wuhan on January 10 to press his demand. But there, the petty bourgeois radicals, Borodin included, momentarily exhilarated by the victory over the British and the strength of the movement behind them, were bold enough to give him a cold reception. Even Borodin at a banquet attended by Chiang made a few pointed sallies about power-seeking militarists, a bit of audacity from which he himself "immediately recoiled in fright," saying: "I am afraid I made a mistake.... Our intervention against Chiang Kai-shek was provoked by the pressure of the general opinion and I do not know whether I acted correctly."[32]

Chiang left Wuhan abruptly. Back in Nanchang he openly announced his intention to smash the Communists. "If the Tung Men Hui (the predecessor of the Kuomintang) failed to construct an ordered republic," he said in a speech on February 19,

> it was because in its ranks were too many disparate elements who did not march together. There were...reactionaries and counter-revolutionaries who compromised the work. Of these people there are still now too many. The time has come to expel them since they are not true comrades.... No more differences or tendencies among us! Being known as a faithful believer in the doctrines of Sun Wen (Sun Yat-sen), I have the right to say that every true member of the party must be just that and nothing else. Whoever goes against the aims and methods indicated by Sun Wen will not be a comrade but an enemy who must not remain among us.[33]

Again, on March 7, Chiang delivered a broadside, directed this time against Borodin and the other Russian advisers, professing, however, continued friendship for the Soviet Union. "It is not (Russia's) policy to tyrannize over us," he said, "and though her representatives have acted otherwise, insulting our every movement, I am convinced that it has naught to do with Russia but (they) are the individual actions of these representatives."[34] Rumors of his negotiations with Mukden and Japan, Chiang laid at the door of "one or two individuals" who were maliciously trying to injure his reputation for revolutionary purity.

The bold mood of the Wuhan radicals found expression in the decisions of the third plenary session of the Kuomintang Central Executive Committee convened by them at Hankow on March 10. Here Borodin and his colleagues put through a series of resolutions which, on paper, restored to the regular party organs the power assumed by Chiang Kai-shek just a year before. The emergency powers delegated to Chiang at that time were revoked and the Military Council re-established. Chiang Kai-shek "resigned" from the chairmanship of the Central Executive Committee and the plenary session abolished the post itself as a gesture against the concentration of too much power in the hands of a single individual. Simultaneously, resolutions were passed arranging for "co-operation" between the Kuomintang and the Communist Party, calling upon the latter to share political responsibility by sending "responsible comrades to join in the Nationalist and provincial governments." It was also resolved that "the Press organs of the Third International, of the Chinese Communist Party, and of the Kuomintang shall not violate the spirit of co-operation in their reports and criticisms of one another."[35]

The decisions regarding the Communist Party, implemented by the nomination of two Communist ministers to the newly created government posts of labor and agriculture, were designed specifically and consciously to tighten the bonds that already strapped the workers' party to the bourgeois Kuomintang. On this point the Kuomintang leaders were perfectly clear. "The present co-operative plan is important," it was explained in the official *People's Tribune,* "because it signifies greater control by the Kuomintang over all the forces participating in the national revolution.... The Communist Party will have to fulfil its obligations to enable the party (the Kuomintang) and the government to exercise full control over the mass movement."[36]

These resolutions took effect. The decisions concerning Chiang Kai-shek remained futile words scribbled on paper. The Communists accepted the authority of the petty bourgeois radicals of Wuhan. Chiang did not and Wuhan dared not take the offensive against him. While the press everywhere buzzed with rumors concerning the growing schism in the Kuomintang, the Wuhan radicals and their Communist allies sought desperately to deny the presence of any rift in the Nationalist lute. "The military organs are willingly and gladly turning over all political functions to the party...the party and the army are in agreement," the Wuhan leaders declared. Asked about the rumor of a split, they said it was "a pure fabrication."[37] The shifts made in the commanding staff of the party were made amid general agreement, it was asserted. "In all these changes there is now complete concurrence. The very individuals and groups which seemed directly aimed at...have now signified their concurrence," reported the Nationalist News Agency.[38]

This whistling in the dark harmonized entirely with Chiang Kai-shek's strategy. He had yet to reach Shanghai. He had yet to conclude and consolidate his new alliances. He wanted no open break so long as he remained in Nanchang. He would break with Wuhan on his own terms once ensconced in the Whangpoo metropolis. In Kiangsi he was already unleashing the terror against the labor and peasant leaders and against the Communists. Press reports almost daily of his negotiations with Mukden for "a reconciliation of north and south to fight the Reds" heralded his course toward a split. For Wuhan, however, the "crisis was over" and the national revolutionary movement was declared to be "in a position to move on unhampered by the slightest suggestion of inner conflict."[39]

> What did the C.C. of our party do….? One would think that it should have conducted a broad campaign among the masses…baring the secret motives behind this conflict and exposing the intriguers, encircling Chiang Kai-shek, and bringing strong pressure to bear on the government and on Borodin to stop camouflaging the conflict as a personal one and to move among the masses on the basis of a political platform of social reforms, and above all agrarian reforms, so that Chiang Kai-shek would have been forced to accept battle (if he wanted it) on the basis of a fixed programme—a fact which would have created grave difficulties for him. But the Central Committee of the Chinese Communist Party and the representative of the E.C.C.I. for a long time "did not notice" this conflict and took no position with regard to it…. We repeat: the leading nucleus of the party took no position and did nothing for two months in the Nanchang-Wuhan conflict…. The Central Committee only hid itself and evaded answering the questions that the situation placed before it. The local organizations of the party in Hupeh developed, at their own risk and peril, a campaign around this question without awaiting the decisions of the Central Committee.[40]

When finally, on March 18, Chen Tu-hsiu took open cognizance of the situation, he confined himself to reproaching Chiang Kai-shek for attacking Wuhan and Borodin. He quoted a headline from a Shanghai Japanese newspaper of March 17: "Nanchang openly proclaims a pro-Japanese policy; Refuses to recognize the results of the Central Executive Committee Conference; Decides to get rid of Borodin." Chiang, exhorted Chen Tu-hsiu, should repudiate these Japanese rumors and not "abuse his own associates." "Our duty, therefore . . ." he wrote, "is earnestly to persuade the Nationalist revolutionary leader, General Chiang Kai-shek, to prove immediately in words and actions that the so-called reconciliation between north and south to oppose the Reds is but the scheming of imperialist Japan."[41]

The advance to the Yangtze and the gigantic upsurge of the mass movement had brought the class contradictions in the Nationalist movement to the breaking-point. Chiang Kai-shek was openly steering for Shanghai to come to terms there with the imperialists. The mass movement would be headed off this time only by the sharper expedient of decapitation. This was the real root of the so-called Nanchang-Wuhan conflict. Yet the Wuhan radicals, flattered by the boldness of their paper resolutions, considered the crisis over. The Communists tried only "earnestly to persuade" the erring general. The issues were kept carefully screened from the masses, and especially from the Shanghai workers who held the key to the crisis in their hands. Unwarned, unprepared, they became first Chiang's pawns and then his victims.

The Shanghai Insurrection

In Shanghai the workers had responded to the victorious advance of the Northern Expedition with a strike wave of unexampled depth and militancy. During 1926 in Shanghai there were, according to one official survey, 169 strikes affecting 165 factories and companies and involving 202,297 workers. Of these, eighty-two, or 49.64 percent, were wholly or partially successful. Another official survey listed 257 strikes, of which 53.89 percent were wholly or partially successful.[1]

A steady depreciation in the value of copper coins during the year had caused a sharp rise in the cost of living. Conditions for the workers worsened accordingly. In most cases the strike demands centered on wage increases, recall of discharged employees, dismissal of offensive foremen, dismissals without reason, strike pay, payment or increase of food allowances, reduction or limitation of working hours, improvements in factory equipment, living quarters, eating-rooms and general working conditions, abolition of corporal punishment of workers, bonuses, release of arrested or detained workers, and compensation for injuries sustained while at work. Other constantly recurring demands, like those for medical service, sick-leave pay, wages for apprentices, six-day week, prompt payment of wages, one month's salary for women workers during confinement, non-replacement of adults by children, and pensions, were eloquent of conditions prevailing in Shanghai industry.

These strike battles were fought and more than half of them won under conditions of the most savage repression by the militarist and foreign authorities. The Shanghai General Labor Union functioned illegally. Few strikes were unaccompanied by arrests and the use of force against the workers. Such measures, however, made little impression on the strike wave. With the Nationalist occupation of Wuhan and Kiukiang, the Shanghai mass movement took on a more directly political coloration. The workers were preparing to intervene in their own way to achieve a political solution of their problems.

An abortive revolt of one of Sun Chuang-fang's subordinates in Chekiang in October was made the signal for an attempted uprising in Shanghai on October 24. The Chekiang revolt failed. The uprising, in which the Communists left the initiative to a Kuomintang committee headed by Niu Yung-chien, was put down with comparative ease by the minions of Sun Chuang-fang. No general strike was called nor were the masses as a whole mobilized for action. Niu, who held a mandate from the central Kuomintang headquarters in Canton and who was an adherent of Chiang Kai-shek, had the double task of disturbing Sun's rear in Chiang's favor and limiting the influence and activities of the Communists. On the night of October 23 news of the defeat of the Chekiang revolt reached Shanghai. Niu did not pass the word along, but simply held himself aloof from the uprising scheduled for the next day. A few small bands of Communist workers attacked police stations during the night but were quickly overpowered. The workers did not fail to draw lessons from this experience and prepared themselves for more effective future action. Huge mass meetings on November 28 and December 12 at which anti-militarist and anti-imperialist feeling ran high proved the heralds of approaching insurrection.

In these months the political situation in Shanghai became exceedingly complex. It revolved around a movement which began as an attempt to agitate for the autonomy of the Shanghai area and which soon developed into agitation for the autonomy of Kiangsu, Chekiang, and Anhwei provinces. This movement became the rallying point for the political activities of all groups and classes. It was the focus for the banking and compradoring bourgeoisie led by Yu Ya-ching and the Chekiang-Kiangsu banking group, the right-wing Kuomintang politicians, led by Wu Chih-hui, Chang Chi, and others, professional intriguers and negotiators like Huang Fu and C. T. Wang, the gangsters under Hwang Ching-yung, Tu Yueh-sen, and Chang Siao-ling, the Kuomintang committee headed by Niu Yung-chien, and the usual host of small fry, hangers-on, go-betweens, job-holders, and job-seekers. Even Sun Chuang-fang, the local warlord against whom the autonomy movement was presumably directed, began poking his finger in the autonomy pie. Hovering in the vicinity was Yang Yu-ting, the special envoy of Mukden, fishing for a deal between Chang Tso-lin and the Kuomintang. Dragging at the tail of all these bourgeois politicians and manipulators were the Chinese Communist Party and the Shanghai General Labor Union to whom the mass of the workers and the city poor looked for leadership.[2]

The worsening of Sun's military position in December helped precipitate this curious and ill-mixed solution. Sun turned in desperation to an erstwhile ally, Chang Tsung-chang, warlord of Shantung and the most notoriously rapacious of his breed. Chang's troops began moving south along the Tientsin-Pukow Railway. Shanghai capitalists heard with consternation reports that Chang was going to force on them ten millions in worthless military paper with a demand for specie payment. The threat of dislocation which accompanied the prospect of the occupation of Shanghai by the Fengtien-Shantung troops of Chang Tsung-chang helped turn the attention of the big banking interests towards Chiang Kai-shek, seemingly the most likely candidate capable of rescuing them from the offensive of the workers and city poor from below and the depredations of the Shantung warlord from above.

The imperialist authorities, the British and American more so than the Japanese, seemed to have found the complexities of the situation somewhat beyond them for the moment. The prevailing attitude among them during those early weeks of 1927 seemed to be to hear and protect the evils they had rather than fly to others they knew not of. For to your foreign businessman, banker, soldier, consul, and missionary, this incomprehensible unrest, these endless slings and arrows for which they were the quivering targets, seemed the blows of a universally outrageous fortune. They could not make out who were the hares and who the hounds. So they barricaded their settlements behind gates and barbed wire. From overseas came regiment after regiment and whole fleets to protect them against all contingencies. Only the keenest among them* understood from the beginning that their bread was buttered on the same side as that of the Shanghai bankers and oriented themselves accordingly. They knew Chiang Kai-shek as a politically minded militarist who wore a coat of many colors. If the Shanghai bankers were ready to back him, they knew they could follow suit. Only the workers of Shanghai stood between them and the consummation of the deal. Chiang's coming would remove this obstacle. Thus by February when Chiang's troops advanced into Chekiang, the situation was vastly clarified for all concerned except the workers and the Communist leaders for whom Chiang still remained the hero-general of the revolution.

The Nationalist troops occupied Hangchow on February 17 and next day advanced to Kashing, less than fifty miles from Shanghai. The vanguard moved up the railway as far as Sungkiang, only twenty-five miles away. In Shanghai all grew taut. The General Labor Union issued orders for a general strike effective the morning of the 19th in expectation of a farther Nationalist advance. The workers answered the call with machine-like precision. Within forty-eight hours more than 350,000 workers were out on the streets.[3] "Pompous Shanghai became like a graveyard. The tram-cars stopped running. Steamships were unable to leave the port. The post office closed down. The department stores ceased business and all the big factories were silent. The sirens could not call a single worker back to work."[4]

The workers carried their fight into the streets. Clashes with the police began to occur. The Communist leadership, instead of placing itself at the head of the workers, looked to the representatives of the bourgeoisie for political direction. The slogans of the general strike were confined to: "Support the Northern Expeditionary Army!", "Overthrow Sun Chuang-fang!", "Hail Chiang Kai-shek!" Even the slogans against imperialism disappeared. Here is the Communist Central Committee functioning, as told by Chiu Chiu-pei, one of its leading members:

* Men like Ferral, the banker in André Malraux's *Mans' Fate*.

> The proclamation of the strike was not an official decision of the party. After the strike broke, it was not regarded as the first step toward an uprising. Not only among the petty bourgeois masses was there no kind of political propaganda, but even among the workers few were clear on the aims and purposes of the general strike....
>
> Although the slogan 'For a Citizens' Delegates' Assembly!' was decided upon, it was not looked upon as a slogan of action which required calling upon all the workers in the factories and unions to elect delegates and inviting the small merchants to send their own representatives. There was no attempt to make this assembly a sort of Soviet of the national revolution, to transform it into an organ of action where issues of the workers' strike, the merchants' strike, and the passage from armed defense to armed uprising could be discussed. In other words, there was no effort to turn it into a de facto provisional revolutionary government.
>
> The party simply organized a provisional revolutionary committee composed of top delegates of the workers and representatives of the big bourgeoisie. Consequently the masses out on the streets had no chance to join in the 'class struggle' between the workers' delegates and the bourgeois representatives.... The natural result was that the workers' delegates yielded to the big bourgeoisie on every question.... Our party sent the masses out into the streets and left them there for three days without paying any attention to them. We did not lead them forward, ordering an offensive along the path of the uprising. We did not even put up any defensive struggle. The workers' capture of rifles and the executions of traitors were mostly spontaneous acts....
>
> What we did was to bend all our efforts to negotiate with Niu Yung-chien, Yang Hsin-fu, Yu Ya-ching, Wang Shiao-lai—simply to negotiate trying to utilize the conflicts among these various (bourgeois) groups. Such tactics amounted to this: The workers were on strike but were waiting for the permission of the big bourgeoisie before going any further. The petty bourgeoisie was left out in the cold, without leadership, without directives. We hoped that after conditions guaranteeing the victory were created (i.e. the successful outcome of negotiations between Niu Yung-chien and Li Pao-chang, the Shanghai garrison commander, on the one hand, and the big merchants, on the other), we hoped after all this to begin preparations for an uprising. This amounted objectively to betraying the working class![5]

Li Pao-chang and the police of the International Settlement and the French Concession did not wait for the outcome of the Communist negotiations with the bourgeoisie to take reprisals against the workers. Students and strikers caught distributing leaflets in the streets were beheaded or shot on the spot. On the very first day of the strike Li sent his execution squads into the streets with their great broadswords. Strike leaders arrested by the foreign police were sent out into Chinese territory for execution. In the concessions and in Chinese territory alike police squads searched pedestrians and shops and created such a reign of terror in the streets that most shops, especially in Chapei and Nantao, boarded up. Hua Kang tells of a peddler in Pootung, the industrial area across the Whangpoo River, who cried his wares, "Mai ta ping!" ("I sell big cakes!") Soldiers shot him dead, claiming he had cried "Ta pai ping!" ("Beat a retreat!") Two metal workers and a tram conductor distributing leaflets were beheaded where they stood. At the West Gate the dread squads grabbed people reading some of the small colored sheets and executed them. Three students caught speaking to crowds in Jessfield, a town on the outskirts of the Settlement, were similarly done brutally to death. The exact number killed was never known. Estimates ran up to two hundred. A foreign correspondent watched the killings:

> After the heads of the victims were severed by swordsmen, they were displayed on the top of poles or placed upon platters and carried through the streets. This sight in a parade through crowded thoroughfares had the effect of creating a veritable reign of terror, because the victims were denied the semblance of a trial. The executions occurred in the densest quarters. The executioners, hearing broadswords and accompanied by a squad of soldiers, marched their victims to a prominent corner, where the strike leaders were forced to bend over while their heads were cut off. Thousands fled in horror when the heads were stuck on sharp-pointed bamboo poles and were hoisted aloft and carried to the scene of the next execution.[6]

Street fighting between the workers and the soldiers and police began on the 21st. The workers had already begun to take arms wherever they found them to put up a defense against the terror in the streets. Skirmishing was already under way when the Communist leaders finally fixed 6 p.m. on February 22 as the time for an uprising, which was supposed to coincide with the arrival of the Nationalist troops, who everyone believed were advancing up the Shanghai-Hangchow Railway. Three days of the general strike had already passed. Workers' heads fell and blood flowed freely in the streets. The Communist leadership continued negotiating with Niu Yung-chien and the other representatives of the bourgeoisie. All this time the Nationalist forces never budged from Sungkiang. There was no military obstacle in the way of their advance on Shanghai. Between them and the metropolis, only twenty-five miles distant, there were only handfuls of demoralized northern soldiers, looting the villages as they fell back in disorder toward the city.

The failure of the Nationalist troops to march was no accident. Following the receipt of a wire from Niu Yung-chien advising "cessation of the advance for the time being,"[7] Chiang Kai-shek had issued sudden orders for the suspension of all operations along the Kashing-Sungkiang front pending the drive on Nanking and the Shanghai-Nanking Railway. Military conditions entirely favored the occupation of Shanghai, but Chiang did not mind giving Li Pao-chang time to slaughter the leaders of the Shanghai workers. This was specifically understood on both sides. "General Li has been trying to get into the Nationalist Party," reported the well-informed *China Weekly Review*, "and, according to report, General Chiang Kai-shek has agreed to take him in.... It is even rumored that conservative Kuomintangists were not altogether displeased at General Li's bloody rampage, because it struck at the power, as well as the heads, of the radical or Communist wing of the Party."[8] Confirmation came a few weeks later when Li was rewarded with the command of the Eighth Nationalist Army.[9]

The attempted uprising was suppressed with bloody slaughter. Fighting continued in the streets until the 24th, growing more sporadic, finally dying out altogether. Meanwhile the strike front had dissipated. Most of the workers, bewildered by the turn of events, had gone back to work. Arrests and executions continued. The foreign eyewitness adds the final touch: "Many persons were arrested because they carried handbills which read: 'Welcome, Chiang Kai-shek, gallant commander of the Cantonese.' These were found guilty and executed on the spot."[10]

Despite the depth and extent of the general strike, despite the savage measures used to suppress the uprising that followed it, despite the continued confusion and vacillation of the Communist leadership, the events of February 19–24 proved to be only the prelude to a mightier spectacle still. Casualties had been heavy, but the workers' organizations were still intact, and the workers had learned how to fight. Yesterday's failure, far from crushing them, tempered them for tomorrow's battles. But had their leaders learned from these fresh experiences? The general strike of February 19 had squarely posed the issue of power. The Communist leadership, guided by the Comintern through Voitinsky, "debated whether or not to make an insurrection while the insurrection was already taking place," and, while the workers fought, sought top combinations with the bourgeoisie. "The result was that we passed up an exceptionally favorable historical moment, an exceptional combination of circumstances. When the power was there in the streets, the party did not know how to take it. Worse, it did not want to take it, it feared to take it," wrote Voitinsky's subordinates in their letter to the Comintern.[11] They compared the failure to the failure of the German insurrection in 1923, adding: "Only there was this difference—that at Shanghai the proletariat had notably greater forces at its disposal and chances on its side. Had it intervened in a determined manner, it could have conquered Shanghai for the revolution and transformed the relationship of forces within the Kuomintang."

If these three Russian delegates believed this to be the case in February, one may be permitted to wonder what they thought of the events that now followed. The February insurrection had failed, but four days after they dispatched their letter to Moscow the workers were going to seize upon a still more exceptionally favorable moment, and this time they would show they had learned how to fight and win their own battles. The Communist leadership, bound fast by its bloc with Chiang Kai-shek, would know only how to turn victory into defeat.

During the two weeks following the crushing of the insurrection, Chang Tsung-chang's Fengtien-Shantung troops came down the Shanghai-Nanking Railway and took over the Shanghai area, Sun Chuang-fang retiring northward out of the picture. In the foreign settlements the imperialists increased their garrisons and fortified their gates and sandbag barricades. By the end of February there were 7,000 British troops, 1,500 American marines, 600 Japanese marines, in addition to landing parties from the growing fleet of foreign warships at anchor in the Whangpoo. Still more troops were en route. On February 25, the diplomatic body issued a bristling statement in which it proclaimed "the necessary steps to ensure the safety of the Settlement and the protection of its nationals."[12]

Meanwhile military operations spread along three fronts. Nationalist forces moved down the Yangtze, occupying Anking and Wuhu and preparing to march on Nanking. A second force faced the Shanghai-Nanking Railway along a Chinkiang-Soochow line. The third point of Nationalist concentration was at Sungkiang, southwest of Shanghai on the Shanghai-Hangchow Railway. This front, quiet after the initial advance that had inspired the uprising of February 19–24, came to life again in March. Pai Chung-hsi, a Kwangsi general subordinate to Chiang Kai-shek, moved slowly down the line toward Shanghai. On the night of March 20 he reached Lunghua on the outskirts of the city. There he stopped. Negotiations were begun with Pi Shu-cheng, the Shantung garrison commander, for the "peaceful occupation" of the city by the Nationalists. The Fengtien-Shantung troops were completely demoralized, and many were already in flight. Their main body, reinforced by White Russian mercenaries, still held strategic positions, however, within the city.

Lunghua became the focal point for a thousand intrigues. Niu Yung-chien rushed to see General Pai. "Delay your entry a day," he advised, "Pi Shu-cheng will surrender."[13] Orders came down the line from Chiang Kai-shek: "Do not attack Shanghai. Do not come into conflict with the imperialists. Wait."[14]

In the city the workers were not interested in waiting. The General Labor Union issued the call for a general strike and insurrection to break simultaneously at noon on March 21. Delegates rushed to Lunghua to ask Pai Chung-hsi to march his troops in to help the workers' offensive. He refused to move. They were still trying to persuade him when the workers struck out for themselves. The echoes of the noon whistles had barely died away before the firing began.[15]

The strike was complete. Practically every worker in Shanghai came out on to the streets. Their ranks were swelled when they were joined by shop employees and the hordes of the city poor. Between 500,000 and 800,000 people were directly involved.[16] Carefully laid plans for the insurrection were based upon a trained workers' militia composed of 5,000 picked men, broken up into squads of twenty and thirty. For arms to begin with they had only 150 Mauser pistols.[17] That meant less than one to a squad. The others came to grips with the police and the Shantung soldiery armed only with clubs, axes, and knives.

Fighting began simultaneously in seven parts of the city: Nantao, including the whole section south of the French Concession; Hongkew, the narrow strip surrounded on three sides by the International Settlement; Woosung, the fortified area near the confluence of the Whangpoo and the Yangtze rivers; East Shanghai, including the vast industrial district known as Yangtzepoo; West

Shanghai, another industrial area adjacent to the Settlement; and Chapei, the most densely populated proletarian district in Shanghai.

Everywhere except in Chapei the fight for control of the police stations and local military posts was won by the workers before nightfall. Many soldiers and policemen tore off their uniforms and surrendered their arms and ammunition. Arms were taken everywhere, and by evening the attacking force of pickets was comparatively well armed. Furniture, boxes, and benches were dragged out into the streets. Doors were torn off hinges to build barricades around the police stations. Hundreds of tiny, smoky restaurants raced the preparation of food which women carried in steaming bowls up to the fighting line. Workers, men and women, bound strips of red rag around their right arms. These were the badges of the new proletarian army. By dark all police stations were occupied. The telephone and telegraph offices were taken. Electric power lines were cut.

"In Nantao . . ." records Hua Kang,

> the uprising began with an attack on the police station, which was entered shortly after 2 p.m. The telephone building and all the branch police stations were taken over in short order. Policemen were all disarmed. Arms were also taken at all the occupied stations. Shortly before four o'clock the workers believed themselves strongly enough armed to march on the arsenal at Kiangnan, at the south end of the city. There the soldiers surrendered without a fight. Exactly at four o'clock the workers came into possession of the rich stock of rifles and machine guns. By that time the soldiers guarding South Station had fled, so it was a simple matter for the railway workers to take over and use the locomotives for the purposes of the battle. At five o'clock, less than five hours after the attack began, the workers massed in the yards of the Chinese Tramway Company. All Nantao was in their hands.
>
> In Hongkew no soldiers had been stationed. The workers had simply to deal with the police. Almost immediately after the uprising had begun, the police station surrendered and Hongkew belonged to the workers. But after the police had been driven out, they instigated gangsters to attack the labor unions and the occupied police stations.... The workers not only had to fight the organized enemy but they had to use their armed power to suppress the gangsters too. . .[18]

Ho Sen's record illuminates this particular incident in Hongkew: "The dispersed police discovered that the attackers were Communists, not members of the Kuomintang. They reassembled, and under the leadership of Niu Yungchien they counter-attacked.... So once more barricade fighting broke out. But eventually the workers won."[19]

In Pootung the workers formed ranks military fashion and marched on the Third Branch police station. It fell into their hands almost painlessly. Soldiers caught in flight were disarmed. Many of them joined the pickets in setting up a Provisional Workers' Bureau of Public Safety, and together they took over the municipal offices of the whole district. Representatives of the Kuomintang crossed the river accompanied by armed gangsters and demanded control of the area.

They were forcibly put back on their launches and ordered to return to Shanghai.

At Woosung the workers had put the soldiery to flight, and one detachment, not knowing the situation in the city, headed for town along the narrow-gauge railway that links Woosung to Shanghai. At Kiangwan they found the rails torn up by workers who had foreseen just such a retreat. The soldiers thereupon entrenched themselves in and around the Tientungan station, the point where the Kiangwan-Hongkew-Chapei districts meet along a contiguous boundary. Meanwhile, in Woosung the workers' pickets assumed full control.

Vanguard detachments of about 50,000 workers marching toward Chapei after successfully taking over Yangtzepoo effected a junction with the fighters in Chapei, and units from both areas joined in an attack on Tientungan station.

Matters took a similar course in West Shanghai, where, after occupying police stations and seizing arms, the workers crossed the creek, joined the pickets at the Pootoo Road police station and forced its surrender after a sharp fight in which the picket leader and several policemen were killed. Then the workers gathered their forces, and from all directions marched toward North Station, in the heart of Chapei, where the fighting was the fiercest.

Resistance everywhere had crumpled quickly and the armed workers triumphed with comparatively little difficulty. At nightfall, however, the battle still raged in all the main streets of working-class Chapei. Chang Tsung-chang's White Russian mercenaries cruised the main streets in armored cars, raking the workers' lines with machine-gun fire. An armored train just back of North Station, also manned by White Russians, dropped shells on the workers' position. From behind the North Chekiang Road gate of the Settlement, which commanded a full view of Paoshan road, across which the workers surged to attack the station, British troops fired whenever the approach of any of the attackers gave them the pretext of "defending" the Settlement. Hundreds of Shantung soldiers were admitted to refuge and were later actually repatriated to Shantung by the foreign authorities.

With their ranks swelling during the afternoon as workers poured into Chapei from east and west, the pickets settled down to a siege of the six main strongholds of the enemy in Chapei—North Station, the Huchow Guild, the Commercial Press, the Fifth police station, the branch police station on Canton Road, and the branch police station on Chung Hwa Road. The seventh and last enemy position was at the other end of Paoshan Road, at Tientungan station. By late afternoon all the police stations and the Huchow Guild had fallen. The remaining three centers, North Station, the Commercial Press, and Tientungan station were strung out along a single line bisecting Chapei. The armed pickets massed between them. The Commercial Press, garrisoned by several hundred soldiers well armed with machine guns and grenades, was entirely surrounded. At all three points fighting continued throughout the night.

> Fiercest fighting of all took place at North Station. Here, in order to drive back the workers, the enemy set fire to near-by houses, over a hundred of which were razed to the ground before the fire could be brought under control.... Pickets left the lines to get water and to haul in disabled fire-engines. The people were so enraged at the soldiers and so grateful to the workers that they joined in the uprising on their own. Old and young, working together, emptied their houses to build up the breastworks.... The soldiers cooped up in the station did not dare sally out, but satisfied themselves with random volleys at the workers. The White Russians opened fire again and once in a while a British shot would come whistling from across the Settlement border.
>
> On the morning of March 22, the enemy was obviously tired, but the workers continued the attack with spirit on all sides.... At noon the soldiers at Tientungan surrendered.... At 4:30 that afternoon some of the soldiers at the Commercial Press tried to escape, but were captured. The rest, seeing that their situation was hopeless, surrendered. The picket command moved in from the Fifth Police Station and from then on all forces were concentrated on capturing the last stronghold of the enemy, North Station.
>
> Since morning many other houses in that vicinity had been burned by the enemy. With water-pipes broken and no fire-fighting apparatus now available, the picket lines bad been forced to fall back five times. Still the enemy did not dare move forward. But by this time scores of thousands of workers were massed behind the attack. Within an hour after the fall of the Commercial Press the White Russians fled into the Settlement, where they were admitted, and the Shantung soldiers dispersed in wild disorder.[20]

A white flag fluttered above North Station at six o'clock.

Such was the position when Nationalist troops of the First Division arrived at Markham Road after coming down from Lunghua. Hsueh Yoh, the division commander, had finally come, under the pressure of his own men, to help the workers despite orders to the contrary. By the time he arrived, the workers had done their job. All of Shanghai, with the exception of the International Settlement and the French Concession, which huddled in hate and fear behind their steel and barbed wire, was in their hands. Along Paoshan, Paotung, and Chingyung roads, the sound of rifle fire gave way to the joyous crackle of fireworks and the shouts of workers celebrating their victory. The railway union issued orders for the repair of destroyed rail sections. The team of 300 workers organized to carry out these orders were the first in all Shanghai to resume work after the victory of the insurrection.

8

The Prodigal's Return

When Chiang Kai-shek landed at Shanghai early in the afternoon of Saturday, March 26, he had at long last arrived home. Here were his first haunts and his early benefactors, his former fellow brokers, and his friends of the underworld. A native of Ningpo, he could here join hands with his fellow provincials, the powerful Chekiang bankers, the Ningpo merchants and industrialists, who shared with the foreigners economic control of China's metropolis.

The bankers and merchants had watched strikes grow into the general strike and the general strike grow into insurrection. The workers' conquest of Shanghai had given them the lever they needed to extract terms from the imperialists. But it also served notice that the time had come to disembarrass themselves of the dangerous weapon of mass power. Their own interests were now at stake no less than those of the imperialists. An essential condition of the impending deal between Chinese and foreign capital was the smashing of the mass movement. They had long known that they could look to Chiang Kai-shek, the prodigal now back in their midst, to carry out this task.

To this end Chiang had already resumed contact in the Yangtze Valley with the secret societies that had flourished there from the earliest days of the Ching Dynasty, now known as the Green and Red gangs. They traded in opium and slaves. They kidnapped for ransom. They trafficked in blackmail and murder. Rare was the shopkeeper or trader, big or small, from the Yangtze's mouth to the Szechwan gorges who did not pay them tribute.

The Green Gang operated out of Shanghai. Its leader, Hwang Ching-yung, known everywhere as Hwang Ma-pi (Pock-marked Hwang), was chief of detectives of the French Concession Police. It was generally believed that he had himself introduced Chiang as a stripling officer of the Shanghai garrison into the closed ranks of the society.[1] When Chiang, the Nationalist general, arrived at Kiukiang in November 1926, it was Hwang Ma-pi who came upriver from Shanghai to reestablish contact in behalf of the Shanghai bankers and merchants. As a result of their conference, the Green Gang was mobilized for the express purpose of breaking up the trade unions. What had been an organization of common criminals now assumed the combined features of the Russian Black Hundred groups and Louis Napoleon's Society of December the Tenth. Yang Hu, one of Chiang's staff officers, was put in charge of operations.[2] Plans were made to set up rival "labor unions." All the scum and riffraff of the treaty ports were quickly recruited as "members." Arms were provided plentifully. Hwang returned to Shanghai. Chiang turned back to Nanchang, where he had set up his headquarters.

The campaign of open repression against the mass organizations began in February 1927. Early that month Chen Tsang-shen, chairman of the General Labor Union of Kanchow, a southern Kiangsi city, was riddled with bullets by Chiang Kai-shek's soldiers. The union was driven underground. In Nanchang on March 17 Chiang ordered the dissolution of the city Kuomintang, arrested its Communist and left-wing leaders, closed down the unions and the students' association, and suppressed the local Kuomintang daily. The same day an attack was launched on the mass organizations in Kiukiang. Several hundred gangsters, described as "moderate unionists," raided the quarters of the General Labor Union, the city Kuomintang, the Peasant Association, the student and women's groups, and the Political Department of the Sixth Army. Resistance was offered. Four were killed and ten wounded. A Chinese account described how the workers held their own against the gangsters until a company of Chiang's own troops appeared, stormed the building, and released several gangsters who had been captured.[3] This is supported by a foreign account which said that when "the raiders appeared to be getting the worst of the battle, the soldiers stepped in and finished off the work they had begun by wrecking the Labor Union's headquarters. Since then," the report went on,

> the heads of the Labor Union have disappeared, and it is said the union is to be reorganized on more conservative lines. Martial law was immediately declared, and an order issued forbidding persons to collect in groups. Civilians may not...carry weapons.... The streets are patrolled by soldiers.... It is said that Chiang Kai-shek, who was himself in Kiukiang at the time of the rioting but has now left for downriver, instigated...the attack. At the time of the trouble he placed a large armed guard in the Concession to protect it.... The new magistrate has returned from Nanchang, whither he retired after the labour extremists had wrecked his yamen and has brought with him a personal bodyguard of 150 of Chiang Kai-shek's picked troops.... The influence of the moderate party represented by Chiang Kai-shek is commencing to be felt throughout the province.... The tide has definitely turned.[4]

Similar events took place wherever Chiang Kai-shek touched port on his way downriver. Organized gangs attacked and occupied union premises at Anking on March 23[5] and at Wuhu a day later. Workers were killed or driven into hiding. Their unions were rapidly "reorganized." Chiang was to have stopped at Nanking, which was occupied by Nationalist troops on March 24.

Whatever plans may have been envisaged for that town were upset, however, by looting and attacks on foreigners on the day the city changed hands. Several consular officials and missionaries were killed. British and American gunboats promptly opened up a bombardment of the city, killing twelve and wounding nineteen Chinese civilians.[6] The remaining foreigners were evacuated. Some foreign journalists quickly developed the theory that the "Nanking outrages" were part of a Machiavellian plot concocted by the Communists and the left-wingers at Wuhan to "embarrass" Chiang and to embroil him with the foreigners. The fact that the whole strategy of the Communists and Kuomintang "liberals" at Wuhan was based on propitiating Chiang Kai-shek is enough to reveal the absurdity of this tale. It was, moreover, a striking fact that the vast movement which had swept South China had been marked by practically no cases of violence against foreigners. Workers and peasants, who did not lack reason to hate the foreign businessmen and missionaries, had in hundreds of towns seized mission property and compelled many foreigners to flee, but "only in a few isolated instances," wrote one of them, "did a foreigner get even a scratch or a bruise."[7] It has since been suggested that the Nanking incident (in which the rape of foreign women was also, of course, alleged, but never proved[8]) had been organized by Chiang himself as an act of deliberate provocation against the Communists. This version has equally little to support it. The only credible documentation on the whole subject is the statement of one foreign investigator who arrived on the scene a few days after the events occurred. Unruffled by the screaming passion into which the foreign community had whipped itself, he assembled impressive and conclusive evidence that the demoralized, retreating Fengtien soldiers were the actual perpetrators of the attacks.[9]

Chiang, therefore, did not disembark at Nanking but continued down the river to Shanghai. Upon his arrival he was whisked from the wharf in a limousine and driven through the foreign barricades to the old Foreign Ministry bureau on Route Ghisi, just outside the French Concession. There his first caller was Pock-marked Hwang. Next to call was T. Patrick Givens, of the Political Branch of the Shanghai Municipal Police, who presented Chiang with a pass for entering the foreign areas, and accorded him the privilege of traveling in those sacred precincts with an armed guard.[10] Chiang was, incidentally, the only Nationalist commander thus honored. Chiang, equally magnanimous, gave assurances that he would "co-operate with the foreign police in Shanghai,"[11] and forthwith plunged into conference with his own aides and supporters to see how "law and order" could be established and maintained.

He met with the right wing Kuomintang "elders," led by Wu Chih-hui, Tsai Yuan-pei, and Chang Ching-chiang. He saw delegates of the bankers and the Chamber of Commerce, led by Yu Ya-ching, his first benefactor, Wang Shiao-lai, and others. He discussed the military situation with his subordinates, Pai Chung-hsi, who had occupied the city for him, and Chow Feng-chi, a new recruit only yesterday with the Northerners. He saw Pock-marked Hwang and his chief aides, Tu Yueh-sen and Chang Siao-ling, and the usual host of lesser lights and satellites.

Their problem was simply posed: How were they going to wrest control of Shanghai from the workers and establish their own government at Nanking? For the job of crushing the workers' organizations and the Communists ample financial support was at hand. But when they looked around them those last grey days of March, Chiang and his friends knew success was by no means certain. The obstacles seemed many and formidable. "It was not at all improbable," wrote one informed foreigner, "that he would be unable to stem the tide of Communist activity on the morrow."[12] And, indeed, for those who did not perceive the gap between the mass of the workers and the Communist leadership, it was difficult to see how victory could fail to fall to the workers' cause.

Shanghai was in their hands. More than half a million workers stood ready to guard what they had conquered by their own arms. To be sure, the workers' pickets, who now patrolled the city instead of the police, numbered only 2,700 men with 1,700 rifles, some machine guns, and a large stock of ammunition seized from the Northern troops,[13] but there appeared to be no serious obstacle to the swift expansion of the numbers and armament of this force. At a word from union headquarters in the Commercial Press building and the Huchow Guild not a working man or woman in the city would have failed to spring into action. Flushed with yesterday's great victory, they presented a formidable force. There was a provisional government set up under what seemed to be full Communist control, which was apparently ready to take over political power throughout the Shanghai area in the name of Shanghai's workers. Nor was there any reason to suppose that the workers would fail to find means of making common cause with the soldiers who now garrisoned the city.

Chiang Kai-shek had only 3,000 troops in the city of whom only a few were "reliable." The nearest reinforcements were at Hangchow, five hours away, where Ho Ying-chin sat with an army of less than 10,000. It was doubtful if many of these, trained in the scorching heat of the mass movement, would have turned their arms against the workers if the issue had been made perfectly plain to them by propagandists from the workers' organizations which they regarded as their main allies. In effect, Chiang did not know whether he dared order his men to march against the workers. In Chapei, the workers' stronghold, was the First Division, which was enthusiastically in sympathy with the unions. Its commander, Hsueh Yoh, had already reflected the temper and pressure of his troops when he marched them into Chapei against Pai Chung-hsi's orders on March 22.[14]

Across the barbed wire barricades fumed the foreigners, all convinced, as one of them put it, that they were going to be murdered in their own beds by their own servants. The British and American communities were thoroughly certain that their fair little islet of foreign justice and rectitude was about to be overrun by insane mobs thirsting for the white man's blood. They were suffering badly from what one writer aptly termed "highly accented funk."[15] They had all heard fantastic atrocity stories of the seizures of the Hankow and Kiukiang Concessions in January and the incidents at Nanking. The tales of fleeing missionaries, which grew taller with every mile they traveled toward Shanghai, made church-going pillars of society shriek hysterically for blood.

"Better a thousand times take a strong line of action now and call a halt to this outrageous villainy that is being perpetrated in the name of freedom, even if it does involve the shedding of a little blood," cried one of the leading lights of the British community.[16] Foreign women palpitatingly distributed their favors among the troops pouring off transports for the defense of the Settlement. Foreign men worried more over the rape of their investments, which they knew would follow when the mob, foaming and frothing crimson and scarlet, rushed in upon them. The Shanghai Municipal Council, governing body of the Settlement, had declared a state of emergency on March 21, establishing rigid martial law. It followed up on March 24 with a manifesto declaring "it realizes the gravity of the local situation and its possible repercussions throughout the civilized world, and will use all the resources at its disposal to retain control of the situation."[17]

These resources were already considerable. Garrisoning the foreign areas were 30,000 foreign troops, nearly one per foreign inhabitant, excluding the White Russians. Counting the British alone, there were two British soldiers for every British civilian in the city. Thirty foreign warships, British, Japanese, American, French, Italian, and even Portuguese, rode at anchor in the Whangpoo River cleared for instant action. Squadrons of British planes were making regular patrol flights over the city and the surrounding territory, a flagrant treaty violation which did not worry the British authorities. Other warships en route would in a few days increase the fleets of all nationalities to forty-five vessels, ranging from gunboats to 10,000-ton battle cruisers. Yet the cry went up for more troops, more ships. The foreigners wanted all Shanghai taken over. They wanted Nanking occupied. They demanded an international force to repeat the ruthless massacres with which allied foreign troops crushed the Boxers in 1900. Their newspapers, notably the *North China Daily News*, conducted frenzied campaigns of alarms, threats, and slanders. They showered abuse on politicians in the chancelleries at home who deemed it wiser to move more slowly.[18]

Any foreigner who by word or deed showed any sympathy for the mildest features of the Nationalist program or was even critical of the prevailing hysteria became the target for the most vicious attacks.* J. B. Powell, an American editor in

---

* In Peking two American journalists, Wilbur Burton and Mildred Mitchell, who worked for the *Nationalist News Agency*, were arrested by the northern military and held incommunicado. Virtually left to their fate by the U.S. Legation, they were freed as a result of the publicity given their case by Randall Gould of the United Press and the efforts of Charles J. Fox, a Tientsin lawyer. Gould was later banned from Legation press conferences by MacMurray, the U.S. minister. William and Rayna Prohme, who edited the *People's Tribune*, were generally regarded as race renegades. Borodin, of course, had horns.

Shanghai, who ventured to doubt that armed intervention would bring the desired results and who perspicaciously urged concessions to the Nationalists, was read out of the American Chamber of Commerce. A lone foreign missionary who joined a handful of Chinese Christians in advocating the peaceful rendition of the Settlement was promptly denounced in the columns of the *North China Daily News* as a betrayer of the faith and a "revolutionary agitator." An article by a Chinese Christian which attempted, under the title "Jesus and the Three People's Principles," to draw a parallel between Sun Yat-sen and Jesus Christ was denounced by high churchmen and low as a "blasphemous outburst." The National Christian Council, a Sino-foreign body which took a pro-Nationalist stand, was renamed the "Bolshevist Aid Society." It was formally repudiated by a group of thirty-two British and American missionaries "as dangerous to and subversive of the best interests of the churches in China." Its appeals in behalf of the Christian spirit were declared to be "a direct violation of the Shanghai Municipal Council's prohibition of documents calculated to stir up animosities, foment trouble, cause public alarm, or incite to a breach of peace." Rodney Gilbert, an Anglophile American journalist, published in the British press daily diatribes which literally shimmered in the pages like white heat. For him a labor union was "an organization of filthy coolies who had never worked and never would." To these people, not only the "filthy coolies," but bankers like Yu Ya-ching and politicians like C. T. Wang, even then working day and night for an entente with the foreigners against the "filthy coolies," were nothing less than "rabid anti-foreignists." The moods of the day are easily sampled:

> *Rabid:* "The big port of Shanghai is a purely foreign creation.... Now the Chinese want it 'returned' and sympathetic understanders run about discussing terms under which all the fruits of several generations of foreign effort can be yielded up to anarchic cooliedom. This strikes me as the exaltation of folly, the apotheosis of imbecility...."[19]

> *Irritated:* "The first thought that comes to one is the bother of it. To have one's home turned upside down, to have to hastily lump a few belongings into a trunk or two and a suitcase and leave the rest behind to be looted or what not, is an unadulterated bother...."[20]

> *Unctuous:* "Coastwards from all directions foreigners are hasting whose only crime is that they are willing to do China good. I say this intending to include not only missionaries, but the many splendid business men who wish China much better than her present behaviour would seem to deserve. We must, however, be merciful. China has some real grievances; many of her present ones, of course, are of her own making, but the innocent have to suffer and are often deceived into thinking that the foreigner is entirely responsible."[21]

> *Selfless:* "Peaceful foreign residents have been driven from their homes, their property destroyed.... Many foreign firms...are now facing ruin.... But these are

really trivial matters.... What is important is the struggle against a political idea whose avowed aim is to destroy present world civilization...hampered by no scruples of conscience...nor regard for established rights, customs, usages.... This is the front line of battle of the conflict between Communism and world civilization."[22]

Spiritual: "In my capacity as a missionary and thinking primarily of the consequences to the Church of Christ throughout the world if the mad dog of Bolshevism is not checked in China, but is allowed to jump across the seas to our own beloved America, I have no hesitation in asserting my conviction that a BOLSHEVIZED CHINA WOULD BE THE WORLD'S GREATEST PERIL."[23]

Chaste: (Quoting a widely published report that the Women's Association in Hankow had called and staged a "naked body procession" of selected women "having snowwhite bodies and perfect breasts.") "Those who are familiar with the modesty of Chinese women during the past centuries require no further or more conclusive proof of the pernicious influence of Russian Communism."[24]

Chivalrous: "The average American gives only passing thought to the vested interests in a foreign country, but he can rise to a high emotional pitch over danger to innocent American women and children at the hands of mobs or soldiers."[25]

Innocent: " In China the Communist appeal is to class hatreds, social antipathies, greed, and envy."[26]

Mocking: " If the present 'barbed-wire' hysteria continues much longer we would not be surprised to wake up some morning to find that our diligent and energetic municipal government had constructed a canopy of barbed-wire overhead in order to keep out the rays of the sun on the grounds that our chief Heavenly body was suspected of spreading Red propaganda."[27]

Forthright: "In times such as these, fine distinctions and legal quibblings lead to nothing. There can be no room for the C.P. (Communist Party) in Shanghai, and it must be fought as the Council would fight bubonic plague.... Chinese and Russian C.P.s should be treated with equal severity—both are enemies of civilization."[28]

Perspicacious: "The Nationalist opportunity—All sympathies with the Kuomintang—But Opposition for the Communists."[29]

Clear-cut: "Chiang Kai-shek...stands at the dividing of the ways.... It is no exaggeration to say that he and Generals Ho Ying-chin and Pai Chung-hsi remain now the only protection of China south of the Yangtze from being submerged by the Communist Party.... But if General Chiang is to save his fellow-countrymen from the Reds, he must act swiftly and relentlessly. Will he prove himself the man of action and decision, the champion of the true principles of Dr. Sun Yat-sen, the defender of his country? Or will he, too, go down with China in the Red flood?"[30]

South of the city at Lunghua, Chiang, too, was pondering this question. In a series of interviews with foreign journalists, he did his best to placate and reassure the foreign community. He deplored the Nanking incidents, promising a thorough investigation and punishment for those responsible. "The Nationalist leaders have always wished to maintain friendly relations with the foreign powers," he declared in an interview on March 31. "The Nationalists are the friends of the foreign powers.... It is the settled policy of the Nationalist government not to use force or mass violence in any form to effect a change in the status of the foreign settlements." He concluded with a promise he hoped the foreigners would not fail to understand: "In spite of the present obstacles to a clearer and better understanding, we hope to remove these so that there will be a clearer and better relationship between China and the foreign powers which will be based upon a mutual friendship and understanding."[31]

A few foreigners nodded hopefully at this unmistakable offer of collaboration between "China" (the property-owners) and the powers against the "obstacles" (the workers). But most of them were still angered more by the protestations Chiang had to make as a "Nationalist" than appeased by his promises to defend their interests. The editor of the *North China Daily News* expressed both views. He called the interview "an extraordinary farrago of assertion...and of brazen pretences contradicted by all experience," but as an afterthought he added: "Apparently General Chiang spoke sincerely, and to do him justice...in the districts under his purview (he) seems to have tried to keep order."[32] It would do no harm to wait watchfully. Not until Chiang proved that he could "act swiftly and relentlessly" would all their suspicions be allayed. A few days later General Duncan, commander of the British troops, felt reassured enough to tell a Chinese newspaperman that Chiang had won his respect "because he not only speaks that way, but really puts it into practice."[33]

The Chinese bankers and industrialists were readier with the faith and trust. They knew their man better. On March 29 more than fifty leading banks and firms and commercial associations banded together into a federation under the leadership of Yu Ya-ching and Wang I-ting, compradore for one of the big Japanese steamship companies whose friendship with Chiang went back at least fifteen years. United in this federation were the various district chambers of commerce, the Bankers' Association, the Native Banks Guild, the Stock Exchange Association, the Cotton Mill Owners' Association, the Flour Merchants' Guild, Tea Merchants' Guild, Silk Merchants' Guild—virtually all the organized propertied interests of Shanghai.

A delegation of the new body waited the same day on General Chiang, "who very cordially received them." Their spokesman

> conveyed the greetings of the Chinese merchants of Shanghai and emphasized the importance of immediately restoring peace and order in this city. They assured him of the whole-hearted support of the merchants. General Chiang responded in a few

> fitting remarks and took full responsibility upon himself for the protection of life and property, both Chinese and foreign, in Shanghai. He also assured the delegation that the relation between capital and labour will soon be regulated.... At the end of the visit the delegation left in good cheer, fully satisfied that they had found in General Chiang a man of sound principles and a leader of singular power.[34]

Several days later all the merchant guilds issued separate declarations of hearty support for Chiang and sent delegations to express their hopes of an early amelioration of the situation. On April 9, representatives of more than twenty commercial organizations met and resolved "for the Kuomintang San Min Principles and for Commander-in-Chief Chiang! Down with all counter-revolutionary elements!"

Naturally the men of money had to be more than vociferous. They had to be generous. The situation demanded more than faith and trust. It required hard cash. The first installment paid over to Chiang was a "loan" of $3,000,000 on April 4.[35] It was widely reported that an additional $7,000,000 was paid over a few days later. "Chinese bankers and merchants," reported a foreign correspondent, "...sent a delegation to Chiang Kai-shek...offering him a fund of 15,000,000 Shanghai dollars on condition that he suppress Communist and labour activities."[36] These advances were quite apart from the $30,000,000 "loan" floated two weeks later to help launch the new government at Nanking.

Chiang at once began to take steps to assure his own control of the city. He installed one of his staff officers as commissioner of police. One of his political henchmen became magistrate of the Shanghai district. He set up a special finance committee, drafting a number of prominent bankers for the purpose, to raise the funds he required. One of his appointees took over the managing directorship of the Shanghai–Nanking and Shanghai–Hangchow railways. He established official contact with the foreigners by naming Quo Tai-chi commissioner for foreign affairs. Martial law was proclaimed on March 28 making all civilian administrative organs in the city responsible to military headquarters at Lunghua. Orders were issued prohibiting "unauthorized persons" from possessing or carrying arms of any description. At the same time appeared on the scene the "Workers' Trade Alliance," sponsored by Pock-marked Hwang, Tu Yueh-sen, and Chang Siao-ling, and presented as a new "moderate" labor union. Preparations went ahead swiftly to repeat in Shanghai the tactics already applied in Nanchang, Kiukiang, Anking, and Wuhu, and, as if Chiang and his gangster aides wanted to make sure these methods still worked, a full dress rehearsal was staged in Hangchow on March 30 and 31.

Here, too, Chiang had seen to the organization of a "Workers' Trade Alliance" in opposition to the Communist-controlled General Labor Union. On the night of March 30 the gangsters broke into the headquarters of the union. Several workers were killed and many wounded in the fight that took place there. Next day, according to a wire from the General Labor Union published in a Shanghai paper,[37] a general strike was called to which, however, only the telephone and postal workers responded. A mass protest meeting was held and a parade formed which marched down Chin Chiao Road. Soldiers were waiting at a strategic crossing. They had been told the union was trying to sabotage the victorious Nationalist advance. No one told them differently. When the workers approached, the soldiers opened fire. Half a dozen marchers fell. More than one hundred were arrested. The pickets, one thousand in number, armed with clubs and staves only, were disarmed and dispersed. The premises of the General Labor Union were smashed. Pickets were arrested. Their denim uniforms were ripped from their backs. Nobody ever knew or recorded how many were killed. The GLU was closed down "pending reorganization" along the now familiar "more moderate" lines. The Hangchow events foreshadowed with deadly accuracy what was about to occur, on a far larger scale, in Shanghai. This was true not only of Chiang's moves but of the Communist reactions as well.

When Chiang put his own men into posts in the civil administration of Hangchow and repressive measures were begun against the workers, the GLU wired to Chiang a respectful request to remove the offending officials. "During the military period I have the power to appoint the chiefs of the Bureau of Public Safety," he curtly replied.[38] To this they acquiesced in silence. After the arrests and massacre of March 31, the union issued a circular telegram which concluded with a request to General Chiang Kai-shek "to come to Hangchow to punish the guilty parties and fight against the reaction."[39] Unfortunately, Chiang happened to be too busy inaugurating the reaction in Shanghai to journey down to Hangchow to suppress it there, and the Shanghai General Labor Union was too busy trying to placate Chiang to learn anything from the Hangchow experience.

Nevertheless, Chiang Kai-shek did not approach the task of breaking up the organizations of the Shanghai workers without showing that he was aware of the magnitude of the task. The mass movement had assumed such proportions that he was compelled to begin a series of gradual maneuvers to bring himself into a reasonably favorable striking position. For every step forward he offered a gesture in the opposite direction. He set out deliberately to befuddle his enemies, confuse the issue, and paralyze all potential opposition to the coup already in view. This course disturbed some of his friends. Just as at Canton on the eve of the March 20 coup many of his militarist allies "were antagonistic toward him on account of their inability to fathom the real aims behind his actions,"[40] similarly at Shanghai there were many, especially among the foreigners, who were impatient with the seeming contradictions in his conduct. "If General Chiang, it is suggested in Chinese political circles, initiated a frankly anti-Communist movement, he would crystallize support for himself, but his half-hearted, apologetic attacks on the Communists leave uncertainty that the rift is irrevocable," complained the *North China Daily News* on April 8.

But Chiang knew better than they exactly what he was doing and precisely where he was going. He neither planned nor sought any compromise whatever with the "Left" Kuomintang at Wuhan. He prepared assiduously to strike down the Shanghai workers; but he needed time to marshal his own forces. Soldiers sympathetic to the workers had to be removed from Chapei and replaced by fresher battalions least touched politically by contact with the mass movement. The mobilization of the gangsters for the anti-Communist offensive was already in full swing. While all this went on Chiang continued to do everything possible to spread the illusion that no conflict impended. This took the form of persistent denials, from the very day of his arrival, of reports that he intended to break with the Nationalist government at Wuhan.

On March 27 he told interviewers "that there was no split, that the members of the Kuomintang were united...that there were no signs or prospects of serious dissension."[41] To a representative of the Japanese Toho Agency two days later he declared that he unreservedly recognized the authority of the Wuhan Central Executive Committee. He made sure to have Moscow reassured along the same lines.

"We know the imperialists hope for a rupture between the Nationalist army and the popular masses," said Pai Chung-hsi to the Shanghai correspondent of *Pravda*, "but that is impossible. Our basic principle is the union of the armed force with the popular masses.... The Chinese revolution forms part of the front of the world revolution. The imperialists are trying to break that front by lies and slander. Sun Yat-sen instructed us to cooperate with the Communists who form part of the Kuomintang and we shall not break the alliance with them. The English Press in China is spreading all kinds of lies on this subject. It ought to be suppressed."[42] It will be seen how eagerly the Communists in Moscow and in China seized upon these assurances—and how much they were really worth.

The arrival of Wang Ching-wei from Europe on April 1 gave Chiang an opportunity to make his words seem even more concrete and convincing. Wang, a typical petty bourgeois radical, flaccid, pliable, and readily submissive to the pressure of stronger personalities, became again, scarce had he set foot on Chinese soil, the tool of the man who had forced him to flee so ignominiously from Canton a year earlier. There were two days of conferences. On April 3 Chiang issued a circular telegram proclaiming his "explicit obedience" to the Central Executive Committee of the Kuomintang at Wuhan.

"I strongly believe," he said, "that his (Wang's) return will result in the real centralization of the party so that we may attain without a split the ultimate success of the Nationalist movement.... Hereafter all matters relating to the welfare of the country and the Kuomintang...will be handled by Chairman Wang or carried on under his guidance.... We will be guided by the Central Executive Committee and we must therefore show nothing but explicit obedience."[43]

Wang, according to his own biographer, "felt very uncomfortable" about Chiang's telegram. He did not approve the methods which Chiang Kai-shek proposed to use in eliminating Communist influence from the ranks of the Kuomintang. To be sure, Wang also "visualized the necessity of separating from the Communist Party," only he was "against any precipitate break...(and)...wanted to settle all the disputes outstanding in a regular, peaceful way."[44]

To avert the direct action he so abhorred (in any form except in flight or in retreat from his own professions), Wang tried to persuade Chiang Kai-shek that they could attain the desired end without resort to violence or "illegality." According to one account Wang promised that Borodin would be dismissed, that the decisions of the Third Plenary Session of the Kuomintang Executive Committee in March, which deposed Chiang from the party chairmanship and the supreme military command, would be revised, that the disarmament of the Shanghai pickets would be approved and Chiang's civil appointees in the Shanghai district sanctioned.[45] Wang tried later to deny that he had come to any such agreement with Chiang, but his own biographer records that he left Shanghai for Wuhan to persuade his colleagues there "to come down to Nanking to hold the plenary session with Chiang and the rest, so as to maintain the unity of the party," adding that Wang "believed that he could get the support of the great majority of the pure Kuomintang members of the C.E.C. to effect a revision of the decisions taken by the Third Plenary Session."[46]

But Chiang Kai-shek and his friends knew that machine guns, not party compromises, had to serve them now. The simulation of the Chiang-Wang accord helped only to thicken the political smoke-screen they needed to cloak their attack. It was further to weaken potential opposition that they reached out through Wang to the Communists, with results that must have far exceeded their expectations, for Wang's services were small indeed compared to the offerings which the Communist leaders of the Shanghai workers were daily laying on the altar of the "national united front."

The Conspiracy of Silence

To the workers of Shanghai the hour of the arrival of the Nationalist troops was represented by their Communist leaders as the hour of liberation for all the oppressed. The central slogan of the victorious insurrection of March 21 had been: "Hail the National Revolutionary Army! Welcome to Chiang Kai-shek!" Quite oblivious of the fact that the advance of the troops had been halted at Lunghua in the hope that the workers' battalions would break themselves in the battle against the Shantung troops, the workers greeted the arrival of the first Nationalist vanguard on the evening of March 22 with delirious joy. Two days later, when foreign correspondents flocked to Lunghua to interview General Pai Chung-hsi, they witnessed a spectacle unlike anything ever seen in China before the revolution. "A striking example of the impression the Cantonese arrival has made on the minds of the labouring classes of Shanghai was furnished during the interview.... A procession of 1,800 factory workers, 300 of them women, entered the yamen bearing a multitude of gifts which they piled outside the door of the inner building as a mark of their pleasure, kettles, teapots, boxes, baskets, cloth . . ."[1]

The day after Chiang Kai-shek's arrival a demonstration of welcome was staged for him at West Gate, where more than 50,000 workers gathered to hear Communist speakers, who "were superlatively laudatory...toward Chiang Kai-shek."[2]

But the workers of Shanghai and the Chinese Communists were by no means alone in saluting Chiang and his army as the saviors of the people. All the parties in the Communist International reacted in the same manner, for everywhere it was understood that Chiang bore with him to the gates of Shanghai nothing less than the standard of the world revolution. Who knew otherwise?

A few days before the insurrection *Rote Fahne,* central organ of the German Communist Party, featured a photo of Chiang Kai-shek, describing him as the heroic leader of the "revolutionary war council" of the Kuomintang.[3] A similar photo appeared in *L'Humanité,* French Communist daily, on March 23, with a report of a great mass meeting at which Chiang's entry into Shanghai was greeted as the inauguration of "the Chinese Commune," opening "a new stage in world revolution." An editorial spoke of the Cantonese victory as the "liberation of Shanghai," which meant "the beginning of liberation for the workers of the world."[4]

This reading of the situation flowed naturally and logically from the whole line pursued by the Comintern up to the very day of Chiang's entry and afterward. If as late as April 10 *Pravda,* the guiding organ of the Communist International, could still proclaim the need, above all else, of maintaining the "bloc of four classes," if leading Soviet spokesmen repeatedly insisted upon the unassailable unity of all classes under the leadership of the Kuomintang,[5] it is not to be wondered that Communists in other countries saw in Chiang Kai-shek's entry into Shanghai the dawning of a new day for the Chinese revolution—the day of the Chinese Commune.

Unfortunately, the facts were the direct contrary. It has been shown how almost from the very outset the elevation of the "national united front," or the "bloc of four classes," into a mystic fetish to be preserved at all and any cost, had served to bind the Chinese Communist Party securely to the bootstraps of the Kuomintang, the workers and peasants to the bourgeoisie. In Canton this policy had already led to the successful establishment of a military dictatorship under Li Chi-sen based upon the savage repression of the workers. It had already made available to the bourgeoisie the fruits of the broad mass movement which made the march to the Yangtze possible. Today in Shanghai, through Chiang Kai-shek, the bourgeoisie was preparing to pluck that fruit. By voluntarily restricting the workers' and peasants' struggles, by limiting their political objectives to those of the bourgeois Nationalists, by yoking the Communists to the task of doing "coolie service" (Borodin) for the Kuomintang, by binding them not to criticize the doctrines of Sun Yat-sen, by forgoing an independent daily press, the Communist leadership had paved the way for the open reaction already established in Canton, in Kiangsi, and in the Yangtze ports.

Toward the end of 1926, and in the early months of 1927, the ruling organs of the Communist International had begun issuing broad, generalized warnings about the forthcoming defection of the national bourgeoisie,[6] which were repeated in a variety of articles during February and March.[7] These articles invariably deprecated the strength of the right wing in the Kuomintang, invariably exaggerated the strength of the left wing, and in no case mentioned Chiang Kai-shek as the actual spearhead of the gathering forces of reaction. On the contrary, when they mentioned Chiang Kai-shek at all, it was to assure their Communist readers that Chiang was "submitting," and that all would be well.

To this end all the press of the Comintern joined in denying and thrusting aside the rumors and reports, growing in number and in plausibility, that Chiang Kai-shek was heading in Shanghai toward a decisive break. It was a veritable conspiracy of silence around an impending catastrophe.

It is impossible to say that the Comintern was unaware of what was happening. In a few weeks its whole press would furiously belch forth denunciations of Chiang Kai-shek, with all the information suppressed for a year pouring out in a hot stream. The letter of the three Comintern functionaries, from which we have quoted, showed that Chiang's orientation was no secret to the men on the spot. But there is evidence still more striking.

Earl Browder, destined to become the generally unrecognized but nevertheless genial and beloved leader of the American proletariat; Jacques Doriot, who was to find his way from Stalin's top staff to fascism; Tom Mann of Great Britain; and a Russian, Sydor Stoler, were the members of a Comintern delegation which arrived in Canton in February and traveled up through Kiangsi at the heels of Chiang Kai-shek during the month of March. They came into direct contact with the terror which had already been laid across the province like a black whip. They were left untouched themselves, for Chiang obligingly left instructions behind that they be dined and wined and sent on. Thus wherever they went, as Browder himself later naively admitted, they "had the experience of actual street fighting being suspended during our visit while leaders of both sides talked to us." As their subsequent reports[8] indicated, the delegates made copious notes of names, dates, and places. They passed through town after town where the unions had already been driven underground, and in Kanchow they received detailed reports on the murder of Chen Tsang-shen, local trade union leader killed by Chiang's orders only a few weeks previously. Knowing, as they did, that everywhere abroad Chiang was believed to be a "revolutionary general" sweeping northward like the avenging angel of the masses, did they rush, on emerging from the hinterland at Kiukiang on March 29, to the cable office to blazon the news to the world? Was it possible that they had missed the significance of what they had seen and heard? No, for listen to Doriot: "The Kanchow incidents taught us a precious lesson. We knew from that moment on—well before the split—that the conflict between the bourgeoisie and the Chinese working class would take on the bloody forms it has since assumed."[9]

Listen to Browder, who says he saw in the Kanchow affair "one whole phase of the deep-going split that was tearing the Kuomintang into two separate warring bodies throughout China."[10]

Nor had anything been left to their imaginations. They had been given explicitly to understand that the showdown was approaching, and would come at Shanghai: "The Marshal (Chiang Kai-shek) cannot speak now," they were told by General Chang Chun at Nanchang on March 26. "He is not free enough. He has not enough territory. He has left for Nanking and Shanghai. There he will speak. There he will have his word!"[11]

In other words, the delegation arrived at Kiukiang with the positive knowledge that the split in the Kuomintang had already taken place, that Chiang Kai-shek had gone to Shanghai specifically and deliberately to smash the workers' organizations there just as he had done throughout Kiangsi on his way north. Was it not necessary for Browder, Doriot, and Mann to sound the alarm, to sound it as loudly and as imperatively as they could? They arrived at Kiukiang only a few days after Chiang Kai-shek arrived at Shanghai. We have already seen how uncertain his strength was there, how immense the strength of the workers. Moscow was counselling retreat, on the theory that Chiang would not attack if he were not provoked. Those were precisely the critical hours of decision. Everywhere the workers were being assured that there was no split in the Kuomintang, that Chiang Kai-shek was "submitting," that there was no possibility of a clash at Shanghai. Who can calculate what effect would have resulted had three responsible representatives of the Communist International at that particular moment broadcast a warning to the workers, and more particularly to the workers of Shanghai, that Chiang Kai-shek was not their friend or their saviour, but their mortal enemy? That they should at all costs keep their arms and prepare to repel the attack which Browder-Doriot-Mann knew was absolutely inevitable? Would such a bold move have changed the course of events? It is, of course, impossible to say. But the fact is that Browder-Doriot-Mann did none of these things.

They arrived at Hankow on March 31. Browder's first statement was anything but an open denunciation of Chiang. Instead: "Everywhere…the contact between army, union, and peasant groups was one of the most pleasing aspects of his visit, Mr. Browder stated.… Everywhere they went…they found that the people, without exception, were solidly in support of the Party (the Kuomintang)…. The peasants were in complete cooperation with all other groups in the Nationalist revolution."[12] The future exponent of twentieth-century Americanism cautiously remarked that in Kiangsi "the movement has been working under difficulties"—but hastened to add that "the workers were not at all discouraged." Except in a single statement, which he claimed to have given to a Chinese newspaper,[13] Browder nowhere mentioned Chiang Kai-shek by name as the author of the "difficulties" in Kiangsi.

In a formal report of their trip published eight days later, Browder-Doriot-Mann affirmed that "almost everywhere the delegation were told that the revolutionary army and its political sections, together with the revolutionary Kuomintang, helped organize and develop new trades and peasant unions." They ventured to remark that they saw "a definite differentiation going on" and mentioned that at Kanchow they found the workers mourning for a leader murdered by "agents of reaction." The identity of these "agents" remained unrevealed. The report concluded with an expression of "the profoundest conviction that the National government and the Kuomintang are determined to crush feudalism and reaction."[14]

Months later the international Communist press was still publishing reports that "the delegation had the pleasure of observing that the peasant masses are organizing everywhere into powerful peasant federations with the aid of the Kuomintang."[15]

These concealing lies sufficed until Chiang Kai-shek struck his blow, in his own time, at Shanghai. Then, and then only, the "agents of reaction" were identified as soldiers "acting in the name of Marshal Chiang Kai-shek." Then it became time to reveal that throughout Kiangsi "the trade unions must hold their meetings secretly, all premises being occupied by troops."[16] So these were the army-union contacts which Browder found so "pleasing"! And now it was time to reveal that in Kiangsi "the Kuomintang represents only the mandarins and the capitalists, as the workers and peasants have no voice whatever."[17] So this was the party "solidly supported by all the people"!

This deliberate concealment of vital information at the most critical phase of the Chinese revolution in 1927 is an index to the atmosphere created throughout the Comintern on the eve of Chiang Kai-shek's coup d'état. A few quotations will evoke it:

"Now that we are on the eve of the taking of Nanking and Shanghai, the imperialists are issuing reports about the so-called splitting tendencies within the Kuomintang. The results of the executive session of the Kuomintang...showed exactly the contrary. The united front inside the Party is today as solid as before.... Far from dividing, as the imperialists say, the Kuomintang has only tightened its ranks...."[18]

Again, under the title, "The Victory of the Shanghai Workers":

> A split in the Kuomintang and hostilities between the Shanghai proletariat and the revolutionary soldiers are absolutely excluded right now.... Chiang Kai-shek has himself declared he will submit to the decisions of the Party. A revolutionist like Chiang Kai-shek will not ally himself, as the imperialists would like to have believed, with the counter-revolutionary Chang Tso-lin to struggle against the emancipation movement. There were, indeed, negotiations last November between Chang Tso-lin and the Cantonese armies—but only for tactical reasons.... The Kuomintang has promised the workers to satisfy all their demands. The only danger for the Shanghai proletariat is in an imperialist provocation.[19]

That same week Paris workers cheered wildly when they were assured of the "indefectible unity" of the Kuomintang.[20]

In Moscow the same reassurance took the form of replies to Trotsky and the Opposition, who were warning of a blow and who demanded the unconditional independence of the Chinese Communists. On March 16 *Pravda* published an article entitled "The Chinese Revolution and the Kuomintang," which declared that "now particularly, the military question is the main political question of the Chinese Revolution." The article went on to describe right-wing elements who "with varying degrees of vacillation" [!] were aiming for a deal with imperialism. On the other hand, it hastened to reassure, "we have a strong left wing in the Kuomintang which reflects the interests of the masses.... For quite understandable reasons, the imperialist press is employing all means to exaggerate the strength of the Right Kuomintang, who are alleged to have already turned the revolution on to 'moderate' lines and concentrated power in their hands. The imperialist Press has predicted the complete degeneration of the Kuomintang, a split, and paralysis of the Chinese revolution." The article then proceeded to lash the Left Opposition for demanding immediate withdrawal from the Kuomintang:

> They see the right fraction of the Kuomintang, but they do not see its kernel and they do not see the masses.... Even the right circles in the Kuomintang, and those who stand near to the right in the Kuomintang Government, and the army, are forced to yield to the pressure of the revolutionary masses.... In this regard, the declaration of Chiang Kai-shek...is a very important document. [This refers to his pledge of discipline.] Chiang Kai-shek is compelled...to maneuver . . to swear his devotion...to submit to the leadership. The plan which the extreme right wing of the Kuomintang hoped to carry out and which the imperialist bourgeoisie regarded as its trump card...has failed. Now even the American capitalist press has been compelled to recognize the failure of the right-wing plot....[21]

Further reassurances came from Martinov, the Menshevik who spoke for the Comintern in the columns of *Pravda*. "The Left wing represents a considerable majority in the Kuomintang," he wrote. "Nine-tenths of the local organs of the Kuomintang are under the leadership of the left wing and the Communists."[22]

Blandest of all were the assurances given by the master-strategist himself, by Joseph Stalin, who rose on April 5 before a meeting of three thousand functionaries in the Hall of Columns in Moscow to answer the warnings of Trotsky and the Opposition. "Chiang Kai-shek is submitting to discipline," he declared in this memorable speech.

> The Kuomintang is a bloc, a sort of revolutionary parliament, with the right, the left, and the Communists. Why make a coup d'état? Why drive away the right when we have the majority and when the right listens to us? The peasant needs an old worn-out jade as long as she is necessary. He does not drive her away. So it is with us. When the right is of no more use to us, we will drive it away. At present we need the right. It has capable people, who still direct the army and lead it against the imperialists. Chiang Kai-shek has perhaps no sympathy for the revolution, but he is leading the army and cannot do otherwise than lead it against the imperialists. Besides this, the people of the right have relations with the generals of Chang Tso-lin and understand very well how to demoralize them and to induce them to pass over to the side of the revolution, bag and baggage, without striking a blow. Also, they have connections with the rich merchants and can raise money from them. So they have to be utilized to the end, squeezed out like a lemon, and then flung away.[23]

Only a few days previously Stalin had told a meeting of Young Communists: "It must be said that until now they [the imperialists] have secured one result: the deepening of the hatred of the Chinese for imperialism, the cohesion of the forces of the Kuomintang and a new swing to the left of the revolutionary movement in China. No one can doubt that right now the imperialists have achieved the exact opposite of what they wanted.... It is said, not without truth, that the gods strike blind those whom they would annihilate."[24]

Not without truth, indeed! It only remained to be determined who, in truth, had been struck blind.

The precise instructions given in this fatal week to the Chinese Communists in Shanghai were the following: "On March 31, when the preparations of the bourgeoisie for the overturn became apparent (!), the E.C.C.I. gave the following directive: Arouse the masses against this overturn now being prepared and conduct a campaign against the right. Open struggle is not to be launched at this time (in view of the very unfavourable change in the relationship of forces). Arms must not be given up, but in any extremity they must be hidden."[25]

These instructions meant an invitation to the Chinese Communists to put their heads docilely on the block, nothing more, nothing less. If they were not to mobilize for "open," i.e. armed, struggle against Chiang Kai-shek, obviously they had to do everything possible to propitiate him. The "campaign against the right" did not mean a campaign against Chiang Kai-shek himself. Was not the whole Comintern press proclaiming his fidelity? It meant angry whimperings against the politicians and generals who now formed Chiang's entourage.

"The Kuomintang is suffering from a lack of revolutionary worker and peasant blood," declared the leading organ of the Comintern in these very days. "The Communist Party must infuse such blood and thereby radically change the situation."[26]

"What an ominous play of words," wrote Trotsky, for it was precisely such a transfusion of blood that was now being prepared—only it was to come in a manner least expected by the bold and confident strategists who sat in Moscow and advised the Shanghai workers to play dead.

It has been necessary to go at this length into the Comintern estimate of the situation in Shanghai in March–April 1927, because after a few half-hearted attempts to defend the policies pursued at this critical juncture,[27] the legend was before long to be created and to persevere in all the literature of the Communist International that responsibility for the Shanghai debacle rested exclusively and indubitably with the Chinese Communist leaders, notably Chen Tu-hsiu, who were to be accused of stubbornly rejecting the instructions from Moscow. We have seen what these instructions were and what was the estimate from which they flowed. They explain why the Chinese Communists in Shanghai faced impending disaster helplessly disarmed.

The rumors of the impending coup were met in Shanghai, as abroad, with indignant denials. "How can the Shanghai workers clash with the army, the same army which they have only to welcome and respect?" asked the General Labor Union in a public statement. "Rumors are being disseminated to the effect that there is a possibility of a breach between the Nationalist army and the laboring classes.... Needless to say, these rumors are groundless and the public is requested not to believe them."[28] These rumors were called "machinations of the enemy to sow discord." Open predictions in the daily press about the forthcoming attack were brushed aside. The Communist organizations replied to all of them by asking Chiang Kai-shek to suppress the newspapers involved for publishing news "prejudicial to the united front"! In accord with Moscow instructions to "conduct a campaign against the right," flaming denunciations of "reactionaries" in general were issued almost daily. On April 4, the GLU even publicly threatened a general strike if any action was taken by the "reactionaries" against the armed pickets and the workers. But Chiang Kai-shek's name was never mentioned in connection with any of these threats, and often the term "reactionaries" was specified to mean only the Western Hills group, the Kuomintang right wingers like Wu Chih-hui and Chang Ching-chiang. The fact that Chiang Kai-shek had openly thrown in his lot with these men was ignored or concealed—or worried about privately.

Every effort was made to propitiate the "revolutionary general." After his arrival the Communists even prepared a pompous reception and banquet in his honor. But neither he nor the other general invited deigned to attend. Swallowing this slight, the Communists greeted with joy every little conciliatory gesture—or every gesture they could interpret as being conciliatory—that Chiang made. His telegram of April 3 endorsing the leadership of Wang Ching-wei brought forth a flood of telegrams from all the Communist organizations, hailing his announcement as a virtual settlement of all disputed issues and expressing pious hopes that he would henceforth faithfully fulfill the obligations he had himself assumed. Chiang's April 3 telegram was followed up, in the same spirit, by a joint manifesto issued over the signatures of Wang Ching-wei and Chen Tu-hsiu, a document which embodies the most complete expression of the self-effacement and class conciliation which characterized the Communist policy. For that reason it is reproduced here in full:

> Comrades of the Kuomintang and the Communist Party:
>
> Although our national revolution has won great victories, our enemies have still not all been defeated. They are watching closely for our weaknesses, in order to attack us and erase our conquests. The consolidation of our ranks is therefore more necessary than ever before. The Chinese Communist Party resolutely recognizes that the Kuomintang and its principles are necessary to the Chinese Revolution. Only those who are unwilling to see the Chinese Revolution advance could advocate the overthrow of the Kuomintang. No matter how misguided it is, the Chinese Communist Party could never advocate the overthrow of its ally, the Kuomintang, to please our imperialist and militarist enemies.
>
> The dictatorship of the proletariat is the maximum aim of the programs of all the Communist Parties. Although it has been realized in the Soviet Union, it is an open question whether in the political and economic situation of the colonial and

semicolonial countries, the transition from capitalism to Socialism must schematically proceed in the same way through the same stages. Moreover, in the present trend of the Chinese Revolution, this question will not only not be raised at the present time, but will not come up in the near future. What China needs is the establishment of a democratic dictatorship of all the oppressed classes to deal with the counter-revolution, not a dictatorship of the proletariat.

There are various forms of co-operation between the two parties. The important thing is that the overwhelming majority of the members of both parties should solve this question with an attitude of mutual goodwill, so that the fundamental spirit of co-operation shall not be violated. Whoever knows clearly the revolutionary theory of the Communist Party and its real attitude toward the Kuomintang will have no doubts of Sun Tsung-li's [Sun Yat-sen's] policy of alliance with the Communist Party.

Now the national revolution has reached the stronghold of the imperialists, Shanghai. This has aroused all the counter-revolutionaries, here and abroad, who are fabricating all sorts of rumours designed to create tension and sow discord between our two parties. Some say the Communist Party will organize a workers' government, will rush into the foreign Concessions in order to embarrass the Northern Expeditionary Army, will overthrow the Kuomintang power. Others say the Kuomintang leaders will expel the Communist Party, will suppress the labor unions and the pickets. It is not clear whence come such rumors. The resolutions of the recent Plenary Session of the Central Executive Committee of the Kuomintang demonstrated to the whole world that such things as the expulsion of the Communist Party and the labor unions can never take place. The Shanghai military authorities have announced that they will obey the Central Government. Although there are dissensions and misunderstandings, none of them is insoluble. The Communist Party is not the last in loving peace and order. It agrees with the policy of the Nationalist government against taking back the Shanghai settlements by force. The Shanghai General Labor Union has also issued a manifesto against any independent action in rushing into the Concessions. The Communist Party also agrees with the policy of the collaboration of all classes in the municipal government. These are hard facts and leave no room for fabricated rumors.

Comrades of the Kuomintang and the Communist Party! Our powerful enemies do not deal with us by force alone. They are also trying to estrange us by rumors, to achieve their aim of "playing red against red." We must stand on the common ground of the revolution, give up mutual suspicions, reject rumor-mongering, and respect each other. Everything must be done candidly, by open consultation. Our political views may be different, but in fundamentals there must be agreement. If there is sincere co-operation between the two parties, as intimately as between brothers, words meant to injure our relations with each other will never take effect. We state here our deepest convictions so that they may be examined by both sides, so that nothing shall be done to disappoint the friends of the revolution and to please its enemies. Then all will be well with both parties and with the Chinese Revolution.

Signed: Wang

Chen.[29]

It was with this attitude that the Communist leadership, in Shanghai and abroad alike, faced the critical tasks of these days. The workers in general believed implicitly in these leaders.

The victorious insurrection had enormously heightened the authority of the Communists. The workers streamed into the unions.[30] For this reason it was not out of mere hysteria that the foreign and Chinese capitalists of Shanghai anticipated imminent expropriation at the hands of the armed workers' power. When all wheels abruptly ceased turning and the workers carried the class struggle from the factories into the streets, it is little wonder that the capitalists thought they heard the knell of property ring, not in tones of measured solemnity, but tapped out in the insistent staccato of machine guns. Stripped of its froth, their fear had meaning in it, for they clearly saw in the armed working class the power capable of destroying them. Warships might protect the foreigners' settlements, but they could not make the wheels go round or make the workers resume their burdens. Their fears, with all their hysteria, rose quite logically from a frank appraisal of the situation. What they misjudged was the caliber of the Communist leadership. They mistook it for the same kind of leadership which had carried out the October revolution in Russia and had destroyed there the system of private property, the base of bourgeois society.

If in the Communist leaders, to whom the workers of Shanghai looked for guidance, there had been the intention to justify even part of these fears, to seize the opportunity which the moment seemed so clearly to offer, there is every reason to believe that Chiang Kai-shek could have been isolated from the army and the bourgeois counterrevolution smothered. But this was not even remotely the case. Gripped in the vise of the "bloc of four classes," struck blind by the gods of the "national united front," the party which had victoriously led the insurrection was quickly to reveal its impotence in the face of reaction. "The keys to Shanghai were handed over by the victorious workers to the Canton army," cried *Pravda* on March 22. "In this fact is expressed the great heroic act of the Shanghai proletariat!"[31] This "heroic act" consisted in handing over to the bourgeoisie, on the morrow of the insurrection, the power won by the workers.

In the Provisional Municipal Government inaugurated under Communist auspices on March 29, a majority was voluntarily given over to representatives of the Shanghai bourgeoisie. Only five of the nineteen government members were nominated by the trade unions. Chiang Kai-shek, who was independently putting his own men into key administrative posts and quickly setting up the framework of his own civil authority, refused to recognize the Provisional Government, declaring through his spokesman, Wu Chih-hui, that it "was contrary to the party system of government."[32]

As soon as Chiang's attitude became known, the elected bourgeois representatives one after another declined the proffered posts. Yu Ya-ching, banker and compradore, ignored the appointment. K. P. Chen, general manager of the Shanghai

Commercial and Savings Bank, declined to take office. Wang Hsiao-lai of the General Chamber of Commerce, who had been elected chairman after he had publicly indicated his unwillingness to participate, said that since he was a silk merchant and the spring was a busy season, he would prefer to cede his position to a wiser man. Wang Han-liang, another prominent merchant, announced that with the occupation of Shanghai all his past efforts were amply rewarded and he had now only to retire and let felicity take its course. Soumei Cheng, a notorious woman lawyer and judge closely connected with the gangs and big business, said she was "too busily engaged with her official duties." Francis Zia, managing editor of the *China Courier*, pleaded illness and inability to assume public responsibility. The remaining bourgeois delegates quickly followed suit.

Thus boycotted by the bourgeoisie, the workers' delegates pleaded helplessness.

> At the fifth delegates' conference on April 3, the chief secretary of the municipal government (Lin Chun, a Communist), said that since the members of the government assumed their positions, petitions from the masses calling upon them to take over local institutions, or reporting local acts in taking over institutions, or urging the government to take measures against the gentry (in the villages adjacent to the city), or to settle school disputes, had been pouring into the government offices like snowflakes. But the members of the government, owing to the fact that they have received a letter from Commander-in-Chief Chiang asking them to postpone doing anything, did not actively conduct their work.[33]

Instead of taking over the local organs of power, the government addressed a letter to Chiang Kai-shek in the form of a *tseng wen*, the form used in the old mandarinate for petitions from lower to higher orders, respectfully asking him to hand over to it the municipal institutions in which he had already placed his own appointees and asking his support for the democratically elected municipal administration.[34] The government did not draw up measures for alleviating the burdens of the masses. It did not call upon the trade unions and pickets to help it carry out a bold social program. It issued a manifesto with a program of demands, but no steps were ever taken to make these demands effective. The only other thing the government did was to devote itself to passing resolutions welcoming Chiang Kai-shek and the Nationalist army, welcoming Wang Ching-wei when he returned, congratulating Chiang Kai-shek for his promise to obey discipline, and greeting with particular joy the Chen-Wang manifesto.

For any measure which actually corresponded to the practical daily needs and interests of the workers and the petty artisans and shopkeepers, the Provisional Government could have counted upon the militant armed support of the trade unions and other mass organizations in Shanghai. By storming the army with the weapons of propaganda and assuring the effective fraternization of the workers and soldiers, the government could have ensured support from the military rank and file. Such measures would have brought forth a resounding echo from the provinces and from other cities where the workers and peasants were already on the march and needed only such an example to free themselves from the vacillation and delays of the Kuomintang regime at Wuhan. None of this was thinkable without the complete independence of the Communist Party functioning consciously as the instrument of the workers. The Chinese Communists, stifling in the Kuomintang straitjacket, were pursuing quite opposite aims.

They dogged the tails of Chiang Kai-shek and the bankers and merchants whose cooperation they deemed vital to the maintenance of the "united front." Without such cooperation they considered themselves helpless. In a few localities, as in Pootung, the workers' power asserted itself more aggressively. There the workers spontaneously took over the local municipal organs, instituted their own tribunals, empowered the pickets to arrest, try, and sentence enemies of the workers. These acts never received the backing of the Provisional Government, but were on the contrary deplored and criticized.

Functioning through the Provisional Government, the Communist leadership failed to take any positive steps in the interests of the workers. Functioning through the leadership of the General Labor Union, the Communists went further. They voluntarily limited the spontaneously rising mass movement and circumscribed the activities of the pickets to bring them within the limits set by the need for maintaining the "national united front." On April 4 the executive committee of the GLU adopted a set of regulations governing strikes. Spontaneous strikes on the initiative of the workers were forbidden. According to the procedure laid down, demands "were not to be too exacting" and were first to be presented for direct negotiations with the employers. If these negotiations failed, no strike was to be called, but the matter was to be referred to the next higher organ in the union, the district committee or the center, which would thereupon take up negotiations with the employers.[35] The effect of the regulations was to sap the initiative of the workers, to scatter and isolate their struggles. When the employers began hitting back at the mass movement by lockouts, the General Labor Union meekly adopted a resolution asking the Provisional Government to ask the employers "not to close their factories without good grounds or on simple pretexts." [!][36]

Strict orders were issued forbidding pickets to make arrests. Their duties were to be confined to "the maintenance of order in cooperation with the army and the police."[37] Heavy penalties were prescribed for pickets exceeding these limits. An attitude of cringing servility toward the military commanders was preserved by the GLU leaders. One evening, for example, some members of the family of General Liu Chih, a notorious enemy of the workers, were arrested on suspicion by a picket patrol. Next morning the GLU executive committee sent a reekingly subservient apology to military headquarters. General Liu was asked to "pardon" the four pickets whose "actions were so reckless and thoughtless as to encroach upon other comrades [!] and to disturb the division commander's family. We have disarmed them and expelled them from membership in the picket corps and will punish them severely."[38]

The same meekness was displayed with regard to the anti-imperialist struggle. The whole situation called for unleashing the most militant and broadest possible action in the form of strikes, boycotts, and demonstrations against the powers whose forces bristled with arms at the border of the Settlement and who were participating directly in the suppression of the mass movement.

The General Labor Union, however, confined itself to issuing reassuring statements and promises that it had no intention of rushing the Settlement gates. Obviously to hurl themselves against the foreign guns would have been foolhardy. But propitiating and reassuring the foreigners was one thing. Carrying on an extensive campaign which would have cut every nerve that linked the Settlement to the rest of the country and sapped the imperialist defenses was quite another. The intention of the bourgeoisie to come to terms with the imperialists was perfectly apparent. Since such a compromise was obviously to be reached at the expense of the workers, it was now more than ever the task of the Communists to dissociate themselves from the bourgeoisie and independently undertake an offensive that would have freed the hands of the workers in the face of the impending union of their native and foreign exploiters. Instead, the Communists announced in advance their unquestioning compliance in any settlement which "the properly constituted authorities" (i.e. the bourgeoisie) might make.

In an advertisement inserted in all the Chinese newspapers, it was stated that "in the question of the rendition of the Concessions, the General Labor Union, jointly with the army and the merchants, will back the foreign policy of the Nationalist government. It will not undertake to rush into the Concessions. In the question of law and order, it will cooperate with the army and the merchants to preserve it."[39]

In a declaration on March 30, the executive committee of the GLU had already promised that it would "await patiently the outcome and a peaceful settlement of forthcoming negotiations in which the Nationalist government and the foreign powers will enter." The GLU deplored the fact that "residents of the International Settlement are considerably agitated" by the rumors of an attack. "While it is our desire to expand our propaganda movement, we desire to remove all unnecessary

* The leading role played by the Americans in the bombardment of Nanking on March 24 came as a rude shock to the many Chinese who still believed that the United States regarded Chinese Nationalism with a benevolent, detached interest. On April 7, a demonstration of workers outside the Oriental Spinning and Weaving Co. was dispersed at the point of bayonets by an American military patrol. On the night of April 8, a detachment of two hundred British soldiers raided the Great China University, wounded eight students, searched the dormitories, seized students' property, and made a number of arrests. Japanese marines repeatedly used bayonets on workers in the Japanese mills.

alarm. The Shanghai GLU strongly supports the movement for the rendition of the Settlement, but the responsibility for this is vested in the proper authorities of the Nationalist government.... Our action with regard to diplomatic affairs will be similar to and will be guided by those who are higher than we, namely, the Nationalist government."[40]

Thus step by step and in the name of the "national united front," the Communist Party abdicated all rights of working-class initiative. Governmental prerogatives could be exercised only with the cooperation of the bourgeoisie—and when the bourgeois delegates refused to cooperate, the Communists declared themselves helpless and did nothing. "Law and order" were to be maintained only "in cooperation with the army and the merchants." The fight against imperialism was to be guided only "by those who are higher than we," by the bourgeoisie, and any settlement they made was to be accepted without question. And if anyone made so bold as to suggest that the bourgeoisie was preparing to smash the unions and the Communist Party, he was charged with circulating tendentious rumors started by "counterrevolutionary elements" for the purpose of driving a wedge into the "national united front."

Writing more than a year later, Mif, the Comintern "expert" on China, described the Chinese Communist leadership in these critical days in the following terms: "The Shanghai comrades still lived hypnotized by the old line and could not imagine a revolutionary government without the participation of the bourgeoisie.... The bourgeoisie, again according to the old tradition, was given the leading role..."[41]

Old line? Old tradition? When had the Communist International proclaimed any new line? Or when had it inaugurated a new tradition? When had it envisaged a revolutionary government without the participation of the bourgeoisie? When and where did it call upon the Chinese Communists to follow their own class course—a course which inevitably required a break with the bourgeoisie? Stalin and Bukharin said that the bourgeoisie would inevitably break with the proletariat. Having sagely made this "prediction," they instructed the proletariat to hang doggedly on to the tails of the bourgeoisie until it was kicked loose. When Chiang Kai-shek openly marched toward the break they had "predicted," Stalin shut his eyes and saw no evil, Bukharin covered his ears and heard no evil, and Borodin-Roy-Browder-Doriot and all the others locked their lips and spoke of none. The clamor and alarm was raised, not against Chiang Kai-shek, but against Leon Trotsky, who in these very days was demanding, unheard, a declaration of independence for the Chinese Communist Party.

On April 3, 1927, Trotsky submitted for publication in the Soviet press an article entitled "Class Relations in the Chinese Revolution." It was refused publication. In this article Trotsky warned against the "Chinese Pilsudski" and declared:

> If the Polish Pilsudski required three decades for his evolution, the Chinese Pilsudski will require a much shorter period for the transition from national revolution to national Fascism.... The policy of a shackled Communist Party serving as a recruiting agent to bring the workers into the Kuomintang is preparation for the successful establishment of a Fascist dictatorship in China at that not very distant moment when the proletariat, despite everything, will be compelled to jump back from the Kuomintang.... To drive the workers and peasants into the political camp of the bourgeoisie and to keep the Communist Party a hostage within the Kuomintang is to carry on a policy equivalent objectively to betrayal.... The Kuomintang in its present form is the embodiment of an "unequal treaty" between the bourgeoisie and the proletariat. If the Chinese revolution as a whole demands the abolition of the unequal treaties with the imperialist powers, then the Chinese proletariat must liquidate the unequal treaty with its own bourgeoisie.[42]

But Stalin said he was engaged in squeezing lemons, that the lemons gave him connections with Chang Tso-lin and the rich merchants which had not yet been fully utilized. Chiang Kai-shek did, indeed, have relations with Chang Tso-lin, but instead of inducing him "to pass over to the side of the revolution," Chiang was trying to negotiate an alliance with him against the Left.[43] Chiang did know, indeed, how to raise money from his connections with the rich merchants, only it was money paid over to finance not the revolution but the counterrevolution. But since Chiang and the other "capable people" in command of the army could not, according to Stalin, "do otherwise than lead it against the imperialists," the question of armed preparation of the workers against an attack by that same army was surely not in order. It was to insure against any such eventuality that Stalin had ordered the workers' arms hidden. It was comprehensible, therefore, that the Communist leaders found themselves helplessly indecisive when the crucial opportunity presented itself to align the whole First Division, then garrisoning the city, aggressively on the side of the workers against Chiang Kai-shek.

The First Division was composed of seasoned, revolutionary troops, schooled in the revolution, and deeply conscious of the firm bonds of unity between themselves and the workers. These were the men who had chafed at Pai Chung-hsi's restraining orders on March 21, and had finally marched into the city the next day in defiance of those orders. One of Chiang Kai-shek's first aims after his arrival was to remove these troops from the scene. During that week he issued orders for them to leave. Hsueh Yoh, the division commander, acting under the pressure of his ranks, came at once to the Central Committee of the Communist Party.

"I have been ordered by Chiang Kai-shek to leave Shanghai," he told them. "What shall I do?" He offered to defy Chiang and to hold his men in readiness to fight him. He offered to arrest and imprison Chiang on charges of plotting counterrevolution.[44] Hsueh's offer put the key to the whole crisis in the hands of the Communist leadership. Chen Tu-hsiu and the others hesitated. There were also Voitinsky and half a dozen other Comintern "advisers." They, too, hesitated. They temporized.

"To this proposition for a decisive attack on Chiang Kai-shek no clear answer was given. They advised Hsueh Yoh to sabotage, to pretend illness." But Chiang accepted no delay. "The moment arrived when it was impossible to put it off. Hsueh Yoh received an ultimatum, and when he addressed himself again to the party there was no other way out: either take up arms against Chiang (he proposed) with the support and under the leadership of the Communist Party, or obey, i.e. take out of Shanghai a large, and from the revolutionary point of view, precious force."[45]

Fearful of the responsibility of advising Hsueh Yoh to remain in Shanghai in defiance of Chiang's orders, the Communist leaders addressed respectful petitions to Chiang Kai-shek and Pai Chung-hsi, humbly requesting them to keep the First Division in the city. To the workers they repeated their assurances that all was well. Individual Communists and working-class leaders who refused to be lulled into somnolence were paralyzed.[46] The decisive moment passed. Hsueh's troops were moved, first out of Chapei, and then up the railway out of the Shanghai area altogether. The soldiers, uncomprehending but still confident in the Communist leadership, moved out without protest.* The working-class districts of Shanghai were occupied by the thoroughly reactionary forces of Pai Chung-hsi, Liu Chih, and Chow Feng-chi, a Sun Chuang-fang renegade.

That same week, the first in April, attacks were begun piecemeal on local Communist centers. Scores were arrested and several picket patrols were disarmed. The city Kuomintang office, under Communist influence, was closed down. Protesting these acts, the staff of the Political Department of the army met on April 5 and adopted a resolution asking Chiang to proclaim again his fidelity to Kuomintang principles and to show it by releasing the arrested men. By way of reply next day Chiang's troops swooped down on the headquarters of the Political Department and arrested nineteen members of the staff. The soldiers were told they were arresting "counterrevolutionaries."

An official communiqué took pains to announce that no ill will against the Communists was to be read into these arrests. "The people in control of the Political Department," it averred, "are secretly fostering reactionary forces and are hindering the development of the Northern Expedition."[47] That same day soldiers of Chang Tso-lin, acting with the permission of the Diplomatic Corps, raided the Soviet Embassy in Peking, arresting twenty Chinese found there, among them Li Ta-chao, a founder of the Communist Party.* Chiang hastened to wire the Soviet Embassy expressing his "indignation" and "regret." He called the raid an "unprecedented outrage" and begged to extend to the Soviet Charge d'Affaires his "sincerest condolences."[48] In Moscow Chiang's telegram was proudly cited as further

---

* Hsueh Yoh became one of Chiang's most faithful lieutenants and one of the most relentless pursuers of the peasant Red armies in 1930-34.

* Li Ta-chao and the nineteen others arrested were later executed by strangulation.

evidence that he could not possibly be contemplating a coup against the workers.[49] But when in Shanghai the foreign authorities responded to the Peking raid by throwing a cordon around the Soviet Consulate-General and searching all who came and went, Chiang remained discreetly silent. "It is suspected in foreign circles," wired a correspondent, "that Chiang Kai-shek's faction may not be averse to the curtailment of the Soviet Consulate's liberties."[50]

At one of the ceremonies arranged for Chiang by the Communists in the days following his arrival, Chiang had actually presented a banner to the pickets inscribed "Common Action."[51] He revealed what he meant by "common action" on April 6 when orders were issued at Lunghua: "All armed pickets of the labor unions are to be under the command of the headquarters of the commander-in-chief, otherwise they will be regarded as conspiratorial organizations and will not be permitted to exist."[52] The time for gestures was fast coming to an end.

While congratulatory telegrams from Communist and left-wing organizations greeting the Chen-Wang manifesto buzzed in over the wires, Wu Chih-hui, Chiang's spokesman, addressed a meeting of right-wing politicians: "The Chen-Wang manifesto was simply diplomatic friendly talk between leaders of the two parties," he told them. "It has no bearing on the policies of the party at all." Wu declared that as far as the Kuomintang was concerned, it was merely tolerating the Communists, not allying itself with them. "As to the acceptance of the Communist Party into the Kuomintang," he said,

> this meant an invitation to individual members of the Communist Party to join the Kuomintang and obey its principles, making them members of the Kuomintang. As to the friendly relations between the Kuomintang and the Communists outside the party, this amounts at most to the same thing as the alliance with Soviet Russia, asking them to aid our party, but not asking them to co-rule with us, still less allowing them to spread Communism.... If they violate the principles of the Kuomintang or endanger the Kuomintang, we must limit their activities.... If they overstep the limits of friendship or try to co-rule China with us, or try to rule China independently, then our support of our own party must become correspondingly strong and vigorous.[53]

To replace the Provisional Government, which had by now become almost extinct, Chiang appointed a "Provisional Committee" headed by Wu Chih-hui to take over and coordinate all organs of civil administration. Almost everything else was in readiness. He had previously sent a force of his own most trusted troops up the line to Nanking to clear that city of forces hostile to him. Later he made a quick trip himself to inspect the results. By about April 9 that operation had been painlessly performed, most of the unreliable units being disarmed.[54] In Shanghai the period of palaver, of maneuvers, and gestures, of negotiations and specious compromises and pronouncements, was drawing to its close. The politicians retired backstage and the gangsters stepped forward for their cues.

The approach of zero hour was perhaps most strikingly reflected in the half-page advertisements run daily in the Chinese press by the Political Department of Pai Chung-hsi's headquarters. In huge black characters during the first few days after the Nationalist occupation, these ads repeated familiar slogans: "Down with Imperialism! Exterminate the Feudal Forces!" But from April 7 on their tone changed, first subtly, soon with brutal directness.

> April 7: "Down with the reactionaries who are wrecking the National revolution!"
> April 8: "Whosoever opposes the Three People's Principles is opposing the revolution!"
> April 9: "Down with the disruptive elements in the rear!"
> April 10: "For the new Shanghai Provisional Committee!"
> April 11: "We, the soldiers, are fighting at the front at heavy cost. Honest workers in the rear will not strike on any pretext whatever or cause any disorder."

Irony crowned the series on April 12, the advertisements that morning reading: "Consolidate the great national united front of peasants, workers, students, merchants, and soldiers to strive for the realization of the San Min Principles!" Irony, for just before dawn that day the blow fell. The spatter of machine-gun and rifle fire crackled over the awakening city. The workers rose to discover the unthinkable, the impossible, coming to pass. Bludgeoned into confusion by the treacherous ignorance of their leaders, they sprang to the arms they still had to defend themselves. One could well ask, hurrying along with Malraux's Kyo some hours before that dawn: "How would they fight, one against ten, in disagreement with the instructions of the Chinese Communist Party, against an army that would oppose them with its corps of bourgeois volunteers armed with European weapons and having the advantage of attack?"[55]

10 The Coup of April 12, 1927

At four o'clock on the morning of April 12 a bugle blast sounded from Chiang Kai-shek's headquarters at the Foreign Ministry Bureau on Route Ghisi. A Chinese gunboat at anchor off Nantao answered with a toot on its siren. "Simultaneously the machine-guns broke loose in a steady roll."[1] The attack was launched in Chapei, Nantao, the western district, in Woosung, Pootung, and Jessfield. It came as no surprise to anyone except the workers because "all the authorities concerned, Chinese and foreign, after midnight were secretly made cognizant of the events which were to take place in the morning."[2]

Mobilized for action at all points, the gangsters, dressed in blue denim uniforms and wearing white armbands bearing the Chinese character kung (labor), "had feverishly worked through the night organizing secret parties to appear at dawn as though from nowhere."[3] The *North China Daily News* called them "armed Kuomintang labourers." The Shanghai Municipal Police Report referred to "merchants' volunteers." The *China Press* contented itself with "Nationalist troops." Franker, George Sokolsky reported: "Arrangements were made with the Green and Red Societies, so that one morning they, as 'white' labourers, fell upon and shot down the Communists."[4] They did not appear from "nowhere," but at the given signal "rushed out of the Concessions,"[5] and, joining forces with picked detachments of Pai Chung-hsi's troops, attacked the headquarters of the working-class organizations scattered throughout the city. In most cases, as at the Foochow Guild in Nantao and the police station in Pootung, the workers' positions were carried directly by the gangsters after brief, sharp battles. Their quarters once occupied, the pickets and their supporters were given short, brutal shrift. Their arms were seized "and even their clothes and shoes ripped from them."[6] Every worker who resisted was shot down in his tracks. The remainder were lashed together and marched out to be executed either in the streets or at Lunghua headquarters.

Where the workers' forces were greater and the resistance likely to be sharper, the attackers employed other tactics. A band of some sixty gangsters opened fire on the Huchow Guild in Chapei at about 4:30 A.M. This building housed the headquarters of the General Labor Union and was defended by several scores of pickets. The surprised guards asked the attackers what union they belonged to. "To the Northern Expeditionary Army," was the reply, and the firing went on. The pickets replied in kind. The street in front of the Guild was alive with gunfire. Twenty minutes later a company of soldiers, headed by an officer named Hsin Ting-yu, appeared. Hsin shouted orders to cease firing. "Do not fire at us!" he shouted to the pickets. "We've come to help you disarm these men." The firing stopped. He proposed from the street that both sides hand over their arms. Ostentatiously he proceeded to disarm some of the gangsters and, under the suspicious eyes of the pickets, even bound some of them securely. At that the gates were opened. Hsin and his men were invited in. Even tea and cigarettes, it is recorded, were laid out for them. The officer told Ku Chen-chung, commander of the pickets, that he had been appointed to conduct "armed mediation" in accordance with the regulations of martial law. He asked Ku to accompany him to headquarters. The picket leader gladly complied and with six of his men left the premises with Hsin. A few steps down the street Hsin turned to Ku.

"We've disarmed those guerrillas. We've got to disarm your squads too," he said.

Ku stopped short. "You can't," he answered, "those men are gangsters. Our pickets are revolutionary workers. Why disarm us?"

Hsin did not answer. Instead his men closed in on the group. Ku and the six were disarmed and brought back to the GLU headquarters. A few minutes later a force of some three hundred gangsters rushed into the building, and while the soldiers stood by they savagely attacked the astounded pickets. In the melée, Ku and the vice-commander, Chow En-lai, escaped. Indignant and frightened, they rushed to the headquarters of the Second Division—to protest the attack! They were thrust aside. Somehow they got out alive and escaped into hiding.* The Huchow Guild meanwhile had fallen to the attackers. Similar methods achieved similar results at most of the other workers' centers in the city. By mid-morning the last stronghold of the workers was the Commercial Press where a band of about four hundred pickets continued to hold out against overwhelmingly superior attacking forces.

When the gangsters attacked and the soldiers came on the scene with their demand for a cessation of hostilities, the workers inside the Commercial Press answered with a renewed fusillade. The soldiers were then ordered to join in the attack. All attempts at deception were discarded. Siege was laid to the building from all sides. Paoshan Road dinned with gunfire for several hours. Armed with but a few machine guns and about fifty rifles, the workers held on. They were worthy of better

---

* Ku remained with the Communist Party until 1931 when he turned renegade, went over to the Kuomintang, and became one of the most rabid killers, and eventually chief of Chiang Kai-shek's anti-Communist organization. Chow En-lai fled from Shanghai and later emerged as one of the political leaders of the Kiangsi peasant Red Armies with whom he fled in 1934–35 to the distant northwest. Today (1938—Ed.) they are reunited in Chiang Kai-shek's camp.

leaders, these anonymous defenders of the Shanghai proletariat. Theirs was a heroism that must have been born not only of desperation but of bitterness, of a sense of having been betrayed that was to live on long after Kuomintang bullets or the broadswords of Kuomintang headsmen had snuffed the lives from their bodies. They fought back until most of them were dead and the rest without ammunition. It was nearly noon before the attackers gingerly stepped inside the bullet-ridden building.[7]

"What action the soldiers took beyond disarming the Communists is naturally not known. It is not going to be advertised by the Chinese authorities," smirked the *North China Daily News*. Early foreign reports minimized the casualties, but the British-controlled Shanghai Municipal Police later came nearer the actual toll when it reported that nearly four hundred workers were killed in the day's operations.[8] Among the missing was Wang Shao-hua, chairman of the General Labor Union. (Not until later was it discovered that he had been kidnapped by gangsters the previous afternoon and carried off to Lunghua Military Headquarters, where he was put to death three days later.) At four o'clock the military authorities announced they had the situation "in hand."

Chen Chuen,* secretary to the gang leader Chang Siao-ling, and political director of Pai Chung-hsi's army, announced plans for the immediate "reorganization" of the General Labor Union along the lines already made familiar by the events in Kiangsi and Chekiang in March. "The policy of the government is to have labor working in harmony with the revolutionary army and the government," he proclaimed, "but when labor becomes a disturbing element, when it arrogates to itself tasks which are detrimental to the movement and disturbing to law and order, labor must be disciplined."

The Workers' Trade Alliance, freshly organized, at once took over the occupied workers' quarters and introduced themselves as follows:

> The Shanghai General Labor Union was manipulated by a few Communist scoundrels. They bullied and deceived the workers and made them sacrifice themselves. Workers who have lost their jobs owing to strikes are daily increasing in number. The General Labor Union wants to starve and ruin the workers to create opportunities for committing crimes against society and the State. The aim of the Workers' Trade Alliance is to realize the San Min Principles of the Kuomintang, to secure for the workers their most concrete interests, to aid in China's reconstruction so as to win freedom and equality in the family of nations.... Now the pickets of the GLU have all been disarmed. They can no longer oppress our workers. Now our workers are completely free. It is hoped that the workers will send delegations to get in touch with us and wait patiently for a settlement.[9]

* Chen Chuen and Yang Hu took personal command of Chiang Kai-shek's execution squads, making side trips to Ningpo and other neighboring cities to complete the "reorganization" of the labor movement by executing hundreds. A saying became current: "In Shanghai wolves and tigers (hu) stalk abroad in packs (chuen)."

But the General Labor Union and the other Communist organizations were not yet wholly destroyed. They still had strength enough and breath enough to address new appeals and petitions to Chiang Kai-shek. The Shanghai *tangpu* (Kuomintang local), long since driven from its headquarters, issued an exhortation: "Our working masses must not shrink from reorganizing their ranks.... The military authorities should also more properly protect the workers' organizations and return their arms to them."[10] The virtually defunct Provisional Government addressed a letter to General Pai: "The workers' pickets made heavy sacrifices to aid the Northern Expeditionary Army and to expel the Chihli-Shantung bandit troops.... After the capture of Shanghai, they cooperated with the army and the police to maintain order and they have rendered no little service to the city. Therefore even Commander-in-Chief Chiang highly approved of them and presented them with a banner inscribed 'Common Action.'" The letter concluded with a respectful request for the return of the arms taken from the pickets.[11] That night Communist speakers addressed the crowds in Chapei. They complained that the workers "had consistently assisted the Nationalist government for years and had only recently captured Shanghai for them.... They had always maintained discipline...and had not only observed the law, but assisted in upholding it." Resolutions were adopted urging "that the authorities be again requested to give back the arms taken."[12]

All this was true, too true. Only now, with the battle lost and the moment for action irretrievably buried in the blunders of the past, the General Labor Union found the sorry courage on April 13 to declare a general strike of protest and to announce: "We shall fight to the death...with the national revolution as our banner. It is glorious to die in such a way."[13]

Having led the workers bound before the guns of Chiang Kai-shek, the Communist leadership could still, on April 13, call upon the workers "to be prepared to sacrifice all, to renew the war against the forces of the right wing."[14]

The workers might well have asked: "WHAT war against the right wing?"

And how were they going to fight now? The instructions of the Communist International had been to play 'possum'—to bury or hide their arms—in hopes of averting "open struggle." Now "open struggle" had been carried to them by the enemy. They were helplessly caught.

Despite the complete collapse of the leadership in the critical hours of April 12, about one hundred thousand workers answered the call for the general strike.[15] What testimony this was to the sustained discipline and courage of the Shanghai working class! The waterfront was paralysed. The tramway workers went out. Most of the textile workers in the western district and about half the workers in the Yangtzepoo answered the strike call.

At noon on April 13 the workers gathered at a mass meeting on Chinyuen Road, Chapei. Resolutions were passed demanding the return of the seized arms, the punishment of the union wreckers, and protection for the General Labor Union.[16] A petition was drawn up embodying these points and a procession was formed to march down to Second Division headquarters to present it to General Chow Feng-chi. Women and children joined. Not a man marching bore arms. They swung into Paoshan Road under a pouring rain. As they came abreast of San Teh Terrace, a short distance from the military headquarters, machine gunners waiting for them there opened fire. Lead spouted into the thick crowd from both sides of the street. Men, women, and children dropped screaming into the mud. The crowd broke up into mad flight. Guns continued streaming fire into the backs of the fleeing workers. The muddy rainwater coursing down ruts in the streets ran red. Waiting squads of soldiers streaked out of adjacent alleyways, slashing into the crowd with bayonets, swinging rifle butts and broadswords. They raced in pursuit of the fleeing demonstrators, chasing many of them right into their houses in Yi Ping Terrace, Paotung and Tientungan roads, streets thick with working-class homes. Men and women were dragged out. "Those who resisted were either killed on the spot or wounded.... Many of the wounded were left to die where they dropped. It was an hour before the street was cleared."[17] One eyewitness saw bodies carted off in vans. "There were more than eight carloads filled with dead bodies." More than three hundred were killed and a far larger number wounded. Not a few of the more heavily wounded "were carried away and buried with the dead."[18]

The workers of Shanghai were shot down as "reactionaries" who were "disrupting the rear of the revolutionary army." Chiang Kai-shek issued a manifesto[19] accusing the Communists "of conspiring with the northern militarists to ruin the cause of the revolution."*

Foreign forces cooperated in the reign of terror now instituted throughout the city. The indirect contribution of the French authorities was the most notable, since the head of the French Concession detective force was Pock-marked Hwang Ching-yung who sent all his men into action against the workers. In the International Settlement foreign municipal police, working in cooperation with detachments of the British and Japanese defense forces, conducted a series of raids beginning on the night of the 11th, several of them in Chinese territory adjacent to the so-called extraconcessional North Szechuen Road. These measures were taken "with permission from the Nationalist military authorities at Lunghua."[20] On the night of April 14, British armored cars cooperated with squads of Japanese

* There is nothing new in the methods of the counterrevolution. The Jacobins were guillotined as "royalists" and "agents of Pitt." Lenin and Trotsky were "agents of the Kaiser." Years later Trotsky would become the "agent of Hitler" and Stalin would shoot thousands of dissident workers as "fascist spies" and "agents of the Mikado." In Spain workers would be shot down for "sabotaging the fight against fascism," and revolutionists would be branded as "agents of Franco." Only in Spain Stalin's party would play the role played by Chiang Kai-shek's executioners and the Mauser-squads of the Green Gang who, in Shanghai, mowed down the "agents of Chang Tso-lin."

marines in minor raids in the extraconcessional area during which machine guns were several times brought into play.[21] Everywhere rigid house-to-house searches were conducted and wholesale arrests made.[22] Prisoners were handed over in batches to the military headquarters at Lunghua. There they faced military courts set up under martial-law regulations issued by General Chiang Kai-shek. Controlled exclusively by military officers expressly empowered to "use their own discretion" in the event of any "emergency," these courts became the instrument for a system of official terrorism which in the coming months claimed the lives of literally thousands of workers, students, and others.

This reign of terror, directed above all at the workers and Communists, likewise for a time crossed the bounds of bourgeois property which it was instituted to keep inviolate. The Chinese bourgeoisie had found it necessary to call in Chiang Kai-shek and the gangsters against the workers. Now it was forced to submit itself to the predatory raids of its own rescuers. Like the French bourgeoisie, which, in 1852, "brought the slum proletariat into power, the loafers and tatterdemalions headed by the chief of the Society of December the Tenth,"[23] the Chinese bourgeoisie in 1927 elevated over itself the scum and riffraff of the cities headed by the chiefs of the Green Gang and Chiang Kai-shek. Like its French prototype, the Chinese bourgeoisie had now to pay heavily for professional services rendered. It "glorified the sword; now it is to be ruled by the sword.... It subjected public meetings to police supervision; now its own drawing-rooms are under police supervision.... It had transported the workers without trial; now the bourgeois are transported without trial...(their) money-bags are rifled.... The words of the bourgeoisie to the revolution were unceasingly those of St. Arsenius to the Christians: *Fuge, tace, quiesce!* The words of Bonaparte to the bourgeoisie are the same."[24]

Likewise spake Chiang Kai-shek to the moneyed men of Shanghai. Only to the admonitions to flee, be silent, and submit, he more explicitly added: "Pay!"

The bourgeoisie had rallied to Chiang's banner solely on the understanding that he would free them of the Communists, of the workers, of strikes and insurrections. With a ruthlessness that should have satisfied the most exacting and worried capitalist he acquitted himself of his task, effecting "such a clean-up of Communists as no northern general would have dared to do even in his own territory." But here came the hitch. "The anti-Communist campaign should have ended there and the people [*sic*] would have been happy. But every form of persecution was resorted to on the pretext of hunting Communists. Men were kidnapped and forced to make heavy contributions to military funds.... No reason or justice was evident...no courts of law were utilized.... Men possessing millions were held as Communists.... No one is safe, even at this moment, from the inquisition which has been established."[25] The bourgeoisie had been kept "breathless with alarm by talking about the menace of Red Anarchy." Now to hasten payment of his bill, Chiang "gave it a taste of the future it had prophesied."

> The plight of the Chinese merchant in and about Shanghai is pitiable. At the mercy of General Chiang Kai-shek's dictatorship the merchants do not know what the next day will bring, confiscations, compulsory loans, exile, or possible execution.... The military authorities have ordered the reorganization of the Chinese Chamber of Commerce and other institutions with new directors, presumably satisfactory to Chiang Kai-shek and Pai Chung-hsi, as they ordered the reorganization of the labor unions.... Outlawry against the better class of Chinese is rampant.[26]

When the raising of the $30,000,000 loan for the new Nanking government lagged, the merchants received "military advice to subscribe, with intimations that arrests may follow failure to do so."[27] Even Yung Chung-chin, the country's leading industrialist, was not exempt. Chiang asked him for half a million dollars. When Yung tried to haggle, Chiang forthwith had him arrested. Yung was thrown into prison and reportedly bought himself out with $250,000. Others had to pay more.[28]

Fascist or military dictators are like ferocious bodyguards who sit at the table of frightened employers and help themselves almost at will to the feast that is spread there. Chiang Kai-shek came forward to serve his class by asserting his mastery over it, remaining in the process, however, nothing but its hireling.[29] If Chiang Kai-shek appeared to be a brigand garbed in the authority of state power, it was only because he had served his masters well. The price they had to pay was nothing compared to what he had saved them by smashing the mass movement. The bankers and merchants proved this when they rallied quickly to the government Chiang set up at Nanking. They thought themselves more than well repaid when within a few days of the Shanghai coup came news of similar blows struck at the workers in Ningpo, Foochow, Amoy, Swatow, and Canton. In these cities under almost identical conditions, Chiang's military subordinates applied the same savage measures of repression against workers equally as confused, disoriented, disarmed, and helpless as their Shanghai comrades.[30]

In the name of the "national united front" and the "bloc of four classes," the Communist International and the Chinese Communist Party had offered sealed in bond the political liberty and independence of the Chinese working class. They had left the workers with nothing more than their lives to offer. "The Kuomintang suffers from a lack of revolutionary worker and peasant blood in its veins," the central organ of the Comintern had said on the very eve of the coup. "The Communist Party must infuse such blood and thereby radically change the situation."[31] What frightful content events had given these words! The Kuomintang had now demanded—and received its pound of flesh.

History was not yet done with its grisly joke. In Hankow Wang Ching-wei had arrived to tell how Chiang had agreed to hold a joint plenary session of the Kuomintang Central Executive Committee for the "peaceful" settlement of all disputes. News now came to Wuhan that Chiang was about to convene his own plenary session in Nanking with his own followers. On April 13, with the bloodletting in Shanghai already in full flow, the delegation of the Communist International in Hankow sent Chiang Kai-shek the following telegram:

> ...The delegation of the Third International is now in China, and has always been eager to visit you; but it could not be done because we have been visiting separately distant parts of the country.... Now comes news that you have decided to convene several members of the Central Committee and the Central Control Committee at Nanking. This act obviously violates your agreement with Wang Ching-wei that all questions of conflict inside the party would be placed before a plenary session of the Central Committee, which should be called at Wuhan and in which you would participate. Your convening a meeting of a few members of the Central Committee at this critical moment will naturally be interpreted by the enemies of the revolution as a rupture in the ranks of the Kuomintang. At this moment when international imperialism unites in an insolent attack upon the Chinese Nationalist revolution, the unity of the revolutionary forces is a supreme necessity.... In view of the dangerous situation, we advise you to abandon the projected Nanking conference, which will practically split the party. And the grave responsibility for breaking the Nationalist front at this critical moment will rest on you. We advise you to stand on the agreement to place all contentions on inner party questions before a plenary session of the Central Committee. If you take this advice, we shall be glad to visit Nanking in order to discuss with you personally all outstanding questions. The Third International will lend all its services to help the formation of a united Nationalist front of all revolutionary forces.—Signed, for the delegation of the Third International, M. N. Roy, April 13, 1927.[32]

Chiang Kai-shek is talking to the workers of Shanghai in the language of machine guns, but the delegates of the Communist International, Roy, Earl Browder, Jacques Doriot, Tom Mann, Borodin, and the rest, can still come scraping before him, begging for the "unity of the revolutionary forces." Perhaps the wires are clogged between Shanghai and Hankow. They are still "propitiating" the haughty general. His acts, they plead, "will practically split the party." Was the calling of a conference at Nanking all the more Chiang had to do to convince the gentlemen of the Comintern that a split in the party was exactly what he wanted and was driving for? Surely he was not loath to oblige! With the workers of Shanghai crushed and bleeding, the "grave responsibility" would rest lightly indeed upon his shoulders. Shanghai streets are running red with workers' blood, workers' bodies are still warm, still unburied, but if, *if* Chiang would only accept the "advice" of Stalin, Roy & Co., the Comintern would continue to "lend all its services" to the Nationalist united front. But if not? If Chiang turns them down? Why, the enemies of the revolution will understand that a rupture has occurred in the ranks of the Kuomintang! Damned clever these enemies of the revolution. This crawling plea to the executioner, who probably did not even stop in the work of slaughter to laugh at it, summed up the whole viciously anti-working class policy dictated by the Comintern to the Chinese Communist Party.

In Moscow, the delegates of the various parties in the International, to say nothing of the national sections themselves, had been kept completely in the dark concerning the developments in China. News of the Shanghai events came like some incredible, shattering catastrophe for which there was no warning. Information circulated in the Soviet capital by rumors alone. A whole day passed before any official statement was made. There is no record available of what went on behind the Kremlin walls during those hours. "After persistently denying reports of serious discord between Chiang Kai-shek and the extremists of the Kuomintang," a bourgeois correspondent was at last able to wire, "the Soviet authorities at Moscow this evening announced it was unfortunately true, and deplored the fact that fighting occurred at Shanghai between detachments of the Nationalist army and 'armed labor fraternities' and that the Nationalist army is busy disarming labor fraternities in other southern towns."[33] Throughout the ranks of the Comintern the surprise was complete, and consternation unbounded. It took days for an appreciation of the realities to sink in. Articles written by Comintern specialists right up to the very day of the coup d'état firmly denying any and all possibility of a coup were still published in the central organs of the Comintern for days after it occurred. On April 16, for example, *La Correspondance Internationale* featured an article by Ernst Thaelmann, the German Communist master-mind, who in a few years would hand his party helpless over to the Nazi executioners, which declared that "the bourgeois right wing in the Kuomintang and its leadership had been defeated"—in 1926! Chiang Kai-shek, he boasted, "must submit...to the supreme military council, whose majority is composed of Communists and members of the Kuomintang." The leadership, left-wingers and Communists together, "are struggling in common accord...for the democratic dictatorship of all the popular classes!" He ended deriding the "illusions" of the imperialists concerning Chiang Kai-shek's defection.[34]

On April 20—a full eight days after the coup— *La Correspondance Internationale* issued an article by Victor Stern of Prague which proudly announced that "the hopes of a split...and a compromise of the right wing with the militarists...are lies and have no chance of succeeding."[35] On the same date it reported in a "special number"—"The Treason of Chiang Kai-shek"![36] Complete failure and complete success for the traitors—all on the same day! On April 23 the same organ unblinkingly declared: "The treason of Chiang Kai-shek was not unexpected."[37]

Then came the first of a stream of documents and theses "justifying" the policies pursued and their results. The tone was set by Stalin himself on April 21 when he solemnly announced that "events have fully and entirely proved the correctness" of the Comintern "line."[38]

From Peking the well-informed Walter Duranty wired his conviction that "the Moscow leaders will do their utmost to restore Kuomintang unity, even at the sacrifice of the more extreme Chinese Communists."[39] He was right. Stalin had not yet finished making sacrifices on the altar of unity with the Chinese bourgeoisie. Events might prove Trotsky right, but the struggle against "Trotskyism" had to go on. In Shanghai, the Central Committee, in Malraux's words, "knowing that the Trotskyist theses were attacking the union with the Kuomintang, was terrified by any attitude which might, rightly or wrongly, seem to be linked to that of the Russian Opposition." So it obediently led the workers to the slaughter. The iron vise of the class struggle was more compelling than papal bulls from Moscow. The workers died for "unity," but the only unity achieved was the unity of the oppressors against all the oppressed. The tawdry, torn cloak of the "bloc of four classes" was ripped away. There was only the crucified body of the Shanghai working class. Under the corpse the militarists and the bankers gambled and bargained for the spoils.

11

Wuhan: "The Revolutionary Center"

Chiang Kai-shek's Shanghai coup d'état dealt a staggering blow to the revolution, but it need not have been mortal. Immense reserves still existed in Hunan and Hupeh where the revolutionary tide was just sweeping in, where the peasants were rising to seize the land and the workers in organization and power were already capable of becoming the leaders of the agrarian revolt and the guardians of its conquests. There was still time to mobilize and weld these forces for a new offensive, to crush the reaction which ruled in the east with Shanghai as its center. Although the organizations of the workers and peasants had been crushed and the ranks of the vanguard decimated in the areas under Chiang's control, nevertheless, on the morrow of April 12 the reaction was by no means firmly in the saddle.

Chiang Kai-shek had struck his blow for the imperialists and the Chinese bourgeoisie, but their full confidence was not yet his. He had slashed the arteries of the national revolutionary movement, but for the sake of maintaining his own position he could not entirely divest himself of its protective covering. He had still to claim for himself and for the Kuomintang the leadership of the "anti-imperialist" struggle. He had still to denounce the "unequal treaties" and demand, at least in form, their abrogation. Imperialist interests concentrated at Shanghai, content for the moment that Chiang had removed the immediate threat of the mass movement, sat back to wait for further proofs of his right to their benevolent guardianship.

"We would not for a moment underrate what General Chiang has done," wrote the *North China Daily News*. "With conditions as they were in this district a fortnight ago the only thing to do was to act ruthlessly and to shoot down the Communists without mercy. And, situated as General Chiang then was, it needed a good deal of moral courage to take this step and to act with the determination that he evinced. Furthermore, we fully recognize the truth of the old saying that 'Rome was not built in a day.' At the same time, much more must be done both by General Chiang Kai-shek and the Kuomintang before their assurances can be accepted at face value."[1]

From the Kiangsu-Chekiang bourgeoisie, Chiang extracted a heavy price for his efforts in their behalf, in extortion, terror, and taxation. Next to his impositions, the burdens of the old militarists must have seemed a dim and relatively pleasant memory. It was by no means a love feast between Chiang and his bourgeois mentors. He had to lash them savagely to him and they, without other alternative but destruction, had to suffer themselves to be lashed. For his plight was desperate. His military position was precarious. Under the counterattack of the Fengtien army Hsuchow fell and the Northerners mockingly dropped shells in his very capital at Nanking from their entrenchments across the river at Pukow. His army was in a state of disunity and demoralization.[2] Chiang, too, had to pay a price for turning on the mass movement. Without the masses who made it real, the legend of Nationalist invincibility waned. Victory came far less easily and the chances of defeat in the field instead loomed large before him.

A counteroffensive of the mass movement would obviously have heightened these chances. Isolated at the mouth of the Yangtze, Chiang could have been engulfed in a venging wave sweeping down the river from the aroused provinces. But this was impossible without a thorough-going reorientation of the Chinese Communist leadership and a drastic revision of the Comintern's policies. It was necessary to understand that the Shanghai disaster stemmed directly from the policy of the "bloc of four classes," from the subordination of the workers and peasants within the stifling framework of the Kuomintang. Step by step, northward from Canton, the execution of these policies had led to catastrophe. Without an understanding of this fact, without an analysis and evaluation of the reasons for the disastrous climax at Shanghai, the resolute turn in word and deed which alone could have cleared the path to a revolutionary triumph was unthinkable. Unfortunately for the Chinese revolution, it was even less thinkable that such a turn could be made by the Comintern under the leadership of Joseph Stalin.

In Moscow, on April 21, *Pravda* published Stalin's theses on "The Questions of the Chinese Revolution," in which he announced that the march of events culminating in the Shanghai tragedy "proved that the line laid down was the correct line."

"This was the line," he wrote, "of the close cooperation of the left-wingers and the Communists within the Kuomintang, of the consolidation of the unity of the Kuomintang...of making use of the right, of their connections and their experiences so far as they submitted to the discipline of the Kuomintang.... The events which followed have fully and entirely proved the correctness of this line."[3]

"We know very well how the bourgeoisie submitted to 'discipline,'" replied Trotsky in a counter-thesis which he tried vainly to get published, "and how the proletariat utilized the Rights, that is the big and middle bourgeoisie, their 'connections' (with the imperialists) and their 'experience' (in strangling and shooting the workers). The story of this 'utilization' is written in the book of the Chinese revolution with letters of blood. But this does not prevent the theses from saying: 'The subsequent events fully confirmed the correctness of this line.' Further than this no one can go!"[4]

The events, said Trotsky, had in reality fully revealed the ruinous nature of the official policy. That the class struggle could not be "exorcised by the idea of the national united front is far too eloquently proved by the bloody April events," he wrote, "a direct consequence of the policy of the bloc of four classes." To refuse to understand this was "to prepare a repetition of the April tragedy at a new stage of the Chinese revolution."

Only a new course, he urged, guaranteeing the organizational and political independence of the Chinese Communist Party and the formation of soviets as organs of dual power to lead and protect the agrarian revolution in the provinces offered any security against new and still greater disasters. The formation of Soviets meant the creation in town and countryside of authentic organs of the mass movement itself. Workers, peasants, and soldiers would democratically elect their own delegates, unite them in common assemblies sitting side by side with the organs of the regular government to guarantee the prosecution of the struggle for the land, the struggle against the militarists and the imperialists. This soldered unity at the base would provide a constant check and a constant threat to the petty bourgeois radicals who occupied the seats of power in Wuhan. It would render the masses independent of vacillation and compromises at the top. It would create, in a word, the dual power as a transition to a further stage in the revolution.

According to Stalin, however, complete reliance was still to be placed in the Kuomintang, in its "left" section, in the Wuhan government which he declared had now become the center of the revolution and on which the workers and peasants were to rely to carry on the fight against militarism and imperialism and to stand sponsor for the agrarian revolt. "Chiang Kai-shek's coup," he wrote,

> means that from now on there will be in South China two camps, two governments, two armies, two centers, the center of the revolution in Wuhan and the center of the counterrevolution in Nanking....
>
> This means that the revolutionary Kuomintang in Wuhan, by a determined fight against militarism and imperialism, will in fact be converted into an organ of the revolutionary democratic dictatorship of the proletariat and the peasantry.... (We must adopt)...the policy of concentrating the whole power in the country in the hands of the revolutionary Kuomintang.... It further follows that the policy of close cooperation between the Lefts and the Communists within the Kuomintang acquires special force and special significance...and that without such co-operation the victory of the revolution is impossible.

The slogan of soviets, therefore, was inadmissible, because it would mean

> issuing the slogan of a fight against the existing power in this territory...of the fight against the power of the revolutionary Kuomintang, for in this territory there

> is at present no power other than the power of the revolutionary Kuomintang. This means confusing the task of creating and consolidating mass organizations of the workers and peasants in the form of strike committees, peasants' leagues and peasant committees, trade councils, factory committees, etc., upon which the revolutionary Kuomintang is already based, with the task of setting up a soviet system as a new type of power in place of the revolutionary Kuomintang.

"These words fairly reek with the apparatus-like, bureaucratic conception of revolutionary authority," replied Trotsky.

> The government is not regarded as the expression and consolidation of the developing struggle of the classes, but as the self-sufficient expression of the will of the Kuomintang. The classes come and go, but the continuity of the Kuomintang goes on for ever. But it is not enough to call Wuhan the revolutionary center for it really to be that. The provincial Kuomintang of Chiang Kai-shek has an old, reactionary, mercenary bureaucracy at its disposal. What has the Left Kuomintang? For the time being nothing, or almost nothing. The slogan of soviets is a call for the creation of real organs of the new state power right through the transitional regime of a dual government.

For Stalin, in the coming period, "the main source of the power of the revolutionary Kuomintang is the further development of the revolutionary movement of the workers and peasants and the strengthening of their mass organizations, the revolutionary peasant committees, the workers' trade unions, and the other revolutionary mass organizations as the elements which are to form the Soviets in the future."

"What should be the course of these organizations?" asked Trotsky.

> We do not find a single word on this in the thesis. The phrase that these are "preparatory" elements for the soviets of the future is only a phrase and nothing more. What will these organizations do now? They will have to conduct strikes, boycotts, break the backbone of the bureaucratic apparatus, annihilate the counter-revolutionary military bands, drive out the large landowners, disarm the detachments of the usurers and the rich peasants, arm the workers and peasants, in a word, solve all the problems of the democratic and agrarian revolution...and in this way raise themselves to the position of local organs of power. But then they will be soviets, only a kind that are badly suited to their tasks.... During all the preceding mass movements, the trade unions were compelled to fulfill functions closely approaching the functions of soviets (Hong Kong, Shanghai, and elsewhere). But these were precisely the functions for which the trade unions were entirely insufficient. They do not at all embrace the petty bourgeois masses in the city that incline toward the proletariat. But such tasks as the carrying through of strikes with the least possible losses to the poorer population of the city, the distribution of provisions, participation in tax policy, participation in the formation of armed forces, to say nothing of carrying through the agrarian revolution in the provinces, can be accomplished with the necessary sweep only when the directing organization embraces not only all sections of the proletariat, but connects them intimately in the course of its activities with the poor population in the city and country.

> One would at least think that the military coup d'état of Chiang Kai-shek had finally hammered into the mind of every revolutionist the fact that trade unions separated from the army are one thing and united workers' and soldiers' soviets on the other hand are quite another thing. Revolutionary trade unions and peasant committees can arouse the hatred of the enemy no less than soviets. But they are far less capable than soviets of warding off its blows.
>
> If we are to speak seriously of the alliance of the proletariat with the oppressed masses in the city and country—not of an "alliance" between the leaders, a semi-adulterated alliance through dubious representatives—then such an alliance can have no other organizational form than that of soviets. This can be denied only by those who rely more upon compromising leaders than upon the revolutionary masses below.

While he rejected the slogan of soviets, Stalin declared that the "most important countermeasure (antidote) against the counterrevolution is the arming of the workers and peasants."

"The arming of the workers and peasants is an excellent thing," answered Trotsky,

> but one must be logical. In Southern China there are already armed peasants; they are the so-called National armies. Yet, far from being an "antidote to the counterrevolution" they have been its tool. Why? Because the political leadership, instead of embracing the masses of the army through soldiers' soviets, has contented itself with a purely external copy of our political departments and commissars, which, without an independent revolutionary party and without soldiers' soviets, have been transformed into an empty camouflage for bourgeois militarism.
>
> The theses of Stalin reject the slogan of soviets with the argument that it would be "a slogan of struggle against the government of the revolutionary Kuomintang." But in that case what is the meaning of the words: "The principal antidote to the counterrevolution is the arming of the workers and peasants"? Against whom will the workers and peasants arm themselves? Will it not be against the governmental authority of the revolutionary Kuomintang? The slogan of arming the workers and peasants, if it is not a phrase, a subterfuge, a masquerade, but a call to action, is not less sharp in character than the slogan of workers' and peasants' soviets. Is it likely that the armed masses will tolerate at their side or over them the governmental authority of a bureaucracy alien and hostile to them? The real arming of the workers and peasants under present circumstances inevitably involves the formation of soviets.... To declare that the time for soviets has not yet arrived and at the same time to launch the slogan for arming the workers and peasants is to sow confusion. Only the soviets, at a further development of the revolution, can become the organs capable of really conducting the arming of the workers and of directing these armed masses....
>
> It is said: The Hankow government is nevertheless a fact. Feng Yu-hsiang is a fact. Tang Sheng-chih is a fact, and they have armed forces at their disposal; neither the Wuhan government nor Feng Yu-hsiang nor Tang Sheng-chih wants soviets. To create soviets would mean to break with these allies. Although this argument is not openly formulated in the theses, it is nevertheless decisive for many comrades. We have already heard from Stalin on the Hankow government, the "revolutionary

centre," the "only governmental authority." At the same time an advertising campaign is launched for Feng Yu-hsiang in our party meetings, "a former worker," "a faithful revolutionist," "a reliable man," etc. All this is a repetition of the past mistakes under circumstances in which these mistakes can become even more disastrous. The Hankow government and the army command can be against soviets only because they will have nothing to do with a radical agrarian program, with a real break with the large landowners and the bourgeoisie, because they secretly cherish the thought of a compromise with the right. But then it becomes all the more important to form soviets. This is the only way to push the revolutionary elements of Hankow to the left and force the counterrevolutionists to retire."

Stalin's theses, therefore, rejected the perspective of the independent initiative of the Chinese masses through the soviets in favor of a bloc which continued to subordinate the masses to the bourgeoisie through the medium of the petty bourgeois radicals of the Left Kuomintang. This was the line which governed the subsequent course of the Chinese Communist Party. Trotsky's position, the demand for the unconditional independence of the Chinese Communist Party, the demand for soviets, the demand "to set the connection with the petty bourgeois masses higher than a connection with their party leaders, to rely upon ourselves, upon our own organizations, arms, and power" were mechanically excluded by the simple expedient of refusing them publication. The Chinese Communists were never given an opportunity to compare notes between the views of the Opposition and their own experience. They vaguely heard of "Trotskyism," a pernicious doctrine which required not arguments but epithets to refute it. The Russian workers and all sections of the Comintern received only the most bowdlerized versions of the Opposition's stand. Meanwhile, the broadest possible publicity was given to a series of articles expounding the official "line" laid down by Stalin.[5]

These articles all reproduced the remarkable argument that the slaughter of the Chinese workers at Shanghai was entirely in accord with the prognoses of the Comintern concerning the "inevitable" defection of the bourgeoisie from the national united front and that it could not have been prevented. With one voice they defended those very actions of the Chinese Communist Party which were later to be made the subject of such bitter attack.

Stalin's April theses said that the events that occurred in China in the spring of 1927 "fully and entirely proved the correctness" of the policies pursued by the Comintern. In the same document Stalin defended the failure of the Chinese Communists to resist Chiang Kai-shek at Shanghai, answering the charges of Trotsky and the Opposition that the debacle there was due directly to policies imposed upon the Chinese Communists by the Comintern.

"The Opposition is dissatisfied because the workers of Shanghai have not undertaken a decisive fight against the imperialists and their lackeys. They do not understand, however, that the revolution in China cannot develop at such a rapid tempo.... They do not understand that one cannot undertake a decisive struggle under unfavorable conditions...that not to avoid a decisive fight under unfavorable conditions (when it is possible to avoid it) means rendering easier the work of the enemies of the revolution."[6]

"It is not true that nothing was done," wrote another defender of the Comintern's strategy.

> The Communist Party undertook a broad campaign to denounce Chiang Kai-shek...and tried to develop the movement for the arming of the masses.... It is possible to discuss whether these measures were adequate, but it is certain that the slogan of an uprising of the workers of Shanghai and Nanking against Chiang Kai-shek would have been a thoughtless step, a beau geste, and nothing more. Only ultra-left loud-mouths could have urged an uprising at Shanghai at a moment when there were tens of foreign warships and tens of thousands of soldiers in the army of occupation. Exactly the opposite had to be done. It was necessary not to permit oneself to be provoked and to await the propitious moment for action. The coup d'état of Chiang Kai-shek, carried out under the pressure and *under the protection of armed foreign imperialism, could not have been prevented.*[7]

In a chapter hastily added to a report made to the Moscow party organization in April, Bukharin defended the policy of "hiding arms and not accepting (?) battle" and declared further that the "authority of the Communist Party will necessarily increase, since long before the armed coup, the Communist Party had conducted a vigorous campaign against the bourgeois 'dictator.'"[8] A little later, even after Bukharin had begun to assail the Chinese Communists for carrying out the policies he himself had dictated, he still added: "It is necessary to affirm that even had they done all that could have been done, we could not, in the present period, have triumphed over Chiang Kai-shek in direct conflict.... The imperialists could have shattered in blood the workers of Shanghai in a single day's armed conflict."[9]

One lengthy article was devoted precisely to proving that the Communist Party of China had unflinchingly followed the directives of the Comintern, and, after citing the progress of the mass movement, it added: "All this proves that the young Communist Party of China has in recent times kept aloof from any vacillations and hesitations and has grasped the fact that the tactics of stimulating the mass movement are the only right tactics for the vanguard of the Chinese proletariat."[10]

They all made it perfectly plain that the Communists would at all costs continue to cling to the Kuomintang ("It would be a great mistake to hand over the Kuomintang banner to the clique of Chiang Kai-shek," cried Bukharin[11]), and would concentrate, primarily and above all, on bringing the masses of workers and peasants into the Kuomintang in support of the government at Wuhan which "is fighting not only the imperialists and the Chinese militarists, but the remnants of the feudal system...to democratize the country, to install the rule of the toiling masses.... It has put the agrarian revolution on the order of the day."[12] All confidence, all support to the "revolutionary government of Wuhan," to the

"Left Kuomintang," which had become nothing more nor less than the "Communist Kuomintang."[13]

These policies and this estimate of the situation, wrote Trotsky, meant "to bring one's head voluntarily to the slaughter. The bloody lesson of Shanghai passed without leaving a trace. The Communists, as before, were being transformed into cattle herders for the party of the bourgeois executioners."[14]

Events with remarkable swiftness soon proved who was right. Even before the Eighth Plenum of the Executive Committee of the Communist International convened a few weeks later to place the rubber stamp of its approval on Stalin's theses, the generals of the "revolutionary Kuomintang" had begun the slaughter of workers and peasants as helpless as the militants mowed down in Shanghai by Chiang Kai-shek. The Wuhan government, nominated by Stalin to sponsor the agrarian revolution, had already endorsed its bloody suppression. To see how this happened, return to Shanghai and there join the exodus of Communists and others fleeing up the Yangtze to escape Chiang's headsmen and with them arrive at the confluence of the Han and Yangtze rivers where the three great cities of Central China, Wuchang, Hankow, and Hanyang, known collectively as Wuhan, hug the muddy banks. Here was Stalin's "revolutionary center," the capital of the "Left Kuomintang," without whose cooperation the victory of the revolution, according to Stalin, was impossible.

Who were these paragons of revolt without whom all was lost? Who were these revolutionary stalwarts who required no workers', peasants', and soldiers' soviets to hold the whip of the masses over their heads? First there was Wang Ching-wei, the most "reliable" ally of all. Wang, whom we have seen bend and fold under Chiang Kai-shek's pressure in Canton and Shanghai, epitomized the petty bourgeois politician, flaccid and fearful, indecisive in all things except his readiness to blench and retreat before his big bourgeois betters. There was George Hsu-chien, one-time Confucian scholar and Christian, who could deliver perorations so scorching as to singe even his Communist colleagues. Today his shouts for imperialist blood were louder than any. Tomorrow, trembling and frightened, he would be the first to seek refuge in flight. There was Ku Meng-yu, who as early as May 1926, had characterized the peasant upsurge as "a movement of vandals, scoundrels, and idle peasants." And Ku was editor of the central organ of the "revolutionary" Kuomintang! There was Sun Fo, son of the dead Leader, who changed his views and allegiances so often that even his own colleagues, themselves scarcely distinguished by qualities of steadfastness, contemptuously called him "Sun Wu-kung" after the mythical Chinese monkey who covered ten thousand miles in a single leap.

Best known to the foreigners was the brilliant Eugene Chen, artisan of the well-turned phrase, master of diplomatic invective but of nothing else, barred by his ignorance of the Chinese language (he was born in Trinidad) from playing any role but that of spokesman to the powers.

Soong Ching-ling, youthful widow of Sun Yat-sen, was nominally among the leaders. Arthur Ransome shrewdly called her "an enthusiast, happier in devotion to her late husband's ideals than, for example, in unravelling a complicated political situation."[15] Of them all, Teng Yen-ta, successor to Liao Chung-kai as head of the political department of the army, was a petty bourgeois radical of the more dynamic type, with a courage of his convictions that lifted him a long notch above his fellows.

These were the principal figures who, with their respective satellites, made up the Wuhan government. These were the main props of the "revolutionary center." Six months later, addressing the Fifteenth Congress of the Communist Party of the Soviet Union, Chitarov, relating the events at Wuhan, said: "One thing was left out of sight in connection with this—that while the bourgeoisie was retreating from the revolution [!] the Wuhan government did not even think of leaving the bourgeoisie. Unfortunately among the majority of our comrades, this was not understood; they had illusions with regard to the Wuhan government. They considered the Wuhan government almost an image, a prototype of the democratic dictatorship of the proletariat and peasantry."[16]

But it was on May 18 at the Eighth Plenum that Trotsky had warned: "The leaders of the Left Kuomintang of the type of Wang Ching-wei and Co. will inevitably betray you if you follow the Wuhan heads instead of forming your own independent soviets. The agrarian revolution is a serious thing. Politicians of the Wang Ching-wei type, under difficult conditions, will unite ten times with Chiang Kai-shek against the workers and peasants."[17]

It was to take less than three months for this prophecy to be fulfilled.

By strapping the Communist Party into a bloc with these leaders, Stalin-Bukharin and Co. considered that they were realizing at Wuhan the "bloc of the workers, peasants, and petty bourgeoisie." In reality these petty bourgeois leaders were infinitely closer to the so-called national or big bourgeoisie than they were to the masses of workers and peasants. Like its prototypes elsewhere, the Chinese petty bourgeoisie is uniform neither in character nor in interests, but is heterogeneous and stratified. The economic interests of the uppermost layers, the small landlords, shopkeepers, master artisans, and petty entrepreneurs, are closely linked to those of the big landlords, the big city capitalists, the banks, and, in the final analysis, with foreign finance capital. Any secondary contradictions pale before the essential agreement on the preservation of existing property relations. Hold a magnifying glass over your upper petty bourgeois and you will observe all the stigmata of his big bourgeois cousin.

Your small landlord not only rents out land, but is probably also the proprietor of a rice shop or pawnshop or some small manufacturing enterprise in town. Your shopkeeper is also an employer of labor, an exploiter of apprentices, who probably invests his small surplus either directly in land from which he extracts interest in the form of rent, or in loans to peasants at usurious rates. Moreover, the links between the petty exploiters in town and country, forged of common and often identical economic interests, are likely to be welded by family and clan relationships of an exceedingly compelling character. As is the case with the big capitalists and landlords, the interests of the upper petty bourgeoisie are bound up with the perpetuation of feudal methods of exploitation in the countryside. Between these two strata there is a difference of scale, not of kind.

On the other hand, the lower strata, the basic masses of the petty bourgeoisie, are the poor of town and country, exploited artisans, handicraftsmen, shop employees, apprentices, middle and poor peasants and agricultural laborers who comprise the overwhelming mass of the rural population. The economic interests of these lower layers are in direct contradiction not only to those of the big bourgeoisie, but even more directly to those of the petty entrepreneurs, landlords, and merchants. This antagonism links them economically and politically to the industrial proletariat in the cities.

Carrying these distinctions to the plane where they find political expression, one must look for the class roots of these Left Kuomintang leaders not among the exploited poor, but in the counting houses of the petty exploiters. That is why the rising demand of the apprentices for liberation from slave-like conditions, the demands of the shop employees for an improved livelihood, the demands of the workers in the factories, and, above all, the demand of the poor peasants for land, appeared to these leaders not as legitimate aspirations to be fought for and espoused, but as shocking "excesses" which threatened to upset the whole economic applecart to which they were accustomed. But it is precisely because these petty bourgeois exploiters occupy a secondary, auxiliary, and often a middleman's, position in the economic scheme of things, that they are dependent upon their big bourgeois brothers and must look to them for protection of their political interests. They may hate their masters, but they cower and cringe before them, for they have an unholy horror of being forced into the black ranks of the exploited below. They know they cannot stand alone and they readily become the middlemen not only in the field of economic exploitation, but in political repression of the masses as well.

Thus it was in Hankow in the spring of 1927. In Nanking the bourgeoisie had found its defender and its tool in Chiang Kai-shek. In Hankow it was likewise compelled to seek the aid of the militarists and found its man in Tang Sheng-chih. Tang was himself a big Hunan landlord, and upon him the Hankow Chamber of Commerce and related gentry relied for protection. In the relations of the Left Kuomintang leaders to Tang Sheng-chih and the other military leaders we will discover, therefore, an almost mathematically perfect expression of the class relationships which have just been described. For a peculiarly apt figure of speech in this connection, history is profoundly indebted to Michael Borodin, high adviser to the National government at Wuhan.

Anna Louise Strong asked him about the civilian and military power in Wuhan. She thought that "if the civil power stood firm, the military would have to yield."

"He laughed. 'Did you ever see a rabbit before an anaconda,' he said, 'trembling, knowing it is going to be devoured, yet fascinated? That's the civic power before the military in Wuhan, staring at the military and trembling.' "

"So he had few illusions," comments Miss Strong, "regarding the courage of the Chinese intellectuals with whom he was working and who made up the Wuhan Government. But he was their chief source of steadfastness and revolutionary purpose to the end."[18]

A fitting epitaph! Stalin, the Comintern, and Borodin confined themselves in China to an attempt to inject into an anemic and frightened rabbit the strength and ability to defeat the anaconda. Instead of responding to the treatment, the rabbit rolled its pink eyes and died, and the anaconda devoured him. But Borodin and the Comintern stood by the rabbit, pumping into it "steadfastness and revolutionary purpose to the end"—to the very end! Not all the pages that must follow could more aptly describe the role and fate of the Left Kuomintang and its Moscow mentors. For it was nothing less than the cooperation with this rabbit that Stalin declared to be indispensable to the victory of the revolution. Somewhat better acquainted with rabbits, Borodin already knew that the anaconda would in the end have his meal. He simply assumed that the revolution was impossible. "You cannot communize poverty," he liked to tell impressed foreign journalists.

One day the same lady remarked in her naive way to Borodin and Chen Tu-hsiu that since she had come to Russia too late for the revolution there, she had come to China earlier "in order to be on time." "Borodin turned to Chen with a smile and said: 'Miss Strong is unfortunate in her dates. She came too late to Russia and now she has come very much too early for China.' A look of prim understanding passed between them which at the time I did not quite understand.* For in common with the rest of the world and with all except the Kuomintang inner committees, I still thought of Wuhan as revolutionary, not knowing how far the swing toward the right had carried it."[19]

---

* Chen Tu-hsiu's idea of the Communist Party's perspectives was illustrated by the story of an interview between him and the arch-reactionary "elder statesman," Wu Chih-hui, as related by the latter: "I said to Mr. Chen: 'Sun Wen (Sun Yat-sen) once said that it would take thirty years for the revolutionary party to make a complete conquest of China.... And you, how long do you think it would require for the Communists to conquer China?' Without a moment's hesitation...Mr. Chen replied 'In twenty years Leninist Communism will be the absolute master of all China.' 'Then,' said I, 'our revolutionary party has only nineteen years to live? He laughed without answering." (Tr. by Wieger, *Chine Moderne,* 138–39.)

This conversation took place on March 6, 1927. Wu could not support the notion of a mere nineteen-year breathing space, and he pressed Chiang Kai-shek to hasten his preparations to smash the Communists once and for all to ward off the evil day well in advance.

The "rest of the world"—and Stalin as well as Miss Strong—thought Wuhan was revolutionary. Only the Kuomintang "inner committees," shying with fear from the mass movement—and Trotsky in Moscow knew otherwise, the one through self-appreciation, the other by virtue of a Marxist analysis.

The world's headlines, including those of the international Communist press, streamed the news of "Red Hankow"—Stalin called Wuhan the "revolutionary center"—because they made the not negligible error of identifying the mass movement with the Wuhan government; because the Wuhan leaders still found it useful and necessary to smear themselves in the protective grease of revolutionary and radical phrases. That the imperialist press, especially the British, which saw red on the least provocation, raved hysterically about Wuhan "Bolsheviks" was natural. That Communists who claimed to speak in the name of Marx, Engels, Lenin, and the October revolution followed suit was monstrous. According to Stalin, Chiang Kai-shek's coup had cleared the field for the "revolutionary center" at Wuhan, and the "revolutionary Kuomintang" would now proceed to carry out the agrarian revolution, expel the imperialists, abolish feudalism, destroy the militarists, and thus ensure the "non-capitalist road of development" for the Chinese revolution. To this end the Communists, and behind them the masses, were ordered to submit to the control and the discipline of the Kuomintang and the Wuhan government.

"The strength of the revolutionary government and the Kuomintang," wrote Jacques Doriot, "resides essentially in the support of the working masses.... With its three million members the General Labour Federation...unreservedly supports the National Government. The Peasant Unions, with their 15,000,000 adherents...also support it.... All these forces are grouping themselves around the Kuomintang banner to realize...the liberation of China from imperialist tutelage, liquidation of the forces of reaction, feudalism, and militarism, and Socialism...the development of its economy on other paths than those of capitalism."[20]

What Stalin, Browder, Doriot, and the other gentlemen from Moscow overlooked was that the rallying of the masses to the Wuhan government was one thing. The rallying of the Wuhan government to the masses was quite another. "The world thought Hankow 'Communist.' But the Left Kuomintang ruled, and the Left Kuomintang was neither Bolshevik nor Socialist, and the generals who shared their condominium in Hankow certainly opposed everything Communist." This was the picture given Louis Fischer by Borodin long after the event.[21] Here was the real Wuhan, not in Moscow's fanciful and over-cunning resolutions, but in fact.

According to the theory of the "revolutionary center," Chiang Kai-shek's coup, by some profound alchemy, resulted in a clear-cut situation in which the forces of the revolution (Wuhan) were diametrically opposed to the forces of the counter-revolution (Nanking). "For the initial moment" (long enough for the ink to dry on Stalin's theses?), "it was characteristic that there was a full contradiction between these two centers," wrote the Comintern "expert" on China, Mif.[22] Or, as the Chinese Communist leaders put it: "The secession of the big bourgeoisie relieved the national revolutionary movement of the causes of internal conflict and disharmony and caused the movement as a whole to be directed to one simple goal."[23] Could anything have been simpler?

But let us see. In just a few weeks startled readers of *Izvestia* would learn that the Left Kuomintang leaders proved to be "playthings in the hands of the generals."[24] Within the same brief space of days readers of the foreign Communist press would suddenly be informed that "in connection with the numerous attempts of the numerous generals and generalissimos to bring the trade unions under their thumb...there is very little, if anything, to distinguish the generals and generalissimos of the counterrevolutionary camp from the generals and generalissimos of the Nationalist Government."[25] Mif himself was forced to record that "in the end...the Wuhan leaders knelt before Nanking."[26]

How did this happen? How did this "full contradiction" so quickly and so completely dissolve? Ah, that was the alchemy of it. And the formula? Elementary, my dear Watson: "The dialectics of the class struggle." There is nothing, after all, quite like "dialectics" to extricate oneself from a tight spot. But let us look for a slightly more honest, more accurate and infinitely more dialectic explanation. For this it is necessary to travel some distance, in time and in space, from the events. Here is what we find in the pages of a work published under the auspices of the Chinese Communist Party in 1931:

> The rupture between Nanking and Wuhan did not bring about the immediate and distinct appearance in Wuhan of the bloc of workers, peasants, and petty bourgeoisie. To the contrary, not only the power of the bourgeoisie, but also that of the landlords and the gentry still existed there. The latter especially held great power. The internal conflict in Wuhan possessed the same social features as that in Nanking, that is, the democratic revolution of the workers and peasants was struggling against the gentry and the landlord class. The internal decomposition of Wuhan had begun even before the Wuhan government was completely organized.[27]

So Stalin to the contrary notwithstanding, there never was a revolutionary center at Wuhan! In Wuhan, as in Nanking, there was the power of the bourgeoisie and the landlords (the latter "especially great") and the Wuhan government was rent by the class struggle and had begun to fall apart, that is, it had begun to fall at Nanking's feet, even before it ever fully came into existence! To advance this view in 1928 or in 1931 was apparently good "dialectics." To breathe it in 1927 was counterrevolutionary Trotskyism.

Between the "Left" Kuomintang in Wuhan and the "Right" Kuomintang in Nanking in the spring of 1927, there was no class contradiction, but a professional rivalry between two groups representing essentially the same class forces. The "Left" at Wuhan, regardless of the phraseology used by its radical leaders, was no less bourgeois in character, no less opposed to the agrarian revolution, than the "Right" at Nanking. This was the basis for Trotsky's view that the subordination of the Communists and the masses to the "Left" Kuomintang, led by Wang Ching-wei and Tang Sheng chih, was no less criminal than the subordination, in the immediately preceding period, to the "Right" Kuomintang headed by Chiang Kai-shek. That is why the Opposition demanded the unconditional independence of the Chinese Communist Party. That is why it demanded the swift and thorough application of the slogans of the agrarian revolution, the formation of workers', peasants', and soldiers' soviets capable of leading the struggle and of snatching the power from the weak hands of Wang Ching-wei and Co. before Chiang Kai-shek did, capable of crushing the counterrevolution by winning over the decisive sections of the soldiery and of disintegrating and destroying the power of the generals.

Struggle had to be waged against the bourgeois Kuomintang because it was unalterably opposed to the agrarian revolution—and the agrarian revolution is the heart and soul of China's future. Refusal to wage this struggle—and it could have been waged only with the weapon of soviets—meant the abandonment and betrayal of the peasants, in a word, the strangling of the revolution itself. But Stalin opposed the course of irreconcilable struggle against the Kuomintang, for he saw in it not the party of the bourgeoisie, but a peculiar kind of "revolutionary parliament" in which hostile classes would learn, under Stalin's tutelage, how to imagine a community of interests where in reality none existed. For Stalin Wuhan was "revolutionary" and its "revolutionary government" would lead and extend the agrarian revolution. Wuhan would overthrow Chiang Kai-shek. Wuhan would in the shortest time become nothing less than the "democratic dictatorship of the proletariat and peasantry"—a phenomenon never seen or known in all history.[28] Wuhan would do all these, promised Stalin, if the Communist Party and the mass organizations supported it with all their might and did not, themselves, prematurely take the road of soviets, the road to power. Thus it was spoken, and thus it had to be. The fate of the Chinese Revolution was laid in the lap of the Left Kuomintang. What came of it there is too soon told.

The "Revolutionary Center" at Work

The Communist International declared that Chiang Kai-shek's Shanghai coup d'état was entirely in accord with its own predictions. It went further. It declared that the slaughter of the Shanghai workers "could not have been prevented."

In Wuhan the Left Kuomintang could not quite approximate this blandness. "A long time ago we knew of this intrigue," said the Kuomintang Executive Committee in a manifesto anathematizing Chiang, "and now we regret that we failed to act until it is too late. For this we offer sincere apology."[1]

"It is to be regretted that the wrong choice of a military commander has led to such difficulties," it also said. "The comrades of the party, prompted by the spirit of leniency, have again and again, for the sake of saving the party, overlooked, though reluctantly, many irregularities."[2]

The fact of the matter was that the Comintern, too, had watched Chiang's progress, paralyzed, helpless, and silent, hoping against hope that he would not take it by the throat. But now, contrary to their best advice, he had done so. Now, and now only, the representatives of the Comintern publicly described the terror launched by Chiang from the very beginning of the Northern Expedition. They listed now as facts the charges against which the Communist press all over the world had hotly defended Chiang as a victim of imperialist slander. Earl Browder, who only three weeks ago had enthusiastically described the idyllic relations between the army and the masses in Kiangsi, now gave names, dates, and places in describing the ruthless terror waged by Chiang Kai-shek throughout the province, beginning as early as February.[3]

"Chiang Kai-shek's counterrevolutionary activities have culminated in the establishment of a rival 'nationalist government' at Nanking," declared the Hankow delegation of the Communist International.

> This act of his is more unpardonable than his previous numerous acts of violation, namely, the coup d'état of March 20, attacks upon the revolutionary wing of the Kuomintang, suppression of the workers' and peasants' movement in Kiangsi and

> Chekiang, and finally the murder of Shanghai workers. We watched all these violent actions of Chiang Kai-shek and his agents with great anxiety, but hoped that he would hesitate to turn a barefaced traitor to the nationalist movement. At this critical period of the nationalist revolution preservation of the united front is so imperative that all crimes of those who fight against imperialism can be temporarily overlooked. But...Chiang Kai-shek's crimes did not stop at the massacre of Kiangsi and Shanghai workers. They culminated in a revolt against the People's party and the People's government.[4]

Like the leaders of the Left Kuomintang, the Comintern delegates were quite prepared to "overlook" negligible backslidings like the repression of the mass movement and the ruthless slaughter of workers and peasants. Had Chiang been willing to preserve the external appearances of "unity," he would have been accorded every support, every concession he demanded. This the Comintern delegation had already made plain in their telegram of April 13, to which we have already referred, and which they now once more cited as proof of their readiness to conciliate. News of Chiang's call for a rump conference at Nanking reached Hankow, apparently, on the eve of the delegation's scheduled departure for a visit to the Generalissimo.

> We immediately telegraphed him to call off the meeting and stand by the agreements he had made in Shanghai with Comrade Wang Ching-wei, to bring all the disputed questions before a plenary session of the Central (Executive) Committee, in which he should participate. In the same telegram we informed him that should he take our advice we would visit him in order to discuss ways and means of preserving the unity of the revolutionary forces in the face of the imperialist attack. He did not answer our telegram and proceeded with his plan to disrupt the party.[5]

Chiang Kai-shek, it seems, did not hesitate to "turn a barefaced traitor." That was his "most unpardonable" crime of all, for on that hinged the entire strategy of the Comintern. They had simply hoped he would not do so. They were wrong. The "hopes" of the bourgeoisie and the imperialists proved to be better founded. The workers of Shanghai paid with their heads for this "error" in judgment.

Wang Ching-wei, too, belonged to the Coué school of revolutionary politics. He now had to explain what had transpired in April during his meeting in Shanghai with Chiang Kai-shek. "I still hoped for the awakening," he related after April 12, "I still hoped that he would sever his connections with reaction.... I promised him to propose to the Central Kuomintang the calling of a conference to settle all outstanding disputes.... When I arrived here, I was still hoping against hope for a change. I made no attack against Chiang in my report."[6]

So Wang also in Wuhan now nursed the shattered fragment of lost hopes. He had left Shanghai apparently convinced that he had persuaded Chiang to put off drastic action and await the "peaceful and legal" liquidation of his grievances. The events of April 12 showed that Chiang had merely used Wang to cover the preparations for his coup, knowing that the time for formal niceties had come to an end. Wang, only two days back in Wuhan, was first confounded and then furious. He too wanted the mass movement checked. Only he wanted it done "lawfully." Now matters had been taken out of his hands.

There was nothing of the irreducible antagonism between Wang Ching-wei ("the revolutionary center") and Chiang Kai-shek ("the counterrevolutionary center"), in which Joseph Stalin now so fondly believed. Wang had been ready enough in Shanghai to bow before Chiang's demand for a further ban on the Communists (i.e. the mass movement), and the recognition of Chiang's virtual dictatorship. But Wang Ching-wei visualized himself as the heir and successor of Sun Yat-sen, as the chief standard-bearer of the national revolution. And nothing smelled sweeter in his nostrils than the prerogatives of office. Chiang's act in setting up a rival government at Nanking mortally affronted these pretensions. Wang was dismayed to discover that the bourgeoisie preferred Chiang's services and Chiang's methods to his own. His chief concern was not the desire gratuitously attributed to him by Stalin and the Comintern, to further the struggle of the masses against imperialism, feudalism, and even the bourgeoisie. Wang was concerned now, as Chiu Chiu-pei later admitted, with ascertaining the ways and means "of competing with Chiang for the sympathy of the south-eastern (Chekiang-Kiangsu) bourgeoisie."[7] Wang, the petty bourgeois radical leader on whom the Comintern now pinned its faith, hoped to prove to the bourgeoisie that Chiang "oppressed" them and that he, Wang, would save them from the mass movement and the impositions of the militarists. For this it was necessary to discredit Chiang, if he could, and it was to this end that the Wuhan Kuomintang issued its mandate of April 17 anathematizing Chiang and all his associates, cataloging their crimes, expelling them from the Party, and depriving them of all their government posts.[8]

But while it was willing to go this far, Wuhan tacitly recognized the essential affinity between itself and Nanking by refusing to reinforce its mandate with a declaration of war against Chiang, the only possible means of making it effective. Indeed, on the morrow of his coup, Chiang Kai-shek was especially vulnerable. His troops were demoralized and his military position was precarious. But when asked if they would smash the rebel, Wuhan leaders blandly indicated that they would leave that task to the workers and peasants in Chiang's own territory. They would soon rise against Chiang and his friends, promised the Kuomintang leader, Tan Yen-kai, "so the Nationalist government does not consider their revolt of serious importance, because they are bound to fail."[9] Borodin, too, dutifully echoed this pious hope. He was asked by a Japanese correspondent if the Nanking militarists would be suppressed by force of arms. "This will hardly be necessary," he answered, "the process of disintegration has already set in in Nanking. Allow them a little time to run their course and they will be finished from within."[10] So sure was Chiang of his seeming enemies in the Wuhan government that he made no attempt, for the time being, to attack them by military means. He had his own ideas about who would be "finished from within."

"All hostility and personal accounts notwithstanding and despite the actual break, some ties with Chiang Kai-shek remained intact." writes Fischer, giving Borodin's post-factum analysis of the relationships that existed on the morrow of Chiang's coup. "Much divided Hankow from Nanking. But something [!] drew them together."[11] To regain the confidence of the bourgeoisie, Wuhan knew it would get nowhere by fighting Chiang. It had first to disembarrass itself of the mass movement and the Communists. Wang Ching-wei, Tang Sheng-chih, and Co., figured that if they could first wrest Honan province from the Fengtien armies, again in the words of Fischer-Borodin, "they could come to terms with Chiang Kai-shek."[12] A military victory culminating in the occupation of Peking, that was the thing. Assuredly it would send their stock up and Chiang's down on the bourgeois exchanges of the country. If they could swing it (and the success of their plan depended entirely, as we shall see, on the military cooperation of Feng Yu-hsiang), they would become the undisputed rulers of the country and Chiang would have to tail along behind. Such were the real calculations of the "revolutionary" leaders of the "revolutionary" Kuomintang. That they jibed perfectly with the private Napoleonic aspirations of Tang Sheng-chih was, moreover, no accident. The Hunan general, now daily protesting his revolutionary loyalty, dreamed of the day when he too would have completely in his hands a movement powerful enough to betray in his own interests. So simultaneously with the expulsion of Chiang Kai-shek, the Wuhan government issued orders for the advance into Honan and troops were immediately set in motion. But Peking could not be taken in a day, and in the interim the Wuhan leaders had to face the multifold difficulties created for them by Chiang's coup and, what was more difficult still, they had to cope with the mass movement.

The Shanghai events had enormously emboldened the reactionary forces throughout the country. They had occurred at the time when the mass movement was reaching its highest point in the central provinces. In Hunan and Hupeh the peasants, in their own plebeian way, were beginning to translate words into action. They were beginning to strike out for themselves. The Wuhan leaders tried to stand between the forces which were coming face to face with each other for the final reckoning. While the issue was being decided in the fields and towns, the petty bourgeois radicals of Wuhan continued to feed upon the delusion that with their committees, their pompous decrees and pronouncements, they were settling the fate of the nation. Actually the gap between the professions and the practices of these flabby politicians was being rapidly closed by events over which they exercised no control. The Wang Ching-weis were not Chiang Kai-sheks. Between these closing clamps they would not strike out boldly, but would squirm and wriggle, check and demoralize, vacillate and temporize—until more aggressive class agents than they seized the reins from their hands.

Even as they declaimed their defiance of the right, the heat of the class struggle scorched the filmy wings of their "Leftism." Before long, they would fly and flit no more. But to the last flutter they would try to prove that they, too, could show pertinacity in one thing, the protection of bourgeois property. Wuhan would try to show the imperialists, the factory owners and shopkeepers, the landlords and the gentry, that not Chiang alone spoke in their name.

The Shanghai events had put an entirely different complexion on things as far as the imperialist powers were concerned. They understood clearly that the balance of forces had shifted in their favor. Until now they had been giving way, step by step, before the advance of a mass movement they knew they could not smash themselves. They probed gingerly for the point at which they could come to terms with the Chinese bourgeoisie. The bombardment of Nanking hastened the bargain. On April 12 it was sealed. Now their tone stiffened. The flow of foreign armed forces to strategic ports increased. On April 21, the 9,750-ton cruiser *Vindictive*, largest British warship in Chinese waters, joined a line of thirty-five foreign warships stretching for a mile and a half along the Hankow Bund. Within a week additional vessels arriving from Shanghai increased the total to forty-two, drawn from the navies of Britain, Japan, the United States, France, and Italy.

In Tokyo the newly-installed premier, Baron Tanaka, "clearly indicated that the period of leaning back in China affairs was at an end."[13] Correspondents in Tokyo reported that "Chiang Kai-shek's successful stroke against the Reds brings that change in the Chinese situation which Japanese observers have been hoping for."[14] In London it was joyfully announced that "the diplomatic situation as regards China...has undergone a change.... The situation has completely changed. [The Wuhan Government] is no longer in the saddle and in a few weeks may have faded from the picture altogether."[15] In the United States an abrupt easing of the official pulse was reflected in the disappearance of China news from the front pages of the metropolitan press.[16]

From an attitude of cool defiance toward the foreign powers, nourished by the diplomatic successes which had followed the seizure of the British concession by the Hankow workers in January, the Wuhan leaders abruptly resumed the posture of respectful supplication. Anti-imperialist posters were torn off Hankow's walls. Foreign missions and church buildings, occupied by workers, peasants, and soldiers, and used as headquarters for mass organizations, were restored to their owners. "The foreign office, instead of being merely courteous and sympathetic, had now become energetic and even decisive in foreigners' difficulties," wrote a delighted Hankow resident.[17] "The topic everywhere," wired the correspondent of the *New York Times* on April 25, "is the metamorphosis which has occurred in the last two or three days."[18]

New edicts were issued by the government and in duplicate by the Hupeh General Labor Union restraining the police powers of the pickets and forbidding any actions which might irritate foreigners or prejudice foreign property and trade. Detailed penalties were prescribed for workers guilty of disobeying these orders.[19]

Foreign Minister Eugene Chen cited these decrees in a personal appeal to the U.S. consul-general and a delegation of businessmen whom he saw on April 23. "The Minister outlined the measures which are being taken to assist the restoration of conditions for the conduct of foreign business and trade, and he emphasized the fact that labor had resolved to impose on itself revolutionary discipline in order to carry out these measures of the government."[20]

The government sharply called to task workers in Changsha who had called a general strike against American enterprises because of the U.S. Navy's role in the bombardment at Nanking. The workers were ordered to evacuate the YMCA they occupied and to suspend their strike against American coal and oil firms in the Hunan capital on the grounds that "any free and unrestrained action, no matter whether in itself good or bad [!], must seriously interfere with the unification policy of the party and at the same time inflict a heavy blow upon the anti-imperialist movement.... Any undue action...must now be rectified and its recurrence in the future must be prevented."[21]

While the Wuhan press began explaining at length the need for "adapting" the government's foreign policy,[22] the Wuhan leaders crudely attempted to apply the traditional Chinese policy of playing off one barbarian against the other. The hopes aroused in Nationalist breasts by the seemingly contradictory zigzags of American policy had been dashed by the events at Nanking, where American guns had spoken louder than all the rest. But Japan's guns had kept silent, and a Japanese subaltern had even sought refuge in hara-kiri from the shame of his government's forbearance. The Wuhan anti-imperialists turned disingenuously to Japan with special appeals.

"Whereas the Chinese revolution is affecting the very roots of British imperialism," wrote the official organ of the Kuomintang Central Executive Committee, "it assists a friendly Japan in stabilizing her position as a world power and can offer her all possibilities for unprecedented development of her trade and prosperity." The British and American imperialists, they went on, were trying everywhere to block Japan's expansion. "The best course for Japan's politicians would be to take sides with the Chinese nation against her enemies, to prove that Japan does not approve or assist either the militarists or the imperialist policy of intervention.... Japan and China must combine to oppose British imperialism."[23]

Within a few weeks Japan replied in her own way to Wuhan's attempt at a flirtation. Japanese troops thrust suddenly into Shantung, occupying Tsinan and taking over the railway to the sea.

Great Britain, on its part, was thoroughly content. On May 9 in the House of Commons, Sir Austen Chamberlain, the foreign secretary, gave official voice to the delight of the powers with Chiang's coup and the subsequent turn of events. Eugene Chen's note sent in reply to the powers' protests concerning the Nanking "outrages" was rejected as "unsatisfactory in substance and detail." When the powers' notes were presented, said Sir Austen, "China south of the Yangtze was apparently united under the Nationalist government, whose seat was in...Hankow.... Within four days after the date of Mr. Chen's reply that united government in South China no longer existed.... Not two months ago it seemed as if the southern party and the Nationalist armies would sweep China from the south to north. Nanking has already checked this victorious career, if it has not wrecked it altogether." The Communists, he exulted, "have been punished by the Chinese Nationalists themselves with a severity and effectiveness of which no foreign Power was capable. In Shanghai, Canton, and other towns the extremist organizations have been broken up and their leaders executed. The Nationalist government at Hankow has lost its dominating position and is at present little more than the shadow of a name."[24]

To the outraged astonishment of the Shanghai British community, which wanted swift and direct and terrible military reprisals, Chamberlain made it plain that British imperialism was content for the moment to let Chiang Kai-shek act as its deputy. A week later the British diplomatic representative at Hankow was withdrawn.*

The same week in London occurred the Arcos raid, and two weeks later, on May 26, Britain severed diplomatic relations with the Soviet Union. Moscow had counted on Chiang Kai-shek to lead the Chinese masses in their struggle for liberation and had counted on that struggle to checkmate Britain, the leader of the anti-Soviet capitalist world. Chiang Kai-shek's coup proved the bankruptcy of all these hopes. Not Britain, but the mass movement in China was dealt a mortal blow, and simultaneously the international position of the Soviet Union was seriously worsened. London understood that Wuhan offered no serious threat, that it was but the "shadow of a name" and acted accordingly in its own interests. Not as much could be said of the Communist International which continued to see substance where, indeed, there was only shadow.

The foreign warships in the Yangtze, which had hitherto seemed only a puny threat when set against the mass movement and had served little better purpose than to supervise the hasty, frightened exit of foreigners, now became grim sea dragons laden with menace. Wuhan's Left Kuomintang leaders acutely felt the new pressure of that long grey line. Roy, the delegate of the Comintern, felt it no less. "Not only Shanghai," he wrote,

> but the entire Yangtze River is packed with war vessels. The Yangtze Valley, the main artery of trade in China, is under the direct control of imperialist puns. This is a "hold up" on a grand scale. The imperialist bandit is crying "Hands up!" to revolutionary China. The seat of the Nationalist government, Hankow, is practically a beleaguered city. A formidable array of cruisers, destroyers, and gunboats arrogantly

* As if to emphasize the nature of this withdrawal, the British government chose the same day, May 17, to announce the award of decorations to the "heroes" of the infamous bombardment of Wanhsien eight months earlier.

> challenges the right of the Chinese people to govern this country in their own way. English, American, French marines crowd the streets of the Nationalist capital. The Nationalist government smarts under this indignity, for on the slightest provocation the bandit will blow out his brains.[25]

Wuhan had indeed lost its "dominating position." Thanks to Chiang's coup and the pusillanimity of the Left Kuomintang, British imperialism which had come to Wuhan in January with hat in hand, left it in May with a contemptuous shrug. What there had been in the Nationalist capital of "youthful optimism, superb confidence, and bold aggressiveness"[26] collapsed. Only fearful uncertainty remained.

"Before three months are ended," blustered Eugene Chen, "we shall conquer our way across Honan to Peking where, in the name of Nationalist China and the Kuomintang, I will speak a language which cannot be ignored by Sir Austen Chamberlain...the revolutionary armies under Feng Yu-hsiang and Tang Sheng-chih, together with the forces under Yen Hsi-shan, are now closing in on the bandit soldiery of Chang Tso-lin."[27]

But Feng failed him. Tang failed him. Yen failed him. Eugene Chen never again had a chance to be ignored by Sir Austen Chamberlain.*

For employers of labor in the factories and shops the emergence of the Nanking government had heralded the appearance of a political instrument which specifically and energetically served their interests against those of the workers. This service was worth whatever it cost. The fact that in Wuhan's territory the trade unions were still legal and the workers still enjoyed at least the opportunity to voice their demands was enough to throw the sympathies of the capitalists, big and small, into Nanking's scales. The Shanghai events gave the employers in Wuhan new heart to resist the shattering wave of strikes in that city. They passed over to the counteroffensive with renewed vigor. They closed down factories and shops. They deliberately organized runs on local banks, accelerated the flow of silver down to Shanghai,[28] and made every effort to sabotage and paralyze economic life.[29] Out in the countryside the usurers hoarded their money or smuggled it down river to Shanghai. The peasants were refused loans on any terms. There was no other ready cash available anywhere, and in many places the peasants were consequently unable to buy seed and other necessary supplies to tide them over the spring months until harvest time. Speculators deliberately drove the price of rice up to unreachable levels. In this economic sabotage the foreigners cooperated by closing down their enterprises, curtailing

---

* Six years later while he was foreign minister of the short-lived and feeble Fukien government, established in Foochow in revolt against Chiang Kai-shek's rule, Eugene Chen ruminated over the past: "Then, then, I could speak with authority because I had the masses with me!" he told the writer. He never understood that he lost that authority because he failed, himself, to go with the masses. Driven to flee from Foochow, as he was from Wuhan, by Chiang Kai-shek, Eugene Chen faded into well-deserved obscurity.

their river-steamer schedules, and instituting a virtual blockade of Wuhan. In May there were nearly 100,000 workers locked out of factories and shops, and within a brief time this figure almost doubled.[30] The bourgeoisie preferred to risk ruin rather than meet the demands of the workers.

This counteroffensive could be met only if the mass movement was carried through to its logical conclusion. The seizure and operation of the closed factories and shops under a system of workers' control could have in large part even under the conditions of civil war alleviated the stringency resulting from sabotage and the blockade. Confiscation of rice hoards, the establishment of peasant cooperatives fed with capital secured by confiscatory measures, and support of the peasants' own drive toward seizure of the land marked the road towards drastic reorganization of village life. But for these measures a revolutionary power was needed. Workers', peasants', and soldiers' councils in town and countryside were needed. For the Wuhan government such measures were unthinkable, because they involved the violation of bourgeois property. The Communist International "advised" the Left Kuomintang to take over the banks, the factories, and shops. But the Left Kuomintang leaders went hat in hand to the Hankow Chamber of Commerce and begged it to let trade resume its normal course, promising to rein in the mass movement. The Communist Party was unable to move on its own. It was bound within the Kuomintang and could not, at any price, dispense with its cooperation. The Wuhan leaders blamed not the sabotage of the capitalists for their economic difficulties, but the "excesses" of the workers. The demands of factory and shop employees were ruining trade and industry, they cried. What were these excessive demands?

Between January and April the strike struggles of the wharf workers had brought their wages up from three to seven Chinese dollars a month. (One Chinese dollar was at that time worth about two shillings or fifty cents in U.S. currency.) In the textile mills women and children workers, who formerly earned twelve cents a day, fought for and won increases to twenty cents a day, that is, a raise from a monthly wage of $3.60 to $6.00. In the match factories the strikers won increases from seventeen to forty coppers for a twelve-hour day.* In the silk filatures they won a twelve-hour day. Formerly they had worked seventeen hours a day. In some dyeing plants, not all, wage increases from eighteen to fifty coppers a day were won. The highest wage paid to industrial workers was still twenty dollars a month. The general average had been raised from about ten dollars a month to about fourteen dollars. Yet a wage and living cost survey conducted under government auspices fixed $27.46 as the minimum subsistence budget for a family of four. In the matter of hours conditions had been little bettered. Children of seven and eight were still working as long as adults for ten cents a day. The demand for an eight-hour day for children remained

* According to *The China Year Book, 1929–30*, in 1925 it took 240 coppers to make up one Chinese dollar in 1928, 285 coppers were equal to one dollar. No figures are given for 1926 and 1927.

on paper. A survey by the labor department of the Kuomintang at the end of June revealed that most shop employees in the city were still working twelve and fourteen hours a day.[31] The workers were asking to have hours reduced from seventeen a day to fifteen, from sixteen to fourteen, from fourteen to twelve. Still unsatisfied were the demands of apprentices for liberation from conditions far worse than bond slavery.

An interviewer saw some union leaders in March when the cry of "unreasonable" demands was already on Kuomintang lips. "At the mention of the word 'unreasonable,' the union leaders smiled. They were mill workers themselves. All their lives they had been wondering about 'reasonableness.' They asked me about it. All their lives, they said, they had been looking for some 'reason' for their existence. So far, unless to starve that others might be clothed and fed, they had found none. Where, they asked, was the reason in this?"[32]

None of the gains made by the Wuhan workers enabled them as yet to come within "reasonable" reach of the minimum cost of minimum living. Was it an "excess," then, when the workers dragged before their own tribunals shopkeepers who speculated in grain and food? Was it an "excess" when the workers of Hanyang decided to meet the sabotage of their employers by forcibly opening the factories and running them? Or when the shop employees of Puchih and other Hupeh towns took over shops which had been deliberately closed down? Or when the peasants in Hunan and Hupeh placed regional embargoes on the export of grain in order to counter the activities of speculators who were trying to starve them into submission? Or when they seized the rice hoards of the landlords to feed their families?

Yes, screamed the leaders of the Left Kuomintang, these were "excesses." They were ruining trade and disrupting economic life. They were attacks on property and they had to stop. One of Wang Ching-wei's first official acts upon his return to Wuhan was to break up the workers' cooperative which was operating fifteen factories in Hanyang, force the surrender of the plants, and order the dissolution of the Hanyang party branch which had supported the workers.[33]

At the end of April regulations were issued abolishing the judicial and police functions assumed by the trade unions, authorizing them to inflict penalties only on their own members. These regulations were issued by the government and the Hupeh General Labor Union in duplicate. Arbitration courts were to be set up and "unjust demands" for money prohibited.[34]

Hsiang Chung-fah, Communist secretary of the General Labor Union, issued a proclamation, posted on all the walls of the city, asking the workers to make a "supreme effort," and ordering that "new struggles against the capitalists should temporarily be suspended."[35]

On May 20, the Central Executive Committee of the Kuomintang published a manifesto on "the all-class nature of the revolution," in which it fully exposed the particular class nature of the Wuhan Left Kuomintang:

> Whether or not the revolution will be a success will depend on the measure of support given to it by the manufacturers and merchants. Whether or not they can effectively support the revolution will depend upon the willingness of the peasants and laborers to treat them as their allies.
>
> Since the Northern Expedition was launched...it is regrettable that the peasant and labor organizations in the Yangtze Valley, by reason of their rapid development, have been unaware of their blunders.... They have not considered the future of the revolution as a whole and have belittled their allies, the manufacturers and the merchants. Excessive demands, for instance, have been made to the employers by the peasant and labor bodies through their own ignorance of the economic aspect of the situation. Factories and shops have been closed by armed pickets and exorbitant demands, impossible to carry out, have been forced upon the employers or owners. Consequently the manufacturers and merchants have felt that they have been denied protection by the government and that they cannot enjoy freedom in respect to both person and property. They have also felt that not only has the revolution failed to benefit them in any way, but that it has endangered and jeopardized their welfare and safety. Therefore they have stayed away from the battle-line of the revolution and bitterly hate the peasants and laborers who should be their revolutionary allies. As a result the peasants and laborers may find themselves in a state of isolation and committing suicide, and the very foundation of the revolution may be shaken.
>
> The party...cannot ignore the isolated condition of the peasants and laborers lacking guidance; and especially cannot neglect the interests of the revolutionary allies, the manufacturers and the merchants, and deny them adequate protection. It is our policy to unite them all on the same battle front, never to be torn asunder, and enable them all to benefit equally from the revolution. In order to carry out this policy, the National government is ordered to put in effect the following:
>
> 1. The Labor Ministry and the provincial authorities shall adopt arbitration rules and organize arbitration boards for the settlement of disputes between labourers and factory owners;
> 2. Enact a labor law, regulate workers' hours,...fix the scale of wages in accordance with living conditions,...and provide for the protection of the laborers;
> 3. Prohibit laborers and employees from making excessive demands and interfering with the administration of factories and shops; all demands made to be examined by a special joint committee to be organized by the labor union and the merchants' union, which committee shall impose suitable limitation on the demands;
> 4. No labor union or picket corps is permitted to threaten, impose fines upon, or adopt any mode of oppression against shopkeepers or factory owners.[36]

Dutifully, in its turn, the Communist General Labor Union "cooperated" with the "revolutionary government." A few days later it proclaimed "revolutionary discipline" for the workers, urged them "not to forget the interests of their allies, the manufacturers and the merchants," and issued the following regulations: (1) Workers who violated revolutionary discipline were to be punished; (2) serious offenders were to be handed over to the government for trial and punishment; (3) unions were prohibited from arresting, fining, "or in any way oppressing persons other than laborers."[37]

It was in the order of things that the exploited should give up their freedom so that the exploiters might feel free. It was also in the order of things, however, that the exploited came unavoidably into conflict with the exploiters. That was the hard fact that insistently intruded itself. The Wuhan government and the Left Kuomintang, with the support of the Comintern, imagined that it was finding common ground for classes in conflict. In practice this meant asking the workers to submit peacefully and in silence to their continued subjection. It never occurred to them to demand and, if necessary, compel the employers to submit to the workers' demands. After all, they represented the bourgeoisie, Joseph Stalin to the contrary notwithstanding, no matter how little confidence the bourgeoisie reposed in them. The economic impasse created at Wuhan by the capitalist counteroffensive could have been met in the workers' interest only by bold revolutionary measures. When the Wuhan government proved incapable of taking the necessary steps, the workers had to find some means of their own of putting them into effect. That meant councils of the workers, peasants, and soldiers (soviets), which would have been prepared to lead the way in applying political and economic policies which guarded the interests of the masses and not the property of the bourgeoisie. But the formation of such councils would have meant "struggle against the revolutionary Kuomintang," the "only governmental authority." That would have been "counterrevolutionary." So in the name of revolution there was no economic policy at all, except the fervid protection of bourgeois property at the cost of the strangulation of Wuhan and the gradual dissipation of the fresh force of the masses who were never shown their own way out.

The same yardstick of property measured the position taken by the Left Kuomintang on the cardinal question of the land. All the determination which Stalin had promised the Left Kuomintang would display in the solution of the agrarian problem came to light in the form of evasions of the land issue, developing into complaints against the "excesses" of the peasants, and passing relentlessly over to forcible repression as soon as the peasants undertook on their own initiative to deal with their problems in their own way.

As petty bourgeois radicals, the leaders of Wuhan were by no means insensible to the motive power of the masses. So long as warmly spoken phrases placed that motive power at their disposal they were more than free with them. Earlier pronouncements from Wuhan on the subject of the agrarian revolution left nothing to be desired—nothing, that is, but their translation into action. For example: "The realization of the aims of the national revolution depends upon the awakening of the peasants of all China. Our party will always defend and struggle for the interests of the peasants in order that all privileged classes oppressing them be deprived of support...in order that the oppressed peasants be really emancipated." Again, as late as March 19, a government manifesto affirmed that the "revolution must work great changes in the village...in order to suppress finally the activities of the local parasites, lawless gentry, landlords, and counterrevolutionaries, under the power of the peasants.... This is the only road.... If the peasants are not given the possibility of possessing their own land they will not be able to support the revolution to the victorious end."[38]

In words no less radical than those employed in the resolutions of the Communist International, the Kuomintang had even proclaimed the slogan: "Arms for the peasants!" In its "declaration to the peasants," the Kuomintang Executive Committee in March had said: "In order to ensure...victory...the peasants will need arms for their protection. The armed forces employed by the feudal landlords...should be disarmed and their munitions should be handed over to the peasants. In addition the party should devise measures to enable the peasants to buy arms at cheap prices. In short, it should enable the peasants to have ample arms for self-protection. This is to ensure the permanence of the victory of the rural revolution and to ensure that democratic influences overthrow the old feudal influences."[39]

These were exciting words, but words alone would not give the peasant his land; and because they were only words and nothing more, the difficulties began for those who uttered them as soon as the peasants of Hunan and Hupeh began to show in action that they took them seriously. To this pitiful little handful of phrasemongers history could not assign the role of Jacobins, not even to please Joseph Stalin. They could not lead, nor support, nor even condone the actual realization of the agrarian revolution because it meant the destruction of the economic and class base to which they were rooted. Their bonds to the "feudal landlords" against whom they railed were infinitely more compelling than the claims of the peasantry whose cause they theoretically espoused. They knew that the victory of the agrarian revolution meant the end of their political power. If they had to go down, they would go down defending property, not violating it.

Sun Yat-sen's program still revolved around the vague and meaningless phrase "equalization of rights in the land." The Kuomintang Platform for Workers and Peasants adopted in October 1926, actually promised the peasants nothing more than a 25 percent reduction in land rent and the "prohibition" of usury with the proviso that interest on loans should not exceed 20 percent per annum![40] Not only was the rent reduction plank still wholly ineffective, but the course of the peasants' own struggle had brought them swiftly to the realization that the issue was not one of partial reforms but of the land itself. The Kuomintang Plenary Session in March 1927, admitted that "the cardinal question in the problem of poor farmers is the land question," but the only practical solution it could offer was a proposal to set up farmers' banks to make loans at 5 percent per annum in order to solve the problem of lack of capital among the poor peasants.[41] The plenary session created a Land Commission which was supposed to marshal statistical and other material with a view to concretizing the Kuomintang's land policy. This Commission began its sessions on April 27. It was composed of the principal Kuomintang leaders, with Tang Ping-shan representing the Communist Party.

Starting out with the general proposition that the peasant had to be made master of the land—to which everyone agreed in principle—the Commission stopped to inquire: Which peasants should be made masters of what land?[42] "Land to the tillers!" had a nice, radical ring to it. But whose land? Certainly not the land of the small landlords, said Wang Ching-wei. The party's duty was to protect the small landlords, for were they not the party of the petty bourgeoisie? Certainly not the land belonging to the officers of the army, said Tang Sheng-chih. The peasants in Hunan, he complained, were already seizing the estates of army officers or of their relatives. Why, in Chienchih, they had even taken a regimental commander who also happened to be the owner of a large local estate, bound him, put a dunce cap on his head, and paraded him through the streets! And the sister-in-law of Chen Cheng, a Kuomintang general, had actually been forced to bob her hair to show her solidarity with the new order of things! This would never do. Maybe the rank and file soldiers, landless peasants all of them, would approve, but the officers would never stand for it. The army, mind you, would be split on the question of the land, and, after all, we cannot afford a split in the army, can we?

No, by no means, quickly agreed the commissioners.

Well, then, the land of the big landlords? Yes, the land of the big landlords! But then again, how are we to know which landlords are big and which small? Moreover, if, as Tang Sheng-chih demanded, "we have to think out concrete means for guaranteeing intact the land belonging to the officers of the national revolutionary army," then we also have to distinguish between those "big" landlords related to the officers and those who are so unfortunate as not to have a son or brother in a Sam Browne belt.

"We must establish the criterion of confiscation," echoed Wang Ching-wei and Sun Fo.

Hsu Chien had a solution all his own. He discovered somewhere that only 15 percent of the land in all China was under cultivation. "Then there is no purpose," said he, "in taking the land from the landlords when we can give the peasants the land which nobody cultivates." But Hsu Chien was unable to verify his figure and, anyway, most of the uncultivated land was out in Tibet and Turkestan and up in the northwest. The wholesale transportation of the peasants of Hunan and Hupeh did not sound like a particularly practicable proposition. So later Hsu Chien agreed with Tan Yen-kai that it might be possible to confiscate only the land of the "especially malicious or evil landlords and the evil businessmen." Now then, which landlords were evil or (we shudder to think of such people) especially malicious?

Hm, said everybody.

When the idea of buying the land from the small landlords was discussed, Tan Yen-kai rubbed his chin. "That will not satisfy the small landlords," he said, "because they still have very little faith in the National government. If we give them our bonds, they cannot live by eating the paper. The land will have to be left in their hands."

On behalf of the Communists, Tang Ping-shan timidly suggested that only the land of the counterrevolutionary landlords be confiscated. Wang Ching-wei leaped into the breach. "Political confiscation!" he snorted, "that is an extremely general phrase which says nothing. If the peasants in any given district are strong enough, they consider every landowner to be counterrevolutionary in order to expropriate his land. Under political confiscation there is no criterion. Where the peasants are strong, they go straight ahead to economic confiscation. Where they are weaker,...they fall first on the small landlords who thus suffer before anyone else, and we want to keep the small landlords on our side."

Completely confounded, the Communists withdrew their proposal.

After three weeks of this it was finally decided, with a general sigh of relief all round, that the revolution was still in its military period and that according to Sun Yat-sen the solution of such problems as the land would have to await the final military victory and the unification of the country which would usher in the period of "political tutelage." A resolution was accordingly adopted recognizing in principle the desirability of confiscating big landed properties, but recommending that for the time being land rents should not exceed 40 percent of the harvest.

This decision represented a retreat even from the plank for a 25 percent rent reduction since land rents averaged from 50 percent to 60 percent, although in places it did amount to 70 percent of the harvest or even more. Nevertheless the Communists accepted the resolution, and when the Commission further decided not to publish an account of its deliberations "for fear of creating confusion," the Communists again concurred. The army was saved. The landlord was saved. The Kuomintang was saved. The issue was settled to the satisfaction of everyone but the peasants. They had to be patient. If they would only keep on supporting the National government, all would be well.

How the peasants would receive this "solution" of their problems remained to be seen. Meanwhile new threats from other quarters rose to plague the "revolutionary center." Inspired by the success of Chiang Kai-shek and directly instigated by him, militarist rebellions against Wuhan's authority rose on all sides. In northern Hupeh, Yu Hsueh-chung defied the government. In the west, Yang Sen started moving his troops against the Nationalist capital. Hsia To-yen, who held the western front against Yang, abruptly mutinied and with a handful of troops careered through the country south and west of Wuhan, burning, looting, and coming to the aid of the landlords and gentry against the peasants. The failure of the Wuhan regime to support the demands of the peasants had already so far alienated their confidence that efforts to recruit them and organize resistance to Hsia brought little or no response.[43] Although Yeh Ting, a Communist officer, by heroic measures was in the end able to stave off Hsia's threat to Wuchang, Wuhan remained beset on all sides, militarist revolts threatening from without and economic stagnation within.

The editor of the *People's Tribune* watched frightened people "with laden carts, bearing household goods, going by our windows," and heard "whisperings of woe in the air." "Disaster is impending, say panic-stricken people in the city.... Foreigners have been half-frenzied, half-elated. They have seen the end of the hated rule of Nationalist Hankow.... Tomorrow morning they expect to see the dawn of a new regime in Wuhan."[44] The editor scoffed at both the frightened and the hopeful and prophesied an early victory for the Nationalist cause on all fronts.

The clamps were, nevertheless, closing in. The revolutionary way out lay in a vigorous unleashing of the masses on the basis of a thoroughgoing agrarian revolt. Such a course alone gave promise of ameliorating the economic difficulties and dissolving the armies of the rebellious militarists. If the Left Kuomintang could not take this course, the Communists had to be ready to do so. The Comintern spoke, too, to be sure, of the agrarian revolution, but in the next breath ordered the Chinese Communists to concede all power to the Left Kuomintang for, in Stalin's words, "without a policy of close collaboration of the Left and the Communists inside the Kuomintang...the victory of the revolution is impossible." It was not at all surprising, therefore, that Wang Ching-wei could appear as guest of honor at the opening of the Fifth Congress of the Chinese Communist Party in Hankow on April 27 and announce that he and his colleagues "gladly accepted the perspectives of the Communist International,"[45] and declare his "complete agreement" with the report of the Comintern delegate, M. N. Roy.[46]

The spiritual leadership of the Fifth Congress of the Chinese Communist Party was provided by the Communist International in the person of the Indian Communist, M. N. Roy. It was Roy, Mif tells us, who gave the young Chinese Party "for the first time"—[Is Mif here, perchance, casting aspersions on the previous directives and resolutions of the Comintern?]—"a really Leninist prognosis" of the events taking place. From Roy the party heard, "for the first time," "a thoroughly thought-out perspective of the movement" and "received directives on a series of cardinal questions." Roy "gave the young Chinese party...the experience of world Bolshevism."[47] Before long the position of the Chinese Communist Party at the time of the Fifth Congress was going to be described in Moscow as being in direct contradiction to the directives of the Comintern. Somewhat later Roy himself was scheduled to become the object of vicious attack. But now listen to Roy's own report of the Congress, published with full responsibility and without adverse comment in the official organ of the Comintern: "The Fifth Congress had a great many complex and difficult questions to solve...a clear perspective for the future development of the revolution had to be traced and firm leadership given to it. It was the historic role of the Fifth Congress to give this perspective, to trace the line of conduct for the proletariat, and to help create clear-thinking, devoted, and energetic leaders indispensable to the victorious march of the revolution. The Congress fulfilled this task."[48]

How did Roy estimate the situation?

> The differentiation of the classes within the Kuomintang has strengthened the bonds between its Left wing and the Communist Party. The departure of the big bourgeoisie has permitted the transformation of the Kuomintang into a revolutionary bloc composed of the industrial proletariat, the peasants, and the petty bourgeoisie (in addition to several strata of the bourgeoisie).... The Chinese revolution continues to develop on the basis of a class coalition and cannot yet be submitted to the exclusive leadership of the proletariat.... The leading members of the Kuomintang participated in the opening meeting of the Congress and declared that they were ready to fortify the bloc with the Communist Party.[49]

What was Roy's practical lead to the Chinese Communists? Listen to Chiu Chiu-pei, a member of the Central Committee of the Chinese Communist Party. Chiu is writing one year after the rude jolt of events had smashed both the revolution and Roy's untouchability in the ranks of the Comintern: "Roy's political view was that the Lefts and the petty bourgeoisie had no other way out but by following us. He did not point out the possibility of new betrayals and the concrete, complicated tasks the Communist Party should have undertaken against the possibility of such new betrayals. Therefore the atmosphere of the Fifth Congress was governed by the slogan: 'Long Live the Cooperation of Communism with the San Min (Three People's) Principles to the End!"[50]

In his report to the Congress, Chen Tu-hsiu admitted that although the peasants were driving forward on their own initiative to the seizure of the land, "we have carried out too pacific a policy." He agreed that large estates should be seized, but added: "At present the alliance with the small landholders is still necessary. We must not fall into extreme leftism, but follow a centrist line. We must also wait for the development of the military movement before seizing the large and middle land-holdings. The only correct solution at the present moment is that the extension of the revolution must take place before it is deepened."[51]

When this extract was published by *Pravda* in Moscow, Trotsky added a postscript to his criticism of Stalin's thesis: "This road is the surest, most positive, the shortest road to ruin. The peasant has already risen to seize the property of the large landowners. Our party, in monstrous contradiction to its program, its name, pursues a pacific-liberal agrarian policy.... The agrarian formula of Comrade Chen Tu-hsiu, who is bound hand and foot by the false leadership of the representatives of the Comintern, is objectively nothing else than the formula of severance of the Chinese Communist Party from the real agrarian movement."[52]

And *Pravda* printed Chen's report without comment. How otherwise? On May 13, Stalin, in full accord with the spirit of Chen's views, declared in Moscow that soviets could be formed in China only "after the strengthening of the Wuhan

Revolutionary Government."[53] Chen's report was published, similarly without criticism, throughout the Communist International. Only later, after events had hit them between the eyes, did Comintern spokesmen begin to echo Trotsky's warning to the Chinese Communist Party.

The deliberations of the Congress on the question of the land followed the course of the discussions at the Kuomintang Land Commission meetings. Like that Commission, the Communist Congress approved, in principle, the confiscation of large landholdings. But, it added, "land belonging to the small landowners and land belonging to the officers of the revolutionary army is not subject to confiscation."[54]

To refuse to touch the land of the officers meant to refuse to touch the agrarian question altogether because there was scarcely a subaltern in the armies of Wuhan, to say nothing of the generals, who was not the kin of landowners in Hunan or Hupeh. In his report, Chen himself pointed out that "the officers (of the Nationalist armies) are young men from the landlord class."[55] But did this resolution differ in any respect from the instructions of the Communist International? Had not Stalin wired, as far back as October 1926, to check the peasants in order not to alienate the generals?[56] Was not the Comintern, in these very days, opposing the creation of workers', peasants', and soldiers' soviets precisely on the grounds that the creation of such soviets "would be consciously to accelerate the conflict with the generals in the most disadvantageous conditions [?] for the Communist Party and its allies?"[57] Would not Stalin, in a few weeks, wire specific directives reiterating, word for word, the same instructions to protect the land of the generals? In Wuhan, at the other end of wires from Moscow, were Borodin, Roy, Mif, Lozovsky, Browder, Doriot, and a host of other "Bolshevik" advisers. Not one among them raised his voice—in time. None of the contemptible evasions and falsehoods with which Moscow later sought to thrust full responsibility for the debacle on the shoulders of Chen Tu-hsiu and the Chinese Central Committee can conceal the identity of the political path designated by the Communist International and followed by the Chinese Communist Party.

The land resolution of the Fifth Congress was the first direct pronouncement of the Communist Party on the agrarian question. It amounted to evasion of the issue which the peasants of Hunan and Hupeh were already taking into their own hands. In practice the Communists were compelled to take up the cudgels of active opposition to the "excesses" of the peasantry. If the victory of the revolution was "impossible" without the collaboration of the Left Kuomintang, as Stalin and the Comintern affirmed, then collaboration with the Left Kuomintang was unthinkable, in terms of agrarian revolt. Therefore the agrarian revolt had to be scrapped and the peasants abandoned to their fate. So long as Stalin's instructions were followed, there was no reason why the Fifth Congress of the Chinese Communist Party, convening at the most acutely critical juncture of the revolution, should not have met under the aegis of the treacherous slogan: "Long Live the Cooperation of

Communism with the Three People's Principles to the End!" It was perfectly in order for the manifesto of the Congress to declare: "Unite all democratic elements under the banner of the Kuomintang. Strengthen this revolutionary alliance. This is the important task of the proletariat in this stage of the revolution. The revolutionary democratic alliance is the leader of the national revolution."[58]

Behind the scenes of the Fifth Congress there were differing tendencies. Here is how Chiu Chiu-pei describes them:

> Borodin's line was retreat and the slackening of the agrarian revolution...concessions to the petty bourgeoisie...concessions to the so-called industrialists and merchants; concessions to the landlords and gentry; ally with Feng Yu-hsiang to overthrow Chiang Kai-shek; and with such a policy lead the left leaders against the right reactionary forces of Wuhan and Nanking.
>
> Roy was for relative concessions to the businessmen...against conceding anything to the landlord and gentry class .. . for small concessions to the small landlords and the revolutionary generals.

The Central Committee of the Party was for "complete concessions to the businessmen, complete concessions to the landlords and gentry, considering that the agrarian revolution could not be realized immediately, but required an adequate period of propaganda...considering it best to let the Left (Kuomintang) lead and for us to go off the path a bit so that the revolution should not be prematurely advanced."[59]

These three tendencies were in reality one—the tendency to retreat. In practice, they became one, for, as Chiu correctly sums them up: "The policy practiced at that time was to make concessions in order to overcome the difficulties after Chiang's betrayal."[60]

"Concede, concede!" cried Borodin, Roy, and all the minions of the Communist International when as never before the Chinese revolution needed to unfurl upon its banners the immortal slogan of Danton, "de l'audace, de l'audace, encore de l'audace." But Moscow ordered the Chinese Communists to bow before the Left Kuomintang. The Left Kuomintang kow-towed before the militarists, the landlords and the bourgeoisie. This treachery would in the end strangle the Chinese revolution, but not all the vacillation and cowardice of these leaders could cloud the grandeur and the might of the masses in action.

13

The Struggle for the Land

Except for the October revolution in Russia, our century has afforded history no spectacle mightier nor more stirring than the rising of the Chinese masses in the spring and summer of 1927. Not since the days of the long-haired Taipings had the Chinese peasant had the chance to hope for more from life than the right to toil and to die. In Hunan and Hupeh now he was beginning to grip the levers of historical hydraulics—drastic and collective action. He was beginning to straighten his back and loosen from his shoulders the burden of centuries. This experience has been described as the dawning realization of the Chinese toiler that he, too, was a man, that he, too, existed. From that, the will to live not as an animal but as a man hurled not one but millions of toilers into a struggle against everything that had made them the packhorses of a civilization thousands of years old.

Ignorant and cowardly leaders had drawn for the peasant moral distinctions among his oppressors. There were "bad" gentry to be overthrown, but there were "good" gentry who were his friends. There were big landlords whose holdings, at some future date, the peasant would be permitted to confiscate, but there were small landlords who were to be regarded as firm and friendly allies. His enemies in the village were the *tuhao*—the local bullies, officials, and hirelings of the landlord; but the officers of the Nationalist army, even if they and their fathers and brothers were also landlords and usurers, were friends and liberators and were not to be offended by injuries to their property. Nothing falls more easily upon the shoulders of the propertied man, after all, than the mantle of moral rectitude. As the movement advanced and the "revolutionary" government displayed no inclination to implement even the mildest of the promises it had made in return for peasant support, it began to dawn on the masses that the slogan: "Down with the *tuhao* and bad gentry!" corresponded not to their interests, but to the interests of classes who wanted their services without paying for them. The villages began to awake. The slogan underwent a process of plebeian face-lifting and soon read: "All who have *tu* [land] are *hao* [oppressive] and there are no gentry who are not bad!"[1]

"Down with the unequal treaties!" said the Kuomintang. The only "unequal treaties" the Hunan peasants knew about were the tenancy agreements under which they were compelled to surrender to the landlord up to 70 percent of their crops, to make non-interest-bearing cash deposits in advance on their rent, to make gifts to the landlords at festival times, to serve without wages when a betrothal, a marriage, or a funeral in the landlord's family required the preparation of ceremonies or the conveying and serving of guests. The slogan for "abolition of the unequal treaties" meant to the Hunan peasant abolition of thraldom on the land. He could not help it if the Kuomintang was talking about China's relations with the powers.[2]

On the Kuomintang banner was inscribed nothing more than a 25 percent reduction in land rent and a "restriction" of interest rates to 20 percent per annum. The Kuomintang also spoke obscurely of "equalization of tenants' rights" without ever clearly indicating what it meant. When the masses started moving and the Left Kuomintang proved unwilling or unable to give point to these mild planks in its own platform, the momentum of their awakening carried the peasants with swift, direct logic to the slogan: "All Land to the Tillers!" And with the draconic simplicity, so terrible to those who stand to lose by it, the peasants proceeded to put their own slogan into practice. By the end of April in an increasing number of *hsien* in Hunan and in a smaller number in Hupeh, confiscation of land and property was the order of the day.

The struggle for land brought nearly ten million peasants within the orbit of the mass organizations in Central China. The accumulated oppression of centuries had laid charges deep in the soil. The upsurge of 1927 only touched the torch to the fuses which meshed through the whole social structure like veins in the human body. Revolution brought a thundering series of explosions which left not a limb of the old society intact. Shaken asunder and trampled upon, all that was old, corrupt, degenerate, and decadent, dissolved in the "inspired frenzy of history." Bandages were torn from the bound feet of women. Young girls, with bobbed hair and an air of defiant energy, streamed into the countryside to awaken their sex and free it of chains that bore the rust of generations.* Confucius, the high priest of privilege and submission, was torn from the shrouds of a vicious and reactionary morality and paraded in effigy through village streets and burned. Buddhist temples were seized and turned into schools and meeting places. Foreign missionaries were packed off, dishevelled, to flee before something they called anarchy, something their creed debarred them from ever

* "I have lived eighty years," said an old woman to a girl propagandist in the field, "without seeing such a short-haired, big-footed, uniformed female creature like you." Sitting in a meadow at Chiayu, south Hupeh, the girl told in a letter to a Hankow friend how she spoke to a group of peasants about the evils of foot-binding. A well-to-do middle-aged woman with three-inch "golden lilies" hobbled up to her and said: "Your feet are so big. Won't your husband get into your shoes some time by mistake?" All the soldiers and peasants who stood around laughed aloud. The girl officer blushed, and then began to laugh herself.—From "A Letter from the Field," *People's Tribune*, June 22, 1927.

understanding. Superstitions were swept away. "The clay and wood gods have already lost their dignity. The people no longer need the Five Classics and the Four Books. What they want is political reports. They want to know the conditions in the country and in the world. The *men sen* (door gods) which used to be pasted on the gates have now been covered with slogans. Inside the houses even the *tsao mu kao pi* (ancestral tablets) have been crowded out by placarded slogans."[3]

Evils which had been blood and stock of the old society were swept away in the flood. "Ever since the last days of the Manchus," reported a Hunan peasant leader,

> the government has repeatedly prohibited opium. But in fact the opium prohibition bureau has always been the bureau for selling opium. Only petty smokers were fined. The greedy officials and gentry, even though they smoked right out in the open, were never touched.... But the ban that was a ban in vain for twenty years became a ban in fact after the peasants rose. The village peasant associations decreed that anyone found smoking would be fined and paraded. After many prominent gentry had been paraded in dunce caps, nobody in the villages of Hunan dared again to smoke. The peasants smashed the pipes of the gentry. To eradicate gambling, the Pioneers [boys of twelve to fifteen] made house-to-house searches. Mah jongg and other gambling paraphernalia were burned on the spot. Footbinding was abolished. Dams and roads were built; waste lands put under cultivation.... The establishment of schools and the smashing of superstitions became the most enthusiastic work in the villages.... The peasants created a peaceful village. No matter how you describe the tumult of the Hunan villages, they have been in fact more peaceful than when the landlords ruled.[4]

The peasant went about his task of cleaning the Augean stables of the past with a grim thoroughness and often not without a certain grim humor. In Hwangkang, Hupeh, the "dunce caps" used for the guilty gentry were the 3-*do* 3-*sen* measuring containers which the landlords had formerly used in dividing the grain after harvest at rent collection time.[5]

Peasant justice was swift and simple in the village. If it erred at all, it erred on the side of leniency. Surprisingly few were the executions ordered and carried out. In most cases heavy fines or sentences of imprisonment were imposed upon the landlords and their followers. Justice was administered by the local peasant committee sitting as the presidium at a mass meeting of the peasants. "We fear nothing but the mass meeting," the gentry used to say. Disputes and claims had previously been settled by the local magistrate or by the local big landlord who enjoyed the privileges of a feudal baron before the law. He used to sit in his courtyard and dispense his own brand of justice according to his own pleasure. This was now all changed. The local peasant associations swept through clogged-up calendars and settled all outstanding cases. They became the courts of appeal in all matters, even including domestic disputes.

The peasant organizations faced the enormous economic problems of the village with a courage and a daring that far exceeded their ability to solve them. Nevertheless, with the funds and other means confiscated from the gentry, in many places they went forward with the establishment of cooperatives and took steps to regulate the movement of grain and to prevent speculation.[6] These cooperatives even issued notes which were accepted in full faith by the peasants of the locality. The problems of interest on loans and land rent were met by the simple expedient of refusal to pay. In the countryside, prostitution, the sale of women and children, stemmed directly from the unbearable poverty of the peasants. Traffic in human lives had become a trade which thrived on human misery, and each year tens of thousands of women and children were sold into brothels or into the homes of the wealthy as slaves. In Yanghsin, the delegates' conference of the *hsien* peasant association voted to appropriate part of the funds confiscated from the gentry to feed the poor "so that they would not need to sell their wives and children in order that all might live." But every partial, crude effort to cope with economic difficulties brought the peasants swiftly to the basic problem of the land itself. No hunger was greater than the hunger for land. Increasingly conscious of his power, the peasant reached out to satisfy his craving.

In the cities, the workers in the trade unions administered justice, maintained local order. Dressed in blue denim uniforms and armed more often with staves than with rifles, the worker-pickets, with their "business-like air of authority," soon became "one of the most noticeable revolutionary features on the streets.[7] In the early stages the prestige and authority of the unions were enormous. "In many of the country towns of Hupeh," writes Chapman, "as I myself saw in Teian and heard from Chinese and foreign colleagues and friends in other towns, the governor of the town, holding his appointment direct from the Nationalist government in Hankow and having Nationalist troops quartered in the town, was yet unable to take any action contrary to the wishes of the two or three leading labour unions."[8]

The unions established schools, protected the rights of women, gave refuge to escaped slave girls, organized unemployed relief, exposed, arrested, and punished counterrevolutionaries where they could. But they were already discharging their functions within the narrow limits prescribed by the restrictive regulations issued by the Wuhan government and approved by the Communist-controlled General Labor Union.[9]

Both in city and country, the mass movement encountered formidable obstacles. The sabotage of the bourgeoisie, the imperialist blockade, the steady refusal of the Wuhan government to cope with the situation by revolutionary measures, had already driven the workers of Wuhan up an economic blind alley. Their own efforts, evidenced in the occupation of the Hanyang factories, were stifled at the outset by the regime to which the Communists told them they owed unquestioning obedience. In Hanyang, the arsenal workers crowded eagerly around a visiting delegation of Russian trade unionists.

"During your revolution," they asked, "what attitude did you take toward sabotage in government industries? Did you encourage it, or tolerate it?"

"During your revolution, when did the metal workers begin to get any benefit? Did they benefit as soon as the exploiters were overthrown, or did they have to suffer long and make many sacrifices before the revolution was finally established?" Reporting these questions, Miss Strong omits to mention what reply was made by the Russian workers, but goes on:

> Many were the sacrifices they were already making for their revolutionary [!] government. They gave up their demand for an eight-hour day to work 13 to 17 hours in the arsenal "because our revolutionary government is menaced." They postponed the demand for a child labor law; I myself saw children of seven and eight working ten hours in Wuchang cotton mills and was told by union organizers, "Wuhan is blockaded; we must not attack production, especially foreign-owned production." They had reason to sacrifice for Wuhan, for elsewhere their situation was far more serious. In Shanghai, Canton, and Hunan, workers were being executed. In Wuhan they still had the chance to raise their heads and argue a little. They were pathetically grateful for his meager privilege.[10]

"Raise their heads and argue a little!" Such were the prerogatives of the workers in the "revolutionary center" of Wuhan! Did the visiting Russian workers tell their Chinese comrades that they indeed had made sacrifices, tremendous sacrifices, for their revolutionary government—but that it was really theirs, really revolutionary, and not the fiction that was "revolutionary Wuhan"? If any of the visitors saw the distinction, it is doubtful if he mentioned it. What was revolutionary in Russia in 1917 was counter-revolutionary in Wuhan in 1927. It must have been. Stalin said so.

Out in the countryside, the first wave of agrarian revolt had rocked the landlords and gentry to their heels. In many places, out of fear for their lives or in hopes that in the nationalization and division of land which they expected to follow they might retrieve a share, landlords even voluntarily surrendered their land to the peasant associations. The original initiative of the peasants, moving toward the seizure of land in villages and *hsien* over wide territories, now needed more than anything else the aid of a centralized power capable of arming the peasants, guarding and extending their conquests. As soon as the landlords and the village gentry realized that in Wuhan no such power existed, that in Wuhan there was only irresolution, vacillation, and a fear of the peasants if anything greater than their own, confidence returned and the reactionary counter-offensive took on an armed, organized character.

"The Hunan peasants at the present time cannot be said to have overthrown the *haosen*,"* reported the provincial peasant association.

> We can only say that they are now rebelling against them. Those who do not know the real conditions say that in Hunan the conditions are terrible, that too many

* A term embracing the landlords, gentry, and their local tools and hirelings.

haosen were killed. But the facts are otherwise.... The *haosen* killed numbered only tens, but the number of peasants killed by the *haosen* is astounding.... Many people know that the peasants are conducting a revolution in Hunan, but few know the cruelty and cunning of the *haosen*.... It has been very common in all *hsien* for the *Min Tuan* (landlord's militia) to lynch peasants.... Torture was freely used.... After being arrested peasants would either be killed outright or mutilated—muscles of the feet extracted, genitals cut away, etc.... The *Min Tuan* in Tsalien burned alive in kerosene a student who had come to the district to work in the peasant movement....

After being driven from the villages by the peasants, the *haosen* and the dregs of the *Min Tuan* often sought alliances with the bandits to fight the peasant associations. Nine reports out of ten coming to the provincial peasant association tell about the gathering of the *tuhao* with the bandits to drink wine and cock's blood* for the overthrow of the peasant associations, for the extermination of the Party commissioner....

They also formed reactionary organizations. In Siangsang, they called it the Association for the Maintenance of Town and Village. In Henyang, it was the White Party. In Liling and Liuyang, the San-Ai Party. In Liling, there was also the Association for Beating Dogs, the dogs meaning the peasants. In many parts of Hunan, there was the Party for the Preservation of Property. These organizations planned and carried out the massacres of peasants and raids on peasant associations.... Sometimes these plots were uncovered by the peasants, but the organizations were never dissolved...

Another method used by the *tuhao* was to mingle in the peasant associations...to disrupt them. Or else they organized their own peasant associations. They also agreed whole-heartedly in words with the peasant movement.... They would organize on a clan basis in order to set one *hsien* against another, one name against another.** They would entice clans-men into the association with promises of cheap grain. They also deceived the higher organs and got themselves recognized as special village or district peasant associations.[11]

The families of the gentry who fled from the *hsien* and villages of Hunan carried rumors like rats carry the plague. Those who could afford to fled all the way to Shanghai. The less wealthy went to Hankow, and the least wealthy to Changsha. Everywhere they brought with them the hoary charges of communization of women which have accompanied every revolutionary movement since 1789*** The Chinese émigrés spread rumors among the soldiers that within six months all their wives and sisters would be "communalized." This accusation came fittingly

* A ceremonial oath of alliance.

** In many *hsien*, most of the inhabitants bear a single name and belong, in varying degrees of relationship, to the same clan.

*** "Nothing could be more absurd," wrote Marx and Engels in the *Communist Manifesto*, "than the virtuous indignation of our bourgeois as regards the official communization of women which the Communists are supposed to advocate. Communists do not need to introduce community of women; it has invariably existed...the abolition of the present system of production will lead to the disappearance of that form of the community of women which results therefrom—to the disappearance of official and unofficial prostitution."

from the Chinese gentry who keep as many concubines as their wealth will allow and whose exactions force the peasants to sell their wives and children into slavery and prostitution. They also tried to appeal to filial sentiments with tales of the wholesale massacre of all men over fifty.

Reports of the Hupeh peasant organizations closely paralleled those from Hunan. In Hupeh, where the movement was slower in getting under way, the gentry had more time to prepare resistance. By May not a few of the peasant associations were entirely in their hands. "In many villages in the peasant associations there are no peasants at all—only the long-gowned and broad-sleeved gentlemen going out and coming in." If the peasants succeeded in retaining control of their own organizations, the gentry concentrated their attention on the local Kuomintang branches. Once in the party, they would set up rival peasant associations under their own auspices and maintain a clear line of demarcation between the peasants and the party. "In Chi-hsui *hsien* there were even such things as refusals to let peasants join the Party."[12] In Hupeh there also sprang up, under various names, reactionary bands like the Ta Tao Hui (Big Sword Society), the Chuan T'o Hui (Fist Society), and others, financed and led by the landlords. The links between the gentry and the revolting militarists were quickly forged.

When Hsia To-yen rebelled in May, his troops marched "from Chianglien to Chenli, Hsienti, Tungyang, everywhere opening the prisons to release the *haosen* who acted as guides to hunt down the commissioners of the peasant associations and the executive committee members and to slaughter them. They killed right and left almost all the way to Wuchang. In the *hsien* adjacent to Honan, the gentry united with the Red Spears (an old reactionary secret society), to massacre the peasants. In western and northern Hupeh they joined with Chang Lien-sen and Yu Hsueh-chung."[13]

The counteroffensive of the gentry was accompanied by the most fiendish tortures—including the kind of refined torture that could have evolved only in the minds of a ruling class entrenched in its seats of privilege for centuries. "In Yangshin they poured kerosene over the peasants and burned them alive. In Hwangkang they used red-hot irons to sear the flesh and to kill. In Lotien they bound their victims to trees and put them to death with one thousand cuts into which they rubbed sand and salt. They cut open the breasts of the women comrades, pierced their bodies perpendicularly with iron wires, and paraded them naked through the streets. In Tsungchang every comrade was pierced twenty times."[14] The revolting masses never displayed one thousandth part of the cruelty shown them by their avenging masters. The barbarism, of which only defenders of property seem to be capable, quickly cracked through their "refined" and "cultured" veneer, so aged, so delicate, so beloved of sentimental sinologues.[15]

The workers and peasants of Hunan and Hupeh faced these enemies with practically nothing but their bare hands and their will to struggle. The movement could go forward only under the leadership of a centralizing force with the demands of the agrarian revolution boldly inscribed upon its banner. They needed local organs of political power. Above all, they needed arms. All these they lacked and without them they were powerless in the face of the reactionary counteroffensive. The Wuhan government did not assume the mantle of revolutionary agrarian leadership with which the Comintern tried to endow it. It was even unable to make a single effective move to enforce its own program of a 25 percent land rent reduction.[16] What it could do was to block at every turn the efforts of the peasants to strike out for themselves.

Reports from peasant associations repeatedly urged the government to define its policies clearly, to set up standards for the solution of the land problem. To these demands the government spokesmen replied only with lectures about the "excesses" of the peasantry.[17]

In Hunan the delegation of the Communist International learned that the Kuomintang program of rent and interest rate reductions could not be realized "because of the resistance of the landlords." A Kuomintang representative told them: "There is a general and loud demand by the peasants of the province for LAND. They want the division of the land. They say that they will be obedient to the Nationalist government, but they at the same time demand that the government do something. They want the land!"[18]

In Moscow Stalin was rejecting the slogan of soviets because that slogan meant struggle against "the revolutionary center" of Wuhan, the "only governmental authority." Trotsky was retorting that the "revolutionary center" was a fiction, that revolutionary organs of power had now to be created and could be created and centralized only through the medium of workers', peasants', and soldiers' soviets. What was the actual situation in the towns and villages of Hunan and Hupeh? The Hupeh Provincial Peasant Association's delegate in Wuhan declared that the most urgent need was "immediately to establish organs for the maintenance of the political system. The political organs now existing are not really a power at all."[19]

In Hunan Stoler-Browder-Doriot were discovering that the peasants were straining with all their might to create precisely the type of local organ of power of which Trotsky spoke, they were discovering that Stalin's "only governmental authority" really did not exist.

> While the militarists have been defeated and driven out...the magistrates and gentry, like the landlords, remained. We saw them everywhere.... They still exercise their feudal dictatorship over the population.... A revolution without the destruction of the old system of local government is unthinkable.... This is keenly felt and understood by the masses everywhere.... In Hunan the process of supplanting the old system has also proceeded further than in any of the other provinces we passed through.... Special commissions are being set up in various districts of the province to take over the administration of local affairs. These commissions are composed of representatives of the Kuomintang, the trade

> unions, and the peasant unions.... While the old magistrates are still officiating in the villages, they are gradually being pushed out and supplanted by so-called Citizens' Councils which are directly elected by the population. In many places the peasant union is the highest authority for all kinds of questions.... But it is appropriate [!] to remark here that all this work of sweeping out the old rotten system...still lacks in system and planfulness. The absence of a definite programme of action for the reorganization of local government is keenly felt. Of course it can be explained [!] by the preoccupation of revolutionary China with the war against the militarists and the struggle against imperialism.[20]

"Citizens' Councils directly elected by the population"—but were these not soviets in embryo? Was the virus of "Trotskyism" strong enough to travel 10,000 miles and at the end of this journey to insinuate itself into the tissues of the Hunan peasants?

Everywhere the Comintern visitors went they heard the cry: "Arms to the peasants! We have no guns or ammunition. The peasants must be armed!"

"We learned," continued Stoler, "that wherever the peasants cannot get hold of rifles, they organize self-defence corps with picks and ploughs.... We were told of many plans and projects for obtaining arms and ammunition for the peasants. Cases were cited where the peasants had captured thousands of rifles from the Northern troops, but invariably these arms were handed over to the National government or the army."[21]

The peasants wanted land and arms. The Comintern imposed upon the Chinese Communists a policy which made the satisfaction of these demands wholly dependent upon the willing collaboration of the Left Kuomintang leaders and their Wuhan government. Without the collaboration, "victory was impossible," decreed Stalin.

"Without solving the land question," wrote the secretary of the Comintern delegation, "the Chinese revolution will not be able to achieve its final victory.... It would be a fatal error for the National government to neglect to tackle the agrarian problem in a most decisive revolutionary manner, or to fail to lend fullest support to the political and economic demands of the peasants." Nor was Stoler going so far as to suggest that the National government give the land to the peasants. "Certain measures are absolutely and immediately necessary.... A radical reduction in rents...tax reforms .. . prohibition of usurious rates of interest...arming of the peasants," he lamely concluded.[22]

This was, textually, the Kuomintang program. But the "revolutionary center" was making no move to implement even this mild program of reform. This was "fatal" for the revolution, but the "fatal error" did not lie with the Kuomintang leaders, who were only defending their own class interests, but with the Comintern, which failed to give the peasants a chance to defend theirs.

According to Browder-Doriot-Stoler, the Wuhan government was too "preoccupied" by the struggle against militarism and imperialism to do anything for the peasants. In reality the Wuhan leaders were preoccupied, deeply preoccupied, by the peasant movement. Only they were concerned not with giving it their "fullest support" but with finding means of checking it and keeping it within the bounds of bourgeois property.

The evasion, the confusion, the lack of any effective policy, exemplified by the deliberations and conclusions of the Kuomintang Land Commission, amounted in practice to passive sabotage of the agrarian revolt. When revolt flared none the less, the Left Kuomintang leaders abandoned their passivity and went over to a policy of direct repression.

When the peasant associations began, in the absence of any other effective force, to assume the functions of political power, the Wuhan leaders cried "Excesses!" and stepped in to limit them. Unable or unwilling itself to deal with the landlords and their hirelings openly marauding through the countryside at the head of counterrevolutionary bands of Min Tuan,[23] the Wuhan government forbade the mass organizations to try and sentence these enemies of the people and, a little later, even prevented them from making arrests or imposing fines.[24]

"Unscrupulous landlords and gentry are denounced by the party for the reason that they have persistently fleeced the peasants by oppressive means," declared the Central Executive Committee of the Kuomintang.

> ...It must be pointed out, however, that it is only after clear and conclusive evidence is established concerning such fleecing and oppressive conduct that landlords and gentry should be dealt with by the legal organs. Those innocent and well-to-do families in the villages and districts who are not opposed to the national revolution are under the protection of the Nationalist government. Our party comrades should definitely instruct the masses against reckless attack on others' liberty of person, property, profession, or religious faith. Anyone who is bent upon disturbing the local public order...is opposed to the revolutionary interests and his conduct is tantamount to anti-revolutionary offences. The party headquarters in the various localities should take heed to check such actions.[25]

"The peasants are glad to give the government this task of judging," said the secretary of the Hupeh Provincial Peasant Association, "but the government has no legal officers in all these districts. Our greatest demand is that the Wuhan government should quickly establish local governments.... Such a government we peasants will still defend with our lives if the government will grant us arms."[26]

But the government did not want a revolutionary power in the villages. Instead it ordered the dissolution of peasant associations which attempted to wield such power. Each peasant association was permitted, in theory, to have only fifty armed militiamen, and there was a decree that said that these fifty might use their arms only against bandits, not against the landlords. In all Hupeh, where by June there were no less than three million peasants organized, the peasant associations possessed seven hundred revolvers, and these were scattered all over the province.[27]

"Many *hsien* have sent people to the capital to request the purchase of rifles," reported the Hupeh Provincial Peasant Association delegate to the Kuomintang. "They have brought sufficient funds, asking only aid in buying them. This is not only the demand of the village peasant associations, but the universal demand of the peasants."[28]

But these delegates were turned back empty-handed and all other appeals went unanswered. "The peasants...were without arms and were continually subject to attack by counter-revolutionaries. Unfortunately it was generally impossible to meet the requests for military aid sent in from the country," said an official report of the Kuomintang.[29] "In the Huang An district, for instance," said the Hupeh peasant secretary,

> reactionaries killed twenty-one of the most responsible peasant leaders. The union has begged the government to send troops to protect them. But the government says the troops are busy at the front. The union then asks for the right to use its own arms; but this also the government forbids, allowing it only against recognized bandits who attack villages, but not for civil conflict within the village. What can we do? The reactionaries recognize no law; they kill as they wish. But we must recognize law, for we are a responsible union. Yet the law cannot help us and only forbids us to help ourselves.... We won the confidence of the peasants by promising relief from bad conditions.... This is not carried out.... The ordinary peasant only cried: "Liars! You did nothing for us. Now we won't listen to your empty words." We are trying to break down feudalism. But feudalism is based on the present economic structure of the village. The gentry have all the money. The poor must borrow every spring for seeds, fertilizer, even for their own food. Now the gentry refuse to lend any more because they hate the peasants' union. Two-thirds of the peasants can get no money for seeds. They begin to blame the union. We promised to organize co-operatives, but for this also we have no money.... The law forbids us to take land from the gentry till the new land policy is settled and the courts decided....

"Against this terrific list of difficulties," adds Miss Strong, "...he told me that the peasants' union made only two simple demands, immediate establishment of local governments with enough militia to support them against bandits and lawless reactionaries; and immediate establishment of co-operative stores and government credits to the peasants.... Such elementary and necessary demands," concluded our lady reporter, "but under the military, financial, and political situation of Wuhan—such Utopian dreams!"[30]

Such was the "revolutionary center!" Not as it existed in the imaginations of Stalin and Bukharin, but as it existed in Central China—in fact. This was where Browder-Doriot-Mann "breathed fresh air again" after their trip through Kiangsi and where "the enthusiasm that we found among the masses in Hupeh and the attitude of the Central Kuomintang and the Nationalist government towards the workers and peasants reassured us once more."[31] This was the government that M. N. Roy called" the emblem of the anti-imperialist fight and struggle of the

Chinese people."[32] Under its sway the most elementary demands of the peasants became—Utopian dreams!

The peasants quickly lost faith in their leaders—("Liars! You did nothing for us—now we won't listen to your empty words!")—and in their organizations. "The peasant unions have gradually lost the confidence and support of the peasant," reported a speaker at a Hupeh conference on June 25, because "what the peasants get from their struggle is often nothing but trouble or massacre."[33]

When Hsia To-yen rebelled in May, it never occurred to him to haul down the blue and white flag. "Because he still put up the Kuomintang banner and did not clearly express his attitude [?], the peasants were attacked off their guard. The onslaught was sudden, arrests were made, many fled, so that the peasants lost their leaders and the organizations collapsed. Therefore they did not help in the fighting nor in transport."[34]

The masses had been taught to regard the Kuomintang banner as their own. When reaction raised its head beneath its folds, it found them entirely unprepared and easily struck them down. That is what happened to the revolutionary movement as a whole. The banner of the Kuomintang had never been the banner of the masses. It was the banner of the bourgeoisie, of the landlords, the gentry, and the militarists. Neither the Shanghai coup nor even the events soon to follow hammered this fact into the heads of the Communist leaders and their Comintern mentors.

In Wuhan, the Communists had assumed full responsibility for the acts of the National government. Communists occupied posts in the national and provincial governments. The leaders of the Communist party sat with the leaders of the Kuomintang in a so-called "Joint Conference" in which all important decisions of policy were made. In a resolution defining the party's duties in these meetings, the Communist Central Committee in the first week of May declared: "The Communists in this joint meeting should discuss all principal questions, set forth concrete proposals, but such concrete proposals should not be based upon the maximum demands of our party, but should keep in mind the interests of the development of the national revolution and the solidarity with the Kuomintang left wing."[35] Let it be remembered that the Communists were functioning in the "bloc" not as the independent representatives of an allied party, but as members of the Kuomintang, subject to its program and its discipline. So when, in one of the first joint meetings, Wang Ching-wei announced that "only the Central Executive Committee of the Kuomintang has the right to ratify and publish the resolutions of the joint conferences," the Communist representatives concurred. Wang Ching-wei, of course, maintained a carefully organized caucus against the Communists. He "secretly got together all the pure Kuomintang members of the different party organs, and secured that before every meeting a preliminary meeting was held at his private residence for the purpose of presenting a united front...against the Communist members."[36]

But he need have had little fear of Communist recalcitrance. The Central Committee of the Communist Party even ordered Communists employed on Kuomintang newspapers "not to turn these papers into Communist organs, but to work in the spirit of the Kuomintang resolutions."[37] Under the conditions of the "bloc" ever since its inception, the Communists had published no daily paper of their own, nor did they have any in Wuhan, nor will one find anywhere in the resolutions of the Communist International instructions to rectify this glaring lack of the most elementary weapon of a revolutionary party. The absence of a Communist press was the final guarantee that the maintenance of "solidarity with the Kuomintang Left" meant the complete subordination of the Communists to the Kuomintang and the soft-pedalling of the Communists' "maximum demands."

Writing of a party so securely strapped and bound as this, Stalin, in his April 21 thesis, said: "While fighting in the ranks of the revolutionary Kuomintang, the Communist Party must preserve its independence more than ever before."[38]

"Preserve?" echoed Trotsky. "But to this day the Communist Party has had no such independence. Precisely its lack of independence is the source of all the evils and all the mistakes.... Instead of making an end once and for all to the practice of yesterday, [Stalin] proposes to retain it, 'more than ever before.' But this means that they want to retain the ideological and organizational dependence of the proletarian party upon a petty bourgeois party, which is inevitably converted into an instrument of the big bourgeoisie."[39]

"Solidarity with the Kuomintang Left" guaranteed that the ideological and organizational dependence of the Chinese Communists on their petty bourgeois and bourgeois allies would continue. Either the Communists would pursue an independent course in defiance of the Left Kuomintang's demand that the mass movement be checked, or else they would capitulate to that demand. So long as the Comintern insisted that satisfaction of the workers' and peasants' demands was possible only through the agency of the Left Kuomintang, the road to independence was barred. The Communists, therefore, traveled the only other path open to them.

> The Central Committee did not develop and push the strike movement, but cooperated with the Kuomintang leaders in fixing compulsory arbitration and left the right of final decision to the government, ordering the labour unions not to struggle for the workers' demands, but to submit to labour discipline.... When the unions arrested a number of factory owners and shopkeepers, the bourgeoisie cried out: "Excesses!" The Central Committee tried to convince the workers not to occupy factories, even when the factory owners deliberately closed them as an act of sabotage, not to close shops even when the shopkeepers deliberately raised prices.[40]

Rising prices were blotting out the meager fruits of a hundred victorious strikes. The workers instinctively moved forward to more revolutionary measures. They occupied the factories and shops and tried to operate them themselves. Their unions took direct punitive action against the saboteurs and the speculators.

But the government stopped them short. Government action, not workers' actions, would solve their problems, they were told. Earl Browder addressed a meeting of trade unionists in Hankow on April 29 and said the government would have to regulate prices. "Failure [of the government] to do this will mean disaster to the revolutionary forces," he said.[41]

Government failure to help the peasants was a "fatal error," said Stoler. Government failure to help the workers meant "disaster," said Browder. And the government failed in both cases.

In this government sat two Communist ministers, holding the portfolios of agriculture and labor, "the classic posts of hostages," to use Trotsky's phrase. The Communists were originally ordered into the National government by the Seventh Plenum of the Executive Committee of the Communist International at the end of 1926. The Kuomintang plenary session in March named Tang Ping-shan minister of agriculture, and Hsu Chao-jen, the Canton trade union leader, minister of labor. Browder wrote on April 10 that "the appointment of Communists to head these two posts signalizes a deepening of the social phase" of the revolution. For Browder the entry of the Communists into the government meant a "turn to the Left" which he felt sure would "undoubtedly come as a surprise and shock to American and British imperialism."[42] Arthur Ransome, a bourgeois journalist, understood somewhat better than Browder what a Communist minister of labor meant in a bourgeois government. "He will not be a tool of the trade unions, but a mediator between the government and labour."[43] In fact, the entry of the Communists into the Wuhan government only thinly disguised a sharp turn to the right which held surprises and shocks only for the masses of workers and peasants.

As ministers, the Communists were required to carry out the policies of the Kuomintang. At the formal induction of Tang Ping-shan on May 20, Wang Ching-wei said: "The peasant movement has grown rapidly.... What we need now is a man who can lead and direct the peasants.... Comrade Tang is such a leader. He is unusually equipped to cope with the peasant problems."[44] He was "unusually equipped" because millions of peasants identified the Communists with the October revolution in Russia and there, they knew, the peasants had been liberated. But Tang was not thinking of the October revolution. "I feel it is my sole duty to work hard to carry out the government's agricultural policy...the agricultural program of the Kuomintang and the late Tsungli (Sun Yat-sen)," said he on assuming his duties.[45]

"The inaugural address of the minister of agriculture, Tang Ping-shan, cannot be called other than shameful," it was charged long after the event. "He was silent on the agrarian revolution, on the confiscation of land, on the elimination of the power of the *tuhao* and the gentry in the villages. He spoke at length about the liberal reform of peasant conditions and inveighed against 'excesses.' After assuming his post, Tang Ping-shan immediately issued instructions to the peasants forbidding 'rash acts' against the *tuhao* and gentry, threatening 'severe punishment.'"[46]

"At present there is a crisis in the peasant emancipation movement," said one of the first manifestoes of the Communist minister of agriculture.

> [It is] a transitional period...a period of much struggle and chaos, of acts that are premature and of deeds that confuse the main issue. Some of this is attributable to excessive demands on the part of the peasants. While excessive demands must be attributed to, and are logical results of, the long suppression of the peasants...it remains a matter of necessity that they be checked and controlled.... The government therefore announces its policy that all irresponsible acts and illegal deeds of the peasants be nipped in the bud in the interests of the majority [?] of the peasants and the larger phase of the peasant movement.... All elements in the village sympathetic to the cause of the revolution must be gathered and organized under its banner and to that end peace must reign in the villages. It must not be annihilated by the peasants' excessive demands. As to the local tyrannical landlords and gentry, these must be left to be dealt with by the government. Free action by the peasants resulting in their arrest or their execution is punishable by law.[47]

In the ministry of labor, the Communist, Hsu Chao-jen, sang the same tune. "There are many evidences of infantile activity on the part of the newly liberated [?] sections of labor and the peasantry. This is causing a serious gap in the revolutionary alliance," he wrote in a circular issued a few days after he took office.[48]

Thus spoke the voice of the landlords and the bourgeoisie through the megaphone of the "revolutionary" government of the "revolutionary" Kuomintang—amplified and carried to the masses by the Communist Party!

> The Ministry of Agriculture and the Ministry of Labor were no different in any respect from the rest of the bureaucratic apparatus...They did not publish a single law to diminish the sufferings of the workers and peasants, not one decree to change the system of exploitation in the cities and villages.... No such decrees were even prepared for submission to the government. The work of these Communist Ministers...in practice turned into the most rotten bourgeois bureaucratic rule. To efface our Communist physiognomy before the masses, we did not make one revolutionary proposal. To cloak the counter-revolution, we did not criticize the errors of the Wuhan government.[49]

Throughout the mass organizations the effort was made to persuade the workers and peasants that their salvation lay in unity with those who oppressed them. Hsiang Chung-fah, head of the Hupeh Provincial General Labor Union, later to become secretary of the Communist Party,* busied himself with the organization of joint meetings between the trade unionists and the merchants and capitalists in an effort to carry out Wang Ching-wei's instruction that the "small capitalists must unite with the labourers."[50] Acting under the orders of the ministry of labor, the Hupeh General Labor Union abdicated the police powers it had assumed.[51]

* He was arrested in Shanghai and shot at Chiang Kai-shek's orders in June 1931.

Jen Hsu, general secretary of the All-China Peasant Association, complained that "the peasant movement in Hupeh developed too rapidly," and announced that the association had decided to "moderate" the peasant upsurge in order to ensure protection of the land of the "revolutionary officers."[52] The Hupeh Provincial Peasant Association obediently followed suit. "In compliance with the instructions of the Central Kuomintang and the Nationalist government," it ordered all branch associations "to prevent immature actions in the peasant movement.... Efforts must be made," it urged, "to consolidate the front and to seek for closer co-operation between the propertyless peasants, the small landlords, the merchants, and the manufacturers.... Confiscation of the property of military men of the revolution or the property of those who are not local rowdies and bad gentry is banned."[53] Wang Ching-wei, it is recorded, complained to Borodin that the peasants were not heeding these instructions and were seizing the land wherever they could. "Borodin denied that he was responsible for the movement.... Wang then asked Borodin what he proposed to do about it. Borodin could only answer to the effect that the only way was to modify the movement."[54]

"Solidarity with the Kuomintang Left wing" was ordained from above. To maintain that solidarity the Communist Party had to abdicate its class role and abandon its historic mission. The impact of the class struggle drove the politicians of Wuhan into the arms of the bourgeoisie and the gentry, whose instrument the Wuhan government had become—and to the Kuomintang and to this government the Communists were bound by the direct instructions of the Communist International. The Communist leaders, "under the influence of the fright and hesitancy of the Kuomintang leaders, were unable to put forward a program of revolutionary action to solve the land problem."[55]

"The infantile acts of the poor peasants," complained the Communist Central Committee on May 15, "are making the petty bourgeoisie go away from us."[56] Borodin, Roy, and the Communist leaders were busy in these critical days—"keeping the petty bourgeoisie with us." By "petty bourgeoisie" they did not mean the great mass of artisans, petty traders, small shopkeepers, and the lower strata of the peasantry who could and would have swarmed to a truly proletarian banner. They meant the small landlords, the "revolutionary" officers, and the politicians of the Left Kuomintang. The great masses of the workers, the peasantry, and the petty bourgeoisie were left leaderless. Reactionary forces in the towns and in the countryside were materially strengthened thereby and they soon moved to reassert their supremacy.

While the Wuhan leaders and the Communists wailed at the "excesses" of the peasants and pleaded for the "restoration of order," militarist forces soon emerged to restore "order" in their own way. The "revolutionary army" moved in to accomplish by force what the Wuhan politicians wanted but could not achieve by persuasion.

A few hours after nightfall on May 21 in Changsha, the capital of Hunan, rifle and machine-gun fire split the darkness. At one o'clock General Hsu Keh-chang, commander of the local garrison and subordinate of General Tang Sheng-chih, ordered his men, the 33rd Battalion of the 35th Army, to tie white bands around their arms. At their head he marched to the headquarters of the Hunan Provincial General Labor Union. Four pickets, two women, and a fifth man were shot down at the gate and the soldiers swarmed into the building. In quick succession raiding squads stormed the provincial Kuomintang headquarters, the party school, and the premises occupied by all the many mass organizations of workers, peasants, and students. The headquarters were smashed and all their occupants either shot out of hand or arrested. The shooting continued almost until dawn.

The next morning the city was plastered with bills: "Down with the extremists!" "Support Chiang Kai-shek!" Hsu Keh-chang announced that he had been "forced" to take action because the pickets and the peasant guards were planning to disarm his men, an explanation that was no longer original after the Shanghai events only six weeks previously. Hsu likewise announced that the Hunan provincial Kuomintang and government would be "reorganized," and a committee, appointed by the military, was set up for that purpose.

News of the events in Changsha on the night of May 21 trickled slowly into print in Wuhan. Not until four weeks later[57] did the press carry full accounts, and that was when a delegation arrived from Hunan to petition the government for protection from marauding troops who had established a reign of terror throughout the province. A whole month had already passed, a month of cowardly indecision and treacherous betrayal in Wuhan.

The raids on May 21 proved to be only the opening phase of the bloodiest chapter in the history of the disasters of 1927 in China. To the open space outside the west gate of Changsha at nightfall and at dawn, arrested workers, peasants, and students were marched and shot down in batches. The soldiers amused themselves with the women victims, despatching them with bullets fired upward into the body through the vagina.[58] The men were subjected to nameless tortures. Many who were not decapitated were sliced through the body at the hips. After the first wave of killings, Changsha settled down to a routine of at least ten, and often as many as thirty, executions daily. Once begun at the provincial capital, the terror spread and took a ghastly toll. Within a few days more than one hundred were killed at Henyang. On May 24, at Sangteh, six hundred active members of the local peasant association were mowed down by machine guns. When the soldiers rose at Liuyang, the peasants fled towards Changsha. There Hsu Keh-chang met them with machine guns, leaving 130 men and women dead and dying in front of the city gate. During the course of the next few months no less than twenty thousand peasant men and women and village workers fell before this juggernaut. For the scores killed by the revolution, the reaction took the lives of thousands.

On the morrow of May 21, an attempt was made to mobilize the scattered guards for a counterattack. Local leaders ordered the concentration of the armed detachments in the hills outside of Changsha. Peasant guards and pickets made their way with their rifles to the appointed place. Within a few days an army of several thousands, bitter with the loss of wives and sisters, fathers and brothers, stood ready to march on Changsha, which Hsu Keh-chang held with 1,700 men. The peasants counted on bottling up the Changsha garrison, reoccupying the city, and organizing their forces on a province-wide scale. They counted, above all, on quick aid from Wuhan.

They were already on the march when word came from the Central Committee of the Communist Party in Wuhan to cancel plans for the attack on Changsha and "to await action of the National government for a settlement of the question."[59] The All-China Trade Union Federation and the All-China Peasant Association sent a joint wire on May 27: "To the Provincial Peasant Union and the Provincial Labor Union, care of the Siangtan and Siangsang unions: The Central Government has appointed a committee of five which left here this morning for the settlement of the Changsha incident. Please notify all peasant and labor comrades of the province to be patient and wait for the government officials in order to avoid further friction."[60] The representative of the Communist Central Committee in Hunan issued orders for the retreat of all the peasant units. They reached all but two detachments of Liuyuanghsien fighters, who marched up to the gates of the city at the time stipulated and were there wiped out by Hsu Keh-chang's machine guns. The delay enabled Ho Chien, who was due to hold the province in fief from Chiang Kai-shek, to send two regiments down from Yochow to reinforce the Changsha garrison. In a few days the opportunity to strike back and mobilize the whole province was lost. Reaction gripped the pommel of the Hunan saddle and would not again be dislodged.[61]

The "committee of five" sent down from Wuhan was headed by Tang Ping-shan. Chiu Chiu-pei records that Borodin accompanied the party[62] that left Hankow on May 26 "to carry out the task of restoring order." But they got no farther than the Hunan border. At Yochow they were turned back by the troops of General Ho Chien. The task of restoring "order" had already been undertaken by abler instruments of counterrevolution.[63]

The "reorganized" provincial government ordered the immediate restoration of the *lien pao* system (collective family and village responsibility for the offenses of individuals). Decrees were issued offering protection to those who would denounce Communists and active leaders of the mass organizations. In the process of "reorganizing" the *tangpus* and other bodies, all the former leaders, wherever caught, were shot without ceremony. All land seized from the landlords or from the temples was ordered restored to the "rightful" owners. The plan for calling a provincial delegates' assembly was cancelled and the hundred-odd delegates already in Changsha awaiting the first session, scheduled for June 1, were executed en masse. Schools were closed down.[64] Girl students were subjected to frightful indignities. Reactionary newspapers which had been suppressed resumed publication. Haosen émigrés who had fled the peasants' wrath returned in droves and filled the posts in the newly reorganized party and government. With them they brought the money with which they filled the private coffers of Hsu Keh-chang and Ho Chien."[64]

14

Moscow and Wuhan

While in Changsha and a hundred other Hunan towns workers and peasants were being led out for execution by soldiers of the Kuomintang, delegates from all over the world were meeting in the Kremlin in Moscow at the eighth plenary session of the Executive Committee of the Communist International. Although Hsu Keh-chang's military coup in Changsha took place three days after the plenum opened, only two or three of those present in Moscow knew that the ensuing days, until the plenum ended on May 30, were the bloodiest days of the terror in Hunan. The plenum itself met, however, in an atmosphere of terror all its own.

Theoretically, the Executive Committee of the Comintern was, after the world congress, the highest policy-determining body in the International. Actually policy was determined by the Russian delegation and the Russian delegation was dominated by Stalin. Stalin's drive for the elimination of the Opposition led by Trotsky was entering its final phases. The sessions of the ECCI revealed the profound cleavage that already separated the contending forces, the nascent petty bourgeois reaction embodied in the Stalinist apparatus, and the Opposition, to which the best of the proletarian Old Bolsheviks adhered. It was revealed in the difference on all the main issues of the day, the internal course in the Soviet Union, the Anglo-Russian Trade Union Unity Committee, the threat of war, and, most sharply of all, the problems and the fate of the Chinese revolution.*

---

* The Opposition was not a homogeneous body. It was composed of a bloc of the original Left Opposition led by Trotsky and the so-called Leningrad Opposition of Zinoviev and Kamenev, who had originally united with Stalin in a "triumvirate" directed against Trotsky and had passed into opposition only in 1926. On the Chinese question important differences existed between the two groups and between Trotsky and Radek. As chairman of the Communist International Zinoviev had stood sponsor, as late as March 1926, for the resolution of the Sixth Plenum of the ECCI which canonized the bloc of classes in China. Stalin, in 1924–25, had produced the idea

The plenum met at a time when events everywhere were directly confirming the crushing correctness of the Opposition's criticisms of Stalin's course. The domestic policy of orienting the regime on the support of the kulaks, or rich peasants, under Bukharin's famous slogan: "Enrich yourselves!" had already undermined the proletarian power to an alarming degree.[1] Far more obvious, especially to the foreign delegates, was the bankruptcy of the Stalinist policies in Britain and in China. The two pillars of the Kremlin's strategy in the struggle against British imperialism had collapsed, the Anglo-Russian Committee, the bloc with Purcell, Hicks, and Citrine,[2] and the Kuomintang, the bloc with Chiang Kai-shek.

The diplomatic break with Britain occurred while the plenum sat. The same week the Anglo-Russian Committee, regarded by Stalin as a prime weapon against the anti-Soviet war plans of Downing Street, dissolved into thin air. While the plenum sat, too, the new articles of faith in Wang Ching-wei, Tang Sheng-chih, & Co., in Wuhan and Changsha were being blotted out by the blood of Hunan workers and peasants.

In these circumstances Stalin was not inclined to provide the Opposition with the public forum to which all the traditions of Bolshevism and the real interests of

---

of "worker-peasant parties" for the East, and had identified the Kuomintang as the model example of such parties. Following him, Radek had regarded the Canton regime as a worker-peasant government. In the subsequent Opposition bloc, these differences intruded themselves.

The Zinoviev group demanded the insertion of the formula of the "democratic dictatorship of the proletariat and peasantry" into the Opposition platform. The Trotsky group, over Trotsky's protest, voted to accept it for the sake of the general agreement on other issues. Trotsky, whose single vote had been consistently cast in the Russian Politbureau against subordination of the Communist Party to the Kuomintang ever since 1923, continued, nevertheless, to present the essential kernel of his own views. The Stalin-Bukharin majority was able to contrast these views, with some effect, to those of Zinoviev, especially on the estimate of the attitude toward the Wuhan government and the question of withdrawal from the Kuomintang. In their speeches and articles on the Chinese question, both Stalin and Bukharin devoted much time and space to baiting the Opposition on the basis of its internal differences.

While the real differences were by no means unimportant, the fundamental logic of the Opposition standpoint as a whole led directly to the demand for withdrawal of the Chinese Communist Party from the Kuomintang, and this was always recognized by its opponents as the essential Opposition demand. On the key question of the creation of soviets there was no difference in the Opposition ranks.

References in the text to the Russian Opposition mean primarily the consistent Left Opposition led by Trotsky. Zinoviev, Kamenev, and Radek capitulated to Stalin in 1928, but this act, and others that followed, did not save them from the fate that awaited them at the hands of the Thermidorian reaction eight years later.

The differences within the Opposition deserve further study which lies beyond the scope of this book. Those relating to the Chinese question are touched on briefly in a letter from Trotsky to Max Shachtman in 1930, published by the latter in his introduction to Trotsky's *Problems of the Chinese Revolution*, pp. 18-20. Zinoviev's views will be found in his "Theses on the Chinese Revolution," printed the appendices to the same volume.

the Soviet Union and the international revolutionary movement entitled it. The plenums of the Executive Committee of the Comintern had previously taken place in Andreyev Hall, the former throne room of the czars inside the Kremlin. Hundreds of Communists, Russian and foreign, used to fill the great hall to listen to the reports and the speeches. These were reproduced verbatim in day-to-day accounts published in the Russian press and in the English, German, and French organs of the Comintern. This procedure, still followed as recently as the two plenums held during the preceding year,[3] was now abruptly scrapped. The Eighth Plenum, contrary to all precedents in the history of the Communist International, met under quasi-conspiratorial conditions. Only a brief, belated, eight-line communique in the press announced that it had convened.[4]

Albert Treint, than a member of the presidium of the Executive Committee of the Comintern, a member of the special subcommittee on China at the Eighth Plenum, and a confirmed opponent of "Trotskyism," described the session in the following words:

> The last plenum of the Executive was held in the small room usually used for meetings of the presidium—and this on the pretext that in Moscow, capital of the world revolution and the proletarian state, there was no other room available for the Executive Committee of the Comintern. In reality, it was a question of preventing the Russian comrades, usually invited to our international sittings, from attending the discussions, where they could have learned some of the things hidden from them. Political documents, bearing no secret character whatever, were delivered to the delegates only on the eve of the opening session of the Executive. Then the sessions of the plenum and its committees went on in unbroken succession, giving the delegates time to read these documents only most superficially if at all.
>
> Delegates were forbidden to take copies of the stenograms of their own speeches or to communicate them to anyone. As soon as the plenum ended, all documents had to be returned immediately, on pain of not receiving permits to leave. They tried to forbid members of the Executive from making declarations when voting, but in the end, following several protests, this decision was applied only to members of the Opposition. For the first time in the history of the International, no record of the discussions was published either in the press of the U.S.S.R. or in the international Communist press. Only the resolutions adopted and a few statements made during the discussion were published, but these lost their real meaning when detached in this way from the discussion from which they emerged.[5]

Beside the resolutions, a brief editorial by *Pravda* on May 31, and a communiqué by the secretariat of the ECCI,[6] the press a month later published Stalin's speech[7] and a report made by Bukharin about the plenum to a Moscow party meeting.[8] It was not until a year later, after oppositionists abroad had begun to publish the speeches made by Trotsky, that the Comintern issued a slim pamphlet in German containing a few of the speeches on the Chinese question at the plenum.[9] The full report of the proceedings was never published.

Yet it was here that the differences on China were brought forward in boldest relief, especially when considered in conjunction with the events that were in precisely those days taking place on the territory of the Wuhan government.

In his speech, delivered on May 24, that is, three days after the Changsha overturn, Stalin reiterated his opposition to the creation of soviets on the grounds that the Hankow government and the Kuomintang were the organs of the agrarian revolution in China.

"The agrarian revolution," he said, "constitutes the foundation and content of the bourgeois democratic revolution in China. The Kuomintang in Hankow and the Hankow government are the center of the bourgeois democratic revolutionary movement."

Again:

> Does the Opposition understand that the creation of soviets of workers' and peasants' deputies now is tantamount to the creation of a dual government, shared by the Soviets and the Hankow government, and necessarily and inevitably leads to the slogan calling for the overthrow of the Hankow government?...It would be quite another matter were there no popular, revolutionary democratic organization such as the Left Kuomintang in China. But since there is such a specific revolutionary organization, adapted to the peculiarities of Chinese conditions and demonstrating its value for the further development of the bourgeois-democratic revolution in China—it would be stupid and unwise to destroy this organization, which it has taken so many years to build, at a moment when the bourgeois democratic revolution has just begun, has not yet conquered, and cannot be victorious for some time.

Again:

> Since China is experiencing an agrarian revolution...since Hankow is the center of the revolutionary movement in China, it is necessary to support the Kuomintang in Wuhan. It is necessary that the Communists form a part of that Kuomintang and its revolutionary government, on condition that the hegemony of the proletariat and its party be secured both within and without the ranks of the Kuomintang. Is the present Hankow government an organ of the revolutionary dictatorship of the proletariat and the peasantry?
>
> No. So far it is not, nor will it be so very soon, but it has all the chances of developing into such an organ in the further development of the revolution.[10]

Stalin wanted the "hegemony of the proletariat" in the Kuomintang and the Hankow government which he expected to carry through the agrarian revolution. Trotsky argued in reply that the Wuhan leaders would break on the issue of the agrarian revolution and that the "hegemony of the proletariat" was realizable only if the masses were mobilized into soviets really capable of leading the peasants in the crucial struggle for the land.

"The bloc of Hankow leaders is not yet a revolutionary government," he warned. "To create and spread any illusions on this score means to condemn the revolution to death. Only the...soviets can serve as the basis for the revolutionary government."[11]

> Again: Stalin has declared himself here against the workers' and peasants' Soviets with the argument that the Kuomintang and the Wuhan government are sufficient means and instruments for the agrarian revolution. Thereby Stalin assumes and wants the International to assume the responsibility for the policy of the Kuomintang and the Wuhan government, as he repeatedly assumed the responsibility for the policy of the former "national government" of Chiang Kai-shek.... We have nothing in common with this policy. We do not want to assume even a shadow of responsibility for the policy of the Wuhan government and the leadership of the Kuomintang, and we urgently advise the Comintern to reject this responsibility. We say directly to the Chinese peasants: The leaders of the Left Kuomintang of the type of Wang Ching-wei and Co. will inevitably betray you if you follow the Wuhan heads instead of forming your own independent soviets.... Politicians of the Wang Ching-wei type, under difficult conditions, will unite ten times with Chiang Kai-shek against the workers and peasants. Under such conditions two Communists in a bourgeois government become impotent hostages, if not a direct mask for the preparation of a new blow against the working masses. We say to the workers of China: The peasants will not carry out the agrarian revolution to the end if they let themselves be led by petty bourgeois radicals instead of by you, the revolutionary proletarians. Therefore build up your workers' soviets, ally them with the peasant soviets, arm yourselves through the soviets, draw soldiers' representatives into the soviets, shoot the generals who do not recognize the soviets, shoot the bureaucrats and bourgeois liberals who will organize uprisings against the soviets. Only through the peasants' and soldiers' soviets will you win over the majority of Chiang Kai-shek's soldiers to your side. You, the advanced Chinese proletarians, would be traitors to your class and your historic mission, were you to believe that an organization of leaders, petty bourgeois and compromising in spirit...is capable of substituting for workers', peasants', and soldiers' soviets embracing millions upon millions. The Chinese bourgeois democratic revolution will go forward and be victorious either in the soviet form or not at all.[12]

The key passages of the resolution adopted at the plenum were the following:

> The Executive Committee of the Communist International deems erroneous the point of view of those who under-estimate the Hankow government and deny its reality, its great revolutionary role. The government of Hankow and the leaders of the Left Kuomintang represent by their class composition not only the peasants, the workers, and the artisans, but also a section of the middle bourgeoisie. That is why the Hankow government, which is a government of the left wing of the Kuomintang, is not yet the dictatorship of the proletariat and the peasantry, but it is on the path toward such a dictatorship and, with the development of the class struggle of the proletariat, losing its bourgeois radicals temporarily travelling the same road, surmounting betrayals, it will inevitably develop toward such a dictatorship....
>
> The Executive Committee of the Communist International particularly calls the attention of the Chinese Party to the fact that now, more than ever, contact between the revolutionary government and the masses is necessary. It is only by this close contact, realized primarily with the aid of the Kuomintang, only

> through determined orientation toward the masses, that it will be possible to strengthen the authority of the revolutionary government and its role as the organizing center of the revolution. The task of the Communist Party is to assure such an orientation on the part of the Hankow government. Without the realization of this task, without the unfolding of a mass movement, without the agrarian revolution, without a decisive improvement in the situation of the working class, without the transformation of the Kuomintang into a large and real organization of the toiling masses, without the future strengthening of the unions and the growth of the Communist Party, without the closest connection between the Hankow government and the masses, it is impossible to lead the revolution to its crowning victory.
>
> In the present conditions in China, the Communist Party is for the war waged by Hankow. It is responsible for the policy of the Wuhan government, into which it enters directly. It is for facilitating the tasks of this government by every means. That is why the Communist Party can have nothing, "in principle," against the tactic of proceeding cautiously. Responsible for the policy of the government, the Communist Party would commit an utter folly if, whatever the circumstances, it rejected the tactic of compromise, that is, it undertook to fight on all fronts at the same time.
>
> That is why the ECCI considers that this question must be settled concretely in conformity with the concrete conditions, which cannot be foreseen in advance.... The admissibility of a tactic of tacking must be reflected in the economic policy of the government, which is under no obligation at all to carry out the immediate confiscation of all foreign enterprises.[13]

Having thus left the door wide open to "proceeding cautiously," the resolution called on the Chinese Communists to "deepen" the agrarian revolution, to arm and to mobilize the masses. These phrases would be cited later to prove that the Chinese Communist leaders had "sabotaged" the instructions of the Comintern. That the agrarian revolution was made wholly dependent upon the Hankow government as the "organizing center of the revolution" for which the Communists, under orders, assumed the fullest responsibility, would be conveniently forgotten, like the orders to mobilize the masses for recruitment into the Kuomintang—("into the hands of the executioners," said Trotsky)—and the orders to "strengthen the authority" of the Hankow government. Without this link between Wuhan and the masses, achieved "primarily with the aid of the Kuomintang," victory, the Comintern decreed, was impossible.

But what if the Hankow government proved unwilling? What if it not only proved unwilling to go along with the agrarian revolt but openly opposed it? This crucial question was neither raised nor answered in the formal resolution adopted by the plenum. Stalin and Bukharin spoke of the "great revolutionary role" of the Hankow government, but they knew perfectly well that the Hankow government would never sanction, no less lead, the agrarian revolution. On the other hand, they regarded the cooperation of the politicians and generals of Hankow as indispensable, and from this they drew the logical conclusion that it was necessary to keep the agrarian revolution within limits that would not frighten away these allies. That is what was really meant by "proceeding cautiously."

This was the point of view set forth by Bukharin at the meeting of the subcommittee on the Chinese question, composed of himself, Ercoli of Italy, and Treint of France. Treint, until that moment a staunch lieutenant of Stalin and a leader in the campaign against "Trotskyism," balked at this perspective, declaring it would lead to the armed suppression of the peasants. Called into the discussion by Bukharin, Stalin declared that failure to check the peasants would "turn the Left bourgeoisie against us," and he displayed telegrams from Borodin "showing that the leadership of the Kuomintang was determined to fight against the agrarian revolution even if it meant a break with the Comintern." "Against this possibility," said Stalin, it was necessary to "maneuver."[14]

"To fight now means certain defeat," argued Stalin. "To maneuver is to gain, with time, the possibility of growing stronger and of fighting later in conditions where victory will be possible. It is possible to maneuver without compromising anything," he went on. "The agrarian revolution frightens the Kuomintang only to the extent that it directly strikes at its own members and the officers of the armies. I propose to send instructions to Borodin to oppose the confiscation and division of land belonging to members of the Kuomintang or officers of the Nationalist army."

When Treint demanded to know whether the Communists would be expected to support Hankow in the armed suppression of the peasants, he says Bukharin replied in the affirmative. At this point, Stalin interjected: "Bukharin is drawing extreme logical conclusions, but things will not happen that way. We have sufficient authority over the Chinese masses to make them accept our decisions."*

Unfortunately, by the time the instructions of the Eighth Plenum and Stalin's telegram arrived in Hankow on June 1, the Kuomintang generals were already exercising their own "sufficient authority" over the masses. Sponsorship of the agrarian revolt led inexorably towards a break with the Left Kuomintang leaders. Yet such a break was expressly forbidden. Creation of soviets, which could provide a framework for the mobilization of the masses to carry through the agrarian revolt, was proscribed, for such a course meant "struggle against the revolutionary Kuomintang," against the Hankow government, the "organizing center of the

* Treint adds that he insisted on having a proviso added to the instructions ordering opposition to any attempt at a use of force by the Hankow regime. "We are agreed in principle," he says Stalin replied, "but it is useless to send instructions relating to problems which are not before us. I repeat that we have enough authority over the masses in China to have no need of using force." Treint made only mild reservations at the plenum itself, but he was shortly afterward expelled from the French Communist Party. It may be apropos to remark, in weighing this evidence, that Treint remains until this day, what he was then, a confirmed opponent of "Trotskyism."

revolution." The public resolution of the ECCI demanded independent action for the "deepening" of the agrarian revolution. Stalin's telegram ordered that it be kept within the limits needed to preserve the alliance with the generals and the politicians. These directives cancelled each other and left the Chinese Communists in hopeless confusion.

Stalin's telegram as given by Chen Tu-hsiu, who received it,* contained the following points:[15]

> 1. "Confiscate the land...not using the name of the Nationalist government, but do not touch the land of the military officers."
>
> This was merely a repetition, in essence, of the formula already adopted in principle by the Kuomintang Land Commission and the Fifth Congress of the Communist Party. Wang Ching-wei had bitterly opposed any form of land confiscation precisely because he realized that "from the gentry of Hunan and Hupeh the majority of the subaltern officers of the Second, Sixth, and Eighth armies were drawn."[16] Wang, on his part, preferred to stay with the generals than to go with the masses. As Chen Tu-hsiu later put it, "not a single one of the bourgeoisie, landlords, *tuchuns* (warlords), and gentry of Hunan and Hupeh provinces but was the kinsman, relative, or old friend of the officers of that time. All the landowners were directly or indirectly protected by the officers."[17] To use Trotsky's phrase, these instructions converted the armies "into mutual insurance societies for the landlords, large and small."[18]
>
> 2. "Check the peasants' overzealous action with the power of party headquarters."
>
> "We did execute this shameful policy," wrote Chen Tuhsiu. The peasants' "overzealousness" was already being "checked," not by the authority of the Communist Party but by the generals of the Kuomintang.
>
> 3. "Destroy the present unreliable generals, arm 20,000 Communists, and select 50,000 worker and peasant elements in Hunan and Hupeh to create a new army."
>
> Who was going to destroy the generals? And how was this to be done so long as the Communists had to remain inside the Kuomintang and inside its government? "I suppose," said Chen Tu-hsiu, "that we should still have pitifully begged the Central Executive Committee of the Kuomintang to discharge them." As we shall see, that was precisely the idea. How was a new army to be created without coming into collision at once with the generals of the Kuomintang? And how could this be achieved if no attempt had been made to organize the ranks of the army into their own soviets, thus bringing them into direct contact with the masses of workers and peasants?
>
> 4. "Put new worker and peasant elements in the Central Executive Committee of the Kuomintang to take the place of the old members."

---

* In a speech on August 1, 1927, Stalin quoted from a directive "relating to May 1927," that was apparently the text or a draft of the June 1 wire. It listed all the points substantially as given by Chen Tu-hsiu. Stalin omitted only to quote the qualification concerning confiscation of officers' land. According to his version, the directive began: "Without an agrarian revolution, victory is impossible." A line further: "*Excesses must be combatted, not, however, with troops, but through the peasant unions.*" Stalin's text italicizes the first sentence. We have italicized the second. Cf. Stalin, *Marxism and the National and Colonial Question*, p. 249.

> Writing of this only a year later, Chiu Chiu-pei did not dare quote directly from Stalin's telegram, but ventured to quote a parallel passage from No. 71 of the *Communist International*: "On the one hand we must consolidate the national revolutionary army and the Kuomintang.... On the other hand...we must seek means whereby, not shaking the united front, we shall change the class groupings within the Kuomintang, in the National government, and in the armies." This, wrote Chiu cautiously, "was indeed extremely difficult because to change the class groupings in the army meant the capture of the army by the Communist Party.... (It meant) a certain social policy [?] had to be put in force boldly to solve the livelihood problems of the soldiers, the peasants, and the broad masses. This not only required encroachment upon the bourgeoisie but also upon the petty bourgeois traders."[19]
>
> 5. "Organize a revolutionary court with a well-known member of the Kuomintang as its chairman to try the reactionary officers."
>
> This was the means proposed for "destroying" the reactionary generals. On this basis the Communists approved the appointment of Tang Sheng-chih to judge Hsu Keh-chang. Perhaps Moscow now wanted Wang Ching-wei to judge Tang Sheng-chih? That was the conclusion Roy drew.

The members of the Communist Central Committee, confused by the accumulated results of their own errors, were dumbfounded and perplexed by these instructions. Chen Tu-hsiu somewhat inelegantly expressed their feelings when he said it was like trying to take a bath in a urinal. Even Stalin's own deputy, he relates, "saw no possibility of carrying them out." The Central Committee wired its thanks to Moscow, pleading only that the designated objectives "could not be realized immediately."[20]

Roy, however, was a sterling World Bolshevik and he understood that cooperation with the Kuomintang was the thing. He promptly showed Stalin's telegram to Wang Ching-wei and asked him to endorse it. "I am quite sure," he is quoted as saying to Wang, "that you would approve of it."[21] Incomprehensibly, Wang did not approve at all. He did not want to "destroy the unreliable generals." He preferred to unite with them to crush both the Communists and the mass movement. Roy learned to his dismay that the Left Kuomintang did have a way out other than "following us." That was the one little detail Stalin had overlooked. His plan needed Wang Ching-wei's approval. And Wang Ching-wei did not approve.

On May 28, in Moscow, Trotsky had written in a letter to the plenum: "The whole revolution cannot be made dependent upon whether or not the pusillanimous bourgeois leadership of the Kuomintang accepts our well-meaning advice. It cannot accept it. The agrarian revolution cannot be accomplished with the consent of Wang Ching-wei, but in spite of Wang Ching-wei and in struggle against him.... But for this we need a really independent Communist Party, which does not implore the leaders but resolutely leads the masses. There is no other road and there can be none."[22]

Trotsky's warnings were brushed aside, however, and a special resolution of the Eighth Plenum condemned him for advocating the creation of soviets.[23] A brief communiqué announced that "the plenum approved the transformation of the Wuhan government and the Kuomintang into a democratic dictatorship of the workers and peasants,"[24] and *Pravda* solemnly proclaimed that "the decisions of the Communist International on the Chinese question give the only correct answer to the most important questions of the Chinese Revolution."[25]

In Hankow the Chinese Communists were trying in their own way not to deny the "great revolutionary role" of the Kuomintang government. That was why they countermanded the peasant attack on Changsha and turned instead to the government with requests for a "settlement." The Hupeh General Labor Union, the Provincial Peasant Association, and the Merchants' Union issued a joint telegram:

> Unfortunately...a misunderstanding has arisen among the workers, peasants, and soldiers in Hunan province. But this will not interfere in our sacred task of revolution. The government has dispatched a special commission for conciliation. A satisfactory settlement may be expected in a few days.... We have decided unanimously to carry out all the policies and orders adopted and promulgated by the government. We shall do our best to strengthen the united front of workers, peasants, and merchants to support the peasant policy of the party. We thoroughly understand that the only way to save the present difficult situation is practical cooperation between the government and the masses of the people.... As regards the incident in Hunan, we hope that the government will settle the case...and will guarantee that hereafter similar incidents shall not occur.[26]

Wang Ching-wei, however, declared that those responsible for the Changsha events were really the peasants, who had dared to seize the land for themselves. "He opposed the proposal of Borodin and the Communists that the Central Executive Committee (of the Kuomintang) should order the attack on the revolting army and the punishment of the guilty officers, as he realized that they had been acting under grave provocation. Instead, Tang Sheng-chih was sent to Changsha to investigate into the affair and restore peace."[27]

To this decision the Communists bowed. Propagandist theses issued for use among the masses counselled "waiting patiently for a settlement."[28] Having tried in vain to "pacify" the Hunan peasants, the Communists now hoped only to "pacify" Tang Sheng-chih, assuring the masses that he was a loyal believer in the Three People's Principles and would see that justice was done. They could cling now only to these vain hopes and false promises because their whole previous course had cut them off from the landless peasants in the army, the rank and file soldiers to whom they might have appealed over the heads of the officers and the generals. That would have been a potent court of appeal. Unfortunately, it did not exist.

In February 1927, that is before Chiang Kai-shek's overturn, the central organ of the Communist International had written: "The Chinese Communist Party and the conscious Chinese workers must not in any circumstances pursue a tactic which would disorganize the revolutionary armies, just because the influence of the bourgeoisie is to a certain degree strong there."[29] What was the result of leaving untouched by propaganda and organizational work this "certain degree" of "bourgeois influence"? Turn again to Chiu Chiu-pei:[30]

> "We did not pay any attention to the soldiers. Even where there were cases of fraternization between the soldiers and the workers, it was only superficial. The concrete demands of the soldiers were not set forth. They were not propagandized. The demands of the worker and peasant and soldier masses were not combined. We paid attention only to the connections with the army and divisional commanders or to the decorative work of the political departments. These political departments beautified the ugly counterrevolutionary faces of the division and army commanders. If the masses were disgusted with the military, they often expressed it in a disgust for the soldiers. The soldier masses were thereby very easily deceived by the militarists and persuaded that the workers, peasants, and Communists were against the armies, seeking only to destroy provisions and cause troubles in the rear."*

It was not surprising, therefore, that the "national revolutionary" armies, which Stalin had called the "armed people," should be transformed into instruments of the counterrevolution as soon as the "revolutionary" generals decided that the time for being "revolutionary" had come to an end. The Communists now could only cling to Tang Sheng-chih's bootstraps, desperately hoping that he would not kick them loose. When Tang arrived from the front on June 14 on his way to Changsha, the Communists issued a leaflet which said that the "Hunan coup was a revolt against Tang Sheng-chih because Tang...has expressed good will towards the oppressed peasants."[31]

An attempt was made to develop a campaign in favor of a punitive expedition against Hsu Keh-chang. Several mass meetings were held and manifestos

---

* A comparison of this passage with several from Trotsky's May 7 Theses is not uninstructive:

"The political leadership, instead of embracing the masses of the army through soldiers' soviets, has contented itself with a purely external copy of our political departments and commissars which, without an independent party and without soldiers' soviets, have been transformed into an empty camouflage for bourgeois militarism."

Again: "One would at least think that the military coup d'état of Chiang Kai-shek had finally hammered into the minds of every revolutionist that trade unions separated from the army are one thing, and united workers' and soldiers' soviets...are quite another thing."

Again: "If we do not want to permit the bourgeoisie to drive a wedge between the revolutionary masses and the army, then soldiers' soviets must be fitted into the revolutionary chain (of workers', peasants' soviets)."—Trotsky, *Problems*, pp. 49, 58, 78.

The difference between Trotsky and Chiu Chiu-pei is that the former wrote these words in May 1927, when corrective action was still possible. Chiu Chiupei's "confession" comes more than a year after the event. This is the difference between Marxism and empiricism.

were issued by various Communist mass organizations calling upon the government to take decisive action to liberate the peasants in Hunan. A group of eighty refugees from Hunan called at Central Kuomintang headquarters. "Although the Hunan delegates have been in Wuhan for more than twenty days...still terror reigns in many districts of Hunan. The Central Kuomintang must send a punitive expedition against Hsu Keh-chang."[32] A still larger party of delegates from Hunan organizations called on General Tang personally to ask for action against Hsu.

"Laborers and peasants will never be suppressed," he promised them, "although some immature actions of the labour and peasant movements should be corrected by the Central Kuomintang.... Long live the revolutionary masses in Hunan!" he cried.[33] The soldiers slaughtering the peasants in Hunan were men under his command.

Assigned by the Eighth Plenum to the task of assuring that the Hankow government would resolutely orient itself towards the masses, the Communist Party on June 16 addressed the following letter to the Kuomintang:

> The moment for carrying out the agrarian policy is the present. This is the historic task of the Kuomintang. The future of the revolution depends upon whether or not the Kuomintang takes decisive steps in this question.... The Central Committee of the Chinese Communist Party proposes the following measures for the suppression of the counterrevolution: The Nationalist government must issue a decree declaring the committee of the insurrectionaries in Changsha to be counterrevolutionary and calling upon all soldiers to overthrow it. This committee must be dissolved and the rightful government of the province re-established. A punitive expedition must be sent immediately to suppress the insurrection. Tang Sheng-chih must be authorized to send troops to overthrow the counterrevolution. The usurping local committee of the Kuomintang must be dissolved.... The workers' and peasants' organizations and the Communist Party must continue to exist unmolested in the province of Hunan. The Nationalist government must order all arms to be returned to the workers' and peasants' guards. The peasantry must be armed to create a guarantee against further reactionary outbreaks. The Kuomintang must now take closer feeling with the masses of the people and lead them unanimously against the counterrevolution. Unless the Kuomintang and the Nationalist government do this, the revolution will be endangered.[34]

Tang made a swift trip to Hunan, not to punish but to "investigate." Naturally his report completely justified the military coup there.

"I have found," he wired from Changsha on June 26,

> that the workers' and peasants' movement, under the misguidance of their leaders, have broken loose from control and precipitated a reign of terror against the people[!]. In defiance of the explicit orders of the Central government for the protection of the revolutionary soldiers' families, they have everywhere extorted taxes and fines, abused people, and even murdered people.... Seeing this state of affairs...the

> soldiers who were stationed in Hunan rose for their self-defense.... Although Hsu Keh-chang's actions were animated by a passion for justice, he has overstepped the limits of law and discipline. He should receive a light punishment in the form of a demerit but should be retained in the army service.

He concluded with a demand that the provincial regime be "reorganized," and asked for power to deal with "a few party members who are...planning to defy the government."[35] Three days later the government obediently responded by naming Tang Sheng-chih chairman of the Hunan provincial government and distributing all the important provincial posts to his underlings.[36]

Moscow had "approved the transformation of the Wuhan government and the Kuomintang into a democratic dictatorship of the workers and peasants," but the Wang Ching-weis of Wuhan, instead of taking this "inevitable" road, preferred to nestle in the bosom of Tang Sheng-chih. Hunan was irretrievably lost to the reaction.

On the same day that the text of Tang Sheng-chih's telegram was published in Hankow, the central organ of the Communist International boasted reassuringly:

"The panic-mongers of the Opposition have made much noise about the Changsha coup. They have spoken of a new defeat for the Chinese Revolution. Their cries will convince no one. Our party is closely following the events in China...confident in the strength of the Chinese Revolution. The uprising of the officers at Changsha, which met with the decided resistance of the workers and peasants [?], has already been suppressed."[37]

Shortly after the Hunan events, General Chu Pei-teh, who held Kiangsi province nominally in behalf of the Wuhan government, expelled all Communists, trade union and peasant leaders, political commissioners, and party workers. Before this new onslaught the Communists again retreated, deciding not to raise the demand for General Chu's dismissal because they "feared to drive General Chu away from the revolution," and they hoped to "neutralize" him by keeping quiet.[38]

"The mass of the poor peasants is the reliable basis of the revolutionary Wuhan government, which can count upon the firm support of the peasant population," the central organ of the Comintern was still telling its readers on June 23.[39] In truth, the masses had counted on the "revolutionary Wuhan government" to support them. "The workers have faith in the Kuomintang leadership," said Tu Cheng-tsu, chairman of the General Miners Union of Hunan. "[They] feel that the Central Party will never sanction the suppression of labor and it is on this basis that they give the party their support."[40] The masses were taught to count on Wuhan. Only Wuhan did not count on the masses. Instead it helped destroy the mass movement.

Kiangsi had been lopped off without a struggle. Hunan was drenched in terror. Within an ever-narrowing circle, right up to Wuhan itself, the mass movement was abandoned to its fate. In Hupeh, "in Chienmen, Yitsang, and other *hsien*, the massacre goes on," ran the somber report of a peasant union official on June 13. "Even ten li (three miles) from Hanyang, the *tuhao* are surrounding and killing the peasants. There used to be fifty-four *hsien* with peasant associations, but last week there were only twenty-three. According to our estimate, the day before yesterday of these twenty-three *hsien* there were only four in which the peasants were holding their own. Today, not one *hsien* is left."[41]

Without the independent organization of the masses into soviets, without the liberation of the Communist Party from its Kuomintang shackles, Trotsky had warned that the peasant revolt would "come to naught and be splattered into froth."[42] Few predictions have ever been more swiftly or more tragically confirmed.

Mif, who helped represent the Comintern in Wuhan, summed up the attitude of the Chinese Communists in these critical days in the following words: "We cannot struggle against the reaction with our own forces. By this we would undermine the authority of the national government and counterpose ourselves to it. We must support the national government; we must wait until it acts. We must push it on that road. But we must not take any measures against the reaction ourselves."[43] Mif is writing a year later. He stigmatizes this attitude as "shameful, cowardly, treacherous." But might he not have been quoting from the documents of Stalin and the Eighth Plenum? Were not soviets, the only road to independent action, proscribed because they would "undermine the authority of the national government"—Stalin's "only governmental authority"? Were not soviets proscribed because this would have meant to "counterpose ourselves" to the Wuhan government—because they were, in Stalin's words, "a slogan of struggle against the revolutionary Kuomintang"?

This course had led directly and swiftly to ruin. The mass movement was being "splattered into froth." While the workers and peasants died under the swords and rifles of the Kuomintang executioners, the Communist Party was still trying to maintain "a determined course towards the masses," "secured primarily with the aid of the Kuomintang," for the purpose of "bringing the masses into the Kuomintang." But the Wuhan leaders shrugged. "The Communists propose to us to go together with the masses," declared Wang Ching-wei at a meeting of the military council. "But where are the masses? Where are the highly praised forces of the Shanghai workers or the Kwangtung and Hunan peasants? There are no such forces. You see, Chiang Kai-shek maintains himself quite strongly without the masses. To go with the masses means to go against the army. No, we had better go without the masses but together with the army."[44]

That Wang Ching-wei would not go with the masses did not prevent the Comintern and the Communist Party from trying to go with Wang Ching-wei. The slogan of soviets had been declared premature in the spring of 1927 because "the possibilities of collaboration with the Left Kuomintang had not yet been completely exhausted."[45] One after another these "possibilities" had been probed, first Chiang Kai-shek, now Wang Ching-wei. It was not yet time, however, to stop "imploring leaders" because not all the "possibilities" had even yet been exhausted. There still remained—Feng Yu-hsiang.

15 The Wuhan Debacle

Feng Yu-hsiang, obese and unscrupulous, was a militarist who had risen to power in the northwest by a series of shrewd and timely betrayals of his superior officers and allies. Originally nurtured on the bosoms of foreign missionaries, he first appeared in the world's headlines as the "Christian General" who taught his hymn-singing soldiers the homely virtues of rustic simplicity. In 1924, he discovered that Moscow made up in generosity what it lacked in spiritual piety. He shed his Christian skin and joined the ranks of that peculiar species, raised exclusively on Chinese soil by Stalin and Bukharin, the "Bolshevized" militarists. The Holy Grail proved no match for Russian arms, Russian money, Russian advisers. Feng was quickly converted to the idea that a Russian gun in hand was worth a dozen haloes in the hereafter, especially when military reverses at the end of 1925 cut his "People's Army" off from all other sources of munition supply.

He left for Russia early in 1926. "Feng Yu-hsiang is coming to Moscow," solemnly said a dispatch to the New York *Daily Worker*, "to work as an ordinary working man in a factory and thus amid labor surroundings to acquire a first-hand education and experience of all phases of economic and political life in the Soviet Republic. He is entering into this self-imposed exile in order to equip himself the most thoroughly to carry out the principles of the Kuomintang."[1] Feng, indeed, wanted to "equip himself most thoroughly" with the goods to be found in Soviet arsenals, and on his arrival at the Soviet capital he found that the open sesame to these riches was a simpler formula than the Lord's Prayer. He had himself and his henchman, Yu Yu-jen, photographed in the center of admiring Russian comrades. He predicted "new battles and new victories awaiting the future of the Chinese nation." Before very long he learned to call "special attention to the labor and peasant movement taking place throughout China" and to declare his conviction that "in the future the proletariat will ultimately gain a victory in China." On August 19, 1926, in an interview with *Pravda*, Feng promised that his army would fight "for the emancipation of the nation" and "the consummation of the national revolution."[2]

Although he had renamed his army the "Kuominchun" or "People's Army," the wily Feng had for years evaded friends who importuned him to throw in his lot with the Kuomintang, "but when he visited Moscow," marvelled a Japanese journalist, "the Christian General allowed himself to be a disciple of Lenin before anyone was aware of it."[3] It was immensely easy, pleasant—and profitable. Delighted with his conquest, Stalin plied Feng with arms and funds and shipped him back to his army, which had already started on a long trek southward from Nankow Pass through Shensi province toward the Honan border. Back among his soldiers, Feng proclaimed on September 17, 1926: "I am the son of a laborer," and announced that it would henceforth be the object of his armies "to awake the masses...sweep away the traitorous military clans, break down imperialism, and secure the freedom and independence of China."[4] Feng was now a full-fledged recruit in the ranks of Stalin's reliable allies and stepped boldly along the path already trod by Hu Han-min, Chiang Kai-shek, Li Chi-sen, Tang Sheng-chih, and Wang Ching-wei. Secure behind the mountains in his great northwestern territory, Feng acquired huge stocks of Russian arms and ammunition, entrenched himself at Tungkwan Pass, overlooking the Honan Plain, listened politely to his Russian advisers, and waited for "der Tag."

It was not long in coming. While he waited, the Northern Expedition swept to the Yangtze. Chiang Kai-shek, who had earlier learned how easy it was to unlock the doors to Russian arsenals, entered Shanghai and there broke, not his faith with Stalin, but Stalin's faith in him. Tang Sheng-chih and Wang Ching-wei were by now also preparing to break, but this was not yet officially admitted in Moscow, for the necessary scapegoat had not yet been selected—and there was still Feng. He, surely, would come like Lochinvar out of his western stronghold and save the day for the "revolutionary Kuomintang!" He was a solid man, closer to the soil, more deeply rooted in it than the thin reeds Moscow had until now leaned upon. Was he not, even now, reiterating by wire his undying fealty to Wuhan?[5] News dispatches reaching Moscow indicating that Feng was in touch with Chiang Kai-shek's emissaries, that Feng would force Wuhan to terms with Chiang, were kept out of the Russian press and elsewhere hotly denied.

"Recently the imperialists have again been circulating rumors that Chiang Kai-shek would be reconciled with Wuhan or that he would collaborate with Feng Yu-hsiang. This is false," declared the central organ of the Comintern. "None of the leaders has any connection with Chiang Kai-shek. Feng Yu-hsiang and his army have no confidence in this traitor either."[6] Feng was Moscow's last trump. To suggest that he would fall down on the job was the rankest Trotskyist heresy, for was not Trotsky warning, once more, that to put faith in Feng meant to court a repetition of the experiment with Chiang Kai-shek?[7]

Wuhan, too, counted, almost piteously, on Feng Yu-hsiang. Wuhan, it will be recalled, had decided to move northward against the Fengtien troops rather than against Chiang Kai-shek, in the hope that a military victory and the occupation of Peking would bring Chiang to heel. The success of this plan rested decisively with Feng Yu-hsiang, sitting tight with his fresh forces back of Tungkwan Pass. In the first part of May the flower of the Kuomintang army had accordingly been moved up the railway into Honan. Led by the famous "Ironsides," it fought its way northward in a series of sanguinary battles which culminated at the end of the month in a Chinese armageddon on the fields north of Chumiatien. Behind the lines in Hankow workers toiled at the arsenal for thirteen, fifteen, and seventeen hours a day. Over their heads fluttered banners: "You are the rearguard of the revolution.... Unless you give your all, there can be no army, no revolution, no struggle to free China from its oppressors.... Our revolutionary soldiers do not fight in eight-hour shifts. Do you want to work only eight hours?"[8] At the front the soldiers, too, thought they were fighting "to free China from oppressors." With unexampled heroism they hurled themselves at the better-fed, better-armed armies of the Northerners, commanded by Chang Hsueh-liang, the young son of Chang Tso-lin. The Fengtien forces were routed, but the victors paid with the destruction of their best forces. They lost 14,000 killed and wounded.[9] The men fought as men had rarely ever fought before in China because they were animated by the hope that in fighting and dying they were helping to put an end to the hated poverty and degradation of their own people. Their sacrifice was futile. They had been sent into battle not for these ends, but to feed the Napoleonic ambitions of Tang Sheng-chih and the hopes of the Wuhan leaders that they could force Chiang Kai-shek to come to terms. These, too, were frustrated. Wuhan had put up the stakes, the flower of its army. It was Feng Yu-hsiang who raked in the winnings.

Feng had remained carefully aloof during the fighting. He now moved down from Tungkwan Pass along the Lunghai railway. Scarcely losing a man, he occupied Loyang and by June 1 was ensconced in new headquarters at Kaifeng. The rout of Fengtien and the decimation of Hankow's armies made him military arbiter of Central China. The march on to Peking depended entirely upon him. As if to underline that fact, he sent telegrams announcing his "victory" with fine impartiality both to Nanking and to Wuhan. The Wuhan leaders he summoned to Chengchow for a conference on June 12. Here they came in a body to learn their fate.

Feng waited until the Wuhan party had arrived at Chengchow before coming down the line to meet them. Miss Strong watched Feng alight, "with ostentatious simplicity," from a freight-car, which he used because his "brother soldiers also travel in freight-cars." She related that "a long time afterward" she heard that Feng had entered the freight-car at the last station before Chengchow, having traveled thus far in a comfortable private car on the same train.[10] Advocates of a bloc with class enemies and dubious allies might have pondered the fact that only a year before Feng had arrived in Moscow in a political freight-car decorated with the name of the Chinese proletariat. Now, "a long time afterward," they were about to learn that he had only temporarily left his own, more comfortable private car labeled: "Reserved for the Chinese bourgeoisie."

When Feng gathered together with the group of Wuhan leaders, he found himself in agreement on one thing only: the workers, peasants, and Communists had to be crushed. "Even the Wuhan government had decided this," adds our lady reporter plaintively.[11] Beyond this, Feng wanted no more truck with Wuhan. He wanted strong allies from whom he could filch advantages, not weaklings from whom he had nothing further to pain. After the formalities of feasting were over and Wuhan had endowed Feng and his principal henchmen with titles to grace his military grip on Honan (from which Wuhan had already voluntarily withdrawn all its political workers),[12] Feng brought the conference to an abrupt close and sent his "allies" packing back to Hankow. "All the forces under Feng Yu-hsiang are pledged to obey the resolutions and orders of the Central Executive Committee at Wuhan and of the Nationalist Government," hopefully reported the *People's Tribune* .[13]

A week later, accompanied by Ku Meng-yu and Hsu Chien, two Wuhan luminaries,[14] Feng Yu-hsiang travelled down to the eastern terminus of the Lunghai railway, Hsuchow, and there met Chiang Kai-shek, with whom he struck an immediate bargain. On June 22 at the Hsuchow station, Feng told eager newspapermen "of his sincere desire to cooperate with the Nationalists and to extirpate militarism and Communism,"[15] and handed them a copy of a telegram he had sent to the leaders of the Wuhan government.

"When I met you gentlemen in Chengchow," it read,

> we talked of the oppression of the merchants and other members of the gentry, of labor oppressing factory owners, and farmers oppressing landowners. The people [*sic*] wish to suppress this form of despotism. We also talked of the remedies for this situation. The only solution which we discussed is, as I see it, as follows: Borodin, who has already resigned, should return to his own country immediately. Secondly, those members of the Central Executive Committee of the Hankow regime who wish to go abroad for rest should be allowed to do so. Others may join the Nationalist Government at Nanking if they desire.... Both Nanking and Hankow, I believe, understand their mutual problems. I do not need to remind you gentlemen that our country is facing a severe crisis. But in view of this I feel constrained to insist that the present is a good time to unite the Nationalist faction in a fight against our common enemies. It is my desire that you accept the above solution and reach a conclusion immediately.[16]

Lochinvar had fallen down on the job.

On the way back from Chengchow, General Galen,* chief Russian military adviser and the real organizer of the Northern Expedition, pointed out from the train some barely distinguishable shapes hugging the ground beneath the trees

---

* The name used in China by Vassily Bluecher, later commander of the Far Eastern Red Army of the USSR.

and in the gullies. These "were the bodies of Cantonese who had died advancing by this pass and railway. It was for this that they had died...boys of Kwangtung and Hunan who had marched forth for a hope that most of them were only beginning to understand. It was for this only—that...their allies who survived might establish a military dictatorship based upon the joint suppression of the workers and peasants."[17]

To come to terms as swiftly as possible with this military dictatorship was now the sole purpose of the Wuhan leaders. At Chengchow they had understood that further collaboration with Feng Yu-hsiang depended upon their ability to disembarrass themselves of the Communists and to put an end to the mass movement. The Feng-Chiang conference at Hsuchow and Feng's ultimatist telegram bade them hasten.

Wang Ching-wei "at once got to work, preparing for the immediate expulsion of the Communists."[18] Tang Sheng-chih made his hurried trip to Hunan and there, as we have already seen, he "confirmed the existence of the Communist conspiracy against the Kuomintang" and advised "the immediate expulsion of the Communists from the Kuomintang."[19] In the press and from public platforms, the Kuomintang leaders opened up a campaign against the Communists to prepare the way for the contemplated split.

Ironically enough, the surge of the mass movement, its tendency to act independently of the Wuhan government, its defiance of Wuhan's restrictive decrees, were all laid at the door of the Communist Party. Before long the Comintern was going to charge the Chinese Communist leaders with sabotaging its instructions by failing to lead and develop this independence of the mass movement. Yet in these days, it is significant and instructive to note, Wang Ching-wei quoted approvingly from Stalin and the resolutions of the Comintern as an argument against the "extremists" in Hunan, the rank-and-file workers and peasants and individual Communists.

In a speech at the Hupeh party delegates' conference at Wuchang on June 26, Wang cited the resolution of the Seventh Plenum of the ECCI "which clearly stated (that) the Chinese Revolution must take its stand on the alliance of the workers and peasants and small capitalists. In view of this fact," said Wang, "members of the Chinese Communist Party itself viewed with disapproval the inconsiderate acts which were recently perpetrated, for example, in Hunan province."[20]

In other words, as Wang saw it, those Communist leaders who "disapproved" the "excesses" of the peasants did so in conformity with, not in defiance of, the instructions of the Communist International! To show how "different" China was from Russia in respect to the problems of the social revolution, Wang quoted "Stalin's admirable comparison"[21] between the China of 1927 and the Russia of 1905 and 1917, a comparison Stalin had drawn in order to refute and deride Trotsky's argument that soviets were needed to carry the Chinese agrarian revolt through to its conclusion.* Wang Ching-wei found common ground with Stalin in his argument against the nameless leaders of the mass movement, whose views, as he quoted them, sounded strangely like lines out of Trotsky's speeches.

"I have heard frequently from those who are conducting the mass movement," wrote Wang Ching-wei,

> the saying: "Don't place your confidence in the strength of the Kuomintang or the Nationalist government. Place confidence in yourself."...As a result the people have refused to accept orders or follow the instructions of the government or party (Kuomintang). It has not only alienated the people from the party, but has also placed the people in the precarious position of conducting an independent war with the counterrevolutionaries without the direction of the party.... As a consequence the masses have been surrounded by counterrevolutionaries and the party has found it impossible to rescue them.[22]

The masses conducted "an independent war" against the counterrevolutionaries, among whom they counted the landlords first and above all. The Kuomintang could not "rescue" the peasants because it was primarily interested in rescuing the landlords. The peasants suffered defeat, not because they ignored the leadership of the Kuomintang, but because the leadership of the Comintern and the Communist Party ignored them to preserve the alliance with the Kuomintang.

"The principle that every peasant should have his own field to plough is indeed clearly stipulated in the third of the Three People's Principles," Wang Ching-wei continued. "But I must point out that when our Tsungli (Sun Yat-sen) drew up the *min sheng* principle (people's livelihood) and made the statement that 'every peasant should have his own field to plough,' he at the same time...said clearly that the land questions should be settled through political and legal channels. He never said that the matter could be settled by taking the lands from the landowners and dividing them among the peasants."

Sun Yat-sen, said Wang, wanted the problem "to be worked out in such a way that the peasants will be benefited and at the same time the landowners will not suf-

* "Can it be stated that the situation in Russia in March–June 1917, was analogous to the present situation in China?" asked Stalin, at the May plenum. "No, it cannot. This cannot be maintained, not only because Russia was then on the threshold of a proletarian revolution, while China is now facing the bourgeois-democratic revolution, but also because the Provisional Government of Russia was then a counterrevolutionary government whilst the present Hankow Government is a revolutionary government in the bourgeois democratic meaning of that word.... The history of the workers' soviets tells us that such soviets can exist and develop only in the event of favorable conditions for the direct transition from the bourgeois-democratic to the proletarian revolution. Was it not because of this that the workers' soviets in Leningrad and Moscow in 1905 came to grief, like the workers' soviets in Germany in 1918—because conditions were not favorable? It is possible that in 1905 there would have been no soviets in Russia had there existed at that time in Russia a broad organization similar to the present-day Left Kuomintang in China.... It follows that the Left Kuomintang in China is playing approximately the same role in the present Chinese bourgeois democratic revolution as the soviets played in 1905."—J. Stalin, "The Revolution in China and the Tasks of the C.I.," *Communist International,* June 30, 1927.

fer." Sun's idea, he went on, was that there would be no class struggle at all in China and that the Kuomintang's job "as a party of many classes of people" was to avoid this class struggle—"otherwise an alliance between the classes is impossible."[23]

In his own way, Wang was right. If you were going to have what Stalin called "a revolutionary parliament," or what Bukharin called a "cross between party and soviets," or what Martinov more simply dubbed the "bloc of four classes," you had to keep the collaborating classes from clashing with each other. Otherwise an alliance was, in truth, impossible. Stalin-Bukharin wanted the class struggle in words and tried to avoid it in deeds. At this point they broke with the workers and peasants, who were not sure of the words, but who performed, with all the sure instincts of the oppressed, the deeds. The only common ground the peasant saw with the landlord was the land which be tilled and whence the landlord drew the profit. His aim in life had become to drive the landlord off that land and make it his own. These were the simple materials of the agrarian revolution. You were either with the peasant or with the landlord. Wang Ching-wei and his friends were now being compelled to swallow all their proud words about the land and the peasant and to place themselves unequivocally with those who were already crushing the revolt on the land.

Stalin had made it the task of the Chinese Communists to strengthen the connection between the masses and the Wuhan government, "the only governmental authority," the "organizing center of the revolution." Yet in China the masses were coming more and more sharply into collision with this government because, Stalin to the contrary notwithstanding, this government did not support but resisted their efforts in their own behalf. The mass organizations went their own way as best they could. "The gulf between the government and the masses is now wide," reported a special Kuomintang commission sent to investigate conditions in the province of Kiangsi.

> The government cannot even participate in or supervise the activities of the public organizations.... Very often we see the districts neglecting the direction of the provincial Kuomintang, or the peasant and labour unions opposing the resolutions of the provincial Kuomintang.... The party branches have made arrests and punished people freely. Public organizations did the same thing. Thus everywhere there have been the phenomena of multiple governments—this is just as dangerous as anarchy.... The greatest fault of the peasant and labor movement leaders is their misunderstanding of the policy: "Support the interests of the peasants and laborers."[24]

The worker and peasant leaders misunderstood the slogan: "Support the interests of the peasants and laborers." They thought it meant to support the interests of the peasants and laborers. Their efforts to do this led them to the creation of "multiple governments." Isolated and scattered in the towns and villages, the local unions of the workers and peasants collided at every point with the district and provincial centers of the Kuomintang and with the "organizing center" at Wuhan. These "multiple governments" completely lacked connection with each other.

They were unable to pursue a uniform policy. The organizations of workers', peasants', and soldiers' councils, rapidly establishing contact with each other, from village to village, town to town, from province to province, offered the only means of overcoming the chaotic disorganization of the mass movement. But these would have been soviets. Stalin opposed this course, urged by Trotsky, on the grounds that it meant "struggle against the revolutionary Kuomintang," against the "only governmental authority." The Left Kuomintang leaders in Hankow opposed it too, and for precisely the same reasons and in exactly the same terms.

In an article entitled "Revolution and the Masses," Sun Fo complained that the masses had proved indifferent to Wuhan's ban on the assumption of civil power by the mass organizations. "Two months have elapsed since these instructions were issued," he wrote. "Various public organizations have continued their free actions in open disregard of the government's decisions, aiming at depredation of the power of the government." Peasants were seizing the land, workers were taking over factories and shops, he complained. "We must call attention to the fact that if the masses are not following the leadership and direction of the Kuomintang and are not prepared to carry out the policy of the party, they are actually acting against the interests of the national revolutionary movement (read: "the revolutionary Kuomintang"). In other words, they are actually committing counterrevolutionary actions.

"If the people can freely arrest, impose fines, confiscate the property of individuals, and carry out executions right under the nose of the government," Sun Fo went on,

> then the political power of the government must be regarded as completely usurped. There is no prestige nor power. On the other hand, if the people regard their actions as proper, then they have openly refused to take the Nationalist government as the only governing organ of the revolutionary movement and the government of the national revolution. They are under the impression that the Nationalist government can no longer enforce its authority and so they must form independent administrative organs.... In opposing openly the revolutionary government, their actions can be taken as being of a counterrevolutionary character.... They refuse to admit that all mass movements in China should be directed and unified under the Kuomintang. They believe the Communist Party should take part in leading mass movements. They have not yet been convinced that the Nationalist government is the only representative organ of the revolutionary movement.[25]

It is doubtful whether Sun Fo in Hankow in July 1927, had read the theses and speeches of Stalin made a few weeks earlier in Moscow. It is certain that he never saw or heard the arguments of Trotsky. Yet here he might have been plagiarizing directly from Stalin. Substitute "Trotsky" or the "Opposition" for the "masses" and Sun Fo's article might just as well have been a document of the Stalin-Bukharin majority at the Eighth Plenum. The Chinese workers and peasants, and Trotsky, rejected the Stalin-Sun Fo dictum that the Wuhan government was the "only governmental authority," "the only governing organ of the revolutionary movement." The masses were convinced that Wuhan could not "enforce its authority" and demanded the creation of "independent administrative organs," just as Trotsky in Moscow warned that Wuhan's power "was nothing or nearly nothing" and demanded the creation of soviets, independent councils of workers, peasants, and soldiers. For this Stalin denounced Trotsky as "counterrevolutionary" and for this his confrère Sun Fo leveled the same charge, more openly, more directly, against the masses themselves. These affinities were not at all accidental.

Prior to striking at the mass movement at Canton in March 1926, and at Shanghai in April 1927, Chiang Kai-shek had laid down a barrage directed at the Communists, charging them with responsibility for the "excesses" of the masses and with plotting against the sovereignty of the bourgeoisie within the Kuomintang. The leaders of the Left Kuomintang now pursued the same tactics. The accusation was no more just now than it had been at Canton or Shanghai. Nothing was further from the minds of the Communist leadership, in Hankow, or in Moscow, than the unleashing of an independent offensive of the masses directed against the sabotage and betrayal of the petty bourgeois leaders of the Kuomintang. On June 29, that is when the Wuhan leaders were already openly taking sides with the militarists against the agrarian revolution, the central organ of the Communist International issued a programmatic article which asked "Who will realize the agrarian revolution?" and answered:

> By its historic past, its social composition and the perspectives of its development, the Kuomintang can and must be transformed into an organ of the democratic dictatorship.... The Kuomintang is a sort of cross between a party and a national parliament....
>
> Soviets will be necessary at the moment when the revolution will be nearing the achievement of its bourgeois-democratic tasks," the Comintern spokesman continued. "At that moment it will be possible and perhaps [?] necessary to split the Kuomintang. This moment cannot be foreseen with precision. Nevertheless, it is clear that it is not close enough for it to be necessary to advance immediately among the masses the slogan of soviets. The Communist International and the Communist Party of China are now responsible for the fate of the Kuomintang, and of the Wuhan government, in other words, for the fate of the Chinese revolution. They cannot therefore permit themselves to issue loose slogans and formulas.
>
> The best illustration of the nonsense of the arch-Left line of the Opposition is in the slogan for soldiers' deputies as one of the forms of the dual power. In proclaiming these slogans the Bolsheviks sought to decompose the army of the czar and of Kerensky. To proclaim it now for the army fighting for the Wuhan government would be consciously to seek to decompose this army.... To proclaim the slogan of soviets of soldiers' deputies would be consciously to accelerate the conflict with the generals in the most disadvantageous circumstances for the Communist Party and its allies. This slogan would mean provoking a conflict which could really cause a lasting defeat for the revolution.[26]

In Hankow the same spirit necessarily dominated the Chinese Communist leaders who clung now to two forlorn hopes, that by retreating still further and conceding still more, they might still preserve the "united front" and, secondly, that by playing on the strings of this or that militarist's ambitions, they might still be able to divert Wuhan in the direction of a punitive expedition against Chiang Kai-shek. They raised the slogan of an "Eastern Expedition" against Nanking, thinking "to fool the 'revolutionary generals' into attacking Chiang first and the Communists later," according to a member of the Communist Central Committee.[27] Meetings were staged and manifestos issued. Appeals were made to the generals believed to be more "reliable." Chang Fah-kwei, commander of the "Ironsides," was most bitter against Chiang Kai-shek and for a while Communist hopes centered in him. Roy went to Wang Ching-wei and tried to persuade him, in the spirit of Stalin's telegram, to permit the expansion of Communist forces under Chang Fah-kwei's command. Roy found Wang cold to his proposal.[28] Representatives of the Shanghai General Labor Union wired an appeal to Feng Yu-hsiang on the same day that the latter was demanding at Chengchow the extermination of all trade union leaders: "We hope that you, who are the true believer in Kuomintang principles and the real supporter of…the policies of the Tsungli, will lead…the revolutionary armies for a punitive expedition against Chiang Kai-shek."[29] All the agitation for a campaign against Chiang was coupled to very fervent demands for continued "cooperation" between the two parties,[30] for everyone already understood that the expulsion of the Communists impended. Wang Ching-wei and Chang Fah-kwei did favor an expedition against Chiang, but only because their own political fortunes required his elimination. Chang actually started moving some of his troops towards Nanking a short while later, but the campaign fizzled into nothing. "We will not fight Chiang Kai-shek for the Communists," sneered Ho Chien and the other generals.[31]

The panic-stricken Central Committee of the Communist Party decided to issue a manifesto to the effect that if the Kuomintang "really" wanted to carry out the policies of Sun Yat-sen, it had to fight Chiang Kai-shek and it had to ally with the Communists. But when the members of the political bureau got together for a meeting, every man present offered a different draft and no agreement could be reached on the terms of the proposed declaration. Finally on June 20 an enlarged meeting of the Central Committee adopted a statement embodying eleven points—the last desperate attempt to convince the "revolutionary Kuomintang" that the Communists were prepared to keep faith with the "national united front." The most important of the eleven points follow:

> 4. The Kuomintang, since it is the bloc of the workers, peasants, and petty bourgeoisie opposed to imperialism, is naturally in the leading position of the national revolution.
>
> 5. Communist members of the Kuomintang, although participating in government work, both central and local, are participating as members of the

Kuomintang and not as members of the Communist Party.... The Communist members now in the government may ask leave in order to reduce the difficulties of the political situation.

6. The workers' and peasants' mass organizations should accept the leadership and control of the Kuomintang. The demands of the workers' and peasants' mass movement should be in accordance with the resolutions of the Kuomintang congresses, the decisions of the Central Executive Committee, and the decrees and laws of the government. But the Kuomintang should also protect the organizations of the workers and peasants and their interests, also in accordance with the party resolutions and government decrees.

7. According to Kuomintang principles, the masses must be armed. But the armed groups of the workers and peasants should submit to the regulation and training of the government. In order to avoid political troubles, the present armed pickets at Wuhan can be reduced or incorporated into the army.

8. The labor unions and workers' pickets may not assume judicial or administrative functions, arrest people, try them, or patrol the streets, without the permission of the tangpu or the government.

9. Shop employees' unions should be organized by the tangpu jointly with the men sent by the General Labor Union. The economic demands of the shop employees shall not exceed the economic capacities of the shopkeepers. The unions shall not interfere with the right of employment or the shopkeeper's right to hire and fire. They shall not insult the shopkeepers with arrests, fines, putting on of dunce caps, etc."[32]

The Chinese Communist Party was making its last effort to obey Stalin's instructions," to strengthen the authority of the revolutionary government and its role as the organizing center of the revolution." When 400 delegates gathered that same week at Hankow to represent 3,000,000 organized workers in eight provinces at the Fourth National Labor Conference, it dared not seize the opportunity thus offered to make a sharp turn and begin the mobilization of the workers against the offensive of the Kuomintang reaction. When Wang Ching-wei appeared on the conference platform on June 23, he was loudly cheered.[33] Nevertheless the delegates repeatedly struck a note of determination to struggle for the interests of the labor movement as such.[34] Even Lozovsky, present as a fraternal delegate of the Russian trade unions, had to make an unusually "radical" speech.[35] "Counterrevolution is gaining strength every day," said the manifesto of the conference, adopted on June 28. "In the territory of the Nationalist government, the labor movement can only be conducted openly at Wuhan. Counterrevolutionaries are now in power in Hunan, Kiangsi, and Honan.... Laborers are still suffering under a new kind of tyrannical rule. Under these circumstances, it is possible for the reactionaries to dominate Wuhan some day. We must struggle hard to maintain the existence of the labor unions. We are now in a reign of white terror."[36] This, however, did not prevent the manifesto from concluding: "Long Live the Nationalist government!"

"Here labor is in a free atmosphere," said the *People's Tribune*. "The heavy hand of unsympathetic or actively antagonistic militarists is absent here. Organized labor in

Nationalist China is loyal to the Wuhan government because it is only under this government that it can confidently count upon holding on to labor's first and most vital right—to work in the open...unafraid and fearless."[37]

Yet on the morning of June 30, the final session had barely ended with the shouting of the slogan, "Long Live the Nationalist Government!" when the "heavy hand of antagonistic militarists" descended sharply and directly on the trade union headquarters. Soldiers marched in and began to loot and destroy the property and records of the All-China Trade Union Federation. Panting protests were made. The offending soldiers were ordered withdrawn. They had acted a little too prematurely. The omnipresent Miss Strong caught Hsu Chao-jen as he raced past her street. She asked him if the recalcitrant soldiers would be punished. "He smiled wearily. He was glad enough to get the building. 'We have it to work in today.... Who knows what will happen tomorrow?' he replied."[38] The federation never did get its building back.

The raid on the union headquarters had followed the announcement that the workers' pickets were being voluntarily disarmed and dissolved. In Shanghai the order had been given to "hide or bury" all arms in hopes of averting the impending blow. In Hankow the Central Committee decided to surrender completely the small stock of arms the workers had and to dissolve the picket forces in advance. On June 29 a delegation of the Hupeh General Labor Union, headed by Hsiang Chung-fah, went to the office of the Kuomintang military council and "stated that in view of the complaints that union pickets were a factor in the reluctance on the part of businessmen to restore normal economic conditions, they wished to offer either to deliver their arms or to be incorporated in the army. It was later decided that they should voluntarily surrender their arms."[39]

"It has been stated that as long as the pickets were armed, the businessmen did not feel safe in resuming business," explained the *People's Tribune* . "Other rumors have been circulated that the pickets were contemplating an attack on the soldiers. In order to aid the government policy and to silence these rumors, the Hupeh General Labor Union decided that the pickets should be disarmed. It was felt that in this way an obstacle to the resumption of business must be removed and also that attempts to alienate workers and soldiers would be circumvented."[40]

Next day the Hupeh General Labor Union issued a further explanatory statement: "For the purpose of consolidating the united front of the troops and laborers, and in order not to give grounds to support the charges made by reactionaries and counterrevolutionaries, the union ordered the dissolution of the armed pickets on the 28th inst. Arms and ammunition were handed to the Hankow office of the Wuhan garrison for custody.... We have petitioned the government for protection in order to show our sincere intention to support it.... As to the reactionaries, we hope the government will mete out strong measures for their punishment."[41]

The Communist Central Committee had also authorized the Communists in the government "to ask leave in order to reduce the difficulties of the political situation." Accordingly on June 30 Tang Ping-shan, the Communist minister of agriculture, petitioned the government for "leave of absence," apologizing for his failure "to put the peasant movement on the right track."

"Ever since I assumed office as minister of agriculture," he wrote, "I have tried my best to perform the important duty of improving peasant conditions. I have consistently done my best to set the peasant movement right. Recent developments have made the political situation so serious that to put the peasant movement on the right track has been too heavy a responsibility for me. Since I am physically unfit to go on with my work, I request leave of absence."[42] Hsu Chao-jen, Communist minister of labor, had long since ceased attending to his office. His letter of resignation, stating that "owing to recent developments in the situation, I can no longer remain in office," was made public a few days later.[43] Hsiang Chung-fah and other Communists who held posts in the Hupeh provincial government had already withdrawn. Panic and demoralization were complete. The Central Committee itself fled across the river to Wuchang. It had done all it could to "strengthen the authority of the organizing center of the revolution." All to no avail, for the decision to expel the Communists had already been made and remained only to be formally adopted at the session of the Kuomintang Political Council on July 15.

It had begun to dawn on Chen Tu-hsiu that the only course left open was complete withdrawal from the Kuomintang. He consulted with Borodin. "I quite agree with your idea," said the high adviser, "but I know that Moscow will never permit it."[44] But in reality Borodin did not agree at all. He was still trying to pump "steadfastness and revolutionary purpose" into the rabbit. According to Tang Leang-li, Borodin had been regarded ever since the Changsha events as merely "an honored guest, no longer...a trusted adviser."[45] Borodin clung fast to the honor of Kuomintang hospitality. He was still probing for "possibilities" of cooperation he might have overlooked. Chiu Chiu-pei says he toyed with the idea of leading Soong Ching-ling (Mrs. Sun Yat-sen), Teng Yen-ta, and Eugene Chen out of the government as a demonstrative act against Wang Ching-wei.[46] But events had already rolled over Borodin's head. The Communist leadership had fallen apart and all but dissolved. The rank and file of the party were scattered and demoralized. Ho Chien's troops had already saddled Wuhan and were riding it their own way. One by one union headquarters were occupied. Arrests were made and executions began to take place. The tide of terror was engulfing Stalin's "revolutionary center." The *Izvestia* correspondent wired that yesterday's reliable allies had today become "playthings in the hands of the generals."[47] The rats began to quit the sinking ship.

On July 6 Bukharin suddenly and desperately advised the Chinese masses that they had to rely on themselves alone: "One of the chief slogans must be: 'Workers and peasants! Trust in your own forces alone! Do not trust the generals and officers! Organize your armed troops!'...Feng Yu-hsiang has gone over to the camp of the opponents of the people's revolution. We must declare merciless war upon him!" Yet Bukharin was still ready to place his trust in Wang Ching-wei: "The friends of Chiang Kai-shek are ready to accept this plan (to expel the Communists)—Wang Ching-wei is not among them. He is firmer than the others,"[48] he added hopefully between parentheses. Less than a week later he discovered that Wang Ching-wei was "firmer than the others" only in his determination to smash the mass movement. Bukharin now proclaimed that "an abrupt turn in the Chinese Revolution" had taken place and solemnly declared that "the revolutionary role of Wuhan is at an end." In a menacing paragraph at the end of the Eighth Plenum resolution and in some of his subsequent articles, Bukharin had already prepared his exit. Responsibility for the debacle, he now declared, lay with the Chinese Communist leadership which "in recent times obstinately sabotaged the decisions of the Comintern...(it) has not stood the fiery test...it has suffered shipwreck."[49]

"The revolutionary role of the Wuhan government is played out; it is becoming a counterrevolutionary force," announced a resolution of the Executive Committee of the Communist International on July 14.[50] "This is the new and peculiar feature which the leaders of the Chinese Communist Party and all the Chinese comrades must fully and clearly take into account."

The Comintern had foreseen and foretold everything. On July 14 it discovered a "new and peculiar" fact which had been known to the simplest Hunan peasant or Wuhan worker for months. Does that mean any mistakes had been made? Not in Moscow! Stalin had not made a mistake, or hardly any, since Lenin died.

"The support given to the Northern Expedition (i.e. to Chiang Kai-shek) was perfectly correct so long as it aroused a revolutionary mass movement. And the support given to Wuhan was equally correct so long as it acted as the opponent of Chiang Kai-shek's Nanking government. But this same tactic of blocs becomes fundamentally wrong in the moment at which the Wuhan government capitulates to the enemies of the revolution. What was correct during the previous stage of the revolution is now absolutely unsuitable."

But the Northern Expedition was the expedition of the bourgeoisie to the Yangtze, where its victories and the Communist policy of retreat enabled Chiang Kai-shek to slaughter the workers and destroy their organizations. That was when his "revolutionary role" ended. It is "perfectly correct" to form blocs with class enemies, but such blocs become "fundamentally wrong" and "absolutely unsuitable" only at the precise moment when your enemy grabs you by the throat. To have mobilized against him in advance, not in words but in deeds, to have armed yourself against the literal certainty of his attack would have been—counterrevolutionary Trotskyism.

> All this involves certain difficulties for the leadership of the party, especially in the case of so young and inexperienced a party as the Communist Party of

> China.... The acute tension of the revolutionary situation requires a rapid grasp of the features peculiar to each moment. It requires skilful and timely maneuvers, rapid adaptation to slogans...and the decided rupture of blocs which have ceased to be factors of the revolutionary struggle, and have become obstacles in its way. If at a certain stage of development of the revolution the support of the Wuhan government by the Communist Party was necessary, such support at present would be disastrous to the Communist Party of China, and would plunge it into the bog of opportunism.

Today, July 14, the "factors of the revolutionary struggle" have suddenly and abruptly become "obstacles in its way." Only now, on July 14, with the Communist Party routed and demoralized, the masses smashed and hurled back from all their positions, it has become "disastrous" to continue supporting Wuhan. Up to their necks in the "bog of opportunism," because from the very beginning they had supported Wuhan and before that Chiang Kai-shek, the Chinese Communists might truly have wondered what the ECCI visualized when it used the word "disastrous." What had become of the "revolutionary center" and the "need for strengthening the authority of the organizing center of the revolution" outlined by the ECCI only six weeks before? Moscow had an answer for that too. Wuhan had been transformed from a "revolutionary center" into a "counterrevolutionary force" because: "In spite of the advice given by the Comintern, the heads of the Kuomintang have not only failed to support the agrarian revolution but have unfettered the hands of its enemies. They have sanctioned the disarmament of the workers, the punitive expeditions against the peasants, and the reprisals of Tang Sheng-chih and Co. They have postponed and sabotaged the campaign against Nanking under various pretexts."

All this had come about because Wuhan spurned Moscow's "advice." The rabbit just rolled over and died. While it lived it blushed pink under Moscow's persistently amorous advances. But now that it was dead its coyness too disappeared. The pink faded into a bloated white, barely visible as the anaconda wrapped it away.

In Canton, Shanghai, Changsha, and finally now in Wuhan, the Chinese masses had seen the standard-bearers of the Kuomintang metamorphose from sterling allies of the revolution into cruel butchers of the workers and peasants. At each new catastrophe the Comintern announced that all had been properly foreseen and the policies pursued perfectly correct. Bukharin was continually discovering "new and peculiar features" in the Chinese Revolution, and he now castigated the Communist Party for being unable to carry through the rupture of "blocs which have become obstacles." The bloc with the Wuhan government was ended. This did not mean an end to the bloc with the Kuomintang. On this score the Comintern's instructions gave unmistakable evidence of blind panic. The Comintern resolution called upon the Chinese Communists "to resign demonstratively from the Wuhan government," but "not to withdraw from the Kuomintang." This was perhaps the newest and most peculiar feature of all.

> The Communists should remain in the Kuomintang, in spite of the campaign carried on by its leaders for the expulsion of the Communists. Closer contact with the mass of the members of the Kuomintang who should be induced to accept resolutions decidedly protesting against the actions of the CEC of the Kuomintang, demanding the removal of the present leaders of the Kuomintang, and to make preparations on these lines for the Party Conference of the Kuomintang.

Still flying the Kuomintang banner, the Communists were now "to intensify the work among the proletarian masses...build up labor mass organizations... strengthen the trade unions...prepare the working classes for decisive action...develop the agrarian revolution...arm the workers and peasants...organize a competent fighting illegal party apparatus."

But how to escape the past? ask the Chinese Communists. The great organizations we built have been smashed. Our comrades are being tortured, killed, and scattered. The mass movement has been destroyed and the workers and peasants rightly look upon us as men who deceived them and led them to the slaughter. We suppose that if you tell us to raise still higher the Kuomintang banner, we must do so; but we doubt whether the masses would follow us now even if we raised a banner of our own. Never mind all that, replies the Comintern. Your own leaders, not we, are responsible.

> The ECCI considers it its revolutionary duty to call upon the members of the Communist Party of China openly to fight against the opportunism of the Central Committee....
>
> Take measures to make good the opportunist errors of the Central Committee of the Communist Party of China in order to render the leadership of the party politically sound...fight decisively against the opportunist deviations of the party leaders...change the character of the leadership...disavow those leaders who have violated the international discipline of the Communist International.

Stalin had acquitted himself of his "revolutionary duty." It would henceforth be the "revolutionary duty" of all the Comintern scribblers to perpetuate the charge that the Chinese Communist leaders, hapless victims of their own gullibility and ignorance, were alone responsible for this immense historical catastrophe. Stalin and Bukharin, however, could impose upon the Chinese Communists a policy which shattered one of the greatest revolutionary mass movements of all time. They could not impose their will upon history by weaving dishonest resolutions. At Wuhan events took their final course. In accordance with Moscow's instructions, the Communists demonstratively "withdrew" from the government they had already left, announcing at the same time that they had "no reason to leave the Kuomintang or to refuse to cooperate with it" and that they would not permit [?] "the generals who have betrayed the revolution and the vacillating politicians to misuse the name of the Kuomintang and hide themselves under the banner of Sun Yat-sen."[51] Unfrightened, the generals proceeded to "misuse" the name of the Kuomintang. On July 15 the Kuomintang Political Council ordered all Communist members of the Kuomintang to renounce their Communist Party membership. Four days later the Military Council ordered a similar purge throughout the army. "Punishment without leniency" was ordered for all recalcitrants.[52] Within a few days execution squads gave due emphasis to the expulsion order. Those Communists who refused to capitulate—and droves of them did—were compelled to flee. Chen Tu-hsiu, overcome by the utter hopelessness of his position, resigned from the chairmanship of the Central Committee. "The International," he wrote, "wishes us to carry out our own policy on the one hand and does not allow us to withdraw from the Kuomintang on the other. There is really no way out and I cannot continue with my work."[53] The remaining Communist leaders, Chiu Chiu-pei, Chang Kuo-tao, Li Li-san, Mao Tse-tung, and the others, stuffed Kuomintang flags into their pockets for future use and precipitately fled. On July 27 the leaders of the Left Kuomintang gathered at the railway station to bid farewell to their "honored guest," Borodin. He left nominally "to confer with Feng Yu-hsiang."[54] Actually he was beginning a long trek across the northwest to the distant Soviet frontier, Moscow's retreat from Hankow.

The military authorities proceeded with the systematic destruction of the trade unions. The Hankow Garrison Headquarters issued a ban on strikes. Between July 14 and 19 soldiers were "billeted" on the premises of twenty-five unions whose archives and effects were confiscated. Simultaneously throughout Honan province Feng Yu-hsiang was conducting a similar drive.[55] "In the last few weeks the Chinese labor movement in the territory of the Wuhan government has lived through a period of the most brazen reaction.... The military...have carried out such enormous work of destruction directed against the mass organizations...that it will require a very long period and gigantic energy to make good the losses and to enable the trade unions to resume their normal functions," reported the Pan-Pacific Trade Union Secretariat.

> Many of the trade union leaders and organizers in the different provinces and districts...have been driven out, arrested, or killed. The other leaders of the Chinese trade unions, among them the most prominent leaders of the All-China Trade Union Federation, were compelled to flee.... At a banquet to the delegates of the Pan-Pacific Trade Union Congress...Wang Ching-wei declared eloquently that he considered the best guarantee for the success of the national revolution to be the development of the mass movement of the workers and peasants and the immediate realization of the basic demands of the toiling masses.... Now we not only hear different speeches and declarations, but we witness quite different actions toward the organizations of the workers and peasants, actions which until now were the exclusive privilege of all militarists and counterrevolutionists of the type of Chang Tso-lin and Chiang Kai-shek.[56]

On July 30, two thousand Hankow ricksha men stormed a police station to force the release of an arrested comrade. Two of them were killed and six were wounded. Police sent a letter to the Ricksha Pullers' Union to send representatives to a parley. But no one was there. The union leaders had fled. There were only the pullers in the streets on strike. Martial law was proclaimed and the death penalty instituted. The strike came to an end. It was the last open manifestation of the Hankow labor movement for a long time to come. A few days later Nanking and Wuhan were exchanging congratulatory telegrams. Nanking wired bouquets to Wuhan for its decisive action against the Communists and invited the leaders to Nanking. "If all feelings of aversion are resolutely given up..." replied Wuhan on August 10, "your former measures devised to meet emergencies will be wholeheartedly excused by us all."[57] Thus ended the "complete contradiction" between the "revolutionary center" at Wuhan and counterrevolutionary Nanking—in an act of touching Christian forgiveness.

Of all the "Leftists" in Wuhan only Teng Yen-ta, and after him Soong Ching-ling, dissociated themselves publicly from the new course. "From Yang Yu-ting (Chang Tso-lin's deputy) to Chiang Kai-shek...all are either Kuomintang members or are going to become members. Kuomintang banners are hoisted everywhere. But is this not the same situation we faced in the 1911 revolution?" wrote Teng on July 6. "Is not all economic, political, and military power still in the hands of the militarists?...We wanted to utilize the military, but we were being utilized by them."[58] A week later Teng resigned as head of the Political Department of the Military Council. Even he saw far more clearly than the "revolutionists" in Moscow that a clean break was occurring between the masses and the Kuomintang. "Those who formerly advocated the full protection of the labourers and peasants have started to massacre them." he declared. "The revolutionary significance of the Kuomintang will be lost.... The natural result will be that the party itself will become counterrevolutionary.... The revolution will be a failure, as it was in 1911."[59]

Following Teng, Soong Ching-ling declared that the Kuomintang had become "a tool in the hands of this or that militarist. It will have ceased to be a living force working for the future welfare of the Chinese people, but will have become a machine, the agent of oppression, a parasite battening on the present enslaving system."[60] Teng Yen-ta and Soong Ching-ling, together with Eugene Chen, fled into European exile. Thus ended the myth of the "Left Kuomintang."*

The revolution which had swept China in three brief and kaleidoscopic years was at an end. The rising of a mighty people had caused the rotten structure of an ancient and outworn and oppressive civilization to totter. The masses had shown more than enough strength to topple it and for ever destroy it to its roots. But today that old society was settling back to its foundations and all the contradictions inherent within it were being renewed and deepened. For having tried to destroy it

---

* Only bitter personal rivalries remained. Chiang Kai-shek temporarily retired from Nanking to permit the unification with the Wuhan group to take place. After trying vainly for five years to displace Chiang, Wang Ching-wei finally became, in January 1932, his minion, along with Sun

and for having aspired to the dignity of human beings, the workers and peasants of China were now paying a ghastly price. Over the prisons and execution grounds flew the banner of the Kuomintang. Under it the Chinese bourgeoisie had been enabled to ride to power. Under it the masses had risen and under it, uncomprehending, they had been struck down. Throughout the revolution that same banner had been tied to the flagstaff of the Communist International and to that flagstaff were lashed the Chinese Communists.

Fo and all the other "Leftists." After a few futile attempts at a comeback, Eugene Chen faded into obscurity. Teng Yen-ta returned from exile in 1930 and organized the so-called "Third Party" in opposition to the Kuomintang and the Communists. He was arrested in the French Concession at Shanghai and handed over to Chiang Kai-shek who shot him. Soong Ching-ling was the last relic of the "Left Kuomintang" to keep faith with the Comintern. After nearly ten years, during which she repeatedly denounced Chiang Kai-shek and the Kuomintang as the butchers of the people, she was led by the Comintern back into Chiang Kai-shek's fold, and today once more ardently supports him in the 1937 revival of the "nationalist united front," making her peace with the "parasite battening on the present enslaving system."

16 Autumn Harvest

Collapse of the Wuhan government completed the victory of the counter-revolution. From Canton to Nanking, from the sea to the hills of Hunan, the generals were in power. Already at war among themselves, they waged in common a ruthless campaign of extermination against the mass movement, its organizations, and its leaders.

"Here are the facts of the suppression," began a contemporary report.

> For four months a systematized massacre has been going on in the territory controlled by Chiang Kai-shek. It has resulted in the smashing of the people's organizations in Kiangsu, Chekiang, Fukien, and Kwangtung, so that in these provinces one finds Kuomintang headquarters, and labor, peasant, and women's unions transformed from forceful, determined organs into docile, spineless organizations, so effectively "reorganized" that they will carry out the will of their reactionary masters.
>
> In the past three months the reaction has spread from the lower Yangtze until today it is dominant in all the territory under so-called Nationalist control. Tang Sheng-chih has proven himself an even more effective commander of execution squads than of armies in battle. In Hunan his subordinate generals have carried out a cleanup of Communists that Chiang Kai-shek can scarcely parallel. The usual methods of shooting and beheading have been abetted by methods of torture and mutilation which reek of the horrors of the Dark Ages and the Inquisition. The results have been impressive. The peasant and labour unions of Hunan, probably the most effectively organized in the whole country, are completely smashed. Those leaders who have escaped the burning in oil, the burying alive, the torture by slow strangulation by wire, and other forms of death too lurid to report, have fled the country or are in such careful hiding that they cannot easily be found.[1]

"The toll of executed trade union leaders and organizers is growing from day to day," reported the Pan-Pacific Trade Union Secretariat.

> Not a day passes without the execution of several workers and trade unionists.... The mass movement is crushed for the moment. All the labour organizations and the peasant unions are being "reorganized," which means that they are first disorganized and broken up, and then what remains of them is put under the whip of some appointee of the militarists.... In Kiukiang, as in Wuhan, all the trade union

> organizations have been dissolved and many trade union leaders executed.... Soldiers have occupied most of the trade union buildings and have worked havoc with the property and the documents and valuable archives of these organizations.... What is happening in Wuhan is an exact repetition of what took place some time ago in Canton, when General Li Chi-sen destroyed and then "reorganized" the trade unions and peasant organizations, and also of the Chiang Kai-shek regime in Shanghai.[2]

The defeat of the mass movement could not be measured merely by the extent of its physical annihilation. The workers and peasants had not merely fallen before a stronger enemy. They had been decapitated by their own leaders, by the men and organizations they had been taught to regard as the standard-bearers of their own revolution. The moral and psychological demoralization that resulted from this fact incalculably deepened the effect of the counterrevolution. In the latter half of 1927 workers in Shanghai and a few other cities still found the strength to strike in attempts to preserve at least part of the fast-disappearing gains made during the preceding years. In these sporadic, unorganized rearguard battles, the workers were easily defeated by the counterrevolution. The masses fell away from the political arena. The brutal and, for them, entirely unexpected assault of the counterrevolution drove them into passivity. They left their shattered organizations. The ranks of the trade unions thinned out. "It will require a very long period and gigantic energy to make good the losses and to enable the trade unions to resume their normal functions," said the Pan-Pacific Trade Union Secretariat as early as July, when only the first blows of the terror had been struck.[3] The peasant unions, that had counted nearly ten millions in their ranks, disappeared almost entirely. Only scattered rebel bands that took to the hills remained to harass the columns of soldiery that went through the countryside like a scourge. In the cities the workers left the ranks of the Communist Party by the thousands. In April 1927, it had been an organization of nearly sixty thousand members, 53.8 percent of them workers.[4] Within a year that percentage fell by four-fifths and an official report admitted that the party "did not have a single healthy party nucleus among the industrial workers."[5] In their own way the workers passed their verdict on the party that had led them to disaster. Had the Communist Party known how to evaluate the reasons for this catastrophic defeat, and embarked on the basis of such an evaluation to reassemble its forces and reestablish itself among the workers by taking command of their defensive struggles, it might have gradually regained their confidence. As it was, never having known how and when to attack, the party never learned how to retreat. Neither then, nor until this day, did the workers ever return to its ranks.

After a heavy defeat, wrote Lenin, referring to the Russian revolution of 1905,

> the revolutionary parties must continue their training. Heretofore they learned to attack. Now they understand that they must add to their knowledge of attack a knowledge of how best to retreat. It becomes necessary to understand—and the

> revolutionary class by its own bitter experience learns to understand—that victory is impossible without a knowledge both of how to attack and how to retreat correctly. Of all the shattered opposition and revolutionary parties, the Bolsheviks effected the most orderly retreat, with the least damage to their "army." They, more than any other, preserved the nucleus of their Party, suffered the fewest splits...felt the least demoralization, and were in the best position to renew work on a large scale efficiently and energetically. The Bolsheviks only attained this by mercilessly exposing and throwing out the revolutionists of phrases, who did not wish to understand that it was necessary to retreat, that it was obligatory upon them to learn how to work legally in the most reactionary parliaments, in the most reactionary trade unions...and similar organizations.[6]

In 1905 the Russian workers were defeated because czarism was still strong enough to stand and the revolutionary forces too weak to dislodge it. In 1927 the Chinese Revolution suffered a crushing defeat not because the workers and peasants lacked the strength and ability to win, but because the leaders they trusted failed to lead them to the victory within their grasp. In Russia the workers had known who were their friends and who their foes. In China the workers and peasants were crushed precisely by those whom they had confidently followed. The Bolsheviks emerged from their defeat with their forces intact. The Chinese Communists emerged with their forces decimated, dispersed, and demoralized. If only for this reason, the effects of the Chinese 1927 were a thousand times more shattering than those of Russia's 1905.

Under Lenin Bolshevism became the science of applying Marxism to practical politics like the navigator uses the compass and sextant in bringing his ship to port. By exposing the internal laws of the social process, Marxism provided the revolutionary leadership with the means of plotting its course in advance, not only in perfect accord with the needs of the objective situation, but with a view to transforming that objective situation in a sense favorable to the proletariat. This method was antithetical to the vulgar empiricism that trailed behind events, veering rudderlessly, helpless in the swirl of shifting currents. The Bolsheviks under Lenin and Trotsky gave the world the most finished demonstration it had yet witnessed of the power of a conscious revolutionary leadership intervening actively in the course of events to give form and direction to the will of great masses of people in motion. The bureaucratic stratum that succeeded them no longer gave conscious expression to the will of the proletariat. It provided instead the channel through which other classes exerted their influence on the proletarian dictatorship and tended to veer between the classes, responding to the pressure first of one and then of the next. Governed primarily by the desire to maintain and increase its own privileges and power, it would proceed "pragmatically," that is, empirically, When its blunders produced their inevitable consequences, it would draw back sharply from the edge of the precipice, rushing pell-mell in the opposite direction where, as a rule, another precipice awaited it.

In this, as in so many other things, Stalin personified the bureaucratic centrist who could not direct but could only tail after the march of events. Only a leadership of this type could have declared, after Chiang Kai-shek's April coup d'état, that the slaughter of the Shanghai workers had been "foreseen" and proceeded lawfully from an entirely correct policy and could not have been prevented. The Stalinist leadership in the Comintern "foresaw" that the bourgeoisie would "abandon" the revolution and saw this as a necessary and unavoidable "stage" in the revolutionary process. It followed from this that the workers had to be taught to cling to the boots of the bourgeoisie until it kicked them loose. No matter if it was ground under the heel of counterrevolution in the process, this was all "foreseen" and in accord with the law of "stages" in the revolution. An inseparable corollary of this type of "leadership" was the idea that the revolutionary vanguard had to wait passively until the bourgeoisie "discredited" itself in the eyes of the masses by openly taking the road of counterrevolution. Only then could it proceed with a bolder revolutionary policy which the masses could thereafter comprehend, having lost all their illusions in the bourgeoisie. This notion was organic with Stalin. Left to himself he would have led the Russian Bolsheviks along this fatal path in 1917 had not Lenin arrived in time to put an end to passive waiting and to galvanize the party into becoming the most active and conscious instrument of masses who were already far ahead of those who were leading them. "We must bide our time until the Provisional Government exhausts itself," said Stalin in March 1917, "until the time when in the process of fulfilling the revolutionary programme it discredits itself...We...must bide our time until the moment when the events reveal the hollowness of the Provisional Government."[7]

Like an echo ten years old, Stalin now wrote on the morrow of the collapse of Wuhan:

> Should the Chinese Communists have set up the slogan six months ago: "Down with the leadership of the Kuomintang?" No, for that would have been a very dangerous and precipitate step and it would have rendered the approach to the masses more difficult for the Communists, for the masses at that time still believed in the leadership of the Kuomintang and this would have isolated the Communist Party from the peasantry. This would have been false, for at that time the leadership of the Kuomintang in Wuhan had not yet achieved its highest point as a bourgeois-revolutionary government and had not yet discredited itself in the eyes of the masses through its fight against the agrarian revolution and by its defection to the counterrevolution. We always said that no attempt should be made to discredit and overthrow the leadership of the Kuomintang in Wuhan as long as it had not exhausted all its possibilities as a bourgeois-revolutionary government.... Should the Chinese Communists now set up the slogan, "Down with the leadership of the Kuomintang in Wuhan?" Yes, of course they must. Now that the leadership of the Kuomintang has already discredited itself by its struggle against the revolution and has created hostile [!] relations between itself and the masses.... Such a slogan will meet with a tremendous response. Now every worker and peasant will see that the Communists are acting correctly.[8]

Stalin overlooked only one thing. In the process of "discrediting itself" and reaching its "highest point" while the Communists passively waited and concealed its real nature from the masses, the Kuomintang counterrevolution successfully crushed the organizations of the mass movement. The workers and peasants, defending themselves as best they could against the blows of the terror, were no longer in a position to perceive that the Communists were now "acting correctly."*

One of the incidental victims of the Kuomintang when it reached its "highest point" and proceeded, arms in hand, to "discredit" itself, was Borodin, midwife-in-chief at the miscarriage of the revolution. He had stood by, pumping steadfastness into Stalin's Kuomintang allies until all their "possibilities" were exhausted. He was now on his way back across the wastes of Northwest China, behind him the wreckage of the revolution he had helped destroy. En route other generals of the Kuomintang, even Feng Yu-hsiang, entertained the parting guest.

"Borodin seemed weary and bored by all these generals," reported Anna Strong, in another of her unintentionally valuable vignettes. "He saw too clearly [!] behind their Nationalist slogans the desire for military assistance. He remarked: 'When the next Chinese general comes to Moscow and shouts: "Hail to the World Revolution!" better send at once for the GPU*.... All that any of them want is rifles.' "

Miss Strong protested that their host for the night "seemed a friendly soul and fond of Russia."

"Borodin answered wearily: 'He's young. They are all good when they are young.'"

A few nights later, sitting on a camp stool beneath a rising Chinese moon, Borodin delivered himself of what Miss Strong called "the most complete and leisurely exposition of the forces involved in China's revolution that I had yet heard him give. There had been no time [!] for such discussion in Hankow. Now, removed by many days and miles from the scene of action, it was as if he summed it up for his own soul also." Spake Borodin: "The big bourgeoisie can never unify China because they are not really against the imperialists; they are allied with them and profit by them. The small bourgeoisie cannot unify China because they vacillate between the workers and peasants on the one hand and the big bourgeoisie on the other and, in the end, go over to the latter. The workers and peasants did not unify China because they trusted too much to the small bourgeoisie."[9]

In Hankow, at the scene of action, there had been "no time" for consideration of these simple propositions. Borodin had been too busy fulfilling Stalin's instructions to see to it that "no attempt should be made to discredit and overthrow the leadership of the Kuomintang." Not until he was removed, many days and miles

---

* At the back of the same issue of the periodical in which this article of Stalin's was published there was reprinted a fragment from Lenin, dating from 1917, in which the following sentence appeared: "It is precisely the first steps which we must learn to recognize, if we are not to fall into the ridiculous role of a dullwitted philistine who cries out at the second step, although he helped to take the first."

from the scene of action, did he find time to conclude that he had "trusted too much to the small bourgeoisie." In Borodin's soul, history is not interested. It is interested in his verdict upon himself and his deeds, here alone expressed, for when he returned to Moscow, he lapsed into the safer obscurity of silence. Had he expatiated on his theme, it would have begun to sound dangerously too much like the ceaseless refrain of Trotsky, before, not after, the debacle. Trotsky had too been "many days and miles from the scene of action," yet he had proved to be infinitely closer to the masses in China than Borodin in their very midst.

Stalin's other acolyte at the altar of the Chinese bourgeoisie was M. N. Roy. A few years earlier, under the vigilant editorial eye of Lenin, Roy had helped draft the historic national and colonial theses of the second and fourth congresses of the Comintern, which had declared that the struggle against bourgeois nationalism was the fundamental task of the Communists in the colonies and semi-colonies. When he left for China, he left these lessons behind. As chief delegate of the Executive Committee of the Communist International in Hankow, Roy turned his back on the masses and devoted himself to the strenuous task of "advising" first Chiang Kai-shek, then Wang Ching-wei, not to "discredit" themselves. When in turn they spurned him he returned solemnly to write:

> Rather than sacrifice the sectional interests of the reactionary landlords and capitalists, the bourgeois Nationalist leaders betrayed the revolution. Class solidarity cut across national solidarity.... Development of the revolution menaced the interests of the capitalist and land-owning classes. Further fight against imperialism would inevitably have caused revolution in the internal social-economic relations. The land should [!] have been given to the peasantry. The peasantry should [!] have been secured against unlimited [?] capitalist exploitation. In short, imperialism could not be overthrown unless its native allies were destroyed. Complete national liberation could be realized...only by seriously encroaching upon the privileged position of the classes whose representatives led the Nationalist movement.... The petty bourgeois radicalism of the Wuhan government went bankrupt. It capitulated...to the counterrevolutionary feudal bourgeois militarist bloc which had already sold the country to imperialism. The nation was sacrificed on the altar of class interests. The democratic (non-class) ideals of the Kuomintang were lost in the fierce clash of class interests. The lessons of these revolutionary and counterrevolutionary events in China are that the Nationalist bourgeoisie in the colonial and semi-colonial countries are essentially counterrevolutionary; that the national revolution to be successful must be an agrarian revolution; that not only the big bourgeoisie but even the petty bourgeoisie, in spite of their radical phrases, cannot and will not lead the agrarian revolution; that the petty bourgeoisie, when placed in power by the support of the workers and peasants, do not share and defend this power with the working class, but hand it over to the counterrevolutionary bourgeoisie, and that the working class operating through its independent political party (Communist Party) is the only guarantee for the success of the national revolution.[10]

Roy's article was entitled "The Lessons of the Chinese Revolution." In the book he published a few years later Roy modestly estimates that 25,000 Communists lost their lives in the first months of the terror in 1927[11] after the "non-class ideals" of the Kuomintang were metamorphosed into the "fierce clash of class interests." Only yesterday Stalin, in his wisdom, was "foreseeing" that the bourgeoisie (not Chiang Kai-shek! not Wang Ching-wei!) would "abandon" the revolution. At the same time he was teaching these 25,000 to believe that the Chiang Kai-sheks and the Wang Ching-weis were the "reliable allies" of the revolution, that Chiang's Canton and later Wang's Hankow were the authentic "organizing centers" of the agrarian revolution, that "no attempt should be made to discredit and overthrow" them until they had "discredited" themselves, that is, until they had snuffed out the lives of the uncomprehending 25,000, and after them the lives of thousands more, and the life of the revolution itself.

Had it really been necessary that this ghastly price be paid before Stalin, Bukharin, Borodin, Roy and their friends could finally realize that the bourgeoisie, big or small, could not lead the agrarian revolution, that "imperialism could not be overthrown unless its native allies were destroyed?"

In a document dated August 9, 1927, Stalin's Central Committee in Moscow summed up what it took all these lives to teach it:

> The experience of the past development shows plainly that the bourgeoisie is not capable of solving the problems of national emancipation from the yoke of imperialism, as it is conducting a fight against the workers and peasants, that it is not capable of conducting a consistent fight against imperialism and is becoming more and more inclined to a compromise...which in fact leaves the domination of imperialism almost completely undisturbed. The national bourgeoisie is equally incapable of solving the inner problems of the revolution, for the reason that it not only fails to support the peasantry, but actively combats them.... It is almost impossible for the bourgeoisie to enter into any compromise with the peasantry, since in China even the scantiest land reform would involve expropriation of the gentry and small landowners, an action of which the bourgeoisie is absolutely incapable.... The Communist Party must declare that the victory over imperialism, the revolutionary unification of China, and its emancipation from the yoke of imperialism are only possible on the basis of the class struggle of the workers and peasants against the feudal lords and capitalists.[12]

Had it really required the physical annihilation of a whole generation of revolutionists to "show plainly" that the bourgeoisie could not fight imperialism, could not lead the peasantry? Was it really only time now, after three years of the "bloc of four classes," for the trade union center to declare: "The Chinese trade unions are confronted with a serious struggle against the theory and practice of class collaboration?"[13]

When Trotsky in the period of the greatest upswing of the mass movement had urged the immediate creation of workers', peasants', and soldiers' councils (soviets), it was precisely in order to provide the broadest and most flexible and self-protective mechanism for the schooling of the masses, for the development of their vigilance with regard to the transient allies from the enemy camp, for the preparation of their defense against the bourgeois reaction, and the transformation of that defense into an offensive in their own behalf, with their own forces, their own organizations, their own banners, their own arms. That road, and that road alone, could have led to the annihilation of the counterevolution. It had been blocked then by the Stalinist leadership that proscribed struggle against "the only governmental authority," against any "attempt to discredit or overthrow" the "revolutionary Kuomintang." Now that events had extracted their remorseless toll for this policy and the bourgeoisie had fulfilled Stalin's "forecast" by "discrediting" itself, the Stalinist leadership announced that the revolution "was striding forward to the highest phase of its development, to the phase of the direct struggle for the dictatorship of the working class and the peasantry."[14] Trotsky had been accused of skipping over the bourgeois democratic stage of the revolution. The leadership now sought only to skip over the disastrous consequences of its own policies.

The Chinese Communist Party, which, in Chen Tu-hsiu's bitter words, had "learned in the past only how to capitulate "[15] was now given no chance to "understand that it was necessary to retreat." In the teeth of the terror, their forces decimated and dispersed, the masses thrust back and their organizations shattered, the Chinese Communists were now ordered to change pace abruptly. Without stopping to discover what had led to catastrophe, nor to measure the magnitude of their defeat, they were compelled to affirm that the policies of the Comintern had been completely correct—(the myth of the infallibility of the leadership had to be preserved at whatever cost!)—that responsibility for failure lay in the "sabotage" of the Chinese Communist leaders, that the final defeat at Wuhan had raised the revolution to a "new and higher stage." Yesterday in the conditions of a rising revolutionary wave, with tremendous mass forces in motion, the Chinese Communists had been taught only how to check and demoralize the masses by subordinating them to hostile classes. Today that wave had been "splattered into froth" on the rocks of the reaction. From the one extreme of opportunism and compromise the remaining Chinese Communists were driven pitilessly to the opposite pole of adventurism in the hope that by belated military action they could retrieve the positions that had now been irretrievably lost. They were compelled to hurl themselves into desperate and hopeless attempts to mend the situation. Under direct orders from Moscow, the Communist Party took the road of insurrection.

The men who embarked upon this course were men who only yesterday, as members of the Central Committee, had been doggedly traveling in the opposite direction. Chen Tu-hsiu, whom the Comintern tried to make the chief scapegoat, was deposed. The new political bureau of the party included Chiu Chiu-pei, Chang Kuo-tao, Li Li-san, Chow En-lai, Chang Tai-lei, and Liu Wei-han, all of whom deeply shared the responsibility for the disasters that had overcome their party and the revolution. It was Chow En-lai who on April 13 had gone to Chiang Kai-shek's Shanghai headquarters to petition for the return of the pickets' arms. It was Liu Wei-han (later better known in the movement as Lo Mai) who, as chairman of the Hunan Provincial Committee of the Communist Party, had ordered the retreat of the peasant detachments from the outskirts of Changsha on the morrow of May 21. All of them now sought to retain the patronage of Moscow by shunting the blame exclusively onto the shoulders of Chen Tu-hsiu and a few others whose principal crime lay in their attempt to carry out faithfully the orders they had received from Moscow. The new "leaders," schooled only in retreat when it had been time to attack, were now ordered to attack when it was time to retreat.

They made the mechanical turn on orders from above, heedless of the objective situation and without changing the basic policies of the party in its attitude towards the Kuomintang or towards the agrarian revolution. When it ordered the Communists out of the Wuhan government, the Comintern had specifically instructed them not to leave the Kuomintang but to continue their efforts in the Kuomintang ranks against the "betrayals" of the Party leaders. That the Kuomintang banner had now become the universal symbol of the terror and flew over the headquarters of every militarist, big and small, in South and Central China, was of no consequence. "The classes come and go, but the continuity of the Kuomintang goes on for ever," Trotsky had written in May.[16] Now, at the end of July, after the going and coming of the classes had transformed the Kuomintang into the open instrument of the terror, the Chinese Communists, faithful to Bukharin's instructions, were going to surrender the blue banner to nobody. On July 29 the new Communist Politbureau appealed to the ranks of the Kuomintang "to rise and oppose the Central Executive Committee."[17] At a conference of the new leadership, hastily convened on August 7 "by the telegraphic instructions of the Communist International and by its new representative (Lominadze),"[18] the Communist Party was called upon "to organize uprisings of the workers and peasants under the banner of the revolutionary Lefts of the Kuomintang." The resolution said that "the organization of the revolutionary Kuomintang, developing to a higher stage, will enable the political power to advance to the Soviet of workers', peasants', and soldiers' deputies in such a manner that the transformation will be easier and without harm."[19]

Disaster had legalized the slogan of soviets—only yesterday Trotskyist contraband. On July 25 *Pravda* abruptly announced that "the crisis of the Kuomintang places the question of soviets on the order of the day. The slogan of soviets is correct now.... The former partisans of the immediate formation of soviets...wanted to force the masses to jump over stages through which the movement had not yet passed."[20]

Stalin phrased it in his own way: "In a new advance of the revolution in the present stage of development, the question of the formation of soviets will be completely ripe. Yesterday, a few months ago, the Chinese Communists could not have put forward the slogan of soviets, because that would have been adventurism [!]...because the leadership of the Kuomintang had not yet discredited itself as an opponent of the revolution."[21] The Moscow strategists staked everything on an early "advance" of the revolution. Stalin wrote that he thought the setback was "probably" comparable to the "July Days" of the Bolsheviks in 1917.[22] At the first sign of a "fresh advance," ordered the Russian Central Committee, it would be "necessary to change the propagandist slogan of soviets into a slogan of immediate fight and to proceed at once to the organization of...soviets."[23] Before this, however, a final attempt had to be made to proceed "more easily and harmlessly" to soviets through the "revolutionary Lefts of the Kuomintang." Not all the "possibilities," even now, had been exhausted. At the August 7 conference the Chinese Communists furiously waved the blue banner over their heads.

"Naturally," commented a Communist Party historian—who after five years was careful to say that this went "too far ahead" of the Comintern's instructions—"naturally this was a great mistake. As a matter of fact, after the Wuhan government turned reactionary, the whole political life of the Kuomintang received its death sentence."[24] As a matter of fact, what had died was not the Kuomintang, which was entrenching itself in the form of a military dictatorship in the seats of political power. What had died was the myth of the revolutionary Kuomintang, the myth of the "bloc of four classes," the cornerstone of Comintern policy. Five years after the event, Hua Kang described the August 7 conference as an "attempt to resurrect the Left Kuomintang!" At the time, however, the Comintern ordered the Chinese Party to hug the corpse. It was not the fault of the Chinese Communists that it failed to come to life.

On the question of the land, the August 7 conference issued the slogan: "Confiscate the land of the big and middle landlords, but ask the small landlords to reduce the rent."[25] As a result, "the local party organizations persisted in the old idea [!] of the agrarian revolution, considering it their task to stop the peasants if and when they tried to seize the land of the small landlords."[26]

The August 7 conference issued a lengthy letter addressed to all the remaining comrades of the party, detailing the "mistakes" of the deposed leadership and declaring that Chen Tu-hsiu had consistently defied or failed to carry out the impeccable instructions of the Comintern. It squeezed every drop of ambiguity out of the cunning, self-insuring phrases of Bukharin to prove that the Comintern, before, during, and after, had been infallibly correct. The "struggle against opportunism" which, according to the official calendar, began on August 7, was in reality nothing but the struggle against any attempt to make the Comintern share responsibility with the Chinese Central Committee for the blunders of the past—and this while the material content of those blunders—the reliance on the Kuomintang—was being carried over, unmodified, into the "new, higher stage" of the revolution. The new crime of adventurism was only added to the catalog of the old. This did not prevent the conference from declaring itself able "to guarantee that henceforth there will be correct, revolutionary Bolshevik leadership."[27] The conference, so goes the official history, "saved the party from impending dissolution and put it on the Bolshevik path."[28] In Moscow it was officially announced that "the right deviation in the leadership of the Chinese brother party has now been liquidated and the policy of the leadership corrected."[29]

Yesterday the "opportunists" had been those who, like Trotsky, had demanded in the period of the rising revolutionary wave a policy of irreconcilable class struggle, the creation of soviets, and the liberation of the Communists from the stranglehold of the Kuomintang. Today the same term had to be applied to those, again like Trotsky and now including Chen Tu-hsiu, who denounced the policy of insurrection in the period of the revolution's ebb as a policy that could lead only to the destruction of the remaining revolutionary cadres and to the complete divorce of the party from the masses. The deposed Chen Tu-hsiu has recorded that he wrote to the new Central Committee, "pointing out that the revolutionary moods of the masses were not then at a high point, that the regime of the Kuomintang could not be quickly or easily overthrown, that untimely uprisings only weakened the power of the party and isolated it the more from the masses.... Of course they never took my opinion into consideration and regarded my words as a joke, repeating them everywhere as proof that I had not corrected my opportunist mistakes."[30]

"Opportunism" became a meaningless epithet with which to wither any opponent of the insurrectionist course. Putschist moods, born of the desperation of failure, were strong within the Communist Party, yet there were still comrades sane enough to doubt the advisability of hurling themselves into mad adventures foredoomed to defeat. Their resistance was smothered by wholesale expulsion of the waverers as part of a program of "Bolshevization" of the party. "After the August 7 Conference...if anybody expressed doubts about the policy of uprisings, he was immediately called an opportunist and pitilessly attacked."[31] Protests were brushed aside. Moscow said that the time for "direct struggle" had come. If the necessary conditions did not exist, they had to be made to order, whatever the cost. The result was a series of adventures in the fall of 1927, known as the "Autumn Harvest Uprisings." Putschism was carried to suicidal extremes. Had the Comintern been setting out deliberately to destroy what was left of the Chinese Communist Party, it could have found no more efficient means. The party seemed intent only upon its own destruction and in this it almost fully succeeded.

The first of the uprisings occurred at Nanchang, capital of Kiangsi province, on August 1. Two Communist officers, Yeh Ting and Ho Lung, raised the banner of revolt. They commanded about three thousand men. Among the members of their "Revolutionary Committee" they listed the names of Mrs. Sun Yat-sen, Teng Yen-ta, and Eugene Chen, then en route to European exile, and Generals Chang

Fah-kwei and Hwang Che-hsiang of the "Ironsides" army, who promptly abandoned their pretense of military action against Chiang Kai-shek for the real business of exterminating the Communist rebels who offered them those unwanted revolutionary honors. "The revolt in Nanchang...is the beginning of the fight against the Wuhan government," reported the Comintern press." Every revolutionist will be of the opinion that a government consisting of elements treacherous to the revolution and supported by officers and big landowners, must in all circumstances be overthrown." Wuhan, it will be recalled, had only begun to answer this description two weeks previously. "A new revolutionary center is being formed."[32] The new "revolutionary center" lasted only a few days. The troops of Yeh Ting and Ho Lung were forced to flee when Chang Fah-kwei approached the city with his army.

Waving their Kuomintang banners in the faces of an apathetic population, the revolutionists evacuated the city and marched southward. They passed among people for whom the Kuomintang banner had long since become the symbol of terror. They had seen Chiang Kai-shek brandish it in March and Chu Pei-teh in June. To them the forces of Yeh-Ho seemed to be only the "armies of Chiang Kai-shek the Third."[33] Yeh and Ho promised to confiscate holdings in excess of 200 *mow*, which amounted to a promise to leave the overwhelming majority of the landlords untouched. Bitter experience had taught the peasants of Kiangsi and northern Kwangtung to distrust armies which came promising to substitute benevolence for the malevolence of their predecessors. There was nothing to distinguish this new "revolutionary army" from the Kuomintang armies that had preceded it. Wherever they could the peasants gave it a wide berth. After fruitlessly careering through the countryside for two months, the Yeh-Ho army attacked the cities of Chaochow and Swatow in northeastern Kwangtung. It was defeated and dispersed. Its remnants fled into the East River districts where an insurgent peasant movement had begun to raise its head in the ebb of the great peasant wave. This was the end of the Yeh-Ho adventure.

The official explanation was that the Nanchang uprising was defeated because of the "superior strength of the enemy," listing incidentally, as it were, a few additional causes under the general heading "errors of the leadership," as follows: "1. Lack of a clear-cut revolutionary policy. 2. Indecisiveness in the agrarian question. 3. Lack of connection with the peasant masses and failure to arm the peasants. 4. Failure to crush the old political organizations and set up new ones. 5. Errors in military judgment."[34] Otherwise all would have been well. The enemy was stronger and we lacked forces, a revolutionary policy, and connections with the masses. The policy of insurrection was nevertheless untouchably correct.

Similar abortions were occurring throughout Central China and even in some districts of the north. All the attempted uprisings had one feature in common: the masses, instead of making the "tremendous response" Stalin predicted, simply refused to cooperate. Perhaps the workers and peasants were "opportunist," or perhaps, as Chiu Chiu-pei was later compelled to admit, "the masses saw before we did that the blue banner had become the banner of the white terror."[35] In most cases the Communists overcame the passive reluctance of the masses by ignoring them altogether and seeking salvation in alliances with little local military satraps. A small force of troops in Hupeh led by a Communist named Chang Fao-cheng tried, for example, to unite with one local militarist against a third who was ravaging the neighborhood. "Because of this opportunist policy," recorded Hua Kang, "the Hupeh uprisings also failed."[36] The same tactics were employed in Northern Kiangsu, where an attempt was made to form a "bloc" with a militarist named Tzo Fung-chi. The results were the same. There were in some *hsien* of Hunan and Hupeh sporadic uprisings of the peasantry who in small bands, armed with pikes and spears, made desperate attempts to seize *hsien* towns. Again and again they were thrust back or wiped out. Even in such cases the Communists on the scene "did not try to arouse and organize the workers and peasants, but relied only on military forces."[37]

In Shanghai the Kiangsu Provincial Committee of the Communist Party found means of its own to "arouse" the masses. Brief peasant outbursts in Yishing and Wusih early in November convinced the committee that "the time for an insurrection has now really arrived." The only difficulty was that the workers, crushed by the terror, were not interested. Undaunted, the party sent bands of "armed Red terrorists to intimidate the workers into striking, factory by factory, thinking that if a general strike could be manufactured [!] in this way, the uprising would surely be successful."[38] In Wuhan after the first series of the Autumn Harvest Uprisings had uniformly failed in the countryside, agitation was begun for the organization of an insurrection in the city. The Yangtze Bureau of the Communist Party at first demurred. Their previous orders for "immediate uprisings" had not turned out so well. The Hupeh Provincial Committee was likewise stricken with the virus of doubt. "Now is not the time for a general uprising," it had the temerity to reply. Whereupon charges of "opportunism" were hurled at it and under this barrage the committee backed down. "In order to avoid the suspicion of being opportunist, the Hupeh Provincial Committee issued new orders for mobilization and general strike." When the time came, however, to put the orders into execution, most of the remaining party members in Wuhan "resorted to flight and panic."[39] The Northern Bureau of the party on October 6 adopted a "General Plan for Uprising" which was so elaborately preposterous that even Hua Kang was compelled to call it "material for an historical joke."

One after another these ill-drawn caricatures of revolutionary uprisings were erased. Some of them may have seemed ludicrous, but only the enemies of Communism might have laughed for in these wild outbursts and wilder plans the Communists were smashing their party to pieces—and the end was not yet.

Only now it began, at long last, to dawn on the Communist leaders that "there was no further basis for the existence of the Kuomintang Lefts."[40] Not until the Autumn Harvest Uprisings had been successively crushed did they finally decide to furl the blue banner of the Kuomintang. The decision of the Political Bureau of the Chinese Communist Party on September 19, 1927, which declared that "the uprisings can under no circumstances take place under the Kuomintang banner,"[41] brought formally to a close the disastrous bloc with the party of the bourgeoisie and terminated the myth that "nine-tenths" of the Kuomintang had been ready to follow an independent Communist lead. The "nine-tenths" had disappeared under the terror. Now, abruptly, Stalin's *Pravda* ordered another 180-degree turn. "The propaganda slogan of soviets," it announced on September 30, "must now become a slogan of action."[42] For the blue banner of the bourgeois Kuomintang flown in the period of the revolutionary upswing the Chinese Communist Party had now to substitute the red banner of the soviets in the period of the revolution's ebb. The November Plenum of the party leadership dutifully proclaimed as the immediate slogan of action: "All power to the delegates' councils of the workers, peasants, soldiers, and city poor—the soviets!"[43] From the collapse of the Yeh-Ho adventure, from the defeats of the Autumn Harvest, the Communist leadership drew the now familiar conclusion: "After the Yeh-Ho defeat, the Chinese Revolution not only did not ebb, but rose to a new, higher stage."[44]

Chiang Kai-shek's coup of March 20, 1926, had elevated the revolution to the "higher" stage of the coup of April 12 which led to the still "higher" stage of Wuhan. The collapse of the Wuhan experiment lifted the revolution to the insurrectionary plane of Nanchang. The failures of the Autumn Harvest ushered it into the dizzy heights of—Sovietism! This remarkable theory of uninterrupted ascent led the November Plenum to declare that "the objective situation in China is such that the duration of a decidedly revolutionary situation is and will be measured not by weeks and months but by years." From this it was but a step to deduce conditions ripe for immediate insurrection: "The strength of the revolutionary movement of the toiling masses of China, far from being exhausted, is only beginning to make itself felt in the revival of the revolutionary struggle, despite the enormous defeats which the revolution has suffered.... All this combined compels the Plenum of the Central Committee of the Chinese Communist Party to declare that a decidedly revolutionary situation exists now throughout China."[45]

This estimate, leading directly to new adventures and new disasters, was based on the premise that in view of the incapacity of the bourgeoisie to solve China's external and internal problems, "stabilization of the bourgeois militarist reaction is impossible."[46] From the fact that the forces of the reaction were split into warring cliques as soon as they had grasped power, the Communists concluded that conditions ripe for insurrection remained. In this they overlooked only one detail: the revolutionary organizations were all but destroyed. The revolutionary moods of the masses, above all of the urban workers, had all but ebbed away. Rent by militarist civil wars, and the consequent dislocation of trade, and bent by imperialist pressure, the bourgeois power would certainly find difficulty in "stabilizing" itself. But were the revolutionary forces in a position to replace it with a power of their own? That was the question the Chinese Communists could not answer correctly because they were unable to understand the causes and the scope of the defeats that had been suffered. They mistook their own putschist moods for the general temper of the people.

The heavy defeat of the revolution guaranteed the relative "stabilization" of the bourgeois power, whatever its inner weaknesses and uncertainties. It would be overthrown only when the masses rose again to topple it. This they could not do in the winter of 1927 when they were still overcome by the shattering defeats to which the blunders of their own leaders had led them. Shackled, they only looked on as the generals fought and the small handfuls of Communists hurled themselves into reckless adventures. The Communists had no interest in organizing the day-to-day defensive struggles of the workers and the slow rebuilding of their organizations and self-confidence. They followed avidly only the smoldering course of intermilitarist clique rivalries and plotted to get arms for the purpose of "transforming the militarist civil wars into an anti-imperialist war of the masses" for the "overthrow of the reactionary rule and the establishment of the Soviet power."[47]

Like Stalin, they looked for an automatic "tremendous response" from the masses. But it never came. In the countryside there were still bands of rebellious peasants and mutinous soldiers, yet the experiences of the Autumn Harvest had clearly revealed the indifferent passivity of the urban workers and the impotence of the scattered peasant detachments. This the Communists were unable to see. Their course toward insurrection, adopted after the Wuhan collapse, had led only to a new series of defeats. "Nevertheless," they concluded, "despite this further partial defeat of the revolution, the enormous [!] experience of the last three months is eloquent [!] testimony that the tactic of the Chinese Communist Party was, on the whole, perfectly correct."[48] The Communists had not learned how to organize victories. They had learned only how to parrot the formulas of the godlike infallibility of Stalin. From Canton to Shanghai to Wuhan, they had moved from disaster to disaster. The cycle had now to be completed. In Canton once more they lurched toward a new catastrophe.

17

The Canton Commune

Kwangtung had been surrendered without a struggle to the militarists after Chiang Kai-shek's coup d'état of March 20, 1926. After the departure of the Northern Expeditionary armies in July that year, the liquidation of the Canton–Hong Kong strike in October, and the transfer of the National Government to Wuhan in December, full control of the province passed into the hands of Li Chi-sen, a southern general.

Li wasted no time in bringing all of Kwangtung under the heel of his military establishment. He rigidly curbed the trade unions and applied Borodin's system of compulsory arbitration with an iron hand. He met with no resistance from the Communists, who had relaxed all their activity, conceding the ground to the general "to preserve the national united front." The Communist policy consisted of "waiting for the success of the Northern Expedition."[1] While they waited, the Northern Expedition was victorious, only the victories fell to Chiang Kai-shek and the Chinese bourgeoisie, culminating in the Shanghai events of April 12, 1927.

Li Chi-sen responded swiftly to Chiang Kai-shek's lead and on April 15 carried out a purge of his own. All the mass organizations which still enjoyed legal existence were raided and closed down. More than 2,000 were arrested and at least one hundred men and women, most of them Communists, were shot. The remnants of the Canton–Hong Kong strike pickets were disarmed after sharp skirmishes and more than 2,000 railway workers under Communist influence were driven from their jobs by Li's soldiers and replaced by workers under the control of the arch-reactionary Mechanics' Union. Taking his cue from Chiang Kai-shek, Li Chi-sen understood the value of preserving the outer forms of working-class organizations. He took over their premises and filled them with gangster-hirelings designated as "Trade Union Reorganization Committees." Similar events took place in cities and towns throughout the province. In the villages peasants often resisted the raids of the military. The peasant unions, however, were crushed.

The Communists now had to pay for their passivity. They proclaimed a general strike on April 24 in protest against Li Chi-sen's attacks on the unions. The strike failed to materialize. In the ensuing months the Communists in Canton and in Kwangtung generally were driven deep underground. Employers launched an offensive against the workers which stripped them of every gain made in wages, hours, and working conditions during the height of the Canton–Hong Kong strike. The famous Kwangtung Workers' Delegates' Council, the embryo soviet that less than a year before represented more than 200,000 workers in all trades, disappeared. In its place functioned an illegal "Special Committee" composed of several former executive members of the Delegates' Council and a smaller number of newly selected delegates. This committee claimed to control about one hundred unions in Canton. In June it claimed credit for bringing nearly 30,000 workers out to a demonstration to commemorate the anniversaries of the Shakee massacre and the beginning of the Hong Kong strike.[2] Even if these claims were justified, they were modest enough, compared to the recent past.

The apathy of the great majority of the workers produced terrorist moods in the ranks of the Communist Party. Incapable of mobilizing the workers for resistance to the capitalist offensive, Communist workers took to bomb throwing in a series of hopelessly futile attempts to frighten and drive away the members of Li Chi-sen's Reorganization Committees. There was even a plot, according to Huang Ping, to assassinate Li Chi-sen. It failed when a planted bomb failed to explode.[3] This resort to individual terrorism by desperate and disillusioned workers and Communists was officially dignified by the Communist Party with the name "Red Terror."

There are times when a Red Terror becomes inescapably necessary to safeguard revolutionary conquests; at such times it is a deliberate measure proclaimed by the government of a victorious working class against enemies who challenge or endanger its rule. The Bolsheviks in Russia did not impose extreme penalties on their opponents until long after they had seized power and not until their enemies made attempts on the lives of the Bolshevik leaders and began actively to organize the forces of the counterrevolution. This has nothing in common with resort to the use of individual terrorist methods against the tools of a reactionary regime in power. Bolshevism grew up in the struggle against these methods which do not aid in the mobilization of the masses but contribute only to their demoralization. The appearance of terrorist tendencies in a revolutionary organization is the deadly symptom of its impotence or its degeneration.*

Just as previously the Kwangtung Communists had rationalized their passivity with the advice to "wait for the success of the Northern Expedition," they now sublimated their helplessness in hopes for the "Eastern Expedition" which all of

* In his two books about the Chinese Revolution, *Les Conquérants* and *La Condition Humaine*, André Malraux described young Chinese terrorists driven to the use of bomb and revolver by the Communist Party's lack of a revolutionary policy. One of them, he relates, tried to blow up Chiang Kai-shek on the eve of the April coup in Shanghai.

them, their leaders in Moscow included, believed would be launched against Chiang Kai-shek by the Wuhan government. When Wuhan capitulated to Chiang instead of attacking him, the cry went up: "Wait for Yeh-Ho!" Towards the end of September plans were hastily improvised for an uprising to coincide with the expected arrival of the Yeh-Ho forces at the gates of Canton. When the awaited saviors were dispersed before Chaochow and Swatow, the plans for the uprising were temporarily abandoned.[4]

In Kwangtung it was not until after the defeat of Yeh Ting and Ho Lung in October that the Communists adopted the slogan: "Down with the Kuomintang!"[5] The slogan was carried out into the streets for the first time in an attempted demonstration on October 14. In other words, exactly one year and four days after the treacherous and unconditional liquidation of the Canton–Hong Kong strike by the Kuomintang government and more than a year and a half after the March coup of Chiang Kai-shek, long months during which the workers of Canton had been shot down by Kuomintang soldiers, imprisoned in Kuomintang jails, deprived of their organizations by Kuomintang decrees, the Communist Party at long last accorded the workers of Canton official permission to cry: "Down with the Kuomintang!" Is it any wonder, then, that the use of the dagger, revolver, knife, or bomb against Kuomintang labor "leaders" seemed to many of them to be more fruitful than the policies of the Communist Party? Is it any wonder that the overwhelming majority of Canton's workers, who had poured with such optimism and hope into their organizations, had in this period, in equal numbers, left the arena of organized activity, bitter, disillusioned, and cynical?

Yet despite the strong play of centrifugal forces which were fast leaving the Communist Party isolated and stranded on the shoals of yesterday's blunders and today's wildcat dreams, there still remained in Canton a small body of workers whose will to struggle had remained firm through all the vicissitudes of the movement. Among them were the best fighters of yesterday's huge mass organizations, a handful of the Canton–Hong Kong strike pickets who had written so brilliant a page into the history of the revolution, remnants of the workers' own Red Guard, and a part of the radical, unemployed railway workers. These were workers who throughout the course of the revolution had made the greatest sacrifices, who had developed the highest degree of conscious political understanding of any in Kwangtung, and whose role in the early rise of the Kuomintang to power in the south had been little short of decisive. The Communist Party possessed in this hardened band of workers a tremendous saving from the wreck of the revolution. Carefully nurtured and properly led, through persistent struggle and with a correct policy, these cadres might have reopened for the Communist Party the road to leadership, now blocked by the debris of the past. Instead, not understanding "that it was necessary to retreat," unable to lead the defensive struggles of the Canton workers—the only path to the reestablishment of its influence, its prestige, and its right to lead—the Communist Party was now preparing to hurl its last proletarian forces into a desperate frontal attack foredoomed by every single circumstance, objective and subjective, to defeat.

Power in Canton was at that time shared by the rival forces of Li Chi-sen and Chang Fah-kwei, between whom civil war impended. Chang's political facade was ornamented by none other than Wang Ching-wei, with whom he planned a coup d'état designed to elbow General Li out of the city. Anticipating this coup, the Central Committee of the Communist Party in Shanghai issued the following instructions to the Kwangtung provincial organization: "The worker-peasant masses of Kwangtung have only one way out...that is, to utilize the opportunity of the civil war resulting from the coup d'état in order resolutely to expand the uprisings in the cities and villages...to agitate among the soldiers to stage mutinies and revolts, and in the time of war swiftly to link such uprisings into a general uprising for the establishment of the rule of the Workers', Peasants', and Soldiers' Delegates' Councils (Soviets)."[6] With the air of a doctor performing a postmortem on a patient he has just negligently killed, Lozovsky a year later wrote: "It is true that there were sharp struggles developing between Chang Fah-kwei and Li Chi-sen, but the insurrectionists should have known that as soon as the banner of revolt was raised, the quarrels in the camp of the counterrevolution would immediately come to an end."[7] Between what the leaders of the Chinese Communist Party should have known and what the Lozovskys and all the other worthies of the Comintern taught them yawned the chasm into which the Chinese Revolution fell to its destruction. The fact that the generals would unite a thousand times against the insurrection before fighting each other was as apparent in December 1927 as it had been during all the previous periods of the revolution. The Comintern had not understood this before and did not understand it now. The Chinese Communists were driven along the course of insurrection under the direct instructions of the Executive Committee of the Comintern and its new representatives in China, first Lominadze and after him the adventurer, Heinz Neumann, who had now arrived in Canton to provide the Chinese Communists with the necessary "guidance" along the insurrectionary path.

The Chang-Wang coup d'état duly took place on November 17 and the forces of the opposing generals squared off for battle in a zone that began forty miles from Canton and stretched from the North River districts to Swatow. On November 26 the Communist Party decided to prepare at once for an insurrection[8]and a few days later set the date for December 13.* According to Heinz Neumann, the

* By a peculiar "coincidence," the Canton insurrection was made to coincide with the Fifteenth Congress of the Communist Party of the Soviet Union at which Stalin completed his conquest of the Opposition and put through the wholesale expulsion of the left wing of the Party. Trotsky has written that the insurrection was timed to give the Stalinist majority a "victory" in

Communist leaders were "profoundly convinced that all the conditions for victory were present and that success...was assured."[9]

In reality, conditions were such that in the country as a whole there was no force left capable of coming to the support of an uprising in Canton, even if it were victorious. More, in Canton and in Kwangtung itself, the existing correlation of forces made such a victory impossible. Only afterward did the Heinz Neumanns and the Lozovskys admit that this had been the case. The Canton insurrectionists counted heavily in their plans on the cooperation of revolting peasants in the East River districts of Haifeng and Lufeng, 150 miles from Canton, where only five years before Peng Pai had cradled the modern Chinese peasant movement. Peng was back there now and with the aid of the fleeing remnants of the Yeh-Ho army had created the first of those peasant "soviets" which became the basis of Communist Party policy during the whole ensuing period. Dating from the end of October, this peasant rising in Hailufeng had stirred scattered sections of the peasantry in two or three other districts, in the North River area, and on the island of Hainan. Viewed in the light of the situation in the whole country, these tiny centers of rural revolt were only belated echoes of past opportunities irretrievably lost; but in Canton the Communists saw them magnified ten thousandfold. They considered them sufficient to guarantee that the whole country would spring to their support. "Obviously," confessed Lominadze—more than a year later—"we far too greatly exaggerated the extent of the development of the peasant uprisings at that time."[10]

The military forces available to the Communists for the insurrection and to the reaction for its suppression, compared even without regard to the prevailing circumstances in the province and in the country at large, offered in themselves a ghastly forecast of what was to come. Assembling the firsthand reports of the participants, Chen Shao-yu* found that "the armed forces of the ruling class stationed in Canton exceeded by five or six times the forces of the insurrectionists."[11] Summarizing the reports of the Communist military commander, Yeh Ting, of "Comrade A" (presumably Neumann), and of the Canton Revolutionary Military Committee, Chen estimated the armaments of the revolutionists, at their highest figures, as follows: "Revolvers and automatic revolvers, at most 30; grenades, at most 200; rifles in the hands of workers, at most 50; rifles in the hands of soldiers,

China "to cover up the physical extermination of the Russian Opposition." —*Problems*, pp. 291–92. Cf. Victor Serge, *De Lenine à Staline*, Paris, 1937, p. 31; Victor Serge, *Russia Twenty Years After*, New York, 1937, p. 160; Boris Souvarine, *Stalin*, Paris, 1935, p. 434. The present writer has been told by members of the little group of left Kuomintang émigrés, which included Mrs. Sun Yat-sen, Eugene Chen, Teng Yen-ta, and others, who were then in Moscow, that they also had reason to believe that events in Canton were deliberately forced to create the necessary "atmosphere" at the Fifteenth Congress.

* Later, better known as Wang Min, secretary-general of the Chinese Communist Party.

at most 1,600."[12] Neumann's report said that the workers' Red Guard had only 29 mausers and about 200 grenades—not a single rifle.[13] The only military detachment at the disposal of the insurrection was the cadet regiment, composed of noncommissioned officers and former Whampoa cadets, of whom about 200 were members of the Communist Party.[14] The actual number of participants in the uprising was given by Yeh Ting as 4,200, including 1,200 men of the cadet regiment, 3,000 Red Guards and others. "Comrade A" estimated only 2,000 in addition to the cadets, giving a total of only 3,200.[15]

According to Yeh Ting the authorities had 7,000 well-armed men available in the city for instant action. These included 5,000 soldiers, 1,000 policemen, and 1,000 gangsters controlled by the reactionary Mechanics' Union. The soldiers included detachments of infantry, machine gunners, and artillery. In all they possessed more than 5,000 rifles, a considerable number of machine guns, thirty-five small trench-mortars and cannon.[16] These were only the forces in the city itself. In the river there were several Chinese and foreign gunboats. On the outskirts of the town there were nearly four full regiments stationed in barracks and only two or three days' travel away there were the combined armies of Chang Fah-kwei and Li Chi-sen, a force totalling no less than 50,000 men, well armed and well trained. Among these troops Communist influence did not exist, not even a trace of it. "The great bulk of the soldiers were completely ignorant of the Communist slogans," admitted Neumann.[17] "We had done no preparatory work to disintegrate the enemy troops," wrote Lozovsky. This "predetermined the outcome of the insurrection."[18] In his subsequent report, Neumann admitted the overwhelming odds. "But if one considers," he feebly added, "that the troops of the bourgeoisie were surrounded on all sides by revolutionary ferment and that the commanding staff could not rely upon them politically, one can say that the military forces, in Canton, were equal." This was Neumann's only attempt at self-defense. The rest of his report is its own refutation.[19]

The "revolutionary ferment" was so great that the Communist Party did not dare issue a call for a general strike. When Neumann and the Communist committee pondered the strategy to be followed, they thought for a moment of calling such a strike, but the idea was abandoned, according to Neumann, "because it seemed to the revolutionary committee that if they did not succeed in taking the enemy unawares by a sudden night attack, the chances of victory would singularly diminish."[20] Huang Ping, a member of the revolutionary committee, records that it decided "unanimously" to stage the insurrection without attempting a strike.[21] The last attempt to call out the Canton workers on October 23 had ended in disaster when Chang Fah-kwei took swift and savage measures which smashed all preparations for the walkout. A further blow had been struck at the remaining forces under Communist influence when a week or so later Wang Ching-wei had secured the forcible eviction of the Canton–Hong Kong pickets from the dormitories which they still occupied on the outskirts of the city. Wang, the late great ally of the Comintern, had carried out the task from which even the militarists, up to then, had shrunk. The pickets bad been dispersed. Only about 500 of them remained at the disposal of the Communists.* After these experiences the Communist leadership ceased even thinking in terms of strikes. Insurrection was the thing. "The Communist Party was not capable of organizing strikes. They could not stop the economic life of the whole city. They could not attract the proletarians in the factories and handicraft shops to the movement.... Only when the roar of guns and rifles was heard and barricade fighting was already in progress did the working masses begin to know that an insurrection was going on.... [The masses] regarded the insurrection as a sudden, accidental thing."[22]

By the same token, equally "sudden" and seemingly "accidental" would be the emergence of the "soviet" whose name was now inscribed on the banner of the Communist Party. Four days before the insurrection fifteen men were selected at a secret meeting, nine of them representing the tiny groups of workers under Communist leadership or influence, three of them representing the cadets' regiment, and three who were supposed to represent the peasants of Kwangtung.[23] These fifteen men constituted nothing less than the "Canton Council of Workers', Peasants', and Soldiers' Deputies!" After the capture of power, it was decided, this "soviet" would be enlarged to a membership of 300.

Like every other revolutionary idea refracted through the Stalinized leadership of the Communist International, the idea of the soviets had been mangled beyond all recognition. What is a soviet? First of all, it is an elected body of workers', peasants', and soldiers' representatives based on the widest suffrage of all sections of the toiling population. It is the embodiment of the broadest proletarian democracy. It rises in times of tremendous revolutionary upheavals. Emerging from strike committees, committees of action, and other local bodies, the soviet brings within the orbit of the revolutionary movement broad sections of the revolting masses which have not yet been reached by any of the political parties. Its virtue lies in that it emerges organically from the mass movement itself and it becomes an extra-governmental authority that directly expresses the will of the masses. In the soviets the masses receive their political schooling, accelerated a thousand times by the heightened friction of the times. In the soviets they are led and trained through every phase of struggle in the rising revolutionary wave right up to the capture of power. Having organized and carried through the insurrection the soviets become the organs of the new revolutionary power. This concept of the soviets, formulated and tested through the experience of the three Russian revolutions, disappeared under the reign of Stalin. Under the new dispensation, soviets were to be regarded not as organs accompanying the whole course of revolutionary

* Neumann says there were only 300.

struggle, but as organs which could rightly appear only on the very threshold of the capture of power itself. This distorted view of the character and role of the soviets found in Canton its correspondingly grotesque expression.[24]

Even supposing for the moment that the Canton insurrection was being planned in the midst of a forward-surging mass movement, reaching out for power—which was not even remotely the case—the hastily improvised election of a soviet would have been an impossible and even unnecessary task. In such an event, the previous rise of the mass movement, if it had not already taken on soviet forms, would necessarily have developed other, equally suitable organizations capable of preparing the masses and leading them to the seizure of power. In Canton none of these conditions existed. There was no rising mass movement and there was no basis for the appearance of an elected soviet—and any other kind is not a soviet at all.

> To create an elected soviet is not an easy matter," wrote Trotsky, who was not entirely unacquainted with the phenomenon. "It is necessary that the masses know from experience what a soviet is, that they understand its form, that they have learned something in the past to accustom them to an elected soviet organization. There was not even a sign of this in China, for the slogan of soviets was declared to be a Trotskyist slogan precisely in the period when it should have become the nerve center of the entire movement. When, however, helter-skelter, a date was set for an insurrection so as to skip over their own defeats, they simultaneously had to appoint a soviet as well. If this error is not laid bare to the core, the slogan of Soviets can be transformed into a strangling noose of the revolution....
>
> The task of the soviets is not merely to issue the call for the insurrection or to carry it out, but to lead the masses toward the insurrection through the necessary stages.... The masses must sense and understand while in action that the soviet is their organization, that it marshals the forces for a struggle, for resistance, for self-defense, and for an offensive. They can sense and understand this not from an action of a single day nor in general from any single act, but from the experience of several weeks, months, and perhaps years.... In contradistinction to this, the epigones have converted the soviets into an organizational parade uniform with which the Party simply dresses up the proletariat on the eve of the capture of power. But this is precisely the time when we find that the soviets cannot be improvised in twenty-four hours, by order, for the direct purpose of an armed insurrection. Such experiments must inevitably assume a fictitious character, and the absence of the most necessary conditions for the capture of power is masked by the external ritual of a soviet system. That is what happened in Canton where the soviet was simply appointed to observe the ritual.... The soviet which was created in a hurry to observe the ritual was only a masquerade for the adventurist putsch.[25]

The stage is set for tragedy. In the face of the countrywide apathy of the masses the Communist Party is conspiring to bring about an insurrection in Canton. Included in the feverish preparations is the "detail" of the appointment of a fifteen-man "soviet" to assume tomorrow's power. Overwhelmingly stronger forces stand ready to crush them. The vast majority of the Cantonese workers do not have the least suspicion of what impends. Against all this there is only the matchless heroism of the workers and soldiers who are about to answer the call to rise.

At the last moment the whole plan almost collapsed.[26] Wang Ching-wei had in the interim gone to Shanghai for a political conference with Chiang Kai-shek. There, according to Huang Ping, he learned of the Communists' plans and wired an urgent warning to Chang Fah-kwei in Canton. Chang immediately wired his chief aide, Hwang Che-hsiang, one of the dashing "revolutionary heroes" of the old Ironsides Army, to return from the front and detach sufficient troops to reinforce the Canton garrison. Hwang arrived in the city on the morning of December 10 with his troops a few hours' march behind him. There developments did not give the conspirators pause. The only conclusion drawn from them by the Revolutionary Committee was to hasten the uprising. The original date, fixed for the 13th, was changed to the 11th.

At 7 p.m. on the evening of the 10th the Red Guards began to gather at their appointed stations. Orders were sped to the barracks of the cadet regiment and within a few hours' time the die was cast. During that night disaster again almost overtook the enterprise. The vigilance of the authorities had been aroused. Heavy police patrols and armored cars were thick in the streets. Pedestrians were searched in all the main thoroughfares. At an early hour in the evening one of the concentration points of the Red Guards was actually uncovered. Ninety of the Guards were arrested and a cache of sixty grenades seized. There was a moment's wavering, but it was too late to turn back now. Orders were issued to the Red Guards to resist arrest if caught. The plan would have to go through now, come what may.

For the next few hours all remained quiet. By midnight most of the police patrols, reassured, were off the streets. At 3:30 a.m. precisely the silence was split by rifle fire in the northern end of the city. The cadet regiment had risen. The regimental commander and several officers were arrested and shot. Climbing into waiting motorbuses the cadets split into parties of one and two companies each and trundled off through the city to the selected points of attack. Simultaneously the squads of Red Guards moved into action.

The first lightning raids were almost all successful. At several points in the city detachments of hostile troops were disarmed or put to flight after brief skirmishes. A considerable number of rifles was added to the slim store of the insurrectionists. In the heart of the city a combined worker-cadet force stormed and quickly occupied the central police headquarters and the headquarters of the military gendarmerie just across the same street. At Chang Fah-kwei's staff headquarters, and at the fortress-like mansion of Li Chi-sen, the attackers were repulsed by a deadly stream of machine-gun fire which proved impassable. By dawn, when most of the city was in the hands of the insurrection, these points still held out and fighting continued there well into the next day.

At six o'clock on the morning of December 11 the Canton "Soviet of Workers', Peasants', and Soldiers' Deputies" formally established itself in the police headquarters and began to function as the de facto government of Canton. There were only thirteen men present to launch the "soviet." Two of the selected peasant delegates did not arrive in time to participate. One of the government's first acts was to release more than 1,000 political prisoners, most of whom immediately joined the forces of the insurrection. Arms seized from the enemy were doled out as fast as they were secured. The city was still crackling with gun fire when the first decrees of the "Soviet Government" began to be issued.

The manifesto of the revolutionary government had been printed a few days before, but the printing plant where the copies still were held was in the line of fire and could not be reached. Hurriedly new handbills were run off in shops located within the captured area. Motorcars were commandeered. Youthful propagandists made off in them to spread the freshly printed sheets among the workers of Canton to let them know that the revolution had at long last taken place, that the blue banner of the Kuomintang had at last been replaced by the red flag of the Soviets. The manifesto called for the confiscation of the property of the big bourgeoisie, of the banks and money exchange shops. The houses of the wealthy were to be turned into dormitories for the workers. The pawnshops were to be taken over and all the articles in them returned freely to their owners. "All our martyrs have struggled and given their lives for such things. We must continue their struggle." Today's struggle would only add to the list of the martyred.

The program of the Canton Commune called for an eight-hour day, wage increases, state aid to the unemployed according to the regular wage scale, nationalization of all big industries, communications, and banks, recognition of the All-China Trade Union Federation as the national organization of the Chinese proletariat. It called for the nationalization of land, the extermination of all landlords and *haosen*, destruction of land deeds, leases, debt bonds, land boundaries, and the establishment of the soviet power in the villages. The city poor were to be relieved by the distribution of property confiscated from the wealthy. All debts to pawnshops and usurers were ordered cancelled and all miscellaneous taxes and contributions imposed upon the toilers abolished, The arming of the workers, the immediate release of all political prisoners, freedom of speech, press, and assembly, and the right to organize and strike were proclaimed for the toiling population.

Regarded in the light of the whole previous course of the Comintern's policy in the Chinese Revolution, the program of the Canton Commune was of the utmost significance. Because the Chinese Revolution was a "bourgeois-democratic revolution," the theoreticians of the Communist International held that the perspective of a proletarian dictatorship was impossible. The revolution, according to the official formulation of Stalin and Bukharin, was to culminate not in the dictatorship of the proletariat but in the "democratic dictatorship of the proletariat and the peasantry." This "democratic dictatorship" was vaguely envisaged as a transitional regime which would carry out the democratic tasks of the revolution and pave the way to the proletarian dictatorship, which was to come in some undetermined manner at a later date. Trotsky held that the democratic tasks could be achieved only by a proletarian dictatorship, because the realization of those tasks was unthinkable without measures of a Socialist character, measures that encroached upon bourgeois property. For this Trotsky had been repeatedly charged with wanting to "skip over the bourgeois-democratic stage of the revolution." When it came to elaborating a program in Canton, however, the Chinese Communists found themselves compelled to proclaim what Trotsky described as "more radical measures than those with which the October revolution began." Trotsky asked: "If these are the methods of a bourgeois revolution, what will the proletarian revolution in China look like? "[27]

This question was not fated to find its answer in Canton. Unconscious of how near they had come to the cardinal crime of "Trotskyism," the Canton Communards did not have time to do more than proclaim their program. By midmorning of December 11, the Kuomintang troops had already begun to strike back. At half a dozen barricades workers and soldiers were already desperately trying to repel the counterattack which grew stronger every hour. The mass of the Canton workers remained passive onlookers. To them the outbreak had come as "a sudden, accidental thing." They were conscious of no identity with this small band of men who were performing miracles of valor before their eyes. They had no idea that the "soviet" which functioned in the Bureau of Public Safety was theirs, an organ of proletarian power. In those strained, desperate hours, who was there even to begin the task of arousing them, of drawing them into the struggle? "The active workers of the unions, the leaders, and the responsible nuclei comrades mostly joined the Red Guards.... They were at the barricades. There was no one to do the work of mobilizing the masses."[28]

The great majority of the workers and artisans of Canton stood apart from the struggle. No general strike call was issued. Only a few handfuls of chauffeurs, printers, ricksha coolies, and some others quit work eagerly to grasp rifles.[29] Railway workers and river sailors continued at their jobs. They transported troops rushing to crush the uprising. They helped Kuomintang officials flee the city.

"The masses took no part in the insurrection," reported Yeh Ting, who had arrived only six hours before the outbreak to take command of the military forces.

> All the shops were closed and the employees showed no desire to support us.... Most of the soldiers we disarmed dispersed in the city. The insurrection was not linked to the difficulties of the railway workers on the three railway lines. The reactionaries could still use the Canton-Hankow line.... The workers of the power plant cut off the lights and we had to work in the dark. The workers of Canton and Hong Kong as well as the sailors, under the pressure of the British imperialists, did not dare join the combatants.... The river sailors placed themselves shamefully at the service of the Whites, whom they helped to cross the river while we were not even able to learn about some of the points of embarkation. The railway workers of the Hong Kong and Canton-Hankow lines transmitted the telegrams of the enemy and transported their soldiers. The peasants did not help us by destroying the tracks and did not try to prevent the enemy from attacking Canton. The workers of Hong Kong did not display the least sympathy for the insurrection.[30]

Neumann, more directly responsible for the debacle, said he felt that Yeh Ting's estimate of the role of the masses in the insurrection was not entirely just, but that he was "in agreement with him on the whole." His own report unavoidably reflected the same facts.

> The great majority of the proletariat and the petty bourgeoisie did not give sufficiently active support to the new power.... The railway workers, the municipal workers, the sailors of Hong Kong, and others did not stop work.... The petty bourgeoisie for the most part adopted a waiting attitude.... At the moment of the insurrection there was no important revolutionary movement among the peasants in the districts adjacent to Canton.... The peasants (of Hailufeng and Hainan) were completely isolated; no aid could be expected from them. The insurrection at Canton was not supported by any intervention of the proletarian masses or revolutionary peasants in the other provinces of China....[31]

That a few, perhaps a few thousand, workers in Canton sprang hopefully into action on the emergence of the Commune there can be little doubt. Yet at most they remained a pitifully small number. "It is true," said Deng Cheng-tsah, "that not all the workers of Canton participated.... But some people say only five thousand men were involved. This is...a slander. Surely more than twenty thousand took part." Even so, Deng, too, stopped to consider "Still we must say that its social basis was not broad. For example, before the betrayal of the Kuomintang, there were about two hundred thousand workers under the Communist Workers' Delegates' Council."[32]

That was less than two years before. With their own forces and their own strength, the workers and peasants of Canton and Kwangtung had demoralized the armies of the old militarists, paralyzed mighty Britain's Hong Kong and made possible the unification of the province and the establishment of a national government—for the Kuomintang and for the bourgeoisie. But at that time the thought of a workers' insurrection, of the expansion of the embryonic soviets (the Workers' Delegates' Council and the Canton–Hong Kong Strike

Committee) into broad democratic bodies embracing the aspirations and the impulses of moving millions was the kind of unthinkable blasphemy that could rise only in the mind of a Trotsky. Today, with their organized forces reduced, to take Deng's figure, to less than a tenth of their former dimensions, with the revolution everywhere shattered, and the reaction everywhere triumphant, the Communist were staging an insurrection under the banner of the soviet power—only the masses were no longer there to follow them. Only two years before the Communists had seemed to see their forces through the broad end of binoculars—minuscule and impotent—when in reality they were mighty beyond belief. Today they were looking at them through the narrow end, magnified multifold. They never saw their forces as they really were. The scores of thousands once with them were now gone, with the hopes in them that had died.

Feverishly the few squads of youthful propagandists operating out of the government's headquarters spread the news, by word of mouth and by handbills, that a monster mass meeting would be staged at noon on December 11. At the appointed time there were a bare 300 men on hand.[33] The leaders swallowed their chagrin and called it a "delegates' meeting." Even a joint conference of all the functionaries and nuclei leaders failed to open at two successively appointed hours. The men were at the barricades or could not be reached. That evening it was decided to hold the scheduled mass meeting at noon the next day, December 12, in front of the Taiping Theatre. Concerning this meeting, Huang Ping, who had been made "Foreign Affairs Commissar" of the Commune, is silent. Deng Cheng-tsah, another participant, says it failed to materialize.[34] Chen Shao-yu, who had the advantage of not having been in Canton but in Moscow at the time, says that 10,000 workers did gather to ratify the decrees of the soviet.[35] Even if Chen's claim were true, a gathering of 10,000 workers to listen to the speeches of a hand-picked soviet could only have been a bitter commentary on the memory of a simple May Day two years before when twenty times that number marched through the city in a mighty display of proletarian strength. According to the agenda of the scheduled mass meeting, the fifteen-man soviet was supposed to have been confirmed in its functions, its measures and decrees ratified, and a proposal adopted for its enlargement to 300 members. Whether these measures were ever actually passed upon is not recorded. Events quickly made the point immaterial, for by the afternoon of December 12 troops were attacking the city in force and a sanguinary battle was raging in which workers and cadets, armed only with rifles, bamboo swords, and spears, stubbornly held their positions under murderous machine gun and light artillery fire.

During the fighting several fires had broken out in the central district of the city. Naturally these were charged to the incendiarism of the Communards.

Actually, the main blazes, which partially destroyed the Central Bank and neighboring buildings, were directly traceable to the bombardment of the city from the river, where Chinese, British, and Japanese gunboats were cooperating to smash the Commune. They went into action to cover the defense of Chang Fah-kwei's headquarters and had also laid down a heavy barrage to cover the crossing of the troops who were now arriving in large numbers to retake the city. The bombardment ignited the powder magazine, starting fires which blazed up and down all the adjoining streets.[36] Moreover the criminal element in the city had taken advantage of the uprising to get into action on its own behalf. "The gangsters took the opportunity to commit arson and to loot."[37] When Li Fu-lin's troops arrived, the two Chinese gunboats poured a rain of steel into the city which, according to the Peking *Yi Shih Pao,* caused fire to break out in ten different places.[38]

Enemy troops converged on the Canton Commune from three different directions. Chang Fah-kwei, Hwang Che-hsiang, and Li Fu-lin directed operations from the safety of a gunboat anchored in the river. Among the commanders marching to the suppression of the Commune was Hsueh Yoh, who only nine months earlier had offered his division to the Communists to oppose Chiang's Shanghai coup. From the West River front, from Kungyi in the north, and from Whampoa and Honan in the east, no less than 45,000 soldiers were being thrown into the fray. Inside the city the gangsters, 1,000 strong, and all well armed, were already in action. The main body of the Red Guards was entrenched behind sandbags at the river bank. It was being attacked by troops from across the river, by the gunboats, and by the Mechanics' Union gangsters in the rear. The Communards were already so isolated from the population that several enemy detachments landed and came within 150 yards of the Revolutionary Committee's headquarters before being spotted.[39] They held out, nevertheless, until ten o'clock on the morning of the 13th. After a final bloody fight at close quarters the workers were forced to retreat from their sandbag barricades. They fell back, fighting from street to street. Some of the leaders gathered part of the cadet regiment and a few Red Guards—Neumann says they totalled 1,500 men—and escaped the cordon of enemy troops, leaving the city to march towards Hailufeng.[40] At noon the remaining Communards were making their last stand at the Bureau of Public Safety where the "soviet" had briefly held sway. Here, after being surrounded on four sides, the last of the Red Guards resisted extermination in a two-hour battle. The enormous superiority in arms and numbers enjoyed by the attackers was matched only by the sheer nerve and courage of the defenders. Huang Mo-sung's Whampoa troops rushed the workers' lines on five occasions and were thrust back every time. Shortly after noon the red flag was finally pulled down from police headquarters.

The Commune, only yesterday risen, today had fallen. In its final hours there was nothing but the desperate heroism of bands of workers who in groups of ten, thirty, and fifty, stood their ground until their ammunition gave out or until they were trampled down and slaughtered by the attackers. By the afternoon of December 13, the last of the defenders of the Canton Commune had been wiped out.

Bourgeois writers like shudderingly to refer to the Canton events of December 11-13 as the "three days of terror." During its brief existence, the Commune had killed only 210 of its enemies and imprisoned only seventy-one.[41] A Chinese bourgeois correspondent put the total deaths under the Commune at 600, including in that figure an estimate of those killed by the Communards while resisting the Kuomintang counterattack.[42] Not until the Chinese Gallifets set to work on the night of December 13 did the real reign of terror begin. Li Chi-sen, Chang Fah-kwei, and Hwang Che-hsiang turned their soldiery loose on the city. Long after actual fighting had come to an end the streets clattered with the gunfire of the executioners and were strewn with the blood and bodies of the worker dead.

A correspondent of the *Ta Kung Pao* saw women Communists "wrapped in cotton-padded blankets, soaked in gasoline and burned alive."[43] Soldiers seized any women they found with bobbed hair, which was regarded as infallible evidence of radicalism. Hundreds of girls were shot or otherwise killed after being subjected to indescribable indignities.[44] "Following the suppression of the worker-peasant uprising," wired a reporter from the scene, "Canton is like hell itself.... Uncleared corpses are piled up along the roads."[45] A correspondent of the Peking *Shuntien Pao* ventured out into the streets.

> The first thing I saw turning out of the small lane was the body of a worker lying face up. It was covered with dirt. On its head was a red kerchief. The forehead and right cheek had been shot away. Flies swarmed on the dead flesh. ... Behind the fallen brick walls, propped up against trees and lying at the street curbs, floating on the surface of the river, wherever you looked, dead men.... In every street everywhere were the corpses of massacred men and women.... Blood seemed to be running in rivers.... There were thick reddish black clots staining the ground, strewn with brains and bowels and entrails. Stones, bamboo swords, and wooden spears still lay about the streets.... The corpses lying stiff in their blood stank horribly.... At the square of the park I saw three trucks piled high with corpses. In the shrubs to the right were ten bodies, seemingly newly shot.... There were mournful shrieks and in the distance there still seemed to be shooting going on.[46]

Under a photo of corpses in a Canton street a Shanghai editor captioned: "The bodies of the dead were collected as so much cordwood and carted away for burial in a common grave."[47] Among them were the bodies of Chang Tai-lei, head of the Revolutionary Committee, killed in battle on the 12th, and of five Russians, shot down by Li Fu-lin's soldiers when they raided the Soviet Consulate General on the 15th. Most of the leaders managed to escape. Heinz Neumann, according to Yeh Ting, had been one of the first to flee. Behind them, grotesquely sprawled on the streets of Canton, they left the flower of the Canton proletariat. The final toll of the counted dead was 5,700.

That the "revolutionary generals" of the Kuomintang were merciless butchers was already a tardily established fact. Who were the real perpetrators of the crime of Canton? The common graves of the nameless dead were still uncovered when bitter voices were raised among the Cantonese Communists charging the Kwangtung Provincial Committee with responsibility for the slaughter.[48] These voices were quickly silenced, for did the Provincial Committee stand alone? Had it not followed the lead of the Central Committee? Had not the Central Committee followed the lead of Stalin? It was not possible to repudiate the policy of insurrection for its source led too directly to the Kremlin. The monstrous crime of Canton would have to be justified in order, once more, to preserve the myth of an infallible leadership. First to leap to do so was the Political Bureau of the Chinese Communist Party. In a resolution entitled "The Significance and Lessons of the Canton Uprising," adopted on January 3, 1928, it declared categorically: "Only cowardly opportunists can call such an uprising a premature act, a putsch, a military conspiracy. Such opportunism did not exist in the Canton section of the Communist Party or among the members of the Central Committee. The Canton uprising in mid-December was an inevitable outgrowth of the development of the class struggle as a whole and the conjuncture of the objective conditions. The working class had no other outlet but to rise directly to capture the revolutionary power."[49]

The resolution went on to show that the insurrection was the "inevitable outgrowth" of the decisions of the Comintern and the Chinese Central Committee. After the collapse of Wuhan, it recalled, "the Executive Committee of the Communist International and the August 7 Conference of the Central Committee considered that a directly revolutionary situation existed in China. This analysis was completely in accord with the facts."[50] The defeats of Nanchang, of the Yeh-Ho adventure and of the Autumn Harvest Uprisings were due, of course, not to any misreading of the situation or the falsity of the insurrectionist course, but to "mistakes of the leadership" which were corrected by the November Plenum. The plenum had also "correctly" pointed out that "the revolutionary forces had not only not diminished but were uninterruptedly growing" and that the question of uprising was still "an issue directly on the order of the day." Thus, early in December, "there was already in existence (in Canton) all the conditions for a victorious proletarian uprising." To have postponed the insurrection at that juncture would have been "to invite a most severe white terror." That the insurrection failed and led directly to the needless massacre of thousands of workers was once more due only to an isolated series of "mistakes," such as the "insufficiency of preparatory work." Thence the conclusion—once more!—that "the general situation in China is still a directly revolutionary situation," that the "perspective of the stabilization of Chinese capitalism after the Canton uprising not only does not improve but infinitely diminishes." Therefore: "The question of insurrection...and the question of Soviet power are the practical, immediate questions." The conclusion was a call to the party "to redouble tenfold" the organization of new uprisings.[51]

A month later the Ninth Plenary Session of the Executive Committee of the Communist International adopted the same position, clothed in a warning against "putschist tendencies" in general. The Canton insurrection was not a putsch but "the heroic attempt of the proletariat to organize soviet power." It suffered only from "several errors of leadership," among them insufficient preparation, "absence of broad political strikes, absence of an elected soviet as the organ of the uprising," for which "Comrade N. and others" were held responsible. "Despite all these mistakes of the leadership, the Canton insurrection must be regarded as the model of the greatest heroism of the Chinese worker."[52] By this cowardly attempt to hide behind the heroism of the Cantonese workers, the authors of the Comintern resolution hoped to cover their past blunders, which they now admitted had "led to the heaviest defeats of the workers and peasants...to the extermination of part of the cadres of the Communist movement." Simultaneously they renewed the call for new sacrifices to justify the official course. They "foresaw" the imminent approach of "a new revolutionary upsurge" which posed before the Communist Party the "practical task of organizing and carrying out the armed uprisings of the masses, since the tasks of the revolution cannot be solved except by uprisings and by the overthrow of the present power." The advice against "putschism" was an injunction to avoid isolated actions. "The Party must consider as its principal task the preparation of general and combined actions in the cities and in the countryside in several adjoining provinces. These actions must be organized on a large scale."[53] On February 7, 1928, Stalin's *Pravda* wrote: "The Chinese Communist Party is heading towards an armed insurrection. The whole situation in China speaks for the fact that this is the correct course.... Experience proves that the Chinese Communist Party must concentrate all its efforts on the task of the day-to-day and widespread careful preparation of the armed insurrection."[54]

During the ensuing five months this policy led the Chinese Communists from disaster to disaster, to scattered adventures which crushed the remnants of its forces. By the time the Sixth Congresses of the Chinese Communist Party and of the Communist International convened in July and August 1928, the fact had at last been impressed on the political strategists of the Kremlin that the "direct revolutionary situation" which allegedly had existed since August 1927, was an unfortunate fiction. This did not mean that the "fundamental line" of insurrection, dictated by Moscow and pursued so disastrously ever since, could now be rejected as false and a clearer light thrown on the period of adventurism as the logical reaction to the opportunist blunders of the past. It simply meant that a new formula of justification had to be found. It was suddenly "discovered" that the Canton insurrection was not the prelude to the immediate establishment of the Soviet power in China, not the climax of a steadily "rising wave" of the revolution, but a rearguard battle which concluded the declining revolutionary wave after the collapse of Wuhan.

"The greatest political mistake of many Chinese Communists and of Communists of other countries [?]...was that for several months after the defeat of the Canton uprising, they thought that this uprising was the direct beginning of a new, higher, revolutionary wave all over China, and accordingly they were for the direct organization of armed uprisings." Who speaks? None other than Lominadze, author of the theory of the "uninterrupted ascent" of the Chinese Revolution.[55]

Recognition of this "greatest political mistake" could not involve recognition of any "mistake" on the part of the ECCI or the Chinese Communist leadership. The Sixth Congress of the Chinese Party, which took place in a Moscow suburb on the eve of the Sixth World Congress of the Comintern, solemnly announced that "the Nanchang uprising, the Autumn Harvest Uprisings and especially [!] the Canton uprising were not putschist in character." The Canton commune was "the necessary [?] heroic attempt to safeguard the revolutionary conquests [?]... But objectively," and here is the new formula, "the Canton insurrection was a rearguard battle in the process of the defeat of the revolution."[56]

The colonial theses of the Sixth World Congress said that after the Wuhan collapse the Chinese Communist Party had "corrected its line"—that is, it took the road of insurrection—"but the revolutionary wave was already falling." So? "Instead of the former gross errors of opportunist leadership, there were now revealed, on the contrary, in various places, extremely harmful putschist mistakes."[57] How could a "correct" policy of uprising in a period of revolutionary decline have led to anything but "harmful putschist mistakes"? What is putschism but the deliberate launching of uprisings in conditions which foredoom them to defeat? These questions were neither asked nor answered, for the Comintern itself had ordered the turn to insurrection and the Comintern was infallible. It could merely be admitted now, in an offhand manner, as if no one had ever spoken differently, that "the revolutionary wave was already falling." The Nanchang adventure, the Autumn Harvest Uprisings and the Canton insurrection were only "attempts to avert the defeat of the revolution." The Canton insurrection was "the last powerful onslaught" of the revolutionary wave which was "near to subsidence."[58]

This casual change of labels only thinly disguised utter bankruptcy. When the Chinese Communist Party took the insurrectionary road and reaped its autumn harvest, it did so in the belief that along this road lay the capture of revolutionary power. No one talked of "safeguarding revolutionary conquests." There were none.

There were only defeats to overcome. The question of conquering power was put belatedly on the order of the day.

When the Opposition in Moscow warned that after the collapse of Wuhan the revolutionary decline had set in, that a defensive retreat had to be made, it was charged with "liquidating" the Chinese Revolution. Only now, after a year of new and catastrophic defeats traceable directly to the Comintern's false estimate of the situation, the Sixth Congress casually remarked that after Wuhan the revolutionary wave was indeed "falling" and "near to subsidence." What was "liquidationism" in August 1927, did not become "Bolshevism" until August 1928, long after events had laid the bodies of 5,700 Cantonese proletarians at the gates of the Kremlin. What defeated general throws his remaining forces into a trap and destroys them in a "rearguard battle" when a road of retreat lies clearly open before him? Only one who is blind or ignorant. The "revolutionary" generals of the Comintern were both.

Fruits of Defeat

The defeat of the revolution placed the Kuomintang in power. It ushered in a period of counterrevolution, terror, renewed militarist wars, deepening economic disintegration and impotence in the face of renewed imperialist invasions.

Unable to offer the masses sufficient economic security to win their voluntary support, the bourgeoisie could not develop or utilize democratic institutions. It could establish its power only in the form of a brutal military dictatorship, shared by groups of rival satraps and wholly dependent upon the military and financial support of the imperialists. Incapable of taking a single effective step toward bettering the condition of the people as a whole, the Kuomintang regime grew into a monstrous parasite on the stricken body of the nation. Its generals and its bankers, its landlords and bureaucrats, its jailers and executioners, inextricably interlaced, mercilessly drained the country. The bright promises of economic and social reforms that had accompanied the Kuomintang's rise to power remained empty phrases. Under Kuomintang rule all the existing means of exploitation were preserved and sharpened to an unprecedented degree. It maintained itself by naked force alone.

No one knows how many have died under the scourge of Kuomintang terror. No one knows how many men and women, boys and girls, have been mutilated, tortured, imprisoned, and killed during the past decade of Kuomintang rule. It is known only that there have been thousands, scores of thousands, slaughtered and maimed during mass butcheries in the countryside and in the cities, in addition to the victims of the day-to-day manhunts carried on unremittingly, year after year. No one has ever known exactly how many political prisoners choked stinking jails from one end of the land to the other, or how many of them died of disease or on the rack.

For the record there are only partial estimates and incomplete figures culled from official announcements and from the daily press. From April to December, 1927, according to one investigation, there were 37,985 known dead and 32,316 known political prisoners. Between January and August 1928, 27,699 were formally condemned to death and more than 17,000 were imprisoned. At the end of 1930 the Chinese Red Aid estimated that a total of 140,000 had been killed or died in prison. In 1931 a study of available figures for cities of six provinces established that 38,778 had been executed as enemies of the regime.[1] From 1932 to 1936 the thousands who were killed or filled the prisons were mainly those who in one way or another challenged the contemptible capitulation of Chiang Kai-shek and the Kuomintang to Japanese imperialism, or who tried to organize resistance to the imperialist invasion of Chinese territory, the seizure of Manchuria and a part of North China. Chiang Kai-shek adopted a policy of "nonresistance" to the imperialist invasion while he conducted a merciless war of extermination against insurgent peasants in Central China, killing thousands and laying waste villages and fields in the provinces south of the Yangtze.

The terror struck hardest at workers and peasants who tried to resist steadily worsening conditions of life under the Kuomintang. When the ravages of the world economic crisis were added to the rapacity of the regime, China was quickly faced with economic stagnation and complete bankruptcy. In five years Chiang Kai-shek's government ran the internal debt up to $1,100,000,000 (Chinese currency), and used all but 1 percent of this huge sum for the military machine upon which Chiang's power rested and its bureaucratic apparatus. When under the blows of the economic crisis Chinese foreign trade suffered a drastic drop, and when Japanese imperialism, goaded by the same crisis, took possession of Manchuria and cut away a substantial portion of the government's revenue, at the same time intensifying its drive on Chinese holdings in the textile and silk industries, the feeble economic structure on which the regime rested threatened to collapse altogether.

The index of foreign trade (1912–100) fell from 277 in 1931 to 118.6 in 1934. The index of the unfavorable balance of trade (1912–100) was 91.92 in 1927 and rocketed to 542.62 in 1932. In the latter year the country's industry and agriculture had declined to a point where food and clothing accounted for more than half the total import. The silk industry, an old mainstay of Chinese economy, was almost entirely wiped out. Of ninety-three filatures operating in Shanghai in 1927 only twenty-three were still working in 1934. In reels this drop was from 22,168 to 5,722. Japanese silk was selling more cheaply on the Chinese market than China's own product. In the textile industry, foreign capital inexorably overtook and absorbed Chinese-owned enterprises. By 1934 Japanese and British textile mills controlled nearly half the spindles and produced half the yarn in China. Foreign weaving mills, although fewer in number, produced 50 percent more pieces of cotton goods than all the Chinese mills put together. Chinese handicrafts, paper-making, match-making, porcelain, went down under the pressure of foreign competition. Prices of agricultural products declined 25 to 50 percent by 1932. Small landowners, swamped by swollen taxes and periodic militarist requisitions many times greater than the total paid in land taxes, could no longer even meet the costs of production. Tenant farmers abandoned the land by the scores of thousands when rents soared 50 to 100 percent. Over vast rural areas thousands of mow of land went to waste. The steady drain of silver, aggravated by the American silver purchasing policy in 1934, destroyed the meager basis of Chinese currency.[2]

Powerless to cope with the economic crisis, aggravated by the inroads of the imperialists, the Kuomintang regime was even more helpless when in 1931 Japanese imperialism began a new, aggressive phase in its program for the conquest of China. Taking shrewd advantage of the strategic vacuum created by the economic crisis and the plans of Britain and France for the creation of a cordon sanitaire around the Soviet Union, Japan moved into Manchuria, terminating the status quo created by the Washington Treaty of 1922. In studied and deliberate stages, separated by pauses for careful consolidation of newly won positions, Japanese imperialism between 1931 and 1935 conquered Manchuria and transformed it into "Manchukuo," forced the demilitarization of Shanghai, occupied Jehol, demilitarized the Hopei border districts, disorganized North China trade by openly sponsoring a large-scale smuggling trade, and drove a wedge westward into the Inner Mongolian province of Chahar.

At each stage the invaders either met no resistance at all or were opposed by isolated detachments abandoned to their fate by Chiang Kai-shek's government at Nanking. The policy of "non-resistance" did not signify mere passivity. While Nanking knocked feebly at the doors of Geneva, it ruthlessly suppressed any attempt independently made in China to organize resistance to the invasion. The whole machinery of the terror was geared to smash the spontaneous anti-Japanese movement that sprang into being in the winter of 1931. It broke up popular anti-Japanese associations and forced the termination of the anti-Japanese boycott. It made no attempt to support the guerrilla detachments of volunteers which continued to harass the Japanese Army in Manchuria. When the soldiers of the 19th Route Army made their historic stand at Shanghai in January–February 1932, Chiang Kai-shek held all but a few of his men and all of his planes and artillery far from the battlefront while thousands fell under merciless attack from land, air, and sea. When the sabotaged defense finally collapsed, Chiang's emissaries signed the Shanghai armistice of May 5, 1932, which demilitarized a 20-kilometer zone around the city.

A year later when the invaders advanced into Jehol they found none of the defenses which Nanking had assured the people it was building. By that time the combined policy of "non-resistance" and appeals to the League of Nations had worn itself thin. No one believed Chiang Kai-shek's repeated assertions that he would "go North" and "lay down his life." The League sent out a commission of ex-colonial administrators, headed by Lord Lytton, whose report proposed dismemberment of China in behalf of all the imperialists instead of for Japan's benefit alone. On the eve of the Jehol march, Nanking executed a clumsy pirouette and announced its intention to resist, but it moved neither men, nor guns, nor food, nor supplies. The "resistance" meant leaving thousands of ill-fed, ill-armed, demoralized soldiers in the path of the Japanese advance. Jehol was taken in a week. A few regiments made brief, spectacular stands at the Great Wall passes, but in a few days they were crushed. In May 1933, when Japanese forces marched to the gates of Peiping, Chiang Kai-shek's representatives signed the Tangku Truce which demilitarized 5,000 square miles south of the Wall and gave Japan a firm foothold in North China. During 1934 agreements were successively signed for resumption of rail and postal connections between North China and Manchukuo and the reestablishment of Chinese customs stations along the Hopei border. Nanking accorded de facto recognition, by these acts, to the Japanese conquest of the northeastern provinces. In 1935 the Chin-Doihara accord recognized Japan's claim to eastern Chahar and Chiang's war minister signed the Ho-Umetsu agreement which cleared Hopei of all central government troops. These were the springboards from which Japan plunged into its further, more extensive campaigns of conquest in 1937.[3]

Born with the aid of imperialist midwives, nurtured on imperialist support, the Kuomintang regime in a few short years brought the country to the brink of economic collapse and dismemberment. For a decade Chiang Kai-shek continued with impunity to massacre revolutionists, suppress and disperse the defensive struggles of the workers, exterminate whole sections of the revolting peasantry, and hand large sections of the country undefended over to imperialist invaders. Throughout, no effective revolutionary force challenged the Kuomintang counterrevolution. These were the fruits of the defeat of the revolution of 1925–27.

After the disasters of 1927, culminating in the Canton insurrection, the Communist Party had plunged into new blind alleys. A party that had suffered a debacle of such dimensions could not hope to re-form its ranks without first thoroughly digesting the reasons for its failures. The lessons of the past had to be the indispensable starting-point of a new course, for they created the premises of the new situation and the new problems it presented. The policies that had led to disaster in 1927, however, were declared to have been infallibly correct. "It is not the main line of tactics that was at fault," Bukharin told the Sixth Congress of the Comintern in July 1928, "but the practical actions and the practical application of the line pursued in China."[4] More, the essential kernel of the "main line," the theory and attempted practice of the "democratic dictatorship," was embodied in the program of the Communist International and reaffirmed as the basic pillar of Communist Party strategy for the future. The triple experience of Canton-Shanghai-Wuhan passed over without leaving a trace.

The Chinese Revolution of 1925–27 had provided, in the form of an antithesis, a new confirmation of the lessons of the October revolution in Russia. It proved again, although this time negatively, that in our times a backward country could realize its democratic revolution only in the form of the proletarian dictatorship, drawing behind it the poor peasant millions. In 1925–27 the Comintern, under Stalin's leadership, rejected the perspective of the proletarian dictatorship and substituted for it Lenin's long-abandoned formula, the nebulous, never-defined intermediate regime of the "democratic dictatorship of the proletariat and peasantry" which again and again in the real life of contending classes turned out to be the dictatorship of the bourgeoisie. First Chiang Kai-shek's Canton and then Wang Ching-wei's Wuhan were described as the budding embryos of the "democratic dictatorship" which would carry out the agrarian revolution and free China of its imperialist yoke. The Chinese proletariat was compelled to pay with its best heads to learn that the bourgeoisie would not destroy the foundations of its own power, that the revolution could advance only in the form of the proletarian dictatorship. To thrust this experience aside, as the Comintern now proceeded to do, was to doom the Communist movement in China to new futility, new defeats.[5]

In line with the general leftward lurch taken by the Comintern in 1928, the sudden discovery of the "third period," the final period of capitalism and the "stormy revolutionary upsurge,"[6] theoretical confusion was multiplied by the tactical madness of ultraleftism, opportunism fused with adventurism. While it continued to dangle before the Chinese Communists the tantalizingly illusory "democratic dictatorship," the Comintern rejected the tactic of agitation for limited democratic demands. Instead the Comintern ordered the shattered Chinese Communist Party to set its course now toward the creation of—soviets.

"At the present time," decreed the colonial thesis of the Sixth Congress,

> the party must everywhere propagate among the masses the idea of soviets, the idea of the democratic dictatorship of the proletariat and peasantry, and the inevitability of the coming revolutionary mass armed uprising. It must already now emphasize in its agitation the necessity of overthrow of the ruling bloc and the mobilization of the masses for revolutionary demonstrations.... It must consistently and undeviatingly follow the line of seizure of state power, organization of soviets as organs of insurrection, expropriation of the landlords and big property owners, expulsion of the foreign imperialists.... The future growth of the revolution will place before the party as an immediate practical task the preparation for and carrying through of armed insurrection as the sole path to the completion of the bourgeois-democratic revolution and to the overthrow...of the power of the Kuomintang.[7]

In the period of the revolutionary rise, when the centripetal tendencies of the masses were in full play, Stalin-Bukharin had substituted the bourgeois Kuomintang for soviets. Now, when a profoundly centrifugal process had set in as a result of the defeat, the slogan of soviets could, in Trotsky's words, be only "doctrinary, lifeless, or what is just as bad...the slogan of adventurists."[8] That the thesis, following Stalin's original concept, regarded soviets as "organs of insurrection" and not as democratic councils accompanying the whole course of the rising mass movement through a period of dual power, served only to emphasize the purely adventurist character of the slogan.

Certainly it followed from the fresh experience of the past that the further development of the Chinese Revolution would have to be toward soviets and through them to the proletarian dictatorship as the only means of winning land for the peasants and freedom from imperialist domination, i.e. the only means of successfully carrying out the tasks of the democratic revolution. This did not mean, however, that the banner of soviets could be waved in the faces of workers who had just been driven back by a series of catastrophic defeats. "Nothing is more fruitless and worthless than to show one's fist after the battle," wrote Trotsky to the Sixth Congress from his exile in Alma Ata. "It must be distinctly understood that there is not, at the present time, a revolutionary situation in China. It is rather a counterrevolutionary situation...transforming itself into an inter-revolutionary period of indefinite duration."[9]

For this transitional period, Trotsky proposed to arm the Communist Party with a program of struggle based upon the most elementary democratic demands as a means of reviving the revolutionary moods of the masses and grouping them together once more on the basis of political demands that corresponded to their simplest daily needs. These were the demands for the eight-hour day, freedom of speech, press, assembly, organization, and strike, generalized in the slogan calling for a thoroughly democratic national assembly, based on universal suffrage. Political agitation along such lines, coupled to the conduct of defensive struggles and the patient reorganization of the trade union movement, could alone, he said, revive the combative moods of the workers, restore their confidence, enable the Communist Party to secure a solid foundation in the key economic sectors, and, with the march of events, to permit it once more to debouch on the revolutionary road. Consistent and audacious championship of a truly democratic national assembly as opposed to the arch-censored and pseudodemocratic pretensions of the Kuomintang military dictatorship could alone help recreate those conditions in which the formation of soviets would once more actually correspond to the moods and needs of the workers.[10]

The Comintern, however, ordered the Chinese Communists to advance against the Kuomintang counterrevolution and in the face of the deepening apathy of the workers with no political weapons other than "the idea of soviets" and the "inevitability of the coming revolutionary mass uprising." Scorning the notion that China had entered a period of the darkest counterrevolution, the Comintern saw itself instead "between two waves" or "in the trough of two waves of the revolution." Momentarily the slogan of insurrection became a "propaganda slogan," but obviously with the swift rise to the crest of the second wave it would "again become the slogan of immediate practice."[11]

"If we find ourselves between two waves of continuous revolutionary progress," warned Trotsky, "then every manifestation of discontent, no matter how small its importance, can be considered as the...'beginning of the second wave.'... From this can grow a 'second wave' of putschism."[12] This tendency had, indeed, already manifested itself at the Sixth Congress where a Chinese delegate cried: "We are marching rapidly toward a new revolutionary wave!"[13] Whereat the other representatives of the party that had just suffered one of the most crushing defeats in the history of the class struggle sprang to their feet and shouted in unison: "Long live the victorious Chinese Revolution!"[14] Holding its own Sixth Congress during the same month in Moscow, the Chinese Communist Party announced that "symptoms of the most elementary kind of the new revolutionary wave can already be perceived."[15] A year later the Executive Committee of the Communist International, excited by a new outbreak of militarist civil war in China, announced the precise moment when the rise from trough to crest began: "This is the initial point of a new revolutionary wave," it wrote in a letter to its Chinese section. "The party should destroy the power of all militarist factions.... 'Turn the militarist war into class civil war,' 'Overthrow the power of the landlord-bourgeois bloc—such should now become the principal and urgent slogans of the party.... Prepare for the political general strike."[16] Thus disoriented, the Chinese Communist Party embarked upon a new series of hopeless adventures that only widened the chasm that already separated it from the working class. It never recovered as a working-class organization from the defeats of 1927.

"The Comintern," a delegate had boasted at the Sixth Congress, "brought forward resolutely the slogan of armed insurrection for the establishment of the soviet regime.... This alone has enabled our party to consolidate our ranks, win new forces, rally hundreds of thousands, nay millions of workers around its slogans."[17] Yet three months later the Central Committee, in an internal document, uncovered the truth behind this hollow extravagance: "The trade union organizations have shrunk to almost nothing. The party organizations in the cities are scattered and smashed. In the whole country there is not one healthy nucleus of industrial workers."[18]

To the enormous task of rebuilding the trade union movement, the Communist Party, led by Li Li-san, came with a program of forming "red unions" in opposition to the "yellow" unions permitted by the Kuomintang to exist after 1927. This was the application in China of the general policy adopted by the Comintern in 1928 of head-on collisions with other sections of the organized labor movement which did not accept the political program of the Communist Party. In China it assumed particularly grotesque forms because the attempt to create Communist unions was made on the morrow of a great defeat when the great mass of the workers had already turned their backs on the party. The "red unions" were, of course, identified, in membership and in program, with the party itself. They presented, full-blown, the party's program of "soviets" which did not attract the workers into their ranks, but instead, in the conditions of white terror, frightened them away.

The great union organizations, built not too solidly during the swift rise of the mass movement, had been swept from the scene. Kuomintang-sponsored unions had replaced only a few of them. A good many of these were unions in name alone, consisting of gangster officials appointed directly by the Kuomintang government to insure the effective repression of the workers. In many cases, however, the workers joined these Kuomintang unions even though they were led by obvious tools of the Nanking regime. It was their natural tendency in seeking to defend themselves to cling to such organizations as the Kuomintang allowed them. Moreover, the regime carried on pseudoliberal propaganda. It adopted enticing labor laws (which, of course, never became operative). It even permitted a number of strikes, especially in foreign enterprises, which helped the "yellow" leaders entrench themselves by sowing new illusions among the workers. These leaders, to be sure, preached class collaboration, compromise, and submission, but had not the workers been schooled only yesterday, by the Communist Party, in the doctrine of the "bloc of four classes"? In North China many unions came into existence for the first time only in 1928, under Kuomintang auspices, after Chiang Kai-shek had completed the march to Peking and the liquidation of the old regime there. In Tientsin and Peking many workers gladly flocked into the unions now set up, most of them still unaware that the alliance of the Communists and the Kuomintang had come somewhat abruptly to an end! These organizations fell largely into the hands of Wang Ching-wei's faction of the Kuomintang ("Reorganizationists") which sought a base among the workers in the interests of its struggle against Chiang Kai-shek's leadership within the ruling party.[19] The attractive force of the Reorganizationists lay precisely in their agitation for a more democratic, civilian regime in the place of the ruthless military dictatorship of Chiang Kai-shek. By disdaining to conduct a struggle on this level, the Communist Party left the field clear to the Wang Ching-wei group, which for four years canalized the democratic aspirations of a considerable stratum of the petty bourgeoisie and of the workers, only to betray those aspirations, as was inevitable, for the sake of a tawdry capitulation to Chiang Kai-shek.*

Under the Kuomintang, however, the organized labor movement was reduced to a shadow of its former dimensions. In 1927 nearly 3,000,000 workers had belonged

---

* Personal breaches were not so easily healed after the reconciliation between Wuhan and Nanking in August 1927. Chiang Kai-shek shrewdly withdrew from the government in September that year while the multiple factions in the Kuomintang scrambled for power. He returned triumphantly early in 1928 to maintain the balance among them. Wang Ching-wei associated himself with various rival militarists, first with Chang Fah-kwei and later with Feng Yu-hsiang and Yen Hsi-hsan, who waged civil war against Chiang in 1930 and were defeated. In January 1932, Wang finally returned to Nanking with Chiang Kai-shek and became the civilian fig-leaf for Chiang's otherwise undisguised military dictatorship. Wang's followers, of the type of Tang Leang-li, who had for years penned passionate indictments of Nanking's brutal misrule, experienced no difficulty in becoming Chiang's humblest apologists once they were favored with fat posts in his government.'

to trade unions. In 1928 this total was cut nearly in half. In 1930, according to official figures, there were 741 unions with 574,766 members, another drop of about 60 percent, and in 1932 there was a further decline to 621 unions with 410,067 members.[20] The overwhelming majority of China's industrial workers remained without any organization at all, even of the most elementary kind.

Neither among the thousands organized in unions nor among the millions of the unorganized could the Communists gain any ground, despite the fact that in 1928 the workers did not entirely abandon the struggle, but fought remarkably stubborn defensive strike battles. The cessation of civil war and a brief economic revival helped restore confidence among the workers in many important industrial sectors. In Shanghai, for example, there were 120 strikes during 1928, involving 213,996 workers. Five-sixths of them were fought for better wages and shorter hours.[21] In these favorable circumstances, the Communists remained impotent onlookers. In 1928 and later, wherever they tried to approach the workers with talk of "political strike," "general strike," "armed uprising," and "soviet power," the frightened strikers rushed back to their jobs. Not until much later, when Li Li-san had been deposed as leader of the party, did some of the facts come to light in the party press. "The workers feared to have the Communists come," it was recorded, "...and implored them not to wreck their struggles. They politely said: 'Your excellencies' words are quite correct, but we cannot carry them out now. It will be a good thing for us if we can get our wages raised a little and not get fired.'" The gulf between what the workers wanted and what the Communists proposed became so wide, according to this same account, that the few Communist workers who remained often concealed news of an impending strike from their party superiors in order to give the strikers a chance to conduct the struggle on their own terms! On one occasion when the party committees in Shanghai sent representatives to the scene of a strike at a textile mill, the workers said: "This is our affair. Why have your excellencies come here so enthusiastically?" Or others said to themselves: "The CP has come again. We had better run away before we lose the more by it."[22]

In the great majority of instances the strikes developed spontaneously in the factories. "Even in Shanghai the workers lacked fighting organizations," said an official Communist Party report. "They were scattered...and defeated. Most of them passed under the leadership of the yellow unions and the Kuomintang." The Communists, on their part, "looked with contempt on the yellow unions. As a result, the work and influence of the red unions shrank to almost nothing and the masses were left under yellow union influence."[23]

The "red unions" had shrunk to "almost nothing" and the party lacked "a single healthy industrial nucleus" at the end of 1928. In the years that followed the Communists made extravagantly preposterous claims to strength. Yet in internal party documents these claims found their own refutation, especially when in accord with the established practice of blaming scapegoats for failures the Comintern would berate the Central Committee, and the Central Committee would in turn lash its provincial and district organizations. The facts revealed on these occasions pitilessly exposed all the propagandist myths. From year to year the leaders had to complain that their followers were failing in their duty, were not properly carrying out the "party line." It was never suggested, of course, that the "party line" was itself responsible in no small measure for the stubborn unwillingness of the workers to follow the party's lead. The party pursued the "new revolutionary wave" which like a nimble elf constantly eluded it. Plunging blindly into scattered and futile demonstrations, planning insurrections that never came off, the Communists succeeded only in divorcing themselves completely from the class they claimed to represent. For evidence of this, one need only briefly scan the party's own press and its own internal documents.

In February 1929, a letter from the Comintern cited the fact that "in most of the cities, even in great working-class centers like Wuhan, Tientsin, and Canton, no work has been done at all.... In the big and important enterprises there are no nuclei whatever."[24] In May an organizational report written by the party leader, Chow En-lai, complained that the members of the party were unable to lead the spontaneous strikes of the workers. "Even where our comrades participated," he added, "our influence and slogans bore no fruit.... Local organizations do not exist...in the important centers."[25] Unable to win the workers to their program on its own merits, the Communists frequently resorted to compulsion, ordering strikes at revolver point or else eliminating "yellow" union leaders by using "terrorist methods" against them.[26] The party leadership complained, to little avail, that such methods were making it even more difficult for the organization to establish contact with the workers in the factories. Han Yin, an old trade unionist and militant, wrote that the party was contenting itself with building an "empty apparatus" composed of national and provincial trade union federations which suffered from the disability of lacking rank and file membership. The "red unions," he wrote, "have been organizations entirely outside the masses."[27] In November 1929, the "empty apparatus" convened what it called the "Fifth National Labor Conference" which claimed, modestly enough, to represent only 30,000 workers.[28] Accepting for a moment even this dubious claim, one might ask: what had happened to the 2,970,000 other workers really represented at the Fourth Labor Conference in Hankow only two years before?

In the summer of 1930 a Communist source claimed for the "red" trade union federation a membership of 64,381. The totals given for all the principal cities, including Shanghai, Wuhan, Hong Kong, Harbin, Tientsin, Amoy, and Wusih, added up to exactly 5,748. The rest were said to be scattered through the countryside where no industrial proletariat existed.[29] A few months later, in February 1931, a party leader wrote: "Now there are no real red unions.... They have been wiped out. All work has been abandoned."[30]

By the end of 1930 the party was threatened with complete collapse and dissolution. Li Li-san was abruptly dethroned and was replaced by a group of students who had passed the revolutionary years in Moscow and who were headed by Chen Shao-yu (Wang Min). The new leaders, imposed upon the party entirely by orders from above, announced their "complete and unconditional devotion and loyalty to the general line of the Leninist Comintern" and declared that "all the severe consequences suffered by the party derive from the fact that Comrade Li Li-san and his adherents ignored the instructions of the Executive Committee of the Communist International."[31] The new "leaders" set out to correct what one party writer aptly called Li's "over-exaggeration" of the Comintern's policies.[32] Under the new dispensation, however, the tendency toward complete abandonment of work in the principal urban centers continued unchecked.

1931 was the year of the Japanese invasion and of a rising strike wave, especially in its closing months. In party reports there was the same refrain: "The struggles were sporadic...spontaneous, lacking organization and leadership.... The great difficulty is that we have no good cadres in the factories.... Our organization does not understand very well what the conditions are in the factories so that we are not able to put forward the most pressing demands of the workers. We have not succeeded in organizing a single anti-imperialist strike." Pleading lack of "complete statistics" on the party-controlled "red unions," the report gave the following membership figures: "Shanghai, 666; Amoy, 72; Harbin, 71; Tsinan-Tsingtao Railway, 20; seamen and longshoremen, 319;...Total: 1,148. In Tientsin, Peking, Hankow, Hong Kong, Kwangtung (i.e. Canton), etc.... we have no organizations."[33]

In March 1932, six months after the Japanese invasion began, the party leadership accused its followers of "abandoning the organization and initiation of strikes, especially in the heavy industries.... Abandonment of the organization of red unions is an unpardonable mistake.... As to penetration of the yellow unions, this work has not even begun. After the Shanghai event (the Japanese invasion of Shanghai, January–February 1932) the All-China Trade Union Federation, the Shanghai Federation, and the provincial committee did not even try."[34]

Yet speaking of this same period, Wang Min later said: "The party organized big anti-Japanese mass movements in practice in the form of strikes, meetings, demonstrations."[35] P. Mif, who had now become the chief Comintern "specialist" in Chinese affairs, wrote in mid-1933 of a "mighty upsurge of the working-class movement on Kuomintang territory," and cited figures alleging that no less than 1,110,170 workers had participated in strikes during the twelve months of 1932.[36] This did not prevent him a year later from claiming that 1,200,000 had struck during the first six months alone![37] These figures respectively trebled and sextupled the total of 301,170 strikers given for the same year by the Communist Party paper in Shanghai,[38] which in turn was half again as high as the findings of more sober surveys. Mif said that a third of his total, or 325,000 strikers, were under the direct leadership of the Communist Party. On the basis of the party's own figure (which somehow overlooked 800,000 other strikers Mif had found somewhere) we are compelled to conclude that the party not only led every single striker who laid down his tools during 1932, but 25,000 more, plucked from the pages of a magazine printed in Moscow!

Despite the "unconditional devotion" that bound the Chinese Communist leaders to their Moscow mentors, there was a lamentable lack of coordination between the propaganda mill in the Kremlin and the editors of the party's paper in Shanghai. Mif boasted, for example, that in September 1932, the Communists organized a textile workers' union which enlisted "the overwhelming mass of workers in the textile factories of Shanghai."[39] Considering that there were 120,000 workers in these plants[40] this meant a rather sudden and spectacular surge in the party's proletarian base. But in this, too, unfortunately, Mif had failed to compare notes with his Shanghai friends who wrote: "The weak industrial basis and the shrinking of the red unions is amazing. Let us take the General Textile Union in Shanghai. Early in December (1932) it had a membership of nearly 1,000 ["the overwhelming majority"?]... This spring when we inspected the work the membership had greatly dwindled. In August this year (1933) it had dropped from twenty units to seven."[41] One more example, involving the 17,445 tobacco factory workers in Shanghai:[42] Wrote Mif in May: "The forces of the revolutionary trade union organization among the tobacco workers have also strengthened and become established organizationally."[43] Said the *Red Flag* in October: "The General Tobacco Union dropped from more than nine hundred [!] to its present intolerable [!] state...and even at that not all its members can be found." Summing up the work in the country as a whole, the same Shanghai report abandoned the attempt to give figures, substituting the cabalistic symbol "xx" in a context, however, whose sense was unmistakable: "Take the three industrial centers of Manchuria—in Harbin there were only xx members.... In Mukden there used to be xx members but now we do not know. In Dairen the work is only at its beginning. In all Manchuria the total was only xx. In Wuhan no work has been started up until now. In Shanghai this spring there were still xx members. Now there are only xx. There was not only no growth, but there was a drop."[44]

At the beginning of 1934 the Central Committee of the Young Communist League took note of a "serious phenomenon" in its ranks: "Our comrades are unaware of impending struggles in the factories.... As a result of this isolation we not only cannot lead the mass struggles but we cannot even grasp them by the tail!"[45]

Six years of "red unions" and "soviet power" proved to be six years of impotence. After 1927 the great mass of the workers turned their backs on the Communist Party, which did not learn how to regain their confidence and reassemble their organized ranks. A class laid prostrate by the treachery of its own leaders could not answer the empty call for "soviets" which corresponded not to reality but only to the adventurist moods in the party's ranks. The result was that the party never reestablished a foothold of any consequence in any of the great urban centers. While the workers, heedless of the party's strident radicalism, departed from the political arena, peasant revolt, stirred to life during 1925–27, continued belatedly to flare. Members of the Communist Party, shot with putschist moods on the morrow of the great defeat, found it easier in the countryside to awaken echoes to their insurrectionist appeals where peasants were taking up arms or where mutinous soldiers were breaking from the armies of the Kuomintang. While some of the leaders, clinging feebly to their proletarian pretensions, resisted the temptation to take the path of least resistance, the repeated failures in the cities, the heavy blows of the Kuomintang terror, helped complete the party's shift from city to countryside, from proletariat to peasantry. This shift found eloquent expression in the transformed composition of the party itself.

At the height of the movement in April 1927, the Communist Party had counted 60,000 members in its ranks, 58 percent of them industrial workers based in the principal industrial cities. Subsequently, despite the shattering series of defeats they suffered, during the Autumn Harvest, at Canton, and afterwards, the Communists nevertheless claimed thousands of new recruits. The party, they said, numbered 100,000 in 1928, 120,000 in 1930, and more than 410,000 in 1933. Reliable figures on party membership have never been available. There can be no doubt whatever that the figures given after 1927 were all more than grossly exaggerated. Yet these exaggerations served only to stress the change that had taken place in the party's class base, for it was officially admitted that workers in the party comprised only 10 percent in 1928, 3 percent in 1929,[46] 2.5 percent in March 1930,[47] 1.6 percent in September,[48] and virtually zero by the end of the year.[49] Actual figures were given less frequently. A Comintern letter in February, 1929, said there were 4,000 workers in the whole party, 1,300 of them in Shanghai and the rest scattered elsewhere.[50] The Kiangsu Committee in December 1929, claimed 6,800 members in the province, of whom only 591 were listed as industrial workers.[51] In September 1930, Chow En-lai told the Third Plenum of the Central Committee that the party numbered 120,000, among them 2,000 factory workers. If at the end of 1933 the complaint was again heard that in Shanghai, greatest industrial center of the country, the party had "not one real industrial nucleus,"[52] what value could be attached to the claim made by Wang Min in Moscow two months later that the party numbered 410,600, and that 25–30 percent, or about 100,000, were workers?[53]

Yet even from this figure, one learned much. Wang Min reported that of the total only 60,000 were in Kuomintang China. Six-sevenths of the party was concentrated in the distant hinterland, hundreds of miles from the principal cities and arteries of communication. What had happened was clear. When the agrarian revolt had drawn tardily on its reserves and marched forward, the Communist Party had rushed to march with it, leaving the working class to its own devices. The Communist Party reemerged from the 1927 debacle at the head of an insurgent peasant movement deep in the provinces of Central China where it established what it called the "Chinese Soviet Republic."

The Rise and Fall of "Soviet China"

Partisan warfare has a tradition in China as long almost as history itself. In great waves rising and lapsing through twenty centuries peasant wars repeatedly convulsed the country and toppled dynasties, only to exhaust themselves while economic relationships were restored and renewed in the ancient grooves of static Chinese society. In times of upheaval peasant armies aroused millions across whole provinces of the Empire. In the intervening periods of the rise and decline of new ruling houses, partisan bands continued in tens and hundreds in a thousand scattered localities to reject the new yokes offered for the old. Chinese economy and the society erected over it were indeed historically static. Yet Chinese history is by no means a placid saga of changelessly unrolling centuries. It has been a history filled with violence and bloodshed, with recurring revolts against the very self-renewing forms of servitude which condemned China to stagnate while the Western world grew.

These were the traditions stirred again to life in South and Central China by the revolution of 1925–27. The millions who unbent from their toil in a new effort to take the land for themselves were less than a century removed from those who had marched with the long-haired Taipings. Yet the peasants who rose in 1926–27 could for the first time hope to succeed where their insurgent forebears had invariably failed. Out of the society dissolving under the impact of imperialist penetration the elements of a new solution had taken form and awaited only to be compounded. By themselves the peasants, scattered, stratified, and backward, could play no independent role. The Chinese bourgeoisie, itself bound to the system of exploitation on the land, could not lead the struggle to smash it. But the new class of urban workers sought in its own interests a fundamental revision of property relations at the base of society, and by linking their fortunes to those of the workers the peasants could now hope for the first time to break through the vicious historical circle to which they had for so long been bound.

It was precisely the failure of the Communist Party to solder the links between the oppressed classes of town and country and to unite them under a bold revolutionary program that had opened the path to the bourgeois counterrevolution. When the proletarian movement was checked, the agrarian revolt was left headless. It lost thousands of its leaders to the terror that scourged the countryside. What was more costly still, it lost the leadership of the city workers who alone could give the peasant revolt the coherence and economic-political framework within which the peasants could regain the land and hold on to it while new productive forms were developed with their help.

As a result, the movement that had for a brief time united ten million peasants was beaten down and its best militants dispersed. Scattered peasant detachments fled to the hills and resumed the role of partisan bands. They joined hands with companies and regiments of Kuomintang soldiers who had mutinied and taken refuge in the mountains. From the towns and cities fleeing the headsmen of Chiang Kai-shek and his allies, Communists—some workers, mostly intellectuals—came to the villages and in many places assumed leadership of the peasant-soldier partisan bands. From a fusion of these elements there emerged in 1928 "Red Armies" which acknowledged the leadership of the Chinese Communist Party, although in many places the peasant revolt continued to flare quite independently of the party's participation.

The first and most important of these armies was formed at Chingkangshan, a mountain on the Hunan-Kiangsi border where many veterans of the abortive Autumn Harvest uprisings of 1927 made their way. Here came the German-educated Communist officer, Chu Teh, at the head of less than two thousand men, mainly the remnants of the army of Yeh Ting and Ho Lung. The Yeh-Ho army, it will be recalled, had revolted at Nanchang in August 1927, and had marched south through Kiangsi to Kwangtung. There it was smashed in October in its attempt to take Swatow. With Chu Teh, many of the soldiers went to Hailufeng, the eastern Kwangtung districts where the peasants had risen in revolt, seized the land, and organized themselves into village soviets. Yeh Ting went to Canton and after the insurrection disappeared from the political scene. Ho Lung set out with a small force and reemerged later at the head of a partisan army in Hupeh province. After Hailufeng was reconquered by the Canton militarists, Chu Teh led a handful of men first to the northern districts of the province and then into Hunan. He recruited some peasants along the line of march and arrived in April 1928, at Chingkangshan.

Here he found peasant detachments from southern Hunan, several companies of insurgent soldiers who had come from Wuhan and other Yangtze cities, and a peasant force from eastern Hunan led by the Communist Mao Tse-tung. In Wuhan Mao had served as head of the Peasant Department of the Kuomintang and there had carried out the policy of keeping the peasants in check while the counterrevolution advanced upon them. When the crash came he had fled to the districts of Pingkiang and Liuyang, in eastern Hunan. There he led the uprisings of the Autumn Harvest. When they failed, he led what was left of his little band to Chingkangshan. They joined there with a local bandit force headed by Yuan and Wang. After Chu Teh's arrival, all the forces were merged and took the name of Fourth Red Army, with Chu as commander-in-chief and Mao Tse-tung as political leader. The official party record describes it as an army of 10,000 men of whom 2,000 had rifles.[1]

This Red force did not spring from any large-scale spontaneous peasant movement. On the contrary, it was for a long time isolated from the peasantry in the surrounding countryside. Peasant committees set up by the guerrilla bands invariably collapsed and disappeared as soon as the armed Red forces passed on. During its months on Chingkangshan the army suffered repeated defections and endured dire hardships because of its isolation. Defeats often caused the peasant partisans to scatter back to their villages. The Hunanese detachments in particular repeatedly drifted away to revisit their homes. Only the most dogged perseverance on the part of the leaders and the harsh lash of necessity managed to keep the partisan force together, especially when winter set in and the strength of surrounding enemies made it impossible to forage for supplies. After nearly a year of aimless guerrilla raids, sorties, and retreats in the vicinity of Chingkangshan, it was decided to march southward in search of a better base. A small force under Peng Teh-huai, a Communist officer who had marched his men from Hunan to Chingkangshan in the fall, was left behind to stand off approaching provincial troops. In January 1929, Chu Teh and Mao Tse-tung led the way down the mountain passes at the head of a starving, freezing, ill-armed, straggling column of a few thousand men.

Out in the countryside they were confronted by the apathy and even the hostility of the peasants. "The masses completely failed to understand what the Red Army was," said a party report. "In many places it was even attacked, like a bandit gang."[2] After nearly meeting disaster in an unexpected clash with Kuomintang provincials near Tayu, the Reds circled towards the Kwangtung border. They marched among peasants who had been cruelly deceived not once but three times by armies that arrived flying revolutionary banners and promising them relief from their burdens. "The Red Army had no support from the masses. There were great difficulties in finding encampments, carrying on military operations, and securing information.... We marched across snow-covered and icy mountains, closely pursued by the enemy. We sometimes covered ninety li (thirty miles) in a single day. Our sufferings increased. We were defeated in battle four times."[3]

On Chinese New Year's Day in mid-February 1929, the exhausted Red force suddenly came upon a division of Kiangsi troops in a valley lying between Juichin and Ningtu in southern Kiangsi. The Reds attacked with desperate fury. When their ammunition gave out, they used their empty rifles, stones, and the limbs of trees. The enemy fled. After that victory the Chu-Mao force won a badly needed rest. In these remote mountain districts they established a new base, where they were joined in March by Peng Teh-huai. Only the hardiest had survived. The whole force totalled 2,800 men. They went to work among the peasants, and when they began driving out the landlords and destroying land deeds, their ranks soon swelled. The territory they occupied they called the "Central Soviet district."

Simultaneously other Red pockets were being similarly formed with even smaller forces in northeastern Kiangsi, where the Communist Fang Chih-min headed a partisan band; in Hupeh near Hung Lake where Ho Lung was already making the lightning-like attacks and forced marches that made him a legendary figure. On the Honan-Anhwei and Hunan-Kiangsi borders and in other scattered mountain districts, small Red forces made their headquarters. These were the component parts, widely separated geographically, of what became known as "Soviet China."

It was upon these partisan forces called Red Armies that the Communist Party, impregnated with adventurist moods on the morrow of the defeat of the revolution, based itself and its activity and its belief in the arrival of the "new revolutionary wave." The party leadership glimpsed the danger of the shift to the countryside and for a time tried to resist it. "If the danger of peasant psychology is not vigorously corrected, the revolution will be liquidated entirely and the party will die," prophetically warned a circular of the Central Committee in November 1928.[4] But these warnings grew more and more feeble as the party's base in the cities narrowed and its proletarian membership and following dwindled and almost entirely disappeared. In October 1929, the Executive Committee of the Communist International described the peasant war as "the peculiarity of the Chinese national crisis and the revolutionary wave." It was still, formally, a "side-current," but a side-current "along which the powerful high wave of the revolutionary movement will grow in the entire country."[5] Admitting the impotence of the Communist Party in the cities* the E.C.C.I. nevertheless proclaimed the arrival of the "initial point of the new revolutionary wave" and laid down a program of insurrection for the Chinese Communists to carry out. While in the cities the revolutionary labor movement was receding and the influence of the Communist Party was being wiped out, the partisan armies in the interior had already come to be regarded as the "determining factor"[6] or the "driving force"[7] of the "revolutionary upsurge." Before long, all reservations were dropped. The "revolutionary upsurge" was "manifested not only in the rising [?] labor movement, but *essentially and basically* in the agrarian movement. The agrarian revolution is the source spring of the new revolutionary wave."[8]

---

* "The ideological and political influence of the Communist Party as well as the state of organization of the working class is still backward in comparison with the growth of mass discontent.... The majority of the Red unions are not yet mass organizations...The Communist Party has not yet gathered around itself the leading revolutionary workers in the factories. Still less has it solved the task of capturing the majority of the working class."—"Letter of ECCI to CCP, October 26, 1929," *Red Flag*, Shanghai, February 15, 1930.

Yet the so-called Red Armies as they emerged in 1928 and 1929 in scattered mountain districts of the central provinces were not even primarily peasant forces. It was only much later that they were able to rally around them sections of the peasantry in the districts they occupied. They were composed in the main of dispossessed peasants, jobless agricultural laborers, mutinous soldiers, local bandits, all declassed elements, playing no direct role even in agricultural production. Their activity for nearly three years consisted exclusively of guerrilla fighting and dart-like raids. They were unable to establish any fixed base. When in 1930 Chen Tu-hsiu, the deposed and expelled leader of the party,* published an article[9] in which he warned the Communist Party that the revolution could not be advanced by abandoning the workers and engaging in military adventures at the head of an army of lumpenproletarians, he was viciously denounced as making common cause with the counterrevolution. Chen borrowed Engels' definition of lumpenproletariat, "the scum of the decaying elements of all classes,"[10] to describe some of the elements that dominated many of the partisan forces. Yet it is not at all difficult to find in the records of the Communist Party ample corroboration of Chen's analysis of the Red Armies of that period. The party had to fight a long and only partially successful struggle to transform these armies into authentic organs of peasant revolt.

The Sixth Congress of the Communist Party in 1928 deplored the tendency of the partisans to engage in "aimless plundering and burning" and described these activities as "the reflection of lumpen-proletarian psychology."[11] Another party report spoke of "bandit psychology, degeneration into a bandit existence of killing and plundering" and even borrowed phrases far stronger than any used by Engels

* After the Conference of August 7, 1927, deposed him from leadership, Chen Tu-hsiu withdrew into retirement while the Comintern laid at his door exclusive responsibility for the disasters that had befallen the revolution. During the period of adventurism that followed, Chen wrote several letters to the Central Committee opposing the policy of staging futile and costly uprisings. In August 1929, he addressed a letter to the Central Committee expressing his opposition to the Party's course and demanding a re-examination of its policies. A few months later he and nearly one hundred others were expelled en masse as Oppositionists. In February 1930, the Comintern asked him to come to Moscow. He refused, demanding that the issues of the revolution be thrown open instead to full discussion within the party. Subsequently he solidarized himself with the Trotskyist Left Opposition that had been formed and was a leading figure in that organization until his arrest by the Kuomintang in 1932. He was sentenced to thirteen years' imprisonment, but was released in the fall of 1937. There appears to be some doubt as to his present political views. See: Chen Tu-hsiu, "A Letter to the Central Committee of the Chinese Communist Party on the Questions of the Chinese Revolution," August 5, 1929, in *The Chinese Revolution and Opportunism*, Shanghai, October 1929; *Letter to All the Comrades of the Chinese Communist Party*, Shanghai, December 10, 1929; Chen Tu-hsiu and eighty others, *Our Political Statement*, Shanghai, December 15, 1929; "Letter of Chen Tu-hsiu to the Communist International," *Le Prolétaire*, Shanghai, July 1, 1930; Chen Tu-hsiu, *Protest to the Kiangsu High Court*, February 20, 1933.

or Chen Tu-hsiu to characterize some of the partisans as "Red bandits, burning, killing, and robbing."[12] A reporter for the Central Committee complained early in 1930 that "in many of the partisan bands, lumpenproletarian ideas persist...often expressing themselves in unorganized burning, plundering, and killing."[13] Even publicly in the columns of no less a paper than *Pravda,* Mif wrote of the "very large percentage of...lumpenproletarian elements" in some of the Chinese Red Armies.[14]

The question, however, did not lie in the precise percentage of lumpenproletarian elements in the Red Armies then or even later. These armies did become the spearhead of a peasant revolt over considerable, if scattered, territories. Such armies had often been known in Chinese history. The important factor was that the Communist Party was tending more and more to look upon these armies as the legitimate basis of its activity and to rationalize through them its growing isolation from the workers in the urban centers. It was the view of the Trotskyist Opposition that the party's lip service to "proletarian hegemony" over the peasant movement was a fraud so long as the party was itself divorced from the proletariat. This hegemony became all the more mythical when the putschist policies in the cities, the attempts to force strikes, to convert them artificially into armed political demonstrations, were stifling at birth the incipient revival of defensive struggles by the workers.

"Proletarian leadership" of the peasant-partisan movement had to be exercised through a living movement and not through a fictional slogan paraded through the party press. It was on this basis that the International Left (Trotskyist) Opposition demanded that the Communist Party keep its roots in the cities and proposed a program of democratic struggle and the slogan of a National Assembly, elected by universal suffrage, as a point of departure for making the Communist Party the truly authentic spokesman and leader of the Chinese workers. Revival of the labor movement under the impetus of a democratic program, declared the Opposition in 1930, could alone provide the peasant revolt with the indispensable leadership of the city workers and lay the basis for worker-peasant collaboration in the march toward the third Chinese Revolution.[15] The Trotskyist Opposition, however, was too weak to make its influence felt. The Communist Party, throwing its main efforts and its best forces into the villages and replacing its disappearing worker-members with peasants, drifted farther and farther away from its work in the cities and finally practically abandoned it altogether. The militarist rivalries that split the Kuomintang camp and the constant economic difficulties which the regime could not surmount were regarded as sufficient symptoms of a ripe revolutionary crisis, and the Red Armies in fact came to be regarded as a sufficient instrument for bringing that crisis to a head.

Having discovered the "initial point of the new revolutionary wave" in October 1929, the Comintern in July 1930 declared that "the new upsurge of the Chinese revolutionary movement has become an indisputable fact." Hence: "The immediate task of the Chinese Communist Party is to prepare and concentrate all forces in the process of struggle to meet decisive battles in the nearest future."

"It is the peculiarity in the new upsurge," the resolution went on, "...that in the initial stage there is a certain [!] weakness, namely, the fighting masses cannot at the very beginning occupy the industrial centers.... Only in the process of the further development of the revolutionary struggles can the peasant war, led by the proletariat, expand to new territory. Then the mutual correlation can improve to better advantage." To this end attention had to be focussed on strengthening the Red Army so that "in the future, according to political and military circumstances, one or several political or industrial centers can be occupied."[16]

While the Comintern, to be sure, surrounded itself with carefully worded injunctions about the need, in general, for organizing the workers and peasants, it laid the basis for all the fatal misconceptions which achieved their most grotesque form in the politics of Li Li-san, who had now become leader of the Communist Party.

Dazzled by the Comintern's commission to him to "overthrow the power of the landlord-bourgeois bloc, to establish a worker-peasant dictatorship...to unfold mass political strikes and demonstrations, to expand the partisan warfare...and to turn the militarist war into class civil war,"[17] Li Li-san began to perceive on all sides the shadows of coming upheavals. When Chiang Kai-shek and a northern coalition headed by Feng Yu-hsiang began a long and bitter civil war in 1930, Li was certain that the earth was ready to swallow up the Kuomintang and all its generals. "Prepare for the establishment of the revolutionary power!" he cried in March.[18] In June his Political Bureau adopted a resolution which saw the masses "marching in seven-league boots toward the revolutionary high wave" and called for active preparation of a countrywide uprising. Taking the Comintern's prattle about the "third period" of the final crisis of world capitalism quite seriously, Li envisaged the Russian Red Army marching in from Mongolia to support the resurgent Chinese Revolution.[19]

Quite in passing, Li deplored the depression of the labor movement, but he was naively confident that the workers were only awaiting the party's call to rise. He was sure that a single puncture in the Kuomintang dam would be enough to precipitate a revolutionary flood. "When the revolutionary high wave arrives," he was later quoted as saying, "90,000,000 can be organized in three days."[20] In the June resolution he wrote: "Long ago the masses said: 'When there is an uprising let us know and we shall surely come.' Now is the time when the party must bravely call upon the masses: 'The time for insurrection has come! Organize yourselves!'"[21] He created what he called a General Council of Action into which he merged the party, the Young Communist League, and the "red" trade unions. In Shanghai he formed a "Red Guard" composed of exactly 176 workers to prepare for the "fourth uprising."[22] He plotted an insurrection in Nanking with a handful of soldiers. To the Red Armies he gave orders to march on the cities. "The aim of the local uprisings is to capture local cities.... The perspective must inevitably be to converge with the central cities to accomplish the victory of the insurrection in the whole country."[23]

In other words both the Comintern and Li Li-san recognized that the proletariat had to lead the peasantry. Many long and even eloquent passages were devoted in all documents to this necessity under the heading "proletarian hegemony." Unfortunately, the proletariat had yet to remarshal its own ranks and collect its own forces, scattered and crushed by the defeat of the revolution and the reign of Kuomintang terror that followed it. The Communist Party tried to substitute itself for the proletariat as a class. In the process, however, it was transformed into a peasant party. Since the revolution could not radiate from the cities to the country, it was necessary to mobilize the country to close in on the cities.

It was with this in view that the Fifth Red Army under Peng Teh-huai marched westward from Kiangsi and on July 28, 1930, succeeded in occupying Changsha, capital of Hunan province. Li Li-san firmly counted on this as the signal for a spontaneous countrywide uprising with its center at Wuhan, where he expected to establish the capital of a "Central Soviet Government." Unfortunately, the Communist Party had at its disposal in Wuhan only 200 party members and 150 "red" trade unionists![24] Contrary to Li's expectations, there was no echo anywhere. There was no insurrection in the rest of the country. The 90,000,000 remained passive. American, British, Japanese, and Italian gunboats, having evacuated frightened foreigners, steamed up the Siang River and mercilessly bombarded the occupied city.[25] The Red Army withdrew. Ho Chien, governor of Hunan, returned with fresh divisions and began a slaughter of the helpless city population that did not pause until more than 5,000 corpses choked open graves and until even the Changsha Chamber of Commerce appealed to Nanking to make him stop. Reinforced by the Chu-Mao Fourth Army, the Reds made another attempt early in September to hammer their way back into the city, but this time they failed and retreated once more toward the mountains of southern Kiangsi.

The Changsha episode bared at a stroke the fatal weakness of the whole Red Army course. The partisan forces had no connection with the workers in the city. When the Red Army marched in and "proclaimed the Soviet power, the power of the workers, peasants, and soldiers,"[26] the great mass of the city's 500,000 people remained inert, frightened, or just curious. The proclamation of "Soviet power" was the gift of a conquering army. It was not the product of mass action in the city itself. "There was insufficient connection between the attack of the Red Army and the mass struggles in Changsha," it was later admitted.[27] The result was a repetition on a different plane of the Canton fiasco. "In Changsha there was no mass soviet elected by factories or streets."[28] Red flags were broken out all over the city and a mass meeting was called, but only 3,000 people appeared. Another effort two days later was only slightly more successful.[29] The army impregnated with the fundamental strategy of the peasant partisan—to strike, seize, destroy, and run—did not regard its occupation of Changsha as a permanent thing. "Its position was not consolidated. No city power was organized."[30] Instead it taxed the Chamber of Commerce for $400,000, which was collected from the people by the merchants, and when the imperialist bombardment began it resisted briefly and withdrew.

When it left, 3,000 workers recruited in the city went with it. In other words, the most advanced of Changsha's workers, the possible nucleus of a revived labor movement, were withdrawn from their factories and shops and converted into partisan-soldiers completely divorced from the town. The job of decapitating the Changsha labor movement, begun in this way by the Red Army, was completed by Ho Chien's executioners. This was the net result of the Changsha adventure.

Sporadic attempts continued through the summer to encircle Wuhan and to take other cities without result. In October the Red Army captured Kian, in Kiangsi, but here again it confined itself to "recruiting new soldiers" and sent off its best forces in an effort to capture Nanchang and Kiukiang. "Organization of the masses was completely ignored."[31] Kian had to be evacuated a few weeks later.

The strategists in Moscow, however, had already begun to realize that the Red Armies could not successfully attack the large cities. At the Third Plenum of the Central Committee in September, Chow En-lai, freshly back from Moscow, cautiously counseled retreat. "The Central Committee," he said, "has had some mechanical conceptions, thinking that the Central (Soviet) Government had to be established in Wuhan, or at least in Changsha or Nanchang.... Of course it would be better to get established in the bigger cities than in the smaller ones, but this is a secondary question." He reminded the Committee that the Comintern had fixed as the "primary task" the consolidation of the Red Armies and the broadening of the mass base underlying them. "We must consolidate the present scattered soviet districts," he reported, "weld them together, strengthen and centralize the leadership of the Red Armies, set broader peasant masses in motion, and establish a Central Soviet Government to develop toward the industrial cities."

Chow sharply denied that this meant retreat or that there was any contradiction between the advice of the Comintern and the policies of Li Li-san. For the cities, he repeated, the central task was still "to prepare actively for armed uprising." Li had merely "overestimated the tempo," made some "isolated tactical mistakes," and had a few "mechanical conceptions," but was otherwise in "complete harmony with the Comintern."[32]

But Li Li-san's "overexaggeration" of the Comintern's line had practically destroyed the party and demoralized its members. It was no longer possible to preserve in Li Li-san the myth of an infallible leadership. Accordingly all the heavy artillery was trundled out and turned on the hapless Li. All the hyphenated invective he had employed against his predecessors was now applied to him. A letter arriving from Moscow on November 16 ordered open warfare against him in the party. Under the personal supervision of Mif, Li Li-san was brusquely deposed. What was called the Fourth Plenum of the Central Committee met on January 7, 1931, and Mif's own protégé, Chen Shao-yu, was elevated into the leadership of the party on a program of "unconditional devotion to the line of the Communist International."

The young men so abruptly enthroned as "leaders" of the Communist Party had all been students in Moscow during the years of the revolution and had won their spurs conducting witch hunts against Trotskyist sympathizers among the students at Sun Yat-sen University. To give them control Mif shouldered aside the group of old militants who had served, not without opposition,[33] under the leadership of Li Li-san. A group of these older party members and trade unionists, and some younger men, led by the veteran Ho Mung-shung, met at a Shanghai hotel on the night of January 17 to consider the new situation with which they were confronted. In circumstances which are still a whispered scandal in the party ranks, that meeting was betrayed to the British police of the International Settlement. Ho Mung-shung and twenty-four others were arrested, handed over to the Kuomintang authorities and executed at Lunghua on February 7. Mif's docile young men became the undisputed leaders of the party.

Other leaders of the party won the right to remain in its ranks only by degrading themselves, by making the self-denying recantations that had already become a fixed feature of Stalinist party methods and which only ten years later flowered into the "confessions" of old Bolshevik leaders put on trial for their lives in Moscow. Chiu Chiu-pei was compelled to denounce his own "cowardly rotten opportunism." Chow En-lai flagellated himself. "I call upon the whole party to condemn my mistakes," he cried.[34] Li Li-san had already left for Moscow and once arrived there had hastily recanted of his sins. Even the hardened cynics in the Comintern apparatus were a little shocked by his eager self-repudiation. At a discussion held by the presidium of the Executive Committee of the Comintern in December, Manuilsky expressed his astonishment: "If Li Li-san here defended his own ideas and disputed with us one article after another," he said, "then I would be easier in my mind. But Li-san so quickly abandoned his views. This alarms me!"[35] Chiu Chiu-pei, Chow En-lai, Han Yin, the trade union leader, and others, were sent to obscure posts in Kiangsi. Li Li-san himself disappeared from view.*

The new leadership had the task of retreating from the disastrous ultra-adventurism of Li Li-san to a more modest adventurist policy that took the party's real strength more soberly into account. There was no intention of making any more fundamental change. The main features of the shift had already been indicated by

* Chiu was captured in Fukien in 1935 and shot by direct order of Chiang Kai-shek. Han Yin was captured and apparently suffered the same fate. Many other leaders were also shot or imprisoned. Deng Cheng-tsah and Lo Teng-hsien, leaders of the Hong Kong strike of 1925, were executed at Nanking in 1933, words of loyalty to the proletarian cause on their lips to the last. See *China Forum*, Shanghai, November 7, 30, 1933. Li-san re-emerged in 1937 at Yenan, Shensi, the new Communist Party center, where he was introduced to a *New Masses* writer as an "old associate of Dr. Sun Yat-sen." —*New Masses*, October 12, 1937.

the Comintern in its November letter. "The military and technical weakness of the Red Army must not be forgotten, the poverty of armament and ammunition, lack of artillery, etc. Such conditions make it impossible to occupy big cities, to attack the modern armies of imperialism, and to conquer the main centers. The experience of the occupation of Changsha and the attack on Wuhan has already shown that such tasks cannot be carried out by the present Red Army." It was necessary now "to concentrate the best forces of the party" to build a "real workers-peasants Red Army" and to establish a central soviet government in one of the existing soviet districts as a basis for future expansion. "Only those who have nothing in common with Bolshevism can interpret this as a line of retreat," the letter said. "It is not a retreat but an offensive. The line of insurrection is fixed."[36]

But a retreat it was, a retreat from the grandiose dreams of Li Li-san. The new party leadership dropped the slogan of "local uprisings" and denounced as "Blanquist" the attempt to organize isolated mutinies in the armies of the Kuomintang.[37] The concentration of the "best forces" of the party for the "primary task" of strengthening the Red Army and creating a central government also signalized the completion of the shift from city to country, from proletariat to peasantry. It was now not so much a question of bringing the urban labor abreast of the peasant revolt in order to lead it. Instead: "Every strike is a rear support for the Soviet districts."[38] Instructions issued to the party in June and again in September 1931 dealt almost exclusively with the problems of the Red Army and the Soviet districts. Where they dealt briefly with the urban labor movement, it was to urge more intensive work in the cities in order "to create powerful support for our worker-peasant Red Army." It was the main task in the "non-Soviet" districts "to intensify support for the great victories of the Red Armies...to recruit soldiers for the Red Armies."[39]

Shanghai, Wuhan, Tientsin, Canton, and all other centers of industrial and proletarian concentration had become, in effect, the "rear" of the mountains of southern Kiangsi. In September 1930, when he was trying to justify his plans for capturing Wuhan and making it the "Soviet capital," Li Li-san had said: "I thought it would be a joke if we established the capital in the mountains."[40] But it was precisely to the mountains that they had to go and stay. Deep in the hills of south Kiangsi in the village of Juichin the Red Armies established their capital and there, on November 7, 1931, they proclaimed the creation of the "Chinese Soviet Republic" and set up a Provisional Soviet Government.

The "Chinese Soviet Republic" consisted in 1932–33, the years of its maximum development, of six widely separated areas scattered along the border regions of the Central China provinces. Wang Min (Chen Shao-yu) boasted at the end of 1933 that the territory of Soviet China occupied "one-fourth of the vast territory of China proper." One-sixth, or one-fifth—both fractions were cited in the same speech—he described as "stable" Soviet domain.[41] Around the world the press of the Communist International boasted that the flag of the Soviets ruled 50,000,000, 75,000,000, 80,000,000 of the Chinese people.[42] In a book that had the misfortune to hail the dawn of "Soviet China" just as twilight descended upon it, one Comintern writer put the population at 90,000,000.[43] The figures never agreed but were all enormous and all enormously exaggerated. The reality was far more modest and the men on the spot who had to deal with realities and not propagandist myths were more soberly truthful.

Because the Red Armies and partisan forces were for the most part, to use a favorite Chinese phrase, "like flowing water and moving clouds," the territory they occupied expanded and contracted according to the fortunes of war. At various times the Red Army, led by Chu Teh, undoubtedly crossed or temporarily occupied at least sixty or seventy of Kiangsi's eighty-one *hsiens* (counties); but there is ample authority for the statement that the most important and most stable Red Army area, the so-called "central Soviet district," held more or less permanently from 1930 to the end of 1934, comprised about seventeen *hsien* astride the Kiangsi-Fukien border, with a total population of 3,000,000. This fact was frequently cited by Mao Tse-tung, president of the "Soviet Republic," and other Communist Party spokesmen, although it was conveniently ignored by the Comintern press abroad.[44] The other Soviet districts, along the Hupeh-Hunan, Hunan-Kiangsi, northeastern Kiangsi, Honan-Hupeh-Anhwei, and Hupeh-Hunan-Kiangsi borders were all smaller, less stable, and more frequently compelled to dissolve under the pressure of repeated attacks.

The Red Armies themselves varied no less in size and strength, both in their more or less regular formations and in the auxiliary corps of peasant Red Guards who functioned with them in the incessant civil war against Chiang Kai-shek's Kuomintang forces. In 1932 one quite carefully checked estimate based on Communist records put the grand total of all armies operating in all districts at 151,000, of whom only 97,500 had rifles.[45] The same creative spirit who from his observation post in Moscow saw one-quarter of China under Soviet rule also expanded the Red Army to a force of 350,000 at the end of 1933.[46] Unfortunately again, a civil war could not be fought with soldiers represented only by digits scratched on Comintern copy paper. Chu Teh, certainly one of the most remarkable military leaders in all history, led a force in 1932 that numbered no more than 40,000 and which, according to the most sober estimates of responsible Communist representatives in Shanghai, never in its best Kiangsi days exceeded 70,000. Ho Lung's wraith-like force never exceeded 10,000. The other scattered forces were even smaller. All of them, of course, were aided by peasant auxiliaries whose number varied greatly from time to time and whose chief uses were in scouting and raids for supplies and creating diversions in the conduct of guerrilla operations.

That these forces and the territory they permanently occupied were in reality so small sharpens into all the bolder relief the quality of their achievements. No more brilliant pages have ever been written in the history of peasant wars than those which must record the exploits of the Chinese Red Armies engaged in a civil war against enemies five, six, and seven times their number and a thousand times their superior in armaments. For more than five years, the Red Armies outmaneuvered and defeated five successive Kuomintang campaigns against them. Because of the incomparable advantage of the support of the population, their superior mobility and generalship, their knowledge of the terrain, the Reds cut off and defeated division after division of Chiang Kai-shek's best troops and armed themselves exclusively with the weapons they captured. The slogans of land to the peasants and freedom from the rapacity of the Kuomintang regime ploughed like tanks through the columns of Chiang's hired soldiers.[47]

Marveling at the many-sided aid given the Reds by the local peasants, a missionary correspondent of the *North China Daily News* found it "a strange thing that so many people are willing to undertake what they know means death."[48] Almost everywhere they went the Red Armies expelled landlords, destroyed land deeds, debt bonds, and contracts. The peasants still suffered from many disabilities, but they understood that the Kuomintang campaigns were waged to restore the landlord his land and his power. All the pompous "rehabilitation" plans announced by the Nanking government with each campaign were designed for this purpose only.[49] Resisting this, the peasants gladly fought and died. This was the heroism, the grandeur, too simple, too elemental for the missionary mind to grasp. It gave its blessing instead to the slaughter, rapine, and wanton destruction with which Chiang Kai-shek scourged the province in his effort to stamp out the peasant revolt.

Ho Ying-chin, Chiang's minister of war, complained in 1931 that the peasants supported the Reds and made it difficult for the invading armies to secure food or transport.[50] Chiang Kai-shek told a Japanese interviewer in 1933 that the punitive forces found it "impossible to draw any line between a good citizen and a Red partisan" and were assailed by the feeling that "the enemy is lurking everywhere."[51] The story of the five anti-Red campaigns is a story of angry and frustrated complaints by Kuomintang generals, of mass desertions by companies, and whole regiments, of shrill threats and reproaches from the missionaries and the treaty port foreign press. In the end Chiang Kai-shek had to put more than half a million men in the field and send aloft a fleet of more than 300 American, British, and Italian bombing planes to lay waste whole districts and to exterminate whole sections of the insurgent peasantry.

The remoteness of the Soviet areas, the mountainous terrain, the absence of roads or rails, were all of great advantage in the military struggle of the Reds against the external enemy. These same factors, when raised from the military to the political and economic plane, became the source of insuperable internal obstacles. "Soviet China" was not only remote from the main urban centers and the principal arteries of communications which are the lifelines of a rural hinterland, but even within its own territory it ruled no cities or sizable towns. The chief cities of the province of Kiangsi—Kiukiang, Nanchang, and even Kanchow—deep in the heart of the Red area, remained in the hands of the Kuomintang, as did the links between them, the Kiukiang–Nanchang railway and the Kian River. Kiukiang was never seriously threatened. Nanchang was approached on several occasions but only for the purpose of creating military diversions. Kian, after the brief occupation of 1930, was never again conquered. Kanchow was repeatedly besieged but never taken. Even the *hsien* towns or county seats constantly changed hands with the shifting fortunes of the civil war. It was still theoretically the aim to capture at least "one or two central or secondary cities,"[52] but this was never achieved. Except for one sortie into Fukien, resulting in the occupation of Changchow for a few days in April 1932, the Red Armies never again took or held any town of consequence. Instead, the increasing pressure of the Kuomintang attacks and the gradual tightening of the economic blockade held them ever more closely confined to their mountain fastnesses along the Kiangsi-Fukien border and along the fringes of other Central China provinces. The "Soviet movement" remained a movement of the villages alone.

The economic self-sufficiency of these villages had long since disappeared. They produced only rice and small quantities of bamboo, paper, and wood oil, which they had to exchange for the most elementary necessities that had to come from the outside, such as salt, cloth, kerosene, farming implements, and matches. This trade was conducted by merchants who preserved contact with the external market. Within the Red areas the merchants were at the same time owners of land, lenders of money, and employers of labor. The peasants themselves were divided into strata with conflicting economic interests. The struggle among them only assumed new forms after the largest and most powerful of the landlords had been driven out. Still dominant in the villages were the rich peasants, who were semilandlords, employers of agricultural labor, and often merchants and moneylenders as well. After them came the middle peasants, who owned barely enough land to satisfy their meager needs and only occasionally hired hands to work in their fields. Finally there were the poor peasants, possessing inadequate land or no land at all and compelled to rent small plots or join the ranks of the agricultural laborers who possessed nothing but their labor power. The poor peasants and agricultural laborers were subjected economically to the rich peasants, while the middle peasants, in various gradations, fluctuated between them.

To these peasant classes, with their complex internal divisions and conflicts, the Communist Party claimed that it brought "proletarian leadership." It based its claims sometimes on the purely abstract view that the Communist Party was by definition the "party of the proletariat" and that consequently its mere presence guaranteed working-class hegemony in the peasant revolt. To strengthen this illusion, the party brought occasional workers in from the cities and gave them leading positions in the Red Army and in some of the governing committees that were established. The effect of this practice, however, was to deprive the workers in the cities of their most advanced representatives. If the vigilant terror of the Kuomintang did not cut them away from the labor movement, the Communist Party did. Once torn from their proletarian environment, these workers ceased to be proletarians and fell inevitably instead under the overwhelming influence of their peasant milieu. Divorced from the productive process, they could become neither the leaders of the proletariat nor the representatives of its leadership over the insurgent peasants.

Only real proletarian leadership of the agrarian revolt could save it from disintegration and dispersal. It alone could knit the poor and middle peasants and rural workers together for a common struggle against the village bourgeoisie. It alone could make this struggle effective by undertaking the complete reorganization of the national economy. But such leadership could be exercised only through the urban labor movement as a whole and through the establishment of its control over the centers of production and distribution on which rural economy so completely depended. In other words, the agrarian revolt had to fuse with a proletarian revolution to have successful issue.

Even under most favorable conditions, the general backwardness of the country meant that great obstacles would be encountered in reorganizing rural life and bringing industry to the direct aid of agriculture in a planned and systematic manner. In this the working classes of the more advanced countries would have to play an important and indispensable role. The scope and complexity of this problem was more than amply demonstrated in Russia where the proletariat holds power but where factors of national isolation and economic backwardness have placed the most severe difficulties in the way of establishing a harmonious balance between urban and rural economy. Reduced to the comparatively microscopic scale of "Soviet China," scattered insurgent villages and mountain communities in a country still dominated as a whole by imperialist and native finance capital, the problem was proportionately more acute and the effort to solve it without a proletarian revolution was utterly hopeless.

The Communist Party had never accepted the perspective of a proletarian revolution in China. It still insisted, after the experience of 1925–27, on the "bourgeois-democratic character of the Chinese Revolution." The theory of the "democratic dictatorship" which had been so thoroughly tested in Russia in 1917 and again in China ten years later remained the chief weapon in the ideological arsenal of the Chinese Communist Party. In 1925–27 it had led them to dependence on the bourgeoisie with disastrous results. Now it provided justification for depending upon a purely peasant movement, for relying, as before, on class interests which collided with those of the proletariat instead of fusing with them. The 1927 defeat had physically divorced the party from the working class. The adventurist course after 1927 converted it into a peasant party without roots or influence among the workers. It had become the Chinese equivalent not of the Russian Bolshevik Party but of the

Social Revolutionary Party, whose example it followed in proposing to carry out an agrarian transformation on the basis of bourgeois property relations. Isolated in purely rural and economically limited pockets, the Communist Party could not even begin to improve the status of the scattered semi-proletarians and agricultural workers in the districts under Red Army control, no less to base a consistent and workable economic policy and political regime upon them. Despite all its pious resolutions and exhortations to the contrary, the Communists had to lean upon the rich peasants and merchants whose contact to the external market was indispensable to the maintenance of even a minimum existence for the Soviet areas. Despite itself, the party became the instrument of the dominant groupings in the villages.

The rich peasants came forward as leaders of the peasant revolt, bent on annexing some of the landlords' wealth and retaining their own. In many places they kept the movement limited to non-payment of rent and taxes. When the peasants drove beyond this to the division of the land, they acquired the best land for themselves and retained their implements and draught animals. The influence of their position in the village clans and the superficial conflict between rich peasant and landlord made it easy for the former to dominate the lower strata of the peasant population. So long as the village remained subject to the operations of commercial capital and the external market, the village bourgeoisie, the rich peasants, and the merchants had to remain the dominant village classes and they took every possible advantage of their strategic position.

The Communists fostered rather than resisted this development. The Sixth Congress of the party in 1928 adopted a conciliatory attitude towards the village bourgeoisie under the slogan of "not deliberately forcing the struggle against the rich peasants because to do so would be to confuse the fundamental contradiction between the peasant and landlord classes."[53] Accordingly, rich peasant land was to be left intact. "Confiscate landlord's land" was to be the principal slogan of the agrarian movement. In other words, the Communists now assumed the same antagonism between rich peasant and landlord as they had formerly assumed between the national bourgeois and compradore-landlord. They sought now to conciliate the rich peasants in the villages just as formerly they had tried, with such disastrous results, to adapt themselves to the national bourgeoisie in the cities. Even the familiar predictions about the "inevitable defection" of the rich peasants to the counterrevolution were dusted off and brought out,[54] and although in words some kind of limited or "secondary "[55] struggle was to be waged against these inevitable counterrevolutionists, in practice, as before, practical leadership was surrendered to them and their economic interests defended. The party found itself compelled to call upon the peasant poor, the rural workers, the artisans, and handicraftsmen to sacrifice their own immediate interests in order not to alienate the rich peasants and the merchants.

"Owing to the alliance with the rich peasants," admitted the Central Committee in 1929, "the interests of the agricultural laborers were sacrificed.... We feared the counterrevolutionary turn of the rich peasants and consequently asked the agricultural labourers to lower their demands."[56] In western Fukien in 1930 the Communists leading the partisan bands had "to compromise with the merchants in order to solve the difficulty of the import and export of supplies. They not only proclaimed protection of the merchants, but exempted them from taxation while the peasants still paid a 15 percent land tax.... They had no means of curbing the raising of prices by the merchants...and sometimes they went so far as to limit the economic struggles of the shop employees and workers."[57]

In May 1930, a secret "Soviet Delegates' Conference" in Shanghai adopted a policy of frank conciliation towards the rich peasants and merchants.[58] The anti-proletarian consequences of this policy were not only pointed out in a brilliant analysis by a young Oppositionist, O Fong,[59] but were dimly realized by some in the Party itself. Chen Shao-yu criticized comrades in the Soviet districts who excused their failure to organize the agricultural laborers by declaring that "the peasants oppose it."

"Shall we fail to organize the agricultural labourers for fear of the rich peasants?" he asked.

> Then we are absolutely not the party of the proletariat.... In many Soviet villages rich peasant psychology dominates. Rich peasants occupy no small position in the mass organizations and in the party. They are aware of rich peasant interests only. This means that we have come to regard rich peasant psychology as the basic psychology of the peasant masses.... For the same reasons they do not organize shop employees, handicraft, and small enterprise workers. In Hupeh-Honan, for example, the slogan "For the interests of the middle and small merchants" was openly proclaimed and as a result not a single demand of the shop employees and handicraft workers was put forward.[60]

At the end of 1930, the Comintern described the situation in the following terms:

> The agrarian revolution's most important tasks have not been solved. Not only rich peasants but even small landlords make their way into the soviets, into the organs of the new power, into the Red Army. The rich peasants seek to steal the fruits of the agrarian revolution. The rich peasant slogan—to distribute land according to productive implements—has not met with adequate resistance. In some places it was proposed to confiscate only the land of landlords holding more than fifty mow. Elsewhere there was a slogan for payment of debts to landlord-usurers owning less than fifty mow.... Equal division of land is the most important task of the agrarian revolution, but it has been carried out in very few places. The organization of the poor peasants has not even begun.... Coolies and agricultural laborers have not been organized into unions.[61]

After Li Li-san was held duly responsible for this state of affairs and Chen Shao-yu put in his place, the situation not only failed to improve but grew steadily worse. "Two-thirds of the government is in the hands of the rich peasants," wrote a correspondent from one of the Soviet districts in 1931.[62] "Rich peasants are in all the party posts," wrote another in August that same year.[63] In 1933, at Juichin, the Soviet capital, a leading spokesman wrote: "The land was divided, but the landlords and rich peasants also received land and better land at that. A number of landlord and rich peasant elements still retain their authority and position in the villages.... Not a few of them are in control of party and government institutions and use them to carry out their own class interests.... In many places the land problem seems to be fully solved, but upon close scrutiny it appears that even landlords are found to have received land and the rich peasants still retain their superior land."[64]

Mao Tse-tung, president of the "Soviet Republic," wrote: "Many landlords and rich peasants put on a revolutionary coloration. They say they are for the revolution and for the division of the land.... They are very active and rely on their historical advantages—'they can speak well and write well'—and consequently in the first period they steal the fruits of the agrarian revolution. Facts from innumerable places prove that they have usurped the provisional power, filtered into the armed forces, controlled the revolutionary organizations, and divided more and better land than the poor peasants." Mao estimated that this was the case in "80 percent of the area of the central district, affecting a population of more than 2,000,000."[65] In his report to the Second Soviet Congress held at Juichin in January 1934, Mao revealed the striking fact that during a land-inspection movement conducted in the summer of 1933, "in the central Soviet district 6,988 landlord families and 6,638 rich peasant families owning a huge excess of land were discovered and their land seized and money taken from them to the total of $606,916."[66] Facts proved harsher and more compelling than party resolutions. Even the attempts made to redivide the land for the greater benefit of the poor peasants had to be abandoned in order not to unsettle crop production. At the end of the year a decree was announced prohibiting further redivision of the land because this practice had become "one of the most serious obstacles to an improvement in peasant agriculture."[67]

The demands of the agricultural laborers, artisans, and other rural workers were no less of a menace to the feeble and limited economic structure in the Soviet districts. In the central district this class was estimated to number about 200,000.[68] Working singly or in twos or threes, scattered on the land, in the villages, or itinerant, these workers occupied a subsidiary position in the peasant economy. The capitalist cannot exist without the factory worker, but the peasant can get along without a hired hand. In the sense that they were divorced from the means of production and sold their labor power for wages, these workers were proletarians. The fact that they were scattered and played no independent role in production meant, however, that they tended to form part of the general petty bourgeois mass of the peasantry. They could not, in any case, play an independent political role. It was impossible to base any consistent policy upon their interests. A proletariat in power will find the means of marshalling rural labor and providing them with the economic means which will raise their level of existence, but here they stood alone, and when they tried to shorten their hours or increase their wages, the peasants resisted sharply or simply discharged them. Operating on the slimmest of all margins, the peasant could not double his workers' wages or the number of hands hired without utterly ruining himself. Similarly, in the shops and small enterprises, the merchants countered employees' demands by the simple threat to suspend activity altogether. This meant slow suffocation of trade and the merchants knew they held the whip hand.

Shortly after it was established in November 1931, the "Provisional Soviet Government" adopted an admirable labor law even more sweeping in its provisions than the labor legislation of the Kuomintang in its early days. It called for a universal eight-hour day for adults, a six-hour day for youths of sixteen to eighteen, and a four-hour day for younger workers, for increased wages and generally improved working conditions. For propaganda purposes outside the Soviet districts and especially abroad, the word was taken for the deed. In "Soviet China" itself, however, it was soon realized that a law "passed for big cities and large-scale production cannot be completely and mechanically applied in the economically backward Soviet districts."[69] Attempts to enforce it had early been abandoned in the face of merchant-peasant opposition. "The comrades consider the labor law impracticable or else purely for propaganda purposes," reported the Hunan-Kiangsi Party committee. "The Provincial Committee has combatted this tendency, but without much effect."[70] Many excuses were devised for the failure to apply the law. One of the most frequent was the plea that the new working hours could not be put into effect "because there are no clocks to reckon time by!"[71] After berating the functionaries of the lower rank for their stubborn "disregard" of the law, the leaders of the top were finally compelled to admit also that it was "impractical."

Lo Fu, a leading spokesman, described the unhappy result of attempts made to double the wages (from eight to sixteen dollars annually!) and cut the hours of farmhands. The workers were simply discharged. "The result was that the peasants were dissatisfied and the laborers were sceptical about our leadership." It was necessary, of course, to improve working conditions for the farmhands, "but such improvements must also be regarded by the peasants as necessary and practicable." The same applied to the apprentices in the shops and the boatmen engaged in the river trade. "I have here the petitions of many merchants and employers from which we can see that the mechanical application of the labor law will inevitably be the decline of industry and commerce." It was necessary, of course, to improve the living standards and working conditions of the apprentices, "but we must make the employment of apprentices profitable, not unprofitable, for the master."[72] The workers were asked to understand that while they were the "masters of the state" they had to consent to remain the "exploited class" at the same time and refrain from making "excessive demands" or conducting strikes whose only effect was "to wreck the worker-peasant alliance."[73] This was the real essence of the "democratic dictatorship" in "Soviet China."

The attempt to organize the rural workers into unions produced in these circumstances either no organizations at all or alleged trade unions which functioned in reality against the interests of the workers. Figures on the "trade unions" in the Soviet districts varied widely. Within the space of a single year different published versions ranged from 14,000 to 30,000, to 150,000, to 229,000, and even to 2,200,000![74] But the character of these unions, whatever their number, was so dubious that even the trade union center of the party at Shanghai had to complain. In its report for 1931 it spoke of the presence of "shopkeepers and rich peasants" in the unions.[75] The next year it addressed a scorching letter to the trade union officials in Kiangsi in which it accused them of admitting "peasants, priests, shopowners, foremen, rich peasants, and landlords," while "on the other hand considerable sections of the agricultural laborers, coolies, employees, and artisans are on various pretexts barred from membership." The party comrades engaged in this work were accused of being "contemptuous of the workers and insolent toward them." The letter described the unions as "anti-proletarian in character, representing more the interests of the landlords, rich peasants, and employers."[76]

"The party in the Soviet districts, generally speaking, ignores proletarian hegemony," wrote one party leader in Juichin. "Everywhere we see the serious phenomenon of the continual ignoring of the trade union movement.... The Committees never even discuss it.... Proletarian leadership exists still for the most part in words in party documents."[77]

This was the hard fact on which the Soviet experiment in Kiangsi broke its back. By driving out the landlords and sponsoring the division of the land, the Red Armies had aroused the enthusiasm of considerable masses of the peasantry. In the absence of effective economic control, however, and in the absence of an effective proletarian mass movement, not only in the great cities, but in the towns nearest the Soviet districts,[78] the rich peasants reemerged as landlords and the merchants reemerged as the dominant class. The poor peasants and rural workers could win and hold not even the smallest material gains. Prices of the simplest necessities rose to unreachable levels. Unemployment became widespread. Peasants and rural workers alike began to wonder why they were fighting and to wish for any kind of peace so long as there was peace. Mass enthusiasm lapsed. Desertions from the Red Army grew in number.[79] A creeping paralysis began at the fringes of the Soviet districts and soon spread toward the centrer. Passivity corroded mass initiative. Pessimism gripped the leaders. This became known in party parlance as the "Lo Min line" because Lo Min, Fukien party leader, was one of the first to capitulate to these moods. "Even if our best leaders were to come, or to bring Stalin himself, or even resurrect Lenin from his tomb, and were to speak all together to the masses for three days and three nights, I do not think it would help change the moods of the masses," said Lo Min.[80]

Through 1933, the "Lo Min line" spread like a virus through the veins of "Soviet China." From Fukien it communicated itself to the Hwei-Hsen-An districts of south Kiangsi where Party functionaries, led by Teng Shao-pin, simply fled from their posts.[81] A Red Army enlistment campaign failed dismally and there was talk of conscription. Whole detachments of the Youth Guard auxiliaries deserted and actually clashed with pursuing detachments of the Red Army.[82] Peasants often fled to the mountains to avoid transport work for the embattled army.[83]

> The partisan bands not only rarely grow but are shrinking daily, as in Hwei-Hsen-An in the past and I-Chung and Nanfeng now. Desertions with rifles and betrayals are constantly occurring.... Corruption and degeneration constantly appear. Some partisan bands showed tendencies to banditry.... These are the conditions not only in the partisan bands but in the independent battalions, as in refusal to take orders, raids for money, etc.... The phenomenon of "soaking the tuhao" (raiding the hoards of the richer peasants) is very widespread.... Party workers going into the districts with small-size baggage soon increase it to large-size baggage. If they go with large-size baggage it soon grows into two loads for a carrying pole.[84]

New Lo Mins cropped up everywhere, even in the Red Army command, and finally in departments of the Central Government at Juichin. Ho So-hen of the workers-peasants inspection bureau was ejected for declaring that of the 3,000,000 people in the Central Soviet district, 2,000,000 were oppressed by rich peasants and landlords and that "the Soviet governments of various grades have become instruments of the landlords and rich peasants for oppressing the masses."[85]

Chow En-lai appealed for "struggle against all kinds of wavering, pessimism, passivity, despair, weariness, and capitulation before difficulties."[86] Other leaders complained that the high turnover in party officials and the frequent changes in the districts were destroying mass enthusiasm, that the approach of any forces sent the peasants fleeing to the mountains. "They do not care if they are Red or White."[87]

The truly heroic effort made by the Red Army in the face of these moods defeated Chiang Kai-shek's drives in the summer of 1933, but the "victories" of those months were the beginning of the end. It was only a question of time before the superior strength of the Kuomintang, unassailed in the centers of its power, prevailed. It was only a question of time before the might of the Kuomintang military machine on land and in the air and the rigid tightening of the economic blockade produced their inevitable results. Chiang's bombers devastated whole districts and his troops inched down the province building fortifications as they advanced. Chiang abandoned the old strategy of sending long columns deep into Red territory, where they were cut off and annihilated. His army of more than 500,000 men, schooled by the German General von Seeckt and armed with weapons of the latest design from the munitions factories of Europe and the United States, closed in on the tiny Soviet districts like a fine-meshed steel net. There were ghastly massacres, violent and swift, by bomb, gun, and torch, slow and agonizing by calculated starvation.[88]

In August 1934, one Red force of about 10,000 men, led by Hsiao Keh, broke through the cordon and escaped westward. They were followed in November by the main force under Chu Teh and Mao Tse-tung. On November 10, 1934, almost exactly three years after the proclamation of the Chinese "Soviet Republic," Chiang Kai-shek's troops triumphantly entered Juichin, the Soviet capital. Chiang had failed to exterminate all the Reds as he had promised, but he had succeeded in winning Kiangsi back for the landlords.

The Red forces marched and countermarched across Hunan, Kweichow, Yunnan, and Szechwan into Shensi, suffering incredible hardships, performing more incredible feats of valor and cunning. That "long trek" will be recorded as one of the most remarkable military exploits of all time, but it carried the Red Army still farther from the political and economic centers of the country. The defeat in Kiangsi could not terminate the peasant war, but it did deal a stunning blow to the organized insurgent peasant movement and consequently to the labor movement in the cities, then at its lowest ebb. New waves of terror, of capitulation and betrayals destroyed most of what remained of the Communist Party apparatus in the principal cities. Events had laid the ghosts of a thousand propagandist myths. Into the sparse desert land of the Chinese northwest the Communists marched toward a new impasse.

20 The New "National United Front"

The Kuomintang regime came to power in 1927 with a mandate from the imperialist Powers to crush the mass movement of the workers and peasants. In the massacres of that year and in the civil war and terror waged with such ferocity in the ensuing decade against the workers, peasants, and radical intellectuals, the Kuomintang performed its essential function as a buffer between the imperialists and the people.

The foreign interests which so completely dominated the political and economic life of the Chinese bourgeosie participated directly and indirectly in the incessant war against the Chinese masses. Armies sent to crush the insurgent peasants in Central China were armed from all the arsenals of Europe, Japan, and the United States. German Fascist instructors trained the troops used against the people. American and Italian officers taught Kuomintang fliers how to bomb the civilian population. American, British, Italian, and German planes made Chinese skies horrible for the defenseless peasants of the Yangtze provinces. American, British, French, Italian, and Japanese gunboats opened fire repeatedly on "bandits"—the official designation for the peasant insurgents—along the banks of Chinese rivers. The $50,000,000 cotton and wheat loan made to the Nanking government by the United States in 1933 provided the final resources needed to consummate the Kiangsi campaigns. In the great urban centers, troops and marines of the United States, Britain, France, Japan, and Italy stood direct guard over foreign interests. British, French, and Japanese police in the foreign areas tirelessly hunted down radical students, strike leaders, and Communists, and handed them over in hundreds to be tortured and executed by the Kuomintang civil or military authorities. The direct attacks of Japanese imperialism which were resumed in 1931 have been accompanied by all the frightfulness of modern predatory warfare, but in this Japan has only continued in its own special interest the no less ghastly war waged jointly by the Kuomintang and all the Powers in their common interest against the exploited and terrorized people. The Japanese invasion, continuing through successive stages into the major war of 1937–38, signified primarily that the leanest and hungriest of the wolves had broken from the pack in a new effort to secure a larger portion of the prey for itself.

Japanese capitalism rests on a light industrial foundation and a feudally backward agrarian system, and has a comparatively weak although highly concentrated financial superstructure. A latecomer into the family of imperialist nations, Japan has sought for forty years to master China in order to create an unimpeded channel for the outward flow of its own products and to secure basic raw materials, mainly coal, iron, and cotton, that it so lamentably lacks. Because of its economic weakness, Japan was less able than its great rivals, Britain and the United States, to withstand the pressure of the world depression that began in 1929. The closing of world markets to Japanese goods led directly to the invasion of Manchuria in 1931. Conquest brought no surcease, but bred only new adventures. The heavy cost of military operations on the mainland and the acute intensification of the crisis increased the strain on Japanese economy. In 1937 Japan resorted again to arms to bring more of China within its orbit and to subject all of Chinese economy to its needs by systematically driving out its imperialist rivals, Great Britain and the United States.

Unlike the Japanese, the British and American imperialist structures are rooted in highly developed heavy industries woven into vast units by a powerful financial mesh. They are capable of ultimately dominating Chinese economy by providing it with capital goods and draining off the necessary super-profits by retaining both direct and indirect financial control. Their mutual rivalries have until now blocked this course, but it is this perspective that makes China the great potential reservoir for capital investment over which the Great Powers will and must eventually come into conflict.

Because it seeks in China to bolster its own frail economic structure through direct and undivided exploitation of the Chinese market, Chinese labor, and Chinese resources, Japanese imperialism not only collides with its great rivals, but cannot tolerate even a relative growth of competing native Chinese industry. It can leave no margin for the development of a semi-independent native exploiting class.* The further exploitation of China by British or American finance capital would not only permit but would absolutely require the services of the Chinese bourgeoisie as agent. For this reason the Chinese bourgeoisie, incapable

* "The incalculably vast damage done to Shanghai's industries by the war is being systematically increased every day. Responsible Japanese officials admit that in Nantao, Pootung, and in other districts still closed to foreigners, Japanese soldiers continue to destroy or take away all machinery found in Chinese-owned factories. In Hongkew and in Yangtzepoo this campaign of destruction has already been completed. And Chapei was just a mass of ruins when the Chinese retreated. The avowed purpose of this industrial wreckage is to put an end to China's industrial development, which was beginning to threaten Japanese domination of Chinese markets. Some Japanese already claim that they have destroyed and wiped out all the industrial progress China had made during the last decade."—Special Correspondence to the *New York Times*, January 30, 1938.

of developing independently, has naturally preferred to be vassal to New York or London rather than to Tokyo.

When Japan attacked in 1931, the Kuomintang looked helplessly for aid from Britain and the United States. Japan, however, had cannily chosen its moment. The invasion of Manchuria occurred at a time when the general preoccupation with the economic crisis and the consequent sharpening of all inter-imperialist rivalries had created a strategic vacuum in which Japan could proceed with little or no fear of immediate interference. Neither of its rivals was prepared or willing to begin an armed struggle for supremacy in Asia. Nor were they entirely unwilling to foster Japan's plan for an eventual attack on the Soviet Union.

More fearful of the masses than it was of the invaders, the Kuomintang regime did not dare mobilize the people for a national revolutionary war. It took instead the alternative course of "non-resistance," conceding as much ground as it had to, in the hope that Japan would content itself with Manchuria, or, at most, with Manchuria and North China. At first it tried to use the boycott weapon, but under the pressure of Japan's attack on Shanghai in 1932 it abandoned and actively suppressed the boycott campaign. It thereafter tried to prove its usefulness to the Japanese by intensifying its drive against the peasants in Central China and by crushing every manifestation of an independent anti-Japanese movement.

It followed almost automatically that as every layer of the population stirred, to one degree or another, under the Japanese lash, those who sought to resist Japanese imperialism found themselves engaged in struggle against the Kuomintang regime. Students, who reacted first and most sharply to the Kuomintang's failure to defend the country's territory, demonstratively trampled on Kuomintang banners. They raided and smashed Kuomintang headquarters. They commandeered trains and streamed to Nanking in thousands to storm the citadels of the government itself. As in 1919, they fought their way into the presence of traitorous ministers. They broke into the Foreign Office, thrashed Foreign Minister C. T. Wang (now ambassador to Washington), and forced him to resign. His successor, V. K. Wellington Koo (now ambassador to Paris), they prevented from taking office. From Chiang Kai-shek they extracted one of his already frequent promises to sacrifice his life on northern battlefields. But a few days later, on December 15, 1931, Chiang engineered one of his strategic resignations. He watched from the sidelines while Sun Fo and Eugene Chen, holding the stage for their sorry moment, took the responsibility for shooting and bayoneting the student demonstrators, who were finally herded from Nanking like cattle. Everywhere with the same reckless heroism the students staged spectacular demonstrations. In Shanghai they held the mayor prisoner and forced him too to resign.

The student movement soon subsided. In 1919 the students had ignited the Nationalist movement that swept workers, peasants, and bourgeois Nationalists into the struggles of the second Chinese Revolution. In 1931 the student spark flickered and went out because the students remained utterly isolated. In 1919 the bourgeoisie, spurred by their gains in the war, encouraged the student rising and stepped forward to lead the broad Nationalist movement that arose. In 1931 the bourgeoisie was fighting the anti-imperialist movement with all its strength. In 1919 the workers, freshly marshalled in the factories, rose swiftly to the struggle, and through them millions of peasants were roused. In 1931 the masses, still passive as a result of the profound defeats of 1927, remained inert.[1]

Nevertheless the boycott momentarily made wheels turn faster in Chinese factories. There was an infant boom which began to stimulate moods of self-confidence among the workers. Strikes began to occur, but everywhere strikers were clubbed and shot and beaten down. The organizations were controlled by agents and gangsters of the Kuomintang. Most of them had no organizations at all. There was no political party with a banner and a program they could recognize as their own.

The same events that so completely exposed the craven role of the Kuomintang no less pitilessly bared the impotence and isolation of the Communist Party. It was utterly unable to rally the forces that the Kuomintang scattered and suppressed. It could not translate into the substance of organized strength the profound hostility that pervaded whole layers of the population, especially those most directly exposed to Japan's imperialist attacks. In Manchuria scores of thousands of soldiers and peasants banded together into volunteer armies, the *hunghudtze* or "bandits," who to this day continue to shake the uneasy throne of Henry Pu Yi. Among them the Communist Party exerted little or no influence.[2]Among the workers in Manchurian cities, the party had no foothold at all.[3] In Shanghai and the other urban centers of China proper, the party was already entirely divorced from the working class and was unable to exploit the opportunity the invasion offered to regain the positions it had lost. Communist intellectuals played some role in the student movement, but lacking contact with the workers, they could not prevent that movement from falling prey to the maneuvers of Kuomintang politicians and disintegrating under the ruthless blows of Kuomintang terror.

From the workers the abstract anti-Japanese slogans issued by the party elicited no response. Mere patriotic appeals could not at a single stroke efface the long series of fatal blunders that had emasculated the party and destroyed its authority and prestige among the workers. As usual the propaganda machinery of the Comintern abroad published glowing reports of Communist successes in the anti-Japanese movement,[4] while on the scene itself the party's own press more accurately reflected the party's real weakness. "Since September 8, the party and the red unions have had absolutely no leadership in the workers' movement," said the *Red Flag* in December 1931. The trade union committee had "failed to establish a single workers' paper" subsequent to the Japanese invasion.[5] Meager efforts made to set up workers' anti-Japanese associations were no more successful.

"The working masses have not yet broadly and actively participated in the struggle," said another Communist organ two months after the invasion began.

> This is due...in part to the fact that the red unions and their vanguard, the Communist Party, were unable to rally the masses around them. In the practical struggle we did not link the anti-Japanese wave to a bold thrust of the class struggle. Therefore the Chinese working class, especially in Shanghai, although consumed with anti-Japanese sentiment, could not immediately react to such slogans as "Down with the Japanese robbers!" "Against the occupation of Manchuria!"...etc., because these slogans have not yet been linked to the urgent demands of the working masses in the localities, such as wage increases, house and rice allowances.... It is clear that purely anti-Japanese slogans cannot give strikers wage increases and improvements in living conditions.[6]

It was also of this period that the labor department of the Central Committee wrote: "We have not succeeded in organizing a single anti-imperialist strike."[7]

Quite independently of the party and despite the savage repressions a strike movement began to gather momentum at Shanghai. Workers at the Chinese Wing On Cotton Mills, which had profited heavily from the boycott of Japanese goods, struck for wage increases in December. Several workers were killed in clashes with Kuomintang police before the strike was smashed. On January 7 a general walkout occurred of the 60,000 workers in Shanghai's thirty-four Japanese-owned cotton mills. The strike was called on purely economic grounds against wage cuts and layoffs.[8] By the end of two weeks all but 7,000 had been forced back to work or to seek jobs elsewhere.

Seven days later, on January 28, the Japanese Navy struck at Shanghai. Unexpectedly and in defiance of direct orders from Chiang Kai-shek, the Nineteenth Route Army put up stubborn resistance. Five weeks of hostilities followed. Seven years earlier the shooting of only thirteen students by British police had precipitated a paralyzing general strike. Now the Japanese attackers freely used the theoretically neutral territory of the International Settlement as a base for the murderous airraids and artillery bombardments which shattered working-class Chapei and brought death to thousands of civilians. Yet the great mass of workers, most of whom were thrown out of employment by the hostilities, looked on passively. Wheels turned in the Settlement and the French Concession much as before. A small band of workers fought side by side with the soldiers at Woosung, and others, kept carefully segregated from the soldiers, were employed behind the lines. The great mass of the Shanghai working class did not intervene.[9] Despite its subsequent claims to a share in the Nineteenth Route Army's glory, the Communist Party played practically no role in the struggle.*

In 1933 the Communist leadership was still deploring "the lack of normal persistance of work" in the cities. It held its local committees responsible for the failure to organize a single anti-Japanese workers' organization in Tientsin or Shanghai.[10]

The Communist Party was unable to rally the masses against Japanese imperialism because it had neither the forces nor the program capable of organizing them for struggle against the Chinese bourgeoisie. It was the triumph of bourgeois Kuomintang reaction in 1927 that had paved the way for Japan's imperialist aggression. It was the defeat of the revolution and the Kuomintang repressions during the ensuing half-decade that disarmed the masses, psychologically and politically, in the face of the imperialist offensive. The Communist Party now had to pay the price of impotence for its role and its responsibility in this accumulation of disasters.

The bourgeois reaction and its military dictatorship was so completely dominant in this entire period that no other party was able to emerge to offer any kind of effective opposition to the Kuomintang. Rival militarists here and there challenged Chiang Kai-shek's rule. They hypocritically wrapped themselves in the banners of anti-Japanism in the hope of exploiting Chiang's patent treachery. But one after another he bought them off or beat them down. Feng Yu-hsiang raised an independent banner in Chahar in August 1933, but made his peace with Chiang rather than face the necessity for carrying out his frequent threats to wage war on the invaders. In November the same year a group of dissident Kuomintang politicians and the commanders of the Nineteenth Route Army joined in a revolt against Chiang that centered for a few weeks in the province of Fukien. They went so far as to flirt tentatively with the Communists, to proclaim the abolition of the Kuomintang and the formation of a new "People's Productionist Party" to take its place. But they, too, were quickly overcome by a single volley of Chiang's silver bullets. The Nineteenth Route Army was dispersed.

Petty-bourgeois radical groupings which tried to take a stand of principled opposition to the Chiang Kai-shek dictatorship were short-lived. Wang Ching-wei's feeble resistance to the dictatorship dissolved completely when Wang passed over to Chiang's camp in January 1932. Teng Yen-ta's Third Party lived only a fitful existence after Teng was executed by Chiang in 1931. The petty-bourgeois opposition was composed of small sects of intellectuals gathered around dissident politicians and ambitious generals in transient conspiracies that never went beyond a scramble for place and pelf. The Kuomintang-military dictatorship of Chiang Kai-shek was a costly and inadequate political instrument, but it was the best the bourgeoisie could devise to serve its interests.

---

* To prove that the 19th Route Army's resistance at Shanghai was "due in no small measure to the work of the Communists," the central organ of the Comintern went so far as to state that the strike in the Japanese mills had been organized at the beginning of February 1932...under the leadership of the Communist Party" (*Communist International*, December 1932). That this was a palpable falsehood could be proved by reference not only to the files of the *China Forum*, but of other Shanghai papers, for January. The author personally covered that strike and met members of the strike committee several times. The strike had already been broken when hostilities began. During the fighting, the workers were simply locked out. It is true, however, that Communists played some part in the refusal of the workers to go back to the Japanese mills until April, more than a month after hostilities ended.

In the Communist movement the only consistent challenge to the Communist Party came from the Trotskyist Opposition. Its nucleus was a group of students who came back from Russia after 1927. While at Sun Yat-sen University in Moscow many of them had found in the documents of the Russian Left Opposition the only coherent explanation of the disaster that had overtaken the revolution. Rapidly expelled from the Communist Party as they began to voice their criticism, they formed small independent organizations which began to issue underground publications. In 1929 Chen Tu-hsiu and a considerable group of his followers were expelled and they too led a separate existence until 1931, when all the oppositional groups merged under the banner of the International Communist League. The Chinese Trotskyist group, like its counterparts in other countries, continued to regard itself as a fraction of the Communist Party. It sought to exert sufficient influence to bring about changes in party policy which would permit its reintegration into the ranks. The Opposition, therefore, remained a tiny propaganda organization, publishing its own periodicals, but was unable to play any role in the class struggle.

The Trotskyists also suffered from the ideological confusion that came as an inevitable aftermath of the great defeats and the recession of the masses from the political arena. The process of political reorientation was a slow and painful one, and because of the conditions of isolation and terror, their discussion went on largely untested in action. After 1933, when the Trotskyists abandoned the attempt to "reform" the Comintern and launched the movement for creation of a Fourth International, the Shanghai group reorganized itself into the Communist League of China, and in 1934 began to win small footholds in some Shanghai factories.

Few in number as they were, the Trotskyists did not escape the heavy blows of the Kuomintang terror. Assailed by their Stalinist foes as "counterrevolutionists" and "agents of Chiang Kai-shek," the Trotskyists nevertheless lost some of their best comrades to Chiang Kai-shek's terror. Two entire central committees were wiped out by arrests. Not a few died of torture and starvation in prison. In 1932 Chen Tu-hsiu and eleven others were arrested and sentenced to long terms. In 1934 the reconstituted Central Committee was again slashed to pieces by the arrests of five of its leading members. The Kuomintang proceeded against its "agents" with the same relentless ferocity it displayed toward all it recognized as revolutionary opponents of its rule.

Although the Trotskyists never gathered enough strength to exert any direct influence on events, they hammered insistently on the need for an elementary democratic program as the indispensable starting-point for the revival of the labor movement. By this means alone, they held, could the labor movement be revived and become, as it had to, the spearhead of struggle against Japanese imperialism. This meant the conduct of the most patient and tireless organizational work in the factories based on the simplest daily demands of the workers. When workers striking for meager improvements in wages, hours, and rice allowances were clubbed, arrested, tortured, and shot, they could readily understand the meaning of agitation for the most elementary democratic rights—freedom of speech, press, organization, and assembly. These slogans flowed with immediate and comprehensible logic from every tiny partial economic conflict in which the workers engaged. Generalized into the slogan for a National Assembly, elected by the universal suffrage of the people, this program offered a common starting-point for all sections of the population oppressed and terrorized by the Kuomintang-military dictatorship.

Events forced the Stalinists to take half a step, despite themselves, in this direction. Their own program of "soviet power" possessed no immediate significance that the workers could grasp. Their slogans, "Support the Red Army," "Support the Soviets," bore no relation to the immediate interests or demands of the workers. Frightened by the impotence to which this condemned it, the Communist Party suddenly introduced in the fall of 1931 the slogan of an "elected people's power" which sounded dangerously like the Trotskyist position of an elected National Assembly. Although it made many efforts to do so, the party leadership was unable to explain adequately, even to its own members, the difference between "people's power" and "soviet power," or between "people's power" and the "National Assembly."[11] It could not follow such a discussion through to its logical conclusion, for even the temporary adoption of the slogan of a "people's power" constituted a dim but unmistakable recognition that the call for "soviet power" could awaken no response from masses crushed under the weight of a bourgeois-military dictatorship. At its Twelfth Plenum in September 1932, the Executive Committee of the Comintern proposed "the establishment of an elected people's government" in Manchuria,[12] but in practice the slogan was quietly abandoned. The Communist Party was going to return later on to this fundamentally correct slogan, but would reissue it in a twisted and misshapen form, transforming it not into a lever for the workers' revolution, but into a noose around the neck of the working-class movement. This would not occur, however, until the experiment with peasant soviets in the hinterland had been carried through to its conclusion and its failure underwritten at the cost of thousands of peasant lives.

Granted a respite by the Shanghai truce, Chiang Kai-shek resumed in the summer of 1932 his war against the Reds in Central China. Hoping to exploit anti-Japanese sentiment in the armies sent against them, the Reds in April 1932, "declared war" on Japan.[13] On January 10, 1933, just prior to Japan's drive into Jehol, the Red Army offered a united front to any armed force that would join it in battle against the imperialist invaders.[14] By the terms it offered, cessation of anti-Red hostilities, the grant of democratic rights to the people, and the arming of the masses, the Red Army leaders again recognized that they had to return to a minimum democratic program if they hoped at all to break through the isolation of their mountain strongholds. Chiang Kai-shek, however, still hoped the Japanese would remain satisfied with the concessions he had made and concentrated upon securing his own power in Central China by stamping out the insurgent peasantry. Lacking mass support in the rear of the Kuomintang armies, the Communists could not impose acceptance of their soundly-principled united front offer. After the Jehol debacle in March 1933, Chiang Kai-shek called his generals together at Kuling and sharply reiterated his basic strategy: "Until the Communists are exterminated, it is useless to speak about resistance against the Japanese!" He threatened "severe punishment" to any of his officers who thought the united front offer merited consideration.[15] The war against the peasant soviets went on, and although it took him until the end of 1934, Chiang finally did reconquer Southern Kiangsi.

For the next year the Red Army fought its way through parts of nine provinces, across rivers, and over the lofty ranges that rim the Tibetan frontier. Chiang Kai-shek sent his best divisions in pursuit, but they never caught up with the elusive foe. Displaying incomparable strategic skill and a fortitude that sustained the heaviest losses and the most grinding hardships, the Red Army finally united with other Red forces that had gone to Szechwan two years earlier, and in October 1935, finally reached Shensi.

The flight of the Reds westward and the enforced liquidation of the Kiangsi "Soviet Republic" was not merely a military defeat for the Reds. Indeed, by escaping through the cordon more or less intact, the Red Army prevented the realization of Chiang's most cherished objective—the physical extermination of the Red forces. The defeat was primarily a political one. It terminated the attempt to establish a revolutionary power based exclusively upon scattered sections of a revolting peasantry. The Reds were not only compelled to abandon the Kiangsi peasants to their fate. They also had to abandon the policies that had led to a hopeless blind alley. Much had been said and written about the imminent victory of the Soviet revolution of the whole of China as the necessary precondition for the waging of a national revolutionary war against Japan.[16] At the Second Soviet Congress held at Juichin in January 1934, "Soviet China" was "steadily growing and obtaining the preponderance" as a result of the "invincible, advancing Soviet revolution."[17] These were the wishful hopes that had to be abandoned along with the Kiangsi Soviet districts when the Red Army marched west.

Having failed to become an instrument in the hands of the working class, the Red Army and the Communist Party now began to move in the direction of the bourgeoisie. Capitulatory moods had already gripped much of the Party apparatus. In the cities, scores of young Communists, demoralized by the defeats in Kiangsi and seeing no new prospect before them, went over to the Kuomintang. Chiang Kai-shek's terror machine absorbed these renegades and used their betrayals to complete the dispersal and destruction of what remained of the Communist Party in the cities.* Their recantations and denunciations of Communism filled the daily press. As spies and police agents they caused the arrest of scores of their former comrades. Party members feared to appear in the streets where they could be spotted. Many fled to other cities. All party activity came to an absolute standstill. The apparatus, feeble at best, fell to pieces. During the final months in Kiangsi desertions occurred not only from the Red Army ranks but from the high command as well. Such veterans as Kung Ho-chung and Chang Yi went over to the enemy, declaring they saw no hope for the Kiangsi soviets.[18] The party assailed all these deserters as cowardly renegades, but it was soon to follow in their footsteps and be reunited with them in the camp of the Kuomintang, for in Moscow the Comintern was already erasing at a single stroke the meager balance of the Chinese soviet experiment.

While the Red Army was marching across West China toward a new turning-point in its own history, the Communist International was consummating at its Seventh World Congress in Moscow (July 1935), a shift in policy that was to mark its final abandonment of the struggle for proletarian revolution. The collapse of the German Communist Party and the victory of Hitler had completely upset international balances in Europe and removed from the scene the powerful organizations of the German proletariat, the most powerful potential revolutionary force in post-war Europe. Hitler reached out for an alliance with Japan and openly bargained with Britain and France for a free hand against the Soviet Union. The Soviet bureaucracy made a panicky turn. Britain and France, yesterday the chief organizers of the anti-Soviet bloc, became "peace-loving" democracies to be wooed and won as potential allies against German fascism. The Communist parties in all countries were converted more openly and unreservedly than ever before into blind instruments of Stalin's foreign policy. The Comintern announced that it struggled now not for the proletarian revolution but for bourgeois democracy. The Communist parties suspended all opposition to the capitalist governments in return for alliances with Moscow, as in France and Czechoslovakia, or became pressure bodies for the conclusion of such alliances, as in the United States and Great Britain.

---

* Among the renegades were some prominent figures, like Huang Ping, "foreign minister" of the short-lived Canton Commune. Wang Min somewhat belatedly discovered, in 1937, that the renegades of 1934 had all been—"Trotskyists." The use of that term as a handy label for all opponents of whatever hue had in the meanwhile been popularized by the purge in the Soviet Union. In his book, *Red Star Over China*, Edgar Snow lightly parroted calumnies to the effect that Trotskyists, because of the "logic of their position"—with which Snow displays no acquaintance whatever—went over to Chiang Kai-shek and betrayed comrades to the police. By the peculiar "logic" of his own position, Snow then goes on enthusiastically to embrace the Communist Party for going over to the same Chiang Kai-shek and betraying the workers and peasants to the bourgeoisie. A little more than a year after Snow gathered the material for the book he called *Red Star Over China*, Nym Wales, to whom he dedicated his volume, saw a Red soldier gingerly fingering his shiny new Kuomintang button. She wondered whether he was thinking of the "tattered old cloth Red Star that he wore from Kiangsi.... But the Red Star," she added, "is no longer visible on the once Soviet horizon" (*Asia*, January 1938).

China naturally occupied a key place in the calculations of the Soviet bureaucracy. The extent to which Japan encountered difficulties in China would in large measure determine the timing and efficacy of its inevitable attack on the Soviet Union. It consequently became one of the prime purposes of Soviet diplomacy to prevent the Kuomintang government from joining Japan in an anti-Soviet pact and, if possible, to swing it to an anti-Japanese position. The defeats in Kiangsi convinced the Moscow strategists that the Chinese Red Army was by itself quite inadequate for this purpose. Having long since abandoned all hope of a Chinese proletarian revolution, the Soviet bureaucracy turned once more to the Chinese bourgeoisie. In return for an alliance against Japan it decided to offer the services of the Red Army and the liquidation of the agrarian struggle.

Along this road the Seventh Congress of the Comintern took only the first step. It drew a line through the debit balance of "Soviet China" and set a new course for the Chinese Communist Party toward a new "national united front." In 1933 Wang Min had posited the "overthrow of the Kuomintang as the government of national betrayal and national disgrace as a condition of the successful carrying out of the national revolutionary war" and had declared that this could be realized "only (by) the Soviet government and the Red Army."[19] This perspective was now abandoned with scarcely a backward look. "The Communist Party," Wang announced at the Seventh Congress, "has no other means for the general mobilization of the entire Chinese nation for the sacred national revolutionary war against Japanese imperialism than the tactics of the anti-imperialist united people's front." This was to be sought by appeal "to all the people, all parties, groups, troops, mass organizations, and to all prominent political and social leaders, to organize together with us an All-China United People's Government of National Defense and an All-China United Anti-Japanese National Defense Army."[20]

This was to be, as events proved, a transitional formula directed toward the recreation of a bloc between the Communist Party and the Kuomintang. The civil war between the Kuomintang and the Red Army had been going on for seven years and was still in progress, the party needed time to reeducate its own forces to the new turn and to begin its courtship of the bourgeoisie. It was necessary to count on the possibility that Chiang Kai-shek and the Kuomintang had already leaned so far in the direction of the Japanese that the "national united front" would still have to be built against them. At the Seventh Congress Wang Min still recognized the "unexampled and infamous national treachery of the Kuomintang" and characterized Chiang Kai-shek as the "arch-traitor to the Chinese people."[21]

For nearly a year after the Seventh Congress, the Chinese Communist Party flirted with various dissident politicians and generals, in the southwest with Chen Chi-tang, Li Tsung-jen, and Pai Chung-hsi, in Nanking with Sun Fo and Feng Yuhsiang, in the northwest, with Chang Hsueh-liang. But none of them was strong enough to prevail over Chiang. Setting out to woo "all" parties, the Communists finally admitted that there was only one, the Kuomintang. Seeking blocs with "all" prominent leaders, they soon had to recognize that only one, Chiang Kai-shek, really counted. Early in 1936 Mao Tse-tung publicly offered "the hand of friendship" to Chiang if he would take up arms against Japan.[22] To the Kuomintang the Communist Party began, in a series of open letters, articles, and telegrams, to offer increasingly specific guarantees to persuade the bourgeoisie that it no longer threatened any essential bourgeois interests, but would instead serve them well.

At the Seventh Congress Wang Min had referred to the "national united front" of 1927 in the following words:

> We know from the history of the struggle of the Communist Party of China that when the opportunists in its leadership, headed by Chen Tu-hsiu, counterposed the tactics of the united national front to the task of the class struggle at the critical moment of the revolutionary movement in 1927, when for the sake of retaining a united national front with a part of the national bourgeoisie, these opportunists renounced the revolutionary struggle of the working class in defense of their vital interests, renounced the agrarian revolution of the peasantry...they brought the 1927 revolution to defeat.[23]

Scarcely a year later, Mao Tse-tung far outstripped the opportunism of Chen Tu-hsiu. He offered the Chinese bourgeoisie the same fatal renunciation of the revolutionary struggle and went one step further: he offered conscious and deliberate guarantees that should the forces of the revolution raise their heads once more, the Chinese Communist Party stood ready to play the role of executioner. Chen Tu-hsiu—guided by Stalin—had destroyed the second Chinese revolution by the bloc with the bourgeoisie. Mao Tse-tung—and Stalin—now sought to renew that bloc by offering in advance to strangle the third.

During the united front negotiations that went forward, the National Salvation Association, a petty bourgeois nationalist body, called upon the Communist Party for unambiguous guarantees of this nature.

> We hope [it wrote] that the Chinese Communist Party will show by concrete acts that it is sincere in its desire to unite with other parties.... In the districts occupied by the Red Army where there are wealthier peasants, the proprietors and merchants must receive liberal treatment. Every effort must be made to avoid conflicts between workers and employers in the big cities so as not to impede the expansion of the united front for the salvation of the country.
>
> ...The committees for national salvation and other mass organizations frequently include young people with unstable ideals who advocate at anti-Japanese meetings...such slogans as "class against class" and "struggle against the Kuomintang and the Kuomintang government," to the great prejudice of the united front.... It is our firm conviction that such action does not originate with the Communist Party.... We consider that the Communist Party ought to rectify the situation immediately. Moreover, detachments appear here and there which call themselves Communist partisans and take the law into their own hands. If these undisciplined detachments are under the control of the Communist Party, the lat-

ter must take stringent measures against them or otherwise declare at the earliest opportunity that it is in no way connected with these detachments.[24]

To each of these points Mao Tse-tung on August 10, 1936, gave an explicit reply. He announced that the "Workers' and Peasants' Government" had been renamed the "People's Soviet Government" and that the "Workers' and Peasants' Army" had become the "People's Red Army." He reported that all previous laws in the Soviet districts placing disabilities on the civil rights of the bourgeoisie had already been repealed and then went on:

> We have already adopted a decision not to confiscate the land of the rich peasants.... We are not confiscating the property and the factories of the big and small merchants and capitalists. We protect their enterprises.... As for the active anti-Japanese officers and big landowners, we can state that their estates and property are not subject to confiscation.
>
> As for the problem of mutual relations between capital and labor in the Soviet districts, we have set up minimum conditions for the improvement of the living standards of the workers. The workers and capitalists have made an agreement the terms of which are based on the actual situation in each enterprise, and are binding on both sides. The agreement does away with unnecessary strikes and sabotage. The former laws about workers' control and leadership in the various enterprises have been repealed. The workers have been advised not to put up demands which may be in excess of what can be granted.... In the non-Soviet districts it is our intention not to accentuate the anti-capitalist struggle,* though we are in favor of improving the standard of living of the workers.... The common interests of both capitalists and workers are grounded in the struggle against imperialist aggression.
>
> The circumstance that the partisans of Hupeh, Hunan, Kiangsi, Fukien, Chekiang, and other localities have up to now failed to abide by the laws which we have lately adopted is due to the fact that our instructions could not be transmitted to them because of various obstacles. Besides the repeated attempts to suppress the partisan movement in these districts, unfailingly accompanied by unspeakable atrocities, might possibly have resulted in the spirit of vengeance [!] gaining the upper hand here and there. However, we are of the opinion that this is a wrong attitude. We are very anxious to have these mistakes corrected at once.

Mao also promised to "correct" the impetuosity of the young men brazen enough to speak of "class against class," and added: "What we are most interested in and consider most important is that all parties and groups should treat us without animosity and bear in mind the objectives of the struggle against Japan for the salvation of the country. We shall hereafter consider of no importance any difference of opinion on other questions."[25]

And what if the workers, without asking the Communists' permission, "accentuated" the anti-capitalist struggle? What if the peasants, without asking leave,

* According to another translation this read: "We similarly do not wilfully intensify the anti-capitalist struggle." —*China Today*, January 1937.

proceeded on their own to seize the land? What, in short, if the masses, as in 1927, swept beyond all parties and all leaders toward the struggle in their own interest? Was it really so easy to forget that in 1927 the cry of "excesses" had been followed by the most brutal repression? At the Seventh World Congress Wang Min could still speak of the "defeat of the revolution" in 1927, but now that segment of history was to be rewritten too:

"We are prepared to form a strong revolutionary united front with you," wrote the Communist Party to the Kuomintang on August 25, 1936,

> as was the case during the...great Chinese Revolution of 1925–27, when there existed a broad united front for struggle against national and feudal oppression, for that is the only proper way to save our country today. You...have not yet forgotten *the glorious history of collaboration* between the Communist Party and the Kuomintang.... It was precisely thanks to this collaboration that all the national and feudal oppressors shook before us. At that time our national oppressors, and Japanese imperialism in particular, were very much afraid that our collaboration might lead to final victory and the complete emancipation of China. Therefore they sowed the seeds of strife between us and set in motion all possible means, threats, and temptations as a result of which one side gave up its collaboration and buried the united front. *Do you feel no pricks of conscience when you recall this today?*[26]

The conscience of Chiang Kai-shek was not pricked by the groveling of his vanquished adversaries. He had by no means forgotten the "glorious" results of his first bloc with the Comintern. It had brought him to power, striding over the prostrate body of the Chinese working class. It had not been a question then—any more than it was now—of conscience, but of political expediency. Chiang Kai-shek, the maker and breaker of a thousand unprincipled alliances, was not concerned with the hypocritical exhortations of a party he had used, smashed with unrestrained brutality, and could now use again if it suited his purpose. If he began to consider the advisability of accepting the capitulation offered to him, it was because a whole pattern of circumstances was forcing the Chinese bourgeoisie toward a decision to begin resisting, however belatedly, the further incursions of the Japanese imperialists.

For nearly two years the Chinese bourgeoisie had been breathing the invigorating air of an economic revival. Starting upward with a bumper crop in 1935, the economic curve rose steadily from the low point it reached in 1934. Proceeding in pace with the world-wide economic upturn, Chinese recovery was featured by new advances in trade, revenue, and production. Chinese currency, badly shaken by the heavy silver drain accentuated in 1934 by Washington's silver purchasing policies, was devaluated in November 1935, and pegged to the pound sterling. Silver stocks were nationalized and subsequently exported for the purchase of foreign exchange. This operation was carried out under the direct supervision of the British Treasury, represented in China by Sir Frederick Leith-Ross. Industry received a new fillip. Chinese banks during 1936 invested $109,000,000 (Chinese currency) in manufacturing enterprises. China's foreign credit position perceptibly improved and negotiations were begun toward the end of 1936 for the £30,000,000 British loan successfully concluded in London the following June. H. H. Kung, the finance minister who went to Europe to close the deal, also arranged substantial credits in other European capitals and a highly favorable gold exchange agreement in Washington. Railway and industrial projects long in the limbo seemed about to be realized.

Economic revival was accompanied by greater political stabilization. Chiang Kai-shek had succeeded in carrying out most of his plans for the military unification of the country. The defeat inflicted upon the Reds in Kiangsi had removed the only important revolutionary threat from his immediate domain. The pursuit of the Reds westward gave Chiang an opportunity to extend his sway for the first time over the provinces of Kweichow, Yunnan, and Szechwan. In 1935 Chiang made a demonstrative air tour to the western provinces, to Shansi, and even to Inner Mongolia. Everywhere he was received as lord of all he surveyed. The last important stronghold of regional authority, the southwest, he conquered almost bloodlessly in July 1936, when his troops marched once more through Canton on the tenth anniversary of his departure from that city for the march northward toward power along the Yangtze.

These improvements in its political and economic position stimulated new and exhilarating moods in the Chinese bourgeoisie. It clearly saw its feeble economic base threatened by the insistent Japanese demand for "Sino-Japanese co-operation." The gradual Japanese conquest of the Chinese cotton industry, continuing in the midst of the revival, was an eloquent foretaste of what that "cooperation" really meant. In Japan's other principal demand for "cooperation against Communism" it was not difficult to see a euphemism for Japan's right to garrison China. Chiang Kai-shek rightly saw in it a threat to his own power. With more firmness than he had yet dared display, Chiang Kai-shek informed the Japanese ambassador in September 1936, that these terms were wholly unacceptable.

Chiang did not yet count upon actually fighting Japan. He calculated rather upon using his strengthened position to force a modification of Japan's demands. To insure the complete consolidation of his power, he still considered it necessary to deal a final blow to the Reds, in whose capitulation he did not yet fully believe. He made this plain in October, when at Sian Chang Hsueh-liang proposed cessation of the civil war, alliance with the Soviet Union, and immediate resistance to Japan. "I will never talk about this until every Red soldier in China is exterminated, and every Communist is in prison," Chiang is supposed to have replied. "Only then would it be possible to cooperate with Russia."[27]

That month a Japanese-controlled army of Manchukuo troops and Inner Mongolian irregulars made a tentative stab across the Suiyuan border. Chiang offered little more than moral encouragement to the provincial forces which successfully resisted the attempted invasion. Several of his divisions were moved into

Suiyuan, but only to make sure that the conflict would be kept within local bounds and that no attempt would be made to advance into Chahar. While the Suiyuan victory had an electrifying effect on the growing anti-Japanese movement among important sections of the bourgeoisie, Chiang was still more concerned with pressing his campaign against the Reds in Shensi. He arrested seven prominent leaders of the National Salvation Association in Shanghai and forcibly broke up new anti-Japanese student demonstrations that began to occur. He was not yet disposed to accept the submission of the Communists and preferred to complete his conquest of them by military means.

When Chang Hsueh-liang's troops balked at breaking their virtual truce with the Reds on the Shensi border, Chiang moved his own First Army into action. When it met defeat at the hands of the Reds in Kansu, Chiang flew to Sian in December determined to force the rebellious northeastern army to obey his orders or to force its withdrawal southward and to replace it by his own forces. These calculations were spectacularly upset when the officers and men of the Sian garrison rose in revolt on the night of December 11 and made Chiang their prisoner, along with most of his closest stall advisers.

Chiang, captured cowering on a hillside in his nightshirt, not only lost "face" immeasurably, he also stood in mortal danger of losing his life. Through the ranks of the Manchurian army rumbled the demand that he be given a "people's trial" for all his crimes. The life of the Kuomintang dictator would not have been worth a copper had the soldiers had their way. At Nanking Chiang's subordinate generals and hangers-on who still favored meeting Japan's terms, were hopefully sure he would never emerge alive. To make sure, they began moving troops toward the Shensi border for a "punitive campaign" against the rebels and ordered planes up for threatening demonstrations over Sian. There Chang Hsueh-liang was urging Chiang to adopt a bold anti-Japanese program. He warned that he could not guarantee control of his younger officers and ranks if Chiang refused to meet their growing demand for cessation of the civil war and a campaign against the conquerors of the Manchurian homeland. The ex-ruler of Manchuria could not have saved Chiang's life by himself. The Communists could and did step in and exert all their "great influence with the Tungpei (the Manchurian army) to preserve Chiang and send him back as national leader to Nanking."[28]

One of the most dramatic and certainly, judging from the sequel, one of the most important incidents of Chiang's enforced stay at the Shensi capital was his meeting with Chow En-lai, who headed the Communist delegation in Sian. The principal actors in what must have been a memorable scene have not yet described it themselves. Chiang in his subsequently published diary did not even mention it.[29] According to another account, however, the generalissimo paled when Chow entered his room. He seemed to think he was about to be surrendered into the hands of the Reds. Chow En-lai, he must have remembered, had been vice-commander of the Shanghai pickets shot and cut down by Chiang's orders that bloody April morning ten years before. It was difficult, even for Chiang Kai-shek, to believe that men he had so ruthlessly betrayed and hounded were genuinely offering to place themselves once more at his disposal. Chow, the account proceeds, came in "with a friendly greeting" and saluting Chiang, "acknowledged him as Commander-in-Chief." He began to explain the Communist Party's new policies. "At first frigidly silent, Chiang gradually thawed as he listened." Other meetings followed. "He became more convinced, not only of the sincerity of his immediate captors, but also of the Reds, in their opposition to civil war and their readiness to assist in the peaceful unification of the country, under his own leadership, provided he defined a policy of positive armed resistance to Japan."[30] What Chiang was finally made to understand at Sian was that the Communists were offering him their unqualified capitulation if he would only adopt a policy upon which he was already half-determined. He realized it was foolish of him to insist upon smashing the Communists by military means when they were fully prepared once more to serve his political ends.* Chiang agreed in substance to the proposals laid before him. He was released on Christmas Day and flown back to Nanking. Six weeks later, after a series of devious and wholly successful face-saving maneuvers, Chiang convened a plenary session of the Kuomintang's Central Executive Committee. To the plenum the Communist Party wired its offers: "To cease armed struggle for the overthrow of the Kuomintang government; to rename the Soviet government the Administration of the Special Area of the Chinese Republic; to call the Red Army the national revolutionary army which

* "It does appear to be more and more generally realized that the Communists of China are not now Communists in any remaining essential," said the American *Shanghai Evening Post* on December 29, 1936. "What is there about this so-called Communist program of the present day which warrants refusal to make peace with a group no longer committed to anything fundamentally Communistic?"

The arch-imperialist British *North China Daily News,* fulminator-in-chief against the Kuomintang-Communist bloc of a decade earlier and the most rabid supporter of Chiang Kai-shek's war on the Reds, also now dulcetly sang the new tune: "It will do well to ascertain," it said on December 28, "how correct is General Chang Hsueh-liang's contention that the so-called Communists are ready to come to terms."

The Sian coup was also the occasion for a striking example of the "flexibility" of the foreign Communist press. On the day Chiang was made prisoner, the New York *Daily Worker* blared forth that Chang Hsueh-liang had raised "the rallying cry of a China united." Harry Cannes wrote that the demands made by the Sian rebels had been "originally proposed by the Communist Party of China." —*Daily Worker,* December 13, 1936. Next day the cables reported that the Moscow Press was denouncing Chang Hsueh-liang as a tool of Japan and was "actually helping Japan to further the sacrifice of his country." The whole plot, said *Izvestia* and *Pravda,* had been fabricated in Tokyo. —Associated Press, December 14, 1936, *New York Times,* December 15, 1936. Next day the *Daily Worker* made a 180-degree turn. Gannes discovered that "the gun was primed in Tokyo," and declared that the first reports, "deliberately filled with anti-Japanese demagogy, were entirely misleading." —*Daily Worker,* December 16, 1936. It was all to prove that Moscow loved Chiang and Chiang alone.

will be subordinated to the Nanking government and the military affairs commission; to introduce a democratic administration in the special area; to discontinue confiscation of land belonging to landlords, and to fulfil the common program of the united anti-Japanese national front."[31]

The Kuomintang plenary session blandly announced that the government would continue, as before, to safeguard the nation's sovereignty, and was determined, as before, to "uproot the Communists." It then laid down its formal terms for accepting the Communists' submission: (1) Abolition of the Red Army and its incorporation into the government armies under the direct control of the Military Affairs Commission. (2) Dissolution of the "Soviet Republic." (3) Cessation of all Communist propaganda. (4) Suspension of the class struggle.[32]

To these terms the Communist Party formally acceded on March 15, protesting that it had already carried out the most important of them and had "proclaimed on its own initiative the cessation of confiscating the land of the landlords" as proof that "the Communist Party is not promoting class struggle."[33] The Red Army was subsequently assigned to a "garrison area" in North Shensi and began receiving a regular subsidy from Nanking. A Communist youth congress held at Yenan, Shensi, in April, elected Chiang Kai-shek and other Nanking generals to its presidium along with Chu Teh and Mao Tse-tung.[34]

"Fushih is the center of activities of the Chinese Communist Party," wrote a visitor to North Shensi. "But here there is no suppression of landlords, no division of land. Not a sheet of Communist propaganda can be found. On the street walls the only posters to be seen are those with slogans calling for war against the aggressor, for national salvation, and for internal unification through peaceful means. The slogan 'Let us support General Chiang to lead in the anti-Japanese war' is the most popular of all and is found everywhere."[35]

What did the Red Army fighters think of these sweeping changes? How did the peasants like the new policies? How easily could the Chinese Communist Party impose the "new line" upon them? Only the future will finally answer these questions. The Red Army in Shensi in 1937 was, in any case, no longer the army that had fought so long and so hard for the land and against the Kuomintang. The army that was placed at the disposal of Chiang Kai-shek numbered about 90,000. Of these fewer than a third were survivors of the long march from Kiangsi. "Of the ninety thousand regular troops here," Chu Teh told one foreign visitor, "only twenty to thirty thousand come from the original Kiangsi district. About thirty thousand were recruited on the way, chiefly in Szechwan, and the rest are from local areas."[36] Another visitor to Shensi in the summer of 1936 caught a few glimpses of the suspicions aroused among these soldiers by the new and unfamiliar commands they had begun to receive. "We must intensify our educational work among our own troops," Peng Teh-huai told him. "In several recent instances, our men have violated the united front by firing on troops that we had agreed to permit to withdraw. In other instances men were reluctant to return captured rifles and had to be ordered several times to do so. This is not a breach of discipline, but a lack of confidence in their commanders' orders, showing that the men do not fully understand the reasons for such actions, some men actually accusing their leaders of 'counter-revolutionary orders.' "[37]

Another journalist some months later asked a Soviet functionary what the people thought. "The people all like the Soviet better," he replied.

> It was simple and easy for them. The landlords will perhaps like the new democracy better, but there are few landlords left here to enjoy it. We find some difficulty in letting the landlord have the right to vote. The people don't understand why it is necessary and the farmers are afraid their land might be distributed back to the landlords.... In general, however, the people give up the Soviet easily. They trust the leadership of the Communist Party to do what is right for them. Yet, they don't see the necessity for such a complex change, and some don't see how it benefited themselves.[38]

These were brief flashes of the doubts and differences that will inevitably grow into future conflicts when the masses "give up" less "easily" and reach out once more to struggle for aims that "benefit themselves." But now these considerations were momentarily obscured by the swift turn of events. In July 1937, Japanese imperialism struck again at North China. Chiang waveringly made a final effort to reach a "local" settlement and on July 11 approved the withdrawal of Chinese forces from the Peiping-Tientsin area. The soldiers of the Twenty-Ninth Army ignored the accord and continued fighting. Japan's drive into the northern provinces went on and in August the Japanese Navy struck once more in full force at Shanghai where Chiang was this time compelled at last to take up arms. A few weeks later the final formal steps establishing the new Kuomintang-Communist bloc were taken. On September 10 the incorporation of the Red Army into the Kuomintang forces as the "Eighth Route Army" was announced at Nanking. On September 22 the Communist Party issued a proclamation at Fushih, Shensi, formally dissolving the "Soviet Republic." Next day Chiang wired them his congratulations. It was almost exactly the tenth anniversary of the day on which Chiang had wired "congratulations" to the Left Kuomintang at Wuhan for its departure from the "national united front" with the Communists and its capitulation to Chiang's government at Nanking. A new "national united front" now took shape at a time when the workers and peasants of China, under the direct impact of a barbarous imperialist onslaught, more than ever needed a party, a banner, and a program of their own with which to lead the struggle against the invader and for their own liberation from the exploiters' yoke.

By coming back into the Kuomintang fold, the Communist Party completed a historical cycle that had been, in all its stages, uniformly disastrous for the cause of Chinese national liberation. The party that had styled itself the "vanguard of the proletariat" had never actually based itself upon the proletariat as the main lever of national revolutionary struggle. In 1925–27 it had subordinated itself and the mass movement it led to the bourgeoisie. The result was the victory of the bourgeois counterrevolution on the basis of a compromise with imperialism which served only to open the road to renewed imperialist invasion. The demoralized party careened after 1927 into the adventures that transformed it into the spearhead of a localized peasant revolt. The defeat and liquidation of the peasant soviets in Kiangsi cut it adrift once more. It rested now exclusively upon a mobile force of peasant warriors most of whom did not have, as Wang Min admitted, "the remotest concept of the working-class movement in the big cities."[39] Having failed to convert that force into an instrument of the proletariat, the Communist Party had now led it back into the camp of the bourgeoisie. When the Comintern failed after the defeat of 1927 to draw the balance of its experiences, it had, Trotsky said, "opened wide the gates for new experiments in the spirit of the Kuomintang course." There would still be, he wrote in 1928, "not a few leftward zigzags in the policy of the Chinese bourgeoisie. There will be no lack of temptations in the future for amateurs of the 'national united front.'"[40] Never having balanced itself on the pivot of a firm proletarian revolutionary policy, the Communist Party toppled back after ten years into the arms of the national bourgeoisie.

The "national united front" was recreated in 1937 on a new historical plane. In 1927 the Communist Party stood at the head of a mighty mass movement. In 1937 it stood at the head of a peasant army of 100,000 men, isolated from the great masses of the people. In 1927 the Communists believed the working class would win "hegemony" in the bloc with the bourgeoisie and would lead the national liberation movement to victory. In 1937 the Communists formed a bloc based upon the Kuomintang's absorption of the Red Army and the conduct of an anti-Japanese struggle which would serve the immediate interests of the Soviet bureaucracy. It was no longer a question of national liberation, for the new bloc, and its Communist supporters in other countries, openly appealed to the British and American imperialists to intervene and to guarantee their own mastery against the Japanese threat to their imperialist interests. The Comintern bothered no longer to weave devious and cunningly over-worded resolutions about the "hegemony of the proletariat," for the proletariat no longer entered into its calculations. In 1927 the Comintern recognized in word, if not in deed, the paramount role of the agrarian revolution in the national struggle. In 1937 to return to their alliance with the bourgeoisie the Communists openly renounced their radical agrarian program and abandoned the land struggle they had led for seven years. They went one step further and promised in advance to "correct "—i.e. to check and suppress—any such movement independently undertaken by the peasantry.

In 1927 the Communists surrendered leadership of the anti-imperialist struggle to the bourgeoisie, with the result that the latter crushed the masses and compromised with the imperialists. The fiction that the interests of all classes coalesced in the fight against imperialism was harshly exploded when the bourgeoisie demonstrated that its interests lay with the imperialists against the masses. That essential fact is as true today as it was then. It constitutes the primary criterion for measuring and understanding the events of 1937–38 and the prospects for the immediate future.

Dissatisfied with the results of the partial surrenders extracted from the Kuomintang regime by diplomatic, economic, and only occasional military pressure, Japan embarked in July 1937, on a large-scale invasion with the object of imposing its domination over the whole of China by force of arms. Faced with the necessity for making a fateful decision, Chiang Kai-shek wavered. A local settlement of the "Lukouchiao incident"—the clash south of Peiping that precipitated hostilities on July 7—was approved by the Nanking government. No Central Government forces were moved to the support of the local troops when the continuing Japanese drive showed that the invaders were determined to take over all of North China. When it became evident, however, that this time the Japanese would accept no temporary accord, and when after the fall of Peiping and Tientsin the Japanese Army and Navy once more invaded Shanghai, the die had finally to be cast. After crawling for six years under the Japanese lash, the Kuomintang was finally compelled to offer resistance because Japanese aggression now threatened to extinguish the Chinese bourgeoisie altogether.

During the opening months of the conflict the Kuomintang carefully left every possible door open to compromise. It avoided taking any irrevocable steps. It abrogated none of its treaties with Japan. It repudiated none of its previous compromise agreements. It desisted from confiscating Japanese property. At the height of the Shanghai battle it even paid over to Japan its regular due instalment of the Boxer Indemnity! It repeatedly announced its readiness to accept the mediation of "friendly" Powers for the termination of the conflict.

But having mounted the tiger, Chiang Kai-shek could not so easily get off. The more extended became the sphere of Japanese operations the dimmer became the prospects of any immediate compromise which offered "reasonable" security to the Chinese bourgeoisie or adequate recompense to the Japanese imperialists. Shanghai, chief center of Chinese-owned industry, was reduced to ruins. What was not destroyed in the battle, the Japanese systematically razed afterward. Within a year the invading armies held all the main centers of the north, almost all of the coastal provinces, all but a few of the principal seaports, and all but two of the principal railways. The Kuomintang confined itself to pitting huge masses of ill-equipped soldiery against the attackers. At Shanghai the flesh and spirit of the Chinese soldiers had to give way in the end to the steel of the invaders after three months of ghastly sacrifices, of incredible courage and doggedness in the face of overwhelming odds. The commanding staff, so efficient in its years of warfare against the people was riddled with corruption, sabotage, and outright treason. With the retreat from Shanghai in November it collapsed altogether, and the retreat turned into a rout across the Yangtze Delta. Nanking was precipitately abandoned while the enemy was still 115 miles away. Chiang Kai-shek fled inland and soon after him went Tang Sheng-chih, hero of the Hunan massacres, who had been left behind to command a futile, last-minute defense. Nanking fell on December 13 amid fearful slaughter.

In the north the Japanese had encountered little resistance from the scattered forces left in their path. They met serious obstacles only in Shansi province where the former Reds, now the Eighth Route Army, gave them a taste of the mobile tactics of which the Red commanders were so completely the masters. Within rigid limits fixed by the central authorities, the Reds succeeded by their guerrilla tactics in harassing Japanese communications across wide areas. Handicapped by shortage of supplies,[41] and even more critically limited by the Kuomintang's strict ban on political mobilization of the masses,[42] the Eighth Route Army guerrillas were able to achieve only a fraction of the results of which they were and still are capable.

On the Central China front, after the Shanghai-Nanking debacle, reorganized forces, most of them newly conscripted provincials from Szechwan and Kwangsi, made a fresh stand around Hsuchow, strategic junction of the Lunghai and Tientsin-Pukow railways. There they punctured forever the myth of Japanese invincibility, inflicting heavy losses and a number of severe defeats upon some of Japan's best divisions. It was not until five months after the fall of Nanking that the Japanese forces, swelled to more than a quarter of a million men, finally conquered the Lunghai railway. Rising waters of the Yellow and Yangtze rivers, flooding through broken dikes, checked their advance at frightful cost to the peasant population, and slowed down their attempt to drive on to Hankow, the provisional Kuomintang capital, from which the government was already beginning to flee. Simultaneously new drives were begun in the south where at Canton, Swatow, and other cities, Japanese bombers, unchallenged, dealt out death to huddled thousands of doomed civilians.

Throughout the first year of the war, the Chinese bourgeoisie dared only to conduct a purely military defensive struggle. It succeeded in making the invasion a costly adventure for Japan, but it also showed that such methods cannot effectively withstand the imperialist attack and will not, certainly, serve the interests of Chinese national liberation. Still fearing the masses more than the imperialists, the bourgeoisie has looked to the United States and Great Britain for aid. These powers, as yet not quite prepared for the eventual showdown in the Pacific, have extended moral and material support to the Kuomintang in cautious doles, while keeping the diplomatic record against Japan clear. Their pressure against Japan, especially that of the United States, is certain to increase in the coming period of struggle for Pacific supremacy. The basis for it, in sharpening notes of protest, in sedulously prepared campaigns of propaganda, and above all in mounting billions of expenditure on a mighty war fleet on the sea and in the air, is already being laid. The Soviet Union, paralyzed by a profound internal crisis, has been able to extend only a thin trickle of aid. Its fate, too, is bound up not only with the outcome of the struggle now raging in China, but with that which is destined to blaze up along still vaster battlefronts.

Meanwhile so long as Chinese leadership remains in the hands of the bourgeoisie, the present war will end at best either in a compromise with Japan or the complete subjection of China to the United States and Great Britain in return for their intervention against their rival. Neither eventuality will free China. Neither will liberate the masses who are bearing the chief burdens of the conflict of which they are also the principal victims. The war against Japanese imperialism will be forced to a victorious and liberating conclusion only when it is clearly linked in the minds of the masses with their own struggle in their own behalf. Only in this way will the technical deficiencies that flow from the backwardness of the country be overcome.

The mobilization of China's vast manpower will be made possible only if the masses are galvanized by bold social measures that will prevent the merchants, bankers, and landlords from passing the costs of the war onto the backs of the exploited. A still bolder revolutionary program that will identify for the peasantry the aims of national liberation from imperialist aggression, and their own liberation from thraldom on the land, will bring forward reserves of strength against which the Japanese invaders will never be able to prevail. Partisan warfare waged by such forces can and will make China as unconquerable as Siberia was when it was overrun by the invading troops of the interventionist powers twenty years ago. But such a war cannot be made to order. In the years when it was a revolutionary peasant force, the Chinese Red Army was able to withstand the infinitely better-armed and more numerous forces sent against it precisely because it had unlocked the simple secret of successful partisan warfare. "Because the masses are interested only in the practical solution of their problems of livelihood," Peng Teh-huai had once said, "it is possible to develop partisan warfare only by the *immediate satisfaction of their most urgent demands.* This means that the exploiting class must be promptly disarmed and immobilized."[43]

In other words, the fight could be carried forward against Japan by rousing the masses to the realization, in word and in action, that this fight was identical with the struggle for the land, by intensifying, not suspending the class struggle. By its capitulation to the Kuomintang, the Red Army abdicated this struggle. In return for a bloc with the bourgeoisie it surrendered its leadership of the peasants and foreswore the mobilization of the working class that it had already long since abandoned. The bourgeoisie, for its part, was no more willing now than it was in 1927 to abdicate its fundamental economic interests. It was just as determined now, as then, to keep the workers and peasants yoked to its wheel, to make them bear the cost of the military struggle which the bourgeoisie felt itself compelled to wage, and to prevent them from rising to struggle in their own interest.

The workers, who had begun under the stimulus of the 1935–36 recovery to reassemble their forces and to conduct bold and militant strikes, were thrust back by the outbreak of the war, which caused such terrific destruction in the chief industrial centers and naturally checked the economic upturn which had begun to revive the labor movement. To insure itself against any attempt by the workers to reject the new loads now laid upon them, the Kuomintang government issued in December 1937, a decree fixing the death penalty for workers who went on strike or even agitated for strikes while the war was in progress.[44] A few days later Wang Min told an interviewer at Hankow that the Communist Party was "fully satisfied" with the Kuomintang's conduct of the war.[45] The further course of that war will be determined by many factors, near and remote from present-day battlefields, but the cause of Chinese national liberation will be served in the coming period only to the degree that the masses cease being as "fully satisfied" as the Communist Party with the continuing domination of the bourgeois exploiters. This will, in turn, depend upon the emergence of a new revolutionary party capable of marshalling the workers and peasants in their own organizations and of embarking with them on the path of revolutionary struggle. Such a party will have to know how to join in the present war side by side with Chiang Kai-shek of the "devil himself," but it will also have to be ready to continue the fight when the Chiang Kai-sheks abandon it, and to carry on the struggle against all who seek to bar the way to the victory of the workers and peasants in the Chinese Revolution of tomorrow.

In any case Japan's temporary superiority in armaments, its transient victories, the apparently broad sweep of its conquests, cannot and will not insure its final triumph. The shadow of ultimate defeat falls across every dearly won "victory" on Chinese battlefields. The fatally frail economic structure of Japan cannot withstand the pressure the war places upon it. Faced always with the threat of a social crisis at home, Japanese imperialism will, moreover, before long, have to face its incomparably stronger rivals when the next world war begins and a new attempt is made by the imperialist Powers to prolong their existence by re-dividing the world's spoils. The warmakers will begin that struggle. The exploited and victimized masses, in China and in Japan and throughout the world, will decide how it is to end. In this respect the present conflict in China can be viewed only as an episode, an opening episode, along with the invasion of Ethiopia and the civil war in Spain, of the greater conflicts that impend.

Notes

1. Seeds of Revolt

1. Karl Wittfogel, *Wirtschaft und Gesellschaft Chinas,* Leipzig, 1931, is still reputed the most scholarly discussion of this subject. Some Russian studies exist, but most of the facts needed for a thorough analysis apparently have yet to be dug out of Chinese records. Chao Ting-chi, *Key Economic Areas in Chinese History,* New York, 1936, is a recent contribution to one aspect of the problem.
2. C. F. Remer, *The Foreign Trade of China,* Shanghai, 1926, p. 26. For tables on the opium trade see Joshua Rowntree, *The Imperial Drug Trade,* London, 1908, p. 344; H. B. Morse, *International Relations of the Chinese Empire,* London, 1910–18, v. I, pp. 209–10.
3. Cf. Wen-tsao, Wu, *The Chinese Opium Question in British Opinion and Action,* New York, 1928, pp. 59–60.
4. "To the Chinese they (opium and Christianity) came together, have been fought for together, and were finally legalized together." —Rowntree, *Imperial Drug Trade,* p. 242.
5. The population rose, according to one estimate, by 237,000,000 or about 190 percent, between 1712 and 1822. —S. Wells Williams, *The Middle Kingdom,* New York, 1882, v. I, p. 283. Another estimate for 1741–1851 showed a rise from 143,000,000 to 432,000,000, or about 200 percent. —E. H. Parker, *China, Her History, Diplomacy, and Commerce,* London, 1901, p. 190. Dynastic records for 1661–1833 indicated an increase of cultivable land of only about 35 percent from 549,357,000 mow to 742,000,000 mow. —Chen Shao-kwan, *System of Taxation in the Ch'ing Dynasty,* New York, 1914, p. 51.
6. "Memorial of Lin Tse-hsu to the Emperor," 1838, tr. by P. C. Kuo, *A Critical Study of the First Anglo-Chinese War,* Shanghai, 1935, pp. 82–84.
7. Prices rose 200 percent from 1830 to 1848 and 470 percent between 1849 and 1851, according to one Russian study. —*Problemi Kitai,* Moscow, No. 1, 1929.
8. H. D. Fong, "Cotton Industry and Trade in China," *Chinese Social and Political Science Review,* Peiping, October, 1932. Table 33.
9. H. B. Morse claims that $500,000,000 in silver was brought to China prior to 1830. —"The Foreign Trade of China," *China and the Far East,* G. H. Blakeslee, ed., New York, 1910, p. 97.
10. G. E. Taylor, "The Taiping Rebellion," *Chinese Social and Political Science Review,* Peiping, January, 1933, p. 558.
11. W. C. Hunter, *The Fan Kwae at Canton before Treaty Days,* 1825–44, London, 1882, p. 48.
12. Taylor, "Taiping Rebellion," pp. 555–56.
13. T. T. Meadows, *The Chinese and Their Rebellions,* London, 1856, p. 33.
14. J. S. Hill, *The Indo-Chinese Opium Trade,* London, 1884, p. 51.

15. Taylor, "Taiping Rebellion," pp. 597–99.
16. K. Latourette, *The Chinese, their History and Culture,* New York, 1934, v. I, p. 379.
17. It is of interest to note that foreign firms engaged in handling commodities other than opium continued to favor the Taipings against the Manchus. They were not yet dominant enough, however, to determine the ultimate policies of the powers. Cf. A. Lindley (Lin-li), *Ti Ping Tien Kwoh,* London, 1866.
18. J. K. Fairbank, "The Provisional System at Shanghai in 1853-4," *Chinese Social and Political Science Review,* Peiping, October 1934 and April 1935, gives an account, based on self-justifying British official records, of how this control was assumed.
19. Taylor, "Taiping Rebellion," p. 612.
20. H. D. Fong, *China's Industrialization, a Statistical Survey,* Shanghai, 1933, p. 2.
21. Fong, "Cotton Industry," Tables 26, 30, 34.
22. For useful documents of this period see M. E. Cameron, *The Reform Movement in China,* 1898–1912, Stanford University, 1931.
23. For brief summary see Latourette, *The Chinese,* v. I, p. 404 ff.
24. Cf. R. Wilhelm, *The Soul of China,* New York, 1928, p. 26.
25. A Peking dispatch to the London *Times* of November 10, 1906, referred, for example, to "the events in Russia and the alarmist telegrams of the Chinese minister in St. Petersburg."
26. For accounts of these boycotts see C. F. Remer, *A Study of Chinese Boycotts,* Baltimore, 1933, Chaps. IV and V.
27. For a picture of these societies at work, see the early chapters of S. Tretiakov, *A Chinese Testament,* New York, 1934.
28. In Shantung, property and literacy qualifications allowed votes only to 119,549 persons out of a population of about 38,000,000. In Hupeh, 113,233 out of 34,000,000 voted. —See *North China Herald,* February 18, 1910.
29. Fong, *China's Industrialization,* Tables 1a and 1b.
30. C. H. Lowe, *Facing Labour Issues in China,* Shanghai, 1933, Tables 6, 7, 8, 10.
31. Fong, *China's Industrialization,* Tables 1 a and 1 b.

2. Problems of the Chinese Revolution

1. Chen Han-seng, *The Present Agrarian Problem in China,* Shanghai, 1933. Useful, although less competently marshalled, facts will be found in J. Lossing Buck, *Chinese Farm Economy,* Shanghai, 1930. Lists of pertinent monographs and various specialized studies will be found in the footnotes to R. H. Tawney, *Land and Labour in China,* New York, 1932.
2. "Report of the Land Committee of the Kuomintang," *Chinese Correspondence,* Hankow, May 8, 1927.
3. Chen, *Present Agrarian Problem,* pp. 2–5.
4. Chen Han-seng, *Agrarian Problems in Southernmost China,* Shanghai, 1936.
5. Cf. Annexes 6 and 7, *Annexes to the Report to the Council of the League of Nations,* Nanking, April, 1934 ; also briefer summary and bibliographical notes in Tawney, *Land and Labour,* pp. 50–54.
6. Wong Yin-seng, *Requisitions and the Peasantry in North China,* Shanghai, 1931 ; Chen, *Present Agrarian Problem,* pp. 15–18; Chen, *Agrarian Problems in Southernmost China,* Chap. V; "Kuomintang vs. Peasants," in H. R. Isaacs (ed.), *Five Years of Kuomintang Reaction,* Shanghai, 1932.
7. Cf. *Chinese Maritime Customs, Annual Report for 1932,* p. 48 ff.; Chen Han-seng, "Economic

Disintegration of China," *Pacific Affairs*, April-May, 1933; C. H. Lowe, *Facing Labour Issues in China,* Table I; Dr. Friedrich Otto, "Harvests and Imports of Cereals," *Chinese Economic Journal,* October, 1934; Louis Beale and G. Clinton Pelham, *Trade and Economic Conditions in China,* 1931–33, Department of Overseas Trade, London, 1933, p. 7 and 149 ff. Food imports were 5 percent of the total in 1918 and 20 percent in 1932. In the latter year it took 43 percent of the total exports to pay for the imported food alone.

8. H. D. Fong, *Cotton Trade and Industry in China,* Table 2b; C. F. Remer, *Foreign Investments in China,* New York, 1933, pp. 69, 86–91, 135; *China Year Book,* 1926, p. 822; Fang Fu-an, "Communications, the Extent of Foreign Control," *The Chinese Nation,* Shanghai, September 10, 1930; L. K. Tao and S. H. Lin, *Industry and Labour in China,* Peiping, 1932, pp. 12, 16–17.
9. Chen, *Present Agrarian Problem,* p. 18.
10. "First Address of the Central Committee of the Communist League to its Members in Germany," in Engels, *Germany: Revolution and Counter-Revolution,* Appendix III, p. 135 ff.
11. Karl Marx and Friedrich Engels, *Correspondence,* 1846–1895, London, 1934 p. 87.
12. For Lenin's 1917 estimate of his 1905 slogan, see V. I. Lenin, *Works* (Eng. ed.), v. XX, p. 118 ff.; for an exposition of these ideas and the polemics that later raged around them, see L. Trotsky, *The Permanent Revolution,* New York, 1931, and *History of the Russian Revolution,* New York, 1932, v. III, Appendix Three.
13. Lenin, *Works* (Russ. ed.), v. VI, p. 30.
14. *Ibid.* (Eng. ed.), v. XX, pp. 33–34.
15. *Ibid.,* v. XX, p. 120.
16. "Theses on the National and Colonial Question," *Theses and Statutes of the Third (Communist) International* (adopted by the Second Congress, July 17–August 7, 1920), Moscow, 1920, p. 70; cf. Lenin, "Preliminary Draft of Some Theses on the National and Colonial Questions," *Communist International,* June–July, 1920.
17. "Theses on the National and Colonial Question," p. 69.
18. *Protokoll des II Weltkongresses der Kommunistischen Internationale,* Hamburg, 1921, pp. 140–42.
19. "Theses on the National and Colonial Question," p. 70.
20. "Supplementary Theses," *Theses and Statutes,* pp. 72–75 ; cf. "Theses on the Eastern Question," *Resolutions and Theses of the Fourth Congress of the Communist International,* November 7–December 3, 1922, London, undated, p. 53 ff.; cf. Safarov, "Report on the National-Colonial Question and the Communist Attitude Thereto," *Proceedings of the First Congress of the Toilers of the Far East,* January 21-February 1, 1922, Petrograd, 1922, p. 166 ff.
21. Trotsky, *History of the Russian Revolution,* v. I, pp. 32 and 53.
22. Lowe Chun-hwa, *Facing Labour Issues in China,* pp. 154–55; for a summary of studies made of the industrial population, see Fang Fu-an, *Chinese Labour,* Shanghai, 1931, Chap. II.
23. "Minutes of the March, 1917, Party Conference," appendix to Trotsky, *Stalin School of Falsification,* New York, 1937, p. 239.
24. Lenin, *Works* (Eng. ed.), p. 207.
25. *Ibid.,* p. 98.
26. *Ibid.,* p. 120.

3. The New Awakening

1. Tsi C. Wang, *The Youth Movement in China,* New York, 1928, p. 100. Wang also quotes portions of Chen's article from *New Youth,* v. I, No. 1, 1915. This book is valuable for its survey of the

Chinese Renaissance and its documented survey of the postwar student movement.

2. Cf. Wong (Wang) Ching-wei, *China and the Nations,* New York, 1927, pp. 91–98.
3. M. T. Z. Tyau, *China Awakened,* New York, 1922, pp. 237, 240.
4. For approximate estimates of the Chinese industrial population, see Fang Fu-an, *Chinese Labour*, Chap. II.
5. Shu-chin Tsui, "The Influence of the Canton-Moscow Entente upon Sun Yat-sen's Political Philosophy," *The Chinese Social and Political Science Review,* Peiping, April-October, 1934, p. 113.
6. Sun Yat-sen, *The International Development of China,* New York, 1922, p. xi ; *Memoirs of a Chinese Revolutionary,* London, 1927, pp. 179–83.
7. Sun Yat-sen, *San Min Chu I* (Three People's Principles), Shanghai, 1927, pp. 431–34.
8. For expositions of Sun's political doctrines, see Shu-chin Tsui, "Influence of the Canton-Moscow Entente," and T. C. Woo, *The Kuomintang and the Future of the Chinese Revolution,* London, 1928, Chap. III.
9. Chen Tu-hsiu, *Letter to the Comrades of the Chinese Communist Party,* Shanghai, December 10, 1929; Eng. tr. in *Militant,* New York, November 15, 1930–January 15, 1931.
10. Chen Tu-hsiu, "The Bourgeois Revolution and the Revolutionary Bourgeoisie," *Essays on the Chinese Revolution,* Shanghai, 1927, p. 60.
11. Speech of Liu Jen-chin at the Fourth World Congress of the Communist International, Session of November 23, 1922, *La Correspondance Internationale,* January 12, 1923.
12. Sun Yat-sen, *International Development,* pp. 251–65.
13. Wang Ching-wei, *China and the Nations,* pp. 108–09.
14. *Izvestia,* Moscow, October 9, 1920, quoted by L. Pasvolsky, *Russia in the Far East,* New York, 1922, p. 87.
15. H. Maring, "Die Revolutionar-Nationalistische Bewegung in Sud-China," *Die Kommunistische Internationale,* September 13, 1922.
16. Louis Fischer, *Soviets in World Affairs,* New York, 1930, v. II, p. 540. Fischer's chapter on China has particular value and will be frequently cited because it gives strong internal evidence of being based almost entirely on conversations with Borodin and throughout attempts to justify and defend the line pursued by the Communist International in China.
17. P. Mif, *Heroic China,* New York, 1937, pp. 21–22.
18. Quoted by Hua Kang, *The Great Chinese Revolution of 1925–27,* Shanghai, 1931, Chap. VI, Section 1.
19. Fischer, *Soviets in World Affairs,* v. II, p. 637.
20. Shu-chin Tsui, "Influence of the Canton-Moscow Entente," p. 97 ; Fischer, *Soviets in World Affairs,* v. II, p. 638.
21. Program of the Kuomintang, adopted at the First National Congress, January, 1924.
22. Fischer, *Soviets in World Affairs,* v. II, p. 640 ; Tang Leang-li, *Inner History of the Chinese Revolution,* London, 1930, p. 183. This work, which will be frequently referred to, has particular importance and authority primarily because it reflects directly the views and attitudes of Wang Ching-wei, Left Kuomintang leader. Tang is Wang's official biographer.
23. For a survey of working-class conditions, see "Kuomintang vs. Labour," *Five Years of Kuomintang Reaction,* Shanghai, 1932 ; see also bibliography given by Lowe Chun-hwa, *Facing Labour Issues in China,* p. 189 ff.
24. Cf. S. Wong and W. L., "La Chine Ouvrière," *La Correspondance Internationale,* September 26, 1923.
25. Lowe Chun-hwa, *Facing Labour Issues,* p. 40.

26. "Proclamation of the National Conference of Railway Workers, February 14, 1924," tr. by L. Wieger, *Chine Moderne,* Siensien, Hopei, 1921-32, v. V, pp. 263–64. For the 1923 events see Lo Chang-lung, *The Massacre of the Peking-Hankow Railway Workers,* Peking, March, 1923. Lo, Communist, organizer and leader of the railway workers, was imprisoned in 1933.
27. Chen Ta, *Analysis of Strikes in China from 1918 to 1926,* Shanghai, undated, p. 5.
28. Wieger, *Chine Moderne,* v. V, p. 266.
29. *Ibid.,* pp. 269–70.
30. Shu-chin Tsui, "Influence of the Canton-Moscow Entente," p. 120.
31. G. Voitinsky, "First Conference of Transport Workers of the Pacific," *International Press Correspondence,* September 11, 1924.
32. Peng Pai, *The Haifeng Peasant Movement,* Canton, 1926; a partial Eng. tr. will be found under the title "Red Haifeng," in *International Literature,* Nos. 2–3, Moscow, 1932. Peng was shot, by order of Chiang Kai-shek, in August, 1929.
33. *Ibid.*
34. Chang, *Farmers' Movement in Kwangtung,* p. 2.
35. "Manifesto of Sun Yat-sen, September 1, 1924," Wieger, *Chine Moderne,* v. V, p. 230; Wang Ching-wei, *China and the Nations,* pp. 111–12; *International Press Correspondence,* September 11, 18, October 2, 1924; *North China Herald,* Shanghai, September 6, 1924.
36. Chang, *Farmers' Movement in Kwangtung,* p. 31.
37. Lowe Chun-hwa, *Facing Labour Issues,* p. 36 ; Hua Kang gives 281 delegates, 166 unions, 540,000 workers. —*Great Chinese Revolution,* Chap. IV, Section 1.
38. Chang, *Farmers' Movement in Kwangtung,* p. 8.
39. *Ibid.,* p. 32.
40. *China Weekly Review,* Shanghai, June 13, 1925.
41. Chen Ta, *Analysis of Strikes,* p. 27. Chen recorded for 1925 as a whole 318 strikes, involving a known total of 784,821 workers, with the number unrecorded for a third of the listed strikes, bringing the probable total to about 1,000,000.
42. H. O. Chapman, *The Chinese Revolution,* 1926–27, London, 1928, pp. 14–15.
43. Chen Ta, *Analysis of Strikes,* p. 28.
44. Deng Cheng-tsah, *A General Survey of the Hong Kong Strike,* Canton, August, 1926. Deng was one of the organizers and leaders of the general strike. He was shot, by order of Chiang Kai-shek, in the summer of 1933. Lo Teng-hsien, one of his chief lieutenants, was shot, by order of Chiang Kai-shek, in August, 1933.
45. *China Year Book,* 1926, pp. 969–70.
46. Chang, *Farmers' Movement in Kwangtung,* p. 38.
47. *China Year Book,* 1926, p. 960.
48. Deng Cheng-tsah, *Survey of the Hong Kong Strike.*
49. *China Year Book,* 1926, p. 977.
50. Chen Ta, *Analysis of Strikes,* p. 35.
51. Quoted by Lowe Chun-hwa, *Facing Labour Issues,* p. 44; see also *Administrative Reports of the Hong Kong Government,* 1925.
52. *China Year Book,* 1926, pp. 974–75.
53. "The Hong Kong Government openly sent 3,000,000 rounds of ammunition to Swatow and the merchants of Hong Kong sent more than $1,000,000 to Chen Chiung-ming." —Hua Kang, *Great Chinese Revolution,* Chap. IV, Section 3.

4. Canton: To Whom the Power?

1. Quoted by Hua Kang, *Great Chinese Revolution,* Chap. IV, Section I.
2. Chapman, *Chinese Revolution,* p. 210.
3. *North China Herald,* June 6, 1925.
4. Chen Ta, "Labour's Part in the New Nationalism," *China Weekly Review,* March 6, 1926.
5. Samuel H. Chang, "An Analysis of Canton Bolshevism," *China Weekly Review,* March 20 and April 3, 1926.
6. *North China Herald,* March 20, 1926.
7. *Ibid.*
8. For the Taku ultimatum, see *China Year Book,* 1926, pp. 1031–32 ; for a graphic description of the massacre, see Oskar Erdberg, "March Eighteenth," in *Tales of Modern China,* Moscow, 1932.
9. *China Weekly Review,* March 27, 1926.
10. *North China Herald,* March 20, 1926.
11. *China Year Book,* 1926, p. 1011.
12. Li Chih-lung, *The Resignation of Chairman Wang Ching-wei,* Wuhan, 1927.
13. "Resolution on the Chinese Question," adopted by the Sixth Enlarged Executive (Plenum) of the E.C.C.I., March 13, 1926, *International Press Correspondence* (No. 40), May 13, 1926.
14. Tang Leang-li, *Inner History,* p. 234.
15. Fischer, *Soviets in World Affairs,* v. II, p. 646.
16. *Ibid.*
17. *The Peasant Movement in Kwangtung* (Report of the Peasant Department of the Kuomintang), Canton, October, 1925.
18. *International Press Correspondence,* January 7, 1926.
19. Stalin, *Marxism and the National and Colonial Question,* New York, undated, p. 216. Cf. Trotsky, *Third International after Lenin,* New York, 1936, pp. 212–22.
20. *International Press Correspondence,* March 18,1926.
21. "Resolution on the Chinese Question," Sixth Plenum of the E.C.C.I. (see Note 13).
22. Katsuji Fuse, *Soviet Policy in the Orient,* Peking, 1927, p. 304; a photograph of Hu Han-min seated with his Krestintern colleagues will be found on p. 305.
23. "Detailed Report of the Session of the Enlarged E.C.C.I." (Sixth Plenum), Opening Session, February 17, 1926, *International Press Correspondence,* March 4, 1926.
24. *Ibid.*
25. *Ibid.*
26. "Resolution on the Chinese Question," Sixth Plenum of the E.C.C.I. (see Note 13).
27. Tang Leang-li, *Inner History,* p. 233; for an illuminating picture, in novel form, of Borodin's role in Canton, see André Malraux, *Les Conquérants,* Paris, 1928 (*The Conquerors,* New York, 1929), and Trotsky's comments on it, "The Strangled Revolution" and "A Strangled Revolution and its Stranglers," in Trotsky, *Problems of the Chinese Revolution,* New York, 1932, pp. 244-66.
28. Fischer, *Soviets in World Affairs,* v. II, p. 647.
29. *Ibid.*
30. Trotsky, *Problems,* p. 254.
31. "First Address of the Central Committee of the Communist League to its Members in Germany," in Engels, *Germany: Revolution and Counter-Revolution,* p. 143.

5. Canton: The Coup of March 20, 1926

1. Tang Leang-li, *Inner History,* p. 231.
2. *Whampoa Year Book,* Canton, December, 1925.
3. *International Press Correspondence,* March 18, 1926.
4. Li Chih-lung, *The Resignation of Chairman Wang Ching-wei.*
5. *La Correspondance Internationale,* February 17, 1926.
6. *China Weekly Review,* April 10, 1926.
7. Hua Kang, *Great Chinese Revolution,* Chap. IV, Section 5.
8. Li Chih-lung, *The Resignation of Chairman Wang Ching-wei.*
9. Tang Leang-li, *Inner History,* p. 246.
10. Li Chih-lung, *The Resignation of Chairman Wang Ching-wei.*
11. Deng Cheng-tsah, *Survey of Hong Kong Strike.*
12. George Sokolsky, *Tinder Box of Asia,* New York, 1933, p. 336.
13. Deng Cheng-tsah, *Survey of Hong Kong Strike.*
14. Li Chih-lung, *The Resignation of Chairman Wang Ching-wei.*
15. Full text of this resolution is given in T. C. Woo, *Kuomintang and the Future of the Chinese Revolution,* pp. 176–78; references and extracts will also be found in Hua Kang, *Great Chinese Revolution,* Chap. IV, Section 5, and in Fuse, *Soviet Policy in the Orient,* pp. 251–56.
16. "Theses on the National and Colonial Question" (Second World Congress), *Theses and Statutes,* pp. 70–71.
17. *Ibid.,* pp. 74–75.
18. "The putsch of Chiang Kai-shek on March 20, 1926, when the Russian Communists were arrested in China, was not mentioned by a single word in our press." —Zinoviev. "Theses on the Chinese Revolution," in appendices to Trotsky, *Problems,* p. 347; "For a whole year, the Stalin-Bukharin group concealed the first coup of Chiang Kai-shek in March, 1926." —Albert Treint. "Declaration du Camarade Treint," *Documents de l'Opposition et la Résponse du Parti,* Paris, November, 1927, p. 76.

18. *International Press Correspondence,* April 8, 1926.

20. *Ibid.*
21. *Daily Worker,* New York, April 21, 1926.
22. G. Voitinsky, "The Situation in China and the Plans of the Imperialists," *International Press Correspondence,* May 6, 1926.
23. G. Sokolsky, *Tinder Box of Asia,* p. 336.
24. Tang Leang-li, *Inner History,* p. 247.
25. A. M. Kotenev, *New Lamps for Old,* Shanghai, 1931, p. 237.
26. Tang Leang-li, *Inner History,* p. 249.
27. Fischer, *Soviets in World Affairs,* v. II, pp. 651–53.
28. In the *Guide Weekly,* Shanghai, end of March, 1926, reprinted with other articles and documents in the Chinese Communist Party pamphlet, *Our Party and the Canton Events,* Peking, July, 1926.
29. "Open Letter of Chen Tu-hsiu to Chiang Kai-shek," June 4, 1926, in *Our Party and the Canton Events.*
30. "Open Letter of Kao Yu-han to Chiang Kai-shek," in *Our Party and the Canton Events.*
31. "Letter of the Central Committee of the Communist Party to the Kuomintang," June 4, 1926,

in *Our Party and the Canton Events.*

32. Reprinted in *Our Party and the Canton Events.*
33. Quoted by Li Li-san in his preface to *The Chinese Revolution* (A Collection of Documents), Shanghai, 1930.
34. Chen Tu-hsiu, *Letter to the Comrades.*
35. "The Fifth Congress of the Communist Party of China and the Kuomintang," *Communist International,* April 15, 1927.
36. Chen Tu-hsiu, *Letter to the Comrades.*
37. Hua Kang, *Great Chinese Revolution,* Chap. IV, Section 3.
38. Quoted by Yuen Tai-ying, *The Kuomintang and the Labour Movement,* Wuhan, April, 1927.
39. "News from South China," *China Weekly Review,* July 31, August 7, August 14, August 21, and August 28, 1926.
40. "Report of the Kwangtung Provincial Peasant Union," February, 1927, *Chinese Correspondence,* Wuhan, May 8, 1927.
41. *China Year Book,* 1926, p. 982.
42. Deng Cheng-tsah, *Survey of Hong Kong Strike* ; *China Weekly Review,* April 24, 1926.
43. "Canton Boycott Negotiations," *China Year Book,* 1926, p. 989.
44. *Ibid.,* p. 998.
45. *China Weekly Review,* August 7, 1926.
46. *Ibid.,* July 31, 1926.
47. *China Year Book,* 1928, p. 976.
48. *Ibid.,* pp. 977–78.
49. Quoted by Fischer, *Soviets in World Affairs,* v. II, p. 645.
50. *China Year Book,* 1928, p. 978.
51. "Strike Regulations in Canton," *Chinese Economic Journal,* Shanghai, March, 1927; cf. "Labour Suppression in Canton," *North China Herald,* December 31, 1926.
52. *North China Herald,* December 31, 1926.
53. "Letter to the Comrades of the Conference of August 7, 1927," published in the appendix to Li Li-san, *Chinese Revolution.* (Hereafter referred to as "August 7 Letter.")
54. P. Mif, *Kitaiskaya Revolutsia,* Moscow, 1932, pp. 97–98.
55. Sydor Stoler, "The Trade Union Movement in Canton," *Pan-Pacific Worker,* Hankow, September 15, 1927.
56. Earl Browder, *Civil War in Nationalist China,* Chicago, 1927, p. 12.
57. "The International Delegation in China," *International Press Correspondence,* April 28, 1927.
58. Tom Mann, *What I Saw in China,* London, 1927, p. 8.
59. Stoler, "Trade Union Movement in Canton."

6. From Canton to Yangtze

1. Chapman, *Chinese Revolution,* p. 20.
2. Quoted by Hua Kang, *Great Chinese Revolution,* Chap. IV, Section 4.
3. *Ibid.*
4. Changsha correspondence to the *Guide Weekly,* quoted by Hua Kang, *Great Chinese Revolution,*

Chap. IV, Section 4.

5. Chen Ta, *Analysis of Strikes,* p. 40.

6. *Ibid.,* p. 41.

7. *La Lettre de Shanghai,* Paris, 1927, pp. 13–18 (Eng. trans. in appendices to Trotsky, *Problems,* p. 397 ff.). The authors of this letter were Nassonov, Fokine, and Albrecht. Although they carefully avoided implicating the Comintern in the errors of the "representative of the E.C.C.I.," the facts they gave were so damaging for the Stalin-Bukharin leadership that the letter was suppressed. It was published by Albert Treint, a member of the presidium of the E.C.C.I.

8. Trotsky, *Problems,* p. 271.

9. Trotsky, "Speech of August 1, 1927," *Stalin School of Falsification,* pp. 165 and 173.

10. Stalin, "Speech of August 1, 1927," *Marxism and the National and Colonial Question,* p. 237.

11. "Thèses sur la Situation en Chine" (adopted by the VII Plenum of the E.C.C.I., November–December, 1926), *La Correspondance Internationale,* February 20, 1927.

12. "Report of Tang Ping-shan" (VII Plenum), *International Press Correspondence,* December 30, 1926.

13. Stalin, "Prospects of the Revolution in China" (speech before the Chinese Commission of the VII Plenum, November 30, 1926), *International Press Correspondence,* December 23, 1926.

14 "Detailed Report of the VII Plenum," First Session, November 22, 1926, *International Press Correspondence,* December 1, 1926.

15. Albert Treint, "La Vérité Qu'on Cache sur la Chine, etc.," *Documents de l'Opposition et la Réponse du Parti,* pp. 77–78.

16. Stalin, "Prospects of the Revolution in China."

17. "Thèses sur la Situation en Chine" (VII Plenum).

18. *Ibid.*

19. Stalin, "Prospects of the Revolution in China."

20. "Speech of Shao Li-tze (Kuomintang)," VII Plenum, Session of November 30, 1926, *International Press Correspondence,* December 30, 1926.

21. Bukharin, "Speech to 24th Conference of Leningrad District, C.P.S.U.," *La Correspondance Internationale,* February 12, 1927.

22. "Speech of Tang Ping-shan," VII Plenum, Session of November 26, 1926, *International Press Correspondence,* December 23, 1926.

23. Stalin, "Prospects of the Revolution in China"; see also "Speech of Petroff (C.P.S.U.)," *International Press Correspondence,* December 30, 1926.

24. Chen Ta, *Analysis of Strikes,* p. 43.

25. *Hankow Herald,* January 5, 1927.

26. Chapman, *Chinese Revolution,* p. 35.

27. Ransome, *Chinese Puzzle,* pp. 106 and 113. Subsequently one of Ransome's British informants at Kiukiang wrote him to complain that his account was "insufficiently lurid"!

28. *Lettre de Shanghai,* p. 4.

29. For texts of these documents and related citations, see *China Year Book,* 1928, pp. 739, 756 ff., 761, 764, 983, 1353.

30. *Lettre de Shanghai,* p. 5.

31. "August 7 Letter."

32. *Lettre de Shanghai,* pp. 7–8. In later years Borodin never wearied of recalling that banquet as evidence that he had struggled against Chiang Kai-shek. For Chiang's own account of the in-

cident, see Wieger, *Chine Moderne,* v. VII, pp. 140–42.

33. Wieger, *Chine Moderne,* v. VIII, pp. 23–24.
34. *North China Herald,* April 2, 1927.
35. *People's Tribune,* Hankow, March 15, 1927; Woo, *Kuomintang and the Future of the Chinese Revolution,* p. 180.
36. *People's Tribune,* March 16, 1927.
37. *Ibid.*
38. *Ibid.,* March 19, 1927.
39. *Ibid.*
40. *Lettre de Shanghai,* pp. 7–8.
41. Trans. from *Guide Weekly,* March 18, 1927, by *North China Herald,* April 9, 1927.

7. The Shanghai Insurrection

1. *Chinese Economic Journal,* March, 1927; *Strikes and Lockouts in Shanghai since 1918*, published by the Bureau of Social Affairs, Shanghai, 1933.
2. "The Fight for Shanghai," *International Press Correspondence,* January 13, 1927.
3. Sources differ on the exact figure. Official foreign reports, which understated strike figures as a matter of policy, gave 106,000 (*China Year Book*, 1928, p. 996). *La Lettre de Shanghai* gives 300,000. Hua Kang in *The Great Chinese Revolution* gives 360,000 with a list of factories and shops to support his figure. Hostile Chinese sources quote much higher totals. The Shanghai Bureau of Social Affairs lists 425,795 (*Strikes and Lockouts*, p. 62). Ho Sen gives 500,000 (*Materials of Modern History*, Shanghai, 1933, v. III).
4. Hua Kang, *Great Chinese Revolution*, Chap. V, Section 2.
5. Chiu Chiu-pei, *Controversial Questions in the Chinese Revolution*, Wuhan, 1927, Appendix I.
6. *New York Herald-Tribune*, February 21, 1927.
7. Ho Sen, "The Three Shanghai Uprisings," *Materials of Modern History*, v. III, p. 170.
8. *China Weekly Review*, Shanghai, March 12, 1927.
9. *North China Herald,* April 16, 1927.
10. *New York Herald Tribune*, February 21, 1927.
11. *La Lettre de Shanghai*, pp. 10–11.
12. *China Year Book*, 1928, p. 1266.
13. Hua Kang, *Great Chinese Revolution*, Chap. V, Section 3.
14. *Ibid.*
15. For striking vignettes of the Shanghai insurrection, see Andre Malraux, *Man's Fate* .
16. Hua Kang and other Communist sources usually give 800,000 as the total involved. *Strikes and Lockouts* gives the number of actual strikers as 329,000.
17. A. Neuberg (Heinz Neumann), *L'Insurrection Armée*, Paris, 1931, p. 141.
18. Hua Kang, *Great Chinese Revolution*, Chap. V, Section 3.
19. Ho Sen, *Materials*, v. III.
20. Hua Kang, *Great Chinese Revolution*, Chap. V, Section 3.

8. The Prodigal's Return

1. Chinese say Chiang belongs to the tung layer, or 22nd generation of the Green Society, which is organized along patriarchal lines. Referring to Chiang's "Connection with the Green and Red societies," George Sokolsky added: "He may even be a member of one or both of these powerful underground groups, but that no outsider can know." —*China Year Book,* 1928, p. 1361.
2. "Shanghai Workers' Delegates' Report," *Hunan Sen Pao,* May 19-20, 1927 (hereafter referred to as "Workers' Delegates' Report"); see also Kuo Mi-lieh's account in the *People's Tribune,* April 16, 1927; and *International Press Correspondence,* June 23, 1927. For a description of the Green gang and its later development see "Gang Rule in Shanghai," *Five Years of Kuomintang Reaction.*
3. Li Chih-lung, *The Resignation of Chairman Wang Ching-wei.*
4. Kiukiang correspondence dated March 23, *North China Herald,* April 21, 1927; see also *People's Tribune,* April 19, 1927. Probably the first of all interested foreigners to learn the facts of Chiang Kai-shek's terror campaign in Kiangsi were Earl Browder, Tom Mann, and Jacques Doriot, delegates of the Communist International. How they deliberately concealed this information until it was too late to be of any use is told in Chap. IX.
5. *People's Tribune,* April 16, 1927.
6. "Report of Political Department of General Cheng's Sixth Army," *People's Tribune,* April 21, 1927.
7. Chapman, *Chinese Revolution,* p. 32.
8. Cf. *China Weekly Review,* May 28, 1927, for absence of proof of rape charges.
9. See report of G. A. Kennedy, *People's Tribune,* April 5 and 16, 1927. Most of Kennedy's findings were also incorporated in a dispatch by William Prohme published by the *Nation,* New York, April 13, 1927. For material on the "Nanking Outrages" presented in the mood and spirit of the Shanghai foreign community, see *China Year Book,* 1928, Chap. XVI.
10. Givens later headed the Special (Political) Branch of the Shanghai Municipal Police which in subsequent years tracked down and arrested hundreds of Communists, handing many of them over to Chiang Kai-shek's government for execution. In 1931, the Nanking Government conferred its First Class "A" Medal of the Military, Naval, and Air Forces upon Givens in appreciation of his cooperation in "preserving peace and order." —*North China Daily News,* December 9, 1931.
11. *North China Herald,* April 2, 1927.
12. George Sokolsky in the *China Year Book,* 1928, p. 1361.
13. "Workers' Delegates' Report," Chen Fo-ta, one of the Shanghai delegates to the Pan-Pacific Trade Union Conference at Hankow, reported that the Shanghai pickets numbered 3,000, had 2,800 rifles, 30 machine guns, 200 pistols, and 16 pieces of light artillery. —*People's Tribune,* May 26, 1927.
14. "There are not more than 3,000 Nationalist troops in Shanghai according to reliable estimates from Chinese sources. General Ho Ying-chin has only 10,000 troops to hold Hangchow. The military forces of Chiang Kai-shek are now so scattered over so vast an area as not to be very valuable...for the suppression of the labourers." —*North China Herald,* April 2, 1927. "Chiang had only 3,000 troops in Shanghai...none of the material elements were in Chiang's favour." —Sokolsky, *China Year Book,* 1928, p. 1361. "Troops sympathetic to the revolution still outnumbered the counter-revolutionary troops. The troops under the direct command of Chiang Kai-shek were also vacillating." —Li Li-san, *The Chinese Revolution,* p. 33.
15. *People's Tribune,* April 28, 1927.
16. A. De C. Sowerby, *North China Herald,* April 2, 1927.
17. *Municipal Gazette,* April 2, 1927.
18. Cf. Arthur Ransome's chapter on "The Shanghai Mind" in *The Chinese Puzzle.*

19. Rodney Gilbert, *North China Herald,* April 2, 1927. An extremely apt reply to this common argument appeared in the *People's Tribune,* July 18, 1927, under the title, "That 'Model Settlement.'"
20. "Thoughts on Evacuation," by a Missionary Refugee, *North China Herald,* April 16, 1927.
21. *Ibid.* Of 8,000 missionaries normally functioning only 500 were still at their posts, according to the *Shanghai Times,* June 24, 1927. For 5,000 who fled home, 1,500 who took refuge at Shanghai, and 1,000 at other ports, the instinct of self-preservation proved more imperative than the mission of propagating the Gospel.
22. "The Real Issue in China," *Constitutionalist,* Shanghai, February, 1927, pp. 321–23.
23. E. E. Strothers, *A Bolshevized China—The World's Greatest Peril,* and other reprints, Shanghai, June, 1927, p. 6.
24. *Ibid.,* p. 18. Unfortunately for this "conclusive proof," Chapman, a resident of Hankow at the time, states categorically that such a parade "never took place." —*Chinese Revolution,* p. 87. This particular report is a typical example of the fantastic notions the foreign press had of what was going on in Hankow. Most of them were deliberately malicious slanders. Several persons were arrested in Hankow for disseminating the rumor about the "naked parade."
25. General Smedley D. Butler, Commander of U.S. Marines in China, *North China Herald,* April 9, 1927.
26. *Constitutionalist,* January, 1927, p. 291.
27. *China Weekly Review,* April 9, 1927.
28. *North China Daily News,* April 7, 1927.
29. *Far Eastern Review,* March, 1927.
30. *North China Daily News,* March 28, 1927.
31. *North China Herald,* April 2, 1927.
32. *North China Daily News,* April 2, 1927.
33. *Sin Wen Pao,* April 7, 1927.
34. *North China Daily News,* March 30, 1927.
35. *China Weekly Review,* April 9, 1927.
36. *New York Times,* April 15, 1927. The sum of $15,000,000 is also given by the "Workers' Delegates' Report," which divides it into $12,000,000 for Chiang, $1,500,000 for Pai Chung-hsi, $1,000,000 for Chow Feng-chi, and $500,000 for the gangsters. It is difficult to ascertain the extent of foreign participation in these "loans." For a description of how the foreigners collaborated through Chinese intermediaries the reader is again recommended to Malraux's *Man's Fate.*
37. *Sin Wen Pao,* April 5, 1927.
38. Peking Chen Pao, April 3, 1927.
39. *Sin Wen Pao,* April 5, 1927.
40. *China Weekly Review,* April 10, 1927.
41. *North China Daily News,* March 28, 1927.
42. Quoted from *Pravda* in a Moscow dispatch to the *New York Times,* April 1, 1927.
43. *North China Herald,* April 9, 1927.
44. Tang Leang-li, *Inner History,* pp. 266–67.
45. *Ta Kung Pao,* Tientsin, April 7, 1927.
46. Tang Leang-li, *Inner History,* p. 268.

9. The Conspiracy of Silence

1. *Shanghai Times,* March 25, 1927.
2. *North China Daily News,* March 28, 1927.
3. *Rote Fahne,* Berlin, March 17, 1927.
4. *L'Humanité,* March 23, 1927. "The confusion created by Stalin-Bukharin… led the leadership of our party on March 23, 1927, to salute telegraphically Chiang Kai-shek, entering Shanghai, as the representative of the Chinese Commune… The policy of the Stalin-Bukharin group led the leadership of the French party astray to the point of confusing Gallifet with the Commune, the butcher with the victim." —Albert Treint, "Déclaration Addressee au C. E. de l'I. C. le 22 Juillet, 1927, sur la Question Chinoise," in *Documents de l'Opposition Francaise et la Réponse du Parti,* p. 67.
5. *Izvestia* pp. a, March 6, 1927; *Pravda,* March 9, 1927, April 10, 1927, etc.
6. See pp. 134–36.
7. Cf. "Thèses on the Situation in China (VII Plenum)," *La Correspondance Internationale,* February 20, 1927; editorial in *Communist International,* February 28, 1927; article by Martinov, *ibid.,* March 15, 1927; "The Chinese Revolution and the Kuomintang," *ibid.,* March 30, 1927; and many others.
8. Earl Browder, *Civil War in Nationalist China*; Jacques Doriot, "A Travers la Révolution Chinoise," *L'Humanité,* Paris, June–August, 1927; Tom Mann, *What I saw in China.*
9. Doriot, *L'Humanité,* July 8, 1927.
10. Browder, *Civil War,* p. 15.
11. Doriot, *L'Humanité,* July 12, 1927.
12. *People's Tribune,* Hankow, April 1, 1927.
13. See *Labour Monthly,* London, July, 1927. It is a fact that the *only* people who were carrying on an open campaign against Chiang were a number of individual Communists in Hankow, who were acting, however, entirely on their own initiative. Cf. *La Lettre de Shanghai,* p. 8.
14. *People's Tribune,* April 9, 1927.
15. "Le Voyage de la Délégation Internationale de Canton à Wuhan," *La Correspondance Internationale,* June 11, 1927.
16. *People's Tribune,* April 22, 1927.
17. *Ibid.*; see also Tom Mann, *What I saw in China,* p. 11.
18. *La Correspondance Internationale,* March 23, 1927.
19. *Ibid.,* March 30, 1927.
20. *L'Humanité,* March 23, 1927.
21. Reproduced in *La Correspondance Internationale,* March 26, 1927; and in *The Communist International,* March 30, 1927.
22. Martinov, "The Regrouping of Forces in the Chinese Revolution," *The Communist International,* March 15, 1927.
23. This speech was never published. Stalin was confronted with these passages by Vuyovitch at the Eighth Plenum of the E.C.C.I. in May, 1927. Vuyovitch had taken them down himself in shorthand. "Comrade Stalin will always have the opportunity of rectifying unintentional inaccuracies by laying his stenogram before us," he challenged (cf. Trotsky, *Problems,* appendices, pp. 388-90). But Stalin offered no corrections, nor did he produce the stenogram because, as Trotsky remarked at the same meeting of the E.C.C.I., "a few days later the squeezed out lemon seized power and the army…. As a member of the C.C. (Central Committee) I had the right to get the stenogram of this speech, but my pains and attempts were in vain. Attempt it now, com-

rades, perhaps you will have better luck. I doubt it" (*ibid.,* p. 91). This speech and its suppression is confirmed not by an Oppositionist, but by one of Stalin's trusted lieutenants, Albert Treint, at that time a member of the Presidium of the E.C.C.I. "Stalin even went so far as to conceal his own speech.... A speech by Stalin himself at the Communist Academy, in the presence of 3,000 officials of the Party, was never published...because the coup d'état of Chiang Kai-shek ten days later brought to his words the shattering refutation of events" (*Documents de l'Opposition Française,* pp. 36, 64). For a projection of Stalin's views on the Chinese scene read the conversation between Kyo and "Vologin" in Hankow in Malraux's *Man's Fate,* pp. 146–55.

24. Stalin, "Speech to the Youth Federation," March 29, 1927, *La Correspondance Internationale,* April 9, 1927.

25. T. Mandalyan, "Why did the Leadership of the Chinese Communist Party Fail to Fulfil its Task?" *La Correspondance Internationale,* July 23 and 30, 1927. Mandalyan was a Comintern delegate in Shanghai at the time. "The International telegraphed us to hide or bury all the weapons of the workers to avoid military conflict between the workers and Chiang Kai-shek." —Chen Tu-hsiu, *Letter to the Comrades.* "Was it not better to hide the arms, not to accept battle and thus not permit oneself to be disarmed...?" —N. Bukharin, *Les Problèmes de la Révolution Chinoise,* Paris, undated (circa May-June, 1927), p. 56. See also Malraux, *Man's Fate,* pp. 209–10.

26. *Communist International,* Russian edition, March 18, 1927; German edition, March 22, 1927; English edition, April 15, 1927.

27. See pp. 222–24.

28. Quoted in *North China Daily News,* April 1, 1927.

29. This translation is made from the original as it appeared in the *Sin Wen Pao* and other Shanghai papers on April 5, 1927. An extremely inaccurate translation appeared in the *People's Tribune,* in Hankow, on April 10, 1927. The essential paragraphs of the manifesto were published the same week, without comment, in the international Communist press. (Cf. *La Correspondance Internationale,* April 13, 1927.) Browder includes sections of it in his pamphlet, *Civil War in Nationalist China,* p. 30, likewise without comment. Not until months later did it become the target of violent criticism.

30. "...at the rate agitators are now enrolling new members, upwards of half a million laborers will be subject to the strike demands of the General Labor Union in the course of the next few weeks." —*North China Herald,* Shanghai, April 9, 1927. Between March 21 and April 12, 1927, union strength in Shanghai grew from 350,000 to 850,000, according to a report by Chen Fo-ta, a Shanghai delegate to the Pan-Pacific Trade Union Congress. —*People's Tribune,* May 26, 1927.

31. *La Correspondance Internationale,* March 26, 1927.

32. Hua Kang, *Great Chinese Revolution,* Chap. V, Section 2.

33. *Sin Wen Pao,* April 4, 1927.

34. *Ibid.,* April 8, 1927.

35. *Ibid.*

36. *Ibid.*

37. *Ibid.,* April 5, 1927.

38. *Ibid.,* April 3, 1927.

39. *Ibid.,* April 2, 1927.

40. *North China Herald,* April 2, 1927.

41. P. Mif, *Kitaiskaya Revolutsia,* p. 98.

42. Translated from the original manuscript.

43. Grover Clark, *China in 1927,* Peking, 1928, p. 13.
44. Yang Tsao-cheng, "Events in Shanghai, Spring, 1927," *Materials on the Chinese Question,* No. 13, Sun Yat-sen University, Moscow, p. 20. "Hsueh Yoh proposed to the Central Committee...to agree that he should not submit to Chiang's order. He was ready to remain in Shanghai and fight together with the Shanghai workers against the military overthrow that was in preparation...." —Chitarov (a Comintern functionary in Shanghai at the time), at the December 11, 1927, session of the Fifteenth Congress of the Communist Party of the Soviet Union. This passage was deleted later from the minutes and is quoted by Trotsky from the original stenographic record. —Trotsky, *Problems,* p. 276. Mif confirms the incident, although in garbled form, in *Kitaiskaya Revolutsia,* p. 99. See also Malraux, *Man's Fate,* p. 207.
45. Yang Tsao-cheng, "Events in Shanghai," p. 20; "...Our responsible leaders...declared that they knew about the overturn being prepared, but did not want a premature conflict with Chiang Kai-shek," —Chitarov, loc. cit.
46. Malraux's Kyo wanted to organize resistance, "but the official speeches of the Chinese Communist Party, the whole propaganda of union with the Kuomintang were paralysing him." —*Man's Fate,* p. 207.
47. *Sin Wen Pao,* April 7, 1927.
48. Reuter from Peking, *North China Daily News,* April 12, 1927.
49. Cf. *La Correspondance Internationale,* April 20, 1927.
50. *New York Times,* April 9, 1927.
51. Hua Kang, *Great Chinese Revolution,* Chap. V, Section 2.
52. *Sin Wen Pao,* April 6, 1927.
53. *Ibid.,* April 6, 1927.
54. Cf. *People's Tribune,* May 7, 1927.
55. Malraux, *Man's Fate,* pp. 266–67.

10. The Coup of April 12, 1927

1. *China Press,* Shanghai, April 13, 1927.
2. *North China Daily News,* April 13, 1927.
3. *Ibid.*
4. *China Year Book,* 1928, p. 1362.
5. *Shun Pao,* Shanghai, April 13, 1927.
6. *Ibid.*
7. Cf. "Workers Delegates' Report," and corroborative accounts in the *Sin Wen Pao* and other Shanghai papers.
8. "Police Report for April," *Municipal Gazette,* May 21, 1927. Shanghai delegates to the Fourth All-China Trade Union Conference at Hankow reported that 140 known union leaders and 500 workers lost their lives in resisting Chiang's coup. —*People's Tribune,* June 30, 1927.
9. *Sin Wen Pao,* Shanghai, April 13, 1927. For a good picture of the "reorganization," see "Chiang Kai-shek's Fascist Trade Unions," *People's Tribune,* June 17, 1927.
10. *Sin Wen Pao,* April 13, 1927.
11. *Ibid.*
12. *North China Herald,* April 16, 1927.
13. *Sin Wen Pao,* April 13, 1927.

14. *China Press,* April 13, 1927.
15. "90,000 workers were out." —*China Press,* April 14, 1927. "An appeal by the Communist Party for a general strike as a protest against the anti-Communist coup was obeyed at noon on April 13 by no less than 111,800 workers." —*Shanghai Municipal Police Annual Report for 1927.*
16. "Workers' Delegates' Report."
17. *China Press,* April 14, 1927.
18. Hua Kang, *Great Chinese Revolution,* Chap. V, Section 2 ; "Workers' Delegates' Report."
19. Chiang Kai-shek, *Manifesto to the People,* Shanghai, April, 1927, p. 11.
20. *North China Herald,* April 16, 1927.
21. *Ibid.*
22. *Peking Morning Post,* April 15, 1927, said official reports gave the number of arrests as totalling 1,000.
23. Karl Marx, *The Eighteenth Brumaire of Louis Bonaparte,* New York, 1926, p. 127.
24. *Ibid.,* p. 128.
25. *China Year Book,* 1928, p. 1374.
26. *New York Times,* May 4, 1927.
27. *Ibid.,* May 19, 1927.
28. *China Weekly Review,* Shanghai, June 25, 1927.
29. "True, this hireling straddles the boss's neck, tears from his mouth at times the juiciest pieces, and spits on his bald spot besides. Say what you will, a most inconvenient hireling! But nevertheless, only a hireling. The bourgeois abides with him, because without him, it and its regime would absolutely go to the dogs.... The dictatorship of the bourgeoisie remains inviolate because all the conditions of its social hegemony have been preserved and strengthened." —Leon Trotsky, *The Soviet Union and the Fourth International,* New York, 1934, pp. 7, 19.
30. A delegation of Soviet trade unionists en route to Hankow arrived at Canton on April 14. They were treated the next day to the spectacle of the raids on the trade unions, mass arrests, and executions in the streets carried out at the orders of General Li Chi-sen who, too, only a few months previously, had been listed in the Stalin-Bukharin directory of "revolutionary generals." —Cf. *People's Tribune,* May 15, 1927. Fleeing Canton trade unionists brought to Hankow the belated message: "We regret to say that the cradle of the national revolution has become a stronghold of reaction." —*People's Tribune,* May 6, 1927.
31. Communist International, April 15, 1927.
32. Released by the official (Wuhan) *Nationalist News Agency* and published in the *China Press,* April 14, 1927.
33. *New York Times,* April 14, 1927.
34. E. Thaelmann, "La Révolution Chinoise et les Tâches du Proletariat," *La Correspondance Internationale,* April 16, 1927.
35. *La Correspondance Internationale,* No. 43, April 20, 1927.
36. *Ibid.,* No. 44, April 20, 1927.
37. Liau Han-sin, "Le Traitre au Peuple, Chiang Kai-shek," *La Correspondance Internationale,* April 23, 1927.
38. Stalin, "The Questions of the Chinese Revolution," *International Press Correspondence,* April 28, 1927.
39. *New York Times,* April 23, 1927.

11. Wuhan: "The Revolutionary Center"

1. *North China Daily News,* April 26, 1927.
2. Cf. Speech of Chiang Kai-shek at Nanking on April 18, 1927, trans. by Wieger, *Chine Moderne,* v. VII, p. 142; James H. Dolsen, "Chiang Kai-shek's Plight," *People's Tribune,* May 25–26, 1927.
3. All quotations from Stalin in this chapter are taken from the official English translation of "The Questions of the Chinese Revolution," *International Press Correspondence,* April 28, 1927.
4. Trotsky, "The Chinese Revolution and the Theses of Comrade Stalin" (May 7, 1927), *Problems,* p. 23 ff. (Unless otherwise noted, all quotations from Trotsky in this chapter are taken from this article.)
5. N. Lenzner, "La Question Chinoise," *La Correspondance Internationale,* June 25 and 29, 1927; A. Stetski, "Un Tournant de la Révolution Chinoise," *ibid.,* April 27, 1927; Stetski, "La Dialectique de la Lutte en Chine," *ibid.,* May 7, 1927; L. Heller, "Apres la Rupture de Front National Révolutionnaire en Chine," *ibid.,* May 7, 1927; J. Pepper, "L'alliance de Chamberlain et de Tchang Kai-chek," *ibid.,* May 21, 1927; etc.
6. See note 3.
7. Lenzner, "La Question Chinoise." (Emphasis in original.)
8. Bukharin, *Problèmes de la Revolution Chinoise,* pp. 56, 59.
9. Bukharin, "Report to the Plenum of the Moscow Committee of the Communist Party of the Soviet Union (June 4, 1927), *La Correspondance Internationale,* July 2, 1927.

   "When is it necessary to conclude a compromise and when must one pass over to the offensive?" asked the resolution of the Eighth Plenum of the E.C.C.I. at the end of May. "That depends on concrete conditions. In particular, the E.C.C.I. considers that the tactic proposed by some comrades at Shanghai at the time of Chiang Kai-shek's coup d'état was absurd. This tactic consisted in arousing in advance an insurrection against the imperialists and against Chiang Kai-shek, and offering them battle on a broad front.... In a broad armed action, the workers of Shanghai would have been exterminated by the bloc of armed forces of Chiang Kai-shek and the imperialists, and the élite of the Chinese proletariat would have perished in a battle in which it had absolutely no chance of success." —"Resolution sur la Question Chinoise," *La Correspondance Internationale,* June 15, 1927.
10. E. Eichenwald, "The Tactical Line of the Comintern in China," *International Press Correspondence,* June 2, 1927.
11. Bukharin, *Problemes de la Revolution Chinoise,* p. 59.
12. Tang Shin-she, "The Play of Forces of Chiang Kai-shek and the Hankow Government," *La Correspondance Internationale,* June 6, 1927.
13. *La Correspondance Internationale,* May 21, 1927.
14. Trotsky, *Problems,* p. 285.
15. Ransome, *Chinese Puzzle,* p. 66.
16. Quoted by Trotsky, *Problems,* p. 280. This and other passages were deleted from the printed minutes of the Congress.
17. Trotsky, "Second Speech on the Chinese Question," *Problems,* p. 103.
18. Anna Louise Strong, *China's Millions,* New York, 1928, pp. 38–39.
19. *Ibid.*
20. Jacques Doriot, "A Travers la Révolution Chinoise," *L'Humanité,* Paris, June 25, 1927.
21. Fischer, *Soviets in World Affairs,* v. II, p. 667.
22. Mif, *Kitaiskaya Revolutsia,* p. 100.
23. "Manifesto of the Fifth Congress of the Chinese Communist Party," *Min Kuo Jih Pao,* Wuhan,

May 23–26, 1927.

24. Official translation, *International Press Correspondence,* July 28, 1927.
25. "Declaration of the Pan-Pacific Trade Union Secretariat," Hankow, July 25, 1927, *International Press Correspondence,* September 2, 1927.
26. Mif, *Kitaiskaya Revolutsia,* p. 100.
27. Hua Kang, *Great Chinese Revolution,* Chap. V, Section 2. This is a re-phrasing of an idea more cautiously expressed by Chiu Chiu-pei at the Sixth Congress of the Chinese Communist Party in July, 1928. Stalin's "revolutionary center" was too freshly in the memory of all for bolder words at that time. (See Chiu Chiu-pei, *The Chinese Revolution*, Chap. 1.)
28. See Trotsky, *The Permanent Revolution* .

12. The "Revolutionary Center" at Work

1. "Manifesto of the Central Executive Committee of the Kuomintang," *People's Tribune,* Hankow, April 24, 1927.
2. "Declaration of the Central Executive Committee of the Kuomintang," *People's Tribune,* April 19, 1927.
3. See Chapter IX, "The Conspiracy of Silence."
4. "Declaration of the Delegation of the Communist International," *Chinese Correspondence,* Hankow, May 1, 1927.
5. *Ibid.*
6. *People's Tribune,* April 17, 1927.
7. Chiu Chiu-pei, *Chinese Revolution,* p. 114.
8. "Declaration of the Central Executive Committee of the Kuomintang," *People's Tribune,* April 19, 1927.
9. *People's Tribune,* May 6, 1927.
10. "Interview of Mr. Borodin with a Representative of the Rengo News Agency," *Chinese Correspondence,* May 8, 1927.
11. Fischer, *Soviets in World Affairs,* v. II, pp. 667–78.
12. *Ibid.*
13. *New York Times,* April 23, 1927.
14. *Ibid.,* April 14, 1927.
15. *Ibid.,* May 5, 1927.
16. The *New York Times* is a fair barometer of the official American pulse. After months as a front-page feature, China disappeared from its front page for the first time on May 6. A few days later the Lindbergh exploit and a sex murder in New York completely engrossed press and public alike.
17. Chapman, *Chinese Revolution,* p. 136.
18. *New York Times,* May 3, 1927.
19. *People's Tribune,* April 24 and 29, 1927.
20. "Communique of the Waichiapu (Foreign Office)," *Chinese Correspondence,* May 1, 1927.
21. *People's Tribune,* April 27, 1927.
22. Cf. *People's Tribune,* April 23, 1927.
23. *Chinese Correspondence,* May 1, 1927.

24. Reuter's (British) News Agency, May 9, 1927, published in the *China Year Book,* 1928, pp. 735–36.
25. M. N. Roy, "Imperialist Intervention in China," *Chinese Correspondence,* May 1, 1927.
26. Chapman, *Chinese Revolution*, p. 129.
27. *People's Tribune,* May 14, 1927.
28. Silver had been flowing to the coast throughout the preceding year. Silver stocks in Shanghai rose from about Tls. 102,000,000 at the beginning of 1926 to Tls. 138,600,000 in April, 1927. Cf. *Capital and Trade*, Shanghai, March 18, 1927, and *China Weekly Review,* Shanghai, April 2, 1927.
29. Cf. "Finance Situation Due to Panic and Sabotage," *People's Tribune,* May 21, 1927.
30. According to a report of the Hupeh Unemployed Bureau, there were 160,000 jobless in Wuhan at the end of June. —*People's Tribune,* July 1927.
31. Cf. Reports to the Fourth All-China Trade Union Congress, *People's Tribune,* June 30, 1927, et seq.
32. *People's Tribune,* March 12, 1927.
33. Chiu Chiu-pei, *Chinese Revolution,* p. 58; Tang Leang-li, *Inner History,* p. 271.
34. *People's Tribune,* April 24, 1927.
35. Text in *Chinese Correspondence,* May 8, 1927.
36. "Manifesto on the All Class Nature of the Revolution," *People's Tribune,* May 21, 1927.
37. "Regulations of the Central Executive Committee of the Hupeh General Labour Union," *People's Tribune,* May 25, 1927.
38. Quoted by Mif, *Kitaiskaya Revolutsia,* p. 101.
39. "Declaration to the Peasants" of the Third Plenary Session of the Kuomintang Central Executive Committee, *Chinese Correspondence,* May 8, 1927.
40. "Kuomintang Platform for Workers and Peasants," (October, 1926), *Chinese Correspondence,* May 8, 1927.
41. "Declaration to the Peasants."
42. "Details of the proceedings of the Land Commission were culled and combined from accounts given in the following: Chiu Chiu-pei, *Chinese Revolution*; Mif, *Kitaiskaya Revolutsia*; "August 7 Letter." All direct quotations used by the author are cited textually by these sources. A vividly stylized account will be found under the title "The Night of August the Fourth," in Oskar Erdberg, *Tales of Modern China,* Moscow, 1932.
43. Chiu Chiu-pei, *Chinese Revolution,* p. 112.
44. *People's Tribune,* May 19, 1927.
45. Mif, *Kitaiskaya Revolutsia,* p. 118.
46. M. N. Roy, "Le Ve Congrès du Parti Communiste de Chine," *La Correspondance Internationale,* Paris, July 13, 1927.
47. Mif, *Kitaiskaya Revolutsia,* p. 118
48. Roy, "Le Ve Congrès"
49. *Ibid.*
50. "Chiu Chiu-pei, *Chinese Revolution*, p. 100 ff.
51. Chen Tu-hsiu, "Rapport au Ve Congrès du P.C. de Chine," *La Correspondance Internationale,* June 4, 1927.
52. Trotsky, *Problems,* pp. 77–78.
53. Quoted by Trotsky, *Problems,* p. 284.

54. Quoted by Mif, *Kitaiskaya Revolutsia,* p. 120 ff. Text also in Asiaticus, *Von Kanton bis Schanghai,* Berlin, 1927, p. 265.
55. Chen Tu-hsiu, "Rapport au Ve Congrès."
56. See p. 133.
57. N. Lenzner, "La Question Chinoise," *La Correspondance Internationale,* June 29, 1927.
58. "Manifesto of the Fifth Congress of the Chinese Communist Party," *Min Kuo Jih Fao,* Hankow, May 23–26, 1927.
59. Chiu Chiu-pei, *Chinese Revolution,* pp. 104–05.
60. *Ibid.,* p. 108.

13. The Struggle for the Land

1. Chiu Chiu-pei, *Chinese Revolution,* p. 53.
2. "Report of the Delegate of the Hunan Provincial Peasant Association," *Min Kuo Jih Pao,* Wuhan, June 12, 1927. (Hereafter referred to as "Hunan Delegate's Report.")
3. Tsai Yi-tsen, "Report of the Delegate of the Hupeh Provincial Peasant Association," *Min Kuo Jih Pao,* May 20–21, 1927. (Hereafter referred to as "Hupeh Delegate's Report.")
4. "Hunan Delegate's Report."
5. "Hupeh Delegate's Report."
6. Cf. Strong, "The People's Food," *China's Millions* .
7. Chapman, *Chinese Revolution,* p. 91.
8. *Ibid.,* p. 91.
9. For accounts of the revolution's cultural achievements, especially in the liberation of women and the destruction of superstitions, see Strong, *China's Millions,* and Chapman, *Chinese Revolution.*
10. String, *China's Millions,* pp. 41–42.
11. "Hunan Delegate's Report"; see also "Resolution of the Hupeh Provincial Peasant Union," *People's Tribune,* July 2, 1927.
12. "Hupeh Delegate's Report."
13. Tsai Yi-tsen, "Difficulties and Recent Tactics of the Hupeh Peasant Movement," *Min Kuo Jih Fao,* June 12–13, 1927.
14. *Ibid.*
15. The Hupeh Provincial Peasant Association estimated that at least 4,700 peasants, including 500 women, were slain in Hupeh province between February and June. Means of execution it listed as follows: "Beheading, burying alive, shooting, strangling, burning...cutting into pieces." —*People's Tribune,* July 7, 1927.
16. "Report of Kuomintang Work in Hupeh," *People's Tribune,* June 24–25, 1927; cf. "Speech of Tung Pi-wu to the Hupeh Party Conference," *People's Tribune,* July 1, 1927.
17. Cf. "Reports to the Conference of Hupeh Kuomintang Representatives," *People's Tribune,* June 26, et seq.
18. Sydor Stoler, "The International Workers' Delegation in Hunan," *Chinese Correspondence,* Hankow, May 8, 1927.
19. "Hupeh Delegate's Report."
20. Stoler, "The International Workers' Delegation in Hunan."

21. *Ibid.*
22. *Ibid.*
23. "The measures for suppression of counterrevolutionary factions were not carried out sufficiently rapidly or carefully. Also it was impossible to induce the government to begin the immediate trial of the corrupt country gentry, local bullies, and other counterrevolutionaries who were under arrest." —"Report of Kuomintang Work in Hupeh."
24. *People's Tribune,* May 12 and July 8, 1927.
25. "Manifesto of the C.E.C.," May 20, 1927, *People's Tribune,* May 22, 1927.
26. Strong, *China's Millions,* p. 166.
27. "Report of the Hupeh Provincial Delegates' Conference, Wuchang, June 25," *People's Tribune,* July 12, 1927.
28. "Hupeh Delegate's Report."
29. "Report of Kuomintang Work in Hupeh."
30. Strong, *China's Millions,* pp. 166–69.
31. Sydor Stoler, "The International Delegation in Hunan," *International Press Correspondence,* July 21, 1927.
32. M. N. Roy, "Revolution and Counter-Revolution in China," *International Press Correspondence,* July 21, 1927.
33. "Report of the Hupeh Provincial Delegates' Conference"; see Note 27.
34. Tsai Yi-tsen, "Difficulties and Recent Tactics."
35. "August 7 Letter."
36. Tang Leang-li, *Inner History,* p. 276.
37. "August 7 Letter."
38. Stalin, "Questions of the Chinese Revolution."
39. Trotsky, *Problems,* p. 43
40. "August 7 Letter."
41. "Remarks of Earl Browder to a Meeting of Trade Union Leaders," *Chinese Correspondence,* May 8, 1927.
42. Earl Browder, "The Chinese Revolution Turns Left," *Labour Monthly,* London, July, 1927.
43. Ransome, *Chinese Puzzle,* p. 92.
44. *People's Tribune,* May 21, 1927.
45. *Ibid.*
46. "August 7 Letter."
47. "Manifesto of Tang Ping-shan," *People's Tribune,* May 29, 1927.
48. *People's Tribune,* June 12, 1927.
49. "August 7 Letter."
50. *People's Tribune,* May 25, 29, 1927.
51. *Ibid.,* June 2, 9, 1927.
52. *Ibid.,* June 11, 1927.
53. *Ibid.,* June 9, 1927.
54. Tang Leang-li, *Inner History,* p. 273.
55. "August 7 Letter."
56. *Ibid.*

57. Cf. *Min Kuo Jih Pao,* Hankow, June 18, 19, 20, 21, 22, 1927; and *People's Tribune,* June 4, 1927.
58. *Min Kuo Jih Pao,* June 18, 1927.
59. "August 7 Letter."
60. *People's Tribune,* May 28, 1927.
61. Cf. "August 7 Letter"; Chiu Chiu-pei, *Chinese Revolution,* p. 112; Chitarov, Speech to XV Congress, C.P.S.U., quoted in Trotsky, *Problems,* pp. 289-90; Mif, *Kitaiskaya Revolutsia,* pp. 139–40.
62. Chiu Chiu-pei, *Chinese Revolution,* pp. 112–13; see also *People's Tribune* May 27, 1927.
63. According to Albert Treint, "Tang Ping-shan…accepted at the beginning of June the command of an armed expedition against the agrarian revolution." —"Déclaration du Camarade Treint," p. 63. This statement also occurs in Max Shachtman, *Ten Years, History and Principles of the Left Opposition,* New York, 1933, p. 50, based upon Treint. When queried by the author on this point, Treint insisted his informant was Bukharin himself. The statement, however, is definitely erroneous.
64. *Min Kuo Jih Pao,* June 18–19, 1927.

14. Moscow and Wuhan

1. See *La Platforme de l'Opposition,* Paris, 1927, pp. 9–24; Trotsky, *The Real Situation in Russia,* New York, 1928, Chaps. III and IV; Trotsky, *The Revolution Betrayed,* New York, 1937, pp. 25–32.
2. See Trotsky, *Problems,* pp. 61–67 ; Trotsky, *The Third International after Lenin,* pp. 128–34.
3. E.g., reports of the proceedings of the Sixth Plenum in February-March, 1926, filled nine numbers of *International Press Correspondence,* occupying 202 closely printed pages. Reports of the Seventh Plenum in November, 1926, were even lengthier, filling sixteen issues of the same publication.
4. *La Correspondance Internationale,* May 25, 1927.
5. "Déclaration de Camarade Treint," Documents de l'Opposition Française, p. 65.
6. "Communiqué de Secretariat de C.E. de l'I.C. sur les Travaux de la Séance Plénière de Comité Executif," *La Correspondance Internationale,* June 8, 1927.
7. J. Stalin, "The Revolution in China and the Tasks of the Communist International," *Communist International,* June 30, 1927.
8. N. Bukharin, "Les Résultats de Plenum de Comité Executif de l'I. C.," *La Correspondance Internationale,* June 29 and July 2, 1927.
9. *Die Chinesische Frage auf dem 8 Plenum des Exekutive der Kommunistische Internationale,* Hamburg-Berlin, 1928.
10. Stalin, "Revolution in China."
11. Trotsky, "First Speech on the Chinese Question," *Problems,* p. 100.
12. Trotsky, "Second Speech on the Chinese Question," *Problems,* pp. 102–04.
13. "Résolution sur la Question Chinoise," *La Correspondance Internationale,* June 11 and 15, 1927.
14. Albert Treint, "Compte Rendu Analytique de la Petite Commission Chinoise, Mai, 1927." This document was written by Treint from notes in August, 1935, at the request of the author. He subsequently published it in Paris and it was reprinted in the *New Militant,* New York, February 8, 1936. Its essential points were included in the "Déclaration de Camarade Treint" (made on July 22, 1927), p. 64.
15. Chen Tu-hsiu, *Letter to the Comrades*; see also Tang Leang-li, *Inner History,* p. 280; cf. Stalin, *Marxism and the National and Colonial Question,* p. 249.

16. Tang Leang-li, *Inner History,* p. 273.
17. Chen Tu-hsiu, *Letter to the Comrades.*
18. Trotsky, "Speech at the Joint Plenary Session of the Central Committee and the Central Control Commission, August 1, 1927," *Stalin School of Falsification,* p. 165.
19. Chiu Chiu-pei, *Chinese Revolution,* p. 90.
20. Chen Tu-hsiu, *Letter to the Comrades.*
21. Tang Leang-li, *Inner History,* p. 280; the fact that Roy showed the wire to Wang Ching-wei is confirmed by Chen Tu-hsiu, *Letter to the Comrades.*
22. Trotsky, *Problems,* pp. 121–22.
23. "Résolution sur les Interventions de Trotsky et de Vouivitch au Plenum de C.E. de l'I.C.," *La Correspondance Internationale,* June 8, 1927.
24. "Communiqué de Secretariat," *La Correspondance Internationale,* June 8, 1927.
25. *Pravda,* May 31, 1927, reprinted in *La Correspondance Internationale,* June 11, 1927.
26. *People's Tribune,* June 2, 1927.
27. Tang Leang-li, *Inner History,* p. 274.
28. Chiu Chiu-pei, *Chinese Revolution,* p. 113.
29. *Die Kommunistische Internationale,* February 25, 1927: Trotsky, *Problems,* p. 292.
30. Chiu Chiu-pei, *Chinese Revolution,* Chap. II.
31. "August 7 Letter."
32. *People's Tribune,* June 12, 1927.
33. *Ibid.,* June 21, 1927.
34. *International Press Correspondence,* June 30, 1927.
35. *People's Tribune,* June 29, 1927.
36. *Ibid.,* July 2, 1927.
37. E. Zeitlin, "La Nouvelle Étape de la Révolution Chinoise," *La Correspondance Internationale,* June 29, 1927.
38. "August 7 Letter" ; Mif, *Kitaiskaya Revolutsia,* p. 141.
39. Sia Ting, "The Peasant Movement in China," *International Press Correspondence,* June 23, 1927.
40. *People's Tribune,* June 30, 1927.
41. *Min Kuo Jih Pao,* June 13, 1927.
42. Trotsky, *Problems,* p. 78.
43. Mif, *Kitaiskaya Revolutsia,* p. 139.
44. *Ibid.*
45. Fischer, *Soviets in World Affairs,* v. II, p. 672.

15. Wuhan: The Debacle

1. *Daily Worker,* New York, April 6, 1926.
2. Katsuji Fuse, *Soviet Policy in the Orient,* pp. 322–26.
3. *Ibid.,* p. 327.
4. *Ibid.,* p. 329.

5. *People's Tribune,* May 8, 1927.
6. *La Correspondance Internationale,* June 8, 1927.
7. Trotsky, *Problems,* pp. 123–24.
8. *People's Tribune,* June 10, 1927.
9. Cf. "Detailed Story of Decisive Campaign in Honan," *People's Tribune,* June 19, 1927.
10. Strong, *China's Millions,* p. 62; M. N. Roy, *Revolution und Konterrevolution in China,* Berlin, 1930, p. 363.
11. Strong, *China's Millions,* p. 62 ff.; Fischer, *Soviets in World Affairs,* v. II, p. 669.
12. *People's Tribune,* June 1927.
13. *Ibid.,* June 13, 1927.
14. Roy, *Revolution und Konterrevolution,* pp. 363–64.
15. *Chinese News Service,* Canton, June 23, 1927.
16. "Marshal Feng Yu-hsiang's Telegram to Hankow, June 21, 1927," *Nationalist China,* issued by the Kuomintang Secretariat, Canton, May, 1927; see also *China Weekly Review,* July 2, 1927.
17. Strong, *China's Millions,* p. 72.
18. Tang Leang-li, *Inner History,* pp. 283–84.
19. *Ibid.,* p. 285.
20. *People's Tribune,* June 29, 1927.
21. *Ibid.*
22. Wang Ching-wei, "The Party Must Lead the Mass Movement," *People's Tribune,* July 8, 1927.
23. *Ibid.*
24. "Report of the Special Kiangsi Commission," *People's Tribune,* July 13, 14, 15, 1927.
25. Sun Fo, "The Revolution and the Masses," *Chung Yang Jih Pao,* Hankow, July 14, 1927.
26. N. Lenzner, "La Question Chinoise," *La Correspondance Internationale,* June 29, 1927.
27. Chiu Chiu-pei, *Chinese Revolution,* p. 114.
28. *Ibid.*
29. *People's Tribune,* June 15, 1927.
30. Cf. *People's Tribune,* July 9, 1927.
31. Chiu Chiu-pei, *Chinese Revolution,* p. 115.
32. "August 7 Letter"; Chiu Chiu-pei, *Chinese Revolution,* p. 115 ff.
33. *People's Tribune,* June 23, 1927.
34. Cf. Sz Toh-li, "The Fourth All-China Trade Union Congress," *Pan-Pacific Worker,* Hankow, July 15, 1927.
35. "Speech of Lozovsky," *Pan-Pacific Worker,* July 1, 1927.
36. "Manifesto of the Fourth Labour Conference," *People's Tribune,* June 29, 1927.
37. *People's Tribune,* June 22, 1927.
38. Strong, *China's Millions,* p. 88.
39. *People's Tribune,* June 30, 1927.
40. *Ibid.*
41. *Ibid.,* July 1, 1927.
42. *Ibid.,* June 30, 1927.

43. *Ibid.* July 18, 1927.
44. Chen Tu-hsiu, *Letter to the Comrades.*
45. Tang Leang-li, *Inner History,* p. 280.
46. Chiu Chiu-pei, *Chinese Revolution,* p. 118.
47. *International Press Correspondence,* July 28, 1927.
48. N. Bukharin, "The Position of the Chinese Revolution," *International Press Correspondence,* July 6, 1927.
49. N. Bukharin, "An Abrupt Turn in the Chinese Revolution," *International Press Correspondence,* July 14, 1927.
50. "Resolution of the E.C.C.I. on the Present Situation of the Chinese Revolution," *International Press Correspondence* July 28, 1927.
51. "Declaration of the Communist Party of China," *International Press Correspondence,* August 4, 1927.
52. *People's Tribune,* July 20, 26, 1927.
53. Chen Tu-hsiu, *Letter to the Comrades.*
54. *People's Tribune,* July 28, 1927.
55. *Ibid.,* July 22, 23, 24, 1927.
56. *Ibid.,* July 29, 1927.
57. Tang Leang-li, *Inner History,* p. 291.
58. *Chung Yang Jih Pao,* July 6, 1927.
59. *People's Tribune,* July 14, 1927.
60. *People's Tribune,* July 18, 1927; the text of Soong Ching-ling's statement will also be found in Woo, *Kuomintang and the Future of the Chinese Revolution,* pp. 270–73.

16. Autumn Harvest

1. Jui Fu-san, "What Has Happened to the Seething Revolution," *China Weekly Review,* August 20, 1927.
2. "The Immediate Tasks of the Chinese Trade Unions in the Present Situation," *Pan-Pacific Worker,* September 15, 1927.
3. *People's Tribune,* July 29, 1927.
4. "Organizational Report of Chen Tu-hsiu to the Fifth Congress, Chinese Communist Party," quoted by Mif, *Kitaiskaya Revolutsia,* p. 117.
5. "Circular of the Central Committee, Chinese Communist Party, November 8, 1928," *Political Work of the Chinese Communist Party after the Sixth Congress,* Shanghai, 1929; Chow En-lai, *Organizational Questions in the Party at the Present Time,* Shanghai, May 15, 1929.
6. Lenin, *Left-Wing Communism: An Infantile Disorder,* London, undated, p. 14.
7. "Minutes of the March, 1917, Party Conference," Trotsky, *Stalin School of Falsification,* p. 239.
8. Stalin, "On Current Questions," *International Press Correspondence,* August 4, 1927.
9. Strong, *China's Millions,* pp. 242, 251–52.
10. M. N. Roy, "The Lessons of the Chinese Revolution," *Labour Monthly,* London, November, 1927.
11. Roy, *Revolution und Konterrevolution in China,* p. 405.
12. "Resolution on the International Situation," by the Joint Plenum of the C.C. and C.C.C.

(C.P.S.U.) after hearing Bukharin's Report, August 9, 1927, *International Press Correspondence,* August 18, 1927.

13. "The Immediate Tasks of the Chinese Trade Unions."
14. "Resolution on the International Situation."
15. Chen Tu-hsiu, "Letter to the Communist International," *Le Prolétaire* (organ of the Chinese Left Opposition), Shanghai, July 1, 1930.
16. Trotsky, *Problems,* p. 52.
17. Hua Kang, *Great Chinese Revolution,* Chap. VI, Section 1.
18. Chiu Chiu-pei, *Chinese Revolution,* p. 122.
19. Hua Kang, *Great Chinese Revolution,* Chap. VI, Section 1.
20. *Pravda,* July 25, 1927, tr. in *La Correspondance Internationale,* August 3, 1927.
21. Stalin, "Concerning Current Questions."
22. *Ibid.*
23. "Resolution on the International Situation."
24. Hua Kang, *Great Chinese Revolution,* Chap. VI, Section 1.
25. Chiu Chiu-pei, *Chinese Revolution,* p. 123.
26. Hua Kang, *Great Chinese Revolution,* Chap. VI, Section 1.
27. "August 7 Letter."
28. Hua Kang, *Great Chinese Revolution,* Chap. VI, Section 8.
29. "Resolution on the International Situation."
30. Chen Tu-hsiu, *Letter to the Comrades.*
31. "Resolution of the Kiangsu District Committee, May 7, 1928," *Materials on the Chinese Question,* Moscow, N. 14, p. 6, quoted by Trotsky, *Problems,* p. 226.
32. *International Press Correspondence,* August 18, 1927.
33. Chiu Chiu-pei, *Chinese Revolution,* p. 124.
34. Hua Kang, *Great Chinese Revolution,* Chap. IV, Section 7.
35. Chiu Chiu-pei, *Chinese Revolution,* p. 135.
36. Hua Kang, *Great Chinese Revolution,* Chap. IV, Section 7.
37. *Ibid.*
38. "Circular No. 8 of the Kiangsu Provincial Committee," quoted in Hua Kang, *Great Chinese Revolution,* Chap. IV, Section 7.
39. Chiu Chiu-pei, *Chinese Revolution,* p. 143.
40. *Ibid.,* p. 134.
41. *Ibid.*
42. *Pravda,* September 30, 1927, tr. in *La Correspondance Internationale,* October 8, 1927.
43. Chiu Chiu-pei, *Chinese Revolution,* p. 136 ff.
44. *Ibid.*
45. "Political Resolution of the November Plenum of the C.C., Chinese Communist Party," *International Press Correspondence,* January 26, 1928. For a discussion of the theory of "uninterrupted ascent" and Lominadze's version of the "permanent revolution," see Trotsky, *Problems,* p. 163 ff., and *Third International after Lenin,* p. 187 ff.
46. "Political Resolution of the November Plenum."
47. Chiu Chiu-pei, *Chinese Revolution,* p. 138 ff.

48. "Political Resolution of the November Plenum."

17. The Canton Commune

1. Chiu Chiu-pei, *Chinese Revolution,* p. 128.
2. Huang Ping, "The Canton Commune and its Preparation," *The Canton Commune (A Collection),* Shanghai, 1930, pp. 77, 80.
3. *Ibid.,* p. 77.
4. A. Neuberg (pseud. for Heinz Neumann), *L'Insurrection Armée,* p. 108; Chiu Chiu-pei, *Chinese Revolution,* p. 128.
5. Deng Cheng-tsah, "The Canton Commune and the Tactics of the Communist Party," *Canton Commune,* p. 43.
6. *Ibid.,* p. 39.
7. Lozovsky, "Lessons of the Canton Commune," *Canton Commune,* p. 5.
8. Neuberg, *Insurrection Armée,* p. 110.
9. *Ibid.*
10. Lominadze, "The Anniversary of the Canton Commune," *Canton Commune,* p. 205.
11. Chen Shao-yu, "The Story of the Canton Uprising," *Canton Commune,* p. 139.
12. *Ibid.,* p. 142.
13. Neuberg, *Insurrection Armée,* p. 114.
14. Huang Ping, *Canton Commune,* p. 85.
15. Chen Shao-yu, *Canton Commune,* p. 142 ; Neuberg, *Insurrection Armée,* p. 112.
16. Chen Shao-yu, *Canton Commune,* p. 142.
17. Neuberg, *Insurrection Armée,* p. 124.
18. Lozovsky, *Canton Commune,* p. 5.
19. Neuberg, *Insurrection Armée,* p. 113.
20. *Ibid.,* p. 115 n.
21. Huang Ping, *Canton Commune,* p. 89.
22. Lozovsky, *Canton Commune,* p. 6.
23. Huang Ping, *Canton Commune,* pp. 89-90; Neumann says the "Soviet" consisted of sixteen men, cf. Neuberg, *Insurrection Armée,* p. 111.
24. Cf. Trotsky, *Problems,* pp. 151–57, 203–06; Trotsky, *Third International after Lenin,* pp. 201–12; "When and under What Conditions Soviets of Workers' Deputies Should Be Formed," *Theses and Statutes of the Communist International* (Second Congress), pp. 62–65; see also above p. 311 n., for Stalin's "theory" of Soviets.
25. Trotsky, *Third International after Lenin,* pp. 201–06.
26. The ensuing account of events of December 11–13 is collated from details in the various articles in *Canton Commune* and Heinz Neumann's account in *Insurrection Armée.*
27. Trotsky, *Problems*, p. 128 ff.
28. Deng Cheng-tsah, *Canton Commune*, p. 55.
29. Neuberg, *Insurrection Armée*, p. 118.
30. "Report of Yeh Ting on the Canton Insurrection," quoted in Neuberg, *Insurrection Armée*, pp. 125–56.

31. Neuberg, *ibid.*, pp. 18, 124–25.
32. Deng Cheng-tsah, *Canton Commune*, pp. 50–51.
33. *Ibid.*, p. 52.
34. *Ibid.*
35. Chen Shao-yu, *Canton Commune*, p. 146.
36. *Peking Morning Post*, December 14, 1927.
37. *Ta Kung Pao*, Tientsin, December 13, 1927.
38. *Yi Shih Pao*, Peking, December 14, 1927.
39. Neuberg, *Insurrection Armée*, p. 118.
40. *Ibid.*, p. 119.
41. Chen Shao-yu, *Canton Commune*, p. 258 ff.
42. *China Weekly Review*, December 31, 1927.
43. *Ta Kung Pao*, December 17, 1927.
44. *Ibid.*, December 19, 1927.
45. *Peking Morning Post*, December 18, 1927.
46. Quoted by Chen Shao-yu, *Canton Commune*.
47. *China Weekly Review*, December 31, 1927; for photos see *Five Years of Kuomintang Reaction.*
48. Chiu Chiu-pei, *Chinese Revolution*, p. 152.
49. *Ibid.*, Appendices, p. 247.
50. *Ibid.*, p. 232.
51. *Ibid.*, p. 246 ff.
52. "Résolution sur la Question Chinoise," *Résolutions Adoptées à la IXE Session Plénière du C.E. de l'I.* C., pp. 53–54.
53. *Ibid.*, pp. 48–51; cf. Trotsky, *Problems*, pp. 216–23 *Third International after Lenin*, pp. 186–212.
54. Quoted by Trotsky, *Problems*, p. 294.
55. Lominadze, *Canton Commune*, p. 205.
56. *Resolutions of the Sixth Congress of the Chinese Communist Party*, Shanghai, 1928, p. 31.
57. *The Revolutionary Movement in the Colonies*, Theses Adopted by the Sixth Congress of the Communist International, New York, 1929, pp. 39–40.
58. *Ibid.*, p. 3.

18. Fruits of Defeat

1. For a graphic and detailed record of Kuomintang terror see Isaacs (ed.), *Five Years of Kuomintang Reaction.*
2. Cf. *Annual Reports*, Chinese Maritime Customs ; *Annual Reports,* Bank of China; Chen Hanseng, "Economic Disintegration in China," *Pacific Affairs*, April–May, 1933; *Annexes*, to the Rajchmann Report, Nanking, April, 1934; *Chinese Year Book*, 1936–37, *China Year Book,* etc.
3. Cf *China Forum,* Shanghai, 1932–34, passim, for week-to-week accounts of Kuomintang nonresistance and suppression of the anti-Japanese movement.
4. *International Press Correspondence,* July 30, 1928.
5. Cf. *Programme of the Communist International,* New York, 1929, p. 58; Trotsky, *Problems,* pp. 173–74; *Third International after Lenin,* p. 196.

6. Cf. Max Shachtman, Introduction to *Third International after Lenin,* p. xix ff.
7. *The Revolutionary Movement in the Colonies,* p. 41.
8. Trotsky, *Problems,* p. 206.
9. *Ibid.,* pp. 175–76.
10. *Ibid.,* pp. 185–86, 203 ff.
11. Bukharin, "The International Situation and the Tasks of the Communist International," *International Press Correspondence,* November 23, 1928.
12. Trotsky, *Problems,* p. 198.
13. *International Press Correspondence,* July 25, 1928.
14. *Ibid.*
15. "Political Resolution, adopted July 9, 1928," *Sixth Congress of the Chinese Communist Party,* Shanghai, 1928.
16. "Letter of the E.C.C.I. to the C.C.P. on the Reorganizationists" (October 26, 1929), *Red Flag,* Shanghai, February 15, 1930.
17. *International Press Correspondence,* July 25, 1928.
18. "Circular of the Central Committee, November 8, 1928," *Political Work of the Chinese Communist Party After the Sixth Congress,* Shanghai, October, 1929, pp. 42–43.
19. "Revolutionary Struggles and the Trade Union Movement in Hopei," *Struggle,* Shanghai, December 12, 1933.
20. Lin Tung-hai, *Labour Movement and Labour Legislation in China,* Shanghai, 1933, pp. 83–84; Fang Fu-an, *Chinese Labour,* p. 74; *Nankai Institute Weekly,* Tientsin, No. 29.
21. Fang Fu-an, *Chinese Labour,* p. 97.
22. Sze Ming, "The Problem of the United Front from Below," *Red Flag,* April 18, 1931.
23. Han Yin, *Development of the Trade Union Movement in the Past Year and Present Tasks,* Report to the Second Enlarged Meeting of the Executive Committee of the All-China Trade Union Federation, Shanghai, February 17, 1929, in *Chinese Worker,* Shanghai, May 15, 1929.
24. "Letter of the E.C.C.I. to the C.C.P., February 8, 1929," *Political Work After the Sixth Congress.*
25. Chow En-lai, *Organizational Questions in the Party at the Present Time,* Shanghai, May 15, 1929.
26. Kuusinen, "Revolutionary Movement in the Colonies," *International Press Correspondence,* October 4, 1928; Han Yin, *Development of the Trade Union Movement*; "Resolution on the Trade Union Question," *Sixth Congress.*
27. Han Yin, *Development of the Trade Union Movement.*
28. Pei Ke-sung, *Present Condition of the Labour Movement,* 1928-30, Shanghai, 1930.
29. *Ibid.*
30. Lo Mai, "Survey of the Work of the Li Li-san Line in Kiangsu," *Truth,* Shanghai, February 7, 1931.
31. *Resolution of the Fourth Plenum of the Central Committee, C.C.P.,* Shanghai, January, 1931.
32. "Practice of the Li Li-san Line in Chihli," *Truth,* December 14, 1930.
33. "Report on the Labour Movement in 1931," by the Labour Department of the Central Committee, *Red Flag,* March 11, 1932.
34. "Against Opportunism in the Labour Movement," *Red Flag,* March 25, 1932.
35. Wang Min and Kang Sin, *Revolutionary China To-day* (Speeches at the XIII Plenum of the E.C.C.I., December 1933), New York, 1934, p. 44.
36. P. Mif, "New Developments in the Revolutionary Crisis in China," *Communist International,*

May 15, 1933.

37. *Sovieti v. Kitai,* Moscow, 1934, p. xiii.
38. *Red Flag,* October 30, 1933.
39. Mif, "New Developments."
40. H. D. Fong, *Cotton Industry and Trade in China,* Table 16.
41. *Red Flag,* October 30, 1933.
42. D. K. Lieu, *Growth and Industrialization of Shanghai,* Shanghai, 1936, p. 294.
43. Mif, "New Developments."
44. *Red Flag,* October 30, 1933.
45. "On the Question of the United Front from Below," *Youth Battle Line,* Peiping, February 1, 1934.
46. Chow En-lai, *Organizational Questions.*
47. *Red Flag,* March 26, 1930.
48. "Chow En-lai, *Report to the Third Plenum, C.C., C.C.P.,* September 24, 1930.
49. *Bolshevik,* Shanghai, May 10, 1931.
50. "Letter of E.C.C.I. February 8, 1929."
51. Chien Sung, *Report of the Kiangsu Provincial Committee to the Second Delegaters' Conference,* Shanghai, December 29, 1929.
52. *Red Flag,* October 30, 1933.
53. Wang Min and Kang Sin, *Revolutionary China To-day,* p. 48.

19. The Rise and Fall of "Soviet China"

1. Tung Li, "Report on the History and Present Condition of the Chu-Mao Red Army, September 1, 1929," *Military Bulletin of the Central Committee,* Shanghai, January 15, 1930.
2. *Ibid.*
3. *Ibid.*
4. "Letter to All the Comrades, November 11, 1928," *Political Work After the Sixth Congress.*
5. "Letter of E.C.C.I. to C.C.P., October 26, 1929."
6. *Political Resolution of the Second Plenum, Central Committee, C.C.P.,* June 1929.
7. *Circular No. 68,* Central Committee, C.C.P.
8. M. James and R. Doonping, *Soviet China,* New York, 1932, p. 10.
9. Chen Tu-hsiu, "Concerning the Question of the So-called Red Armies,"*Le Prolétaire,* Shanghai, July 1, 1930.
10. Engels, *Peasant War in Germany,* New York, 1926, p. 18.
11. "Resolution on the Peasant Question," *Sixth Congress.*
12. Chien Sung, *Report of the Kiangsu Provincial Committee.*
13. "A Discussion on the Peasant-Partisan War," *Military Bulletin of the Central Committee,* January 15, 1930.
14. P. Mif, "Toward the Storm of the Chinese Revolution," *Pravda,* April 28, 1930, tr. in *Red Flag,* June 25, 1930.
15. Cf. L. Trotsky, "The Chinese Political Situation and the Tasks of the Chinese Bolshevik-Leninists, June, 1929," *Le Prolétaire,* July 1, 1930; "On the Chinese Revolution," *Militant,* New

York, January 25, 1930; "The Slogan of the National Assembly in China," *Militant*, June 14, 1930; "Perspectives and Tasks of the Chinese Revolution, Manifesto of the International Left Opposition," *Militant*, October 1, 1930.

16. "Resolution on the Chinese Question, by the Political Secretariat of the E.C.C.I., July 23, 1930," *Truth*, October 23, 1930.
17. "Letter of the E.C.C.I. to C.C.P., October 26, 1929."
18. *Red Flag*, March 26, 1930.
19. "The New Revolutionary Wave and the Victory in One or Several Provinces, adopted by the Political Bureau, June 1930," *Red Flag*, July 19, 1930.
20. *Truth*, December 9, 1930.
21. "New Revolutionary Wave, etc."
22. Lo Mai, *Speech before Shanghai Activists*, Shanghai, December 3, 1930.
23. "New Revolutionary Wave, etc."
24. "Letter of E.C.C.I. to C.C.P., received November 16, 1930," *Truth*, December 14, 1930.
25. *China Weekly Review*, September 6, 1930.
26. *International Press Correspondence*, August 7, 1930.
27. "The Political Situation and the Tasks of the Communist Party, Resolution of the Third Plenum, Central Committee, C.C.P. (September, 1930)," *Truth*, October 30, 1930.
28. Speech of Kuchiumov, "Discussion on the Li Li-san Line, by the Presidium of the E.C.C.I., December 1930," *Bolshevik*, Shanghai, May 10, 1931.
29. *Ibid.*
30. *Ibid.*
31. Chiu Chiu-pei, "Capture and Loss of Kian," *Truth*, December 9, 1930.
32. Chow En-lai, "Report to the Third Plenum on Transmitting the Resolution of the E.C.C.I., September 24, 1930," *Materials of the Third Plenum*, No. 9.
33. Ho Mung-shung, *Statements to the Central Committee*, September 8, October 2, 9, 1930, Shanghai, January 6, 1931.
34. "Statement of Comrade Chiu Chiu-pei, January 17, 1931," *Materials of the Fourth Plenum; Statement of Comrade Chow En-lai*, January 3, 1931 (Prefatory Note to leaflet containing text of Chow's report to the Third Plenum).
35. *Bolshevik*, May 10, 1931.
36. "Letter of E.C.C.I. to C.C.P., received November 16, 1930."
37. "The Present Political Situation and the Central Tasks of the Party," *Truth*, February 2, 1931.
38. "Letter of E.C.C.I. to C.C.P., received November 16, 1930."
39. "Instructions to the Red Armies and All Party Organizations, June 10, 1931"; "Resolution of the Central Committee on Urgent Tasks," *Bolshevik*, November 10, 1931.
40. "Speech of Li Li-san to the Third Plenum," *Materials of the Third Plenum*, No 10.
41. Wang Min and Kang Sin, *Revolutionary China To-day*, pp. 8, 28.
42. *International Press Correspondence*, September 8, 1933, April 20, 1934; *New Masses*, New York, March 13, 1934.
43. Agnes Smedley, *China's Red Army Marches*, New York, 1934, p. xx.
44. Cf. Liang Pin, "May 1 and Several Important Questions of Red Army Building," *Struggle*, Juichin, May 1, 1933; "Summary of Conference of Kiangsi Party Organizations," *Struggle*, May 20, 1933; Lo Fu, "Fire Against Right Opportunism," *Struggle*, July 5, 1933; Liang Pin, "The Question of Cash in the Soviet Districts," *Struggle*, August 5, 1933; Mao Tse-tung,

"Smashing the Fifth Campaign and Tasks of Economic Construction," *Red Flag,* November 20, 1933.

45. Isaacs (ed.), *Five Years of Kuomintang Reaction,* p. 129.
46. Wang Min and Kang Sin, *Revolutionary China To-day,* p. 9.
47. *China Forum,* Shanghai, January 20, 1932.
48. *North China Daily News,* August 19, 1931.
49. Cf. "Survey of Certain Localities in Kiangsi," *Annexes,* to the Rajchmann Report.
50. *Shanghai Evening Post,* November 10, 1931.
51. *Chung Yang Kung Lien,* June, 1933, quoted in *Revolutionary China To-day,* p. 40.
52. "Resolution on Urgent Tasks," *Bolshevik,* November 10, 1931.
53. "Political Resolution," *Sixth Congress.*
54. *Political Resolution of the Second Plenum,* June, 1929.
55. *Letter of the E.C.C.I. to the C.C.P. on the Peasant Question,* June 7, 1929.
56. *Resolution of the Central Committee on Accepting the Directives of the E.C.C.I. on the Peasant Question,* August, 1929.
57. Yuen Tai-ying, "Past and Future of the West Fukien Soviet," *Red Flag,* March 26, 1930.
58. Cf. Special Issue of the *Red Flag,* June 4, 1930, on the Soviet Districts Delegates' Conference ; "Propaganda Thesis on the First Delegates' Conference," *Red Flag,* June 21, 1930.
59. O Fong, "Results of the Soviet Districts Delegates' Conference," *Our Word,* Shanghai, August 30, 1930.
60. Chen Shao-yu, "Why Not Organize Agricultural Labourers' Unions?" *Red Flag,* May 17, 1930.
61. "Letter of E.C.C.I. to C.C.P., received November 16, 1930."
62. *Party Construction,* Shanghai, March 8, 1931.
63. "Correspondence from the Hunan-Hupeh Soviet District, August 14, 1931," *Workers and Peasants' Correspondence,* Shanghai, March, 1932.
64. Lo Fu, "Class Struggles under the Soviet Power," *Struggle,* Juichin, June 5, 1933.
65. Mao Tse-tung, "Re-Examination of Land Distribution in the Soviet Districts is the Central Task," *Red Flag,* August 31, 1933.
66. Mao Tse-tung, *Red China,* London, 1934, p. 22.
67. Wang Min and Kang Sin, *Revolutionary China To-day,* p. 10.
68. *Struggle,* Juichin, May 10, 1933.
69. Lo Fu, "May 1 and the Examination of the Execution of the Labour Laws," *Struggle,* May 1, 1933.
70. "Report of the Hunan-Kiangsi Party to the Central Committee," *Red Flag,* March 11, 1932.
71. *Red Flag,* March 11, 1932; *Struggle,* February 4, 1933.
72. Lo Fu, "May 1 and the Labour Laws."
73. Lo Fu, "Class Struggles under the Soviet Power."
74. *Red Flag,* March 11, July 10, 1932; *Struggle,* February 4, 1933; Mao Tse-tung, *Red China,* p. 20; *Communist International,* September 15, 1933.
75. *Red Flag,* March 11, 1932.
76. "Letter to the Labour Unions in the Soviet Districts on the Question of Labour Union Membership, from the Standing Committee of the All-China Trade Union Federation," *Red Flag,* November 15, 1932.

77. Teng Yen-tsao, "Examination of the Struggle for Strengthening the Proletariat," *Struggle,* February 4, 1933.
78. "The Political Situation in China and the Tasks of the Chinese Communist Party," *Communist International,* September 15, 1933.
79. *Struggle,* April 5, 25, 1933.
80. Quoted by Po Ku, "For a Bolshevik Line in the Party," *Struggle,* February 23, 1933.
81. Lo Fu, "The Lo Min Line in Kiangsi," *Struggle,* April 15, 1933.
82. *Struggle,* May 1, 1933.
83. *Ibid.,* August 29, 1933.
84. Lo Mai, "For a Bolshevik Turn," *Struggle,* August 22, 1933.
85. Lo Fu, "Fire Against Right Opportunism," *Struggle,* July 5, 1933.
86. Chow En-lai, "Smash the Fifth Campaign," *Struggle,* August 29, 1933.
87. *Struggle,* October 21, 1933.
88. For a detailed description of the blockade in Kiangsi, see the report of its special correspondent with the Kuomintang armies, *Ta Kung Pao,* Tientsin, September 2, 3, 4, 1934.

20. The New "National United Front"

1. Cf. *China Forum,* Shanghai, January 13, 1932.
2. *China Forum,* May 21, 1932; "Letter of the Central Committee to the Manchurian Organizations, June 9, 1933," *Struggle,* Juichin, August 15, 1933; Lo Mai, "The Manchurian National Revolutionary War," *Struggle,* September 15, 1933.
3. See Chap. XVIII, Notes 33, 44.
4. Cf. "Examples of Bolshevist Work and Revolutionary Struggle," *Communist International,* December, 1932.
5. *Red Flag,* December 17, 1931.
6. "The Manchurian Events and the Fundamental Tasks of the Anti-Imperialist Movement," *Bolshevik,* Shanghai, November 10, 1931.
7. See Chap. XVIII, Note 33.
8. *China Forum,* January 27, 1932.
9. *Ibid.,* March 15, 1932.
10. "Letter to Party Organizations and to all Comrades from the Central Committee on the Question of the United Front in the Anti-Imperialist Movement," *Struggle,* Shanghai, June 10, 1933; "Resolution of the Central Committee on the 5th Campaign and the Tasks of the Party, July 24, 1933," *Struggle,* Juichin, August 12, 1933.
11. Cf. Lo Fu, "On the Soviet Power and the People's Power," *Red Flag,* February 15, 1932.
12. *Theses and Resolutions,* XII Plenum of the E.C.C.I. (September, 1932), Moscow, 1933, p. 16.
13. *China Forum,* May 21, 1932.
14. *Ibid.,* April 13, 1933.
15. *Ibid.*
16. Wang Min, *Revolutionary China To-day,* p. 33.
17. "The Second Soviet Congress of the Chinese Soviet Republic," *International Press Correspondence,* June 1, 1934.

18. *Shanghai Evening Post,* August 25, 1934; *China Press,* September 2, 1934.
19. Wang Min, *Revolutionary China To-day,* p. 33.
20. Wang Min, *Revolutionary Movement in the Colonial Countries* (Report to Seventh Congress of the Comintern), New York, 1935, pp. 15, 20–21.
21. *Ibid.*, pp. 13, 20.
22. *Daily Worker,* New York, March 30, 1936.
23. Wang Min, *Revolutionary Movement,* pp. 51–52.
24. "Essential Conditions and Minimum Demands for United Resistance," *China: The March Toward Unity,* New York, 1937, pp. 66–67.
25. Mao Tse-tung to the Members of the All-China National Salvation League, August 10, 1936, *China: The March Toward Unity,* p. 70 ff.; cf. *China To-day,* New York, January, 1937.
26. *China: The March Toward Unity,* p. 30.
27. Edgar Snow, *Red Star Over China,* New York, 1938, p. 398.
28. Harry Gannes, *When China Unites,* New York, 1937, p. 265; Snow, *Red Star Over China,* p. 414.
29. Chiang Kai-shek and Mme Chiang Kai-shek, *General Chiang Kai-shek,* New York, 1937; see also James Bertram, *First Act in China,* New York, 1938. The position of the Communist Party in these events will be found in various telegrams reproduced in *China To-day,* March, 1937; see also "Concerning Events in Sian," *Communist International,* January, 1937.
30. Snow, *Red Star Over China,* p. 417.
31. *Sunday Worker,* New York, February 21, 1937.
32. *New York Times,* February 20, 1937; *New York Herald Tribune,* February 22, 1937; Gannes, *When China Unites,* p. 279; Snow, *Red Star Over China,* p. 427.
33. *China To-day,* May, 1937.
34. *New Tork Times,* April 30, 1937.
35. *China To-day,* July, 1937.
36. Philip Jaffe, "China's Communists Told Me," *New Masses,* New York, October 12, 1937; Cf. Snow, *Red Star Over China,* p. 194.
37. Snow, *Red Star Over China,* pp. 342–43.
38. Nym Wales, "The Passing of the Chinese Soviets," *Asia,* New York, January, 1938.
39. Wang Min, *China Can Win!* New York, 1937, p. 45.
40. Trotsky, *Third International After Lenin,* pp. 177, 196.
41. *New York Times,* January 24, 1938.
42. *Shanghai Evening Post,* October 18, 1937.
43. Snow, *Red Star Over China,* p. 275.
44. *Havas News Agency,* December 23, 1937.
45. *Shanghai Evening Post,* December 27, 1937.

Index